# DECISIVE BATTLES OF
# THE WESTERN WORLD

# DECISIVE BATTLES OF THE WESTERN WORLD

*and their influence upon history*

## VOLUME I

*From the earliest times
to the Battle of Lepanto*

MAJOR GENERAL
# J. F. C. FULLER
CB CBE DSO

CASSELL&CO

Cassell & Co
Wellington House, 125 Strand
London WC2R 0BB

First published in 1954
This edition 2001

British Library Cataloguing-in-Publication Data
A catalogue record for this book is available from the British Library

ISBN 0-304-35867-3

Printed and bound in Great Britain by
Creative Print & Design (Wales), Ebbw Vale

*To*

FRANCIS NEILSON

# Contents

# Maps and Diagrams

# Preface

Whether war is a necessary factor in the evolution of mankind may be disputed, but a fact which cannot be questioned is that, from the earliest records of man to the present age, war has been his dominant preoccupation. There has never been a period in human history altogether free from war, and seldom one of more than a generation which has not witnessed a major conflict: great wars flow and ebb almost as regularly as the tides.

This becomes more noticeable when a civilization ages and begins to decay, as seemingly is happening to our world-wide industrial civilization. Whereas but a generation or two back war was accepted as an instrument of policy, it has now become policy itself. Today we live in a state of "wardom" – a condition in which war dominates all other human activities. How long this tension will last, whether there is a definite answer to it, or whether it is destined blindly to work out its own end, no man can say; yet one thing is certain, and it is that the more we study the history of war, the more we shall be able to understand war itself, and, seeing that it is now the dominant factor, until we do understand it, how can we hope to regulate human affairs?

It was shortly after the first World War that I began to consider this problem, and when, in 1923, I became an instructor at the Camberley Staff College, I found that, beyond the reading up of a campaign or two, the study of the history of war was sadly neglected by the very people who should be most interested in it. As one reason for this was that there was no single book in English covering the whole subject, I decided to supply its want. In order to condense so vast a task, the method I elected was to concentrate on what I believed to be the decisive battles fought between Western peoples; next, to weave round them the wars and campaigns in which they were fought, and lastly to deduce from them their influence on history. Further, in order that the story of war might be as continuous as possible, I decided to preface each Battle Chapter with a Chronicle of preceding events, describing in it how the wars, campaigns and battles arose and how they were shaped by their political origins. Taken as a whole, the book I had in mind may be compared with the surface of a wind-swept sea: the Battle Chapters are the crests of the waves and the Chronicles the dips between them, the one linked to the other in the flow and ebb of 3,500 years of warfare.

From 1923 on I set out to collect data, and this led in 1939-40 to the publication of two volumes on Decisive Battles. But as I was far from satisfied with the book as it then stood, when shortly after the second volume appeared the whole stock was destroyed by enemy action, in no way did I regret its loss, because it presented me with the opportunity to rewrite the work. Since then I have devoted ten years to the task; have extended the book from two to three volumes; have rewritten twenty-eight of the original twenty-nine chapters; omitted one and added twenty-three new ones. Further, all the Chronicles are new, as also is the Introductory Chapter. The book is, therefore, not a revised edition, but a new work.

In the selection of my battles I have relied on my own judgement. Nevertheless, I am well aware that others could be added; but of not a few so little has been recorded as to make an extended study of them impossible, and others I have been compelled to omit if only because of linguistic difficulties.

A more complex problem has been the selection of sources. Whenever possible I have relied upon the accounts given by participants, eyewitnesses, and contemporary historians, checking them with the works of recognized modern authors. But at times I have found that war–that "impassioned drama" as Jomini calls it–is more fully and understandingly dealt with by historians of past ages, now long superseded, than by those of the present day. I think the reason for this is that, whereas in past times historians looked upon war as a natural process, today some are apt to regard it as an infernal nuisance, and therefore of secondary interest. However, my main difficulty has been to discover reliable sources for the most recent war of all–World War II–for since it ended there has been such an outpouring of undigested history larded with war propaganda, such a want of political veracity, and in certain cases, more particularly in that of Russia, such a lack of reliable information, that it is still impossible to obtain anything like a clear picture of several of the great battles fought.

Two small points remain to be mentioned. The first is that of numerical strengths of fighting forces and their battle losses. Seldom are they reliably reported, and as often as not they are

twisted to fit some propaganda motive. This holds as good today
as it did 3,000 years ago. Therefore I cannot vouch for the accuracy
of many of the figures in this book. The other point is, that all
foreign and ancient money values, when converted into pounds
sterling, refer to the value of the sovereign in 1913.

Finally, my thanks are due to all those who have assisted me
with advice and criticism. Among those to whom I am especially
indebted are Professor David Douglas, M.A., F.B.A., Professor
of History, University of Bristol; Mr. J. P. V. D. Balsdon, M.A.,
Fellow of Exeter College, Oxford; Professor Edouard Perroy,
Professor of Mediaeval History at the Sorbonne; Mr. G. Stephen-
son, B.A., Oxford; The Rev. R. Trevor Davies, M.A., Lecturer
in Modern History, Oxford, and my friend and publisher Mr.
Douglas Jerrold, who has given me unstinting assistance over
many years and whose advice has been invaluable to me. In
addition, I wish to tend my grateful thanks to Mr. Anthony S. F.
Rippon, who spent infinite trouble in preparing the typescript
for the press. While it would be difficult to exaggerate the value
of the assistance I have received from all those I have mentioned,
I am alone responsible for the text as it stands and for such errors
as it may contain.

*Crowborough,*                                            J. F. C. FULLER.
  *September,* 1953.

# The rise of imperialism

The wars discussed in this book may be divided into three geographical groups: those which from the earliest times to the battle of Lepanto, in 1571, were mostly fought in the Mediterranean lands and south-western Asia; those which from then on to the battle of Waterloo were for the most part fought in the lands bordering or dependent upon the Atlantic, and those which since 1815, because of the progress of industry, science, and locomotion, have claimed increasingly the whole world for their stage.

In the first group, the supreme political event was the emergence of the Roman Empire; in the second, of the British Empire, and in the third it has still to appear. That it will run true to precedent and assume the form of yet another imperialism would seem probable. And because to-day the only two great war-powers left in the world are the United States and Russia, should, in the conflicts of to-morrow, one or the other gain supremacy, then the next empire is likely to be global. Kant suggests this in his treatise on *Perpetual Peace* (*Zum Ewigen Frieden*): wars, according to him, tend in the long run to unite the human race, because grouping lessens their incidence. It would appear that though Nature's goal is concord, her driving force is discord. Thus, the tribe, by striving to remain a tribe, through inter-tribal warfare becomes a multi-tribal community or people. Similarly, a people, striving to remain a closed community, through inter-community wars becomes a nation, and a nation, striving to remain a nation, through international wars grows into an empire. So it comes about that the unit, at any particular time, through striving to remain single, inevitably is duplicated through absorption until ultimately the biological and economic frontiers of the globe are reached.

Though warfare is primeval, as the disappearance of Mousterian man after the arrival of Aurignacian man suggests, organized warfare would seem to have been unknown before the advent of civilization, which sprang from two roots: the discovery that certain grass seeds could be cultivated and that certain grass-feeding animals could be domesticated. From these roots sprouted two very differently organized human communities, the agricultural and the pastoral. The former first arose in the Nile valley and in the "Fertile Crescent" linking Palestine to the upper Euphrates and then followed that river to the Persian Gulf; the latter is thought by some to have been located mainly in the Eurasian steppelands of the Caspian region.

In the one case the first step taken towards civilization was the appearance of the village, a fenced area protecting the tillers of the soil and their stores of food; and in the other the domestication of the horse and the invention of the wheel and wagon. Thus arose two ways of life, the settled and the wandering, and throughout history they have been in opposition.

In time, and frequently to gain security from the attacks of the wagon folk, villages grew into walled cities, each becoming a small world of its own. The wall challenged the wagon, and defence becoming the stronger form of war, the civilization of the city men soon outstripped that of the wagon folk. Not only did the wall protect the growth of civilization, but also it forced a differentiation between weapons of war and the instruments of the hunt and the field. In their turn, weapons dictated the form military organization should take, the most primitive being that of the citizen phalanx. One such, a line of men six ranks deep, is to be seen depicted on the fragment of a Sumerian monument of 2900 B.C. Each hoplite is armed with bow and spear, wears a leathern helmet, and carries a square shield which covers his entire body.

In both civilizations the fundamental causes of war were biological and economic. The more prolific the herds and flocks, the more frequently had new grass-lands to be sought for: at any moment a drought might precipitate an invasion. Similarly, the more prolific the city population, the more food was needed and the more land was necessary for its cultivation. War, accordingly, was constant in both civilizations; for stomachs, whether animal or human, dictated its necessity and *Lebensraum* (living space) became and has since remained the one great problem in the struggle for existence.[1]

Plato discusses the city's problem in his *Republic*. In a conversa-

---

[1] *Cf.* Hobbes's remark, "And when all the world is overcharged with inhabitants, then the last remedy is Warre; which provideth for every man, by Victory, or Death" (*Leviathan*, pt. II, chap. 30).

tion between Socrates and Glaucon he shows that war is endemic in civilization. Starting with the city in its simplest form, he points out that as civilization advances the call for man-power becomes greater, and that the lands which were sufficient to sustain a primitive civilization are insufficient to support an advancing one. The gist of his argument is contained in the following extract:

*Socrates:* "Then we must enlarge our borders; for the original healthy State is no longer sufficient . . . and there will be animals of many other kinds, if the people eat them."
*Glaucon:* "Certainly."
*Socrates:* "And the country which was enough to support the original inhabitants will be too small now, and not enough."
*Glaucon:* "Quite true."
*Socrates:* "Then a slice of our neighbour's land will be wanted by us for pasture and tillage, and they will want a slice of ours, if, like ourselves, they exceed the limit of necessity, and give themselves up to the unlimited accumulation of wealth?"
*Glaucon:* "That, Socrates, will be inevitable."
*Socrates:* "And so we shall go to war, Glaucon. Shall we not?"
*Glaucon:* "Most certainly. . . ."
*Socrates:* "Then, without determining as yet whether war does good or harm, thus much we may affirm, that now we have discovered war to be derived from causes which are also the causes of almost all the evils in States, private as well as public."
*Glaucon:* "Undoubtedly."[1]

The first great clash known to us between the pastoral and agricultural civilizations occurred during the third millennium B.C. From the northern grasslands of the Caspian region came a vast outpouring of a warrior people, known as the Indo-Europeans, which continued for centuries. Horde after horde moved eastward, south-eastward, westward and southward. What set these migrations in motion is not known exactly. It may have been a change of climate resulting in periods of drought, or, as some historians have suggested, the adoption of a superior breed of horse combined with the invention of the sword.

In the West, many of the nomadic bands had crossed the Danube before the year 2000 B.C. to become the ancestors of the Greeks, Romans, and other European peoples; others, called Aryans, broke into two groups about 1800 B.C., one moving south-

[1] *The Republic of Plato,* trans. B. Jowett (1888), pp. 54–55.

eastward into India and the other south-westward into the mountainous lands to the north of the "Fertile Crescent." The latter group became known as the Iranian, and its two most powerful tribes were the Medes and the Persians.

About the same time as these incursions a people, probably of Semitic origin, known as the Hyksos (princes of the desert), appeared in western Asia and overran Upper Egypt. They brought with them the horse, until then unknown to the Egyptians. Their success mainly would seem to have been due to their horse-drawn chariots and superior weapons. The first may have been adopted from the Babylonians, into whose lands the horse had been intro-duced from the north in about 2100 B.C.

Though Upper Egypt put up a stout resistance to the Hyksos, it was from Thebes (Karnak and Luxor) in Lower Egypt that a national revolt against them began, to end in their final expulsion by Ahmose I (1580–1557 B.C.), founder of the XVIIIth Egyptian Dynasty. The old Egyptian militia was transformed during these wars into a well-organized army of two grand divisions, one garrisoned in the delta and the other in the upper country. The soldiers were armed with bows and spears and carried shields, but wore no armour. The quiver was introduced from Asia and "fire" was by volleys. Though cavalry was not yet employed, the chariot was adopted. Thousands of horses were bred in Pharaoh's State stables and chariot-making became an art.

Ahmose died in 1541 B.C. He was succeeded by Amenhotep I, and then by Thutmose I, both warrior kings who carried war into Syria, as far north as the Euphrates; but neither attempted to organize his conquests. On the death of the latter, his elder son, also named Thutmose, reigned for a few years, and was succeeded by his half-sister Hatsheput, the first great woman in history, who would appear to have married his younger brother – yet an-other Thutmose – in 1501 B.C. He remained no more than her con-sort until her death in about 1481 B.C. Her rule was so peaceful and unmilitary that when he succeeded her as Thutmose III,[1] the king of Kadesh headed a revolt of all the city kings of Syria and Palestine against him. In answer, on about April 19, 1479, B.C., after he had assembled his army at Tharu (Kantara), Thutmose marched by way of Gaza to Yehem (Yemma), a town on the southern slopes of the Carmel range, and arrived there on May 10.

Meanwhile the forces of the city kings, under the command

[1] He dated his reign from his marriage day and not from the death of his wife.

of the king of Kadesh, had occupied the fortress of Megiddo
(Armageddon) which lay on the northern slope of the Carmel

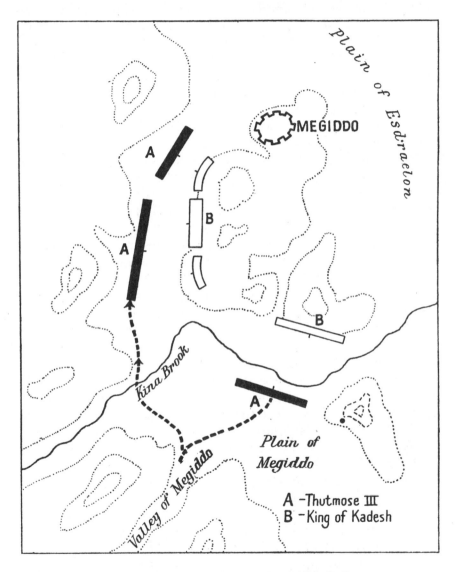

I. BATTLE OF MEGIDDO, 1479 B.C.

ridge and which blocked the main road from Egypt to the
Euphrates. Moving along this road on Megiddo, on May 14 Thutmose led his army through the pass traversed by Lord Allenby

3,397 years later. He debouched on the Plain of Megiddo, south of the fortress, and the next day he advanced with his army in battle order against the king of Kadesh, whose forces were encamped outside Megiddo. With the southern horn of his army resting on a hill south of the brook of Kina, and the northern pointing toward Megiddo, Thutmose, "like Horus armed with talons", in a shining chariot of electrum, led the attack, and in one charge he scattered his enemy, who fled headlong toward Megiddo "as if terrified by spirits". The men of Kadesh abandoned their chariots of gold and silver and, finding the city gates closed to them, were hauled up its walls by the citizens.[1]

Unfortunately for Thutmose, instead of assaulting the city when all was in confusion his soldiers pillaged their enemy's camps and, in consequence, Megiddo had to be invested. The siege was a short one; but when the city was surrendered it was found that the king of Kadesh had escaped. The spoil taken was immense. It included 924 chariots, 2,238 horses, 200 suits of armour,[2] the king's household furniture, and a vast quantity of gold and silver.

Immediately after the victory, unlike any of his predecessors, Thutmose began to reorganize the reconquered territories. First, he replaced the city kings by those of their leading nobles who were likely to prove loyal to him. He gave them a free hand in governing their cities as long as they promptly paid tribute to him. Secondly, he sent their eldest sons to Egypt to be educated in loyalty to him so that when they succeeded their fathers they would prove reliable rulers. He returned to Thebes in October when these things had been done.

Two years later he set out on his second campaign. In all he undertook fifteen. In the fifth, so that he might land an army on the Syrian coast and establish a base of operations against Kadesh and the interior, he built a fleet. In the sixth he disembarked his army at Simyra, a little north of Tripoli on the Syrian coast, and advanced on Kadesh, a fortress of great strength on the left bank of the Orontes, not far from Homs. After a lengthy siege he took it. In the seventh campaign he subdued a series of revolts to his rear, and in the eighth he invaded the country of the Mitanni,

---

[1] *A History of Egypt*, W. M. Flinders Petrie (1896), vol. II, pp. 107–109.
[2] "One excellent suit of bronze armour" and a "bronze suit of armour of the chief of Maketa [Megiddo]" are also mentioned (*ibid.*, vol. II, p. 110). These were coats of scale armour. Soon after they were adopted by the Egyptian kings and nobles (*ibid.*, p. 146).

an Aryan people who had occupied the region within the great bend of the Euphrates. Also he took Aleppo.

His fame by now had so spread that most of the local princes brought him tribute and even distant Babylon sent him gifts, as did the great Hittite Empire, which now for the first time is mentioned in history. What is even more remarkable was that his fleet was so feared that he was able to establish naval command over the eastern Mediterranean as far as the Aegean Islands, bringing Crete and Cyprus under his sway.

In his last campaign he destroyed Kadesh, which city had once again raised a coalition against him, and with its end the last vestige of Hyksos power disappeared. Sixteen years later, in the spring of 1447 B.C. and in the fifty-fourth year of his reign, he died. He was buried in the Valley of the Kings, and his body still survives in the museum at Cairo.

Breasted writes of him:

"He was the first to build an empire in any real sense; he was the first world-hero. He made, not only a world-wide impression upon his age, but an impression of a new order. His commanding figure, towering over the trivial plots and schemes of the petty Syrian dynasts, must have clarified the atmosphere of oriental politics as a strong wind drives away miasmic vapours. The inevitable chastisement of his strong arm was held in awed remembrance by the men of Naharin [the Mitanni] for three generations. His name was one to conjure with, and centuries after his empire had crumbled to pieces it was placed on amulets as a word of power. And to-day two of this king's greatest monuments, his Heliopolitan obelisks, now rise on opposite shores of the western ocean, memorials of the world's first empire-builder."[1]

By 1400 B.C., under Amenhotep III, Egypt reached the height of her imperial power, and Pharaoh having by then become an international ruler for the first time in history the conception of a single universal world god arose. He was called Aton, and his worship was established by Amenhotep IV, who succeeded Amenhotep III in 1375 B.C.

[1] *The Cambridge Ancient History*, vol. II, p. 87. The obelisks are in London and New York. In his *A History of Israel* (vol. I, p. 4, 1945) Theodore H. Robinson said of his reign: "Modern history properly begins with the year 1479 B.C., and treats of that epoch in the story of our race which we may call territorial imperialism. For thirty-four centuries, all political ambition, whether of the individual or of the race, has aimed at geographical extension, and at the subjugation of neighbouring tribes and peoples."

Amenhotep IV hated Amon, the god of Thebes, and all the other ancient gods. He changed his name to Ikhnaton ("He-in-whom-Aton-is-satisfied"), closed the old temples, and turned out their priests.

This religious revolution shook the empire to its foundations, and in the confusion Egyptian hold of the Asiatic dominions became little more than nominal.

Ikhnaton died about 1360 B.C. and was succeeded by his son-in-law, Tutenkhaton, who, as soon as he had ascended the throne, was forced by the old priesthood to reinstate the worship of Amon and to change his name to Tutenkhamon ("Living-image-of-Amon"). On his death, probably in 1354 B.C., anarchy followed, until, in about 1350 B.C., an Egyptian named Harmhab made himself Pharaoh and the old order was restored completely. During these disturbances Palestine was overrun by nomadic tribes of the eastern desert, among which were the Hebrews, and Syria was occupied by the Hittites.

In 1315 B.C., Harmhab was succeeded by Ramses I with his son Seti I as co-partner. Thus was the XIXth Dynasty founded.

Seti reorganized the army and reconquered Palestine, but was unable to shake the power of the Hittites in Syria; Kadesh on the Orontes and all Syria north of Palestine remaining in their hands. His son, Ramses II, succeeded him in 1292 B.C. and set out to regain Kadesh. He might have equalled the exploits of Thutmose III had not two things been against him. The first was that the old national Egyptian army had given way to a mercenary one, consisting largely of Nubians and men drawn from the northern Mediterranean lands. The second was that the Hittites were armed, in part at least, with weapons of iron, whereas his soldiers were still armed with those of bronze.

In the spring of 1288 B.C. Ramses advanced on Kadesh; fell into a trap; was surrounded; cut his way out; and, while the Hittites were plundering his camp, turned the tables upon them and won a Pyrrhic victory, for Kadesh remained in their hands. This battle was the last won by the Egyptian Empire.

In his old age—he lived to be over ninety, reigning sixty-seven years—Ramses became senile, and before his death in 1225 B.C. the Libyans and their allies invaded the western Egyptian desert and extended their settlements to the walls of Memphis (12 miles south of Cairo). With him the empire ended, and until the rise of Assyria, three centuries later, Egypt was hard put to it to protect her frontiers, north, south, and west.

Though the Assyrians first appear in 3000 B.C., when as a wandering Semitic tribe they settled at Assur on the upper Tigris and there founded a small city kingdom, it was not until the tenth century B.C. that their star began to rise in the western Asiatic firmanent. A century later, under Ashur-nasirpal II (884–859 B.C.), they set out on their imperial way and created a vast empire which, in the days of Shalmaneser V (727–722 B.C.) and Sargon II (722–705 B.C.), reached the border of Egypt.

The Assyrians were essentially a warrior people, for their army was the State. It was a highly disciplined and organized force, and for its age superbly armed. Already, in the tenth century B.C., it is known to have employed powerful battering rams, an essential in city warfare. These instruments were mounted in wooden towers, roofed and shielded in front with metal plates, and moved on six wheels. Under the roof was a platform for archers to pick off the defenders on the walls. Through contact with the Hittites iron weapons had been introduced.[1]

The army was composed of archers supported by spearmen and shield bearers, and the mobile arm was the chariot. But its main weapon was "terror". Cities were stormed, sacked and systematically demolished, and prisoners were often impaled or flayed alive.

Under Sennacherib (705–681 B.C.), Tarsus was plundered and Babylon obliterated; and his successor, Esarhaddon (681–669 B.C.), conquered Egypt from the delta to Thebes, sacking and burning its cities in 671 B.C. This conquest, when added to the lands already won, made the Assyrian Empire the most extensive yet seen in the world. But in her effort to establish universal dominion Assyria overreached herself. Her destructive wars obliterated the wealth of the countries she won and led to their constant revolt, so making necessary an immense network of garrisons. In the end her imperial commitments exceeded her power to hold them.

Meanwhile the nomads were on the move again: Aramean hordes drifted in from the desert; from the head of the Persian Gulf came the Kaldi, or Chaldeans, and from the northern moun-

---

[1] "The Assyrian forces", writes Breasted, "were . . . *the first large armies equipped with weapons of iron*. A single arsenal room of Sargon's palace was found to contain two hundred tons of iron implements. To a certain extent the rise and power of the Assyrian Empire were among the results of the incoming of iron" (*The Conquest of Civilization*, 1926, p. 173).

tains hordes of Indo-European peoples, led by Medes and Persians, swept down on the Assyrian homelands.

Egypt was then abandoned, but Pharaoh Psamalik I (Psammetichus), who feared an invasion by the northern barbarians, came to terms with Assyria and sent out an army to support her tottering empire. Its fall was imminent. In 614 B.C. the Medes, under Cyaxares, took Assur, and the Chaldeans, under Nabopolasser (625–604 B.C.), having conquered the Babylonians, linked up with them, and in 612 B.C. the two together stormed Nineveh and utterly destroyed it.

"Thy shepherds slumber, O King of Assyria; thy nobles shall dwell in the dust; thy people is scattered upon the mountains, and no man gathereth them.

"There is no healing of thy bruise; thy wound is grievous; all that hear the bruit of thee shall clap the hands over thee; for upon whom hath not thy wickedness passed continually?"[1]

Seven years later, the Chaldeans, under Nabopolasser's son, Nebuchadrezzar II (604–562 B.C.), who had rebuilt Babylon, met the army of Necho, King of Egypt, at Carchemish on the Euphrates, and routed it.

"They did cry there, Pharaoh king of Egypt is but a noise; he had passed the time appointed."[2]

Later, Nebuchadrezzar, the greatest of the Chaldean kings, overran Judea. In 586 B.C. he stormed Jerusalem, carried the Jews into captivity, and then advanced to the threshold of Egypt.

Though the fall of Assyria was swift and dramatic, once again the rule of a single sovereign had been enforced on a great group of peoples. In spite of Assyrian destructiveness, this gave increasing strength to the idea of a universal monarchy and no sooner had the empire of Assyria vanished than another people was ready to take up the task; this time neither African nor Semitic, but Indo-European—the Persians.

It is now necessary to leave Asia for Europe to trace events in the south-eastern corner of that continent during the centuries which followed the arrival of the Indo-Europeans; for it was their descendants who were destined to halt and to ruin the third attempt to create a universal empire.

At what date the first Greek tribes percolated into Greece is unknown. Professor Bury suggests that by 2000 B.C. "Zeus, the great Indo-European lord of Heaven, was probably invoked

---

[1] Nahum iii. 18, 19.                    [2] Jeremiah xlvi. 17.

throughout the length and breadth of the land".[1] Gradually their van, a people known as the Achaeans,[2] moved southwards into the Peloponnese, to overwhelm and mingle with its highly civilized Aegean dwellers. Later came a second wave of people, called the Dorians, who reached the Peloponnese by 1500 B.C. and subdued the Achaeans. Next, the Dorians took to the sea and conquered Crete and the Aegean Islands, and by 1325 B.C. we find Eteokles, who called himself an Aeolian, so firmly established on the western coast of Asia Minor that he entered into friendly relations with the Hittite Emperor, whose chief city was Hatti (Boghaz Keui) to the east of the river Halys (Kizil Irmak). Two generations later these relations were broken by yet another series of migrations of Indo-European peoples, the Phrygians from Thessaly and the Armenians from the region of Lake Van, who overwhelmed the Hittite Empire which, by 1200 B.C., disappears. A band of Phrygians also occupied the ancient mound of Hissarlik on the eastern side of the Dardanelles, and there built Troy, which in 1184 B.C., after a nine-year siege, fell to the Achaeans under Agamemnon, king of Argos. By the year 1000 B.C. the Greeks had gained possession of the entire Greek peninsula and of the whole of the Aegean coast of Asia Minor; the Dorians occupying the south, the Ionians the centre, and the Aeolians the north.

Between 1200 and 1000 B.C. the whole western world was in turmoil. Hordes, tribes, and peoples were moving in all directions to conquer or to escape conquest. Waves of fleeing Aegeans broke on the Syrian coast and swamped the Egyptian delta. Some, called Philistines, established themselves in Palestine, giving to that country their name. This period of chaos coincided with the introduction of iron weapons, and possibly also of the horse as a cavalry charger and not merely as a draught animal.

Those who settled in the conquered lands built villages in the form of groups of family hutments, which grew into cities. The peculiar topography of Greece, a small country split by numerous mountain ranges and possessing few land communications, led to the creation of separate city states, each becoming the only nation the Greeks ever knew. Each was a sovereign power, having its own king, its own laws, gods, and field lands. Within the city amity was the governing principle; without its walls, it was enmity.

[1] *A History of Greece*, J. B. Bury (1916), p. 6. In the 1951 edition, revised by Russell Meiggs, is substituted: "At some time near 2000 B.C. there are signs of a new people entering Greece. A new style of pottery . . . is introduced. . . ." (!)
[2] The common designation for Greeks in Hittite and Egyptian texts and in Homer.

Thus in Greece itself and along the coast and in the islands of the Aegean, hundreds of city states arose: self-interested communities and jealous of each other, they were constantly at war. Frequently, when the cities became overcrowded, they threw off colonies, and it was the shortage of good agricultural land more than the desire to conquer and plunder that made of the Greeks the greatest colonizing people in classical history.

In 750 B.C. the first Greek colonies appeared in the central Mediterranean, where the Phoenicians were already established. There were three main groups: the Euboean in Sicily and Italy; the Achaean in southern Italy, which was called "Great Greece"; and the Dorian in Sicily, of which the most important was Syracuse. Others were established in Cyprus, Lydia, southern Gaul, and eastern Spain, and soon the coasts of the Black Sea were girdled with them. This extraordinary expansion, which lasted until the middle of the sixth century B.C., would have made Greece the first great maritime empire in the world had the Greeks been a united nation under a single ruler. As it was, their colonies, well over a hundred in all, were no more than duplications of their city states, the existence of which depended on their military strength.

In the early days of the city kings, battles were little more than duels between selected heroes, as depicted by Homer, in which valour was the supreme virtue, valour and virtue being expressed by the same word. It is out of valour that European history rises; the spear and sword, and not, as in Asia, the bow and arrow, are its symbols. The bravest and not the most crafty are the leaders of men, and it is their example rather than their skill which dominates battle. Fighting is a contest between man and man more than between brain and brain. The spearman Achilles, and not Paris the archer, is the typical hero. Psychologically the *arme blanche* dominates the missile.

Later, as had happened in Egypt and Asia, the phalanx appeared, Sparta being the first fully to develop it. With its appearance, largely due to the progress in working metals and the consequent fall in the cost of armour, the nobles, hitherto the warriors of the city, gradually were ousted by the people. With armour at a reasonable price, each well-to-do citizen could pro-vide himself with a complete panoply, comprising a metal helmet, breast-plate, greaves and thigh-pieces, a round shield, spear, and heavy two-edged sword – the bow was seldom carried. This trans-formation was both levelling and democratic because it placed the noble and the ordinary citizen on a footing of equality in the field. "It is significant", writes Bury, "that in Thessaly, where the system of hoplites was not introduced and cavalry was always the kernel of the army, democratic ideas never made way. . . ."[1] Wherever they did, the development was one which was to become normal throughout history.

Incapable of ruling themselves, the people became easy prey to those who were capable of leading them and it frequently came about that a leader of an aristocratic faction would place himself at the head of the dissatisfied citizens, and having expelled his rivals by their aid would make himself sole ruler of the city. Such rulers were called "tyrants", a "tyranny" being an office and not a term of abuse.

By 650 B.C. tyrants began to appear in Greece and soon became so numerous that the following hundred and fifty years has been called the "Age of the Tyrants". They flourished in the Ionian cities and islands, in Corinth, Sicily, Euboea and Athens, but not in Sparta, where, to avert a tyranny, a dual monarchy was established, one king acting as a check to the other. The Spartans feared the growth of the tyrannies, and in the last half of the sixth century B.C. they established the Peloponnesian League. It was a loose alliance of the Peloponnesian states under the leadership of Sparta, coupled with the autonomy and territorial integrity of the members of the league: a kind of Monroe Doctrine. Although the members were free to fight each other, should anyone be attacked by a non-member all were bound to coalesce against him. By the end of the sixth century B.C. the league included the whole of the Peloponnese, except Argos and Achaea. Of all organizations it was the most permanent in Greek politics.

When the Peloponnesian League was being formed, an event occurred in Asia which in the years to come was destined to endow the league with a significance of overwhelming importance. The prelude to this event was as follows:

When Nebuchadrezzar was conquering Judea, Cyaxares, king of Media (634–594 B.C.), his recent ally, overran the lands east of the Halys. This conquest brought Media into contact with Lydia, and a war between the two countries followed. It was an inconclusive affair and ended in a peace cemented by the marriage of the daughter of Alyattes, king of Lydia (617–560 B.C.), and Astyages, the son of Cyaxares.

[1] *A History of Greece*, J. B. Bury (1951 edit.), p. 129.

Alyattes's eastern frontier was now secure and he determined to push his western frontier to the Aegean. To do this he set out to conquer Miletus (Palatia), the most important city of the Ionian Confederacy. A long indecisive war followed which was only brought to a successful issue by his son Croesus (560–546 B.C.), who reduced all the Ionian and Aeolian cities and compelled the Dorian cities to become subject to him. Next Croesus conceived the idea of raising a fleet to conquer the Aegean Islands. Then the above-mentioned event occurred – his brother-in-law, Astyages (594–549 B.C.), was hurled suddenly from his throne by an obscure Persian prince called Kurush, the Cyrus of the Greeks.

Cyrus was Prince of Anshan, a country subject to Media. About 552 B.C. he revolted against Medish rule. His soldiers were hardy peasants and expert archers, and it would appear that he was the first great captain to possess a body of really efficient cavalry. Within three years of the start of his revolt the whole of Media was his; a success largely due to the troops of Astyages changing sides.

This event alarmed Croesus. Because he feared that Cyrus would next cross the Halys he abandoned his Aegean project and went into alliance with Egypt, Babylonia (Chaldea), and the Spartans, to check the new conqueror. He crossed the Halys in 547 B.C., near Pteria (site unknown), and fought an indecisive battle with the Persians; after which, as winter was near, he retired to his capital, Sardes (Sart), and sent envoys to his allies to ask them to be prepared to carry out a combined advance against the Persians the following spring.

No sooner had Croesus retired than Cyrus, bent upon making the most of his interior position, advanced across the Halys and defeated the Lydian army in a great battle outside Sardes. Next, he took Sardes and made Croesus his prisoner. Leaving his general, Harpagus, to reduce the Greek coastal cities, which, because of their disunity, he did easily, Cyrus established himself in Lydia, then, in 540 B.C., marched eastward and defeated the Babylonian army under Belshazzar at Opis (near Ctesiphon). Two years later he took Babylon, the fall of which is poetically referred to by the prophet Daniel in his fifth chapter.

The surrender of Babylon brought with it the submission of all the countries from northern Syria to the borders of Egypt. Cyrus left his son Cambyses to prepare an invasion of Egypt, and organized his conquests, taking the title of "King of Babel, Sumer

and Akkad, and the four quarters of the world." Thus he claimed
dominion over all the lands of the East–Hyrcania,Parthia, Bac-
triana and Sogdiana–which had formed part of the Median
Empire. Of the campaigns which followed in these countries and
beyond them nothing is known, except that in his last one Cyrus
was warring against the Massagetae, a Scythian people in the
region of Lake Aral. During this campaign he was either killed in
battle or died in 528 B.C. His body was taken to Pasargadae
(Murghab) and buried there.

Three years after his death, Cambyses (528–522 B.C.) invaded
Egypt, and won so decisive a victory at Pelusium (at the eastern
mouth of the Nile) that Egyptian resistance virtually collapsed.
Next, he set out up the Nile to conquer Ethiopia, but because of
the difficulty of supplying his army, he abandoned the project.
Meanwhile the Greek colony of Cyrene submitted to him, and he
was declared king of Egypt.

When he died in 522 B.C., the Persian Empire stretched from
the borders of India to the Aegean, from the Black Sea to Nubia,
and from the Caspian Sea to the Indian Ocean. Four great kingdoms had disappeared–Media, Babylonia (Chaldea), Lydia and
Egypt. Such were the fruits of thirty warring years.

The heir to this vast and as yet undigested conglomeration of
kingdoms was Hystaspes, satrap of Parthia, but as he made no
attempt to secure the succession the throne was seized by a pre-
tender who posed as the dead brother of Cambyses. His reign was
a brief one: soon after his usurpation, Darius (521–483 B.C.), son
of Hystaspes, killed him and assumed the sovereignty.

The first years of his reign were spent in quelling widespread
rebellion, and once order was reinstated he began organizing his
empire. First, he divided the whole realm into twenty satrapies,
placing over each a governor, who was a true civil servant and
not, as hitherto, a mere tax collector. Next, he raised a powerful
Phoenician fleet to command the eastern Mediterranean and
built a network of roads linking the satrapies with his capital
Susa (Suster, Biblical Shushan). Posting-stations and inns were
established every four parasangs (about 14 miles), making possible
so rapid a postal service that a royal messenger took less than a
week to travel by relays from Sardes to Susa, a distance of some
1,600 miles. Also he reopened the Suez Canal, which existed in
the days of Seti I, and explored the Indian Ocean.

Darius placed the army on a divisional basis. Each division was

10,000 men strong and consisted of ten battalions of ten companies each, and each company of ten sections. His royal bodyguard, known as the "Immortals", also 10,000 strong, was exclusively Persian, as was his cavalry. Nearly all superior officers and garrison commanders were either Persians or Medes. His army in this way closely resembled the recent British Indian Army. Taken as a whole, Breasted speaks of Darius's imperial organization as "one of the most remarkable achievements in the history of the ancient Orient, if not of the world",[1] and Robinson states that "it proved to be the model for all latter empires",[2] and in particular the Roman.

With his empire secure from internal disturbances, Darius's next problem was to secure it against dangers from without–that is, to provide it with secure frontiers. Of these, the two more important lay in diametrically opposite directions–in the east and in the west. To establish the first, in a series of campaigns he pushed the eastern frontier beyond the Indus, so that that great river and the mountains to the west of it together would form a moated wall against invasion. The second problem was more complex. With the exception of the gap between the Caspian and the Hindu Kush, the weakest section of the Persian frontiers lay along the shores of the Aegean and the Propontis (Sea of Marmara). The reason for this was that the peoples on each side of these narrow seas were of kindred race, and in times of trouble were always liable to support each other. The only practical solution was to establish an ethnic frontier by pushing the western frontier westward until it included all the Greeks. This idea, it would seem, led him to the Danube in or about 512 B.C.

He assembled a fleet of possibly 200 to 300 ships and an army 70,000 strong,[3] bridged the Bosphorus in the vicinity of Chalcedon (Kadikoy), and having crossed his army over reached the Danube while his fleet, sailing up the mouth of that river, threw a bridge of boats over it near Galatz or Braila. Next, he pushed on north of the Danube, possibly to reconnoitre the country and to impress the Scythians with his power. How far he advanced is not known; but the Scythians, wasting the land, compelled him to turn back, and as he did so they attacked his rearguard and captured his baggage train.

[1] *The Conquest of Civilization*, p. 199.
[2] *A History of Israel*, vol. i, p. 5.
[3] These are the figures given in *The Cambridge Ancient History*, vol. iv, p. 212. Those of Herodotus are 600 and 700,000–800,000 respectively.

The Asiatic Greek detachment he had left behind to guard the boat bridge was incited by Miltiades, tyrant of the Thracian Chersonese (Gallipoli peninsula), to break it and thereby to cut off Darius from his base; but Histiaeus, tyrant of Miletus, persuaded the Greeks not to do so, for should Darius meet with a catastrophe the chances were that the Ionian cities would revolt, expel their tyrants, and become democracies. Darius crossed the bridge and withdrew to Sardes, leaving behind him his lieutenant, Megabazus, and a powerful army to reduce Thrace. This Megabazus successfully did from the sea of Marmara to the river Strymon (Struma), and though he failed to reduce Macedonia, Alexander, its king, acknowledged allegiance to Darius.

Thus opened the two hundred years' struggle between Greece and Persia, and though it was between two Aryan peoples it is the first recorded contest between Europe and Asia–the West and the East–a struggle which stands apart from the innumerable internal wars between European peoples and nations and which from that day to this has constituted the major war problem of Europe as a whole.

While the above events were taking place, equally important ones were perplexing the Greeks. In the year in which Cyrus died in distant Sogdiana, in Athens, Peisistratus, tyrant of that city, also died and was succeeded by his two sons, Hippias and Hipparchus. The latter was murdered in 514 B.C., and four years later the former made himself so unpopular that the people, helped by a body of troops under Cleomenes (540–491 B.C.) king of Sparta, expelled him and he fled to the court of Darius to seek assistance. To pay Sparta for their deliverance the Athenians were compelled to enter the Peloponnesian League and Sparta so acquired a certain right to interfere in Athenian affairs.

Freed of their tyrants, the Athenians, under Cleisthenes, a noble friendly to the people, established a democracy; but no sooner had Cleisthenes gained power than Isagoras, another noble and his rival, appealed to Cleomenes to eject him. Again the Spartan king entered Athens; but the people rose against him and he and his small army, and Isagoras, were blockaded in the Acropolis and forced to capitulate–a disgrace no king of Sparta had suffered hitherto.

Again in power, Cleisthenes set about reforming the Athenian state, and one of the first laws he introduced was that of ostracism, by which any prominent citizen considered dangerous to the state

ethnic western frontier, and in Hippias he saw a tool which would help him to do so. He determined, directly he had reorganized Asiatic Greece, to reconquer Thrace and Macedonia, which had been lost during the rebellion, and to restore Hippias to his tyranny as his vassal, after which Sparta and the rest of Greece could be swallowed piecemeal. His goal then was the occupation of Athens, which, when occupied, would isolate Sparta.

In 492 B.C., Mardonius, the king's son-in-law, was sent with an army to Thrace. He reduced Thrace, compelled Alexander, king of Macedonia, again to submit to Persia, and was on the point of advancing into Greece when most of his fleet was wrecked in a storm off Mount Athos and he was compelled to return to Asia. This set-back in no way affected Darius's decision, for at once he ordered another expedition, this time to proceed across the Aegean, but not by the land route, and as Mardonius had been disabled by a wound its command was given to Artaphernes, son of the satrap of Sardes, and Datis, a Median admiral. What its strength was is not known; perhaps 25,000 infantry and 1,000 cavalry.[1] As the entire force was moved by sea, it could not have been much larger.

What was the Persian plan of campaign? Here we must rely on conjecture, based on what happened and not on what was proposed, because the account set down by Herodotus is devoid of any clear strategical idea. Following Munro's speculations,[2] which in part are adopted by Grundy,[3] it was as follows, and it in no way contradicts what Herodotus says:

Through Hippias, Darius learnt that the Alcemaeonidae[4] in Athens were violently opposed to Miltiades and were now willing to reinstate him. Further, to obtain a pardon for the part Athens had played in the Ionian revolt, they were prepared to toe the Persian line. In other words, there existed in Athens what to-day would be called a powerful "fifth column" which favoured Persia. If the Athenian army could be lured away from Athens, and simultaneously a Persian force landed at Phalerum (Phaleron) to support the Alcemaeonidae, Athens could be carried by revolt instead of by battle. How to reinforce the morale of the con-

---

[1] *The Cambridge Ancient History*, vol. IV, p. 234.
[2] "The Campaign of Marathon", J. Arthur R. Munro, *The Journal of Hellenic Studies*, vol. XIX (1899), pp. 185–197.
[3] *The Great Persian War*, G. B. Grundy (1901), pp. 171–172.
[4] A noble Athenian family which played a leading part in Attic politics in the seventh, sixth, and fifth centuries B.C.

spirators in Athens, and how to entice from Athens the Athenian army, which kept them in check, were the two main problems the plan had to solve.

The solution of the former was sought in first subduing Eretria – which could offer little resistance–because its reduction would strike terror into the Athenians and drive them into the conspirators' arms. The solution of the latter problem was to land an army in the Bay of Marathon–25 miles north-east of Athens–and by threatening a land advance on Athens to draw the Athenian army out of the city.

In late August or early September, 491 B.C.,[1] all was ready to carry out this astute plan, and the Persian transports under escort of the fleet sailed from Samos to Naxos, and after operating in the Cyclides, reached Carystus (Karysto) on the south coast of Euboea (Negropont). From there the expedition sailed up the Euboean channel to Eretria, when the Persian aim became apparent to the Greeks. Determined to resist attack, the Eretrians sent an urgent message to Athens for help. Agreeing, but also realizing that single-handed they were not strong enough, the Athenians immediately sent a courier, Pheilippides, to solicit the support of the Spartans, and presumably, another messenger to the Plataeans. Pheilippides covered a hundred and fifty miles in forty-eight hours and arrived at Sparta on September 9. As Athens was a member of the League the Spartans at once promised aid, but pointed out that as the Carneian festival forbade them going to war until after the full moon on the night of September 19-20, they could not move until then.

Artaphernes, with part of the Persian army, laid siege to Eretria, and Datis, with the remainder, crossed the Euboean channel and landed in the bay of Marathon. Simultaneously the Athenian army, 9,000 to 10,000 strong, marched north from Athens under the command of Callimachus, the *polemarch*, accompanied by his ten tribal generals, among whom was Miltiades. They had not gone far when, hearing that the Persians had landed in the Bay of Marathon (Marathona), Callimachus wheeled to the right and gained the valley of Avlona where he encamped the army at the shrine of Heracles. There he was joined by 1,000 Plataeans.

When the Athenians arrived at the shrine of Heracles–somewhere to the north of Vrana–presumably the Persian fleet was

---

[1] The traditional date is 490. The date 491 was maintained by J. A. R. Munro. The argument for the correction is strong, but has not been universally accepted.

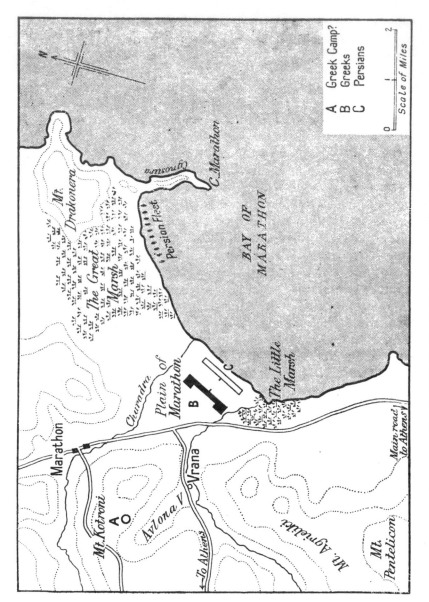

2. BATTLE OF MARATHON, 491 B.C.

at anchor on the western side of the promontory of Cynosura, and the army[1] was ashore, encamped under cover of the Great Marsh which flanked this section of the coast. To the south of it lay the Plain of Marathon, cut into two by a small river, Charadra,[2] and south of the plain was a stretch of swampy ground, known as the Little Marsh, lying between the coast and the foothills of Mount Agrieliki.

The position the Athenians had occupied was virtually un-attackable, and it must have been clear to them that because the Persians had not seized the passes leading from the plain towards Athens—namely, by way of the Little Marsh and the valleys of the Charadra and Avlona—they did not intend to make an overland advance on Athens. Their sole risk in not attacking the Persians was that while Athens lay undefended, treachery might work its will within the city. Otherwise there was every reason for them to delay an attack until the Spartans arrived after the full moon. The issue was that for eight days the opposing armies peacefully confronted each other, and it was not until the ninth day, when the fall of Eretria through treachery became known to the Athenians, that it was imperative for Callimachus and his generals to arrive at a decision. Clearly the reason was that as Artaphernes was now free to move, and were he to do so under cover of Datis's holding operation, he might slip round by sea to Athens. A council of war was assembled at which Miltiades pressed for an immediate attack. Because five generals were against him and four for him, he appealed to Callimachus, who gave him his vote and settled the question: attack it was to be. But no action was taken until it became known that Artaphernes was embarking his troops, and as it happened, the receipt of this information coincided with Miltiades's turn to assume tactical command of the army.[3]

It was probably on September 21 that Miltiades, the general of the day, drew up the Athenian army in order of battle, and it would seem that he must have marched his 10,000 or 11,000 men in two parallel columns, each about half a mile in length, and

[1] Possibly 15,000 strong (*The Cambridge Ancient History*, vol. IV, p. 243).
[2] The word means "torrent" or "stream".
[3] The whole question of command is obscure. The *polemarch* was titular commander-in-chief and the ten generals were his council. Tactics in the fifth century B.C. consisted in little more than drawing up the order of battle. From Herodotus it would appear that each general had the honour of doing so in turn. This in no way infringed the authority of the *polemarch* because it was no more than a question of drill which any general could carry out. It was as if to-day a colonel had ten sergeant-majors and employed them in rotation.

then, on entering the plain of Marathon, to have wheeled them outwards into line. The Persians, seeing this, immediately deployed their army between the right bank of the Charadra and the Little Marsh so that their front must have been parallel to the shore. The interval between the two armies is stated to have been less than eight stades, or slightly less than a mile.[1] Next, to prevent the Persian front overlapping the Greek, Callimachus, or Miltiades, reduced the Greek centre to possibly four ranks, maintaining eight on the flanks.[2] The right wing of the Greeks – the post of honour – was led by Callimachus; the Plataeans were on the left, and Miltiades, presumably, was at the head of his tribal regiment. Among those present was Aeschylus, the tragic poet.

Tactically Callimachus and Miltiades were faced by a difficult problem. It was that the bulk of the Persian infantry consisted of archers. At close quarters, the two generals could rely on their armoured hoplites breaking the Persian front; but the assault would have to be rapid directly arrow range was reached. Once the "beaten zone" was entered – that is, 200 yards in front of the Persian archers – the assault would have to be carried out at the double. For a mile long phalanx to maintain its dressing at this pace was impossible; disorder had to be risked.

As soon as battle order was formed and the sacrifices proved propitious, the advance in slow time began, to be followed by the double as the "beaten zone" was approached. Though what now happened is conjectural, it is common sense. It would be normal in the advance of a long line under frontal fire for the wings to sweep forward faster than the centre. This must have happened, with the result that the Greek front became concave, and as the centre was, presumably, four ranks deep, and the wings in eight ranks, gaps began to appear in the former through which the Persians broke, driving the centre back in rout. The Greek retreat in the centre, besides drawing the Persian front into a convex line, drew the Greek wings inwards and thereby reduced the original length of the front. This reduction automatically led to an inward wheel of the Greek wings against the flanks of the Persian line. The result was a double envelopment, very similar to that intentionally effected by Hannibal three hundred years later at Cannae, and the battle ended when the whole Persian army, crowded into confusion, in panic broke back to the ships and was pursued by the Greeks. A fight then took place on the

[1] *History of Herodotus*, trans. George Rawlinson (1880), VI, 112.    [2] *Ibid.*, VI, 102

shore, but Datis, at a loss of seven ships and 6,400 killed,[1] escaped.

Only 192 Athenians fell, we are told. These included the gallant *polemarch*, Callimachus, one other general, and Cynegirus, the brother of Aeschylus. The losses of the Plataeans are not recorded. The dead were buried under a mound which still marks the site of the battlefield.

When Datis hastily embarked the remnants of his army, Artaphernes must have been at sea, and his van may well have been passing the headland of Cynosura. At this juncture, a signal was flashed from a shield by someone on Mount Pentelicon.[2] Who held the shield and what the signal conveyed are unknown; but the later day explanation is that it was an invitation to the Persians to sail straight for Athens to support the conspirators.[3]

For the Greeks there was not a moment to lose. As soon as Datis had put to sea they marched for Athens, arriving there in time to prevent Artaphernes securing a footing at Phalerum. Artaphernes saw that his chance had gone, set about his fleet, and steered for Asia. That same evening the Spartan van entered Attica, and learning that the battle had been fought and won, marched on to Marathon to view the Persian dead.

Marathon was a remarkable battle, both from the point of view of Persian strategy, which was admirable, and of Grecian tactics, which were no less so. Though it wrecked Darius's punitive expedition it was in no sense a decisive victory. It did not end the contest for supremacy between Greek and Persian; rather it prepared the way for the conflict which was to do so. "It was", Munro writes, "a brilliant prologue to a grand drama."[4] For the first time in their history the Greeks had beaten the Persians on their own element, the land, and Marathon endowed the victors with a faith in their destiny which was to endure for three centuries, during which western culture was born. Marathon was the birth cry of Europe.

---

[1] Herodotus, VI, 117.                          [2] *Ibid.*, VI, 121 and 124.

[3] Regarding this signal, it would seem in all probability that the intention was to give it when the *coup d'état* was on the point of being carried out, but for some reason the uprising was delayed, and when the conspirators learnt that the Spartans were approaching they sent it out in desperation, for were the Spartans to go straight to Athens the revolt would at once be quashed.

[4] *The Cambridge Ancient History*, vol. IV, p. 252.

# CHAPTER I

# The Battles of Salamis, 480 B.C., and Plataea, 479 B.C.

"Now there was at Athens", writes Herodotus, "a man who
had lately made his way into the first rank of citizens: his
true name was Themistocles; but he was known more
generally as the son of Neocles."[1] More clairvoyant than most of
his contemporaries, he saw that Marathon was no more than the
beginning of the war with Persia and not its ending as many
supposed. He also saw that unless Athens built a strong enough
fleet to win the command of the Aegean her doom was virtually
sealed.

When great men appear, and Themistocles is among the
greatest, it frequently happens that events play into their hands.
This was so in his case. Firstly, a war between Athens and Aegina
showed clearly the need for a stronger Athenian navy. Secondly,
though Darius was more determined than ever to prosecute the
war against Greece, he was diverted from his purpose by a revolt
in Egypt. Thirdly, a rich bed of silver was discovered at Maroneia
in the mining district of Laurion, and though at first it was proposed to divide the bullion among the citizens of Athens, in the
end Themistocles persuaded the Assembly to spend it on the
building of one hundred triremes. Lastly, before Darius could
suppress the rebellion in Egypt, he died, and was succeeded by
his son Xerxes (485–465 B.C.). This gave Greece yet further breathing space; for not only had Xerxes to end the revolt, but at the
same time he had to establish himself securely on the throne.

Once order had been re-established in Egypt, as it was in 484
B.C., Xerxes began preparing for the now long delayed invasion
of Greece, and in spite of Herodotus's exaggerations the four
years spent in preparing it prove that the expedition was a
formidable one. Each satrapy was called upon to provide its
quota of fighting men. "For was there a nation in all Asia", writes
Herodotus, "which Xerxes did not bring against Greece?"[2] Sir

---

[1] *History of Herodotus*, trans. George Rawlinson (1880), VII 143.
[2] *Ibid.*, VII, 21.

Frederick Maurice estimates the strength of the levy at 150,500[1] and Munro at 180,000 combatants,[2] which are small figures compared with Herodotus's 2,641,610. Whatever the actual figure, it was far too large to allow of another approach by sea; the land route had to be followed, and this time the crossing into Europe was to be made at the Hellespont instead of the Bosphorus. To avert a disaster such as Mardonius had suffered in 492 B.C., Xerxes ordered the cutting of a canal through the narrow isthmus which connects Mount Athos with the mainland of Chalcidice. Also he ordered the river Strymon to be bridged and depôts to be established along the coastal road the army was to follow.

The bridging of the Hellespont between Abydus and Sestus was for its day a phenomenal undertaking; even to-day it would be no mean task. The first attempt failed, but the second, directed by the Greek engineer Harpalus, was successful. Two boat-bridges formed of triremes and penteconters (fifty-oared galleys) were built. They were linked by six long cables, two of flax and four of papyrus, and over the vessels was constructed a wooden roadway. In all 314 ships were used for the western bridge and 360 for the eastern.

By the winter of 481 B.C. the preparations ended. Xerxes established his headquarters at Sardes and sent heralds to all the Greek states, except Athens and Sparta, to demand earth and water—the symbols of submission. In the spring the advance began and the army set out for Abydus, where, according to Herodotus, 1,207 warships and 3,000 transports were assembled already. At Abydus Xerxes reviewed his army, after which it crossed over to Sestus, marched up the Thracian Chersonese, rounded the bay of Melas, and so reached Doriscus, where it was joined by the fleet, which later passed through the Mount Athos canal. Xerxes reviewed the fleet, then left for Therma (Salonica) where the expedition rested, the king going ahead by ship to explore the pass of Tempe, which lies south of Mount Olympus and north of Mount Ossa.

Before the events which followed are described, it is as well briefly to consider the art of war in Greece at this period, and, to complete the subject, to carry its development to the end of the fifth century.

By now the phalangial organization had reached its highest

---

[1] "The Size of the Army of Xerxes", *Journal of Hellenic Studies* (1930), pp. 210–235.
[2] *The Cambridge Ancient History*, vol. IV, p. 273.

perfection in Sparta, where by law the citizen soldier was required "to conquer or die." To him war was a festival and battle a competition of courage. Each Spartan soldier was accompanied by a shield-bearer, for his equipment weighed some seventy-two pounds. At the battle of Plataea, in 479 B.C., the hoplite had seven helots, or serfs, who formed the rear ranks, making the depth of the phalanx eight in all. These men clubbed to death the enemy wounded and attended to their masters should they be injured. To maintain line of battle the hoplites kept step to the music of flute-players.

In these ceremonial battles, tactics were limited to push of pikes, and remained so until light troops were added to the phalanx. Had it not been for the religion of valour there can be little doubt that this would have been done from the start. Yet, even so late as the Peloponnesian War (431–404 B.C.), except among the northern semi-Greek tribes, light troops were held in disdain. Nevertheless, in 426 B.C., the Athenians under Demosthenes were severely defeated by Aetolian javelin-men who, refusing to close, destroyed the phalanx from a distance. Through force of circumstances, this change was imminent, for early in the fourth century B.C. the Athenian general Iphicrates raised a body of true light infantry, called peltasts, who were trained for rapid movements. They wore a quilted or leathern jerkin and carried shields, javelins, and swords. In 390 B.C. he proved their worth by annihilating a Spartan *mora* (battalion).

It is strange that the Athenians, an intelligent people, should have been so slow in creating this essential arm, because for long past they had maintained a highly efficient body of naval bowmen, recruited from the second richest class, those not wealthy enough to keep a horse. During the Peloponnesian War these archers were so successfully employed in sea raids on Sparta that, according to Thucydides, the Spartans took the unusual step of raising four hundred horse and a body of bowmen to meet them.

At the time of the Persian invasions the sole true cavalry soldiers in Greece were the Thessalians, but they played no part in the defence of Greece for they were completely outclassed by the Persian cavalry. In spite of the mountainous nature of their country, it is strange that the Greeks should have been so backward in this arm; for twenty years earlier, in 511 B.C., the Spartans had experienced its value and to their cost, for they had been defeated by Thessalian horsemen not far from Athens. According to Delbrück, the whole course of the Persian Wars was determined by the Greek fear of Persian horseman.

The point to note in this brief summary of Greek warfare is that changes in armament were due solely to compulsion, because, throughout, valour disdained inventiveness. Only in siege operations do we find play given to imagination. At the siege of Plataea, in 429 B.C., the Plataeans would seem to have used fire arrows to burn the besiegers' engines; at the siege of Delium a gas attack with sulphur fumes was made; and, in 413 B.C., it would appear that the Syracusans defended their walls with liquid fire.

Long before Xerxes arrived at Therma, many Greek cities had sent delegates to a Panhellenic Congress to discuss his advance. It met at the Isthmus of Corinth under the presidency of Sparta. Many states were absent, the more important being Thessaly and most of the Boeotian cities.

The scheme of defence discussed was first of all governed by the fact that, as the Peloponnese was held by its states to be the "citadel of Greek independence", the defence of the Isthmus of Corinth was for them imperative. The second consideration was that were the isthmus alone held, all northern and central Greece would be abandoned, and once occupied by the enemy the isthmus defences could be turned by sea; therefore, to avert this risk it was also imperative to hold the enemy as far north of the isthmus as possible. The army and navy, because of their numerical inferiority, could only hope to do so, the one in the narrow passes and the other in the narrow seas. Except for the isthmus itself, the vale of Tempe and the pass of Thermopylae offered such localities for the army, and except for the strait of Salamis, the Euripus, or Euboean Channel, offered an equally good one for the fleet. Further, because the last mentioned narrow stretch of water flanked all practical landing places on the east coast of Greece between Tempe and Thermopylae, a fleet operating in it could cooperate with an army holding either Tempe or Thermopylae. Nor need the army be large; only strong enough to hold up the Persian land advance sufficiently long to induce the Persians to outflank the position held by means of their fleet and thereby to bring on a naval engagement in the Euboean Channel, where their numerical superiority would be at a discount. Were the Persians to be decisively beaten in these waters, then the isthmus would be secured against an outflanking sea attack.

When the above strategy was being discussed and Xerxes was

still at Abydus, the Thessalians appealed to the Greek Congress to block the vale of Tempe. This resulted in a Greek fleet carrying 10,000 hoplites in two divisions, one a Spartan, under Evaenetus, and the other an Athenian, under Themistocles, being sent through the Euripus to Halus in Achaea Phthiotis. From Halus, Evaenetus, who was general-in-chief, marched to Tempe, but when there he found that there were several passes and that he had not sufficient men to hold them all, so he returned to the isthmus. This retreat on the threshold of the war greatly discouraged the northern Greeks; also it reinforced the opinions of those members of the Congress who were for holding the isthmus only.

The situation was further complicated by the Oracle at Delphi. Impressed by the vastness of the Persian preparations, which Xerxes in no way attempted to conceal, it prophesied evil of the Hellenic cause: "Wretches why sit you here? Fly, fly to the ends of creation. Quitting your homes, and the crags which your city crowns with her circlet."[1]

This advice was given to the Athenians alone, apparently because the Oracle thought that Athens was the sole object of the expedition, and that, were she punished, the other states would be spared so long as they did not support her.

The Athenians were so depressed by these gloomy words that they consulted the Oracle for a second time,[2] when they received another utterance, ending with the famous lines:

Safe shall the wooden wall continue for thee and thy children.
Wait not the tramp of the horse, nor the footmen mightily moving
Over the land, but turn your back to the foe, and retire ye.
Yet shall a day arrive when ye shall meet him in battle.
Holy Salamis, thou shalt destroy the offspring of women,
Where men scatter the seed, or where they gather the harvest.[3]

Were these words ever uttered? If so, then it would seem that the Oracle had fairly accurately gauged the probability that a decision must be sought on the sea and not on the land. Be this as it may, soon after Evaenetus returned, the Congress appealed for help to the then greatest power in the Greek world: to Gelo, tyrant of Syracuse, whose fleet in size equalled the Athenian.

Though, according to Herodotus, Gelo would have been

[1] Herodotus, VII, 140.
[2] See *A History of the Delphic Oracle*, H. W. Parke (1939), chap. IX.
[3] Herodotus, VII, 141.

pleased to help, he was unable to do so, for he was threatened by an impending Carthaginian invasion of Sicily on a vast scale.

Here an interesting question intrudes. Were the Persian and Carthaginian invasions parts of one combined operation aimed at wrecking not only Greece, but the entire Greek world?

According to Diodorus, Xerxes, "desiring to drive all the Greeks from their homes, sent an embassy to the Carthaginians to urge them to join him in the undertaking and closed an agreement with them to the effect that he would wage war upon the Greeks who lived in Greece, while the Carthaginians should at the same time gather great armaments and subdue those Greeks who lived in Sicily and Italy".[1] Grundy considers that this is probable; firstly, because the Phoenicians were both subjects of Persia and blood relations of the Carthaginians, and secondly, because each invasion would clearly assist the other.

The Tempe fiasco, coupled with the failure to obtain Gelo's help, compelled the Greek Congress to decide on one of two courses of action: whether to seek a naval battle in the Euboean Channel, which carried with it the holding of Thermopylae; or whether to stand at the isthmus and await a naval battle in the strait of Salamis. The Spartans urged the latter and the Athenians the former; but in the end the Spartans had to give way, for were Attica abandoned the Athenians might prefer to medize than see their country wasted, and were they to do so their fleet would pass into Persian hands and without it the isthmus would lose its defensive value.

So it came about that the Congress sent the allied fleet to Artemisium (Potaki?) which lay on the north-western coast of Euboea, and an army under Leonidas, the Agiad king of Sparta, to Thermopylae. The latter consisted of some 7,000 to 8,000 hoplites and light armed troops, and included the royal bodyguard of 300 Spartans. The former consisted of 324 triremes and nine penteconters, of which the Athenian contingent was 180 ships under Themistocles, and though the Spartan contingent, commanded by Eurybiades, numbered only ten ships, because he represented the leading member of the League he was given supreme command.

Although the disproportion between the sea and land forces indicates that the primary object was a naval battle, the holding

[1] *Diodorus Siculus*, trans. C. H. Oldfather (1946), XI, 2.

of Thermopylae was of equal importance, because the halting of the Persian army was the most likely operation to compel the Persian fleet to fight. As we shall see, the weakness in the Greek plan was that Leonidas–like Evaenetus before him–had not sufficient troops to carry out his task. This was because the

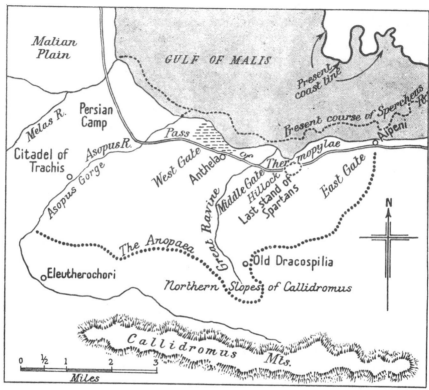

3.  DEFENCE OF THERMOPYLAE, 480 B.C.

Spartans insisted that the garrison of the isthmus could not be too strong.

The Persian plan was that the army and the main fleet were to arrive simultaneously before Thermopylae and the northern entrance of the Euboean Channel, the latter engaging the Greek fleet. At the same time, the Phoenician squadron of 200 ships was to sail round the east and south coasts of Euboea and to block the southern entrance of the channel: thus the Greek fleet would be bottled up.

On the twelfth day after the Persian army marched south from Therma, the main Persian fleet and the Phoenician squadron put to sea. Eurybiades heard of the squadron's movement and sent fifty-three Attic ships to Chalcis to hold the waist of the Channel. Meanwhile the fleet sailed down the east coast of the Magnesian Peninsula, and before the roadstead of Aphetae could be reached it was caught in a south-easterly gale—the *Hellespontias*—and, according to Herodotus, 400 warships were wrecked and provision craft "beyond count".[1]

Eurybiades assembled a council of war to discuss the disaster, during which—following Diodorus—all the commanders except Themistocles favoured the defensive; nevertheless he persuaded them to take a contrary course, pointing out that that party ever had the advantage who, in good order, made the first onset upon an enemy in disorder.[2] An obstinate and indecisive fight followed, and the day afterwards news from Chalcis was received at Artemisium that the Phoenician squadron had been caught in the gale and for the greater part wrecked, and that the fifty-three Attic ships were returning. Probably they were back at Artemisium on the evening of the day of the battle.

The next day it was the Persian fleet which assumed the offensive. The Greeks ranged their ships in a crescent, with the cusps pointing to the land to prevent their flanks being turned, and at a signal charged the oncoming Persians. The battle at once developed into a close quarter mêlée; but again no decision was reached. A council of Greek admirals met after the engagement to consider a retreat. As they were arguing, a triaconter (thirty-oar galley) arrived from Thermopylae with the portentous news that the pass had been lost, that Leonidas had fallen, and that the Persians were marching towards Athens.[3] This left no choice but to retire, and under cover of darkness the Greeks sailed south for Salamis.

Before outlining the events which led up to this disaster, it is essential briefly to describe the pass. In 480 B.C. it skirted the southern shore of the Malian Gulf and was divided into three "gates", the West, Middle, and East. The first lay a little east of the mouth of the Asopus river; the third on the western side of the town of Alpeni, and the Middle half way between the two. To the south lay Mount Callidromus, over the northern slopes of which a track, called the Anopaea, ran from near the East Gate to close by a place in the mountains called Dracospilia and thence westwards to the Asopus gorge in the vicinity of the citadel of Trachis.

---

[1] Herodotus, vii, 190–191.    [2] Diodorus, xi, 13.    [3] Herodotus, viii, 21.

By way of this track the coastal road running through the three gates could be turned either from the west or east.[1]

On his arrival at Thermopylae Leonidas occupied the Middle Gate, and to secure his left flank he posted 1,000 Phocians on the Anopaea, not far from Dracospilia.[2] Soon after he had done so Xerxes entered the Malian plain and encamped his army west of the West Gate and the Asopus. There he remained for four days, expecting, so Herodotus says, that the vastness of his army would frighten the Greeks away; but it seems more probable that he was waiting to give his fleet time to win a naval battle and then to turn the Greek position.

On the fifth day he launched his first assault against the Middle Gate; but only to find that his unarmoured men were no match for armoured. The next day the assault was repeated, and again it was beaten back. The Persian king's position was now becoming critical. Neither his army nor his fleet could force a passage, and we may assume that the supply of the former was running short. At this juncture, had the Greeks numbered 16,000 men instead of 8,000 the probabilities are that Xerxes would have been forced to retreat, and had he done so it is more than likely that the Greek fleet would have attacked all out.

Xerxes was at a loss what to do when a man of Malis, Ephialtes, told him "of the pathway which led across the mountains of Thermopylae".[3] Xerxes saw the possibility of turning the Middle Gate by moving along this path and sent Hydarnes and the Immortals at "about the time of the lighting of the lamps"[4] to make the attempt. They marched all night and at daybreak surprised the Phocian detachment near Dracospilia and drove it into the mountains; after which Hydarnes pushed on. Some time later, scouts—presumably Phocians—reached Leonidas and told him of the disaster. What next happened is obscure. Grundy's reconstruction is that Leonidas divided his army into two divisions. Keeping the Spartans, Thebans, and Thespians at the Middle Gate, he sent the rest back "to seize the forest path before the Persians had time to debouch from it in any strength"[5] so that his line of communications might be kept open. What occurred after this is unknown, but it would seem that either the rear half of the army arrived too late to stop the Persians or took panic and re-

---

[1] This track has been discussed by nearly every historian of the campaign and few agree on its location.
[2] The *Cambridge Ancient History* (vol. IV, p. 296) suggests at Eleutherochori.
[3] Herodotus VII, 213.   [4] *Ibid.*, VII, 215.   [5] *The Great Persian War*, p. 309.

treated through the East Gate to Elataea. Whatever happened, Leonidas was soon after attacked in front and rear, and, scorning surrender, fell fighting. Thus the pass was cleared for the Persians and the road to Athens was opened.

At once Xerxes struck south to impose his will on the Athenians and Spartans and to end the war in triumph. His universal kingship demanded nothing less, and nothing now seemed to stand in his way to prevent him adding the whole Grecian peninsula to his empire.

In Athens consternation reigned. Its citizens expected to see their Peloponnesian allies march into Boeotia and there halt the barbarian descent. Instead, they heard that they were still busily fortifying the isthmus. Rather than surrender, they made the most heroic decision in their history. They stockaded and garrisoned the Acropolis, evacuated Athens and Attica, and transported their families to Aegina, Salamis, and Troezen.

In spite of the confusion that this migration must have caused, and in spite of Spartan self-interest, Themistocles still held the ace of trumps—the Athenian fleet. If the defence of Thermopylae had depended on the fleet, doubly now did the defence of the isthmus so depend. But how should the fleet act? At Artemisium, and more particularly in the second naval battle, the error had been to engage a numerically superior enemy in open water. As he was bent on not repeating this mistake, Themistocles's thoughts now fixed on the strait of Salamis. But, as Grundy points out: ". . . if the Persians chose to ignore the Greek fleet at Salamis, and to sail straight to the Isthmus, the situation would be dangerous to the last degree."[1] Therefore, how to induce the Persians to attack at his chosen point became the heart of Themistocles's problem.

The island of Salamis lies to the south of the bay of Eleusis, which is approached from the west and east by two narrow channels: the one between Salamis and Megara and the other between the promontory of Cynosura and the mouth of the Piraeus. The latter is separated by the island of Psyttaleia into two sub-channels, the western being half a mile in width and the eastern a little more than three-quarters of a mile.

To persuade the Persians to carry out the same manœuvre they attempted at Artemisium—namely, to bottle up the Greek fleet and to capture rather than to destroy it—Themistocles took the tremendous risk of leaving the channel between Salamis and

[1] Herodotus, p. 352.

4

Megara unguarded. For the defence of the two eastern sub-channels he could rely on 366 triremes and seven penteconters.[1]

For a moment we will look at this great man through the eyes of Thucydides. He says:

". . . Themistocles was a man who exhibited the most indubitable signs of genius; indeed, in this particular he has a claim in our

4.  CAMPAIGNS OF SALAMIS AND PLATAEA, 480–479 B.C.

admiration quite extraordinary and unparalleled. By his own native capacity, alike unformed and unsupplemented by study, he was at once the best judge in those sudden crises which admit of little or of no deliberation, and the best prophet of the future, even to its most distant possibilities. An able theoretical expositor of all that came within the sphere of his practice, he was not

---

[1] Herodotus, p. 354.

without the power of passing an adequate judgement in matters in which he had no experience. He could also excellently divine the good and evil which lay hid in the unseen future. In fine, whether we consider the extent of his natural powers, or the slightness of his application, this extraordinary man must be allowed to have surpassed all others in the faculty of intuitively meeting an emergency."[1]

While Themistocles planned, Xerxes marched. He reached Athens, lay siege to the Acropolis, took it after a severe fight, and slaughtered its defenders. This seemingly unexpected disaster threw the crews of the Greek fleet into a panic which precipitated a council of war. But the alarm was so great that some of the captains "did not even wait for the council to come to a vote, but embarked hastily on board their vessels, and hoisted sail as though they would take flight immediately".[2] Themistocles heard of this and persuaded Eurybiades to "quit his ship and again collect the captains to council".[3] Then Themistocles spoke as follows:

"With thee it rests, O Eurybiades! to save Greece, if thou wilt only hearken unto me, and give the enemy battle here, rather than yield to the advice of those among us, who would have the fleet withdraw to the Isthmus. Hear now, I beseech thee, and judge between the two courses. At the Isthmus thou wilt fight in the open sea, which is greatly to our disadvantage. . . . The land and sea force of the Persians will advance together, and thy retreat will but draw them towards the Peloponnese, and so bring all Greece into peril. If, on the other hand, thou doest as I advise, these are the advantages which thou wilt so secure: in the first place, as we shall fight in a narrow sea with a few ships against many, if the war follows the common course, we shall gain a great victory; for to fight in a narrow space is favourable to us—in an open sea, to them. . . . Nay, that very point by which ye set most store, is secured as much by this course as by the other; for whether we fight here or at the Isthmus, we shall equally give battle in defence of the Peloponnese. . . . When men counsel reasonably, reasonable success ensues; but when in their counsels they reject reason, God does not choose to follow the wanderings of human fancies."

He was opposed by Adeimantus the Corinthian, who called on

[1] *The History of the Peloponnesian War by Thucydides*, trans. Richard Crawley (1874), I, 138.
[2] Herodotus, VIII, 56.    [3] *Ibid.*, VIII, 58.

Eurybiades to reject Themistocles's plan. Turning to Eurybiades, Themistocles then played his ace of trumps:

" 'If thou wilt stay here and behave like a brave man', he said, 'all will be well. . . . If not, we will take our families on board and go, just as we are, to Siris (? Torre di Senna), in Italy, which is ours from of old. . . . You then, when you have lost allies like us, will hereafter call to mind what I have now said.'

"At these words. . . . Eurybiades changed his determination . . . because he feared that if he withdrew the fleet to the Isthmus, the Athenians would sail away, and knew that without the Athenians the rest of their ships could be no match for the fleet of the enemy. He therefore decided to remain, and give battle at Salamis."[1]

The next day, September 22, 480 B.C., the eve of the battle, Aeschylus, who was present at it, relates that a message came to Xerxes from the Greek fleet. In Lewis Campbell's translation it reads:

> Let but the shades of gloomy Night come o'er
> The Hellenes will not bide, but, each his way,
> Manning the benches with a rush, will seek
> By covert flight to save themselves alive.[2]

When he received the message–probably during the early afternoon–Xerxes, who had already ordered his fleet to put to sea, cancelled the order and postponed the movement until nightfall. Who sent the message and why? The story, as given by Herodotus, is as follows:

There was so much dissatisfaction with Eurybiades's decision to fight at Salamis that a third council of war assembled on the morning of September 22 at which the same old subject was again discussed. But "Themistocles, when he saw that the Peloponnesians would carry the votes against him, went out secretly from the council, and, instructing a certain man what he should say, sent him on board a merchant ship to the fleet of the Medes". And this is what the messenger said to Xerxes:

"The Athenian commander has sent me to you privily, without the knowledge of the other Greeks. He is a well-wisher to the king's cause, and would rather success should attend on you than on his countrymen; wherefore he bids me tell you that fear has seized the Greeks and they are meditating a hasty flight. Now then it is open to you to achieve the best work that ever ye wrought, if only ye will hinder their escaping. They no longer agree among them-

---

[1] Herodotus, VIII, 60–62.          [2] Aeschylus (1890), "The Persians", p. 63.

selves, so that they will not now make any resistance—nay, 'tis likely ye may see a fight already begun between such as favour and such as oppose your cause."[1]

That Xerxes fell into the trap is understandable; for all along he must have heard from his spies of the dissensions in his enemy's camp. As has been mentioned, he immediately modified his plan, now deciding secretly and simultaneously to block the western and eastern straits of Salamis and so to bottle up the Greek fleet. According to Aeschylus, these operations were to be put into force at nightfall.[2]

The Egyptians' contingent of 200 ships was instructed to sail round Salamis to block the western passage, while the remainder of the fleet formed a triple line from south of the promontory of Cynosura to the Piraeus. The island of Psyttaleia was to be occupied by Persian troops. These movements, so it would seem, were completed shortly before daybreak on September 23.

While they were under way, oblivious of what was happening, the Greek captains were still arguing when they were suddenly cut short by the appearance of Aristeides, the rival of Themistocles. He had just come from Aegina, and calling Themistocles apart, he told him that "however much the Corinthians and Eurybiades may wish it, they cannot now retreat; for we are all enclosed on every side by the enemy".[3] Then Themistocles asked him to speak to the Council. This he did, but the Spartans refused to believe him and it was not until the arrival of a Tenian trireme, which had deserted from the Persians, confirmed what Aristeides had told them that they realized that their problem was solved and without their assistance.

Compelled now to fight, the Greek admirals hastily prepared for battle. First, it may be assumed, the Corinthian squadron was sent to hold the western channel against the Egyptians. Next, they drew their ships in line of battle across the channel between the town of Salamis and the shore under the Heracleion on the southern slope of Mount Aegaleos. It was in the following order: on the right, Eurybiades and sixteen ships; on the left, the Athenians with more than half the ships present; and in the centre the remainder of the allies.

As yet hidden from view, the Persian fleet lay in three lines. Soon it began to break into columns of ships in order to pass

---

[1] Herodotus, VIII, 75.                    [2] Aeschylus. "The Persians", line 364.
[3] Herodotux, VIII, 79.

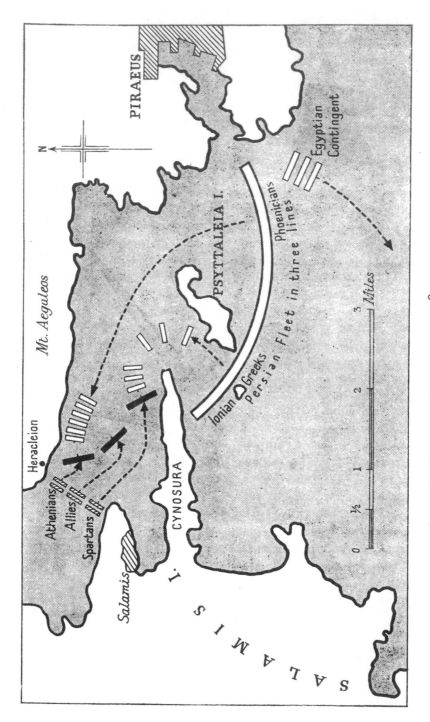

PIRAEUS

N

Egyptian Contingent

Mt. Aegaleos

Heracleion

Athenians
Allies
Spartans

Salamis

CYNOSURA

S A L A M I S   I.

SALAMIS I.

PSYTTALEIA I.

Phoenicians

Persian Fleet in three lines

Greeks

Ionian

0    ½    1    2    3
Miles

5. BATTLE OF SALAMIS, 480 B.C.

Psyttaleia, the Phoenicians on the right and the Ionian Greeks on the left. As soon as this manœuvre began, then either because of the number of the ships, the ineptness of their crews, or the roughness of the sea—possibly all three combined—the columns were thrown into confusion and were still in disorder when the Greeks rowed upon them and a mêlée began in which the heaviest and not the fastest ships held the advantage. Soon the leading Persian ships were forced back on those in the rear, doubling the confusion, while the Athenian ships, more strongly built, shaved close past their enemy's vessels, sheering away their oars on one side to render them unmanageable, and then hauled round to ram them amidships. On each Athenian trireme there was a boarding party of eighteen marines—fourteen hoplites and four bowmen.

The decisive action was fought on the Greek left. There the Athenians and Aeginetans, rowing close to the shore, and in full view of Xerxes—who had taken up his position on a hill north of the Piraeus to watch the surrender of the Greek fleet—turned the Phoenician right and drove it back towards the Persian centre, where the fighting was as yet more even, while the Greek right, having advanced too rapidly, like the Phoenician had been attacked in flank. Gradually the wave of victory advanced from the left to the right of the Greek line until the encirclement of the Persian centre by the Athenians and Aeginetans threatened a rear attack on the Persian left. The Ionian Greeks then began to fall back and their withdrawal brought the battle to an end after a hotly contested fight of some seven to eight hours.

There would appear to have been little or no pursuit; probably the Greeks had had enough. Psyttaleia was cleared of its defenders by Aristeides; the defeated Persians returned to Phalerum and the victorious Greeks to Salamis. There is no reliable account of losses. According to Diodorus,[1] the Greeks lost forty ships and the Persians 200, not counting those captured.

Tactically, Salamis was not a superlatively great victory, but strategically it was shattering. It knocked the bottom out of the Persian plan, which, for success, depended on the closest co-operation of fleet and army. It was not the loss of ships which was so serious for Xerxes, it was the loss of prestige. The one could be replaced, the other could not be in a conglomerate empire held together by the autocracy of its universal monarch. It was a loss

[1] Diodorus, XI, 19.

which heralded revolt in the rear and more especially among the Ionian Greeks.

Up to the date of Salamis, Persian naval power had been supreme in the Aegean because of the number of ships the Persians could muster and because, since the failure of the Ionian revolt, the Persian naval bases along its eastern shore had been secure. Now they were no longer so; for the Greek triremes at Salamis not only shattered the Persian fleet but simultaneously shivered the loyalty of the Ionians to Persia. Though at the time it was not appreciated by both sides, Salamis spelt the end of Persian naval command of the Aegean, and without it the Persians were unable to maintain a great army in so poor a country as Greece. The vast forces they had carried there, as Grundy states, had now to be reduced to a point which enabled the Greeks successfully to challenge them in the field. As he says, "Salamis was the turning-point of the war. Plataea was the consummation of Salamis."[1]

The battle ended, Xerxes's all-mastering anxiety was for the security of the bridges over the Hellespont. He had lost his nerve and he magnified the danger: were they destroyed either by the victorious Greeks or by the Ionians, it appeared to him that his whole army must perish. So he at once sent his fleet back to Asia to hold the eastern coast of the Aegean, and a few days after he set out northward with his army.

Meanwhile the Greeks, seeing the Persian army in position, supposed that the Persian navy was still at Phalerum, and it would appear that not until the army began to withdraw did they set out to make certain. They found that the fleet had gone, and failing to catch up with any Persian ships, they proceeded no farther than the island of Andros, where they disembarked and held a council of war. Themistocles proposed that they should sail on to the Hellespont and destroy the bridges. But this suggestion was opposed by Eurybiades, for were it carried out the Persian army would be cut off from Asia, and, in consequence, if only to live, it would waste all Greece. As the majority declared itself of the same mind the project was abandoned.

When he found that the Greek navy was inactive, it would seem that Xerxes regained his nerve. He now realized that to withdraw the whole army from Greece would be nearly as calamitous as were it to perish there—for it would be an acknowledgement of so overwhelming a defeat that the very foundations of his empire

[1] *The Great Persian War* .p. 407.

would be upheaved – and decided to hold on to Greece. He left Mardonius and Artabazus, the one in Thessaly and the other in Thrace and Macedonia, with one part of the army, for in those countries supplies had been accumulated and the lines of communication with Asia were short, and with the other part he withdrew over the Hellespont to be in a position to suppress any rebellion that might break out.

According to Herodotus, 300,000 of the best troops in the Persian army were left with Mardonius, and though this is an exaggerated number,[1] whatever the actual figure was it was sufficient to enable Mardonius to renew the offensive whenever he chose. But as the Persian fleet had been withdrawn this did not solve the problem of the isthmus. That this was apparent to him is clear; for instead of advancing on it he attempted to turn the never ceasing discussions within and between the Greek city states to his advantage.

In Athens the year 479 B.C. opened with a new board of generals. Themistocles – we do not know for what reason – had not been re-elected, but two of his political opponents, Aristeides and Xanthippus, had been. This was fortunate for Mardonius because their past suggested that they would prefer a reconciliation with the Persians to an alliance with Sparta. Could he but win them over, the problem of the isthmus would be solved.

In the early summer of 479 B.C. he sent Alexander of Macedonia to the Athenians with an offer of a free pardon for the past and an alliance with Persia on equal terms. This became known to the Spartans, who at once took alarm, and the Athenians agreed to reject the offer on the understanding that the Spartans would join them in an offensive against the common enemy.

Mardonius then began stirring up trouble within the Peloponnese. Knowing that the Argives were hostile to the Spartans, he intrigued with them to attack the latter so that when the two were engaged he might suddenly march down from the north and carry the isthmus by a *coup de main*. The plot miscarried.

Mardonius then returned to a modified edition of his first plan. This time it was to bring the Spartans into the open by putting pressure on the Athenians. On his way down from Thessaly, he changed his direction accordingly and marched on Athens, at the same time sending an envoy to Salamis to reopen negotiations with the Athenians in the hope of alarming the Spartans. It succeeded

[1]Munro, in *The Cambridge Ancient History* (vol. IV, p. 317), suggests 120,000.

in doing so; Aristeides at once sent representatives to Sparta urging immediate action should the Spartans wish to retain the loyalty of the Athenians. The result of the threat was that after considerable delay a field army of 5,000 Spartan hoplites and 35,000 armed helots was sent to the isthmus under the command of Pausanias, regent for Pleistarchus, the young Spartan king. Mardonius, who had thus far refrained from damaging Athens, then fired the city and withdrew to Boeotia to draw the Spartans and their allies into country more suitable for his cavalry to operate in.

When he arrived at the isthmus, probably in July, Pausanias first assembled the Peloponnesian contingents there, and then passed over to Eleusis, where Aristeides joined him with 8,000 hoplites and a considerable body of archers. From Eleusis he marched to Erythrae (site uncertain) where from the northern foot-hills of Cithaeron, he could view Mardonius's stockaded camp on the river Asopus.

Though the Greek position was unsuited for cavalry to operate against, the ground being hilly and broken, Mardonius, eager to attack his enemy before he could be reinforced, launched the whole of his cavalry, under Masistius, against the Greeks, and with disastrous results. Masistius was unhorsed by an Athenian arrow and then killed. A fierce fight for his body followed in which the Persians were worsted, and then withdrew.

Though the action was little more than a big skirmish it had important tactical results. The Persians were taught the lesson that on broken hilly ground it does not pay cavalry to chance a fight at close quarters with close-ordered heavy infantry. But the Greeks were so elated by their success that they made the error of assuming that they could defeat cavalry on any ground. As we shall see, the results were that in the next operation the Persians were over-cautious and the Greeks over-bold.

The success against the Persian cavalry, the lack of an adequate supply of water at Erythrae, and, seemingly, the difficulty of assuming an offensive against the Persian right wing, which if turned would lay bare Mardonius's communications with his base at Thebes, persuaded Pausanias, under cover of the hills and so out of view of the Persians, to move out of his good defensive position into the Plataean plain between Plataea and the Asopus. There he drew up his army, the Spartans on the right, the Athenians on the left, and the remainder of the allies—nineteen contingents–between the two:[1] in all, according to Herodotus, his army numbered 108,200.[2]

From his new position, so long as he struck before his enemy could conform with his move, Pausanias was well placed to manœuvre against the Persian right flank. So it is surprising to learn that once the position was occupied he did not attack at once. Whatever the reason may have been, Mardonius soon discovered his opponents' change of position, drew his army out of its stockaded camp, and brought it into parallel order on the opposite (northern) bank of the Asopus–directly facing the Greeks. On the left were the Persians proper, opposite the Spartans; the Asiatic contingents were in the centre, and the Boeotians and other medized Greeks on the right, facing the Athenians, Plataeans, and Megarians.

For eight days, so Herodotus states, the two armies faced each other inactively, and the question "why" has been asked.[3] There are two probable reasons: (1) that the Persian cavalry had been so roughly handled at Erythrae by close-ordered heavy infantry that Mardonius was waiting for his enemy to move over the Asopus which, even if half-dry, would have disordered the Greek ranks before he attacked, and (2) that as Pausanias was now unable to turn the Persian right flank, and as he had won his last success when in a stationary position and so in perfect battle order, he was waiting for his enemy to move first.

At length, on the eighth day, a Theban, Timagenidas, advised Mardonius to keep a watch on the passes of Cithaeron, telling him how supplies of men kept coming in day after day, and assuring him that he might cut off large numbers. These were the passes through which Pausanias's supply columns moved, the most important being that of Dryoscephalae ("oaks-heads"). The advice was accepted and a cavalry raid was made on Dryoscephalae with immediate success: a Greek provision train of 500 pack animals was caught in the pass and destroyed, not a man or beast being spared.

What the raid actually showed was that Pausanias's position was untenable; possessing no cavalry, he could only protect his line of communication by falling back on the passes. Further, it

---

[1] For the complete order of battle see Herodotus, IX, 28.

[2] *Ibid.*, IX, 30. Munro's estimate is about 80,000, of whom about two-fifths were hoplites (*The Cambridge Ancient History*, vol. IV, p. 324).

[3] See *The Cambridge Ancient History*, vol. IV, p. 331. Is it however a coincidence that an eight-day pause also occurred at Marathon?

woke up the Persians, for during the next two days much skirmishing between the armies took place, and to the disadvantage of the Greeks, whose bowmen were vastly outnumbered by those of their enemy.

Impatient now to take advantage of his enemy's intolerable position, and probably also because the supply of his army—particularly of his cavalry—was becoming increasingly difficult, Mardonius contemplated a full-out offensive in spite of Artabazus's suggestion that he should withdraw to Thebes and bribe the Greek commanders. Having more faith in his army than in his colleague, Mardonius decided on a cavalry attack; but this time at long range with missiles, and not at close quarters.

At the time, the Greeks were in line south of the Asopus, the Athenians on the left and the allies in the centre. Both depended for their water on the river, whereas on the right the Spartans drew theirs from the spring of Gargaphia. The river supply was a precarious one, because the Asopus flowed between the Greeks and Persians; but the spring was secure enough, for it lay in rear of the Spartan wing. When the Persian cavalry advanced, so formidable a missile attack was opened on the Athenians and allies that both were cut off from the Asopus and were compelled to draw their water from Gargaphia. Next, the Spartans must have been driven back, though this is not actually stated, and before they could advance again the Persians "choked up and spoiled" the spring, with the result that when it was retaken it was found to be useless.[1]

The position of the Greeks, which, since their communications had been raided, had become critical, with the loss of their water supply became impossible, and on the morning of the second day of the attack a council of war was held at which it was decided to move by night back to a position called the "Island", a tract of ground about one mile east of the ruins of Plataea and lying between two head streams of the Oëröe river to the south of Gargaphia. "It was agreed likewise", writes Herodotus, "that after they had reached the place . . . they should dispatch, the very same night, one half of their army . . . to relieve those whom they had sent to procure provisions, and who were now blocked up in that region."[2]

From this and what actually happened, it would appear that the withdrawal was planned as follows: The whole army to with-

---

[1] Herodotus, IX 49.　　　　　　　　　　[2] *Ibid.*, IX, 51.

draw to Mount Cithaeron, where it would cover the three passes:
Plataea–Megara Pass; Plataea–Athens Pass, and Athens–Thebes
Pass (Dryoscephalae). It was complicated by three factors. The
first was that the provision parties were still besieged and had to
be relieved *at the earliest moment*. The second, that the movement
had to be carried out by night and so would be slow, too slow for
the left and centre of the army to reach Mount Cithaeron and to

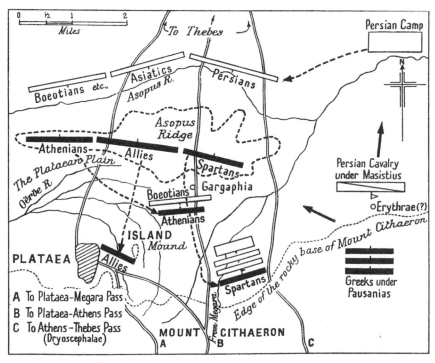

6. BATTLE OF PLATAEA, 479 B.C.

form line before daylight. Because of this it was decided to send
back the right wing (Spartans)–the closest to the passes–to
relieve the besieged provision parties, and at the same time to take
up an intermediate position on the Island with the centre and
left wing. Tactically this position must have stretched from the
Citadel of Plataea to the Megara–Thebes road, a distance of two
miles–about one mile each side of the mound which marks the
centre of the Island. Now enters the third factor. Clearly the
simplest thing to do was to withdraw the centre (lesser allies) to
the east of the mound and the left wing (Athenians) to the west of

it; but this would have violated military etiquette, so the lesser allies were ordered to the new left and the Athenians to the new right. This meant that the Athenians could not withdraw until the lesser allies and Spartans had cleared their rear; they had to move last.

At the second watch of the night the withdrawal began. The Greek centre fell back to its position between Plataea and the mound and would seem to have accomplished its task in spite of Herodotus's strictures.[1] When he heard that the centre was in movement Pausanias ordered his right wing to withdraw, when one of his divisional commanders, Amompharetus–a typically stupid Spartan–holding that a retreat in face of the enemy was disgraceful, refused to budge. The upshot was that the best part of the night was spent in the customary Greek wrangling and it was not until day was breaking that Pausanias, leaving Amompharetus behind, got under way. Meanwhile the Athenians, who had been waiting for the centre to clear their rear, were further delayed by having to wait for Pausanias to do the same.

Soon after Pausanias had begun to withdraw, Amompharetus–the source of all these delays–found himself abandoned and set off after the right wing just in the nick of time, for as he caught up with it the Persian cavalry attacked. Unfortunately for the Spartans, the delay had prevented them gaining the hilly ground and they were caught on a gentle open slope in every way favourable for the Persian horse, whose aim evidently was to pin the Spartans down before they could gain the rocky slopes of Cithaeron and to hold them until the Persian infantry came up.

Leaving his right wing to move against the Athenians–still far behind–Mardonius ordered up his Persian infantry to support his cavalry, and behind them he set in motion the whole of his Asiatic centre. Pausanias saw that most of the enemy's army was moving directly against him and sent an urgent message to the Athenians to come to his aid. They were unable to do so because the Persian right wing was marching on them. Thus it came about that Pausanias and his men were left to face the bulk of the Persian army.

The Persian cavalry by adhering to missile tactics soon placed the Spartans in an intolerable position; and when the fight was in progress the Persian infantry came up, took over from the cavalry, and built up a "rampart of wicker shields, and shot from

[1] Herodotus, IX, 53.

behind them such clouds of arrows, that the Spartans were sorely distressed".[1] Now Mardonius made the crucial blunder, which was to cost him the battle and his life. Instead of leaving plenty of room in rear of his bowmen to give them space to withdraw and advance in again and thus to maintain an elastic tactical front, he jammed behind them the mass of his Asiatic troops and so rendered the bow-front rigid.

At length the omens proving propitious, or, in other words, when Pausanias saw that with the closing up of the Asiatics the decisive moment had come, he launched his counter-attack. His hoplites scattered the rampart of shields and drove the bowmen back on the Asiatics. A fierce contest followed. "The barbarians," writes Herodotus, "many times seized hold of the Greek spears and brake them; for in boldness and warlike spirit the Persians were not a whit inferior to the Greeks; but they were without bucklers, untrained, and far below the enemy in respect of skill in arms. Sometimes singly, sometimes in bodies of ten, now fewer and now more in number, they dashed forward upon the Spartan ranks, and so perished." Herodotus continues:

"The fight went most against the Greeks, where Mardonius, mounted upon a white horse, and surrounded by the bravest of all the Persians, the thousand picked men, fought in person. So long as Mardonius was alive, this body resisted all attacks, and, while they defended their own lives, struck down no small number of Spartans, but after Mardonius fell, and the troops with him, which were the main strength of his army, perished, the remainder yielded to the Lacedaemonians, and took to flight. Their light clothing, and want of bucklers, were of the greatest hurt to them: for they had to contend against men heavily armed, while they themselves were without any such defence."[2]

Thus "did Pausanias, the son of Cleombrotus . . . win a victory exceeding in glory all those of which our knowledge extends".[3] The day of his victory was in all probability August 27, 497 B.C.

Meanwhile, what of the Athenians? When they received Pausanias's urgent message they at once changed direction and started out for where the Spartan wing then was. But no sooner had they done so than the Boeotians and other medized Greeks swept down on their left flank and compelled them to form front against them. A stiff fight followed, which ended in the Boeotians being routed and driven in disorder towards Thebes. At the same time the

[1] Herodotus, IX, 61.        [2] *Ibid.*, IX, 62–63.        [3] *Ibid.*, IX, 64.

Greek centre, which had been holding the left flank of the Island position and which so far had been unengaged, seeing the enemy in flight, moved rapidly forward in two columns, and in the plain below, the left column was routed by Theban cavalry, losing 600 men killed. It was the only disaster the Greeks suffered in this extraordinary battle.

Of the casualties little is known. Herodotus says, "of the 300,000 men who composed the [Persian] army . . . no more than 3,000 outlived the battle", and that the Spartans lost 91 killed, the Tegeans 16, and the Athenians 52.[1] In his life of Aristeides, Plutarch says that in all the Greeks lost 1,360 men killed.[2]

Ten days after the victory the Greeks invested Thebes, and on the twentieth day of the siege Mardonius's base surrendered to them on terms.

On the day Thermopylae was being fought, according to Diodorus,[3] Gelo of Syracuse decisively defeated Hamilcar at Himera (near Termini), a victory which gained for Sicily immunity from Carthage for seventy years. Also the Greek fleet, which we last heard of at Andros, was not idle. Some time in the summer of 479 B.C., when an appeal was received from Samos that if the Ionian Greeks were supported they would again revolt, the fleet was ordered to carry war into the enemy's waters.

It was at Delos at the time under the command of the Spartan king, Leotychidas. When he sailed to Samos the Persian fleet retired to Mycale, where Xerxes had posted a considerable army under Tigranes to watch the Ionian cities. At Mycale the ships were beached and fortifications were built to protect them. Leotychidas rowed past the enemy fleet, disembarked his marines and hoplites some twenty miles from Mycale, marched upon the position and carried it by assault, the Ionian Greeks helping him by turning on the Persians. Leotychidas then burnt the Persian fleet–or found it burnt–and returned to Samos.

Next, it was decided to sail to the Hellespont to impound the bridging cables and to take Sestus, the key to the Thracian Chersonese and the Persian tête-du-pont in Europe. But as it was strongly fortified and the Spartans disliked sieges, Leotychidas returned home, leaving it to the Athenians under Xanthippus to besiege it. Though the siege was begun in the autumn it took the

---

[1] Herodotus, IX, 70, a worthless estimate.
[2] *Plutarch's Lives*, trans. Bernadotte Perrin (1914), XIX.
[3] Diordorus, XI, 24; Herodotus, VII, 166, says on the day Salamis was fought.

Athenians most of the winter to reduce the fortress through starvation. Artabazus, instead of coming to its relief, withdrew to Byzantium and crossed the Bosphorus into Asia.

Thus ended the first great struggle between Asia and Europe of which a full record has been preserved. And so far as war is concerned, the first thing which strikes us is that in the fifth century B.C., in all its essentials the art of war was almost as highly developed as it is to-day. Secondly, that the mistakes made during war are as common now as they were then.

To create a diversion in the central Mediterranean by stirring up the Carthaginians against the Sicilian Greeks shows that the Persians were fully aware of the meaning of grand strategy, and the Greek appeal to Gelo goes to prove that the Persians knew exactly what they were doing. Even should this diversion be set aside as uncertain, the combination of fleet and army leaves no doubt whatsoever that the relationship between sea and land power was as clearly understood as it is to-day, and not only by the Persians but by the Greeks also. Further, the administration of the fighting forces of both sides must have been of a remarkably high order; even should the army Xerxes brought to Europe have numbered no more than 100,000 men, that it was able to operate in a roadless country 800 miles from its Asiatic base is proof positive that its system of supply must have been superbly organized. And for Pausanias, in a mountainous country, to have maintained in the field an army of 80,000 strong—or even considerably less—was in itself no mean feat of administration.

In tactics, the mistakes made were those which have since pursued the soldier over many a battlefield, notably reliance on masses of semi-trained men, expecting that quantity can make good a deficit in quality, and a lack of appreciation of weapon power as well as the misapplication of weapons to ground and the tactical conditions of the moment. But above all, the whole war shows that the psychological factor, loss or gain of morale by the soldier and loss or gain of prestige by the supreme command was, as it still remains, the determining factor in war.

It was loss of prestige which not only checked the expansion, but undermined the foundations of the Persian Empire, and, like most empires before or since, led to its eventual ruin. Also it was the prestige won by the Greeks at Salamis and Plataea which started them on their astonishing course, for as Professor Bury writes: "Men seemed to rise at once to the sense of the high

5

historical importance of their experience. The great poets of the day wrought it into their song; the great plastic artists alluded to it in their sculptures. . . . The idea was afloat in the air that the Trojan war was an earlier act in the same drama, – that the warriors of Salamis and Plataea were fighting in the same cause as the heroes who had striven with Hector on the plain of Troy."[1]

With these battles we stand on the threshold of the western world to be, in which Greek intellect was to conquer and to lay the foundations of centuries to come. No two battles in history are, therefore, more portentous than Salamis and Plataea; they stand like the pillars of the temple of the ages supporting the architecture of western history.

[1] *A History of Greece*, J. B. Bury (1951 edit.), pp. 284–285.

# The struggle for supremacy within Greece

Though Salamis gained for the Athenians the command of the Aegean, it did not win for them full naval power. Their fleet had saved Greece from conquest, but it had not secured their city from invasion, which could only have been done had it been fortified and had the fleet been based on a near and strongly defended harbour. At the time, lacking both, strategically the Athenians had to appease Sparta, a situation Themistocles determined they never should be placed in again. When, after Plataea, the Athenians returned to the ashes of Athens, under his guidance they set to work to rebuild the city as a fortress and to develop the Piraeus into a strongly fortified naval base. In any case, because of ever-increasing oversea trade, the latter work had become imperative, for trade was essential to pay for the food of the rapidly growing population of Attica.

Because the bulk of their corn came from the steppes of the Ukraine, it was also vital for the Athenians to keep the Pontic route open. To guarantee this, under the inspiration of Themistocles, in the winter of 478–477 B.C., a naval league, led by Athens, was formed with the Greek city states of Asia Minor and the Aegean islands, the treasury of which was placed in the temple of Apollo on the island of Delos: hence the Confederation became known as the Delian League. Because the treasurers were all Athenian citizens, from the first Athens possessed the means gradually to transform the naval union into a naval empire.

Fully to establish the League, which was to become the rival of the Peloponnesian, it was essential to liberate all those Greek cities in Asia Minor and on the coast of Thrace still under Persian rule. The war with Persia was continued accordingly, the League taking the offensive.

This policy of expansion was opposed by Cimon, son of Miltiades, who favoured a stronger attachment to Sparta. He carried the Assembly with him, and about 470 B.C. Themistocles was ostracized. Next, he was accused of high treason, and to evade arrest he fled to Corcyra (Corfu) and later to Susa.

Meanwhile the war of the Delian League against Persia had

been entrusted to Cimon. First, he cleared the remaining pockets of Persians from the Thracian seaboard, and, in 468 B.C., at the river Eurymedon in Pamphylia, he overcame the Persian army and navy in a remarkable double battle by land and sea, in which his enemy lost 200 ships. This decisive victory won for the League a number of the coastal cities of Caria and Pamphylia.

Cimon's policy was to continue in alliance with Sparta; but the people were now opposed to this, and, in 462 B.C., he was dismissed and ostracized. Thus the anti-Persian Confederacy, which Athens had joined in 481 B.C., was ended to make way for an alliance with Thessaly and Argos, and the latter was Sparta's most powerful rival in the Peloponnese. War between Athens and Sparta now became certain and its outbreak was accelerated by the trade competition between Athens and Corinth and Aegina.

With the ostracism of Cimon, the democratic party found its leader in Pericles, son of Xanthippus, the victor of Mycale. Pericles held that it was more profitable to base political power on freemen he could cajole than on slaves compelled to obey his will. His overmastering desire was to build the Athenian Hegemony of which Themistocles had dreamed, and to transform Athens into a memorial to the victory of Greeks over Persians by making her the most beautiful city in the world. Of his many projects, probably the most important was the replanning of the Piraeus, which he laid out on the rectangular system now so largely favoured in modern cities. Equally important, he linked the Piraeus with Athens by a four and a half mile corridor protected on either flank by a fortified wall. This vast work was not completed until 457 B.C., and when it was, a naval base of great strength and including Athens was provided for the Athenian navy and merchant fleet.

The first warlike act came in 458 B.C. That year Athens wrested Naupactus (Lepanto) from the Ozolian Locrians to gain command of the Corinthian Gulf and to establish a stranglehold on Corinthian trade with Italy and Sicily. Next, the Megarians broke away from the Peloponnesian League and placed themselves under Athenian protection, which gained for Athens a strong outwork against a Spartan land invasion of Attica. Pericles had at his command at this time 13,000 hoplites, besides 16,000 troops to garrison the home fortifications, 1,200 horse, 1,600 bowmen, and 300 triremes fit for war.

War now broke out and Athens struck the first blow, an unsuccessful one, in Argolis, which was followed immediately by a naval victory in the Saronic Gulf and the blockade of Aegina by land and sea. Shortly before this siege was undertaken, Inaros, king of Libya, had raised an insurrection in Egypt, and hard pressed he appealed to Athens for aid. It was readily granted by Pericles who, having two wars on his hands, hoped by helping Inaros to compel the Persians to come to terms with the Delian League. Two

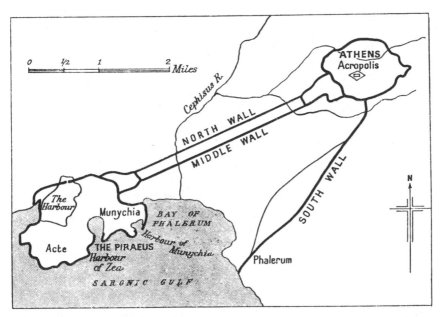

7.  FORTIFICATIONS OF ATHENS AND THE PIRAEUS

hundred sail were sent to Egypt and with their help Inaros captured the whole of Memphis, except its citadel.

The moment had come for Sparta to intervene, and to induce the Boeotians to enter the Peloponnesian League and to threaten Athens from the north, an army of 1,500 Spartan hoplites and 10,000 Peloponnesian allies was sent to Boeotia. After it had succeeded in its task, early in 457 B.C., on its return this army advanced on Athens and at Tanagra defeated an Athenian army sent out to meet it. Nevertheless, the battle saved Athens; for immediately after winning it the Peloponnesians retired to the isthmus. Two months later the Boeotians were defeated by the Athenians at Oenophyta, and, except for Thebes, the whole of Boeotia passed under Athenian control. Before the year was out the Long Walls were finished and the siege of Aegina brought to a successful issue. Thus the power of Athens reached its zenith: all the land from the Isthmus of Corinth to the Malian Gulf had been subdued, and north of the gulf Thessaly was still a nominal ally.

The tide of conquest turned rapidly. In 456 B.C. disaster overwhelmed the expedition to Egypt. Driven out of Memphis by the Persians, the insurgents were invested in the island of Prosopitis, which lay between two channels of the Nile linked by a canal. There they were besieged for eighteen months, and in 454 B.C. they were annihilated, the Greeks losing some 250 ships and 50,000 men. It was the greatest naval disaster the Athenians had so far suffered, and to secure the treasury at Delos against a Persian raid, and probably also to establish a firmer grip over the members of the League, it was moved to Athens. Lastly, a revolt between factions broke out in Thessaly and the Athenian forces sent to quell it were repulsed.

All parties were by now so weary of the war that, in 452 B.C., Cimon, whose ostracism had expired, returned to Athens and negotiated a five-year truce with the Peloponnesian League. Next, in 448 B.C., peace with Persia, known as the peace of Callias, brought the struggle of thirty-two years to an end.

A year before the truce expired, a revolt broke out in Boeotia, which led to the Athenians withdrawing from that state. Next Euboea rose in revolt, and then Megara. The former was subdued, but the latter, except for the ports of Nisaea and Pagae, was lost. These mishaps persuaded Athens to seek peace, and by offering to surrender Nisaea and Pagae, together with Achaea and Troezen, in return for Sparta's recognition of the Athenian Empire in the Aegean, a thirty-year peace was agreed in 445 B.C.

The first sixteen years of the peace were spent by Pericles in consolidating the commonwealth and in making Athens the queen of Hellas, his ultimate aim being to unite all Greeks in a religious union under Athens as its spiritual head. Thus, again, the ideal of a universal monarchy was reborn; but it was an impossible dream, for not only did the tributes which Pericles was exacting for the beautification of Athens exasperate the tributary states, but the conditions of a universal empire were entirely wanting. Hostility between Sparta and Athens was in no way allayed, and to this was now added the fear of most of the Greek states, who saw in the Athenian Empire a challenge to their independence. This fear needed but an incident to precipitate a second Peloponnesian war.

In 435 B.C. trouble began. That year Corcyra broke away from Corinth and sought Athenian aid. Because Corcyra was the eastern key of the Italo-Sicilian trade route, it was clear to Athens that, could she obtain control of the powerful Corcyraean fleet, the command of the Ionian Sea would be assured to her and by this means she could at any time bring pressure to bear on the Peloponnesian states by threatening to cut off the Sicilian corn upon which they depended. Accordingly, she sent to Corcyra thirty ships, which, in 433 B.C., at the battle of Sybota, saved the Corcyraean fleet from destruction.

Next, Potidaea, a former Corinthian Colony, but at the time a tributary ally of Athens, revolted and the Corinthians urged the Spartans to declare war. In 432 B.C. representatives of the states hostile to Athens assembled at Sparta to consider the suggestion and sent an embassy to Athens. Diplomatic exchanges followed and the second Peloponnesian War was in the balance. In March that year the incident came which tipped the scales. The Thebans surprised and took Plataea by treachery, and though they were at once ejected by the Plataeans, Athens sent an army into Boeotia and war became general.

Throughout his conduct of the war Pericles relied upon the strategy of exhaustion: a defensive on land and an offensive at sea. The former was based on the Athens-Piraeus fortifications, which were virtually impregnable; the latter on the fleet which, to all intents and purposes, was invincible if skilfully handled. Whenever threatened by land the inhabitants of Attica sought refuge between the Long Walls while the fleet ravaged the enemy's coasts and decimated his trade. By these means Pericles hoped to maintain the Empire intact and to wear down his enemies.

No sooner had the war started than an unforeseeable event upset all calculations. In 430-429, and again in 427-426 B.C., a fearful plague, which for some time had been ravaging the East, reached Athens, and among its victims was Pericles, who died in 429 B.C. Irreplaceable, for he was indispensable in his particular system of government, the destiny of Athens passed into the hands of Cleon, a man of the people who made the fatal mistake of converting what in essence was a defensive war into a war of aggression.

In 428 B.C. Mytilene revolted, and the following year, after a long siege, Plataea fell to the Boeotians. Next, the war was extended to Sicily and an Athenian fleet was sent there to interrupt the Sicilian corn trade with the Peloponnese. According to

Thucydides, its purpose was also "to test the possibility of bringing Sicily into subjection".

The war continued with its ups and downs until in 425 B.C. Cleon added to his prestige by capturing a force of Spartans on the island of Spacteria (Sphaghia). Two years later he was given command of an army to oppose Brasidas and his Spartans in Thrace, and under the walls of Amphipolis Cleon was routed and he and Brasidas were killed.

The deaths of Cleon and Brasidas removed the chief obstacle to peace, and in Athens, Nicias, leader of the aristocratic party, was commissioned to meet Pleistoanax, King of Sparta, and to discuss terms. The result was the Peace of Nicias, according to which Athens undertook to restore nearly all the conquests she had made during the war, and Sparta undertook to relinquish Amphipolis and some other cities which, though declared independent, were nevertheless to pay tribute to Athens. The Corinthians, Boeotians, and Megarians came off so badly that their dissatisfaction was intense.

# CHAPTER 2

# The siege of Syracuse, 415-413 B.C., and the Battle of Aegospotami, 405 B.C.

No sooner had the Peace of Nicias been concluded than Argos refused to renew her treaty with Sparta, and the Spartans, fearful that Athens would combine with Argos, persuaded Athens to enter into a fifty-year alliance. The Boeotians took alarm and demanded a similar alliance. Sparta agreed to it and the Argives, frightened by this combination of the two most formidable military powers in Greece, sent envoys to Athens to cement a quadruple alliance between them and Elis and Mantinea. When the Spartans heard this they also sent envoys to Athens.

When these two embassies arrived, Nicias, who had persuaded the Athenians to form the alliance with Sparta, now urged them to abide by their decision. But he was opposed by a young aristocrat, Alcibiades, who, in spite of his youth, had been elected a general.

Born in 450 B.C., Alcibiades had been brought up in the household of Pericles. He was arrestingly handsome, and though a man of outstanding abilities and great wealth, was self-willed, reckless, dissolute, and contemptuous of goodness in his fellow men. The projects he championed were invariably in his own interest, for the public good meant nothing to him. He cleverly tricked the Spartan envoys into making fools of themselves. He won the people by his astuteness, and in July, 420 B.C., a hundred-year treaty of alliance was agreed between Athens, Argos, Elis, and Mantinea. In recognition for this Alcibiades was re-elected a general. Secure for another twelve months, his first step was to visit the Peloponnese to persuade the Argives to pick a quarrel with the city of Epidaurus, then a member of the Peloponnesian League.

This aggressive act was in part mitigated by the return of Nicias to power. Nevertheless, the alliance with Argos was maintained and the Spartans, in no way satisfied, sent an army to help Epidaurus. The Athenians then protested that they had broken the peace. Undeterred by this, the Spartans sent a powerful army under King Agis into the Argive lands; but he sought no decision until an Athenian army arrived to support Argos. In 418 B.C. a battle was fought at Mantinea, in which the Argives and Athenians were routed.

This decisive victory restored Spartan prestige. The Athenians withdrew from Epidaurus, the quadruple alliance was dissolved, and Argos was compelled to enter into a fifty-year alliance with Sparta. These mishaps and others led to a proposal to ostracize Nicias. Alcibiades, alarmed, carried his followers over to Nicias's side.

In the early spring of 417 B.C. Sparta overthrew the democracy in Argos and forced an oligarchy on the Argives; but immediately afterwards the oligarchs were expelled and the democracy re-instated, and through the persuasions of Alcibiades the treaty between Athens and Argos was renewed, this time for fifty years.

In June the following year, an embassy arrived in Athens from Segesta (not far from Alcamo) in Sicily, to plead for Athenian intervention in their war with the city of Selinus, at the same time suggesting a greater project–arresting the expansion of Syracusan power in Sicily. After guarantees that the cost of assistance would be met by Segesta, Athenian envoys were sent there to inspect the treasury, and after they were given sixty talents and shown other treasures they reported that the cost could be met. Seeing in the project an opportunity to distinguish himself, Alcibiades was so persuasive that the Assembly voted to send sixty ships to Sicily under three generals, Nicias, Lamachus, and himself.

Nicias opposed the resolution, pointing to the unwisdom of embarking on so distant a campaign when at any moment war might again break out in Greece. But Alcibiades, being "exceed-ingly ambitious of a command by which he hoped to reduce Sicily and Carthage, and personally to gain in wealth and reputation by means of his successes",[1] supported the project, and appealing to the emotions of the people he said: "Men do not rest content with parrying the attacks of a superior, but often strike the first blow to prevent the attack being made. And we cannot fix the exact point at which our empire shall stop; we have reached a position in which we must not be content with retaining but must scheme to extend it, for, if we cease to rule others, we are in danger of being ruled ourselves."[2]

Nicias thought that by exaggerating the size of the projected

---

[1] *The History of the Peloponnesian War*, by Thucydides, trans. Richard Crawley (1874), VI, 15.          [2] *Ibid.*, VI, 18

expedition he would divert the people from their purpose, and he pointed out that it would have to be exceedingly powerful. But the people became more eager than ever and their enthusiasm was so great that "the few that liked it not, feared to appear unpatriotic by holding up their hands against it, so kept quiet".[1]

Preparations were at once put in hand, when shortly before the expedition was due to sail, all the busts of Hermes, which stood in the shrines and at the entrances of private houses, were mutilated in a single night. Though no one knew who had committed this outrage, suspicion fell on Alcibiades, who at once demanded a trial; but his enemies, who feared that were he tried the army would side with him, succeeded in getting the trial postponed until he had arrived in Sicily, "their plan being to have him sent back and brought home for trial upon some graver charge, which they would the more easily get up in his absence".[2]

In June, 415 B.C., when all was ready, the battle fleet stood out from the Piraeus for Corcyra, where the rest of the allied forces had assembled already. From there the expedition sailed to Italy; it comprised 134 triremes (100 Athenian); 130 transports; 5,100 hoplites (1,500 Athenian); 1,300 archers; javelin–men and slingers; and 30 horses.[3] In all, there were probably 27,000 officers and men.[4] Its supplies were carried in 30 corn ships and 100 other vessels, "besides many other boats and ships of burden which followed the armament voluntarily for purposes of trade".[5] At Rhegium (Reggio) the troops were landed, and there news was received that the Segestans had no more than thirty talents in their treasury, and that the Athenian envoys had been completely hoaxed.

In Syracuse little credence was given to the report that the expedition was aimed at Sicily, though Hermocrates, one of the generals, thinking otherwise, urged immediate action:

"If we Siciliots, all together, or at least as many as possible besides ourselves," he said, "would only launch the whole of our actual navy with two months' provisions and meet the Athenians at Tarentum (Tarento) and the Iapygian promontory (Cape Leuca), and show them that before fighting for Sicily they must first fight for their passage across the Ionian sea, we should strike dismay into their army. . . . In my opinion this consideration alone would be sufficient to deter them from putting out from Corcyra

[1] Thucydides, VI, 25.    [2] Ibid., VI, 29.    [3] Ibid., VI, 43.
[4] The Cambridge Ancient History, vol. V, p. 287.    [5] Thucydides, VI, 44.

. . . or, confounded by so unexpected a circumstance, would break up the expedition, especially as their most experienced general has, as I hear, taken the command against his will, and would grasp at the first excuse offered by any serious demonstration of ours . . . besides the first to attack, or to show that they mean to defend themselves against an attack, inspire greater fear because men see that they are ready for the emergency . . . and remember all of you that contempt for an assailant is best shown by bravery in action, but that for the present the best course is to accept the preparations which fear inspires as giving the surest promise of safety, and to act as if the danger was real."[1]

Few listened to him, least of all Athenagoras, the leader of the people, and it was only when to their consternation the Syracusans learned that the Athenians were at Rhegium that they threw themselves heart and soul into the work of preparation.

After the exposure of the Segestan hoax, a council of war was held at which Nicias proposed that a demonstration in force be made, and that after the power of Athens had been displayed the expedition should return to Greece. Alcibiades considered that this would be a disgrace and urged that opposition to Syracuse should be stirred up in Sicily and a political war fomented against her. Lastly came the turn of Lamachus, who urged an immediate attack on Syracuse while the city was still unprepared and her citizens fearful. In a memorable speech he said: "Every armament was most terrible at first; if it allowed time to run on without showing itself, men's courage revived, and they saw it appear at last almost with indifference. By attacking suddenly, while Syracuse still trembled at their coming, they would have the best chance of gaining a victory for themselves and of striking a complete panic into the enemy by the aspect of their numbers—which would never appear so considerable as at present—by the anticipation of coming disaster, and above all by the immediate danger of the engagement."[2]

In spite of these bold words, the opinion of Alcibiades prevailed, and a series of attempts was made to win over the Sicilian cities, each to end in a dismal failure, for no city of importance was found to be friendly to Athens and even the semi-friendly Catana (Catania), at which it was decided to gain a foothold in Sicily, had to be occupied by a *ruse de guerre*.

Soon after the Athenians established themselves at Catana,

[1] Thucydides, VI, 34.                    [2] *Ibid.* VI, 50.

a dispatch boat, the *Salaminia*, arrived from Athens with orders for the immediate return of Alcibiades to stand his trial. To this he agreed; but when on the return journey the ship put into Thurii, a city of southern Italy, he gave his guard the slip, and not long after crossed in a boat to the Peloponnese and deserted to the Spartans; "and the Athenians passed sentence of death by default upon him and those in his company".[1] Nicias and Lamachus were now free to conduct the campaign on their own lines.

The Syracusans, because they had not been attacked, had recovered from their surprise, and growing contemptuous of their enemy they "called upon their generals, as the multitude is apt to do in its moments of confidence, to lead them to Catana, since the enemy would not come to them".[2] Nicias heard of this and determined to indulge their fancy. His intention was, directly their army set out for Catana, to embark his troops and under cover of night sail into the Great Harbour of Syracuse and occupy a position immediately east of Olympieum. He bribed a native of Catana who was held in high esteem by the Syracusans, and sent him to them with false information regarding the careless watch the Athenians kept.

Catana lay some thirty miles north of Syracuse, which latter city was built on a promontory between the bay of Thapsus and the Great Harbour, the entrance of which, between Ortygia and Plemmyrium, was half a mile in width. On Ortygia, once an islet but now a peninsula, the original city had been built, and immediately north of it lay the Little Harbour. When the city was extended to the mainland the eastern end of the promontory, called Achradina, was walled in, the two cities—one now named the inner and the other the outer—being separated by a burial ground in which stood the statue of Apollo Temenites. West of Achradina—of which it was the eastern part—stretched the plateau of Epipolae, the northern and southern flanks of which were so precipitous that an army could only approach the plateau by three "gates": from Trogilus in the north, Temenites in the south, and Euryalus in the extreme west. South of Epipolae and west of the Great Harbour lay the plain of Anapus, named after the river which traversed it.

When all was ready for the surprise attack on Catana, the Syracusan army set out, and immediately its departure was signalled to Nicias, he embarked his army, slipped round by night

---

[1] Thucydides, VI, 62.  [2] *Ibid.*, VI, 64.

to the Great Harbour, and landed south of the Anapus river. There he established his camp, and built a palisade round his ships before the Syracusan army could return. When it did, it

8.  SIEGE OF SYRACUSE, 415–413 B.C.

went into camp opposite him.

The next day both armies prepared for battle. The Syracusans drew up their heavy infantry in a sixteen-rank phalanx with 1,200 cavalry on its right flank; Nicias, still without cavalry and fearing the enemy horse, formed half his army into an eight-deep phalanx in advance, and close to his camp in rear of this division he marshalled the other half in a hollow square of eight-deep sides. with the camp followers inside it. This reserve corps was ordered "to look out and be ready to go to the support of the troops hardest pressed".[1] It was clearly an anti-cavalry formation.

The battle opened with a skirmish between the archers and slingers, under cover of which the heavy infantry closed in on each other. The Argives drove in the enemy's left; the Athenians penetrated his centre, and the Syracusans were only saved from annihilation by their cavalry slowing down the Athenian pursuit.

Soon after the battle winter set in, and Nicias, not daring to remain in the Anapus plain in face of the enemy's cavalry, sailed back to Catana, where he went into winter quarters, sending a galley to Athens with a request that a force of cavalry should be sent to him in the spring. The Syracusans, having learned the folly of pitting a hastily raised rabble of troops against trained soldiers, began exercising their heavy infantry. Also they sent envoys to Corinth and Sparta to seek help. Further, they set to work to wall in Temenites, in order to impede their enemy building a wall of contravallation west of the city and to secure for themselves the southern gate of the Epipolae plateau.

When the Syracusan envoys arrived in the Peloponnese they at once found their advocate in Alcibiades, who not only divulged the Athenian plans to them, but urged the Spartans to action. As the Spartans did not yet want to break the peace with Athens, on Alcibiades's suggestion they agreed to send Gylippus to take command of the Syracusan army; and the Corinthians, then at war with Athens, promised to send reinforcements.

In May, 414 B.C., Nicias and Lamachus having received 280 horsemen from Athens, and by then having recruited 400 from Naxos and Segesta, were ready for the summer campaign.

As he expected that the next blow would be struck where the first had fallen, Hermocrates garrisoned Olympieum, and to prevent an advance on Epipolae from the north, by way of Trogilus and Euryalus, he raised a picked force, 600 strong, under Diomilus, to guard these approaches. On the very morning upon which he was reviewing this corps on the plain of Anapus before it was to take over the approaches, Nicias and Lamachus struck. Instead of attempting to gain the shore of the Great Harbour they made a night fleet movement; disembarked their forces at Leon, and seized the Euryalus gate before the 600 could man it. When Diomilus, followed by Hermocrates, came up, a battle was fought

[1] Thucydides, VI, 68.

in which the Syracusans were worsted and driven back into their city. Free of them, Nicias and Lamachus at once established a fortified base at Labdalum, and near Syke they began to build what Thucydides calls "the Circle", a central fort from which a wall of contravallation was to be pushed northwards to Trogilus and southwards to the Great Harbour. The wall, when finished, would completely invest the landward side of Syracuse. To impede the building of the Southern wing of the wall the Syracusans started to erect a counter-wall west of Temenites. But one day, when they were off their guard, the Athenians rushed the half-finished work, pulled it down and appropriated the material. They also destroyed the underground pipes which carried drinking water into Syracuse.

Next, the Syracusans began building a counter-wall–a stockade and ditch–from the city across the middle of the marsh southwest of Temenites, in order to prevent the Athenians carrying their wall down to the sea. Again the Athenians attacked. Ordering their fleet to sail round from Thapsus (on the peninsula of Isola degli Magnesi) into the Great Harbour, Lamachus, with a strong corps, descended from Epipolae and, "laying doors and planks over the marsh, where it was muddy and firmest, crossed over on these and by daybreak took the ditch and the stockade".[1] Again a battle followed in which the Syracusans were routed; but the Athenian loss was an irreparable one, for in the fight for the marsh Lamachus was killed. Simultaneously, the Syracusans attacked the Circle, which they hoped to take while denuded of its defenders. Though they failed to occupy it, they succeeded in pulling down about a thousand feet of the wall.

So desperate was the situation the Syracusans were now placed in that privately they opened negotiations with Nicias and, accusing their generals of treachery, they dismissed Hermocrates.

Sometime before this occurred Gylippus and the Corinthian reinforcement had arrived at Leucas (Santa Maura), an island in the Ionian Sea. Gylippus left the fleet to follow and sailed on to Locri in Calabria. There, learning that Syracuse was not yet completely invested, he pressed on to Himera in Sicily. Persuading the Himerians to join in the war, in a short time he recruited an army of more than 2,000 hoplites and light armed men and 100 horse.

Meanwhile the Corinthian fleet at Leucas put out for Syracuse,

---

[1] Thucydides, VI, 102.

and in the first ship that arrived was a general named Gongylus, who, on landing, found the Syracusans on the point of holding an assembly to consider whether they should not put an end to the war. This he at once prevented, and when they heard what he had to say they plucked up courage and made ready to cooperate with Gylippus directly his army approached.

Once ready, Gylippus marched on Syracuse and had the surprising good fortune to find Euryalus unguarded. He occupied it and he pressed on over Epipolae, soon joining hands with the Syracusan army at a point north of the Circle where the Athenian wall had not yet been built. He found the Syracusans in much disorder, and instead of attacking he surprised and took Labdalum, and next set to work to build a counter-wall from Syracuse westwards across Epipolae and through the gap between the completed end of the Athenian wall and Trogilus. This work, when finished, not only blocked his enemy's land communications, but added the northern half of Epipolae to the defences of Syracuse, so linking the city with the hinterland.

Why Nicias did not at once attempt to reopen his land communications is not recorded. But by not doing so he became more than ever dependent on his fleet to supply his army, and in order to gain a freer access to the Great Harbour, he occupied Plemmyrium, fortified it, and established his naval base there.

Meanwhile Gylippus went on building his wall, using the stones the Athenians had collected for theirs. Two engagements followed. In the first the Syracusans were worsted, and in the second the Athenians were so severely repulsed that Gylippus was able to carry his wall past the Athenian works, and so "deprived them, even if victorious in the field, of all chance of investing the city for the future".[1]

Immediately after this important engagement the Corinthian fleet from Leucas, under Erasinides, arrived. It eluded the Athenian guard ships off Plemmyrium and sailed into the Great Harbour where it landed its reinforcements.

Summer was now over and Nicias sent a long and gloomy dispatch to Athens. He wrote that, on the land side it was he who was being besieged and not his enemy; that his ships were becoming rotten and their crews wasted; that every sortie for fuel, forage, and water had to be fought for; that he had no means of recruiting his crews; and that should the Italian markets cease to supply

---

[1] Thucydides, VII, 7.

6

him, famine would compel him to abandon the campaign. Further, as a general Sicilian coalition was being formed against him and a fresh enemy army was expected from the Peloponnese, ". . . you must promptly decide," he wrote, "either to recall us or to send out to us another fleet and army as numerous again, with a large sum of money, and someone to succeed me, as a disease in the kidneys unfits me for retaining my post. . . . But whatever you mean to do, do it at the commencement of spring and without delay. . . ."[1]

Rather than sacrifice prestige by abandoning the siege, the Athenians decided to send out a second expedition under Eurymedon and Demosthenes; the former to leave in December for Sicily with ten ships and 2,000 seamen while the latter recruited the expedition. The Spartans reopened the Peloponnesian war in March, 413 B.C., to frustrate this. Urged on by Alcibiades, they sent an army under Agis into Attica to seize Decelea, which he did. Meanwhile, during the winter, twenty-five Corinthian ships masked the twenty Athenian at Naupactus "until the heavy infantry in the merchant-men were fairly on their way from the Peloponnesus".[2]

The spring offensive was opened by Gylippus. He had won the initiative on land and was now determined to win it at sea by seizing his enemy's base at Plemmyrium. He decided to feint with his fleet and to attack with his army. Under cover of night he moved the latter to a position where it could be secured by his cavalry and could wait unobserved until a signal was given it to assault the defences of the Plemmyrium. Next, he divided the fleet into two squadrons of forty-five and thirty-five ships, the former based on the Little Harbour and the latter on the Great. Both were simultaneously to put to sea, to link into line, and to attack the naval base; their aim was to draw the enemy out of his land defences to the shore, which done, the signal for the assault would be given.

In clockless days, combined operations from separated bases were always risky. Further, in the present case, the skill of the Syracusan crews was inferior to the Athenian. The result was that before the two squadrons could link up the Athenians manned sixty triremes and a long-drawn struggle in the mouth of the Great Harbour followed. During this, as Gylippus had calculated, many Athenians came down from the land defences to watch the fight,

---

[1] Thucydides, VII, 12–15.  [2] *Ibid.*, VII, 20.

and when he judged that the main forts largely had been emptied, he ordered the signal for the assault to be given. At once the Syracusan army emerged from its hiding place, and swarmed up the slopes of Plemmyrium and stormed its defences. Meanwhile the Athenian fleet routed the Syracusan, sinking eleven of its ships.

For the Athenians, the loss of their naval base was catastrophic: Thucydides calls it "the first and chiefest cause of their ruin".[1] They lost with it their supplies of corn, masts, and naval tackle. The mouth of the harbour was no longer theirs, and now daily it would have to be fought for to keep their sea communications open. Worse still, as they were compelled to return to their old base within the Great Harbour, in future they would have to operate in waters so narrow that their superior naval skill would be at a discount.

Immediately after the battle both sides set to work to strengthen their naval bases within the Great Harbour by driving piles into the sea bottom, behind which their fleets could shelter. This led to what may be called "pile-warfare". "The Athenians", we read, "brought up to them [the Syracusan piles] a ship of ten thousand talents burden [275 tons] furnished with wooden turrets and screens, and fastened ropes round the piles from their boats, wrenched them up and broke them. . . ." And because many of the piles did not appear above the water, divers were employed to saw them off. "Indeed there was no end of the contrivances to which they resorted against each other."[2]

When they learned that Demosthenes had put out from Aegina with the second expedition, the Syracusans decided on another fleet action before he could arrive. And as it would have to be fought in the Great Harbour, where for want of room the Athenians would be unable to employ their favourite tactics, they strengthened the prows of their ships in order to meet their enemy's in head-to-head collisions. Once again Gylippus's plan was to attack simultaneously on land and sea, this time the land attack providing the feint.

He opened the battle with a dual advance on the Athenian entrenched camp and naval base from the city and the Olympieum, and so drew the enemy's attention away from the sea. Next, he launched his fleet, when in great confusion the Athenian crews rushed down to the shore and hastily manned seventy-five triremes against the enemy's eighty.

[1] Thucydides, VII, 24.                    [2] *Ibid.*, VII, 25.

A three-day operation followed. The first day was taken up with skirmishing, apparently in order to tire out the Athenian crews. On the second no fighting took place, and Nicias refitted his damaged ships and formed an "enclosed harbour" in front of his sea stockade by mooring a line of merchant ships at two hundred feet intervals. Its purpose was to provide any ship which was hard pressed with a secure refuge.

On the third day the Syracusans renewed the attack both by land and sea, but with so little success that a Corinthian pilot, Pyrrhicus, suggested the following ruse: First, to send back to the city and bring the dinners of the crews down to the shore; next, to break off the naval engagement, retire to the harbour and rapidly refresh the rowers, and lastly, once the enemy had withdrawn to his harbour, to put to sea and renew the battle before he could feed his crews.

The ruse was adopted and the Athenians, seeing their enemy backwater and withdraw, assumed that he had had enough, disembarked, and set about getting their meals, imagining that they had done with fighting for the day. Next, we read:

"Suddenly the Syracusans manned their ships and sailed against them; and the Athenians in great confusion and most of them fasting got on board, and with great difficulty put out to meet them." For a time both sides refused to engage. At length the Athenians resolved not to let themselves be worn out, and with a cheer went into action. "The Syracusans received them, and charging prow to prow as they had intended, stove in a great part of the Athenian foreships by the strength of their beaks; the darters on the decks also did great damage to the Athenians, but still greater damage was done by the Syracusans who went about in small boats, ran in upon the oars of the Athenian galleys, and sailed against their sides, and discharged from thence their darts upon the sailors."[1]

These surprise tactics proved so successful that the Athenians turned about and sought refuge behind their merchant craft, the Syracusans pursuing until stopped by the dolphins[2] mounted on their decks. Though the Athenians lost no more than seven ships, the battle was decisive, for it knocked the bottom out of the morale of their fleet and won for the Syracusans the initiative at sea.

---

[1] Thucydides, vii, 40–41.
[2] A mass of iron or stone hung from the yard arm and dropped on the deck of an enemy ship. In the battle two Syracusan triremes were sunk by this machine.

In July, 413 B.C., to the joy of the Athenians and to the consternation of the Syracusans, the second expedition under Demosthenes and Eurymedon, comprising 73 triremes, 5,000 hoplites,
3,000 bowmen, slingers and javelin-men, in all some 15,000,
sailed into the Great Harbour. As Nicias was now a sick man, the
conduct of the war was at once assumed by Demosthenes, who
lost not a moment in drawing the utmost profit out of the enthusiasm his arrival had created. He decided at once that the siege
could not continue unless the counter-wall Gylippus had built
across Epipolae were mastered. First, to clear the approach to the
plateau, he drove the Syracusans out of the Anapus plain. Next, he
brought up his battering rams and made a full-scale attack on the
counter-wall; but the attack failed, for the enemy burnt his
engines. Lastly, he decided on an outflanking movement by night,
his aim being to regain Euryalus and turn the right flank of the
counter-wall. The attack was to be carried out at the time of
the full moon, and, once Euryalus was occupied, an advance
was to be made towards Achradina so that the work on the
Athenian wall to Trogilus could be resumed.

The first part of the programme was successfully carried out.
Euryalus was surprised and occupied; but while the Athenians
were busily engaged upon demolishing the counter-wall, the
Syracusan army came up. It was repulsed, but when it advanced
again, both lines got mixed up in an indescribable confusion. A
common incident in night fighting now occurred. A part of the
attacking Athenian forces fell back in panic on the reserves coming
up in the rear. These fell prey to the contagion, took to their heels,
and Demosthenes's attack failed disastrously.

He now decided that the only thing to be done was to raise the
siege and return to Greece, and though Nicias agreed that no
further headway could be made, he counselled delay on the
ground that he was in touch with "a party in Syracuse who wished
to betray the city to the Athenians, and kept sending him messages
and telling him not to raise the siege".[1]

The departure was deferred for nearly a month; but when
further enemy reinforcements arrived a decision became imperative. Secretly it was made and plans for the withdrawal were prepared. But when the expedition was on the point of sailing the
moon, which again was at its full, was eclipsed (August 27, 413
B.C.). The troops and seamen took it as an ill omen and refused to

---

[1] Thucydides, VII, 49.

embark, urging their generals to wait for a more propitious day. Unfortunately, Nicias, "who was somewhat over-addicted to divination", agreed with them "until they had waited the thrice nine days prescribed by the soothsayers".[1]

When this suicidal decision was reported to Gylippus he at once turned it to his advantage; for though he could only muster seventy-six sail to his enemy's eighty-six, he again attacked the Athenian naval base. Eurymedon, in command of the Athenian right, tried to manœuvre round the Syracusan left, got separated from the centre, was surrounded, and perished with his squadron. Then the centre was penetrated and the whole Athenian fleet was driven back in confusion all along the shore of the Great Harbour; but the army rescued many of the crews by driving back the enemy troops sent to capture them. Eighteen Athenian ships were lost, and those which had returned to the naval base the Syracusans tried to destroy by means of fire-ships; this attack failed.

It was clear to Gylippus that the sole course now open to his enemy was to break out of the Great Harbour; to prevent this, he blocked its mouth with a line of triremes and merchant craft anchored and chained together.

The Athenians lacked provisions, the country was hostile and infested with enemy cavalry, and a council of war, as Gylippus foresaw, decided that a break-out by sea offered the only practical chance of escape. So the Athenians shortened their land defences, loaded as many troops as they could in their triremes, determined to "fight it out at sea, and if victorious, to go to Catana; if not, to burn their vessels . . . and retreat by land for the nearest friendly place they could reach. . . ."[2] Nicias, as senior general, claimed the honour of remaining behind with the reduced land garrison, while Demosthenes, Menander, and Euthydemus led the retreat by sea. In all they had 110 ships fit and unfit for action.

On September 10 the three Athenian generals set out on their desperate adventure. They made straight for the boom across the mouth of the Great Harbour, in front of which was a Corinthian squadron in the centre with the main Syracusan fleet drawn up in crescent formation on either of its wings. In all the Syracusans had seventy-six ships. Thrusting the Corinthians back, the Athenians reached the block-ships, but before they could master the obstacle the Syracusans bore down on them from all directions.

[1] Thucydides, VII, 51.　　　　　[2] Ibid., VII, 61.

A confused mêlée followed, of which Thucydides gives little information, save that: "as many ships were engaged in a small compass (for these were the largest fleets fighting in the narrowest space ever known, being little short of two hundred), the regular attacks with the beak were few, there being no opportunity of backing water or of breaking the line; while the collisions caused by one ship chancing to run foul of another, either in flying from or attacking a third, were more frequent".[1]

The battle ended in an overwhelming Syracusan victory; the Athenians lost fifty ships to their enemy's twenty-six.

In no way daunted by this disaster, the Athenian generals, who saw that they still had sixty triremes to their enemy's fifty, decided to make yet another attempt; but the crews refused to embark and demanded a retreat by land. Instead of setting out at once, while their enemy was celebrating his victory, a pause of thirty-six hours was made because Hermocrates had spread a false report abroad that their line of retreat was blocked. He had done this to gain time until the rejoicings in Syracuse had ended.

At length, leaving the sick and wounded behind, the retreat began. The army marched in a hollow square, "the division of Nicias leading, and that of Demosthenes following, the heavy infantry being outside the baggage-carriers and the bulk of the army in the middle".[2] The army crossed the Anapus, but on the first day, because of persistent cavalry attacks, less than four miles were made. Next day it was less than two, and then only to find the line of retreat blocked by strong forces. On the two succeeding days the Athenians attempted to drive back the Syracusans, but they failed to do so and sought another line of retreat by way of the river Cacyparis (Cassibili). They left their camp fires burning, set out by night, and reached the coastal road to Helorum (near Noto). Nicias and his division were still leading, but Demosthenes had been delayed by a panic and was far behind. By noon the two divisions were five or six miles apart, when the one in rear was surrounded in a walled enclosure – the "Homestead of Polyzelus" – by the enemy cavalry. There Demosthenes and his men were offered freedom if they would desert. This he refused to do, and fought on until the situation was so hopeless that on receiving a guarantee that his men's lives would be spared he surrendered – 6,000 men in all.

The fate of Nicias and his division was much the same. On the

[1] Thucydides, VII, 70.  [2] *Ibid.*, VII, 79.

river Erineus he found his path blocked by the enemy. He fought his way on for some three miles and reached the Assinarus River where his men, breaking their ranks, rushed into it to quench their thirst. There they were surrounded and butchered, "especially those in the water, which was thus immediately spoiled, but which they went on drinking just the same, mud and all, bloody as it was, most even fighting to have it".[1] Only 1,000 still survived when at length Nicias surrendered to Gylippus.

The 7,000 survivors of the 45,000 to 50,000 soldiers and sailors whom Athens had sent against Syracuse were relegated to the quarries where "no single suffering to be apprehended by men thrust into such a place was spared them".[2] And, against the will of Gylippus, "Nicias and Demosthenes were butchered".

"This", writes Thucydides, "was the greatest Hellenic achievement of any in this war, or, in my opinion in Hellenic history; at once most glorious to the victors, and most calamitous to the conquered. They were beaten at all points and altogether; all that they suffered was great; they were destroyed, as the saying is, with a total destruction, their fleet, their army—everything was destroyed, and few out of many returned home."[3]

Absolute as the disaster was, its cause was not faulty strategical conception, but inept tactical execution. When the pretexts of war are set aside, the former appears brilliant: it was to make good the lack of Athenian man-power, which prohibited Athens from gaining supremacy over her enemies on land, by depriving the enemy's superior man-power of its means of subsistence—its corn, oil and trade. Though Sparta, unlike Corinth and Athens, was not an overpopulated city state, according to Thucydides, a definite cause of the war was "to prevent the exportation of Sicilian corn to the Peloponnese".[4] It can only be assumed that Sicily as a source of supply was as important to the Spartans and Corinthians as the Ukraine was to the Athenians, and the command of the strait of Messina was as vital to the first two as the command of the Hellespont was to the latter. Therefore, when in the summer of 415 B.C. the decision was made to seize Syracuse, the essence of the operation became one of tactical time: to effect the occupation as rapidly as possible, so that the forces engaged could return to Attica as early as possible and confront Sparta. Had the advice of Lamachus been followed, there can be little doubt that Syracuse would have fallen at the first onset and that

[1] Thucydides, VII, 85.    [2] Ibid., VII, 87.    [3] Ibid., VII, 87.    [4] Ibid., III, 86.

immediately afterwards the main Sicilian cities would have submitted to the victor. This would have resulted in so complete a strangulation of Peloponnesian food supplies that, faced by the returned and triumphant Athenian army, Sparta and Corinth would have been unable to maintain sufficient men in the field to wage a successful war against Athens. Athens would, consequently, and in spite of her inferior man-power, have been able to impose her will on both without resorting to battle.

If one accepts this argument, then the origins of the disaster are directly traceable to Alcibiades who, at the outset of the campaign, in defiance of Lamachus, by imposing his will on Nicias, won over his support to substitute a political war for a tactical operation. Now he was to play a leading part in an even greater Athenian disaster, this time centring in the Hellespont—the umbilical cord of the Athenian Empire. The events leading up to it were as follows:

As was inevitable, the annihilation of the Athenian fleet and army in Sicily shook the Athenian Empire to its core and went far to undo what Salamis and Plataea had accomplished. Euboea, Lesbos, and Chios revolted; Sparta turned to the sea and built a hundred warships; and Persia set out to regain her lost Ionian dominions.

Darius II (424–404 B.C.) was king of Persia at this time, Tissaphernes, satrap of Sardes, and Pharnabazus, satrap of Hellespontine Phrygia. The latter two sent envoys to Sparta for purely self-interested reasons, the one urging support of Chios and the other action in the Hellespont. Alcibiades was then in Ionia, stirring up revolt against Athens. Largely because of his machinations Sparta went into alliance with Tissaphernes and recognized the rights of Darius to all Greek cities in Ionia. Alcibiades next returned to Sparta, and as he had earlier seduced the wife of Agis, the outraged king ordered his execution. Alcibiades heard of this in time and fled to Tissaphernes whom he urged to abandon Sparta and to come to an understanding with Athens. He hoped that if this were effected the grateful Athenians would call him back to his native land.

His suggestion was that if the Athenians changed their government to an oligarchy the Persian king would supply them with money, and as this was the one thing they needed the Athenians were persuaded to acquiesce in a change of constitution. Although the fleet, then at Samos, remained loyal to the democracy, as it also favoured an alliance with Persia, it called in Alcibiades, pardoned him and elected him a general. Pharnabazus invited the Peloponnesian fleet to the Hellespont about the same time, and there, in 411 B.C., in a battle fought off Cape Cynossema (N. of Rhodes) it was defeated by the Athenians. The repulse of his ally so annoyed Tissaphernes that when Alcibiades paid him his next visit he had him arrested. But again he escaped, and in 410 B.C., in cooperation with Theramenes and Thrasybulus, in a considerable naval battle he took or destroyed sixty Spartan ships off Cyzicus (in the Sea of Marmara), and raised the siege of that city.

After this disaster Sparta sought peace, but Athens refused to consider it; for meanwhile the democracy under Cleophon – a man of the people and leader of the war party – had been restored. Operations were continued in the Propontis, and the Athenians, under the able leadership of Alcibiades, steadily gained ground until the complete command of the Bosphorus was rewon and the umbilical cord restored.

This setback, coupled with the incompetence and mutual jealousies of his two satraps, led Darius to appoint his younger son Cyrus to take control of affairs in Ionia, and about the same time the Spartans appointed Lysander admiral of their fleet. He was a man who appealed to Cyrus, the Oriental, because he could not be bribed.

While these two were negotiating, in 407 B.C. Alcibiades returned to Athens, where he was received with tumultuous enthusiasm by the people, who again elected him general and placed the direction of the war in his hands. But no sooner had they hailed him as their saviour than the Athenian fleet, then at Notion, watching Ephesus, was defeated by Lysander and the people replaced him by Conon. Alcibiades scented personal danger and withdrew to a castle on the Hellespont, with which he had had the foresight to provide himself as a refuge.

The Peloponnesian fleet was greatly strengthened during the following winter, and when Lysander's twelve-month appointment as admiral expired, Callicratidas, who succeeded him, was in command of 140 triremes. He carried all before him, at length forced Conon to battle outside Mytilene, and defeated him, sinking thirty of his seventy ships and blockading the remaining forty in Mytilene.

This defeat placed Athens in so critical a position that the gold and silver in the Acropolis temples were melted down to equip another fleet and all slaves who volunteered to man the ships were promised manumission. A fleet of 150 triremes was raised by these methods and sent to relieve Mytilene. When he learned of its approach, Callicratidas, now in command of 170 ships, left fifty to continue the blockade, and with the remainder met the Athenian fleet near the islets of the Arginusae, south of Lesbos. In the battle which followed (406 B.C.) he was decisively defeated and lost seventy ships and his life. His whole fleet in all probability would have been annihilated had not a sudden storm put an end to the Athenian pursuit; but it also prevented the Athenians from rescuing those of their sailors clinging to the wreckage of the twenty-five ships they had lost.

The victory rewon for Athens the command of the eastern Aegean and led Sparta again to seek peace. But, through the influence of Cleophon, for a second time it was refused, and was followed by an astonishing incident. In Athens a furious clamour broke out against the commanders of the fleet for not having rescued the shipwrecked sailors at Arginusae. The question was placed before the Assembly and eight commanders were condemned to death. Six, including the son of Pericles, were executed; the remaining two prudently kept out of the way. Shortly after, as is common in democracies, the Athenians repented and passed a decree that those who had been the deceivers of the people should give securities until they were brought to trial. Five were seized and later escaped.[1]

The Athenian refusal to consider peace led Cyrus to urge the reappointment of Lysander to the command of the Peloponnesian fleet, and as Spartan law prohibited the same man holding the office of admiral for a second time, the difficulty was overcome by appointing a nominal commander-in-chief with Lysander as his second in command. Lysander then went to Ephesus, and Cyrus, called to the bedside of his dying father, entrusted Lysander with the administration of his satrapy, with full powers to levy his tribute. With these resources Lysander soon doubled the number of his triremes.

He put out from Ephesus in 405 B.C., sailed to Rhodes, doubled back, and then followed the Asiatic coast to the Hellespont. He laid siege to Lampsacus (Lapseki), which he found unguarded, in order to intercept the Athenian Pontic trade.

Conon was then attacking Chios, but when he heard that Lamp-

[1] *Xenophon. Hellenica*, trans. Charleton L. Brownson (1918), I, VII, 34.

sacus was besieged he at once set sail with a fleet of 180 ships to relieve it; but before he reached Sestus, Lampsacus had fallen. Determined to force Lysander to battle, Conon sailed to Aegospotami, which lay a few miles north of Sestus and opposite Lampsacus. There his crews prepared their evening meal.

On the following day Lysander, who had about 200 ships, made full preparations for battle; but ordered his crews not to put to sea. The Athenians also made ready and rowed up to Lampsacus; but when Lysander refused their challenge they returned to Aegospotami, followed by enemy scouting ships, the captains of which had been instructed by Lysander to observe what the Athenians did on landing.

These challenges and refusals were repeated on four consecutive days, when Alcibiades, who knew from experience how crafty Lysander was, came down from his neighbouring castle. When he learnt that the Athenians were lying at anchor on an open beach and had to fetch their provisions from Sestus, whereas the Spartans could obtain everything they needed from Lampsacus, he suggested to Conon and his captains "that they were not moored in a good place", and advised them to shift their anchorage to Sestus and thereby gain a harbour and a city; for "if you are there", he said, "you will be able to fight when you please". But the generals told him to go; "for they said that they were in command now, not he".[1]

When on the fifth day the Athenians put out from Aegospotami, Lysander ordered his scouts to signal to him by means of a shield flashed in the sun immediately they saw them on their return set out for Sestus to obtain provisions. When the signal was given Lysander put to sea at top speed. Conon saw his enemy's fleet advancing and immediately ordered his own ships to be manned. "But since his men were scattered here and there, some of the ships had but two banks of oars manned, some but one, and some were entirely empty; Conon's own ship, indeed, and seven others accompanying him, which were fully manned, put to sea in close order, and the *Paralus* [a dispatch-boat] with them, but all the rest Lysander captured on the beach. He also gathered up on the shore most of the men of their crews; some gained the shelter of the neighbouring strongholds. But when Conon, fleeing with his nine ships, realized that the Athenian cause was lost, he put in at Abarnis, the promontory of Lampsacus, and there seized the

Xenophon, ii, i, 25–26.

cruising sails that belonged to Lysander's ships;[1] then he sailed away with eight ships to seek refuge with Euagoras in Cyprus, while the *Paralus* went to Athens with the tidings of what had happened."[2]

There was no battle; such was the Battle of Aegospotami, in which 170 Athenian ships were captured while beached. Of the three to four thousand prisoners taken, all were slaughtered because of the outrages they had already committed and because, if victorious, they had determined to cut off the right hands of all their prisoners.[3]

Immediately after the victory Lysander sailed to Byzantium and Chalcedon (Kadikoy) and these cities opened their gates. Their garrisons, as well as all Athenians settled or serving abroad, he sent to Athens under safe conduct, "for he knew that the more people were collected in the city and Piraeus, the more quickly there would be a scarcity of provisions".[4]

The arrival of the *Paralus* at Athens, bearing news of the disaster, spread such consternation throughout the city that no one slept that night.[5] Next morning the Assembly met, when it was resolved to block the harbours, repair the walls, and place the city in a state of siege. Eucrates, the brother of Nicias, was chosen general.

Pausanias, the second Spartan king, levied the troops of the entire Peloponnesian coalition except Argos and joined Agis at Decelea, from where they moved on to Athens and besieged the city on its land side. Later Lysander arrived with a fleet of 150 ships and blockaded it from the sea. Athens was surrounded and all her enemies had now to do was to wait until starvation won the city for them.

Negotiations were opened, the Athenians offering to join the Spartan alliance on condition that their city was left in possession of its walls and homelands. The offer was refused and a demand made that 2,000 yards of each "leg" of the Long Wall should be demolished. Cleophon, who had already twice rejected peace when it might have been made with honour, now did so again. Theramenes then undertook to visit Lysander to obtain more favourable terms; his real intention was, however, to gain time for the people to come to their senses. He remained away for three months, and during his absence hunger worked its course. In-

---

[1] Normally, the Greek ships unshipped their sails when prepared for battle.
[2] Xenophon, II, 1, 28–29.   [3] *Ibid.*, II, 1, 31.   [4] *Ibid.*, II, II, 1.   [5] *Ibid.*, II, II, 3.

furiated by Cleophon's obstinacy, the people revolted and slew him.

Meanwhile the fate of Athens was being decided by the Peloponnesians and their allies. Corinth and Thebes urged that the city should be utterly destroyed and the whole people sold into slavery. The Spartans rejected these barbarous proposals and substituted for them the following terms: The Long Wall and the fortifications were to be demolished; all foreign possessions were to be relinquished and Athenian rule confined to Attica and Salamis; the whole fleet was to be forfeited; all exiles were to be granted freedom to return; and Athens was to enter into alliance with Sparta and accept her leadership.

These terms were accepted, because in the circumstances they could not be rejected. So it came about in April, 404 B.C., that Lysander sailed into the Piraeus and the exiles were restored. Then "the Peloponnesians with great enthusiasm began to tear down the walls to the music of flute-girls, thinking that that day was the beginning of freedom for Greece".[1]

Thus ended the first attempt at empire building in Europe; an empire built on force and destroyed not by force or by internal decay, but by crowd psychology. After the disaster in Sicily, the most the Athenians could do was to stave off defeat; therefore they should have sought peace at the first opportune moment. But the demos would not have this, and incapable of judging events, they proved themselves incapable of holding fast to their empire. Not only did they lose it, but what was more catastrophic, by losing it the cultural and political leadership of Hellas were divorced.

[1] Xenophon, II, II, 23.

# The rise of Macedonia

Though, in the Peloponnesian wars, Sparta's avowed aim was the liberation of the states Athens had subjected, no sooner did the Athenian Confederacy collapse than the Spartans resolved to bring the states they had freed under their own dominion. For the age-old policy of isolation was substituted a policy of aggrandizement beyond the confines of the Peloponnese.

The first step taken was to repress the Athenian democracies and establish oligarchies in their stead, and the next was to banish their political opponents and confiscate their estates. Added to these exiles, many of whom sought refuge in Persia, were many soldiers; for during the long struggle, through constant service in the field, the old city militias had grown into standing armies, and with the coming of peace the professional soldiers were thrown out of work.

Among these mercenaries, who sold their services to the highest bidder, was Xenophon, an Athenian knight and friend of Socrates, who, with the Spartan general Clearchus, entered the service of Cyrus, satrap of Asia Minor, who was then planning to oust his elder brother Artaxerxes from the throne of Persia. Cyrus instigated the Ionian cities to revolt against their satrap, Tissaphernes, collected together an army of some 30,000 Oriental troops and 13,000 Greek mercenaries, 10,600 of whom were hoplites commanded by Clearchus, and in 401 B.C. set out from Sardes. After a march of some fifteen hundred miles he reached Cunaxa, sixty miles north of Babylon, and there came face to face with Artaxerxes and his army. In the battle which followed the initial onslaught of the Greeks carried everything before it. Cyrus thought the battle won—which it virtually was—and accompanied by a small body of horsemen, and over-eager to slay his brother with his own hand, recklessly galloped forward and was killed. His Asiatic troops were then seized with panic and fled. Nevertheless, the Greek mercenaries, though soon surrounded, refused to surrender, and Artaxerxes, fearing to attack them, yet wishing to be quit of them, agreed to provide them with guides and an escort, under Tissaphernes, to lead them back to Greece.

On the way home, by means of a ruse, the crafty satrap separated the Greek generals from their men, seized the former and sent them to Artaxerxes, who put them to death. Because he expected that the now leaderless Greeks would surrender and he still feared to attack them, Tissaphernes held back; but they, largely because of the exertions and exhortations of Xenophon, rapidly recovered from their dismay, appointed new generals, and set out on what to history is known as the "Retreat of the Ten Thousand", so fully described in Xenophon's *Anabasis*. Early in 400 B.C., and after one of the most famous retreats in history, they reached the coast of the Black Sea at Trapezus (Trebizond).

This remarkable feat electrified every Greek city. Never before had a Greek army marched to the centre of the Persian Empire, fought a great battle, and in face of hostile multitudes marched safely home again. These things clearly showed that no Oriental forces could hope to withstand an army of well-trained Greek soldiers. As Professor Bury writes of this campaign: "It is an epilogue to the invasion of Xerxes and a prologue to the conquest of Alexander."

Its consequences were immediate. The Greek Asiatic cities, fearing the return of Tissaphernes, appealed to Sparta for protection, and a Spartan army under King Agesilaus was sent to their aid. They carried war into Phrygia and Lydia with considerable success and were dreaming of marching on Babylon and dethroning Artaxerxes, when, in 394 B.C. the Spartans were rudely awakened by the reappearance of Conon, the Athenian admiral who had escaped at the battle of Aegospotami. Now in command of the Persian navy, in August Conon decisively defeated Agesilaus's fleet, commanded by Peisander, in the battle of Cnidus (Kirio-Burnu) and thereby destroyed Sparta's maritime power.

Meanwhile war had broken out in Greece between Sparta and her allies. Exasperated by Spartan exactions and supported by Persia, Thebes revolted and was joined by Athens, Corinth, and Argos, and a battle was fought near Corinth, in July, 394 B.C., in which the Spartans were victorious. Thus opened an eight-year struggle known as the Corinthian War, in which, soon after the above battle, though the Spartans under Agesilaus – now back from Asia – beat the Confederates again at Coronea (S.E. of Lake Kopias), they were compelled to abandon Boeotia and to withdraw to the Peloponnese, where they were blockaded.

The Spartans ascribed the success of their enemies to the support given them by Persia, and in 392 B.C. they sent Antalcidas to the Persian commander, Tiribazus, to propose that for Persian support they were willing to recognize the Great King's rights over all the Greek cities in Asia. Nothing definite came of this proposal until 386 B.C., when Persia's fears that Athens might rise again in the ascendant compelled her to accept the shameful "King's Peace", dictated to the Greek states by Artaxerxes. Under its terms, the Asiatic Greek cities and Cyprus were abandoned to Persia; the leadership of Sparta within Greece was acknowledged; and any state which did not accept the peace was to be compelled by Persia to do so. Thus the Great King became the arbiter of Greece with the right of perpetual interference.

Supported by Persia and now freed from her complications in Asia, Sparta returned to her despotic policy. In 378 B.C. this led Thebes again to revolt and to enter into an alliance with Athens, who meanwhile had begun to build up a second naval league on the Delian lines. War with Sparta followed, in which the Thebans successfully defended themselves and Athens gained considerable advantages at sea. In 371 B.C. a mutual agreement was arrived at between the contending parties to discuss peace; but because Sparta refused to allow Thebes to represent the whole of Boeotia, the latter decided to carry on the war single-handed, and in the eyes of all the Greeks her doom appeared sealed.

Had it not been for the Theban commander, Epaminondas, there can be little doubt that Thebes would have succumbed. But he realized that the Spartans would never change their traditional shock tactics, the success of which depended on an advance in perfect order, all spears of the phalanx striking the enemy's front simultaneously, and devised a tactics which would prevent this and throw the phalanx into confusion. Instead of drawing his troops up in parallel lines to the Spartan army, he formed them into oblique order to it, with his left leading and his right drawn back. At the same time he massed on his left wing a column of troops fifty ranks deep. Its object was to meet shock by super-shock and simultaneously to have enough reserve force in hand to lap round the enemy's right wing. In July, 371 B.C., he met King Cleombrotus and the Spartan army at Leuctra (near Domvrena) in southern Boeotia, and by means of these tactics decisively defeated him, Cleombrotus being killed. This battle not only broke the charm of Spartan prestige, but brought the short-lived Spartan hegemony to its end.

7

Thebes now rose in the ascendant, and between 369 and 362 B.C. had the chance of accomplishing what both Athens and Sparta had failed to do–namely, to weld the Greek states into a nation. She built a fleet and weakened Athens at sea, and under Epaminondas and Pelopidas gained the leadership of Greece. But her supremacy hung on the mortal life of one man–Epaminondas–who, in the summer of 362 B.C., at Mantinea in Arcadia, with the same tactics he had employed at Leuctra, again defeated the Spartans. Nevertheless, it was the death blow to the supremacy of Thebes, for in the pursuit Epaminondas was killed, and the light which had guided the Thebans since 379 B.C. was extinguished–her power by land and sea collapsed. Thus three great states, Athens, Sparta, and Thebes, each in turn had failed to establish a federated Hellenic world, and Hellas was ready to fall before a conqueror from the outside. His name was Philip of Macedon.

Born in 382 B.C., Philip, the third son of Amyntas III, on the death of his brother Perdiccas III, in 359 B.C., seized the throne of Macedonia, and from then to his death in 336 B.C. by sheer force of personality he dominated events. Restless and energetic, far-seeing and crafty, according to Polyaenus he won the land "by wiles rather than arms", and Hogarth, his best biographer, says of him: "Fraud before force, but force at the last" was his principle of empire.

In 367 B.C. he had been a hostage in Thebes, and during his three years there he had learnt much of war from Pelopidas and Epaminondas. This knowledge he put to good account once he had established his authority over the turbulent Macedonian clans. Next, he did something no ruler had yet done: out of his feudal bands he created a professional army endowed with a national spirit. He evolved, as Hogarth says, "the first European Power in the modern sense of the word–an armed nation with a common national ideal".

The wars he fought fall roughly into four groups: those to the west, north, and east of Macedonia, to establish his base of operations; those to the south of Macedonia, to gain control of Thessaly; those to establish his dominion over Thrace and to win the command of the Bosphorus; and those fought to impose his authority over the whole of Greece south of Thermopylae.

In 358 B.C. he warred against the Illyrian tribes, and in 357 occupied the former Athenian colony of Amphipolis on the river

Strymon and the gold mines of Pangaeus, which were of the utmost value to him. About this time he married Olympias, daughter of the Epirote king, and, in 356 B.C., she bore to him his son Alexander. Four years later he invaded Thrace and Thessaly, which led Lycophron, tyrant of Pherae (W. of Volo), to call to his help a body of Phocian mercenaries who had profaned Delphi. Philip was checked by them and retired; but he returned in the following year and proclaiming himself the champion of the outraged Apollo, he routed them in a battle fought near Volo. Other campaigns followed, when in 346 B.C., bent on gaining the command of the land route leading into Greece, he marched on Thermopylae and bribed the Phocian commander to surrender the famous pass to him. Sensing which way the wind was blowing, the Delphic Amphictyony[1] received him into the innermost circle of the Hellenes, and under his presidency the Pythian games of 346 B.C. were celebrated at Delphi in honour of its deliverance. For Philip, this was a political victory of the first order.

Of the next six years little is known, other than that Philip marched into the Peloponnese, warred on the Adriatic coast, and led his army to and beyond the Danube. During these years his final ambition took shape, "for it was coming to be his desire", writes Diodorus, "to be designated Captain-General of Hellas and to wage war against the Persian".

This grand project was in the air; for others besides Philip saw in Persia the standing danger to a divided Greece. It was almost forty years since Isocrates first urged the Greeks to bury their differences and unite as a nation. In an inspiring address given at the Olympic Games, he had said: "Anyone coming from abroad and observing the present situation of Greece would regard us as great fools struggling among ourselves about trifles and destroying our own land, when without danger we might conquer Asia."

Before he finally established his dominion over Greece, Philip determined to gain control of the Hellespontine corn route; once this was in his hands he would possess a powerful economic weapon with which to coerce the Greeks. Further, he would gain the key to the Asiatic door. He carried war into the Propontis and met with a signal failure; in 340 B.C. he failed to take by siege both Perinthus (Eregli) and Byzantium. This setback was

[1] The Delphic Amphictyony was originally a league of twelve ancient Greek tribes inhabiting the country round Thermopylae, which assumed the protection of the temple and worship of Apollo at Delphi and the direction of the Pythian games.

short-lived; early in 338 B.C. a herald came to him at Pella (near Janitza) from the Synod of the Amphictyons with a request that he should coerce Amphissa, a town near Delphi. Philip at once agreed, and some have credited him with having invented the invitation to efface the memory of Perinthus and Byzantium. Thebes and Athens went into alliance to oppose his advance and took the field against him. Philip then crossed into Boeotia and, late in August or early in September, 338 B.C., met them at Chaeronea (E. of Mt. Parnassus). He had with him 30,000 infantry and 3,000 cavalry, and probably his opponents were not inferior to him in numbers. But theirs was a mixed force of mercenaries and civic militias under a dual command, whereas Philip's army was a highly trained national one under his single direction.

Though little is known of the battle which followed, it would appear that the first onslaught was stubborn, and that Philip's aim was to wear down his enemies' resistance before he delivered the decisive blow. When it came, it was dealt by his son Alexander, in command of the Macedonian cavalry who shattered the Theban flank. The whole of the Theban-Athenian line then gave way and a general rout, including Philip's implacable enemy Demosthenes, the Athenian orator, followed.

Chaeronea made Philip lord of the Hellenes *de facto*, and to become so *de jure*, he first secured Corinth and next he invited all the Greek states within Thermopylae to send delegates to a Congress at the isthmus; all sent delegates except Sparta, which refused. He spoke at length at the congress of his resolution to make war on Persia and to liberate the Greek cities in Asia. The Confederacy elected him Captain-General with supreme powers, and Parmenio, Amyntas, and Attalus, with a strong force, were sent to hold the Hellespont and to win a footing in the Troad and Bithynia, while the main Panhellenic army of invasion was being assembled.

In the autumn of 336 B.C., immediately before he intended to set out to join Parmenio, he was assassinated while attending in Pella the marriage of his daughter. Thus the great project became the inheritance of his son, whose work – the expansion of the Macedonian hegemony into one of world-wide empire – is the most authentic testimony of his father's genius.

# CHAPTER 3

# The Battle of Gaugamela or Arbela, 331 B.C.

Imperialism was an essentially eastern conception and foreign to Hellenism. In idea it was theocratic and not aristocratic or democratic. Nor was it purely autocratic, as were the Greek tyrannies; instead it was mystical, because in eastern eyes the king was more than an absolute monarch, above all he was the vicar, or son of the gods, and their priests were his ministers. He ruled his empire, not so much by the right of the sword as by the will of the gods, and when many lands were concerned, as an instrument of government it became clearly convenient that there should be one god who gave to their common ruler power and authority over all men irrespective of race. Further, should this expansion of divinity be carried a step farther, so that it embraced the whole of the known world, then it followed that the right to conquer the lands of a neighbouring god could be expanded into the right or even duty to establish a world-wide empire, the secular domain of the one and only god. Aton, as we have seen, was probably the earliest example of this divine evolution.

This idea was totally foreign to Philip, for the Corinthian League he created, like all the Greek leagues which had preceded it, was no more than a confederation of city states under his military leadership. We may, therefore, conclude that, had Philip lived, though he might have avenged Greece upon Persia, because he neither believed himself to be, nor was accepted as a vicar of the gods, he could never have carried the idea of a world ruler into his conquests, and thereby have leavened them into a world empire—that is, an empire extending over the known world of its day.

This supreme idea of divine conquest was left to his son, and though Dr. Tarn is probably right when he says that Alexander never contemplated becoming a world ruler,[1] the fact remains, which will be discussed later, that he conceived the idea of a divine world ruler, out of which the conception of a universal world empire took shape. It was because he discerned a new relationship between God and man, the aim of which, as we shall see, was

---

[1] *Alexander the Great*, W. W. Tarn (1948), vol. II, Appendix 24.

to establish harmony between man and man–undermining the principle of enmity which separated city from city and people from people, and exalting the principle of amity which united them into a single city and a common brotherhood–that it was possible for Droysen to open his history of him by saying: "The name of Alexander betokens the end of one world epoch and the beginning of another." Equally it made possible what one of his latest biographers, Wilcken, has written: "The whole subsequent course of history, the political, economic and cultural life of after times, cannot be understood apart from the career of Alexander."[1]

More than a world-conqueror, he established a world idea which ever since has reverberated down the ages, and because of this, no man in history approaches him in the span of his fame. In Rome he was glorified by the early Caesars; in Jewish folk-lore he was acclaimed the precursor of the Messiah; and in Turkestan and Badakhshan chieftains of note still seek in him their ancestor. The "Romance"[2] which emanated from his life swept from Iceland to the Yellow Sea; it transformed him into the son of the last Pharaoh, Nectanebo; a scion of the Achaemenid house; a fervent Moslem; a Christian saint; and an all-powerful magician. Fabulous though these legends are, each contains a grain of truth, that Alexander was a prodigy among men.

Born in 356 B.C., probably in the month of October, though it was his father, whose legendary ancestor was Heracles, who impregnated him with the idea of vengeance against Persia, it was from his mother, Olympias, that he inherited the passion which fructified it. A remarkable woman, savage, mystical and domineering, she was the daughter of Neoptolemus of Epirus, who traced his descent from Achilles. At Dodona (Dramisos) in her native land, she had worshipped at the most ancient oracle of Zeus,[3] and was aware that the more mysterious oracle of Amon was situated at the oasis of Siwa. Besides Heracles and Achilles, Dionysus, son of Zeus and Semele, a daughter of Cadmus king of Thebes, was also one of Alexander's legendary ancestors, and in Macedonia a day was set apart for his worship.[4] He was a man-god who,

[1] *Alexander the Great*, Ulrich Wilcken (1932), p. 265.
[2] *The Romance of Alexander*, attributed to "Pseudo-Callisthenes" (Aisopos) is the work of many hands. There are several versions of it, the original appearing in Egypt in the second century A.D. The Ethiopic Version has been translated by Sir Ernest W. Budge under the title *The Alexander Book in Ethiopia* (1933).
[3] Its greatest influence was during the heroic age; later on it was supplanted by the oracle of Delphi.
[4] *Arrian's Anabasis Alexandri*, trans. E. Iliff Robson (1929), IV, VIII.

tradition affirmed, had journeyed through Lydia and Egypt to India, spreading the mystical cult of the vine and conquering the nations as he went. These myths, which were spiritual realities in the age in which Olympias lived, had a profound influence upon her and through her upon her son.

Next to the influence of his father and mother came that of Aristotle, whom Philip engaged as his tutor when his son was thirteen years old, and with whom he remained in the little village of Mieza for three years. Under him he became inspired with love of Greek culture and a deep veneration for Homer, a copy of whose works, annotated by Aristotle, it is said he carried with him throughout his campaigns. While under his tutorship there can be little doubt that Aristotle instilled into him hatred of the Persians, for they had murdered Aristotle's friend and relative, Hermeias tyrant of Atarneus.

With such parents and such a tutor, coupled with his native genius and inexhaustible energy, it is not to be wondered at that everything Alexander did took upon itself the superlative mood. He was incredibly brave and yet profoundly cautious. Both as realist and idealist, a doer and a foreseer, he stood out above all his fellows, whether as a man of action or man of thought. He was both mystical and practical, and to all who came into contact with him infinitely magnetic. Though imaginative in the extreme, his imagination seldom ran away with his reason, and he was as meticulous in detail as he was expansive in general ideas. In his eulogy of Alexander, Arrian says it seemed to him that a hero so totally unlike any other human being could not have been born "without some divine influence".[1]

We are told that Alexander was of medium height and of fair complexion; he had, says Plutarch, a habit of inclining his head "a little to one side towards his left shoulder". A swift runner, he despised professional athletes, and on his campaigns, when he was free from employment, "he would spend the day in hunting, or administering justice, or arranging his military affairs, or reading. . . . Often too, for diversion he would hunt foxes or birds. . . ."[2] "He was also by nature", Plutarch further relates, "a lover of learning and a lover of reading . . . and when he could find no other books [except the *Iliad*] in the interior of Asia, he ordered Harpalus to send him some. So Harpalus sent him the books of

[1] *Arrian's Anabasis Alexandri*, VII, xxx.
[2] *Plutarch's Lives*, trans. Bernadotte Perrin (1919), "Alexander", XXIII.

Philistus", and "a great many of the tragedies of Euripides, Sophocles and Aeschylus. . . ."[1]

But it was his moral outlook which, above all his qualities, distinguished him from his contemporaries. He could, in an age in which compassion was considered to be unmanly, show compassion to others and pity to those in misfortune. At Ephesus he stopped the Ephesians slaughtering the oligarchs, for he knew if the people were not checked, they "would put to death, together with the guilty, certain others, some from hatred, and some for plunder of their goods".[2] At the siege of Miletus, when some of the besieged had sought refuge on an island, Alexander, seeing that they "were going to fight to the death, he felt compassion for them; as noble and loyal soldiers, and made terms with them that they should join his forces".[3] After the battle of Issus he showed compassion to the Theban ambassadors, partly out of pity for Thebes[4] which he regretted having destroyed. And when on his return from India, during the march through the desert of Gedrosia (Makran), some of the famishing soldiers placed on guard over the magazines of corn, pilfered from them, Alexander, "on learning of the grave necessity pardoned the offenders".[5]

But it was in his outlook upon women—in nearly all ages considered the legitimate spoil of the soldier—that Alexander stood in a totally different moral world compared with the one inhabited by his contemporaries. Not only did he treat the captive wife and daughters of Darius with a royal respect, but he held in abhorrence rape and violence, which in his day were the universal concomitants of war. On one occasion, "when he heard that two Macedonians of Parmenio's regiment had outraged the wives of some of the mercenary soldiers, he wrote to Parmenio ordering him, in case the men were convicted to punish them and put them to death as wild beasts born for the destruction of mankind".[6] On another occasion, when Atropates, viceroy of Media, presented him with a hundred girls equipped and armed like horsemen, "Alexander sent them from the army, lest they should meet any roughness from the Macedonians or foreign troops. . . ."[7] And at the sack of Persepolis he issued the amazing order that the women were not to be touched. Yet, in spite of this extraordinary respect for womanhood, his highest moral virtue is to be discovered in one of the final remarks Arrian makes in The Anabasis. In his

---

[1] Arrian, VIII.    [2] Ibid., I, XVII.    [3] Ibid., II, XV.    [4] Ibid., I, XIX.
[5] Ibid., VI, XXIII.    [6] Plutarch's "Alexander" ,XXII.    [7] Arrian, VII, XIII.

apology for Alexander's errors he writes: "But I do know that to Alexander alone of the kings of old did repentance for his faults come by reason of his noble nature."[1]

Of his generalship much has been written; but of all the summaries Arrian's is probably the most true, because the main source of *The Anabasis* was the lost history of Alexander's general, Ptolemy, written after he had become king of Egypt. It runs as follows:

He was "of much shrewdness, most courageous, most zealous for honour and danger, and most careful of religion . . . most brilliant to seize on the right course of action, even where all was obscure; and where all was clear, most happy in his conjectures of likelihood; most masterly in marshalling an army and in arming and equipping it; and in uplifting his soldiers' spirits and filling them with good hopes, and brushing away anything fearful in dangers by his own want of fear – in all this most noble. And all that had to be done in uncertainty he did with the utmost daring; he was most skilled in swift anticipation and gripping of his enemy before anyone had time to fear the event. . . ."[2]

On his accession Alexander found himself menaced on all sides and acted with startling rapidity. First he advanced into Thessaly and by turning the flank of the Thessalian garrison at Tempe he won so decisive a bloodless victory that he was at once elected head of the Thessalian League. Next, he descended on Thermopylae and was recognized by the Amphictyony as Philip's successor. So rapid was his southward advance that Athens, then preparing to break away from Macedonia, at once submitted to him and the Congress of the Corinthian Confederacy elected him Captain-General in his father's place. Thus, within a few weeks of Philip's death, he had so firmly established his position within Greece that he was able to set out and secure the northern and western frontiers of his realm by imposing his will on the wild tribes bordering upon them. In two astonishing campaigns, the one on the Danube and the other in Illyria, he established his authority, and, immediately he had done so, set out southward at top speed, for again trouble was brewing within Greece, this time fostered by Persia.

In 338 B.C. Artaxerxes III, son of Artaxerxes II, the victor of Cunaxa, was assassinated and succeeded by Codomannus, a distant relative, who, adopting the name Darius, became Darius III. He feared the rise of Macedonia, and when Alexander was en-

[1] Arrian, VII, XXIX.          *Ibid.*, VII, XXVIII.

gaged in the north seized the opportunity to send 300 talents to Athens as a bribe. Though the Athenians refused it, it was accepted by Demosthenes, and about the same time rumours came in that Alexander and his army had perished in the wilds of Illyria. The Thebans did not wait to verify these reports and laid siege to the Macedonian garrison holding the Cadmea, the Athenians supporting the former with a contingent. Then, suddenly, the Thebans learnt that instead of being dead Alexander was at Onchestus, a town some fifteen miles north-west of Thebes. He had marched there with such speed that his coming fell like a thunderbolt on the Thebans. The next day he was before the walls of their city, and seizing one of its gates in a surprise attack, 6,000 Thebans were slaughtered; after which the city was levelled with the ground and its lands divided up among the members of the Confederacy. Terrified by this catastrophe, the Athenians at once submitted and were treated with great leniency, not only because Alexander recognized Athens to be the cultural centre of Greece, but because he did not want the powerful Athenian fleet to go over to the Persians. Thus, in little more than twelve months he had securely established a base of operations in Europe from which he could launch his attack against Persia.

Alexander left Antipater with some 9,000 foot and a small body of horse to hold Greece and to watch Sparta and assembled his fleet of 160 triremes at Lake Cercinitis–the lower waters of the Strymon river. Late in 335 B.C., or early in the following year, he set out from Pella with his army for Sestus. While it was being ferried over to Abydus, he sailed down the Hellespont and visited Troy, so that he might lay a wreath on the tomb of Achilles and propitiate the genius of the most human of his traditional ancestors. At Arisbe, a few miles east of Abydus, he rejoined his army, which now numbered 30,000 foot and 5,000 horse,[1] and, to clear his left flank before marching into central Persia, he advanced on the river Granicus (Bigha Tschai), where lay an army of 20,000 Asiatic horse and 20,000 Greek mercenaries under Memnon of Rhodes.[2] On the Granicus, in May or June, 334 B.C., he won the first of his four major battles. It was followed by the submission of the whole of Hellespontine Phrygia. Turning south, he marched on Sardes, which capitulated; next to Ephesus, which submitted; and

---

[1] Arrian, I, XI.
[2] *Ibid.*, I, XIV. Tarn (*Alexander the Great*, vol. I, p. 16) says the cavalry must have been considerably less.

then to Miletus, which refusing to do so was besieged and occupied in July. There he made his first great decision since the campaign had opened. It was to wrest the command of the sea from the Persians, not by destroying their fleet, for he had not the means to do so, but by occupying all its ports and bases on the shores of the eastern Mediterranean. This formidable task took him two years to accomplish.

The first of these bases was Halicarnassus (Bodrum). When he found that its reduction would be a long task, Alexander left 3,000 foot and 200 horse under Ptolemy to besiege it while he pressed on to Gordium (Bela-Hissar), in two columns, one under Parmenio moving through Lydia, and the other, under himself following the Lycian coast. From Gordium he marched by way of Ancyra to Tarsus, and thence to where Alexandretta now stands, arriving there in October, 333 B.C.

Meanwhile Darius had assembled an army at Sochoi, to the east of the Amanus Mountains, and learning that Alexander was advancing southward along the coast, he abandoned the plain lands, crossed the Amanus range, came down on Issus, at the northern extremity of the Gulf of Alexandretta, and cut the Macedonian line of communications and supply. Immediately this became known to Alexander he doubled back and fought the second of his major battles – the Battle of Issus – on the banks of the river Pinarus (Deli Tschai). There the Persians were routed and Darius put to flight.

Alexander held fast to his aim – the occupation of the Persian naval bases – and instead of pushing inland after his beaten enemy he continued his advance down the Syrian coast. Aradus (near Tripoli), Byblus (Jebeil), and Sidon opened their gates to him, and Tyre would have done likewise had not he demanded the right of sacrificing to the Tyrian god Melkarth, whom the Greeks called the Heracles of Tyre. The request was refused, the island city was besieged, and after one of the most famous and extraordinary sieges in history, which lasted from January to August, 332 B.C., it was stormed. Thus, not only did all the Persian naval bases, but also all the Phoenician city fleets, including that of Cyprus, pass into Alexander's hands. Together, they gave him absolute command of the eastern Mediterranean and made Macedonia the greatest naval power in the world.

He moved on through what to-day is Palestine, and Gaza, after a two-month siege, was stormed and Egypt cut off from any possible Persian assistance. Alexander sent his fleet to Pelusium, marched on to Memphis, and entered the capital of the Pharaohs where, according to the "Romance", he was placed on a throne in the temple of Ptah, and invested as King of Egypt. From Memphis he sailed down the Nile to Canopus, and close by Rhacotis he chose the site of Alexandria, the most famous of the many cities which bore his name.

Early in 331 B.C. he marched two hundred and twenty miles over the desert to visit the oracle of Amon at Siwa, which legend affirmed had been conquered by his ancestors Perseus[1] and Heracles. According to Plutarch (though modern scholarship disputes the story), as he approached the shrine in the oasis he was met by a priest who, wishing to give him a friendly greeting in the Greek language, said, "O my son", but being a foreigner, mispronounced the words so as to say "Son of Zeus", a mistake which pleased Alexander and as a story caused men to say that the god himself had addressed him as "O son of Zeus".[2] Together they went to the god; but what was revealed to Alexander is unknown, except that it was so great a secret he dared not even communicate it to his mother in writing.[3]

Whatever it was, it would seem to be more than a coincidence that, immediately after the priest addressed Alexander as "Son of Zeus", Plutarch relates the following incident: That while in Egypt, he attended the lectures of the philosopher Psammon, and was especially pleased when he pointed out that God is King over all men, "since in every case that which gets the mastery and rules is divine. Still more philosophical, however, was his own opinion and utterance on this head, namely that although God was indeed common father of all mankind, still He made peculiarly His own the noblest and best of them."[4]

---

[1] Perseus was the grandfather of Alcmena, the mother of Heracles.

[2] Plutarch's "Alexander", xxvii. Alexander never claimed to be son of Zeus, though he acquiesced in people calling him so. But in Egypt, having been crowned Pharaoh, he automatically became son of his divine father Amon-Re as well as of his actual father Philip.

[3] In all probability it was that Amon declared Alexander to be his beloved son, on whom he bestowed "the immortality of Ra, and the royalty of Horus, victory over all his enemies, and the dominion of the world," etc., etc. In this the important point is that this declaration "was the only formula known by which the priests could declare him *de jure* King of Egypt, as he already was *de facto*" (*A History of Egypt under the Ptolemaic Dynasty*, J. P. Mahaffy, 1899, p. 16).

[4] *Ibid.*, xxvii. ". . . what he had in mind was presumably his own adoption by Ammon, for his whole career illustrates his conviction that Ammon had made him 'peculiarly his own' " (*Alexander the Great and the Unity of Mankind*, W. W. Tarn, 1933, p. 25).

From this we may hazard that, whatever the priest or god actually said to him, he came away from the shrine with the idea in his mind that, because the sun-god Amon-Re shines upon all men, good and evil, alike, the conception of *Homonoia*–"unity in concord" or "being of one mind together"–without which there could be no true peace within a city state, should be expanded to include the whole world as the City of God, and, therefore, to all human beings irrespective of race. According to Dr. Tarn, this was an advance far beyond the idea of *Homonoia* held by either Plato, Aristotle, or Isocrates.[1] Professor Wright holds the same opinion. He says: "To Aristotle he owed much, but he went far beyond his master when, casting aside the distinction between Hellene and barbarian, he boldly proclaimed the universal brotherhood of man."[2] On this question, possibly the most important intellectual event in the history of the world, Tarn writes:

"What Eratosthenes says amounts to this. Aristotle told Alexander to treat Greeks as friends, but barbarians like animals; but Alexander knew better, and preferred to divide men into good and bad without regard to their race, and thus carried out Aristotle's real intention. For Alexander believed that he had a mission from the deity to harmonize men generally and be the reconciler of the world, mixing men's lives and customs as in a loving cup, and treating the good as his kin, the bad as strangers; for he thought that the good man was the real Greek and the bad man the real barbarian."

Commenting on this, he continues:

"It is obvious that, wherever all this comes from, we are dealing with a great revolution in thought. It amounts to this, that there is a natural brotherhood of all men, though bad men do not share in it; that *Homonoia* is no longer to be confined to the relations between Greek and Greek, but is to unite Greek and barbarian; and that Alexander's aim was to substitute peace for war, and reconcile the enmities of mankind by bringing them all–all that is whom his arm could reach, the peoples of his empire–to be of one mind together; as men were one in blood, so they should become one in heart and spirit."[3]

Xenophon, in his *Cyropaedia*, had in Cyrus presented Alexander with the picture of the ideal world ruler. Plato had written of the

---

[1] *Alexander the Great and the Unity of Mankind*, pp. 4–5.
[2] *Alexander the Great*, F. A. Wright (1934), p. 2.
[3] *Alexander the Great and the Unity of Mankind*, p. 7.

philosopher-king, and, as Henri Berr has pointed out: "Being accustomed to leave the circle of facts to soar into the sphere of ideas, he [Alexander] rose to the principle that there must be one single ruler for men, just as there is only one sun to light the earth."[1] Thus, in his mystical metamorphosis at Siwa, the philosopher-taught king became the god-king. So it came about that through Alexander the West received from the East the ideas of the theocratic empire and king worship, the one to find its blossoming in the Roman Empire and its successor, the Empire of Christendom, and the other to be transmuted into the divine right of kings.

This extended interpretation of *Homonoia*–"one of the supreme revolutions in the world's outlook"[2]–afterwards became the goal of all his conquests, and it lead him from Siwa towards the ends of the world, as they seemed to be in his day.

When he returned to Memphis and found reinforcements from Greece awaiting him, Alexander hastened to organize his control over Egypt. He appointed his garrison commanders and ordered them to allow the governors to rule their respective districts according to ancient custom; but to collect from them the tribute due to him.[3] His method throughout his reign was invariably the same: he separated civil administration from military control. The former he handed over to the representatives of the conquered people, and the latter he placed in the hands of one of his chosen Macedonians.

In the spring of 331 B.C., he bridged the Nile and marched back to Tyre, where he found his fleet had already arrived. From there he sent a strong squadron to the Peloponnese to counteract the intrigues of the Spartans, and thence, by way of the valley of the Orontes, he marched towards Antioch. Turning eastward he debouched on the Euphrates at Thapsacus (the ford of El-Hamman), and in its vicinity founded the city of Nicephorium (Rakkah) as a strong point and depot on his line of communications. At first he intended to cross the Tigris near Nineveh, at the spot where Mosul now stands; but when he learnt that Darius was in this region with a large army he decided to cross the river north-west of the old Assyrian capital and to march down its left bank towards Arbela (Erbil).

The army which was now destined to win what was to be the

[1] In Foreword to *Macedonian Imperialism and the Hellenization of the East*, Pierre Jouguet (1928), pp. xiii-xiv.
[2] *Alexander the Great and the Unity of Mankind*, p. 28.　　　　[3] Arrian, III, v.

most epoch-making of all the decisive battles of the western world was the creation of Philip, and as a military organizer his greatness springs from his appreciation that mobility is the governing tactical element in army organization. Up to his day battles had been looked upon as competitions of endurance, in which victory went to the side which won the battlefield and erected a trophy upon it. In any case, because of its rigidity, the phalanx could not pursue without breaking its order, when it became easy prey to light-armed and mounted troops. What Philip saw was that the tussle on the battlefield was only a means to an end, the tactical end being the annihilation of the enemy in the pursuit. He organized his army with this aim in view and combined all classes of fighters in one tactical instrument. While his infantry clinched with the enemy and held him, his cavalry manœuvred and struck the decisive blow: the first was the bow from which the arrow was shot.

Long before his day the Macedonian cavalry had consisted of nobles called *Hetairoi*, or the King's Companions. It was a very ancient title, dating back to the *Iliad*, in which the 2,500 Myrmidons of Achilles are called by the same name. In Philip's day the infantry was already in the process of being transformed from a mere gathering of armed peasants into organized regular infantry called *Pezhetairoi*, or Foot Companions. Philip divided the cavalry into regiments (*Ilae*), each from 1,500 to 1,800 strong, one of which was constituted the *Agema* of the Companions, or the Royal Horse Guard. The Companion (heavy) cavalry were armed with the sword and wore helmets and corselets, but their chief weapon was the lance. Because stirrups were not introduced until the sixth century A.D., the lance was used as a thrusting weapon and was not couched for shock as in the Middle Ages. For the old hoplite Philip substituted a soldier who was a cross between the hoplite and the light armed *peltast*, armed with a long pike and small round shield (*pelta*), introduced by the Athenian general Iphicrates in 392 B.C. The new hoplite was armed with a fourteen-foot spear, the *sarissa*,[1] and a light shield carried on the right arm; he wore greaves and a metal protected jerkin of leather. Philip organized the infantry of the phalanx in regiments (*taxeis*) each normally containing 1,536 men divided into battalions and companies. The smallest unit was the file of sixteen men, but by Alexander normally it was reduced to eight men.

[1] See Tarn's *Alexander the Great*, vol. II, pp. 170–171.

Besides the phalangites, Philip raised three battalions of light-armed infantry, the Hypaspists, each 1,000 strong, to act as a link between the faster moving cavalry of the right wing and the slower moving phalanx. The three together may be compared to a slow moving wall on the left, a fast moving door on the right, with a hinge in between. The hinge, or flexible link–Hypaspists–was essential to an advance in oblique order, for without it contact between the cavalry and phalanx would almost certainly be lost, and in all ancient fighting the maintenance of an unbroken front was always the aim. One battalion of the Hypaspists was known as the *Agema*, or Royal Foot Guard.

In addition to the above, which were wholly Macedonian, Philip raised a considerable body of light allied cavalry, mainly Thessalian. And in addition to the Macedonian infantry, Alexander had a large force of Confederate infantry and also a force of mercenaries.

Up to Philip's time, sieges in Greece had depended upon starving out the besieged garrisons. To speed this slow process, Philip introduced siege engines from Sicily, where for long they had been used by Greek and Carthaginian engineers.

Of Alexander's artillery and engineers[1] we know next to nothing, and nothing whatever of his baggage and supply trains. The artillery was provided with *ballistae* (guns) and catapults (howitzers) which threw stone shot and javelins, and the engineers were provided with the necessary tools and materials for building battering-rams, siege-towers, ramps, bridges, and encampments. All these arms and services were commanded by Alexander, who was helped by an organized staff, comprising a Secretariat; the Keepers of the Diary; Keepers of the King's Plans; Surveyors; the Official Historian; and many specialists and scientific research workers. As a whole, the army, unlike any which had preceded it, was not solely an army of conquest, but above all an army of occupation, organized for scientific exploration as well as for fighting.

Darius recruited another army after his defeat at Issus, and since we are told that he armed certain of his divisions with swords

[1] Tarn (*Alexander the Great*, vol. II, pp. 39–40) gives the names of the following engineers on the headquarters staff: Diades of Thessaly, Charias and Poseidonius, siege engineers; Gorgos, water and mining engineer; Deinocrates, town planning expert; Aristobolus, architect and engineer; Baeton, Diognetos and Philonides, bematists (steppers), who dealt with routes and camps and kept geographical records. Besides these, Nearchus and Onesicritus were naval experts, and Eumenes head of the Secretariat.

and longer spears, the better to cope with the *sarissa*, it is apparent that he was not beyond learning a lesson. He marched northward from Babylon, crossed to the left bank of the Tigris, and proceeded to Arbela, the "city of the four gods", where he established his magazines and harem. From there he moved forward to Gaugamela (Mound of Tel Gomel) on the river Bumodos (Khajir), a tributary of the Greater Zab; which place is about eighteen miles north-east of Mosul and thirty-five west of Arbela. The reason why he selected this locality was that it consisted of an extensive plain (near Keramlais), and, therefore, favoured his large forces of cavalry.

Alexander crossed the Tigris while this was being done and, on September 20, when resting his army on its eastern bank, a partial eclipse of the moon occurred, so he sacrificed to Selene, Helios, and Ge (Moon, Sun, and Earth).[1]

A few days later, after his scouts had informed him that the Persians were approaching, he at once prepared for battle, and at the head of a picked force of cavalry marched with all speed towards his enemy, having ordered the rest of his army to follow at walking pace.[2] From captured prisoners he learnt that the Persian king was at Gaugamela at the head of 40,000 cavalry, 1,000,000 infantry,[3] 200 scythe-bearing chariots[4] and a few war elephants.[5] Meanwhile Darius, by levelling the land and removing obstacles, converted the plain of Gaugamela into an immense parade ground, on which he drew up his army in the following order of battle:

"The left wing the Bactrian cavalry held, and with them the Dahans [a Scythian tribe] and the Arachotians; next to them were arrayed the Persians, cavalry and infantry mixed, and after the Persians Susians, and after the Susians Cadusians. This was the

---

[1] Arrian, III, VII. As Alexander selected these gods, it may be concluded that he understood the cause of a lunar eclipse.

[2] *Ibid.*, III, VIII.

[3] These figures are Arrian's and clearly are exaggerated. What the actual strength was is unknown. Justin gives 400,000 foot and 100,000 horse; Curtius 45,000 cavalry and 200,000 infantry; and Diodorus and Plutarch 1,000,000 all told.

[4] Chariots at times could be very effective, see Xenophon's *Hellenica*, IV, I, 18. Lucretius (*On the Nature of Things*, III, 660–662) gives a dramatic description of their use: "Reeking with indiscriminate slaughter, they lop off limbs so instantaneously that what has been cut away is seen to quiver on the ground before any pain is felt. One man perceives not that the wheels and devouring scythes have carried off among the horses' feet his left arm, shield and all; another while he presses forward sees not that his right arm has dropped from him; a third tries to get up after he has lost a leg, while the dying foot quivers with its toes on the ground close by."

[5] The first recorded instance outside India of the employment of elephants in battle.

disposition of the left wing up to the centre of the entire phalanx. On the right were marshalled the troops from Lowland Syria and Mesopotamia; and next on the right were Medes, and with them the Parthyaeans and Sacians, then Tapurians and Hyrcanians, and then Albanians and Sacesinians, right up to the centre of the entire phalanx. In the centre, where was King Darius, were posted the king's kinsmen, the Persians whose spears are fitted with golden apples, Indians, the 'transplanted' Carians, as they were called, and the Mardian bowmen. The Uxians, Babylonians, Red Sea tribes, and Sitacenians were in deep formation behind them. Then, in advance, on the left wing, facing Alexander's right, were the Scythian cavalry, some thousand Bactrians, and a hundred scythe-chariots. The elephants were posted ahead of Darius's royal squadron and fifty chariots. In front of the right wing were posted the Armenian and Cappadocian cavalry and fifty scythe-chariots. The Greek mercenaries, close by Darius, and his Persian troops, on either side were stationed exactly opposite the Macedonian phalanx as being the only troops able to meet the phalanx."[1]

From this discription it is not possible to make out how the various bodies of men were actually marshalled. The accompanying diagrams show what Colonel Dodge[2] considered to be the probable distribution. According to Tarn, the whole of the first line was composed of cavalry "with a second line of infantry behind them".[3] The right wing was commanded by Mazaeus and the left by Bessus.[4]

After he had ascertained the dispositions of his enemy, Alexander spent four days in resting his army and in strengthening his camp with a ditch and a stockade. About the second watch of the fourth night after crossing the Tigris he broke camp and marched towards Darius, "so as to meet the enemy at dawn".[5] When some three and a half miles distant from the Persians, he halted and assembled his generals. Parmenio, his second in command, suggested that they should encamp where they were and reconnoitre the ground and the enemy. Alexander agreed to this, and while the camp was being fortified he "took the light infantry and the Cavalry Companions and rode all round surveying the ground which was to be the battlefield".[6]

[1] Arrian, III, XI.　　　[2] *Alexander*, Theodore Ayrault Dodge (1890), vol. II, p. 371.
[3] *Alexander the Great*, vol. II, p. 183.
[4] *Quintus Curtius*, trans. John C. Rolfe (1946), IV, XVI, and IV, XV, 2.
[5] Arrian, III, IX.　　　　　　　　　　　　[6] *Ibid.*, III, IX.

He again called together a conference on his return at which
he discussed what he had seen and urged upon his generals the
importance of the immediate execution of orders.

On September 30, the night before the battle, when Darius was
holding a kind of midnight tattoo, Alexander's army rested.
Parmenio came to the king's tent to suggest a night attack, but

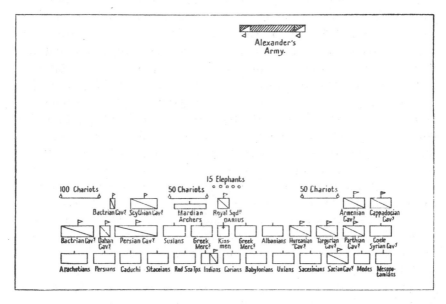

9. DARIUS'S ORDER OF BATTLE AT ARBELA, 331 B.C.

(See footnote 3, page 99.)

Alexander refused to consider it.[1] In the forthcoming battle he had
planned to deliver a decisive blow, and he realized well the difficulties coincident with night operations. Alexander drew up
his army as follows:

The right wing was held by the Companions, the Hypaspists,
and presumably, three *taxeis* of the phalanx. Thus, to the right
front stood the Royal Squadron of Clitus; slightly to his left the
squadrons of Glaucias, Aristo, Sopolis, Heraclides, Demetrius,
Meleager, and Hegelochus. The whole of the cavalry was under
the command of Philotas, son of Parmenio. Next came the *Agema*,
and then the Hypaspists under Nicanor. The phalanx was
marshalled as follows: the brigade of Coenus on the right, then

[1] Arrian, III, x.

those of Perdiccas, Meleager, Polysperchon, Simmias, and Craterus; Craterus, as usual, commanded the infantry of the left wing. On the left came the Greek cavalry under Erigyius, then the Thessalian cavalry under Philip. The whole of the left wing was under the command of Parmenio, around whose person were ranged the Pharsalian horsemen.[1]

So far there was nothing unusual in this order of battle. The array was normal and similar to that at the battles of Granicus and Issus; but the tactical problem was different, and in idea it closely resembled the one which, as described by Xenophon, faced Cyrus at the battle of Thymbra.[2] Alexander probably was acquainted with Xenophon's *Cyropaedia*; in any case he applied the tactics of this semi-mythological battle to the present one, for behind his front he posted "a second line, so as to duplicate his phalanx".[3] Directions had been given, writes Arrian, to the commanders of this reserve line, "if they should see their own front line being surrounded by the Persian host, to wheel round to receive the Persian attack".[4] This rear or reserve line consisted of two flying columns, one behind each wing. They were posted "angular wise"—that is, at an angle to the front—in order to take the enemy in flank should he attempt to sweep round the wings; or, if he did not, they were to wheel inwards to reinforce the front of the army.

On the right were drawn up the following: half the Agrianians under Attalus; half the Macedonian archers under Briso, and the Veteran Mercenaries (infantry) under Cleander. In front of the first two were posted the light cavalry under Aretes and the Paeonians under Ariosto, and to their front the Grecian mercenary cavalry under Menidas. The rest of the Agrianians, archers and javelin-men of Balacrus, was drawn up in front of the Companion cavalry to oppose the charge of the Persian scythe-bearing chariots. Instructions had been given to Menidas and the troops under him to wheel round and attack the enemy in flank if they should ride round their wing.[5] The left column was similarly marshalled at an angle to the front. First the Thracians under Sitalces, then the cavalry of the Greek allies under Coeranus, next the Odrysian cavalry under Agatho. In front of these were drawn up the Greek mercenaries under Andromachus. The baggage guard consisted

---

[1] Arrian, III, XI.    [2] *Cyropaedia*, VII,I.
[3] Arrian, III, XII. See Arrian's *Tactics*, 29, for this arrangement.
[4] *Ibid.*, III, XII.    [5] *Ibid.*, III, XII.

of Thracian infantry. In all, Alexander's army numbered 7,000 cavalry and 40,000 infantry.

Of Alexander's grand tactical formation Colonel Dodge writes: "This disposition has been called a grand hollow square, but it

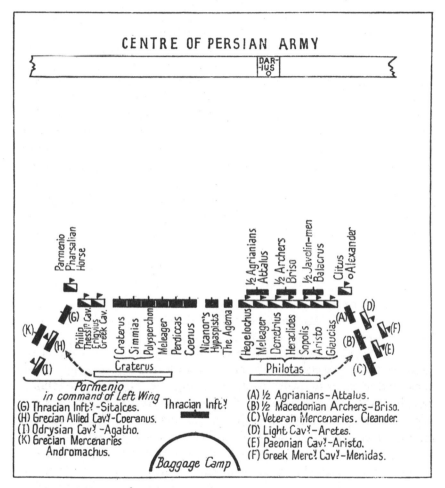

10. ALEXANDER'S ORDER OF BATTLE AT ARBELA, 331 B.C.

was more than that. The arrangements were such as to ensure greater mobility than a square is capable of possessing. For the flying columns were so organised and disposed that they could face in any direction, and were prepared to meet attacks from front, flank or rear. Indeed, the left flying column met an attack from within, and beat it off. 'In fine', says Curtius, 'he had so disposed his army that it fronted every way'—he should have said could front every way—'and was ready to engage on all sides, if attempted to be encompassed; thus the front was not better secured than the flanks, nor the flanks better provided than the rear!"[1]

Such was Alexander's order of battle, and it is important to bear it in mind; for, as will now be shown, in the battle itself, because he had gauged his enemy's intentions and had prepared to meet them, he was able to develop his tactics in accordance with his own idea. It was his foresight which gained him the victory.

As the Macedonians approached the Persians, Alexander, instead of moving directly upon them, inclined towards their left wing, and seeing this Darius marched along parallel with him,[2] his Scythian cavalry galloping forward to the attack. Alexander continued his oblique approach and gradually began to get beyond the ground which had been cleared and levelled by the Persians.[3] Fearing that his chariots would become useless, Darius ordered the front units of his left wing to ride round Alexander's right wing and compel it to halt. To meet this attack, Alexander moved forward the Greek mercenaries under Menidas, but they were driven back in confusion. Next, the Paeonians under Aristo and Cleander's mercenaries were ordered forward; and, in reply, Bessus sent in the Bactrian and Scythian horsemen. These broke the ranks of the Companions and heavy losses resulted, the Scythians and their horses being "better protected by defensive armour".[4] In spite of this, Macedonian discipline and valour began to tell as squadron after squadron charged home, and Bessus's attack was driven back. Apparently to take advantage of the confusion into which the Companions had been thrown, Darius launched his chariots to throw the phalanx into disorder; but, as soon as they approached, they were met by showers of arrows and javelins from the Agrianians and the men of Balacrus who had been drawn up in front of the Companion cavalry. Thus ended the first phase of the battle on the Macedonian right wing.

The second opened by an order to Aretes to attack those who were riding round the Macedonian right wing. Next, placing himself at the head of the Companion cavalry, Alexander wheeled it round, formed it into a wedge, and with the four right *taxeis* of

---

[1] *Alexander*, vol. II, p. 372.
[3] *Ibid.*, III, XIII.
[2] Arrian, III, XIII.
[4] *Ibid.*, III, XIII.

the phalanx, led his horse towards a gap formed in the Persian front by the advance of their own cavalry. Lastly, he galloped forward making straight for Darius–the decisive point. The

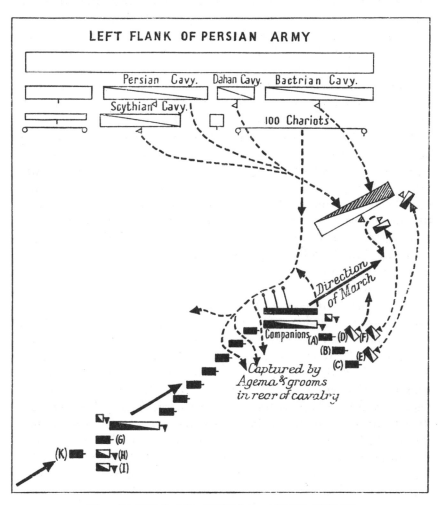

**LEFT FLANK OF PERSIAN ARMY**

Persian Cavy.   Dahan Cavy.   Bactrian Cavy.

Scythian Cavy.

100 Chariots

*Direction of March*

Companions (A)   (D) (F)
(B)
(C)   (E)

*Captured by Agema & grooms in rear of cavalry*

(6)
(K)   (H)
(I)

II.   BATTLE OF ARBELA, FIRST PHASE

charge, closely supported on its left by the dense array of bristling pikes of the phalanx, smote such terror into the Persian king that he fled the field. Meanwhile the enemy cavalry on Alexander's original right, finding their rear threatened by Aretes, took to flight, and the Macedonians followed and slaughtered them. The scene must have been an extraordinary one, for both Curtius and Diodorus say: "That so thick a cloud of dust was raised by the mighty mass of fugitives, that nothing could be clearly distinguished, and that thus the Macedonians lost the track of Darius. The noise of the shouting and the cracking of whips served as guides to the pursuers."[1]

When the battle on Alexander's right was in progress, another was being fought on the left. The left wing, because of the oblique approach march, was in rear of the right, and Alexander's impetuous advance appears to have created a gap between it and the right wing. Through this gap the Indian and Persian cavalry burst and galloped towards the Macedonian baggage camp to rescue Darius's family. Here, as Arrian states, the action became desperate. "However the commanders of the troops which formed the reserve to the first phalanx, learning what had happened, smartly turned about face, according to previous orders, and so appeared in the rear of the Persians and slew large numbers of them. . . ."[2] While this action was being fought the Persian cavalry on Darius's right wing rode round Alexander's left wing and attacked Parmenio in flank. Parmenio was now surrounded.

At this juncture, Parmenio sent a messenger to Alexander to inform him of his critical situation. He received it at the time when he was pursuing the fragments of the Persian left wing. At once he wheeled round with the Companion cavalry and led them against the Persian right. The Persian cavalry, now falling back, finding their retreat menaced, fought stubbornly. They struck and were struck without quarter, and at length were routed by Alexander.

Parmenio freed, the pursuit was renewed and pressed until midnight, when a forced march was made on Arbela. About thirty-five miles were covered, but in vain, for Darius made good his escape.

The casualties suffered in this battle are impossible even to guess. Arrian states that 300,000 of the Persians were slain, and that far more prisoners were taken.[3] Alexander's losses are given as 100 killed and 1,000 horses lost. Curtius says that 40,000 Persians were killed and 300 Macedonians, and Diodorus 90,000 and 500 respectively.[4]

Instead of pursuing Darius farther Alexander marched on Babylon, which was not defensible as its walls for long had been

[1] Diodorus, xvii, 5, and Curtius, iv, xv, 33.    [2] Arrian, ii, xiv.
[3] *Ibid.*, iii, xv.    [4] Curtius. iv, xvi, 26, and Diodorus, xvii, 61.

destroyed. When he entered it he ordered the restoration of the temple of Marduk (the Semitic Bel). Thence he advanced on Susa where he seized 50,000 talents in bullion (£12,000,000 at £3 17s. 10½d. the fine ounce); next to Pasargadae where he seized 120,000 talents (£29,000,000), and from there to Persepolis,

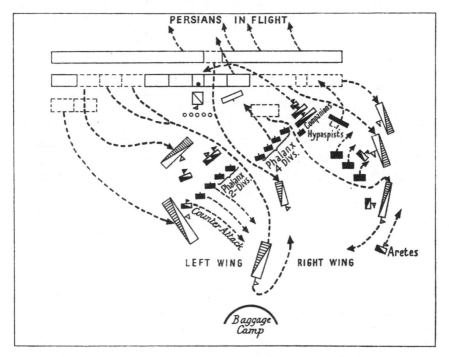

12.  BATTLE OF ARBELA, SECOND PHASE

where, as an act of ritualistic vengeance, the palace of Xerxes was burnt. It was at Persepolis that Alexander heard from Antipater that in a great battle before Megalopolis he had defeated and slain Agis, king of Sparta, and that the Peloponnesian League had been dissolved and Sparta compelled to enter the Corinthian League.

Alexander left Persepolis during the winter of 330 B.C., and set out for Ecbatana (Hamadan) where he seized 180,000 talents (£43,785,000). But once again Darius eluded him. At length, covering 390 miles in eleven days, he caught up with Darius, only to find that he had been murdered by Bessus. With his death, Alexander's political object was attained, by right of the sword he had become King of Kings. As such it was imperative that he should impose his will on his empire by establishing his authority over its eastern satrapies and, if possible, by providing them with secure frontiers.

He subdued the Caspian region and then marched eastward to Herat, where he founded Alexandria in Aria; next southward to the river Helmand, on the northern borders of Gedrosia; and thence north-east, founding Alexandria in Arachosia at Ghazni. From Kabul, near which he built Alexandria of the Caucasus, in the early spring of 329 B.C. he and his army climbed the Khawak Pass and scrambled over the Hindu-Kush. He descended into Bactria, crossed the Oxus, marched into Scythia (Tartary), and established a chain of forts as his northern protective frontier, the most important being Alexandria Eschate (Khojend) on the Jaxartes (Syr Daria).

He formed an alliance with the Scythians and, in order to bind Bactria to him, he married Roxana, the daughter of Oxyartes, chief of that country, and in the late spring of 327 B.C., he followed the line of advance which legend affirmed had been trodden by Dionysus and Heracles, and set out for India at the head of some 27,000 to 30,000 men. At Kabul he divided his army, sent one half under Hephaestion and Perdiccas down the Khyber, and led the other half through Chitral, conquered various hill tribes, and then descended through Swat to Attock, on the Indus, where he rejoined Hephaestion. He crossed the Indus and marched to the Hydaspes (Jhelum) and there, in 326 B.C., in the last of his four major battles, tactically the most brilliant of all, he defeated the Indian king Porus. He reinstated him for his bravery, reduced Sangala (near Lahore), crossed the river Accsines (Chenab), and led his army towards the Hydraotis (Ravee) and then on to the Hyphasis (Sutlej), his intention being to reach the Ganges and to move down to the sea, which he supposed, and rightly so, would provide him with his eastern frontier.[1] Here it was that his army,

[1] Though it may be true, as Tarn points out, that the Ganges was unknown to the Greek world before Megasthenes–that is, until the close of the fourth century B.C. (*Alexander*, vol. II, Appendix 14), it is incredible that Alexander did not know of its existence; for it was only 150 miles from the Sutlej, and then as now it was the most sacred river in India. That he considered the "Eastern Sea" (Bay of Bengal) far closer than it actually was is probably true, and that he minimized the distance to encourage his men is also possible. Though his projects of future conquests, as related by Arrian (v, xxvi), have been shown by Tarn to be later interpolations (*Alexander*, vol. II, pp. 287–290), their strategical aim–namely, to establish an unattackable empire—is common sense, and is one which must have occurred to Alexander, more especially so as it is alleged that he said: "But if you flinch now, there will be many warlike races left behind on the far side of the Hyphasis up to the Eastern Sea, and many too stretching from these to the Hyrcanian Sea towards the north wind, and

having marched some seventeen thousand miles and having gained the eastern border of Darius's empire, refused to go farther. Most reluctantly he halted and prepared for the homeward journey. Before turning westward he built twelve altars on the bank of the river Hyphasis "as thank offerings to the gods" and "as memorials of his labours".[1] While they were being erected, there was with him in his camp an exiled Indian chief named Sandrocottus (Chandragupta), who a few years later, in emulation of Alexander, founded the great Mauryan empire with its capital at Palibotha (Patna), on the Ganges.

As he was unable to secure his eastern frontier by the ocean, it must have been apparent to him that the next best line of defence was the Indus, and more particularly so were it possible by sea to link its mouth with that of the Euphrates; for then the deserts of Persia and the western mountains of India would be circumvented.

Alexander began his return journey, and on the Jhelum built a fleet. When, in November 326 B.C., it was ready, he poured out libations to his forefather Heracles, to Amon, and other gods,[2] and then set out. On his way southward he fought a campaign against the Malli (Mahlavas), in which he nearly lost his life, and eventually arrived at the delta of the Indus. After he had explored the mouth of the river down to the sea, he built a naval station at Patala (? Haiderabad) and next decided that his admiral Nearchus, with a fleet of perhaps 100 to 150 ships, should sail westward in search of the Persian Gulf. He divided his army into two divisions and ordered Craterus with the larger of the two to return by way of the Bolan Pass and Kandahar to Persepolis, while he and the smaller, 8,000 to 10,000 men, marched homeward through the coastal region of the desert of Gedrosia in order to establish depôts of food on the shore of the Arabian Sea for the provisioning of Nearchus's fleet. He lost most of his baggage and many of the non-combatants during the march, but extricated his forces without great loss. All three expeditions ended happily, and the sea route to India was established.

In the spring of 324 B.C. he was back in Susa, where, in

not far from these, again, the Scythian tribes, so that there is reason to fear that if we turn back now, such territory as we now hold, being yet unconsolidated, may be stirred to revolt by such as we do not yet hold. Then in very truth there will be no profit from our many labours; or we shall need once more, from the very beginning, more dangers and more labours" (Arrian, v, xxvi). In the circumstances, this seems exactly what Alexander should have said.

[1] Arrian, v, xxix.  [2] *Ibid.*, vi, iii.

celebration of his conquests, he held a great feast during which he and many of his officers, as well as 10,000 of his men, married Persian women.[1] Soon after this symbolic act of fusion of victors and vanquished, and to remove a danger that ever since the days of Xenophon had threatened Greece–the floating mass of home-less Greeks who were ever ready to sell their services as mercen-aries–he ordered the cities of the League of Corinth to readmit their exiles and their families. Because this order exceeded his rights as Captain-General, Tarn has suggested that to correct the anomaly he sent instructions to the cities of the League to recognize him as a god, for as such he would not be bound by the League's rules. They did so and the exiles returned.

Soon afterwards he determined to send back to Greece all veterans past service. This common-sense decision was taken at Opis and was strongly resented by the Macedonians, who suspected that his aim was to oust them in favour of the Persians and to transfer his seat of government from Macedonia to Asia. Soon discontent led to the mutiny of the whole army, except the *Agema* of the Hypaspists. The soldiers demanded to go home and told Alexander to prosecute the war in company with his father Amon.[2] Alexander arrested the ringleaders and took the mutineers at their word. He dismissed the whole army from his service and began forming a Persian one. This drastic action broke the back of the mutiny, which was followed by a remarkable reconciliation. A vast banquet was held to which 9,000 guests were invited, the feast being symbolic of the peace he intended to establish in his empire. Macedonians and Persians–the two great antagon-ists in the war–sat at his own table, and every race of the empire was represented. Arrian informs us that Alexander "and his comrades drank from the same bowl and poured the same libations, while the Greek seers and the Magians began the ceremony".[3] During this banquet, writes Tarn, Alexander "prayed for peace, and that Macedonians and Persians and all the peoples of his Empire might be alike partners in the common-wealth (*i.e.* not merely subjects), and that the peoples of the world he knew might live together in harmony and in unity of heart and mind–that *Homonoia* which for centuries the world was to long for but never to reach. He had previously said that all men

[1] Arrian, VII, IV.                              [2] *Ibid.*, VII, VIII.
[3] *Ibid.*, VII, XI, and Plutarch's *Moralia*, trans. Frank Cole Babbit (1926), vol. IV "on the Fortune and Virtue of Alexander", pp. 327–330.

were sons of one Father and his prayer was the expression of his recorded belief that he had a mission from God to be the Reconciler of the World. Though none present could foresee it, that prayer was to be the crown of his career. . . ."[1]

In the spring of 323 B.C. he returned to Babylon, which he selected as his capital, and there was met "by embassies from the Libyans, who congratulated him and offered him a crown on his becoming King of Asia [the Persian Empire]. From Italy also Bruttians and Lucanians and Tyrrhenians [Etruscans] sent envoys for a like purpose."[2] Other envoys are also mentioned by Arrian, but are discounted by Tarn as later additions.[3]

At Babylon he busied himself with the planning of a number of expeditions. One was to explore the Hyrcanian (Caspian) Sea, to discover whether it was a lake or a gulf of the ocean; others were to explore the Persian Gulf. For the latter expedition he built a great harbour at Babylon, from which ships could set out to colonize the eastern coast of the gulf; to explore the sea-route between Babylon and Egypt and so link the latter to India by the way Nearchus had discovered; and also to circumnavigate Arabia, an expedition he intended to lead in person. While the fleet was being built, he remodelled the phalanx by incorporating Persian light armed troops with the Macedonian hoplites.

None of these projects was destined to see fruition, for while the preparations were under way, on June 2 he was taken ill with malaria. He grew steadily worse and was carried into the palace of Nebuchadrezzar. There, on June 12, his veterans filed past him in silence as he lay speechless, "yet he greeted one and all, raising his head, though with difficulty and signing to them, with his eyes".[4] The following day, June 13, 323 B.C., towards evening, he died in his thirty-third year, after a reign of twelve years and eight months. He was buried in Alexandria.

Though under his successors, the Diadochi,[5] the empire he founded split into fractions, four great monarchies arising in its stead—Egypt under the Ptolomies, Asia under the Seleucids, Macedonia under the Antigonids, and in India the empire of Chandragupts[6]—his idea of world unity as the brotherhood of man

[1] *Alexander the Great*, vol. i, pp. 116–117.          [2] Arrian, vii, xv.
[3] *Alexander the Great*, vol. ii, Appendix 23.          [4] Arrian, vii, xxvi.
[5] More especially Antigonus, Ptolemy, Seleucus and Lysimachus.
[6] ". . . Chandragupta saw him and deduced the possibility of realizing in actual fact the conception, handed down from Vedic times, of a comprehensive monarchy in India; hence Alexander indirectly created Asoka's empire and enabled the spread of Buddhism" (*Alexander the Great*, W. W. Tarn, vol. i, p. 143).

was never extinguished. The fusing of races, which on his return to Susa from India he had symbolized by mass-weddings between Macedonians and Persians, became a daily occurrence in the great cosmopolitan cities he had founded. In these the various races mingled and out of their mingling arose a common culture—the Hellenistic.

Soon after his death, Alexandria, the greatest of these cities, became the power-house of the new culture. It was "the meeting place of the world". There, writes Reinach, an indefatigable curiosity "drove men's minds to multiply inquiries and information in every direction. They wanted to know everything, to explain everything. They interrogated old texts. . . . They travelled over the inhabited earth. . . . They carried to a very high pitch the study of the sciences properly so-called, which tended to become definitely separated from philosophy. . . . What is all this, if it is not the very principle of the scientific spirit?"[1] There steam-power was discovered, mathematics extended, mechanics developed, and new faiths and cults compounded, to flow east and west.

The process of fusion was much accelerated by the financial system Alexander introduced. Before he set out on his great adventure he most certainly must have realized that his father's strength was derived largely from his gold mines in Thrace. Further, when in Egypt, he must have realized that gold was looked upon as a divine substance which gave immortality to its kings, masking them in their tombs. He seized the hoarded wealth of Persia and de-sterilized it by minting it into coin. When Alexander carried off the treasures of Asia, writes Athenaeus, "the sun of 'wealth, with far-flung might', as Pindar has it, verily rose".[2] Not only did he issue coin, but he unified the financial system by introducing a uniform standard. After his death the Ptolomies monopolized the whole of the banking business in Egypt, and through "their central bank at Alexandria they . . . transacted business in money with foreign countries".[3] Wilcken further writes:

"In Alexander's wars, the previous barriers between East and West were removed, and in the next generation thousands of Greek traders and artisans entered the new world, to seek their

[1] *L'Hellénisation du Monde Antique*, A. J. Reinach (1914), p. 270.
[2] *Athenaeus*, trans. Charles Burton Gulick (1929), vol. III, "Deipnosophistae," VI, 231, e.
[3] *Alexander the Great*, Ulrich Wilcken, p. 292.

fortunes in the new Greek cities, which shot up out of the ground like mushrooms. In this way the two previously detached circles came more and more to coincide and form a single economic circle; and when the Western Mediterranean was attracted into the orbit of the great revolution that occurred in the East, there was finally created a world commerce, which embraced the whole inhabited world, and extended from Spain to India, and beyond through Central Asia to China. This development was completed only under the Roman Empire, but its basis was the conquest of Asia by Alexander."[1]

In the great monarchies which arose after his death not only was an aristocracy of wealth created, but the divine right of kingship became the corner-stone of the state. "Hardly was he dead", writes Professor Tarn, "when legend became busy with his terrible name. . . . Around him the whole dream-world of the East took shape and substance; of him every story of a divine world-conqueror was told afresh. . . . He lifted the civilized world out of one groove and set it in another; he started a new epoch; nothing could again be as it had been."[2] As we shall see in succeeding chapters, the effects of his work were to reach far and wide. In the middle of the third century B.C., immediately after the ending of the First Punic War, Greek culture began to influence Roman society, and during and after the Second Punic War it expanded steadily under the Scipios. Wilcken says: "It was the Romans who first gave Alexander the title of 'The Great' (Magnus)", and that "it was left to Greek historians to draw a parallel between Alexander and the great Scipio Africanus, the conqueror of Hannibal, and the founder of the Roman world-empire; they made Scipio the son of Jupiter Capitolinus, and transferred to him the legend about Alexander that he was the offspring of a sacred snake. . . ."[3]

Later, when Augustus, a fervent admirer of Alexander, and under whom the worship of the emperor as the divine world-ruler was established, placed his effigy upon the imperial signet, Alexander's dream, in part at least, came true; for under the *Pax Romana* the western world tasted for the first time the blessings of a prolonged peace. It was but a step from this idea—Alexander as god-king—coupled with what Plutarch attributed to him as

---

[1] *Alexander the Great*, Ulrich Wilcken, p. 284.
[2] *The Cambridge Ancient History*, vol. VI, pp. 435–436, and *Alexander the Great*, W. W. Tarn, vol. I, p. 145.
[3] *Alexander the Great*, Ulrich Wilcken, p. 277.

saying: "God is the common father of all men, but he makes the best ones peculiarly his own", to the establishment of Christianity and later to the transference of the temporal rule of the Roman emperors to the spiritual rule of the medieval Popes. Further, strange as it may seem, Islam, the great opponent of Christendom, was only rendered possible by the contact of Arabianism with Hellenism in Egypt, Syria, and Asia Minor.

CHRONICLE 3

# The rise of Rome and her conflict with Carthage

During the great migratory movements which took place between the years 1200 and 1000 B.C., two peoples of Asiatic stock appeared in the central Mediterranean. They were the Phoenicians of Tyre who, about 1100 B.C., established the first of their North African colonies at Utica and founded Carthage (Kart-hadasht or "New Town") in the second half of the ninth century B.C., and the Etruscans, who settled in Italy, north of the Tiber, before 1000 B.C. South of the Tiber lay Latium, a small gathering of villages inhabited by the Latins, tribes of Indo-European stock grouped about Alba Longa, who, about 753 B.C.– the traditional date of the founding of Rome by Romulus—were overrun by the Etruscans. Under the latter the villages in the neighbourhood of the Palatine Hill gradually merged into the city state of Rome.

Two hundred and fifty years later–that is, about 500 B.C.– while the Etruscans were busily engaged with the Gauls in the north, the Latin tribes drove their Etruscan kings out of Rome and invaded Etruria. Eventually the Gauls overran Etruria, crossed the lower Tiber, and about 390 B.C., Rome, as yet unwalled, was occupied by them and burnt. Only the citadel on the Capitoline Hill held out, and soon weary of besieging it, they accepted a ransom in gold and departed northward.

At this early period the Roman military unit was the legion, levy, or· "gathering of the clans". It was recruited from the burgesses of Rome, those who belonged to one of the original tribes, who alone had the right to bear arms. They formed the "spear-armed body of warriors upon whom the blessing of Mars was invoked", and because service in war was the sole road to civic honours it was these men of hereditary valour who shaped the character of the Roman people.

Originally the legion was a phalanx armed in the old Doric style. At an early date it consisted of 3,000 to 4,000 men in eight ranks. The first six were hoplites and the last two *velites*–the light armed. Like the Greek phalanx its tactical principle was shock; it had no reserves, and as it was supported by a mere handful of cavalry, pursuit was difficult.

According to tradition, immediately after the burning of Rome this primitive military organization was completely transformed by Marcus Furius Camillus, the most celebrated Roman general of the Gallic Wars. For arrangement by census he substituted arrangement by age, in order to make the most of individual capacity and experience. The heavy infantry, which were the real legionary troops, were organized in three bodies, *hastati, principes,* and *triarii*: the first comprising the youngest men and the third the oldest. The *velites* were maintained, but continued to be recruited on the census.

Next, to gain the necessary elasticity to meet the highly mobile Gauls, the phalangial legion was divided into three divisions ordered in depth: the *hastati* in front, the *principes* in rear of them, and behind the latter the *triarii*–veterans. Each of these divisions was organized into ten companies (*manipuli*), the first two of 120 men each and the third of 60. A cohort consisted of one maniple of each class and 120 *velites* and a squadron (*turma*) of cavalry 30 strong: in all 450 soldiers. Ten cohorts made a legion. In battle order the maniples were drawn up chequer-wise, so that those of the second division covered the intervals in the front of the first, and the third those of the second. The cavalry, ten *turmae*, formed a wing (*ala*).

The growth of this new organization probably was gradual. The armament is fully described by Polybius in sections 19-42 of his Sixth Book.[1] The *velites* carried a sword, spear, and a target (*parma*) three feet in diameter. The spear was for throwing and had so slender a point that, once cast, it bent and became useless in the hands of the enemy. The *hastati* carried a large shield (*scutum*), semi-cylindrical in shape. It was two feet six inches wide and four feet long, and was made of two layers of wood glued together, covered with hide and bound with iron. They were armed with a short thrusting sword (*gladius*) and two javelins (*pila*) and wore a brass helmet and greaves and a brass plate on their breasts (*pectorale*), or, if they could afford it, a cuirass (*lorica*). The *principes* and *triarii* were armed and armoured in like manner, except that instead of *pila* they carried long spears (*hastae*).

---

[1] For a full account of the developments of Roman armament see *Les Armes Romaines*, Paul Couissen (1926).

The cavalry, it would seem, was completely neglected, for even at the opening of the Punic Wars cavalrymen had no armour; their shields were of leather and their swords and lances indifferent. Normally, they preferred to fight on foot.

Collective fighting was discouraged in favour of single combats. The one great shock of the phalanx gave way to a series of shocks in rapid succession. The entrenching of camps was also introduced, even when a halt was made for a single night. The old discipline, always severe, was unaltered, and drill and training were prolonged. Tactically, these changes were radical. Close and distant fighting were combined; a reserve came into being, and the offensive and defensive were closely knit together. Mommsen writes of the manipular legion:

"The Roman combination of the heavy javelin with the sword produced results similar . . . to those attained in modern warfare by the introduction of bayonet muskets; the volley of javelins prepared the way for the sword encounter, exactly in the same way as a volley of musketry now precedes a charge with the bayonet. Lastly, the thorough system of encampment allowed the Romans to combine the advantages of defensive and offensive war, and to decline or give battle according to circumstances, and in the latter case to fight under the ramparts of their camp just as under the walls of a fortress."

After the Gallic invasion Rome was turned into a walled city and the Romans, who now had a secure base from which to operate, set out on their path of conquest. In 325 B.C. their expansion brought them into conflict with the Samnites to the south of them, and a series of wars followed which, in 295 B.C., was ended by the decisive battle of Sentinum (near Fabriano), in which the combined forces of the Samnites, Etruscans, and Gauls were routed by the Romans. This victory made Rome the leading power from the river Arnus to the Gulf of Salerno and, as Breasted says, "decided the future of Italy for over two thousand years". Within Italy, Rome's only potential enemies were, in the north the Gauls, and in the south the Lucanians, and, if they opposed her, the Greek city states on the coast.

Tarentum (Taranto) was the foremost of these cities, and the Tarentines, thoroughly alarmed by the rapid expansion of Rome, called to their assistance Pyrrhus, King of Epirus and kinsman of Alexander the Great, a leading soldier of his day. He landed in Italy in 280 B.C. and defeated the Romans in two battles, at

Heraclea on the Gulf of Taranto, and near Asculum, east of present-day Venosa. His losses in these battles were so great that when the Syracusans asked him to help them against the Carthaginians he transferred his army to Sicily. From there, after several brilliant campaigns and because of the normal dissension between the Greek cities, he returned to Italy in 276 B.C., and was so badly beaten by the Romans at Beneventum (Benevento) that he withdrew to Epirus, exclaiming: "What a battlefield I am leaving for Carthage and Rome." A true prediction, for as soon as he had left, one by one the Greek cities surrendered to the Romans, and with the occupation of Rhegium, the two great powers were left to face each other over the Strait of Messina.

Between 310 and 289 B.C. most of Sicily had been subdued by Agathocles, tyrant and king of Syracuse: a remarkable soldier and the first European to carry war into Carthaginian Africa. The prolonged disorders after his death, which were used by Carthage to her advantage, were the reason why Syracuse had sought the assistance of Pyrrhus, who had married a daughter of Agathocles. When Pyrrhus left Sicily, Hiero II, then king of Syracuse, became involved in a war with a body of Agathocles's former mercenaries, called Mamertines after Marmar the Oscan Mars, which had seized Messana (Messina). Hard pressed by him, the Mamertines appealed to Carthage and Rome for assistance at the same time. Both answered the call and a clash followed which, in 264 B.C., detonated the First Punic War.

When they found that without a fleet they could not prevent the Carthaginians from sending over reinforcements from Africa, in 261 B.C. the Romans decided to build one and become a naval power: a singularly daring resolution, since they had little knowledge of the sea and at the time Carthage was the leading naval power in the Mediterranean. After they had built ships and manned them with partially trained crews, in 260 B.C. they attempted to seize Messana and were defeated. In no way discouraged by the reverse, and realizing that they could not hope to equal the Carthaginians at sea as long as they themselves adhered to the conventional tactics of the day, they set about devising an altogether new tactics which would enable the superiority of their soldiers in hand-to-hand fighting to have full scope. To effect this they fitted their galleys with wooden boarding-bridges called *corvi* ("crows"), each provided with a spike under its fore-end. By means of a pole fixed in the prow of each ship, the bridge could be raised vertically, swung to right or left, and dropped on the deck of an enemy ship and the ship firmly grappled. The boarding party would pass over the bridge.

They put to sea again and met the Carthaginian fleet off Mylae (Cape Milazzo), when the Carthaginians steered straight for them. "But the engines", writes Polybius, "swung round to meet them in every direction, and dropped down upon them so infallibly, that no ship could come to close quarters without being grappled. Eventually the Carthaginians turned and fled, bewildered at the novelty of the occurrence, and with it a loss of fifty ships."

The victory of Mylae made Rome a naval power, and its immediate results were the evacuation of Corsica by the Carthaginians and the invasion of Sardinia by the Romans.

The Romans now, like Agathocles, resolved to transfer the war to Africa. Their fleet consisted of 330 ships, and though the Carthaginians assembled a considerably larger fleet at Heraclea Minoa, west of Agrigentum (Agrigento), in order to take the Roman advance on Africa in flank, when the two fleets met the *corvi* once again proved decisive and the Carthaginians lost ninety-four ships to the Romans' twenty-four. The battle of Heraclea won for the Romans the command of the central Mediterranean.

The Romans refitted their ships and the fleet steered straight for Hermaeum (Cape Bon), where the army, under M. Atilius Regulus, was landed. First he occupied Tunes (Tunis) to establish a base of operations against Carthage. But while he was doing so a force of Greek mercenaries, under a Spartan named Xanthippus, reinforced the Carthaginians. Xanthippus was an able soldier. Polybius says of him: "For it was one man, one brain, that defeated the numbers which were believed to be invincible and able to accomplish anything; and restored to confidence a whole city that was unmistakably and utterly ruined, and the spirits of its army which had sunk to the lowest depths of despair." He selected a battleground on which the superior Carthaginian cavalry would have full scope and defeated and captured Regulus. The Romans abandoned the invasion and returned to Sicily. In July, 255 B.C., they met with a terrible disaster. In a storm they lost 284 ships out of 364. Through this mischance the Carthaginians regained command of the sea and at once reinforced Lilybaeum (Marsala). In 249 B.C. another storm virtually annihilated the Roman fleet, and so discouraged were the Romans by its loss that they abandoned the idea of fighting at sea. Two years later the Carthaginians sent Hamilcar Barca, the father of Hannibal, to Sicily.

When they had recovered their nerve, in 242 B.C. the Romans once again set to work and built another fleet, and in the following year, when they had 250 quinqueremes ready, they surprised the Carthaginian seaports of Lilybaeum and Drepana (Trapani). This caused high alarm in Carthage because they were the nearest of the Sicilian ports to Cape Bon. They at once put to sea to regain them, and the two fleets met at the Aegates (Egadi) islands. The Roman fleet was victorious, seventy Carthaginian ships were captured and fifty sunk. Carthage was now exhausted and so was Rome, and in 241 B.C. peace between the two was re-established on condition that Carthage evacuated Sicily. Sicily thus became the first province of the Roman Empire.

For the Carthaginians the cessation of war was immediately followed by general unrest and widespread mutinies among their mercenaries. In Sardinia, they revolted from Carthage, and on being expelled by the Sardinians they appealed to Rome to re-establish order. The Romans agreed, and in 238 B.C. they intervened; Carthage abandoned Sardinia and the island passed into Roman hands.

When the Romans were reducing the wild tribes in Sardinia, which took many years, they were also engaged in a grim frontier war with the Gauls in northern Italy, and between 229-219 B.C. in a series of punitive operations against the Illyrian pirates in the Adriatic. In 225 B.C. the Gauls were brought to a temporary halt in a great battle in which 40,000 are said to have been killed and 10,000 captured. After this victory, Roman colonies were established at Cremona and Placentia (Piacenza), and to reinforce these and other northern garrisons the Via Flaminia was made fit for the passage of troops as far as Arimini (Rimini). The Illyrian war, which for the first time brought the Romans into diplomatic contact with Greece, roused the fears of Philip V of Macedonia, who from then on took up a position of hostility to Rome.

Meanwhile Carthage, to make good her losses in the central Mediterranean, sent Hamilcar Barca to Spain to extend her dominion over that country. In 229 B.C. he died, and was succeeded in command by his son-in-law Hasdrubal who, in 228 B.C., founded Nova Carthago (Cartagena). Apparently in answer to this extension of Carthaginian power, Rome made an alliance with the wealthy Greek city of Saguntum (Sagunto), and being fully occupied with the Gauls, and so for the time being not desiring another war with Carthage, a treaty was agreed upon between the Romans and Hasdrubal by the terms of which the Iberus (Ebro) river was fixed as the boundary between the Carthaginian and Roman spheres of interest in Spain. In 221 B.C. Hasdrubal was assassinated, and was succeeded by his brother-in-law Hannibal, son of Hamilcar Barca.

# CHAPTER 4

# The Battles of the Metaurus, 207 B.C., and Zama, 202 B.C.

Rome all but accomplished what Alexander attempted, for Rome, as we shall see, absorbed his idea. But this was not done in a purposeful way, because history grows by force of circumstances. The imperial urge was now in the bones of Rome, and rightly Livy says: "No great state can long be in peace. If it lacks an enemy abroad it finds one at home, just as powerful bodies seem protected against infection from without, but are of themselves weighed down by their very strength."[1] Thus it comes about that in the life history of every virile nation two events control its destiny, inner and outer conflicts, which are called revolutions and wars. Not until nations grow old is peacefulness established, and what ages them the more rapidly is the feeling of security. In no way was this true of Rome, for when the Second Punic War broke out she was in her early youth and confronted by two great powers—Macedonia in the east and Carthage in the south. Before security could be gained, these powers had to be eliminated, for the goal of a virile nation is the establishment of unattackable frontiers—the Alexandrian drive.

In Spain such a frontier did not exist, for the Ebro was little more than a geographical expression, and once the Gaulish war was ended, Rome, with an eye on the Spanish silver mines and markets, brought into power a party within Saguntum which attacked the Torboletae, who were subjects of Carthage. Hannibal took action and was warned by the Romans to leave the Saguntines alone. He refused to do so, and in 219 B.C. attacked their city and after an eight-month siege took it by storm. Though the Romans had made no effort to help the Saguntines, in March the following year they sent envoys to Carthage demanding the surrender of Hannibal and his assessors. The ultimatum was rejected and a formal declaration of war followed.

That Hannibal had every right to retaliate seems clear; yet there can be little doubt that, when he laid siege to Saguntum, he

---

[1] *Livy* (trans. Frank Gardner Moore, 1949), xxx, 44.

did so in full knowledge of the probable consequences. That his idea was to revenge himself on Rome may be true; though not in the sense of fulfilling the "Wrath of the house of Barca", but rather to cancel out the results of the First Punic War and thereby to reinstate the supremacy of Carthage. He possessed a high political instinct and realized that Rome was as yet no more than a patchwork power. She had won her supremacy by force and not by persuasion; the Gauls were permanently antogonistic to her, and during the incursion of Pyrrhus several of her allies had deserted her cause. Strategically the moment seemed propitious, and tactically Hannibal was in a strong position; for so far the revolution in the art of war created by Alexander's use of cavalry, which he understood, was little appreciated by the Romans.

The situation was also clear to the Roman Senate and the moment seemed equally propitious. In northern Italy the Gauls had been defeated and Latin colonies had been established to control them; Tarentum and other southern ports had been garrisoned, no danger threatened across the Adriatic and the command of the seas was in Roman hands. Not only were Roman sea communications with Spain safe, but from Sicily a direct attack could be launched against Carthage. But war is always a game of chance and the plaything of the unexpected. The senators calculated all things correctly enough except one imponderable factor. They could measure up the Carthaginians, but the genius of Hannibal was hidden from them. They could not see, as Dodge says, that from beginning to end Hannibal was to be the pivot around which all things were to revolve;[1] and that before them lay a war of over sixteen years, during which one man was to fight Rome and to teach her how to conquer the world. What manner of man was he?

Little is known of Hannibal, except for what may be learnt from his campaigns, and none of these is described by a friendly pen. He was born in 249 B.C., and at the age of nine left Carthage with his father for Spain. There he remained until his great adventure began, and though he must have accompanied Hamilcar on many of his campaigns, in which he was schooled in the art of war, his education was in no way neglected. We are told that he could speak Greek fluently as well as read and write it, and that he was deeply versed in the history of Hellenistic warfare. He was lightly yet firmly built, an excellent runner and fencer and

[1] *Hannibal*, Theodore Ayrault Dodge (1891), vol. II, p. 638.

a fearless rider. Possessed of an iron constitution, he could support hardship, and endowed with a quick and calculating brain he was able to sum up situations. In his living he was simple and little addicted to wine or women. "To his reckless courage in encountering dangers", says Livy, "he united the greatest judgement when in the midst of them", nevertheless, he attributes to him inhuman cruelty, more than Punic perfidy, "no regard for truth, and none for sanctity, no fear of the gods, no reverence for an oath, no religions scruple".[1] Also Polybius says that he was "extraordinarily cruel" and "exceedingly grasping for money".[2] These vices, we think, may be largely discounted; as we shall see, his "perfidy" was no greater than that of his great adversary Scipio, and his cruelty in no way abnormal in his age.

When, in the spring of 218 B.C., he set out from Nova Carthago for the Ebro, his object was clear. It was not to conquer Italy, but instead to break up the Italian Confederacy and to force Rome to make peace as once Agathocles had forced Carthage to do. After his victory at Lake Trasimene he said: "I am not come to fight against Italians, but on behalf of Italians against Rome."[3] He moved forward not as a conqueror, but as a liberator. With this idea as the linchpin of his strategy he advanced on modern Perpignan at the head of 90,000 foot, 12,000 cavalry and 37 elephants.[4] The reason why he took the land route in preference to the sea route was not only because the Romans held command of the sea, but because it was essential for him to rouse the Gauls against them and to establish a supply base and recruiting ground as close to Cisalpine Gaul as he could; for his line of communications with Spain could readily be cut.

From the Pyrenees he moved to a little north of Avignon without opposition, because the Roman Senate had failed completely to fathom his intentions. When they had assembled one army under Tiberius Sempronius in Sicily for an expedition against Carthage, the Senate ordered another under Publius Cornelius Scipio to march by way of Massilia (Marseilles) to the Ebro. When Scipio got to Massilia he learnt that Hannibal was fifty

---

[1] *Livy*, trans. B. O. Foster (1929), XXI, 4.

[2] *The Histories of Polybius*, trans. Evelyn S. Shuckburgh (1889), IX, 22. This translation is quoted throughout and as regards the "fragments" does not follow the rearrangement by Büttner-Wobst in his Teubner edition of 1914.

[3] *Ibid.*, I, III, 85.

[4] *Ibid.*, I, III, 35. These numbers would appear to be exaggerated, for Polybius says: "The army was not so much numerous as highly efficient, and in an extraordinary state of physical training. . . ."

miles to the north of him and so out of his reach, and instead of bringing his army back to Italy by the coast road he sent it on under his brother Gnaeus to Spain to attack Hannibal's base, while he himself returned with a few men to Pisa.

Directly the whereabouts of Hannibal became known, word was sent to Sempronius to transfer his army to the north. Meanwhile Hannibal, by a manœuvre very similar to Alexander's on the Hydaspes, forded the Rhône and headed his army for the Maritime Alps. Where he crossed them is unknown, though it was somewhere between the little St. Bernard and Mt. Genèvre. His main difficulty was not the mountains,[1] but the hostility of the Allobroges, who constantly attacked his rearguard. His losses from these affrays were so considerable that, though he crossed the Rhône with 50,000 foot and 9,000 horse,[2] he entered the plains of Cisalpine Gaul with no more than 20,000 and 6,000 respectively; that is almost exactly one quarter of the strength accredited to him by Livy on leaving New Carthage.

Whether this heavy loss of men was due to faulty generalship it is not possible to say; but it certainly does not point to a high state of discipline in his army, and this, in its turn, throws into relief the amazing series of victories he was to win with it during the next few years.

In December, 218 B.C., on the banks of the Trebia, he lured Sempronius into battle.[3] He bewildered him, held him in front, and with half his cavalry outflanked him and fell upon his rear, when Sempronius was utterly routed. In April the following year, on the northern shore of Lake Trasimene, by deliberately placing himself between the armies of Servilius and Flaminius he surprised the latter and all but annihilated his army.[4]

Hannibal then moved south towards the Adriatic coast and captured a Roman supply depôt at Cannae on the river Aufidus (Ofanto). But it would seem that his main reason for going there was to gain suitable country for his cavalry. At the time there were four double legions at Gerunium (to the south of Termoli), under command of the Consuls Aemilius Paullus and C. Terentius Varro.

---

[1] Napoleon says: "Les éléphants seuls ont pu lui donner de l'embarras" (*Commentaires*, VI, p. 163).

[2] The difference between this and the original strength was due mainly to Hannibal leaving behind him in Catalonia 22,000 men. To account for the remaining 21,000 points to considerable desertions.

[3] Polybius gives the strength of the opposing forces as – Carthagians, 28,000 infantry and 10,000 cavalry; Romans 36,000 infantry and 4,000 cavalry (*The Histories*, III, 72).

[4] *Ibid.*, III, 84. The Roman losses were 15,000 killed and 15,000 prisoners.

When Hannibal's whereabouts were known, they marched to the Aufidus and camped on its right bank three miles above Hannibal.

Because of the superiority of the Carthaginian cavalry, Aemilius was against giving battle, but Varro thought differently, and because the two consuls were in chief command on alternate days, and the day after their arrival it was Varro's turn to command, he ordered an immediate advance. An indecisive skirmish followed; but on the next day, August 2, 216 B.C., Aemilius could no longer draw off his army as he wished and, probably realizing this, Hannibal drew out his in a crescent formation. In the centre he marshalled his Spaniards and Gauls, with his Africans on their flanks. On each wing of the infantry line he posted a powerful force of cavalry. Faced by the Romans drawn up in parallel order, he first routed the Roman cavalry, and next awaited the advance of the Roman infantry. They pressed the Carthaginian crescent back until it became concave. Then, suddenly, Hannibal advanced his two divisions of African infantry, wheeled them inwards, and closed on the flanks of the Romans engaged in the pocket. Lastly, the Carthaginian cavalry returned from the pursuit and fell upon the Roman rear. The Roman army was swallowed up as if by an earthquake.[1]

When the battles of the Trebia, Lake Trasimene, and Cannae are examined, there is not the slightest doubt that victory was won by the tactical genius of Hannibal and that his genius was able to achieve what it did because of the Roman outlook upon war. It was purely mechanical and depended solely upon valour, discipline, and drill. Of generalship there was next to none, a general still being looked upon as a drill-master, a man who could successfully carry out a number of parade evolutions with little reference to ground or to tactical requirements. Because they had won innumerable battles against undisciplined and poorly drilled barbarians through discipline and drill, and because they had learnt nothing from the wars of Alexander and his successors, the Romans invariably were surprised, as much by their ignorance and tactical blunders as by Hannibal's insight, foresight, and imagination. Nor was it the fault of the generals themselves, who

---

[1] Polybius (iii, 107) gives the Roman strength at 80,000 infantry and 9,600 cavalry. In *The Cambridge Ancient History* doubt is thrown on this (see vol. VIII, p. 53), and the Roman strength is calculated at 48,000. According to Polybius (iii, 117) the Roman casualties were the whole of their cavalry less 370, 10,000 infantry captured (who were not actually engaged in the battle) and 70,000 killed; the Carthaginian casualties were 5,700 in all.

seldom lacked courage, but of the Roman military system. Each citizen was considered fit to be a general, because each citizen was supposed to know his drill. As Mommsen says: "It was simply impossible that the question as to the leadership of the armies of the city in such a war should be left year after year to be decided by the Pandora's box of the balloting-urn."[1] This was largely because of party politics, arising out of rivalries between the great families. Livy, perhaps with some exaggeration, tells us that "All the tribes voted for Publius Scipio. In spite of that, the consuls cast losts for Africa as a province, for so the Senate had decreed."[2] The result was the creation of a stolid, static army, in which the generals were elected, not because of their experience or ability, but because of their devotion to party interests.

In contrast, Hannibal was a general who could adapt himself to every circumstance except one—siege warfare—and who, by an act of will, could pass from the unequalled boldness shown during the campaigns of his first three years in Italy to the obstinate and closely circumscribed defensive he adopted during the thirteen which followed. It was his ability to adapt his actions to changing circumstances which justifies the remark of Polybius: "Of all that befell the Roman and Carthaginians, good or bad, the cause was one man and one mind, Hannibal. . . . So great and wonderful is the influence of a Man, and a mind duly fitted by original constitution for any undertaking within the reach of human powers."[3] He further says of him: "For sixteen continuous years Hannibal maintained the war with Rome in Italy, without once releasing his army from service in the field, but keeping those vast numbers under control, like a good pilot, without any sign of disaffection towards himself or towards each other, though he had troops in his service who, so far from being of the same tribe, were not even of the same race. . . . Yet the skill of the commander was such, that these differences, so manifold and so wide, did not disturb the obedience to one word of command and to a single will."[4]

To quote a modern historian, Mommsen says: "He was peculiarly marked by that inventive craftiness, which forms one of the leading traits of the Phoenician character; he was fond

_____

[1] *The History of Rome,* Theodor Mommsen (1921), vol. ii, p. 126.

[2] *Livy,* xxx, 27. On this question see *Roman Politics 200–150* B.C., H. H. Scullard (1951), pp. 79-80. Behind it was the divided strategical aims of Fabius and Scipio. The former wanted to drive Hannibal out of Italy and end the war; the latter to force Hannibal out of Italy by attacking Carthage, and winning peace in Africa (*ibid.*, pp. 75-76).

[3] Polybius, ix, 22.                                    [4] *Ibid.,* xi, 19.

of taking singular and unexpected routes, ambushes and strata-
gems of all sorts were familiar to him; and he studied the character
of his antagonists with unprecedented care. By an unrivalled
system of espionage–he had regular spies even in Rome–he
kept himself informed of the projects of the enemy; he himself
was frequently seen wearing disguises and false hair in order to
procure information on some point or other. Every page of the
history of the period attests his genius as a general; and his gifts
as a statesman . . . He was a great man; wherever he went, he
riveted the eyes of all.''[1]

What could the Roman military system accomplish against
such a man? Nothing; yet in the end it was the Roman character
which won through. After Cannae, what do we see? A general
disruption of the Republic as Hannibal had hoped for? No–not
a single Latin city revolted; all held fast to Rome paralysed though
she was, and had Hannibal been Alexander Rome would have
fallen. Realizing, as he must have done by now, the strength of the
Roman Confederacy, it was Rome or nothing. Maharbal, his
cavalry general, urged him to advance on the capital–but he
would not. Then Maharbal cried: ''In very truth the gods
bestow not on the same man all their gifts. You know how to gain a
victory, Hannibal; you know not how to use one.'' As Livy
comments: ''That day's delay is generally believed to have saved
the City and the Empire.''[2]

Why did not Hannibal advance on Rome? Mr. Hallward's
answer is, because he conceived a new strategy: ''The whole
strength of Carthage was to be employed in extending the war
to new areas to produce the encirclement of Italy.'' While he was
detaching city after city, the home government was to prepare the
way for peace ''by pushing the Romans out of Spain, by regaining
Sardinia and above all by re-establishing themselves in Sicily''.[3]
To that end, in 215 B.C., Hannibal had already received and
accepted an offer of alliance and cooperation from Philip V of
Macedonia.[4] Yet was this the more speedy way of gaining his end?

---

[1] *History of Rome*, vol. II, p. 88.                    [2] *Livy*, XXII, 51.
[3] *The Cambridge Ancient History*, vol. VIII, p. 61.
[4] On learning of Hannibal's victory at Lake Trasimene, Philip V of Macedonia
set about to prepare to attack Italy, and after the battle of Cannae entered into
alliance with Hannibal. This led to the Roman Senate, supported by Attalus, King of
Pergamum, engaging in war with him in 214 B.C., which became known as the First
Macedonian War. In 211 B.C. a treaty was concluded between the Romans and the
Aetolian League, and in 205 B.C. the war was brought to an end by the Peace of
Phoenice, according to which Philip agreed not to molest the states in alliance with
Rome.

Had Rome capitulated or been stormed, all Spain, Sardinia and Sicily would have fallen with her into his lap. It was not because the "new strategy" was best, but because it was forced upon Hannibal by his lack of a siege train. He knew he could not storm Rome, therefore he was compelled to abandon the offensive and, like his opponent, Q. Fabius Cunctator, to assume the defensive and henceforth rely upon attrition.

Why had no city revolted? Not only because each was loyal to Rome, but because all were walled and connected by roads. They were not only safe against Hannibal's field army, but they could readily be supplied. It was the walled cities which now formed the pivots of the Roman strategy, and it is strange that Hannibal did not realize this. Had he done so when, in 215 B.C., he established himself at Capua and the greater part of southern Italy became his, surely he would have organized a siege train to knock the props out of his enemy's tactics. For four years onwards the war became a matter of marches, counter-marches, threats and withdrawals, and in 211 B.C., when Fulvius besieged and took Capua, all Hannibal could do was to advance across the Anio, approach the walls of Rome, and wave his sword outside the Colline Gate: an heroic gesture, but five years too late.

While this dual defensive was being waged in Italy, largely because of Hannibal's diplomacy the war was vigorously conducted in other quarters. In Spain Hannibal's brothers, Hasdrubal and Mago, as well as Hasdrubal, son of Gisgo, were fighting the two Scipios–Publius and Gnaeus. In 215 B.C. an insurrection broke out in Sardinia, and the following year the Consul, M. Claudius Marcellus, went to Sicily, where Syracuse had gone into alliance with Carthage, and his siege of that city became for the time being the dominant event in the war. As a military episode it is of marked interest, for then was displayed the inventive genius of Archimedes, of whom Polybius says: "In certain circumstances, the genius of one man is more effective than any numbers whatever."[1] Syracuse held out until 211 B.C., when by treachery it was delivered to the Romans, after which all resistance in Sicily was stamped out.

Though success crowned Marcellus in Sicily, disaster shrouded the Scipios in Spain; for this year, their Celtiberian troops deserted them and both were defeated and killed. Again Rome lay paralysed, and once again the selection of a commander was left

[1] Polybius VIII, 5.

to the popular vote. Since no man of mark, such as had been consuls or praetors, came forward, at length a youth of twenty-four, who had held the minor offices of military tribune and aedile, presented himself for election, and because of the clamour of the people was somewhat reluctantly accepted by the Senate. He bore the same name as his father–Publius Cornelius Scipio–and later became known to history as Scipio Africanus, conqueror of Hannibal.

Born in 235 B.C., he is first heard of during the Trebia campaign, when, though still a boy, he saved his father's life;[1] and next, at Cannae, as a military tribune. He escaped from the slaughter and, learning that Metellus and a number of young nobles intended to fly from Italy, he went to the lodgings of that officer and standing over him with a drawn sword made him swear that he and his followers would never desert Rome. Though a man of remarkable courage, his character is not an easy one to gauge. Mommsen's estimate of him is as follows:

"He was not one of the few who by their energy and iron will constrain the world to adopt and to move in new paths for centuries. ... Yet a special charm lingers around the form of that graceful hero; it is surrounded, as with a dazzling halo, by the atmosphere of serene and confident inspiration, in which Scipio with mingled credulity and adroitness always moved. With quite enough of enthusiasm to warm men's hearts, and enough of calculation to follow in every case the dictates of intelligence, while not leaving out of account the vulgar; not naïve enough to share the belief of the multitude in the divine inspirations, nor straightforward enough to set it aside, and yet in secret thoroughly persuaded that he was a man specially favoured of the gods–in a word, a genuine prophetic nature; raised above the people, and not less aloof from them; a man steadfast to his word and kingly in his bearing, who thought that he would humble himself by adopting the ordinary title of a king, but could never understand how the constitution of the republic should in his case be binding; so confident in his own greatness that he knew nothing of envy or of hatred, courteously acknowledged other men's merits, and compassionately forgave other men's faults; an excellent officer and a refined diplomatist without presenting offensively the special stamp of either calling, uniting Hellenic culture with the fullest national feeling of a Roman, an accomplished speaker and of

[1] Polybius, x, 3.

graceful manners–Publius Scipio won the hearts of soldiers and of women, of his countrymen and of the Spaniards, of his rivals in the Senate and of his greater Carthaginian antagonist."[1]

His record of unbroken successes from the day he was appointed to command the forces in Spain until the final act of the war was due to his Hellenic open-mindedness. Whereas other generals learned little from the Roman defeats, he learned far more from them than from his own successes. Hannibal, though his enemy, was simultaneously his master, who taught him not only the art of war, but the art of leading and governing men. His most remarkable gift was his insight into crowd psychology. When in Spain his men mutinied, he commented on this mishap as follows: ". . . a crowd is ever easily misled and easily induced to any error. Therefore it is that crowds are like the sea, which in its own nature is safe and quiet; but, when the winds fall violently upon it, assumes the character of the blasts which lash it into fury; thus a multitude is ever found to be what its leaders and counsellors are."[2]

Scipio sailed from the Tiber and landed at Emporium (Ampurias) late in 210 B.C. The situation which faced him on his arrival was far from an encouraging one. He found that, except for the fortified cities of Castulo (Cazlona) and Saguntum, hold had been lost on all the country south of the Ebro. This situation merely stimulated his generalship. His first move was one of the most daring and dramatic in the history of the war, and it was only possible because of his command of the sea. It was, while the forces of the two Hasdrubals and Mago were divided, to seize New Carthage by a *coup de main* and so to establish himself on the eastern flank of his enemies and to attack them in rear as well as to threaten their sea communications.[3] He did this, displaying high tactical skill in the storming of that city. Once it was in his hands he established a terror by sacking the town, and then behaving kindly to the Spanish hostages he found impounded there, he released them and loaded them with presents, "the girls with ear-rings and bracelets, the young men with daggers and swords",[4] which had a marked influence in winning the good will of the people.

Once New Carthage was his and his fleet and army had been refitted, he marched into Andalusia and, in 208 B.C., defeated but

[1] *History of Rome*, vol. II, pp. 148–149.  [2] Polybius, XI, 29.
[3] See Polybius, x, 8.  [4] *Ibid.*, x, 18.

by no means annihilated Hasdrubal's army at Baecula (? Bailen); for that skilful soldier withdrew towards San Sebastian, crossed into France, and eventually passed into Italy. Though several historians have blamed Scipio for allowing him to escape, there is no justification for their criticism, because to have plunged after Hasdrubal through an unknown and most difficult country, leaving behind him the forces of Mago and Hasdrubal, son of Gisgo, intact, would have been an act of tactical folly.

Next, he concentrated his army at Castulo and advanced on Hasdrubal, son of Gisgo, and Mago at Ilipa (near Seville), and by remarkable tactics,[1] which resembled in part those used by Hannibal at Cannae, he decisively defeated them, Hasdrubal fleeing to Mauritania (Morocco) and Mago to the Balearic Isles, where he set about recruiting a new army to help Hannibal. The battle decided the fate of Carthage in Spain; by the autumn of 206 B.C. the whole country had submitted to Rome.

Meanwhile, in the spring of 207 B.C., Hasdrubal had crossed the Alps, followed the same road taken by his brother eleven years earlier, and debouched into the valley of the Po, where, after he had recruited 10,000 Gauls,[2] he laid siege to Placentia. He failed to take the town and pushed on to Fanum Fortunae (Fano), a small port on the Adriatic at which the Via Flaminia strikes the coast. There he came into contact with the outposts of the combined armies of the praetor L. Porcius and the consul M. Livius, which were encamped at Sena Gallica (Senigallia) a few miles south of Fanum Fortunae. Hannibal was still in winter quarters in southern Italy at the time, watched by 40,000 Roman infantry and 2,500 horse, under the consul C. Claudius Nero and Q. Fulvius Flaccus. His intention was to effect a junction with his brother's army in central Italy; but because he had also to keep an eye on his bases in Bruttium (the toe of Italy), he did not want to move north until he was certain where Hasdrubal was. According to Livy, he did not expect him to cross the Alps as rapidly as he did, and when he heard that he had laid siege to Placentia, and knowing how long sieges generally take, he moved no further north than Canusium (Canosa) and awaited a message from his brother.

While there, one of those incalculable incidents occurred which

---

[1] Polybius, XI, 20–22.
[2] What the strength of his army was is uncertain. B. H. Hallward in *The Cambridge Ancient History* (vol. VIII, p. 93) suggests 30,000.

in war have so frequently decided the fate of nations. When he raised the siege of Placentia, Hasdrubal sent four Gallic and two Numidian horsemen with a letter to Hannibal. These men traversed the whole of Italy, but unaware that Hannibal had moved to Canusium they sought him near Tarentum, missed their way and were captured by a party of Roman foragers. Claudius Nero learnt from them that Hasdrubal proposed to cross the Apennines to meet his brother in Umbria, and, as Livy writes, he "judged that the situation of the state was not such that they should carry on the war by routine methods, each consul within the bounds of his own province, operating with his own armies against the enemy prescribed by the Senate. Rather must he venture to improvise something unforeseen, unexpected, something which in the beginning would cause no less alarm among citizens than among enemies, but if accomplished, would convert great fear into great rejoicing."[1] He therefore sent Hasdrubal's letter to Rome and informed the conscript fathers that while Hannibal remained in doubt, he, at the head of 6,000 picked infantry and 1,000 cavalry, would move north to reinforce Porcius and Livius, leaving Quintius Catius in command of his army to watch Hannibal. He suggested also that the legion at Capua should be moved to Rome and that the troops in Rome should move to Narnia (Narni). He sent messengers in advance through the territories he intended to traverse with orders that "they should carry from the farms and the cities provisions, ready for the soldiers to eat, down to the road, and should bring out horses and mules as well, that the weary might have no lack of vehicles."[2] He knew that there was not a moment to be lost and did not wait for a reply but set out northward.

This unprecedented step threw the senators into high alarm. They saw Hannibal again unleashed, and "The earlier disasters in that war, the deaths of two consuls in the preceding year, were still terrifying. And they said that all those misfortunes had befallen them when the enemy had but a single general, a single army, in Italy. At present it had become two Punic wars, two mighty armies, two Hannibals, so to speak, in Italy. . . ."[3]

Nero and his 7,000 set out at top speed, marched day and night, and when they approached Sena Gallica messengers were sent forward to Livius to tell him of their approach and that they would enter his camp secretly by night. So that their arrival

[1] Livy, xxvii, 43.          [2] Ibid., xxvii, 43.          [3] Ibid., xxvii, 44.

should not become known to Hasdrubal by an enlargement of Livius's camp, each of Nero's officers and soldiers doubled-up with one of Livius's and together shared the same tent.

Immediately after Nero's arrival a council of war was assembled, and though many wanted to defer the engagement until Nero's weary men were thoroughly rested, Nero urged an immediate attack while Hasdrubal was unaware of his arrival and Hannibal of his departure. On his proposal being accepted, the signal for battle was displayed and the troops marshalled.

In spite of the precautions taken to assure secrecy, through a foolish mistake on the part of the Romans, Hasdrubal learnt that Livius had been reinforced. A reconnoitring patrol reported on its return that though the signal had sounded once in the praetor's camp, it had sounded twice in the consul's. Hasdrubal judged from this that there must be two consuls in Livius's camp, suspected that Livius had been reinforced and decided to refuse battle. That night he slipped away up the valley of the Metaurus (Metauro) river to gain the Via Flaminia; but in the darkness his guides deserted him and he lost so much time in striking the road that the Romans, who discovered his withdrawal, caught up with him and forced him to accept battle.

Hasdrubal drew up his army as follows: In the centre he deployed the Ligurians covered by his elephants, with his Spanish troops on their right and his Gauls on their left. The Gauls occupied a hill overlooking a ravine—possibly that of San Angelo— and would appear to have been separated from the Ligurian left by a considerable distance. Opposite the Gauls, on a height overlooking the ravine, Nero took up his position, with Livius also separated from him and well away on his left, facing the Spaniards, who were under the direct command of Hasdrubal. We are told by Livy that Hasdrubal's line was "rather long than deep" and that the Roman right wing extended beyond the line of battle.

The battle was opened by the Spaniards. "There both [Roman] generals were engaged, there the greater part of the Roman infantry and cavalry, there the Spanish troops, the old soldiers, acquainted also with the Roman mode of fighting, and the Ligurians, a hardy race of warriors. To the same place came the elephants, which had thrown the front lines into confusion by their first charge and had by this time forced the standards back. Then as the conflict and the shouting increased, they were no longer under control and roamed about between the two battle-

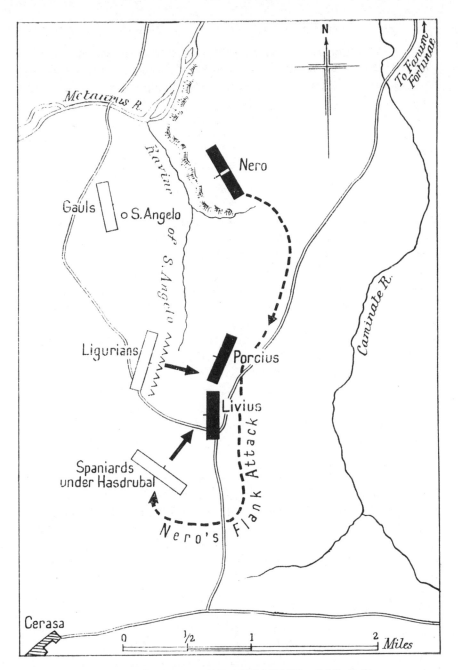

13. BATTLE OF THE METAURUS, 207 B.C.

The "Ravine of S. Angelo" is, of course, a modern name, but as, according to Hallward, "the evidence does not permit any reasonably certain certification of the precise site of the battlefield" it has been used, although out of historical context, as a guide.

lines, as though uncertain to whom they belonged, not unlike ships drifting without their steering-oars.''[1] Eventually, many had to be killed by their mahouts, who were equipped with a long knife and mallet for that purpose, the latter used to drive the former into the elephant's spinal cord.

Meanwhile, on Hasdrubal's left, the formation of the ground prevented an engagement and Nero, who saw that a furious battle was being fought away to his left, decided to take part in it. He left a force to demonstrate against the Gauls and led "several cohorts" out of sight of his enemy and round the rear of Livius's army, much as centuries later Marlborough did at Ramillies. To the surprise of Hasdrubal he charged the right flank of the Spaniards and then fell upon their rear, pushing them on to the Ligurians.

When he saw that the battle was lost, Hasdrubal spurred his horse and "rushed upon a Roman cohort, where he fell fighting, as was worthy of the son of Hamilcar and the brother of Hannibal''.[2] Of this incident Polybius remarks that "as long as there was any hope of being able to accomplish anything worthy of his former achievements", Hasdrubal "regarded his personal safety in this battle as of the highest consequence; but when Fortune deprived him of all hopes for the future, and reduced him to the last extremities, though neglecting nothing either in his preparations or on the field that might secure him the victory, nevertheless considered how, in case of total overthrow, he might face his fate and suffer nothing unworthy of his past career".[3]

The casualties, as given by Polybius, were "not less than 10,000 in killed for the Carthaginians, including the Celts, and about 2,000 for the Romans".[4]

On the night after the battle Nero set out on his return, and marching even more rapidly than when he came, he arrived at his camp before (Hannibal) on the sixth day.[5] Meanwhile a vague report of his victory reached Rome. At first the people "rather heard than credited the news"; but when it was confirmed, the whole city was swept by a wild joy—for the victory was the greatest yet won against their deadly enemy.

When he heard of his brother's defeat and death, Hannibal retired to Bruttium. Still the Romans did not dare to attack him, so great was the terror of his name. Yet it must have been apparent

---

[1] Livy, xxvii, 48.     [2] *Ibid.*, xxvii, 49.     [3] Polybius, xi, 2.
[4] *Ibid.*, xi, 3.                                    [5] Livy, xxvii, 50.

to them that their victory was in every way a decisive one. It ended Hannibal's last desperate hope of breaking the Roman hold on Italy; it restored confidence to the Roman soldiers, and it assured the loyalty of Rome's allies and subject peoples. Hence onwards the initiative passed into Roman hands.

If it be a fact that, after his victory of Cannae, Hannibal abandoned his advance on Rome because he believed that the encirclement of Italy would prove more profitable, after his brother's defeat on the Metaurus he must have realized his mistake; instead it was he who was encircled. By 205 B.C. he was isolated in the toe of Italy; Sicily had been lost and so had Spain, and peace had been agreed between Rome and Philip V of Macedonia.[1] So it came about that because Hannibal was reduced to a passive defensive, the initiative passed into the hands of the Romans. Their intention was slowly to strangle him; but Scipio thought differently, and, it would seem, had done so from the moment he took over command in Spain. His idea was to carry the war into Africa with Spain his stepping-stone. Polybius tells us that, after he had driven the Carthaginians out of Spain, he was advised "to take some rest and ease". He answered that, instead, he was "more than ever revolving in his mind how to begin the war with Carthage".[2] All along, it would appear, he had the campaign of Agathocles in his head, a man whose boldness he greatly admired.[3] So convinced was he of the necessity of carrying the war into Africa that, shortly after the battle of Ilipa, he had risked his life to visit Mauritania in order to win over Syphax, king of the Masaesylli, and to obtain from Masinissa, king of Numidia, a body of cavalry.[4]

After this mission, in 205 B.C., he returned to Italy, where he was acclaimed by the people and opposed by the elder generals who, because of his youth, were jealous of his success. He was chosen consul and Sicily was assigned to him as his province, more to get rid of him than to make use of his services. There he found himself in command of two legions formed from the

[1] The Roman operations in Illyria have not been examined because they were but a by-product of the war, and inglorious on both sides. Their importance lies in the future, namely the intervention of Rome in Greece and the declaration of the Second Macedonian War in 200 B.C. For the First Macedonian War see F. W. Walbank's *Philip V of Macedon* (1940), chap. III.

[2] Polybius, XI, 24.    [3] *Ibid.*, XV, 35.

[4] Mommsen (*History of Rome*, vol. II, p. 152) calls this "a foolhardy venture", and Captain B. H. Liddell Hart (*A Greater than Napoleon*, 1927, pp. 64–66) "a mission of diplomatic importance". Masinissa's capital was at Cirta (Constantine) and Syphax's at Siga (west of Oran).

remnants of the army of Cannae, and was refused all further help; yet, instead of being dejected, he set to work to recruit, organize, and train the army of the great revenge.

He sent his lieutenant, C. Laelius, over to Africa during 205 B.C., and in the spring of the following year he embarked his army at Lilybaeum, landed it at Cape Farina, near Utica, and was at once joined by Masinissa, who had been driven from his territories by Syphax. Scipio's expeditionary force consisted of his two legions and such volunteers he had been able to recruit, about 25,000 men in all, 40 warships and 400 transports. Meanwhile, since his return to Africa, Hasdrubal, son of Gisgo, had raised a Carthaginian army of 20,000 foot, 6,000 cavalry and 140 elephants, and was expecting the arrival of a corps of Celtiberian mercenaries. Syphax also was engaged in raising a large body of horsemen in his support.

Because Scipio's first need was to secure a base of operations, he laid siege to Utica, but on the approach of Hasdrubal and Syphax he was compelled to raise the siege and to retire to a rocky promontory some two miles distant, which he called Castra Cornelia; there he wintered. Syphax thought him cornered, which he very nearly was, and offered terms of peace. Scipio, with a cunning surpassing anything as yet done by a Carthaginian, prolonged the negotiations so that he might reconnoitre the enemy's camps which were but six miles distant from his own; his intention was suddenly to attack them under cover of night.

This craftiness has rightly been condemned by many as sheer treachery; yet, in mitigation, it should be remembered that Scipio's situation was a critical one, more particularly so because his enemy's numerous cavalry seriously restricted his foraging. But whatever view is taken, the fact remains that what Scipio was about to do was so decisive that, had he not done it, the probability is that his final victory would have been impossible. By "appearing excessively eager for peace" he lured his two opponents, Syphax and Hasdrubal, into a false sense of security, suddenly concluded the truce, and further to mislead them he began preparing to reopen the siege of Utica. He then hastily marshalled his two legions, set out at sunset, and ordered Laelius and Masinissa to fall upon Syphax's camp "and throw fire upon it", while he went to Hasdrubal's to do the same.

The Carthaginian outposts seemingly were negligent or asleep when suddenly flames shot up into the night and pandemonium followed. The accounts given by both Livy and Polybius are dramatic in the extreme. The latter writes: "It is . . . impossible for the imagination to exaggerate the dreadful scene, so completely did it surpass in horror everything hitherto recorded"; and the former informs us that 40,000 men were slain or destroyed by the flames and 5,000 were captured as well as 2,700 Numidian horses and six elephants. In short, if Livy's figures are not a gross exaggeration, though Hasdrubal and Syphax escaped, their combined armies were all but annihilated.[1]

Utica still held out, and instead of marching on Carthage, which would have been a risky operation, Scipio returned to Utica and pressed the siege. Meanwhile Hasdrubal and Syphax, now joined by 4,000 Celtiberian mercenaries, began to organize a new army. Scipio realized the danger of the probable withdrawal of Hannibal to Africa and the urgent need to smash Hasdrubal before he could arrive, and with one legion and the whole of his cavalry, now much strengthened, again took the field. On the great plains of the Bagradas (Mejerda) river he met Hasdrubal and Syphax, and by a tactical manœuvre similar to the one he had made use of at Ilipa, for the first time in Roman history the enemy was defeated by cavalry charges alone. Hasdrubal was overwhelmed, and Syphax, who broke away with a remnant of his horse, was pursued by Masinissa to Cirta and taken prisoner. For Scipio this action was of the utmost value, not only because it enabled him to reinstate Masinissa, but because it simultaneously deprived Carthage of its most valuable cavalry recruiting ground and won it for himself.

The result of the battle was panic in Carthage; peace was once again proposed, and Mago, then operating in the valley of the Po, and lastly Hannibal, in Bruttium, were recalled. Scipio thus gained his first objective, the evacuation of Italy by Hannibal, and, by offering a generous peace settlement, he hoped to gain his second, the victorious termination of the war.

Mago slipped away, while peace was being debated, but though his army gained the African shore he died of a wound during the voyage.

Hannibal was at Croton (Cotrone) when he received his orders to withdraw. He first killed his horses, then on June 23, 203 B.C.,

---

[1] For full accounts of the burning of these camps see Livy, xxx, 4–7, and Polybius, xiv, 1–6. Though it would seem to go unnoticed, there is little doubt that this ruse was inspired by Scipio's readings of the campaigns of Agathocles, during which a very similar incident occurred. (See Diodorus, xx, 64–66; also xx, 18.)

under protection of the armistice, he embarked his army, some 15,000 to 20,000 men, and landed it at Leptis Minor (Lemta). Thence he moved to Hadrumentum (Susa) to collect such cavalry as he could, which action so encouraged the patriot party in Carthage that its adherents refused to ratify the peace and seized the Roman envoys. Indignant at this treachery, early in 202 B.C., Scipio struck his camp at Tunes and marched up the valley of the Bagradas, burning the villages as he went to terrorize the people and to cut off the food stocks upon which Carthage largely depended. This struck such fear into that city that its inhabitants urged Hannibal to act without further delay. So it came about that a few days later he struck camp at Hadrumentum and marched inland to Zama (Zowareen), which lies five days' march southwest of Carthage. There he was received with foreboding news that Masinissa, at the head of 6,000 infantry and 4,000 cavalry, had joined Scipio.

He realized that with so great a preponderance of cavalry against him his chances of victory were slight and he sought an interview with his adversary. It was granted, and on the following day "both commanders advanced from their camps attended by a few horsemen. Presently they left their escorts and met in the intervening space by themselves, each accompanied by an interpreter."[1] Hannibal pointed out how fickle in war fortune could be and urged that a settlement should be agreed whereby Sicily, Sardinia, and Spain should be retained by Rome, the Carthaginians engaging never to go to war for these territories. Scipio, who realized full well his military superiority, brushed these proposals aside and said that because of the breaking of the recent truce he could no longer trust the Carthaginian word. The conference ended, both returned to their camps, and at dawn the following day they drew out their respective armies in order of battle.

In quality and training Hannibal's army was vastly inferior to his opponent's, and the order in which he marshalled it shows that he understood this. He had three divisions of infantry: his own army, Mago's, and a body of Carthaginian and African troops hastily raised by the Carthaginian Senate. The first and second he could rely upon, the third he could not; therefore he drew up the second, composed of Ligurian and Gallic auxiliaries, in front, presumably in open order of units, for he intermixed with it Balearic slingers and Moorish light infantry. The third, consisting

[1] Polybius, xv, 6.

of Carthaginian and African troops, he formed in second line immediately in rear of the first. The first he held in reserve some 200 yards in rear of the second line; it consisted mainly of Bruttians. In front of his first line he drew up in extended order eighty elephants; lastly he posted on the wings of his army his 2,000 cavalry, the Carthaginian on the right and the Numidian on the left. Because the weakness of his cavalry prohibited him from turning his enemy's flanks, as he had done at Cannae, his idea was to break the Roman front, a gamble which depended on the behaviour of his elephants. Were they to behave themselves well, the Roman front would undoubtedly be thrown into disorder, and this would not only facilitate the assault of his first line, but also encourage his second line, the hastily raised Africans. Lastly, with his veteran third line, he hoped to deliver the knock-out blow.

Scipio maintained the normal legionary organization, but adapted it to the tactical situation as it faced him. Instead of drawing up the maniples of the three lines chequer-wise, so that those of the second covered the intervals in the first–the usual formation–the maniples of the second line were marshalled immediately behind those of the first to create lanes for the Carthaginian elephants to pass along. Further, the *triarii* were held back well in rear, so they would not be thrown into confusion should the elephants break through, and the *velites* were posted in the lanes with orders to fall back should they be unable "to stand the charge of the elephants". On the left flank he posted Laelius with the Italian cavalry, and on the right Masinissa with the Numidian.

The battle may be divided into four phases: (1) The charge of Hannibal's elephants and the rout of his cavalry; (2) the fight between Hannibal's first two lines and Scipio's *hastati* supported by his *principes*; (3) the fight between the opposing reserves; and (4) Masinissa'a rear attack on Hannibal's veterans.

According to Polybius's account, though Livy's is the more dramatic,[1] the battle opened with a skirmish between the opposing forces of Numidian cavalry, during which Hannibal ordered his elephants to charge. But as they approached their enemy, the noise of the Roman horns and trumpets so terrified them that those on the left wing rushed backwards and threw Hannibal's Numidian horse into confusion. Masinissa seized the oppor-

---

[1] Polybius, xv, 12–14; Livy, xxx, 33–35.

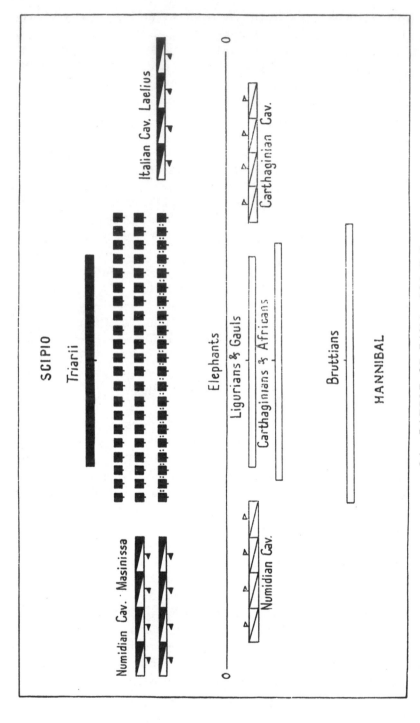

14. BATTLE OF ZAMA, 202 B.C.

tunity, charged home, and drove the Numidians from the field. In the centre the elephants drove the *velites* down the lanes and punished them severely. Next came Laelius's opportunity, and he seized it; for while the elephants were surging towards the Roman rear, he charged Hannibal's Carthaginian cavalry and drove it back in rout, and, emulating Masinissa, he set out on a vigorous pursuit.

Not until the cavalry of both sides were off the field did the infantry action begin, and it proved to be, as Polybius says, "a trial of strength between man and man at close quarters". At first it would appear that the advantage was with Hannibal; but because his second line failed to support the first, the latter was slowly forced back until it felt that it had been abandoned, broke to the rear, and not being allowed to pass through the second line, its panic-stricken men tried to hack their way through it. A general mêlée followed in which the first and second lines, pressed by the *hastati* who had been reinforced by the *principes*, fell back on Hannibal's third lines, and being refused admittance its men disappeared in rout round its flanks.

The third phase then opened. It is a grim picture, for the ground was now encumbered with the dead, the wounded "lying piled up in bloody heaps". Scipio ordered the wounded to be carried to the rear to clear the ground for his final assault, withdrew his *hastati* to the flanks, and between them he advanced the *principes* and *triarii* in close order. And "when they had surmounted the obstacles [the corpses] and got into line with the *hastati*, the two lines charged each other with the greatest fire and fury. Being nearly equal in numbers, spirit, courage and arms, the battle was for a long time undecided, the men in their obstinate valour falling dead without giving way a step."[1]

Had the action now remained solely an infantry one, it is possible that Hannibal might have won it; but most fortunate for Scipio, "in the very nick or time" Masinissa and Laelius returned, and "charging Hannibal's rear, the greater part of his men were cut down in their ranks; while of those who attempted to fly very few escaped with their life. . . ." This led to a total defeat of the Carthaginian forces. "On the Roman side there fell over fifteen hundred, on the Carthaginian over twenty thousand, while the prisoners taken were almost as numerous."[2] Hannibal, accompanied by a few horsemen, escaped to Hadrumentum.

[1] Polybius, xv, 14.                    [2] *Ibid.*, xv, 14.

Scipio did not march upon Carthage after the battle because, as Livy informs us, he thought that were he to lay siege to it and be recalled before it finished, his successor would come in for the glory of finishing the war,[1] and Polybius says that the dignity of Rome demanded lenity and magnanimous behaviour.[2] Both these reasons are suspect because undoubtedly the true reason is that Scipio was in no way prepared to carry out a prolonged siege. Like Hannibal, though a master of fieldcraft, his siegecraft was indifferent. Besides, the war had now lasted for sixteen years and Rome was weary and exhausted. In any case a siege was likely to absorb much time, for Carthage was superlatively well fortified.[3] Peace with Carthage rather than its occupation was, therefore, essential, and so it came about that the peace terms offered by Scipio were both generous and wise. The main clauses agreed upon were:

(1) The handing over of all ships of war and all elephants.

(2) Agreement to carry on no future war without the consent of Rome.

(3) The reinstatement of Masinissa in his former kingdom.

(4) The payment of 10,000 talents of silver (£2,970,000) spread over fifty years.

These terms were accepted by the Roman Senate and people. "Thus", writes Mr. Scullard, "the conqueror of Hannibal having vindicated his military strategy, triumphed also in the political field; he negotiated a wise peace such as could never have been made if Hannibal had been defeated in Italy. . . . His success owed much to the enthusiastic and loyal support of the People of Rome."[4] Mommsen remarks: "It is . . . probable that the two great generals, on whom the decision of the political question . . . devolved, offered and accepted peace on such terms in order to set just and reasonable limits on the one hand to the furious vengeance of the victors, on the other to the obstinacy and imprudence of the vanquished. The noble-mindedness and statesmanlike gifts of the great antagonists are no less apparent in the

---

[1] Livy, xxx, 36.  [2] Polybius, xv, 17.

[3] The citadel or Byrsa of Carthage was built on a hill near the extremity of a peninsula connected with the mainland by an isthmus about three miles broad, defended by a triple line of fortifications, the outer wall of which was forty-five feet high with towers at intervals of 200 feet. The whole peninsula thus enclosed was about thirty miles in circuit. Carthage was in fact a vast and immensely strong entrenched camp stored with all the necessaries for sustaining a siege.

[4] *Roman Politics 220–150 B.C.*, p. 81.

magnanimous submission of Hannibal to what was inevitable, than in the wise abstinence of Scipio from an extravagant and insulting use of victory."[1]

Though, at the time, no doubt, neither of the two great men fully realized the supreme importance of the event, in part at least the words which Livy and Polybius wrote in later years must have found an echo in Scipio's heart. Livy, when about to describe the battle of Zama, writes that, "before nightfall they would know whether Rome or Carthage should give laws to the nations. . . . For not Africa . . . or Italy, but the whole world would be the reward of victory."[2] And Polybius says: "To the Carthaginians it was a struggle for their own lives and the sovereignty of Libya; to the Romans for universal dominion and supremacy."[3]

These words are true, for Zama, by deciding who should rule supreme in the western Mediterranean, decided the coming struggle for supremacy in its eastern half. Even during the war the alliance between Carthage and Macedonia had compelled the Romans to glance eastward; but now that they were freed of Carthage they could, and of necessity were compelled to, stare in that direction.

"The immediate results of the war out of Italy were, the conversion of Spain into two Roman provinces – which, however, were in perpetual insurrection; the union of the hitherto dependent kingdom of Syracuse with the Roman province of Sicily; the establishment of a Roman instead of a Carthaginian protectorate over the most important Numidian chiefs; and lastly the conversion of Carthage from a powerful commercial state into a defenceless mercantile town. In other words, it established the uncontested hegemony of Rome over the western region of the Mediterranean."[4] The battle of Zama constitutes one of the great turning points in history; it led the Roman people across the threshold of a united Italy to the high-road of world dominion.

---

[1] *History of Rome*, vol. II, pp. 175–176.        [2] Livy, XXX, 32.
[3] Polybius, XV, 9. Appian writes, "Hannibal said that the battle would decide the fate of Carthage and all Africa", and Scipio "that there was no safe refuge for his men if they were vanquished" (*The Punic War*, VIII, 42).
[4] *History of Rome*, vol. II, p. 176–177.

# The rise of Roman imperialism

The Second Punic War influenced the Romans as profoundly as the wars of Alexander had influenced the Greeks. Not only did the Roman Empire emerge from it, but, coupled with the first, it arrested the development of Roman democracy by placing tremendous administrative powers in the hands of the Senate which, in the main, was recruited from the *nobiles*— that is, from the members of the old families. In the second century B.C. this led to issues being settled by a kind of tug-of-war between the different family groupings, both patrician and plebeian. Further, large fortunes were being made by a new class of people, who later on, as the *equites*, were to appear in Roman politics.

In the meantime the devastation of the farms had driven large numbers of free labourers into the cities and the enrolment of freemen in the legions, by further depleting the farms of workers, had led to an ever-increasing demand for cheap slave labour. Abroad, the opening up of vast wheat regions in Africa, Sicily, and Sardinia brought with it a further need for slaves, and the slave markets could be supplied by war. War thus became a necessity of Roman civilization. After expansion southward and westward it was only logical that the next great series of wars should be fought in the East, where, by 306 B.C., out of the general confusion after the death of Alexander, five great powers had emerged, the rulers of which had assumed the title of king. These powers were Egypt, under Ptolemy, son of Lagus (323–283–2 B.C.); Syra, under Antigonus (323–301 B.C.); Upper Asia, under Seleucus (312–280 B.C.); Thrace, under Lysimachus (323–281 B.C.); and Macedonia, under Cassander, son of Antipater (319–297 B.C.).

War between these kingdoms was incessant, and in 301 B.C. when the ambitions of Antigonus, then in his eighty-first year, and of his son, Demetrius Poliorcetes (the Besieger), had provoked a general combination against them, they were decisively defeated at Ipsus, in Phrygia, by Lysimachus, supported by a contingent of Cassander's and by Seleucus at the head of 480 elephants and a vast force of cavalry. So ended the last serious attempt to conquer the whole empire of Alexander.

After the battle, Antigonus's kingdom was divided and the five great powers were reduced to four; Macedonia was the weakest, because during the following ten years it was in a state of anarchy, a confusion rendered all but hopeless by waves of Gauls sweeping in from the north. At length, in 276 B.C., Antigonus Gonatus, grandson of Antigonus, obtained the crown, and in a reign of thirty-eight years he re-established order and prosperity. He died in 239 B.C. and in 221 B.C. his grandson Philip V became king. As we have seen, between 217 and 205 B.C. he came into conflict with the Romans in the First Macedonian War.

In 281 B.C., Lysimachus, at the age of eighty, was defeated and killed by Seleucus in the battle of Korupedion, and with his death Syria and Thrace disappear as independent kingdoms. The following year Seleucus was assassinated, and in 241 B.C. Attalus succeeded his uncle Eumenes as ruler of Pergamum, and took the title of king.

The general result of these changes was that by 202 B.C., when Hannibal was defeated at Zama, the East was divided between three great powers: Syria (or Asia) under Antiochus III, the Great (223–187 B.C.); Egypt, under Ptolemy V, Epiphanes (205–180 B.C.), and Macedonia, under Philip V (221–179 B.C.). There were also some lesser kingdoms – Pergamum, Bithynia, Cappadocia and Pontus, and in the region of the Halys, called after them, was Galatia, the final home of the Gauls who had invaded Macedonia and Thrace in 278 B.C.

It was with all these kingdoms that Rome was now to contend for what remained of Alexander's empire, and the first step taken was the Second Macedonian War.

After the Peace of Phoenice, in 205 B.C., Philip V turned toward the Aegean, an area in which he thought that the Romans would have little interest, and he made a secret treaty with Antiochus III for seizing and sharing the possessions of Egypt, whose king, Ptolemy V, was a child. Attalus and the Rhodians, who bore the brunt of Philip's first efforts at expansion, then appealed to Rome and grossly exaggerated the menace for Rome involved in the secret treaty. Though war weary, the Romans were frightened by the Rhodian envoys into declaring war against Philip in order to forestall any attempt by him and Antiochus to seize Greece as a jumping-off ground for an invasion of Italy. Actually, nothing could have been farther from Philip's plan or from Antiochus's.[1] The upshot was that in 198 B.C., the consul T. Quintius Flamininus was sent to Greece to take over command, and on his arrival the Achaean League threw in its lot with him.

In the spring of 197 B.C., when Philip with a powerful army was at Larissa, covering the vale of Tempe, Flamininus, who had invaded Boeotia, marched on Pherae in south-eastern Thessaly. Philip moved southward from Larissa into the plain of Scotussa when he learned of his approach, and when Flamininus entered the plain from the south the two armies met near a range of hills called Cynoscephalae (Dogheads). As the ground was unfavourable for the manœuvring of his phalanx, Philip wished to avoid battle, but unfortunately for him the two armies met in a fog, and though his right wing drove back the Roman left, his left wing, because of the broken ground, could not keep in line with it and became separated. It was charged and routed by the Roman right wing led by Flamininus in person and preceded by a number of elephants. Probably the battle would have ended in a draw, had not one of Flamininus's tribunes on his own initiative led some twenty maniples against the rear of the victorious Macedonian right wing. This bold move decided the battle, and Philip, with the survivors of his army, retired to Tempe.

As Polybius points out, it was superior Roman mobility which won the day, for though the phalanx was unbeatable on its own ground, once gaps appeared in its front it was an easy victim to the legion.

The immediate effect of the battle was to end Macedonian dominion in Greece. Though the Aetolians loudly demanded the extinction of Macedonia, Flamininus would not consider it. Not only did he want to maintain a balance of power within Greece, but also a bulwark against the northern barbarians who were the real danger. Besides, Rome wanted a speedy end of the war because of her commitments in northern Italy, which were not brought to a successful issue until 191 B.C. Accordingly, at the peace conference, which met at the pass of Tempe, all Flamininus demanded of Philip was the withdrawal of his garrisons from the Greek cities and towns.

The Aetolians were dissatisfied with this settlement and entered

---

[1] See A. H. Macdonald and F. W. Walbank, "The Origins of the Second Macedonian War", *Journal of Roman Studies*, vol. XXVII (1937), pp. 180–207.

into negotiations with Antiochus the Great, at whose court Hannibal was then residing. Hannibal saw in this approach a possible means of revenging himself on Rome and suggested to the king that while he (Hannibal) with 100 ships, 10,000 infantry and 1,000 cavalry, sailed to Carthage to induce the Carthaginians again to invade Italy, Antiochus should invade Greece, and when opportunity offered cross the Adriatic and invade Italy also.

When it heard this, the Senate sent envoys to Antiochus, but gained no satisfaction. Next, in 192 B.C., when the Aetolians broke away from Rome, Antiochus set Hannibal's bold plan aside and landed an army at Demetrias (Volo) in Thessaly. The Senate accepted the challenge and in the spring of the following year sent an army under Acilius Glabrio to Greece. When he sought to hold the pass of Thermopylae, Antiochus was worsted, abandoned Greece and withdrew to Ephesus. Even there he was not safe; for after he had won a naval battle off Phocaea (Foca), the northern-most of the Ionian cities, Acilius passed over to Asia, and for the first time in history a Roman army wintered on its soil.

In 190 B.C. Acilius was succeeded by the consul L. Cornelius Scipio, and with him came his brother Africanus as *legatus* to lend him his brains. In October the two Scipios arrived with their army at the Hellespont, where they found everything prepared for their passage by Eumenes II, King of Pergamum. Antiochus then attempted to negotiate; but the answer he received was that peace would only be considered were he to agree to pay the entire cost of the war and to surrender the whole of Asia west of the Taurus Mountains. He refused these terms and withdrew to the plain of Magnesia ad Sipylum, south of Ephesus.

The two Scipios followed the coastal road from the Hellespont and gained Elaea (near Candarli), where they were joined by Eumenes with a large force of cavalry. There Africanus was left ill and his place was taken by Cn. Domitius Ahenobarbus. From Elaea the army marched south, caught up with Antiochus, and after some manœuvring by the latter, the decisive battle of Magnesia (near Ephesus) was fought on a misty winter morning either in December, 190 B.C., or in January, 189 B.C.

Antiochus led the cavalry on his right wing, broke through the Roman left and threatened the Roman camp in its rear. Meanwhile his own left and centre met with disaster; for Eumenes, who commanded all the cavalry on the Roman right wing, hurled back the Syrian left wing cavalry, came in on the rear of

Antiochus's phalanx in the centre, and violently attacked it while Ahenobarbus assaulted it in front. The victory was complete and chiefly due to Eumenes's bold manœuvre. Thus in Asia, as in Greece, a single battle decided the issue.

After his defeat, Antiochus asked on what terms he could be admitted to the friendship of Rome, and the answer given him by Africanus, now recovered from his sickness, was that, (1) all Asia west of the Taurus must be abandoned; (2) 15,000 Euboic talents (£3,600,000) must be paid as indemnity; (3) all elephants must be surrendered and his fleet reduced to ten ships; and (4) Hannibal must be given up.

These terms were accepted by Antiochus, but suspecting that a demand would be made for Hannibal, he had already seen to his escape. The great Carthaginian had fled, first to Crete and later to Prusias, king of Bithynia, with whom he remained until about 183 B.C., when he ended his life by taking poison to avoid falling into Roman hands.

The Senate confirmed the treaty, but the real difficulty was the settlement of the country surrendered by Antiochus. The general principle adopted was that all Greek states should be free, and that the remainder of the territories annexed should be divided between Pergamum and Rhodes, the latter to obtain Lycia and Caria south of the Maenander (Menderes), and the former the rest. This made Eumenes the most powerful monarch in Asia, and so powerful that soon he incurred the jealousy of Rome.

The next problem was to secure the peace from the depredations of the Gauls, and the consul Cn. Manlius Vulso carried out this task. The Aetolians, who already had been forced to submit unconditionally, were bound to follow Rome in peace and war.

These two wars, the first with Macedonia and the second with Syria, were struggles in the first place for security, though they led the way to wealth and power. They did not add a square foot to Roman territory; for with constant war in northern Italy and Spain, Rome had not the men to hold the conquered lands. Their main influence was that they further stimulated the rising monied nobility and corrupted both the people and the army. The effects of this will be seen in the three campaigns which preceded the battle of Pydna, for never before had the consuls and their legions proved themselves less competent than in these.

CHAPTER 5

# The Battle of Pydna, 168 B.C.

The settlement of 188 B.C., which the Romans had hoped would keep Greece divided and power in Asia balanced, soon began to creak and crack. First, Eumenes quarrelled with Prusias, king of Bithynia, and next with Philip of Macedonia. The Romans saw in this an attempt on the part of Eumenes to extend his power and set out to check him by favouring his brother Attalus. Secondly, the Lycians fretted under Rhodes, and the increasing strength of the Rhodians at sea aroused the fears of the Romans, who saw in it a threat to the Aegean. Thirdly, the Aetolians were continually quarrelling among themselves, and the unwilling addition of Sparta to the Achaean League had become a source of constant friction. These discords led to frequent appeals to Rome and to the dispatch of embassies and commissions to investigate them; but so little did they accomplish that Philip, who had never abandoned hope of regaining his former dominance, judged that the power of Rome was weakening, grew contemptuous of her authority, and in 187 or 186 B.C. seized the Thracian coastal cities of Aenus (Enos) and Maroneia (Maronia). As this threatened the Hellespont – the shortest passage to Asia – Eumenes took alarm, and in 185 B.C. a Roman commission was sent to investigate and to report on the situation. Its decision was that Philip should withdraw his garrisons from Aenus and Maroneia as well as those in Thessaly. On hearing this, Philip in a passion exclaimed that "his days had not yet set",[1] but, as he was in no way ready for war, he withdrew the offending garrisons and soon after, to gain time for preparations, he sent his younger son, Demetrius, to plead his case before the Senate in Rome.

Demetrius was no stranger in Rome, he had for several years resided there as a hostage. He was liked and he was well received, and every effort was made to introduce division into the Macedonian royal household by treating him with special honour, Flamininus even flattering him "by suggesting that the Romans meant before long to invest him with the kingdom".[2] The issue

[1] Livy, trans. Evan T. Sage (1936), XXXIX, 26.
[2] *The Histories of Polybius*, trans. Evelyn S. Shuckburgh (1889), XXIII, 3.

151

was that, on his return to Macedonia, as he brought with him a most favourable answer, he was joyfully received by the people, who "had looked upon war with Rome as all but at their doors, owing to the provocations given by Philip".[1] This popularity roused the jealousy of his elder brother Perseus, who feared that he might be ousted from the succession and by means of a forged letter purporting to come from Flamininus, so worked upon his father's imagination that at length he persuaded him to have Demetrius poisoned.[2] This happened in 181 B.C., and immediately after, learning that he had been tricked, Philip, haunted by his conscience and forsaken by his courtiers, who flocked to Perseus, died at Amphipolis within two years of the murder and sank into a dishonoured grave.

Though, on his accession in 179 B.C., Perseus was determined to continue his father's hostile policy towards Rome, his first act was to ask for a renewal of the alliance Rome had made with Philip. Once this was agreed, he set about strengthening his hold on Thrace,[3] and simultaneously he exploited the land question, which for so long had been at the bottom of most of the trouble in Greece. Pauperism was rampant, and was largely so because the Romans had put a stop to the lucrative mercenary wars between the Hellenistic sovereigns. The destitute and the outlawed, no longer able to sell their services as soldiers, turned their attention to despoiling the rich, who for self-preservation were driven to seek the protection of Rome.

Perseus now set out to win over all those who desired a revolution in matters of property and of debt, and not only issued edicts in favour of Macedonian bankrupts, but also summoned all Greeks who were exiled because of political or other offences or because of their debts, to come to Macedonia and to expect full restitution of their former honours and estates.[4] This was an astute move, for it established in nearly every Greek state and city, whether friendly or hostile to Macedonia, an anti-Roman "fifth column". The issue was that the social revolution, which for long had been smouldering throughout northern Greece, burst into flames, and each "national social" faction, to quote Mommsen's words, sent to Perseus for help.

---

[1] Polybius, xxiii, 7.                                    [2] Livy, xl, 24.
[3] "The great reservoir of available man-power", see *Philip V of Macedon*, F. W. Walbank (1940), p. 236.
[4] See *The History of Rome*, Theodor Mommsen, trans. W. P. Dickson (1921), vol. ii, p. 274.

This upheaval threw the Roman Senate into high alarm and at once a commission was sent to Macedonia, but only to be slighted. At length, in 172 B.C., Eumenes went to Rome and laid before the Senate proofs of the hostile intention of Perseus. The Rhodian ambassadors, who were present, retorted that Eumenes was pursuing a policy in Asia similar to that of Perseus in Greece. Ignoring this accusation, but not altogether forgetting it, the Senate showed Eumenes every mark of honour, and satisfied with this diplomatic victory he set out on his return. At Delphi, where he broke his journey to sacrifice to Apollo, an attempt on his life was made by hirelings of Perseus.[1] Such was the pretext which detonated the Third Macedonian War, and early in 172 B.C. the praetor Gneius Sicinius was sent to Apollonia (Pollina) in Illyricum to establish a bridgehead on the eastern shore of the Adriatic for the future disembarkation of troops.

Had Perseus then acted with boldness the Romans would have been placed in a critical situation, for he was in a far stronger position than his father had been at the outbreak of the Second Macedonian War. "The power" of Macedonia, writes Mommsen, "was in all respects at least doubled: with a power in every point of view far inferior Hannibal had been able to shake Rome to its foundations."[2] In his treasury Perseus had sufficient money to pay for his existing army and 10,000 mercenaries for ten years, and in his magazines were stores of grain for as long a period and equipment for an army three times the strength of the one he put into the field–namely 39,000 infantry and 4,000 cavalry. Knowing that the Romans were unprepared, had he assumed a bold offensive, the probability is that he would have detonated a general Hellenic insurrection against Rome's allies and supporters in Greece; but, lacking the courage of his father, he adopted a purely defensive strategy and awaited his adversary's attack.

The army Perseus commanded was very different from the one Philip of Macedon had created and which Alexander the Great and his successors had developed. In it cavalry played a subordinate and the phalanx the decisive part, and a return was made to the pitched battles of heavy infantry, possibly because of the mountainous nature of Macedonia. But by the second century the phalanx had become less mobile, for by then it was ranged in sixteen ranks, its men carrying a twenty-one foot long *sarissa*. The first five ranks and its rearmost consisted of fully trained men,

[1] Livy, XLII, 15.          [2] *The History of Rome*, vol. II, p. 271.

whereas those between were composed of half-trained men whose task was to push on those in front. The files were so closely packed that they could only move straight forward, and each of the front line spearmen was covered by the shield of the man on his right. In battle the phalanx may be compared to a slowly moving fortress, from which the spears of the first five ranks protruded beyond the front. On level ground the front was virtually un-attackable, but on rough it was liable to crack, and as both hands were required to wield the *sarissa*, when disordered the phalanx became extremely vulnerable to the more mobile legion.[1] Besides the phalanx proper, the Macedonian army contained a body of 5,000 hypaspists, but actually they were heavy infantry, and at Pydna formed the phalanx of the Leucaspides.

It was not until midsummer 171 B.C. that the Roman army, under command of the consul P. Licinius Crassus, crossed from Brundisium to Apollonia. It consisted of the normal two consular legions, each of 6,000 infantry and 300 cavalry, and 16,000 allied foot and 600 allied horse. To cooperate with the Romans, Eumenes put his army and fleet on a war footing about the same time.

Licinius left a strong division in Illyricum to harass Macedonia from the west and marched over the mountains from Apollonia on Larissa in Thessaly. When approaching that city he was met by Perseus near the hill of Callicinus and severely defeated; he lost 2,000 infantry and 200 cavalry killed as well as 200 of the latter captured, and withdrew across the river Peneus (Salambria) which flows through the vale of Tempe.

Instead of at once exploiting the prestige the victory won for him throughout Greece, Perseus clung fast to his defensive strategy. Not only did he renounce all ideas of raising a Hellenic insurrection and of starting a guerilla war, for which his enemy was in no way prepared, but he even sent envoys to the Romans to discuss terms of peace. This suggestion was at once rejected, for the Romans could not possibly consider peace immediately after a defeat, and the answer he received was that the sole terms they were prepared to consider were those of unconditional surrender.

In spite of these bold words, never had a Roman army shown worse discipline than in this campaign. The soldiers were disorganized by defeat and demoralized by pillage. Friendly peoples were treated in the most shameful way and allied states like conquered enemies. Had Philip instead of Perseus been in command

---

[1] See *Hellenistic Military and Naval Developments*, W. W. Tarn (1930), pp. 24–30.

there can be no doubt that Licinius's army would have been destroyed and the whole of Greece lost to the Romans for the time being.

In 170 B.C., Licinius was replaced by Aulus Hostilius Mancinus, who attempted again an advance in Thessaly and, like his predecessor, was repulsed. Next, in 169 B.C., came Q. Marcius Philippus, an equally incompetent soldier, who set out to cross Mount Olympus by the pass of Lapathus, westward of Tempe, and at length, through all but impracticable defiles, reached Heracleum to find that it was impossible for him to supply his army. Again the Romans were saved from destruction by the pusillanimity of Perseus. When he saw his enemy on Macedonian soil he imagined that all was lost, flew in a panic to Pydna, and ordered his ships to be burnt and his treasure to be sunk. After a further advance of four days, his fleet was unable to supply him and Philippus was forced to retire. Perseus, regaining his nerve, advanced southward from Pydna and occupied a position on the Elpeus river,[1] south of Dium, which could be so strongly defended that Philippus abandoned all hope of attacking it.

As we shall see shortly, had Perseus's avarice not stood in the way, there is little doubt that he could have manœuvred Philippus out of his camp into the open and have beaten him decisively. Had he done so, he would have retrieved everything his father had lost at Cynoscephalae. Rome's prestige would have collapsed; Greece would have thrown off the Roman sway, and, in all probability, Egypt would have fallen to Antiochus IV, who had succeeded to the Syrian throne in 175 B.C., and in 168 B.C. was about to invade her. It is these possibilities which give to the Third Macedonian War an importance far exceeding that of the second. It was the testing ground upon which was to be proved whether Roman prestige in Greece, Asia Minor, and Egypt was to stand or fall.

At length, under popular pressure, the Roman Senate was brought to understand that the war could no longer be entrusted to incompetent consuls who saw in it no more than a means to enrich themselves. This accounts for the election to his second consulate of Lucius Aemilius Paullus, to whom was entrusted the campaign of 168 B.C. He was a son of the consul of the same name who had fallen at Cannae, a man of the old nobility, a brother-in-

---

[1] Also called the Macedonian Enipeus, and not to be confounded with the Thessalian Enipeus fifty miles to the south of it.

law of Scipio Africanus, and he had greatly distinguished himself in Spain and Liguria. At the time of his appointment he was sixty years old, and, according to Polybius–his contemporary–one of the few Romans of note who could resist the temptation of money.[1]

His first action was to request the Senate to appoint a commission to investigate affairs in Greece, and wisely the choice of commissioners was left in his hands. He selected three, including Cn. Domitius Ahenobarbus, the victor of Magnesia. How little the situation in Greece was appreciated at the time may be gathered from the list of questions to which the commissioners were instructed to provide answers: What were the requirements of the army and fleet and the state of the Macedonian forces? How much of the country was in Roman and enemy hands? Where were the Romans encamped; among the mountains or on the plains? Which of the allies were to be trusted and which not? What provisions and supplies were needed, and whence could new supplies "be brought by land carriage" and "whence by the fleet?" And lastly, "What had been achieved during the campaign either by land or sea?"[2]

Within two days of their appointment, the three commissioners were on their way; and when soon after their departure the senators impatiently pressed Paullus to tell them what his plans were, they received the prompt reply that until the commissioners returned he could not say.

On their return, Ahenobarbus and his two colleagues reported that the Roman and Macedonian camps faced each other across the Elpeus river; that Perseus had no intention of attacking and that Philippus was not strong enough to do so; that his troops were in a state of idleness and that there was only sufficient corn for a few days; that in Illyricum, where Appius Claudius was in command, the situation was critical, but were his army reinforced, Perseus might be caught between two attacks; that the fleet was in a deplorable condition, many sailors had died of sickness, others had deserted, and those who remained had received no pay or clothing; and lastly, that the loyalty of Eumenes was suspect.[3]

This suspicion would appear to have been well founded, for since he had established himself on the Elpeus, Perseus had been

---

[1] Polybius, xviii, 35.
[2] Livy, trans. William A. M'Devitte (1862), xliv, 18.    [3] *Ibid.*, xliv, 20.

intriguing with Rome's allies–Genthius of Illyricum, Eumenes, and the Rhodians. Also, he had entered into negotiations with a certain Clondicus, a Celtic chief who had offered him for hire 10,000 Gallic horse and as many foot. But, except for the Rhodians, in each case a wrangle occurred over the amount of money to be paid for treachery or assistance. Genthius was inveigled into an alliance by the promise of 300 talents, and on the strength of this he impounded two Roman ambassadors, only to find that the money was not forthcoming. With Eumenes there was so much haggling that, at length discovering that "his own craftiness was no match for the meanness of Perseus",[1] negotiations were broken off. But Perseus's worst mistake was his attempt to cheat Clondicus; as Livy points out, had he bought the Celtic horde, it could have been led through the passes of Perrhaebia–the region immediately east of the Cambunnian and the Pindus mountains and north of the river Europus–into Thessaly, where, by devastating the country, "the Romans, indeed, would have been obliged to look out for their own safety, since they could neither stay where they were, after losing Thessaly, whence their army drew sustenance, nor move forward, as the camp of the Macedonians stood in their way".[2]

Once the commissioners had been heard, Aemilius Paullus was given authority to select the tribunes of his two legions, which together consisted of 14,000 Roman citizens and Latin confederates and 1,200 horse. Another two legions, each of 5,000 foot and 200 horse, were raised for service in Illyricum under Lucius Anicius Gallus. When these arrangements had been made, Paullus went out from the senate house into the assembly of the people and spoke to them. The speech which Livy attributes to him is of considerable interest, because it shows that hitherto the direction of the war had largely been influenced by armchair strategists whose suggestions, schemes, and criticisms had paralysed commanders in the field.

"In every circle", he said, "and, truly, at every table, there are people who lead armies into Macedonia; who know where the camp ought to be placed; what posts ought to be occupied by troops; when and through what pass Macedonia should be entered; where magazines should be formed; how provisions should be conveyed by land and sea; and when it is proper to engage the enemy, when to lie quiet. And they not only determine

[1] Polybius, XXIX, 8.                          [2] Livy, XLIV, 27.

what is best to be done, but if anything is done in any other manner than what they have pointed out, they arraign the consul, as if he were on his trial . . .''

Next, after pointing out that he was "not one of those who think commanders ought never to receive advice", he said that he welcomed it so long as it was given by those "who are skilled in the art of war, or are present in the field". He concluded his address by saying:

"If, therefore, any one thinks himself qualified to give advice respecting the war which I am to conduct, which may prove advantageous to the public, let him not refuse his assistance to the state, but let him come with me to Macedonia. He shall be furnished by me with a ship, a horse, a tent; and even with his travelling charges. But if he thinks this is too much trouble, and prefers the repose of a city life to the toils of war, let him not, on land, assume the office of a pilot. The city, in itself, furnishes abundance of topics for conversation; let it confine its passion for talking, and rest assured, that we shall be content with such councils as shall be framed within our camp."[1]

In the early spring of 168 B.C. Paullus set out for Greece, and his journey was a rapid one, for on the fifth day after leaving Brundisium he arrived at Delphi. There he sacrificed, and four days later joined the army on the Elpeus. At the same time the praetor Anicius went to Illyricum, and within thirty days of his arrival the war there "was announced at Rome as finished before it was known to have been begun".[2] Genthius and his household fell into Roman hands.

On his arrival Paullus found the army short of water—which points to the Elpeus being dry at the time—and at once ordered wells to be dug. "The great height of the mountains", we read in Livy, "gave him reason to suppose that they contained hidden springs of water, the veins of which flowing through to the sea, mingled with the waves; and the more so, as they discharged no streams above ground. Scarcely was the surface of the sand removed, when springs began to boil up . . . as if through the favourable interference of the gods. This circumstance added greatly to the reputation and influence of the general in the minds of the soldiers."[3]

---

[1] Livy, XLIV, 22.    [2] Ibid., XLIV, 32.
[3] Ibid., XLIV, 33. In several parts of the world water is still obtained in this way, notably at Quetta in Baluchistan.

Next he ordered that "everything should be done regularly and without noise"; he forbade sentinels to carry arms because their object was not to fight, and organized the outposts in accordance with a roster of regular reliefs. He did these and other things to rouse the army out of the lethargy into which it had fallen, and soon "in the whole camp, not one person was to be seen idle".[1]

After he had set his men to work he assembled his officers, more to find out what they thought than to seek their advice. Some were for a frontal attack on Perseus's camp; others for a fleet flanking movement which would turn it. The first suggestion he at once discounted because the works on the Macedonian side of the Elpeus were exceedingly strong and well furnished with war engines – catapults and *ballistae*. The second he viewed more favourably, and when he had heard what his officers had to say he dismissed them and secretly set to work on his plan.

His idea was, while holding Perseus in front and distracting his attention by a fleet movement against his northern communications, to send a strong column westward across the southern slopes of Mount Olympus by way of Pythium and Petra to Dium, which would come in on the rear of the Macedonian camp. Not certain of the country, before he made up his mind he sent for two Perrhaebian merchants who were well acquainted with the mountain tracks, and questioned them in private about the nature of the passes leading into Perrhaebia.[2] They said that the passes were not difficult, but they had heard that they were occupied by detachments of the king's troops.

Paullus kept the two merchants for guides and sent for the praetor Octavius whom he instructed to assemble the whole fleet at Heracleum and to provision it for 1,000 men for ten days. Next he ordered to Heracleum 8,200 picked infantry and 200 cavalry, under the command of Publius Scipio Nasica – the son-in law of Scipio Africanus – and his own son Quintus Fabius Maximus,[3] still a very young man, in order to give the impression that they were to embark and turn the Macedonian position by sea. To Nasica alone he divulged his plan. He handed over to him the two guides and instructed him, by a series of night marches, to move west of Heracleum and to occupy Pythium at the fourth watch on the third day, and then to advance to north

---

[1] Livy, XLIV, 34.                    [2] *Ibid.*, XLIV, 45.
[3] So named, because he had been adopted by Q. Fabius Maximus; his brother was adopted by P. Cornelius Scipio, son of the elder Africanus, his maternal uncle.

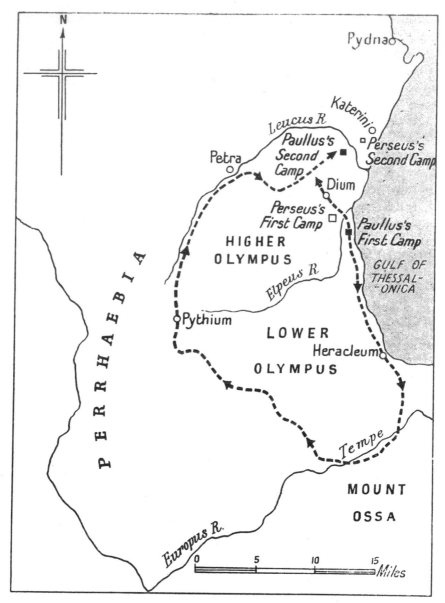

15. THE PYDNA CAMPAIGN, 168 B.C.

of Dium. He told him that in order to divert Perseus's attention, he himself with the rest of the army would attack the Macedonian outposts.

Nasica set out, and at dawn on the following day Paullus

launched the first of these diversionary attacks against the Macedonian posts in the middle of the channel of the Elpeus, "while the king on one side, and the consul with his legions on the other, stood spectators on the ramparts of their camps. At a distance, the king's troops had the advantage in fighting with missile weapons; but in close fight the Roman soldier was more steady, and was better defended, either with a target or a Ligurian buckler. About noon, the consul ordered the signal of retreat to be given, and thus the battle ended for that day. . . ."[1] The next day the same action was repeated, and on the following, instead of attacking, Paullus moved a column down to the coast as if he were about to attempt a crossing of the river at its mouth. Obviously, this was done to draw the Macedonians as far as possible away from Nasica's outflanking march.

From Heracleum Nasica set out under cover of night "in the opposite direction of the sea"–that is, westwards; but, unfortunately for him, one of his Cretan soldiers deserted when on the march, gained the Macedonian camp, and told Perseus what was in progress.

It would seem that the two merchant guides had been misinformed, for at the time the passes were unheld. But when he received the news of Nasica's march, Perseus at once sent 10,000 mercenaries and 2,000 Macedonians, under Milo, to block the Roman approach. According to Plutarch, in his biography of Aemilius Paullus, Nasica came up with Milo in the mountains and after a sharp and severe struggle routed him. When he heard of this defeat, Perseus, rightly fearing that he would be caught between two attacks, slipped out of the trap and fell back towards Pydna, taking up a position a little to the south of Katerini (Katerina) on a plain well suited to the manœuvring of his phalanx and bounded by two small rivers, the Aeson and Leucus (Pelicas and Mavroneri), which, though nearly dry, were likely to give the Romans some trouble. Immediately this withdrawal became known to Paullus, he advanced and without difficulty linked up with Nasica north of Dium, and from there the combined forces pressed on towards Katerini to find the Macedonian army ranged for battle immediately to the south-west of the town.

Scipio Nasica feared that Perseus would once again slip away under cover of night and urged an immediate attack; but Paullus, a far more experienced soldier, set the suggestion aside. His men

[1] Livy, XLIV, 35.

were exhausted by the march, it was now midsummer; and as he had as yet no defended camp from which to operate, to risk a battle would have been folly. Later in the day, and apparently to silence criticism, he pointed out to his men that "A camp is a residence for the victorious, a refuge for the conquered. How many armies, to whom the fortune of the fight has been adverse, when driven within their ramparts, have, at their own time, and sometimes the next moment, sallied out and defeated their victors? This military settlement is another native country to every soldier; the rampart is as the wall of his city, and his own tent his habitation and his home."[1]

Why, in circumstances so favourable to him, Perseus did not bring his enemy to battle can only have been because Paullus had halted his army on Mount Olocrus, a hill some four hundred feet high and west of the Leucus stream, which ran close by the western side of the Macedonian camp. It was unsuitable ground for the phalanx to attack over, and it must never be overlooked that the pike phalanx was an instrument designed for dead level ground, and that even quite minor obstacles disorganized its ranks. This is why, with one exception – the battle of the Hydaspes – Alexander never used his phalanx as a weapon of assault. But, since his day this had been forgotten, in spite of the fact that the phalanx was now more cumbersome.

When the Roman camp had been built a certain Caius Sulpicius Gallus, one of the tribunes, informed the soldiers that "on the following night, the moon would be eclipsed, from the second hour to the fourth". To calm their fears he explained to them that it was purely a natural phenomenon, and gave the correct reasons for it. Nevertheless, when it took place, ". . . the Roman soldiers thought the wisdom of Gallus almost divine; but the Macedonians were shocked as at a dismal prodigy, foreboding the fall of their kingdom and the ruin of their nation. . . . There was shouting and yelling in the camp of the Macedonians, until the moon emerged forth into its full light."[2] As the eclipse

---

[1] Livy, XLIV, 39.
[2] *Ibid.*, XLIV, 37. Shouting at an eclipsed moon was an ancient magical practice. Robert Stapylton mentions it in his tragi-comedy "The Step Mother" (1664), Act II, p. 23:

> "But hark
> Brasse Basons and Trumpets are sounding;
> See, see, how soon
> They thunder the Moon
> Out of the Eclipse she was droun'd in."

took place on the night of June 21-22, 168 B.C., and as the battle of Pydna was fought on the day following, its exact date is known.

According to Livy and Plutarch, both camps drew their water from the Leucus river, which at that time of the year cannot have been much more than a trickle, and to protect their watering parties the Romans had posted a detachment of two cohorts and two troops of horse on the western bank of the Leucus, as well as another of three cohorts and two troops to watch the Macedonian camp. Presumably the Macedonians had done likewise; therefore, considerable numbers of men were facing each other, and as so often happens on such occasions, it would seem that a gentlemen's agreement existed between the opposing detachments not to interfere with each other's watering parties.

On the afternoon following the eclipse and at about the ninth hour (3 p.m.) a Roman horse broke loose and galloped off towards the Macedonian bank, to be followed by three soldiers; the water was but knee deep. At the same time two Thracians of the Macedonian army set out to catch the animal and one of them got killed. This so enraged a body of 800 Thracians–presumably the Macedonian picket–that they intervened, and at once the two Roman cohorts did likewise and a skirmish started, the noise of which brought Paullus out of his tent. So considerable was the fray that "it seemed neither easy nor safe to recall or stop the impetuosity of those who were rushing to arms"; therefore "he thought it best to avail himself of the ardour of his soldiers, and to turn an accident into an opportunity. He therefore led out his forces from the camp."[1] At the same time Nasica, who had ridden out to the skirmish, came in and reported to Paullus that Perseus was leading his army out of his camp and was forming order of battle.

It is unfortunate that, except for fragments, the sections of Polybius's History describing the battle of Pydna have been lost, because Livy's account is obscure. Plutarch in his "Aemilius", quoting a report of Nasica's, gives Perseus's order of march as follows:

"First the Thracians advanced, whose appearance, Nasica says, was most terrible–men of lofty stature, clad in tunics which showed black beneath the white and gleaming armour of their shields and greaves, and tossing high on their right shoulders battle-axes with heavy iron heads. Next to the Thracians, the

[1] Livy, XLIV, 40.

mercenaries advanced to the attack; their equipment was every variety, the Paeonians were mingled with them. Next to these came a third division [phalanx of the Leucaspides], picked men, the flower of the Macedonians themselves for youthful strength and valour, gleaming with gilded armour and fresh scarlet coats. As these took their places in the line, they were illumined by the phalanx-lines of the Bronze-shields [phalanx of the Chalcaspides] which issued from the camp behind them and filled the plain with the gleam of iron and the glitter of bronze, the hills too, with the tumultuous shouts and their cheering."[1]

What the actual order of battle was is not given, but bearing in mind that the phalanx proper normally held the centre of the line, all one can conjecture is that the Macedonian battle order was probably as follows: Thracians on the right, then the phalanx of the Leucaspides, next that of the Chalcaspides, and lastly the mercenaries on the left, with the cavalry either on one flank or both.

Of the Roman order of battle nothing definite is known. But, again, it may be assumed that the two legions were in the centre, with the Latin allies on their right and the Greek allies on their left, with cavalry on one or both wings. It is stated that a number of elephants were at first held back, and eventually, as we shall see, were engaged on the right of the Roman line.

Perseus's attack was unexpectedly swift, for Livy states "that those who were first slain fell at two hundred and fifty paces from the Roman camp".[2] If so, and should the plan of battle given by Kromayer and Veith in their *Schlachten-Atlas Zur Antiken Kriegsgeschichte* be correct, then the whole of the Macedonian line must have crossed the Leucus stream and advanced up the lower slopes of Mount Olocrus.

At the sight of "the bristling rampart of outstretched pikes", Aemilius Paullus "was smitten at once with astonishment and terror"; never before had he seen so fearful a spectacle.[3] But he concealed his agitation and "with his head and body undefended he drew up his line".[4] Should this be true, then it looks much as if he had been surprised by the attack and caught unprepared, in which case it was Perseus and not he who seized the initiative.

The initial Roman counter-attack was made by the Pelignians

---

[1] *Plutarch's Lives*, trans. Bernadotte Perrin (1918), "Aemilius Paulus", xviii.
[2] Livy, xliv, 40.      [3] *Ibid.*, xliv, 40, and Polybius, xxix, 17.
[4] Livy, xliv, 40.

(soldiers of Sabine origin) who, as conjectured, were on the right of the Roman line, and as they could make no impression on the spear-wall, their commander, Salvius, seized a standard and threw it among the enemy. This excited a prodigious conflict in which the Pelignians were worsted and broke back in disorder towards

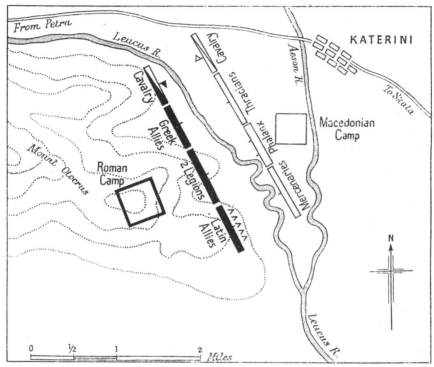

16. BATTLE OF PYDNA, JUNE 22, 168 B.C.

Mount Olocrus. This retrograde movement would seem to have carried the rest of the front line back with it and the whole army sought to gain the slope of the hill. If so, then it is clear that so long as the ground suited the phalanx the Romans were unable to make any impression on the hedge of steel. Next, as the ground became more and more unfavourable to the phalanx, its front began to bend and crack until gaps opened in it, "either on account of the unevenness of the ground, or on account of the very length of the front . . . while those who attempted to occupy higher ground were necessarily, though unwillingly, separated from those who occupied lower positions. . . ."[1]

[1] Livy, XLIV, 40.

Fortunately for the Romans, Perseus was no Alexander, and he would appear to have had no comprehension of Alexander's tactics; for at this crisis, instead of attempting to push his phalangites up the slope of Mount Olocrus, he would have moved forward the whole of his cavalry and light armed troops against his shaken enemy, and under their cover have re-dressed his pike front.

At Arbela, it will be remembered that Alexander's victory was because he took advantage of a gap in the Persian front. The same thing now happened at Pydna, but with the difference that besides one big gap there were a considerable number of smaller gaps.

Plutarch's account of the battle gives a clear picture of how the smaller gaps were dealt with. He says: Aemilius, "dividing up his cohorts, ordered them to plunge quickly into the interstices and empty spaces in the enemy's line and thus come to close quarters, not fighting a single battle against them all, but many separate and successive battles. These instructions being given by Aemilius to his officers, and by his officers to the soldiers, as soon as they got between the ranks of the enemy and separated them, they attacked some of them in the flank where their armour did not shield them, and cut off others by falling upon their rear, and the strength and general efficiency of the phalanx was lost when it was thus broken up."[1]

Livy's account, though confused, makes it clear that besides the small gaps an extensive one had developed between the left of the centre and the right of the left wing of the Macedonian army. The probable reason for this was that, when following up the routed Pelignians, the left wing got some distance ahead of the centre, which, at the time, was still engaged with the two Roman legions. This is what Livy says: After Aemilius had ordered his cohorts to insinuate themselves like wedges in the gaps, he placed himself at the head of one of his two legions and led it forward into the space between the Macedonian mercenaries and the phalanxes, and "thus disunited the enemy's line. Behind him were the targeteers [mercenaries] and his front faced the shielded phalanx of Chalcaspides."[2] Simultaneously, Lucius Albinus led the "second legion" against the phalanx of the Leucaspides, and the elephants with cohorts of allied cavalry were moved forward against the now isolated Macedonian mercenaries; but as they proved useless, their

---

[1] Plutarch's "Aemilius Paulus", xx.          [2] Livy, XLIV, 41.

attack was followed by the Latin allies, "who forced the enemy's left wing to give way".[1]

Meanwhile "in the centre, the second legion [? Aemilius's] charged and dispersed the phalanx [of the Chalcaspides]; nor was there any more evident cause of the victory, than there being many distinct fights, which first disordered that body, when it wavered, and at last quite broke it".[2]

When he saw the battle was lost, Perseus with his cavalry, which had sustained scarcely any casualties, fled to Pella and thence to Amphipolis. The slaughter following the battle was appalling. According to Livy, the Macedonians lost 20,000 killed and 6,000 captured; and another 5,000 taken during the pursuit, which was pushed for fourteen miles. The Roman losses are given at "more than one hundred, the greater part of whom were Pelignians", and "a much greater number wounded".[3]

Thus, writes Mommsen, "perished the Empire of Alexander the Great, which had subdued and Hellenised the East, 144 years after his death".[4] And thus, writes Polybius, "within a period of not quite fifty-three years (219–167 B.C.) . . . almost the whole inhabited world was conquered and brought under the dominion of the single city of Rome".[5] A period in which, as he says, world history passed from a series of "disconnected transactions" into "a connected whole".[6]

As soon as the battle had been won the Roman Senate resolved that all states in question, whether friend or foe, should for ever be rendered impotent. Macedonia was abolished and recast in the form of four federated republican leagues in which no inhabitant of any one was permitted to acquire property or to marry into another. The kingdom was disarmed and stripped of all its better classes, including every official, and all these people were transported to Italy to live in captivity. Trials for high treason were held throughout Greece, for in every city there was to be found a Macedonian party, and whoever had served in the army of Perseus was, to use a present-day expression, "liquidated". Illyricum was similarly treated, and in Epirus, though against his will, Aemilius Paullus gave up seventy townships to plunder and sold 150,000 Epirotes into slavery.

When their enemies were crushed, the Romans set out to crush their allies. The Achaean League had behaved correctly in the

[1] Livy, XLIV, 41.                [2] Ibid., XLIV, 41.        [3] Ibid., XLIV, 42.
[4] History of Rome, vol. II, p. 283.    [5] Polybius, I, I.        [6] Ibid., I, 3.

war; nevertheless 1,000 of its leading men, including Polybius the historian, were deported to Italy, where they were kept for seventeen years without trial. Eumenes was deprived of his Thracian possessions, and, if we are to believe Polybius, "Caius Sulpicius Gallus [the Roman envoy] on arriving in Asia, put up notices in the most important cities, ordering anyone who wished to bring any accusation against Eumenes to meet him at Sardis, and, taking his seat in the Gymnasium, gave audience for ten days to those who had such accusations to make: admitting every kind of foul and abusive language against the king, and, generally, making the most of every fact and every accusation. . . ."[1] The Rhodians were similarly treated; they were deprived of all the territories on the mainland granted to them by the Romans after the battle of Magnesia, and their commerce was systematically crippled so that Rome might monopolize the trade of the eastern Mediterranean.

Thus Rome became a world power and an empire all but in name. "The Hellenistic world", writes Mr. Scullard, "lay in broken pieces at her feet and it owed any independence that it still enjoyed entirely to the patronage of a Power which fifty years before had appeared to Philip V as only 'a cloud in the West'. That cloud now filled the sky over the whole Mediterranean, bringing to some fertilizing showers, but to others destructive storms."[2]

Yet, this vast extension of power was not planned. It was the outcome of the growth of a virile people in the conditions which prevailed in an age in which the balance of power was unknown. In such an age each nation, once it has attained internal unity, is for self-preservation compelled either to subdue its neighbours or emasculate them. The Hellenic states attempted the first course, Rome the second; but it was only a slower process toward the same end, because abject weakness whets the appetite of conquest. Thus it came about, as Mommsen says: ". . . all the other richly endowed and highly developed nations of antiquity had to perish in order to enrich a single people, as if the ultimate object of their existence had simply been to contribute to the greatness of Italy and to the decay involved in that greatness."[3]

Nevertheless, once this ruthlessness ended, the result was not the decay of Greece, but the victory of Hellenism; for the Greeks

[1] Polybius, xxxi, 10.       [2] Roman Politics 220–150 B.C., p. 218.
[3] History of Rome, vol. ii, p. 294.

were the Chinese of the ancient world and always conquered their conquerors. What they needed, in order to exorcise the excessive individualism which had kept them fractionized and mutually antagonistic, was the authority of a strong and stable world-government. And what Rome needed, in order to become a civilizing world power, was the culture of the Hellenistic world.[1] These two things and not plunder and tribute were the true booty of Pydna and the Third Macedonian War.

---

[1] For its rapid growth see *Roman Politics 220-150 B.C.*, H. H. Scullard, p. 246, and *The Cambridge Ancient History*, vol. VIII, chap. XIII.

# The struggle for supremacy within the Roman Empire

Though the Roman Senate had obtained much experience in waging war, it was not so successful in the technique of establishing peace within an empire. The result was that the government of the conquered territories was left to magistrates and ex-magistrates, whose short terms of office, normally one year, encouraged their rapacity. Besides, vast tributes yearly had to be raised from the provinces and territories because the citizens of Rome were no longer directly taxed, and the demands of an ever-increasing, indolent and pleasure-loving proletariat had to be satisfied as well as legitimate expenditure. The result was constant discontent and unrest, which at times gave way to open rebellion.

The first rising of importance came in 152 B.C., when a certain Andriscus, who claimed to be a son of Perseus of Macedonia, gathered an army of Thracians and invaded Thessaly. Suppressed by Q. Caecilius Metellus in 148 B.C., he was followed by two other pretenders, and in 146 B.C., when they had been crushed, the four leagues into which Macedonia had been divided were turned into a Roman province.

Meanwhile Sparta had broken away from the Achaean League, and when the Achaeans broke the peace, early in 146 B.C. Metellus marched on Corinth, where their army had assembled, and laid siege to the city. He was succeeded by Lucius Mummius who, in July, after he had defeated the Achaeans at the isthmus, entered Corinth unopposed, looted the city and razed it to the ground. The Achaean League was then dissolved with other surviving leagues in Greece. Henceforth Greece was a part of the general administrative responsibility of the Governor of Macedonia.

Simultaneously with the subjection of Greece came the obliteration of Carthage. Since their defeat at Zama, in 202 B.C., the Carthaginians had so far recovered their former prosperity that the jealousy and greed of Rome were again aroused. Porcius Cato, the celebrated censor, ceaselessly thundered that Rome would never be safe so long as Carthage existed, and, toward the end of his long life, whatever the subject might be, whenever he was called upon to vote in the Senate, his words were *"Delenda est Carthago"*. In 149 B.C., the year of his death at the age of eighty-five, war was determined upon, and to make it certain a series of ultimatums was presented to Carthage, each more outrageous than the last. First, a demand was made for 300 boys of noble birth as hostages, and when complied with, next came a demand for the surrender of all arms. This order was also obeyed, and 200,000 stands of arms and 2,000 catapults were delivered up. Lastly came a third demand, which revealed the true purpose of the Senate: the Carthaginians were informed that Carthage must be abandoned and its inhabitants moved inland to some spot not less than ten miles from the sea. As war could bring nothing worse than this, the Carthaginians resolved to fight. They converted their city into an arsenal, laboured night and day, and each day produced a vast amount of weapons; the women even sacrificed their hair for the torsion cords of the catapults.

In 147 B.C., Publius Scipio Aemilianus, the younger son of the victor of Pydna, was sent to conduct the war. He invested the city, cut off its supplies, and in the spring of the following year, through starvation forced its surrender. Once it was his he received the order to destroy it so utterly that a plough could be drawn over its site. When he gave the order to fire the city, he turned to his old friend and tutor, Polybius, and said: "Oh, Polybius, it is a grand thing; but I shudder to think that someone may one day give the same order to Rome." So were Cato's words fulfilled, and the territories of the city made a Roman province, the Province of Africa.

The obliteration of cities had now become the seal of Roman power. Yet, as Polybius remarks: "To destroy that for which a war is undertaken seems an act of madness, and madness of a very violent kind." Corinth, Carthage, and later Numantia (Guarray near Soria) in Spain (133 B.C.) were destroyed to show the might of Rome and also to sate her greed for plunder. Also, the sale of their citizens as slaves was profitable, and many of these rebellions and so-called wars were little more than slave hunts.

In Sicily, in particular, the brutal treatment meted out to these unfortunate people became so unbearable that it led to a revolt known as the First Servile War. In 135 B.C. the slaves rose against their masters. They were led by two remarkable men, Eunus, a

Syrian, and Achaeus. They raised an army, estimated at 70,000 strong, and won several pitched battles; but in 132 B.C. were suppressed ruthlessly by Publius Rupilius.

The war against them was in full swing when Tiberius Gracchus, a grandson of Scipio Africanus, entered on his tribunate and espoused the cause of the people, more especially the landless farmer class. "The beasts", he said, "that prowl about Italy have holes and lurking places, where they may make their beds. You who fight and die for Italy enjoy only the blessings of air and light. These alone are your heritage. Homeless, unsettled, you wander to and fro with your wives and children. . . . You fight and die to give wealth and luxury to others. You are called the masters of the world; yet there is no clod of earth that you can call your own." As tribune, he placed before the Assembly a motion for the reassignment of the public lands, and after it became law in 133 B.C., in his effort to secure re-election so that he might assure its enforcement, he was assassinated: a deed which unlocked a century (133–31 B.C.) of revolution and civil war which ended in the destruction of the Republic. In 123 B.C. his brother Caius Gracchus gained the same office and set out to champion the same cause, as well as to demand that the Italian allies should be given full Roman citizenship. In 121 B.C. he also was assassinated in a riot.

Though the two brothers did not achieve their full aim, they taught the people to look up to a leader, and, as Breasted says: "This tendency was the beginning of one-man power." But the next leader to whom the people turned was a soldier and not a magistrate.

Ten years after the death of Caius Gracchus and during the war with Jugurtha, king of Numidia and grandson of Masinissa, the corruption and misrule of the Senate became so scandalous that the people elected a new man consul and proceeded to appoint him by popular vote to the command in Africa, establishing a precedent for popular military appointments which was followed several times in the following century. The man they selected was Caius Marius. Born in 157 B.C., he was of humble origin, had served under the younger Scipio Africanus at the siege of Numantia, and at the time was on duty in Africa as legate of the consul Q. Caecilius Metellus. He replaced Metellus in 107 B.C., and in the following year he brought the war to a successful end when Jugurtha was captured by one of Marius's officers, L. Cornelius Sulla.

Meanwhile a far more formidable danger threatened Italy. In 113 B.C., hordes of barbarians, known as Cimbri, occupied the valley of the Drave and were joined there by the Teutones. The consul Cn. Papirius Carbo was sent against them and was defeated, and during the following five years each consular army engaged with them met with the same fate. In 106 B.C. they burst into Gaul and took Tolosa (Toulouse). The following year they routed Cn. Manlius, who lost his camp and 80,000 men, and crossed the Pyrenees into Spain when they were driven back into Gaul by the Celtiberians. The Cimbri left the Teutones and Ambrones in Provence to move on Italy by way of the Maritime Alps, and turned northward to pass through Switzerland in order to come over the Brenner, the two hosts intending to meet in Cisalpine Gaul.

Never since the days of Camillus had Rome been so threatened; the people were in panic, and to save the Republic, Marius, now consul for the fourth time, was given command of Transalpine Gaul (South-Eastern France) and Lutatius Catalus of Cisalpine.

Marius posted himself in a fortified camp on the lower Rhône and awaited the barbarians. They failed in an attempt to storm his camp and passed it by; but immediately they did so he followed them, and in 102 B.C. he brought them to battle at Aquae Sextiae (Aix in Provence), and slaughtered them; the village of Pourrières (Putridi) still recalls the memory of the massacre.

With Transalpine Gaul so secured, Marius returned to Rome and was again elected consul. While he was there news was received that Catalus had been defeated near Verona and had retreated to the Po, and, in 101 B.C., Marius set out to his assistance. With Catalus he crossed the Po and found the Cimbri near Vercellae (Vercelli) awaiting the arrival of the Teutones and Ambrones. Instead, they met Marius and were utterly destroyed.

Though an able leader of the brutal type, Marius was so blinded by hatred of the nobility that he was an indifferent statesman. The year after Vercellae he was elected consul for the sixth time. But in the riots which followed, the Senate regained the upper hand, and he was forced to retire in disgrace. Further trouble came. The Italian allies now demanded full citizenship and found their leader in a noble named Livius Drusus, who was assassinated in 91 B.C. Then the leading peoples of central and southern Italy revolted and formed a state of their own with its capital at Corfinium, which they renamed Italica. This caused the

Social War of 90-88 B.C., which ended when their demand for citizenship was granted.

Trouble also was brewing in Asia Minor, and the plutocrats, when they saw their financial interests threatened, forced the Senate to appoint Sulla in command. But the leaders of the people refused to accept him and elected Marius. To frustrate his rival, Sulla occupied Rome and forced a law through the Senate whereby the Assembly was compelled in future to obtain the consent of the Senate before it could vote any measure; after which Sulla left for Asia Minor. Immediately, the people rose, and during the rioting Marius returned from Africa at the head of a body of troops and with the consul Cornelius Cinna entered Rome and massacred the senatorial party. Without going through the form of an election, Marius and Cinna named themselves consuls for the year 86 B.C. Soon after Marius died.

The war which had called Sulla to Asia was against Mithridates, king of Pontus, and such was the discontent of the Greek cities under Roman rule that soon the conflict blazed over the Aegean and set fire to Greece. Sulla laid siege to Athens, and recovering European Greece, he drove Mithridates back into Asia. He then returned to Italy, overthrew the Marians in a decisive battle fought outside the Colline Gate, entered Rome, and in 82 B.C. by means of his army forced his appointment as dictator. His first action as such was to carry out a systematic slaughter of the leaders of the people. A reign of terror was established, under cover of which he deprived the Assembly of all power and re-established the leadership of the Senate. In 79 B.C. he retired into private life and in the year following died of pediculosis.

In 70 B.C. the people found another soldier leader of ability in Cn. Pompeius—generally called Pompey—a former officer of Sulla's, born in 106 B.C. He agreed to repeal the laws of Sulla and was elected consul. In 67 B.C. the Assembly passed a law which placed him in supreme command of the Mediterranean in order to extirpate the pirates which then infested it and preyed on Roman shipping. No Roman general before him had been given so far-reaching a command.

In forty days he cleared the western Mediterranean, sailed eastwards, and in seven weeks exterminated the pirate strongholds in the Aegean. In the following year he was appointed to succeed L. Licinius Lucullus in the third war against Mithridates, which had been declared in 74 B.C. He crushed what remained of the kingdom of the Seleucids, marched up the Euphrates and gazed on the Caspian Sea. On his way back he entered Jerusalem and brought the Jews under Roman rule. In 62 B.C. he returned to Italy and there were fears in the Senate that he might march with his army on Rome and seize supreme power. Instead, when he landed at Brundisium, he dismissed his soldiers to their homes.

# CHAPTER 6

# The siege of Dyrrhachium and the Battle of Pharsalus, 48 B.C.

When, in the year 62 B.C., Pompey returned in triumph from the East, the Republic, like a lump of well-saturated sugar, though still maintaining its form, was approaching dissolution. Constituted as a city council, the Senate was incapable of discharging its imperial functions, and though antagonistic to the idea of autocracy, its incapacity to grasp the meaning of the world-wide problems which now faced the universal empire sterilized its imagination and palsied its will.

Radical economic changes caused by the increase of wealth and the vast number of slaves imported had followed the Hannibalic wars. Business now meant banking more than trading – the undertaking of state contracts, the financing of games, the raising of taxes, and the collecting of indemnities and booty each amounted to £6,000,000 in modern money.[1]

Rapidly the desire to make money replaced the idea of duty to the state. Taxation impoverished the people, who increasingly were compelled to resort to the money-lenders, and who through debt were reduced to either potential or actual slavery, which in ancient history reached its high-water mark during the last century of the Republic. In the days of Cicero Rome was the great emporium for slaves and war was the principal source of supply. Further, slaves bred slaves, until slave-farming became a highly lucrative business. With the extinction of the peasantry the land passed into fewer and fewer hands, and the general replacement of free by slave labour sent the landless flocking into the cities, which, to quote W. Warde Fowler, became largely composed of "human beings destitute of all natural means of moral and social development. The ties that had been once broken", he writes, "could never be replaced. There is no need to dwell on the inevitable result – the introduction into the Roman State of a poisonous element of terrible volume and power."[2]

---

[1] See *Social Life at Rome in the Age of Cicero*, W. Warde Fowler (1908), p. 66.
[2] *Ibid.*, p. 232.

Simultaneously, among the wealthy, the money accumulated through conquest was spent, not on productive work, but on pleasure and excitement.

At bottom, usury was the cancer of the Republic, and though the resultant degeneracy was of surfeit rather than of senility – a violent indigestion and not a mortal disease – seldom had a people sunk so low. Bereft of religion, morality, and all the social virtues, the dole-fed masses wallowed in vice. Luxury begot brutality and brutality licence; licence led to celibacy, and childlessness became more and more prevalent. To these degenerates licence spelt liberty, but to the plutocrats liberty spelt power, profit, and an unlimited scramble for wealth, until money became the sole link between man and man. To many it seemed as if a total eclipse, if not collapse, of civilization was at hand, and that only a Hercules could wrestle with such a problem. So it came about that instinctively all eyes searched the horizon for a man, and when, on September 29, 61 B.C., dressed, it was said, in the costume of Alexander,[1] Pompey entered Rome in triumph, the people acclaimed him their hero. When, in 66 B.C., Pompey superseded Lucullus in the East, he cannot have failed to have measured himself with the great Macedonian. Like him he carried the war beyond the Euphrates, annexed vast lands and founded cities and towns. The power of a conquering army was his, also the command of great treasure. Money meant donatives, donatives meant sycophancy, and out of hero-worship emanated first the shadow and later the substance of a returning monarchy.

When all eyes were focused on Pompey, a second man appeared, a man of noble birth, born in 102 B.C.,[2] who traced his descent from Aeneas, the son of Venus and Anchises. His name was Caius Julius Caesar.

Though most of his family belonged to the senatorial party (*optimates*), he was of the people's party (*populares*), possibly because his aunt, Julia, had married the great Marius. In 68 B.C. he had served in Spain as quaestor (financial secretary) and when at Gades (Cadiz) "noticing a stature of Alexander the Great, in the temple of Hercules, he heaved a sigh and as if out of patience

---

[1] "Pompey himself was borne in a chariot of studded gems, wearing, it is said, a cloak of Alexander the Great, if any one can believe that. It seems to have been found among the possessions of Mithridates that the inhabitants of Cos had received from Cleopatra" (*Appian's Roman History*, trans. Horace White, 1912, "The Mithridatic Wars", XII, XVII, 117).

[2] The year is in doubt, some authorities accept 100 B.C.

with his own incapacity in having as yet done nothing noteworthy at a time of life when Alexander had already brought the world to his feet, he straightway asked for his discharge, to grasp the first opportunity for greater enterprises at Rome".[1]

When, in 60 B.C., Caesar returned to Rome to stand for the consulship, he found the situation dominated by three men–M. Porcius Cato, Pompey and M. Licinius Crassus, the latter two opposed by the former. By denying Caesar the triumph he rightly expected for his successes in Spain, Cato added him to his political enemies, a blunder which led to the first triumvirate of Pompey, Caesar, and Crassus, between whom the compact was that Pompey and Crassus would support Caesar's candidature for the consulship, and that Caesar, when consul, would secure the settlement of Pompey's disbanded veterans and revise certain taxes concerning which Crassus, a banker of immense wealth, was interested.

In 59 B.C., when Caesar had been elected consul, these undertakings were carried out, and in all probability the triumvirate would then have come to an end had not a serious uprising of the Helvetii occurred. To deal with this threat to the northern frontier, Caesar was given as his province Cisalpine Gaul and Illyricum, to which shortly afterwards Transalpine Gaul was added. He assumed command in 58 B.C., defeated the Helvetii at Bibracte (Autun), and when he found the Celts in central Gaul threatened by a horde of Germans under Ariovistus, he advanced through the Belfort Gap and near Mülhausen routed the latter in a great battle on September 2. During the next year, as will be related in Chapter 8, by conquering the Belgae and Nervii he concluded the first stage of the conquest of Gaul.

In 56 B.C., a conference of the *Triumviri* was held at Lucca, at which it was agreed that Caesar's rule in Gaul should be renewed for a further term of five years, that Pompey should be given the government of the two Spanish provinces for a similar period, and that Crassus should take over Syria so that war might be made upon Parthia.

Had Caesar not grasped it already, he must now have realized that Gaul was not only a bulwark against the warlike Germanic tribes and a magnificent recruiting ground[2] for his army–his

[1] *Suetonius*, trans. J. C. Rolfe (1914), "The Deified Julius", VII. Plutarch tells the story in a different context.

[2] See Jérôme Carcopino in his essay "Rome et la Gaule" in his *Points de Vue sur L'Imperialisme Romain* (1934), pp. 203–256.

political as well as his military weapon—but that it was also the most certain base for a political attack upon Pompey. Not only did the province of Cisalpine Gaul flank the entire north of Italy, but that of Transalpine Gaul cut across Pompey's land communications between Italy and Spain, and, therefore, in the event of a clash with Caesar, would put him at a decided disadvantage.

Meanwhile Crassus, fabulously wealthy, sixty years of age, physically deaf and spiritually blind, set out for Syria to rival Alexander[1] and to prepare his campaign against the Parthians, whose western frontier bordered the Euphrates.

The Parthian Empire was founded by Mithridates I, who set out on his conquests about 160 B.C. First he occupied Media, next Syria, then Bactria (Bokhara) and Gedrosia (Makran). The army he created was a formidable one, composed almost entirely of horse-archers, and it was this type of army which Crassus was to meet, led by an able young general, Surenas, who, though he painted his face like a girl, feared nothing and was a man of imagination. He realized that bowmen rapidly expend the arrows they carry and attached to his 10,000 horse-arches 1,000 munition camels, each carrying a vast supply of arrows, and by this means was able to increase their fire-power a hundredfold. It was against this formidable man that, in 53 B.C., Crassus marched eastwards.

After he had occupied Nicephorium, where Alexander had crossed the Tigris, Crassus turned northward towards Edessa, and in June was surrounded by Surenas at Carrhae (Haran) and his army was virtually annihilated. He was killed and of his 40,000 legionaries 20,000 were killed and nearly 10,000 were captured.

Carrhae was the most disastrous defeat Rome had suffered since Cannae, and though her citizens took little notice of it, its effects placed Caesar in a most difficult position; for now that Crassus had been removed, Pompey was left without a counterpoise. To render Caesar's situation still more perplexing, in 52 B.C. Gaul, under the able generalship of Vercingetorix, revolted. The siege of Alesia (Auxois) followed, and it was not until the next year that the rebellion was crushed and the conquest of Gaul finally accomplished.

[1] Plutarch in his "Crassus" says: "But now being altogether exalted and out of his senses, he would not consider Syria nor even Parthia as the boundaries of his success, but thought to make the campaigns of Lucullus against Tigranes and those of Pompey against Mithridates seem mere child's play, and flew on the wings of his hopes as far as Bactria and India and the Outer Sea" (xvi).

It had been an amazing task, for in all, as Plutarch writes, Caesar "took by storm more than eight hundred cities, subdued three hundred nations, and fought pitched battles at different times with three million men, of whom he slew one million in hand to hand fighting and took as many more prisoners".[1] It was his amazing energy which had accomplished this, and not only did it give Rome Gaul, but its conquest made Caesar both the hero of the people and master of the most powerful Roman army. Pompey entered his eclipse. This meant war, yet it was, as Mommsen says, "not a struggle between republic and monarchy . . . but a struggle between Pompey and Caesar for the possession of the crown of Rome".[2]

Here one may digress to inquire into a subject of considerable importance – the changes in military organization which had taken place since the battle of Zama; for they had a pronounced influence upon the politics as well as the strategy and tactics of this period.

The legion of the Second Punic War was, to repeat, a body of burgesses divided into *hastati*, *principes*, and *triarii*. But as wealth percolated into Rome a profound change took place: the burgesses growing richer increasingly avoided military service, with the result that about 104 B.C. Marius threw the army open to volunteers outside the propertied classes, and later on recruited men from the servile and criminal classes as well as many foreigners. Further, to lessen the danger inherent in the many intervals in the front of the manipular system, he reorganized the legion in three lines of cohorts, each cohort consisting of five maniples, when all distinction between *hastati*, *principes*, and *triarii* disappeared. The tactical unit was thus increased from 120 to 600 soldiers, and as there were ten cohorts in the legion, normally four in the first line, three in the second and three in the third, the strength of the legion was raised from 4,500 to 6,000 men. The legionary cavalry was abolished, their place was taken by foreign cavalry (*auxilia*). By degrees the intervals between the cohorts were diminished, until, to all intents and purposes, the phalangial order was re-introduced.

The old militia system thus gave way to a professional army with a mercenary spirit, and where in former days the soldier swore allegiance to the Republic, he now swore to serve his general.

[1] *Plutarch's Lives*, trans. Bernadotte Perrin (1919), "Caesar", xv. These figures are obviously exaggerated.  [2] *History of Rome*, vol. IV, p. 322.

Such an army demanded highly educated and skilful generals, and when these were forthcoming success was assured. When they were not, discipline was apt rapidly to break down.

The exact structure of the legion in Caesar's day is unknown, but probably it was much as Marius had left it. Its arms and armour would appear to have been little changed, except that light troops, slingers and bowmen were increased.

The most remarkable innovations were the increase in cavalry, artillery, and engineers. The first was largely brought about by contact with the Numidians and other mounted foreigners, and the increases in the latter two through wars with the Carthaginians and Greeks, as well as by contact with the engineers of Alexandria.[1] The following examples will give some idea of the progress made.

In 53 B.C., during the siege of Avaricum (Bourges), Caesar apparently made use of some form of quick-firing engine,[2] and in his campaign against the Bellovaci (a tribe round Beauvais) in 51 B.C., we find that he used veritable bombardments of projectiles in the open field. We read: "Having . . . drawn up his army in order of battle he marched to the furthest hill, from which he could, with his engines, shower darts upon the thickest of the enemy."[3] A similar operation is mentioned when he attempted to hem in Pompey at Dyrrhachium. When his ninth legion gained a hill and began to fortify it, Pompey seized a neighbouring hill and brought such concentrated fire to bear on Caesar's men that they were compelled to abandon their work and withdraw.[4]

Later, we learn from Plutarch that Antony, in his expedition against the Parthians, had a siege train of 300 wagons. The smaller field-pieces were transported in carriages called *carroballistae*, examples of which may be seen on Trajan's Column, erected in Rome between A.D. 105–113. This field artillery was probably in use a hundred years earlier. Mules were harnessed to these vehicles, and the pieces carried on them could be discharged over the heads of the animals. According to Vegetius, every cohort was equipped with one catapult, and every century with one *carroballista*. Therefore, at some time after Caesar's day the legion pos-

---

[1] For a fuller account see "The Artillery of the Carthaginians, Greeks and Romans", *Journal of the Royal Artillery*, vol. LVIII, no. 1, April, 1931, and *Projectile-Throwing Engines of the Ancients*, Sir Ralph Payne-Gallwey (1907).

[2] *Caesar's Commentaries on the Gallic War*, trans. T. Rice Holmes (1908), VII, 25.

[3] *Caesar's Commentaries*, trans. W. A. M'Devitte (1927), "The Gallic War", VIII, XIV (written by Aulus Hirtius).

[4] *Caesar*, "The Civil War", trans. A. G. Peskett (1914), III, 45.

sessed an artillery train of sixty *carroballistae* and ten catapults, the equivalent of sixty field guns and ten howitzers.

Hand in hand with increasing missile power went progress in fortification and siege work, and in these branches of the art of war Caesar is without a rival. In 52 B.C., at the siege of Alesia (Auxois), it has been calculated that his men shifted 2,000,000 cubic metres of earth from the trenches they dug.[1] Four years later, at the siege of Dyrrhachium, much the same must have been done, and at the siege of Massilia in 49 B.C., all manner of engines were employed.

Though the advancing technique of war may have saved lives, it led to the defensive becoming the stronger form of war and thereby cramped initiative and exorcised valour. Further, the big professional armies and the formidable development in their fighting power, as well as the big provincial appointments beyond control of the home government, endowed the generals with ever-increasing independence which, as it grew, weakened in direct proportion the authority of the Senate and the people. Also, one of the great troubles was that the new professional soldier had no assured terms of service; no assurance of discharge after a fixed number of years' service, and no assurance of a gratuity on discharge. When combined, these changes and circumstances led to civil war and the establishment of dictatorships.

With the final conquest of Gaul, the situation which faced the Roman world was one of change or dissolution; the Senate and the people were impotent, all power was in the hands of Caesar and Pompey. Both were democrats, the one believing in a *démocratie royale*, the other in a *laisser-faire* system. On the one side there was energy, on the other lethargy; neither wanted war, yet war was inevitable, for a new idea confronted an old feeling or tradition which was so lacking in vigour that it no longer possessed the power to reform itself.

In these circumstances the Senate supported Pompey, the country towns and the people generally favoured Caesar who, hoping to be elected consul in July, 49 B.C., to deprive his enemies of the opportunity to prosecute him on some trumped-up charge during the interval between giving up his command and entering upon his consulship, decided to remain in Gaul until the end of 49 and to enter Rome as consul at the beginning of 48. After this, so he expected, he would be given command of the war against

[1] *Revue des Deux Mondes*, May 1, 1858, p. 113.

the Parthians. But when, in 51 or 50, Pompey went over to the side of the Senate, the opposition to Caesar took the line that though he had been given leave by the law of the ten tribunes to stand in absence for the consulship of 48, he had not been given leave to stand while keeping his military command. As the plot thickened, and Caesar was fully aware of it, he suggested that he was willing to resign his army and provinces if Pompey would do likewise. Pompey refused; the die was cast. The country was declared by the Senate to be in danger and, on January 7, 49 B.C., all the burgesses were called to arms and the magistrates instructed to form them into legions.

Although the citizens of Rome were no longer a disciplined force, this muster placed Caesar in a precarious position; Pompey and the Senate had supreme control of the sea, eight veteran legions in Spain, two in Italy, and others in Syria, Macedonia, Africa, and Sicily; he had at immediate call but one, the 13th Legion, some 5,000 infantry and 300 cavalry at Ravenna, which by road was 240 miles distant from Rome. Opposed to it were Pompey's two legions, 7,000 strong, at Luceria (Lucera). Of Caesar's remaining forces half was on the Saône and Loire and half in the north of Gaul.

In spite of his numerical inferiority, Caesar decided to strike before Pompey and the Senate could mobilize their forces, and by January 14, 49 B.C.,[1] news reached Rome that he had crossed the Rubicon (Rugone) and had entered Ariminum (Rimini). Pompey realized that the people favoured Caesar, decided to abandon Rome and Italy, and set about concentrating his troops at Canusium (Canosa) and Brundisium (Brindisi) under cover of fourteen cohorts at Luceria. He ordered the levies of Campania, thirty cohorts in all, to Canusium, and he expected a like number to join him from Corfinium (San Farino), where L. Domitius Ahenobarbus, the new governor of Transalpine Gaul, then was. Though formally not under Pompey, on about February 6 Pompey urged him, while yet there was time, to march south with the levies, but although Ahenobarbus had heard that Caesar was advancing on Castrum Truentinum (Tronto), he decided to stand his ground.

Caesar seized the opportunity thus offered him to inflict a blow on his enemy and on February 13 he crossed the Aternus (Perscara) river and prepared to lay siege to Corfinium, which,

[1] Or according to the Julian calendar, November 26, 50 B.C.

however, surrendered to him on February 19. He did not pause a day, but marched on Brundisium, where Pompey had concentrated the whole of his available troops. The next day, the latter transported more than half of them across the Adriatic to Dyrrhachium (Durazzo).

On March 1 Caesar arrived before Brundisium, and his first step was to open negotiations with Pompey. But the latter refused to consider terms, and on the return of his transports skilfully embarked the remainder of his army and carried it over to Epirus. Then Caesar decided upon his strategy.

The situation which faced him was as follows: by abandoning Italy Pompey had split his forces into two main groups, one in Epirus and the other in Spain. Nevertheless, as he held the command of the sea, it was possible for him to crush Caesar between them. Caesar realized that time was again the crucial factor and decided with all speed to move on Spain, where Pompey's main strength lay. Meanwhile, to forestall an economic attack upon Italy, he sent one legion to Sicily and another to Sardinia to protect the corn supply. Then he ordered nine of his best legions in Gaul and 6,000 cavalry and a body of archers to assemble in the neighbourhood of Massilia.

Two days after Pompey sailed from Brundisium, Caesar set out for Rome and arrived there on March 29. At once he placed Marcus Antonius, commonly called Mark Antony, in command of the troops in Italy; seized 15,000 pounds of gold bullion, 30,000 bars of silver, and about 30,000,000 sesterces in coin;[1] passed a variety of laws, and, about April 5, set out for Massilia with a small escort. He sent on five legions and 6,000 cavalry to Spain, laid siege to Massilia, and, in June, leaving Decimus Brutus and Trebonius to push the siege, crossed the Pyrenees with 900 cavalry, rejoined his army, and advanced on Illerda (Lerida) where the Pompeian forces under Afranius lay encamped.

Afranius's strategy was to refuse battle, in order not to risk defeat during the campaigning season; Caesar's was to bring one about at the lowest possible cost to himself, and he did this in a series of astonishing manœuvres which were concluded by cutting off his enemy from his food and water and so forcing his capitulation; a victory so complete that all Further Spain fell into his hands. He treated his foe with great magnanimity, returned to Massilia about the end of September, pressed the siege, and

---

[1] The value of a sestertius was about twopence farthing.

received the surrender of the city. Again he showed the highest restraint, a tribute, as he said, to its citizens, out of regard to the renown and antiquity of their state rather than for anything they had deserved of him.[1] Leaving two legions as garrison, and hearing that he had been appointed dictator, he left for Rome, and on his arrival rectified the law between debtor and creditor, recalled various exiles, and granted full citizenship to all freeborn inhabitants of Cisalpine Gaul. After he had held office for eleven days, he resigned his dictatorship and did not wait formally to enter upon his consulship but pressed on to Brundisium where, towards the end of December, he rejoined his army. Thus ended the most astonishing politico-military campaign in Roman history.

Though in Spain Caesar had struck a deadly blow at Pompey's prestige, and by overwhelming his forces there had relieved himself of the necessity of protecting his rear, and though through his wisdom he had established a fairly stable political and social base in Italy, the position in which he found himself at Brundisium was an exceedingly anxious one.

Pompey still held the eastern half of the Empire; his fleet, over 300 sail, was supreme; he could draw vast supplies from Egypt and the Levant; his army was daily being reinforced; he had now under his command nine legions, in all about 36,000 men; and Metellus Scipio was on his way with two legions from Syria. He also had 7,000 cavalry, 3,000 archers and 1,200 slingers, and his base, Dyrrhachium, was but a day's sail from the Italian coast.

At once Caesar realized that Dyrrhachium was the key to the whole situation, and that it was of the utmost importance to occupy it; but the question was, how? Because Pompey's fleet commanded the Adriatic, the sea voyage was likely to prove exceedingly dangerous; yet Caesar decided to risk it, not only because the land journey through Illyricum would take weeks, possibly months, but also because should he get entangled in that difficult country, Pompey might invade Italy and overrun his base. Fortunately for him, it was midwinter and Pompey, never dreaming that so audacious a venture would be made, was away in Macedonia recruiting. Again, as on the Rubicon, the die was cast; Caesar decided on what appeared to be the impossible, not because the operation he had determined upon was strategically sound, but because it is the seemingly impossible which of all things surprises most.

[1] Caesar, "The Civil War", II, 22.

When he had assembled in all twelve legions at Brundisium, though there were transports for only seven, Caesar would not wait. He embarked seven legions, about 20,000 infantry and 600 cavalry, without corn, slaves or pack animals, left Mark Antony in command of the rest to await the return of the transports, and on January 4, 48 B.C., he stood out to sea. The next day he landed at Palaeste (Paliassa) on the Acroceraunian coast, one hundred miles south of Dyrrhachium, and from there immediately sent an ambassador to Pompey with proposals of peace. Next he completed the disembarkation of his troops and set out for Dyrrhachium, ordering his transports to return to Brundisium the same night. Though on the outward journey, Marcus Bibulus, the Pompeian admiral, had been caught napping, he was now awake, and while Caesar pushed on to Oricus and Apollonia, he destroyed thirty of his enemy's ships on their return journey and their crews were offered no quarter.

When he heard of Caesar's landing, Pompey, who was nearer to Dyrrhachium than Caesar realized, advanced on it by forced marches, and short-headed him; he then took up a strong position on the northern bank of the Apsus river (Semani) at Kuči, and confronted his adversary who had occupied its southern bank.

How long the armies faced each other is not known exactly; but growing more and more impatient, probably towards the end of February Caesar sent Antony a peremptory order to sail. The latter slipped off secretly one evening with four legions and 800 cavalry; his ships were carried by a south-westerly wind past the two armies on the Apsus to Nymphaeum (S. Giovanni di Medua) north of Dyrrhachium, and from there he sent back his transports to fetch the remainder of his troops. At once Pompey struck camp and marched north to waylay him; Caesar moved north-east on Tirana, and warned Antony of Pompey's approach; Antony avoided the ambush set to trap him and linked up with Caesar at Scampi (Elbasan) on the Genusus river (Skumbi). After his failure to prevent the junction of his enemy's forces, Pompey fell back on Asparagium (near Rogozina), and Caesar, now that he had been reinforced by Antony, decided to extend his area of operations. First he sent Domitius Calvinus with two legions and 500 horse to Macedonia to head off Pompey's lieutenant, Metellus Scipio, who was then advancing northward from Thessalonica (Salonica). Next, he sent one legion, five cohorts, and 200 horse to Thessaly and Aetolia to seek supplies of grain. Shortly after

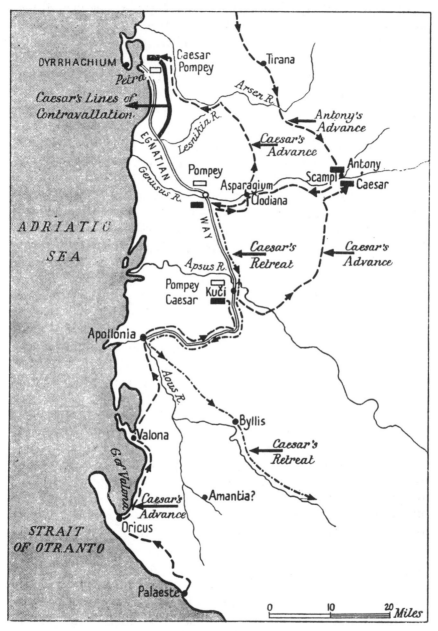

DYRRHACHIUM
Caesar
Pompey
Petra
Caesar's Lines of
Contravallation.
Tirana
Arsen R.
Antony's
Advance
Caesar's
Advance
Lesnikia R.
EGNATIAN
Pompey
Asparagium
Antony
Scampi
Caesar
Clodiana
Genusus R.
ADRIATIC
SEA
WAY
Caesar's
Retreat
Caesar's
Advance
Apsus R.
Pompey
Caesar
Kuči
Apollonia
Aous R.
Byllis
Caesar's
Retreat
Valona
G. of Valona
Amantia?
Caesar's
Advance
Oricus
STRAIT
OF OTRANTO
Palaeste
0      10      20 Miles

17.   THE DYRRHACHIUM CAMPAIGN, 48 B.C.

these detachments had moved off, news was received of a serious disaster.

Caesar had left M. Acilius in command of his sea base at Oricus, at the southern extremity of the Gulf of Valona. To block the mouth of its harbour, in which Caesar's transports lay, Acilius had sunk a merchantman and had anchored to her another which immediately rode over her and upon which a turret for artillery had been built. In spite of this defence, Pompey's elder son Gnaeus, who commanded the Egyptian squadron, determined to seize Caesar's ships. He did this, first by overpowering the floating blockship by volleys of missiles, and next, after removing the sunken vessel, he brought his galleys into the harbour and under cover of their artillery scaled the walls of Oricus and seized the galleys. Simultaneously D. Laelius, who commanded Pompey's Asiatic fleet, sailed to Antony's base at Lissus (Alessio) near Nymphaeum, and though he failed to storm its acropolis he burnt all Antony's transports. Thus Caesar's entire fleet in Greek waters was destroyed, not a single ship was left even to communicate with Italy.

Though this disaster would have paralysed a lesser man it made Caesar more determined than ever to bring his enemy to battle. Marching down the Genusus, he encamped on its southern bank immediately opposite Pompey's camp at Asparagium. There he drew out his army in battle array. But when Pompey refused the challenge, he decided to make a dash for his enemy's base at Dyrrhachium, and either to cut off Pompey from it or to blockade him there should he reach it first.

Caesar struck camp and advanced from Asparagium up the Genusus. Pompey supposed that he was in search of supplies, but when Caesar's troops reached Clodiana (Pekinj), crossed the river and moved northward, he realized that they were making for Dyrrhachium and marched at top speed up the Egnatian Way toward his base. Caesar descending into the valley of the Arzen, moved down it and encamped his army on a ridge a few miles east of Dyrrhachium, from which he could see to the south of him Pompey's advanced guard winding along the Via Egnatia. Finding himself cut off from his base by land, Pompey encamped his army on a rocky plateau, called Petra (Sasso Bianco), immediately to the south of Caesar's camp and separated from it by a torrent.

Although unable to storm Dyrrhachium, since Pompey's army was so close, Caesar had no intention of loosening his grip on his enemy; besides his own safety depended upon holding fast to him. Were he to march inland, Pompey would be free to cross to Italy or to advance against him and manœuvre him into open country where his more numerous cavalry would be at an advantage. Caesar therefore decided to invest him where he was although his own strength, since he had sent out the detachments, had fallen to 22,000 men. Further, by investing Pompey he would be able to secure his own foragers against his enemy's cavalry, and simultaneously to confine Pompey's horses to the meadows along the coast, the grass of which would speedily be exhausted. Caesar accordingly set his army to work to draw a line of contravallation right round the position Pompey was fortifying, which extended from Petra in the north to the river Lesnikia (Gešnike) in the south, and in this he was favoured by a continuous hilly ridge which encircled the greater part of it. In all, the line of contravallation was fifteen miles long; probably the most extensive field work constructed during classical times. Immediately west of it ran Pompey's defences, about eight miles long and built from one mile to a mile and a half eastward of the coast.

Though by means of his fleet Pompey could supply his men, soon his forage and next his water began to give out, for Caesar had either diverted all the rivers and streams which ran to the sea, or had dammed them up with strong works.[1] Rapidly his situation became so difficult that he had to decide whether to invade Italy or to attack Caesar. Because the former choice would entail the abandonment of Dyrrhachium, in which his supplies and siege engines were stored, he decided on the latter, and, so it would seem, in order to facilitate the attack, he arranged for news to be conveyed to Caesar that within Dyrrhachium was a party of traitors who would help him to enter the city.

Caesar presumably accepted this information without further question, and leaving Publius Sulla in command of the army, by night he led a small force to the outskirts of Dyrrhachium, fell into a trap and nearly lost his life. At the same time Pompey launched four legions against a redoubt situated on a hill in the centre of his enemy's line of contravallation; yet, although it was held by a single cohort—and although 30,000 arrows were shot into it—its garrison held it until two legions came up, when Pompey's attackers retired.

[1] Caesar, "The Civil War", III, 49. Running water had now to be obtained from the Lesnikia alone, which was five miles to the south of Pompey's camp at Petra.

Pompey next decided to attack Caesar's extreme left, and while he was engaged on the plan, two Allobrogian officers of Caesar's Gallic contingent deserted and joined him. For Pompey this was a piece of unforeseeable good luck because they were able to supply him with a detailed description of all Caesar's field works.

To complete his line of contravallation, Caesar was carrying his

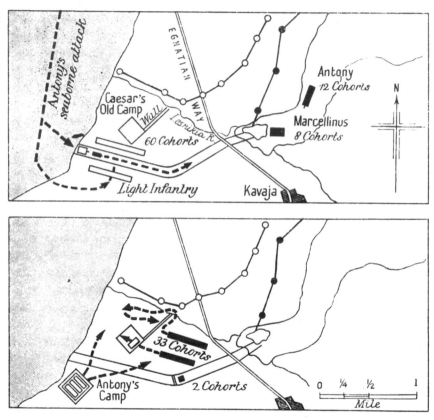

18. SIEGE OF DYRRHACHIUM, 48 B.C.

entrenchments across the plain south of the Lesnikia, and to protect his army's rear from attack he was also building a line of circumvallation. The two lines were 200 yards apart; the first consisting of a ditch fifteen feet wide, and a rampart ten feet high, and the second was of lesser proportions. These works were not finished, and ". . . the transverse rampart facing the sea and joining the two lines had not yet been completed. This fact was known to Pompey, who had been informed of it by the Allobrogian deserters.''[1] By this must be meant that no transverse rampart linked the two lines of entrenchments together at their coastal end.

To face Caesar's line of contravallation over the plain, Pompey had swung the right of his own line of entrenchments westward along the right bank of the Lesnikia, and to the south of the river he had occupied a camp which, though built by Caesar, had since been abandoned by him, and to secure its communications with the river, Pompey had an entrenchment dug back from its north-eastern corner to the Lesnikia.

When he had gathered all the information he could from the two deserters, Pompey decided to carry out a combined land and sea attack on Caesar's left. While 60 cohorts moved south of the Lesnikia – with Caesar's old camp in rear as a base of operations – to assault Caesar's wall of contravallation, a force of light infantry was to move by sea and to land in two parties: the larger south of the wall of circumvallation to assault it from the south, and the smaller on the coast between the two walls – that is, where the transverse wall had not yet been built. In short, Caesar's left was simultaneously to be attacked in front, in rear and in flank. In every way it was an admirably planned operation.

On or about July 9 the attack was launched under cover of night and the light infantry were landed a little before daybreak. The two cohorts holding Caesar's left were relieving the guard at the seaward end of the two lines at the time, and the nearest reserves, eight cohorts, under Lentulus Marcellinus, were in camp some two miles inland. Though the two cohorts at once manned the defences, the sudden landing on the coast between the two lines – the weak point indicated by the deserters – enabled the Pompeians to take the defenders of both lines in flank, and seized by panic they fled inland between the lines and hindered the advance of the reinforcements Marcellinus had sent to help them.

The Pompeians were on the point of storming Marcellinus's camp when Mark Antony arrived with twelve cohorts and drove them back. He was followed by Caesar with thirteen cohorts. Meanwhile Pompey was busily engaged in building a new camp on the coast, immediately south of his enemy's wall of circumvallation. Its object was a twofold one – to enable his ships to approach the coast in safety, and to secure the plain to the south as a grazing ground for his cavalry. Thus Pompey broke the blockade.

[1] Caesar, "The Civil War", III, 63.

To secure his left flank as best he could, Caesar drove back the Pompeians to within about a mile of the coast to regain more than half of his lines of contra- and circumvallation, and then linked them together by a transverse trench. Next, when he heard that Pompey was moving troops into the camp south of the Lesnikia (Caesar's old camp), he decided to seize it before it was fully occupied. He had thirty-five cohorts on the spot, but apparently was unaware that the camp had been linked by a rampart with the Lesnikia.

He left two cohorts to hold the transverse wall, then organized the remaining thirty-three into two columns and advanced on the camp under the cover of the woods. The left column made for its eastern face and the right for its northern. The former broke into the camp and drove its garrison towards its western gate, but the latter struck the connecting rampart, assumed it to be the wall of the camp, moved down it seeking a gate, and eventually broke through it close by the Lesnikia and entered a broad plain between the rampart, river, sea and camp.

Immediately he heard of the attack on the camp, Pompey marched to its succour, his cavalry sweeping down over the plain to the east of the camp. Then Caesar's right column, seeing its rear threatened, attempted to withdraw, but was impeded by the rampart it had so recently broken through. Seized by panic, the soldiers scrambled over it. At the same time the Pompeian garrison, who had been driven back by Caesar's left column, saw Pompey advancing and charged Caesar's left column, and its men, then descrying the right column in rout, also were swept by panic and a general émeute followed. Fortunately for Caesar, Pompey did not pursue, and when he collected his beaten men, the former found that he had lost 32 tribunes and centurions, 960 rank and file and 32 standards. We are told that most of these perished without wound, having been trodden to death in the panic and flight of their comrades.[1]

Caesar realized that with shaken troops he could no longer hold his over-long lines, and soon after sunset on the evening of the battle he withdrew his army, and by a rapid night march to avoid Pompey's cavalry, on the following morning he reached his former camp at Asparagium. At noon he set off again, shook off Pompey's horsemen and arrived at Apollonia on July 14.

While the investment of Dyrrhachium was in progress, Domitius

[1] Caesar, "The Civil War", III, 71.

had checked Scipio in Macedonia; but as his rear was now uncovered by Caesar's retreat, Caesar decided to unite with him.
His idea was, either by threatening Scipio to compel Pompey to
draw away from the sea and to be separated from his stores at
Dyrrhachium, and so be obliged to fight him on equal terms; or,
should Pompey cross to Italy, he would join Domitius and march
his united army through Illyricum to its relief.[1] Meanwhile
Pompey set aside the Italian project, for he realized that there
could be no peace until Caesar was defeated, and he decided to
join up with Scipio. Both junctions were effected, Caesar united
with Domitius at Aeginium (near Kalabaka in Thessaly) and
Pompey with Scipio at Larissa. From these two cities the opposing
armies–why it is not revealed–marched to the Pharsalian plain
below the hills of Cynoscephalae, and there at length the ghost
of the past faced the spirit of the future, as two hundred and
eighty-three years before it had done on the plains of Gaugamela.

The actual site of the battlefield of Pharsalus has been much
disputed. Appian, Plutarch, Polyaenus, and Suetonius place it
between Pharsalus (Pharsala) and the Enipeus river, but Hirtius,
Frontinus, Eutropius, and Orosius agree that it was fought near
Palaepharsalus (? Koutouri), and as the latest criticism tends to
accept the latter rather than the former,[2] it is accepted here.
According to this, Caesar marched south-eastward from Aeginium,
crossed the Enipeus near Pharsalus and encamped on its northern
bank almost immediately north of Palaepharsalus, which lay on
the southern side of the river. Soon after Pompey came up and
encamped some three miles north-west of Caesar on the slopes
of Mount Dogandzis, and, as convention dictated, Caesar formed
up his army in line of battle outside his own camp. This was
repeated daily, and each time the line was advanced nearer to
Pompey's position. But Pompey was not to be enticed to leave
the favourable ground he occupied, and when Caesar found
that his granaries in Pharsalus were becoming exhausted he
decided to withdraw from his camp and march north-east to
Scotussa, immediately south of Cynoscephalae, so that by
threatening Pompey's communications with Larissa he might
force him to abandon his position.

On the morning of August 9, when the tents had been struck

[1] Caesar, "The Civil War", III, 78.
[2] See *The Roman Republic*, T. Rice Holmes (1923), vol. III, pp. 452–467; *The Cambridge Ancient History* (1932), vol. IX, p. 664; and "The Battle-field of Pharsalos", F. L. Lucas, in *Annual of the British School at Athens*, vol. XXIV (1919–1921).

and the march was about to begin, Caesar noticed that Pompey was forming up his army, not close to his camp, as had hitherto been the case, but at a considerable distance in advance of it, turned to his soldiers, and said: "We must put off our march for the present, and think of giving battle, as we have always demanded. Let us be prepared in heart for a conflict; we shall not easily hereafter find an opportunity."[1]

Of his 80 cohorts (eight legions), in all 22,000 men, he left two cohorts to defend his camp and wheeled the remaining 78 into three lines, the left wing resting on the Enipeus river, to face Pompey's 110 cohorts (eleven legions) which, he states, were 45,000 strong. But numbers are not everything in war, and in discipline, training, and morale, Caesar's men in every respect outmatched their opponents, for as Warde Fowler says: "On one side the disunion, selfishness, and pride of the last survivors of an ancient oligarchy, speculating before the event on the wealth or office that victory was to bring them; on the other the absolute command of a single man, whose clear mental vision was entirely occupied with the facts and issues that lay before him that day."[2] As Colonel Dodge remarks: "The defect in Pompey's army was the lack of one head, one purpose to control and direct events. Caesar, on the other hand, *was* his army. The whole body was instinct with his purpose. From low to high all worked on his own method. He controlled its every mood and act. He was the mainspring and balance-wheel alike."[3]

Pompey's plan was to secure his right on the Enipeus, and with his vastly superior cavalry to outflank Caesar's right, sweep round it and attack him in rear. His order of battle was:

Six hundred cavalry from Pontus he placed on his right, and on their left drew up his infantry in three lines and in three main divisions, the right under Lentulus, the centre under Scipio, and the left under Domitius Ahenorbarbus. On the left of the line he marshalled all his cavalry, less the above 600, with his archers and slingers; the whole he placed under Labienus. Further, he detailed seven cohorts to protect his camp and interspersed some of his auxiliaries between the lines to act as light infantry.

As Pompey marshalled his line of battle, Caesar, watching it closely, grasped what his opponent's intentions were. He saw

[1] Caesar, "The Civil War", III, 85.
[2] *Julius Caesar*, W. Warde Fowler (1935), p. 299.
[3] *Caesar*, Theodore Ayrault Dodge (1892), vol. II, p. 552.

that Pompey intended to turn his right wing and brought up his
1,000 cavalry, supported by the light infantry on his right, to face
Labienus's 6,400 horsemen. The right wing he placed under the
command of Publius Sulla, the centre under Cn. Domitius
Calvinus, and the left under Mark Antony. Then, as he says,
"fearing lest his right wing should be surrounded by the multitude
of cavalry, he hastily withdrew individual cohorts from the third
line"[1] and formed them into a fourth line, obliquely to his front
and immediately in rear of his cavalry, so that it should not be
seen. He explained to these men what his object was and reminded

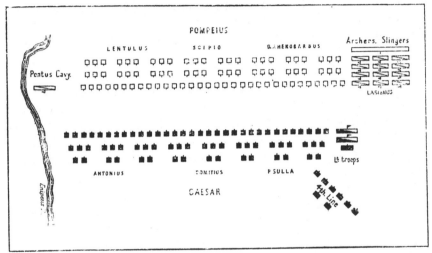

19. BATTLE OF PHARSALUS, 48 B.C.

them that the day's victory depended upon their courage. At the
same time he ordered the third line (reserve) and the whole army
not to join in battle without his orders.[2] The battle-cry was to be

---

[1] As each of the eight legions was marshalled in three lines, and according to
Appian ("The Civil War", II, 76) the number of men withdrawn was 3,000, it is
generally accepted that Caesar withdrew one cohort from the third line of each of the
eight legions.

[2] Caesar, "The Civil War," III, 89. It would appear from Book III, 84, that Caesar
had for some time trained his light troops to operate with his cavalry. He says: "But
in the case of his cavalry he retained his previous custom . . . since they were many
times inferior in number, he gave orders that lightly equipped youths from among the
first-rank men, with arms selected with a view to fleetness, should go into battle
among the cavalry. So that by daily practice they might win experience in this kind
of fighting also. The result of these measures was that one thousand horsemen even
in the more open ground, ventured, with the experience they had gained, to sustain
the attack of seven thousand Pompeian horse, and were not greatly terrified by their
multitude."

14

"*Venus Victrix*", and that of the Pompeian army was—"*Hercules Invictus*".

Though Pompey's numerical superiority was overwhelming, he none the less awaited the attack in order that his line might not become disordered and that it might meet Caesar's men when exhausted. Caesar, a far shrewder general, thought otherwise. He says: "Now this seems to us to have been an irrational act on the part of Pompeius, because there is a certain keenness of spirit and impetuosity implanted by nature in all men which is kindled by the ardour of battle. This feeling it is the duty of commanders not to repress but to foster, nor was it without good reason that the custom was instituted of old that signals should sound in every direction and the whole body of men raise a shout, by which means they thought that the enemy were terrified and their own men stimulated."[1]

Caesar launched his attack, and as Pompey did not advance to meet it, when his men had traversed about half the distance which separated the two armies (less than 200 yards), he halted them that they might regain their breath. Soon after, when he renewed his advance, Pompey launched his cavalry, archers and slingers, and when Caesar's horse was forced back, Pompey's pressed forward all the more eagerly and began to surround Caesar's exposed flank. "Caesar, observing it, gave the signal to his fourth line, which he had composed of six cohorts [? eight]. These advanced rapidly and with colours flying attacked Pompeius' horse with such fury that not one of them stood his ground, and all, wheeling round, not only quitted the position but forthwith in hurried flight made for the highest hills. When these were dislodged all the archers and slingers, left defenceless, without support were slain. With the same onslaught the cohorts surrounded the left wing, the Pompeians still fighting and continuing their resistance in their lines, and attacked in the rear."[2] Simultaneously Caesar launched his reserves and they broke through Pompey's front.

Directly his cavalry was routed, Pompey, like Darius at Gaugamela, fled the field, sought refuge in his camp and there awaited the issue of the battle; but Caesar urged his exhausted men on and stormed his enemy's camp, which was found loaded with every luxury. And, as his men broke through its ramparts, Pompey, throwing aside his general's cloak, hastily mounted and

[1] Caesar, "The Civil War", III, 92.　　　　[2] *Ibid.*, III, 93.

fled to Larissa. Yet, even now, Caesar refused to pause, and forbidding his men to plunder he pressed on into the mountains. First, he drove the remnants of Pompey's broken army from one hill, and next, at the head of four legions, surrounded them on another. He cut them off from their water and forced them to treat for surrender. They did this on the following morning, when he showed them the greatest magnanimity and at once pressed on to Larissa.

In casualties what did this memorable day, August 9, 48 B.C., cost? Caesar, according to Appian, lost 30 centurions and 200 men killed, "or, as some authorities have it, 1,200", and Pompey in killed 6,000.[1]

From Larissa Pompey fled to the coast, and from there took ship to Egypt. Caesar followed him, and, when early in October he landed at Alexandria, he learnt that Pompey had been assassinated: a most fortunate event for the dictator, for such he had been appointed for the second time

In Egypt Caesar became entangled with the last of the Ptolemies, the intriguing Cleopatra, daughter of Ptolemy Auletes, born in 69 B.C. She and a small war kept him busy until the summer of 47 B.C., when he returned through Syria and Pontus and subdued Pharnaces, son of the great Mithridates, at Zela, in his famous *"Veni, Vidi, Vici"* campaign, and thence proceeded home. Again in Rome, he tackled the financial problem and set about preparing an expedition to Africa, where Pompey's lieutenants Scipio and Labienus had fled after Pharsalus.

In the last week of December, with six legions and 2,000 cavalry, he sailed from Sicily and landed at Hadrumentum on December 28. At Ruspina, though surrounded by the forces of Labienus, he cut his way through, and, on April 6, 46 B.C., met Scipio and Juba, king of Numidia, at Thapsus (Demas) and annihilated their forces. After which Labienus fled to Spain and a dictatorship for ten years was conferred upon Caesar.

He left Utica on June 13, returned to Rome, and remained there for several months, while Labienus and others roused Spain against him. At once he decided to quell the revolt, and, early in November, he drove out of Rome and in twenty-seven days reached the Spanish front to fight his last campaign around Cordova and in the valley of the Guadalquiver. After much

---

[1] *Appian's Roman History,* "The Civil War", II, XI, 82, quoting Polli, who was one of Caesar's officers in this battle.

manœuvring, on March 17, 45 B.C., he forced Labienus to stand and fight at Munda, where Labienus was defeated decisively and killed. Thus ended the Second Civil War. In September he was back in Rome with six months of life before him, and brief though this period was, in events it is as crowded as any equal space of time in history. Most remarkable of all, Caesar was no longer a young man, for he was now in his fifty-seventh year.

Caesar contemplated Herculean reforms and projects. By his conquest of Gaul he had extended the western frontier of Rome to the Atlantic and the North Sea, but as the northern and eastern frontiers still lay open, in his last six months his one idea was to render them unattackable. First, he planned a campaign against the Getae and Dacians on the Danube, and secondly, the conquest of Parthia, which stretched from the Euphrates to Bactria and Indo-Scythia, in order to revenge the defeat of Crassus. As Plutarch tells us: He intended to march "around the Euxine by way of Hyrcania (Asterabad), the Caspian sea and the Caucasus, to invade Scythia; and after overrunning the countries bordering on Germany and Germany itself, to come back by way of Gaul to Italy, and so to complete this circuit of his empire, which would then be bounded on all sides by the ocean".[1]

Shortly before he proposed to set out on this vast adventure, and after having ruled Rome for five and a half years, during which fifty-one months were spent in seven great campaigns, he was assassinated on March 15, 44 B.C.

Suetonius tells us that he was tall, of fair complexion, with keen black eyes; that he was "highly skilled in arms and horsemanship, and of incredible powers of endurance".[2] Certainly his energy and activity were phenomenal, and in these qualities he compares with Alexander. Intellectually, he was a realist endowed with profound common-sense. A student, an artist and man of action, his practical imagination and well-balanced mind never failed to lead to lightning-like decisions. Cicero once called him "a portent of incredible speed, application and insight". His self-control was as remarkable. Sentiment and mysticism were not in him, and routine and traditions were to him but means to an end and never ends in themselves. He was generous, but his generosity was purposeful, as was his power to suborn. On the field of Pharsalus he called out to his soldiers to spare their fellow-citizens[3]

[1] Plutarch's "Caesar", LVIII.
[2] Suetonius, "Julius Caesar", XLV and LVII.        [3] *Ibid.*, LXXV.

because it suited his policy, as also did his wholesale donations of corn and of money. All means were his instruments; the rabble he won by bribery, the middle classes by debt remission, and the cultured by fostering the arts and sciences.

As a leader of men Caesar was not only the brain but the soul of his army; in this respect he equals Alexander and Hannibal. The well-being of his soldiers was his constant concern, and though, when on service, he enforced the strictest discipline, when not, he relaxed it as occasion demanded; for he knew that vice as well as virtue is a component of human contentedness. Suetonius tells us that "he valued his soldiers neither for their personal character nor their fortune, but solely for their prowess",[1] and, as Mommsen says, he treated his soldiers "as men who are entitled to demand and were able to endure the truth".[2] He so fully won their respect and fidelity that, when present among them, defeat seemed to them to be impossible.

As a commander of armies he excelled in three main respects: Firstly, with Alexander and Hannibal he possessed the skill to fashion an instrument of war which fitted his own genius. He was a marvellous organiser and his faith in his genius was unshakable. Secondly, he grasped the nature of war in his age. It was national: not merely the contending of armies, but the struggle of an entire people yearning for something new. In such wars grand strategy – the utilization of all means towards the end – predominates: men, money, trade, political reactions and propaganda must all be canalized and lead to the one goal. Lastly, his amazing boldness and seeming rashness were founded on his grasping of the secret that in war, as in peace, most difficulties are self-suggested – that, generally speaking, because opponents are equally fearful of each other, he who first brushes the terrors of the moment aside is the first to set his foot on the high road to victory. Caesar, like Alexander, possessed that spirit of audacity which raises generalship to its highest level. He divined his enemy's intentions and he set aside his own fears.

Gifts such as these could not fail to fashion him into a statesman of outstanding ability. He understood what the conditions of the Republic were and in what direction they tended. He read the inner meaning of the times as clearly as he fathomed the heart of Pompey. He saw that they demanded a monarchical democracy: freedom under discipline and not licence under greed; in short,

[1] Suetonius, LXV.    [2] *History of Rome*, vol. IV, p. 243.

what the Duke of Wellington once called a *démocratie royale*. Keeping his mind on this goal he became, as Warde Fowler has so truly said, "a great schoolmaster of mankind".[1]

Though it would be out of place here to enter into the details of his political reforms, it is relevant to mention their foundations. They may be summed up in three words–authority, order, and discipline. Firstly, he changed the character of the central government by reducing the oligarchic powers of the Senate to those of a council of state under his supreme control, making Rome the denationalized capital of the many nations. Secondly, he began to establish a new political order which would give life to Rome and the provinces, and weld them into one being. He set about limiting the Money Power which had been the ruin of the Republic; relieved the provinces of money-making governors; sent out to them no fewer than 80,000 colonists,[2] and thereby permitted democracy to expand more freely. Thirdly, he aimed at creating a new social order, which can best be explained by quoting from a speech he made at Placentia in 49 B.C. He is reported to have said to some mutinous soldiers:

"For no society of men whatever can preserve its unity and continue to exist, if the criminal element is not punished, since, if the diseased member does not receive proper treatment, it causes all the rest, even as in our own physical bodies, to share in its affliction. And least of all in armies can discipline be relaxed, because when the wrong-doers have power they become more daring, and corrupt the excellent also by causing them to grow dejected and to believe that they will obtain no benefit from right behaviour. For wherever the insolent element has the advantage, there inevitably the decent element has the worst of it; and wherever wrong-doing is unpunished, there self-restraint also goes unrewarded. . . . For it is not by any characteristic of birth that what is friendly is distinguished from what is hostile, but it is determined by men's habits and actions, which, if they are good, can make that which is alien like unto itself, but if bad can alienate everything, even that which is alien."[3]

Though in his short reign he could do no more than sow the seed of the autocratic empire, much of which was trampled into the mire by his successors, he changed Rome from a municipality

[1] *Julius Caesar*, W. Warde Fowler, p. 329.
[2] Suetonius, "The Deified Julius", XLII. For a discussion of this colonizing see *An Economic Survey of Ancient Rome*, edit. Tenny Frank (1933), vol. I, p. 316 ff.
[3] *Dio's Roman History*, trans. E. Cary (1916), XLI, 29–30.

into a world-kingdom, and extended it in idea until the hub was swallowed by the circumference. He breathed into the Republic a new life, and thereby not only gave life to the *démocratie royale* of Augustus, the first true world ruler, but blazed the trail for a still higher conception, that of unity in concord, which became the ideal of the universal Church.

# The passing of the Roman Republic

The tyrannicides' hope that Caesar's death would revivify the dying Republic was swiftly dispelled. Clamour and not rejoicing at once swept Rome, and to secure their lives from the infuriated people, Caius Cassius and Marcus Brutus, with many of the sixty-odd conspirators, sought refuge in the Capitol. At the same time Mark Antony, consul and trusted lieutenant of the dead dictator, received an assurance of support from M. Aemilius Lepidus, Master of the Horse, and so fully secured his position that Caesar's widow, Calpurnia, entrusted to him her husband's papers and his fortune, valued at 4,000 talents (nearly £1,000,000). The excitement subsided and towards the end of April, 44 B.C., Antony left Rome for Campania, where large numbers of Caesar's discharged veterans had been settled by him, to induce them to uphold the dictator's acts and to urge them to arm.

As the distribution of forces stood—a problem to which the tyrannicides do not seem to have paid much attention—it definitely favoured Antony and not the Republic. The support of Lepidus, Governor of Southern Gaul (Provence) and Near Spain was already his; Asinius Pollio, who held Further Spain, was a devoted adherent of Caesar's; from Munatius Plancus, who governed all Gaul north of Provence, there was no reason to expect hostility; only Decimus Brutus and Quintus Cornificius would definitely support the Senate, the one was Governor of Cisalpine Gaul and the other of Africa.

When Caesar's will was opened, it was found that he had named his grand-nephew, Caius Octavius, his adopted son and heir to three-quarters of his estate. He was born on September 23, 63 B.C., and when he accepted his adoption, became known as Octavianus—Octavian. At the time of Caesar's assassination he was at Apollonia, and toward the end of March he received a letter from his mother conveying to him the news. At once he crossed over to Brundisium, where he was welcomed by the troops and where he received letters from his mother and step-father, Marcius Philippus, urging him to decline the adoption and legacy. This advice he rejected, and wrote to the latter that he intended to avenge Caesar's murder and succeed to his authority. From Brundisium he went on to Rome. Antony heard of his arrival and hurried back from Campania to meet him. When they met at the end of April, Octavian reproached him for not having punished the assassins. Next, in July, under the influence of Antony, in order to be quit of them, the Senate assigned Crete to Brutus and Cyrene to Cassius; but they refused to be shelved in second-rate provinces and sailed to Macedonia and Syria.

Though the meeting between Octavian and Antony had on the whole been amicable, soon a breach between them occurred. One of the tribunes died, and Octavian presented himself as a candidate for the vacant post; but because of his youth and his patrician descent, Antony, as consul, forbade the appointment, for the Senate feared that were he to obtain the office he would forthwith prosecute the tyrannicides.

Early in October Antony left for Brundisium to meet the Macedonian legions for which he had sent in order to expel Decimus Brutus from Cisalpine Gaul, for Decimus had taken possession of that province on the strength that it had been promised to him by Caesar.

With extraordinary promptness Octavian made up his mind. He sent agents to Brundisium to distribute conciliatory leaflets among the legions arriving there and set out for Campania to win over the Caesarian colonies of veteran soldiers. By promising each man who joined him 500 drachmas (about £20) he recruited 3,000. Meanwhile Antony was badly received at Brundisium, the legionaries upbraided him for not having punished the assassins, and only after he had promised to pay each man a sum equal to Octavian's in Campania, did he succeed in persuading a Gallic legion to set out with him for Rome.

Octavian knew that he could count on the support of Decimus Brutus, whom he intended eventually to destroy, but he did not yet feel sufficiently strong to meet Antony in the field, so on November 10 he left Rome for Cisalpine Gaul. A few days later Antony entered Rome, where he learnt that two of his legions had deserted to Octavian. Nevertheless, with two legions he marched to Ariminum and ordered Decimus Brutus to evacuate Cisalpine Gaul. He refused, shut himself up in Mutina (Modena) and prepared to stand a siege.

While Antony was besieging Mutina, Octavian prepared to

relieve it. He now held the rank of propraetor, and as such supported the consuls A. Hirtius and C. Vibius Pansa, who were preparing to take the field. Hirtius joined him at Ariminum, from where, with four legions, they marched to the relief of Decimus Brutus. Antony left his brother Lucius to continue the siege of Mutina and set out to encounter them; but Octavian and Hirtius refused battle and awaited the arrival of Pansa.

On April 14, 43 B.C., Antony heard that Pansa, with four newly raised legions, was on his way to join Octavian, and set out with two veteran legions to destroy them. But, the day before, Hirtius, who was fully aware that Pansa'a recruits were no match for Antony's veterans, had sent the Martian legion and two praetorian cohorts to reinforce him. In spite of these reinforcements Pansa was defeated and mortally wounded in the battle of Forum Gallorum. But later the same day, Hirtius came up with two legions, caught the Antonians in complete disorder while they were celebrating their victory, and routed them. Again on April 21, Hirtius defeated Antony outside Mutina, but at the cost of his life; after which Antony, on May 3, crossed the Apennines and linked up with Vendidius Bassus, who was commanding three Antonian legions at Vada Sabatia, some thirty miles southwest of Genoa.

Though Decimus Brutus urged pursuit, Octavian refused because he did not want to destroy Antony while Brutus and Cassius were still alive. He had before this determined on his policy: it was first to reduce Antony's power, then to ally himself with him to destroy Brutus and Cassius, and lastly to destroy Antony, when he would be left without an enemy or rival. As a step toward an alliance, he treated Antony's prisoners with great consideration and would have nothing to do with Decimus Brutus.

In spite of this, Decimus set out after Antony; but the latter got safely into Provence, where Lepidus ruled, and though Lepidus had professed loyalty to the Senate he threw in his lot with Antony, while Plancus, Governor of Northern Gaul, retired over the Isère to await the arrival of Decimus Brutus.

When these movements were taking place, Octavian was occupied in gaining one of the consulships rendered vacant by the deaths of Hirtius and Pansa, because the time was rapidly approaching when he intended to enter into alliance with Antony, and then he would need all the prestige a consulship could give him. Early in July, he sent a party of centurions to Rome to demand the appointment, and, according to Suetonius, when the senators hesitated, one of the centurions drawing his sword called out: "This will make him consul, if ye will not!" When the centurions returned, Octavian with eight legions set out for Rome, and at once the Senate agreed that he could stand for election; but immediately afterwards it heard that the legions which had been summoned from Africa were on the point of arriving, and the senators rescinded their resolve. Octavian then occupied the suburb outside the Quirinal Hill, and the next day, when he entered Rome with a bodyguard, at once three legions deserted to him. On August 19 he and his kinsman Quintus Pedius were proclaimed consuls; the adoption of Octavian was confirmed by the assembly of the people and laws were passed providing for the prosecution of Caesar's assassins. Octavian then marched toward Cisalpine Gaul to win over Antony.

Meanwhile Asinius Pollio and Plancus had joined Antony, and Decimus Brutus, now condemned as an assassin, set out to join Marcus Brutus in Macedonia and was killed on the way by brigands.

Joined by Pollio and Plancus, Antony and Lepidus were superior in strength to Octavian, but they welcomed an alliance with him because their soldiers were devoted to the Caesarian cause. A meeting with Octavian near Bononia (Bologna) was agreed upon, and there it was arranged that a Triumvirate should be formed, each member possessing proconsular powers for a term of five years; that Octavian should be given Sicily, Sardinia, and Africa; Antony, all Gaul; and Lepidus, Spain. Also it was decided that for the time being Lepidus should hand over his province to a subordinate and assume the government of Italy while plans were made by Antony and Octavian to make war on Brutus and Cassius.

One thing was lacking, the funds necessary to defray the expenses of the war, and because it was necessary to prevent Republican leaders from fomenting opposition during the absence of Antony and Octavian, it was decided to hold a proscription and to confiscate the property of the proscribed. A list of the names of 300 senators, including Cicero's, and 2,000 Roman knights was drawn up, many of the victims being marked down because of their wealth. Among them was Sextus Pompeius, younger son of Pompey the Great. At the time of the battle of

Forum Gallorum, when in Spain, he had been appointed by the Senate to command the fleet, and when the proscription list was published and he learnt that his name was on it, he sailed with his ships to Sicily and added to their crews by recruiting pirates and proscribed fugitives. In Sicily he subdued Syracuse and other cities, and at sea he defeated Salvidienus Rufus whom Octavian sent to bring him to heel.

The proscription was carried out with brutal ruthlessness, and the estates of the victims were confiscated and sold. While the massacre was under way, on January 1, 42 B.C., the Triumvirs did honour to the memory of Caesar, vowed to maintain his acts, and the Senate and the people resolved that he should be recognized as divine. Thereafter Octavian found it politic officially to call himself "*Divi filius*" – "Son of the Deified" – a claim which gave him immense prestige among the common people and the soldiers.

# CHAPTER 7

# The Battles of Philippi, 42 B.C., and Actium, 31 B.C.

When Octavian and Antony were contending for the mastership of Italy, Brutus and Cassius were engaged in Macedonia and Syria preparing for the inevitable struggle with one or the other, and, as fate was to decide, with both. Like Octavian and Antony they were short of funds, and another initial task was to secure their rear once the campaign opened. Unable to carry out a proscription, which would at one and the same time fill their war chest and eliminate the danger of a rear attack, they resorted to its equivalent. Knowing that Ariobarzanes, king of Cappadocia, the Rhodians, and the Lycians were sympathetic to the Caesarian cause, they decided to dispose of them and to seize their wealth.

To begin with, after his fleet under L. Statius Murcus had defeated the Rhodians at sea, Cassius occupied Rhodes, seized the Rhodian fleet, confiscated all gold and silver in the treasury and the temples as well as private fortunes, amounting to 8,000 talents, and Tarsus was fined 1,500 talents. Next, on a pretext of treason, he had Ariobarzanes put to death, and then seized his treasure and military equipment. Meanwhile Brutus, who had carried his army over to Asia, received the surrender of nearly all the Lycian cities. Xanthus (near Esen), one of the most famous cities in Asia, refused to open its gates, and after a desperate resistance was stormed and sacked, all public and private treasure was seized, also the Lycian fleet, which was sent to Abydus to await the arrival of the army.

Once these acts of brigandage were at an end, Brutus and Cassius met at Sardes, where they assembled their forces, in all 19 legions, comprising 80,000 infantry, 13,000 cavalry, and 4,000 bowmen. About the middle of July the army set out from Sardes and in September reached Abydus, from where, crossing the Hellespont, it marched up the Gallipoli peninsula, skirted the Gulf of Saros and arrived at Doriscus. Fearful of its loyalty, for many of the men had served under Julius Caesar, Cassius addressed the army in one of those speeches Roman historians are so fond of attributing to the leading characters of their histories. It ended with the sole point his soldiers were interested in—namely, that each was to receive a present of "1,500 Italic drachmas, to each centurion five times that sum, and to each tribune in proportion".[1]

Meanwhile Antony and Octavian also were engaged on preparing their campaign. In all the Triumvirate had at its command forty-three legions, besides cavalry and auxiliaries, of which, after providing for the security of the provinces, twenty-eight were available for the campaign in Macedonia. Eight of these were sent ahead as an advanced guard, under Decidius Saxa and Norbanus Flaccus, and Antony took up his headquarters at Brundisium to superintend their embarkation. In transit they suffered such considerable losses from attacks made by sixty of Cassius's galleys under Murcus that Antony sent to Octavian at Rhegium for assistance. At the same time, Octavian was engaged with Sextus Pompeius in Sicilian waters, and though it was highly important to hold him there, Octavian sent his fleet to Antony. Murcus drew off and the whole of the army got safely over the Adriatic.

From Apollonia, Decidius and Norbanus marched through Macedonia and Thrace to Philippi, and then eastward through the pass of the Sapaei (east of Kavala) to that of the Corpili (near Chirka, north of Dede Agatch) who inhabited the lands of a Thracian chieftain named Rhascuporis. Their object was to hold the latter of these passes, to delay the advance of Cassius and Brutus, and so enable Antony and Octavian to get well established in Macedonia.

When they arrived at Doriscus, Cassius and Brutus learnt that the Corpili defile was held and sent their fleet with one legion and a body of archers westward along the coast toward Neapolis (Kavala) to turn the pass. Norbanus feared that the pass of the Sapaei would be occupied and his line of communications cut, so he hurried back to it, and when the Republicans arrived and found it strongly held, discontent broke out among the soldiers. The difficulty was solved by Rhascuporis, who was with Cassius at the time. He explained to the latter that by striking north over the mountains it was possible to outflank the pass. It was a hazardous journey, but by sending sappers ahead to cut a track

---

[1] *Appian's Roman History*, trans. Horace White (1912), "The Civil Wars", IV, XII, 100. An Italic drachma (a denarius) was worth eightpence; therefore 1,500 represented £50.

through the forests, after a four-day march the army debouched to the north of Philippi, and Norbanus withdrew from the Sapaei pass and retreated towards Amphipolis (near Orphani).

Cassius and Brutus descended Mount Pangaeus and entered Philippi, which had been built by Philip of Macedon on one of its southern spurs. On its southern side for several miles it was flanked by marshes, which surrounded lake Bere-Ketli, as it is now called. South of the lake a range of hills skirted the sea, and on the north-west and south-west of the city the ground was undulating; over it ran the Egnatian Way. To the north of the road and close to the mountains, Brutus built his camp, and south of it, a little to the north of the marshes, Cassius built his. Both camps were strongly fortified and on the western face of Cassius's camp the streamlet Gangites formed a moat. The Republican fleet was beached or at anchor in the harbour of Neapolis, and the main supply base was established on the island of Thasos.[1]

Meanwhile Antony and Octavian landed their combined armies at Dyrrhachium, and there Octavian, seized by one of his periodic attacks of illness, was left behind, while Antony pushed on to Amphipolis, which he intended to make his base. When he found that Norbanus had already fortified it, he left a legion and his heavy baggage there, then continued his advance and encamped in the plain north of the marsh, less than a mile from the rampart which connected the camps of Brutus and Cassius. He surrounded his camp on all sides with a ditch, wall and palisade, and built some towers. Cassius then "extended his fortifications at the only place where it was still wanting, from the camp to the marsh, a space which had been overlooked on account of its narrowness, so that there was now nothing unfortified except the cliffs on Brutus's flank and the marsh on that of Cassius and the sea lying against the marsh. In the centre everything was intercepted by ditch, palisade, wall, and gates."[2]

There were nineteen legions on both sides, but those of Antony and Octavian were up to establishments, and Brutus's and Cassius's were not. Of cavalry the latter two had 20,000 and the former two 13,000.[3]

Some cavalry skirmishes followed, and when Octavian received a false report at Dyrrhachium that Antony had been repulsed, sick though he was, he set out in his carriage and joined him, and

---

[1] *Appian's Roman History*, trans. Horace White. "The Civil Wars", IV, XIII, 106.
[2] *Ibid.*, IV, XIV, 107.          [3] *Ibid.*, IV, XIV, 108.

was carried along the ranks of his men in a litter. Both he and
Antony were eager to bring the Republicans to battle, not only
because their own men were better soldiers and more trustworthy, but because the resources of Macedonia were insufficient
to sustain the army, and the Republican command of the sea,
under Sextus Pompeius, Murcus, and Domitius Ahenobarbus,
rendered it most difficult to obtain supplies from Italy. As they
realized this, and were not sure of their men, Brutus and Cassius
were as eager to refuse battle as Antony and Octavian were to seek
it. They trusted on starvation to compel the Caesarians to retire.

Days passed and supplies dwindled. Antony–the brains of the
expedition–decided to force the Republicans to battle by operating against their communications. We read: "He formed a plan of
effecting a passage through the marsh secretly, if possible, in
order to get in the enemy's rear without their knowledge, and cut
off their avenue of supply from Thasos. So he arrayed his forces
for battle with all the standards set each day, so that it might seem
that his entire army was drawn up, while a part of his force was
really working night and day cutting a narrow passage in the
marsh, cutting down the reeds, throwing up a causeway, and
flanking it with stone so that the earth should not fall away, and
bridging the deeper parts with piles, all in the profoundest silence.
The reeds which were still growing around his passage-way
prevented the enemy from seeing his work."[1]

This went on for ten days, when the entrenchment was
occupied. Meanwhile Antony had built a line of redoubts at
right angles to his camp in the space between it and the marsh;
its purpose clearly was to protect its southern side and to link the
camp with the marsh.

When he discovered the new enemy entrenchment in the marsh
Cassius hastily set to work to extend the rampart he had built
south of his camp still farther southward and through the
marsh, in order to strike his enemy's entrenchment in its centre.
Apparently before the work could be completed, Antony wheeled
part of his army which had been facing east so that it faced north
behind the entrenchment he had built through the marsh. His
men were equipped with ladders as well as tools to break down the
palisade which had been built on Cassius's transverse work, while
the other part of his army attacked the western front of his camp.
When this attack was in full swing, Brutus's troops suddenly and

[1] Appian, IV, XIV, 109.

without being ordered to do so, charged across the plain and took Antony's left wing in flank. They rolled it up, then charged the troops belonging to Octavian, pressed them back, stormed their enemy's camp, and all but captured the sick Octavian.[1] Meanwhile Antony "continued his charge, as he had begun it, on the run and advanced under a shower of missiles, and forced his way till he struck a body of Cassius's troops, which had not moved from its assigned position and which was amazed at this unexpected audacity. He courageously broke this advance guard and dashed against the fortification that ran between the marsh and the camp, demolished the palisade, filled up the ditch, undermined the works, and killed the men at the gates, disregarding the missiles hurled from the wall, until he had forced an entrance through the gates, and others had made breaches in the fortifications, and still others had climbed up on the debris. All this was done so swiftly that those who had just now captured the fortification met Cassius's men, who had been at work in the marsh, coming to the assistance of their friends, and, with a powerful charge, put them to flight, drove them into the marsh, and then at once wheeled against the camp of Cassius itself. These were only the men who had scaled the fortification with Antony, the remainder being engaged in conflict with the enemy on the other side of the wall."[2]

Rapidly Antony broke into the camp, which because of its strength was weakly guarded, and when Cassius's soldiers outside the camp saw that it was taken, they scattered in flight.

"The victory was complete and alike on either side," writes Appian, "Brutus defeating the enemy's left wing and taking their camp, while Antony overcame Cassius and ravaged his camp with irresistible courage. There was great slaughter on both sides, but by reason of the extent of the plain, and the clouds of dust they were ignorant of each other's fate. When they learned the facts they recalled their scattered forces."[3] But before this happened, Cassius, unaware of Brutus's success on the right, in despair committed suicide, and later was buried by Brutus on the island of Thasos.

The casualties in this, the first of the two battles of Philippi, are stated by Appian to have been 8,000 on the side of Cassius, and 16,000 on that of Antony, which appears to be a wild guess.

Though the first battle of Philippi ended in a draw, the gain was Antony's; for as Cassius was dead, Brutus was left in sole

[1] Appian, IV, XIV, 110.      [2] Ibid., IV, XIV, 111.      [3] Ibid., IV, XIV, 112.

command, and he lacked the forceful personality of his colleague. As Appian informs us, whereas Brutus was "of a gentle and kindly disposition", Cassius "was austere and imperious in every way, for which reason the army obeyed his orders promptly, not interfering with his authority, not inquiring the reasons for his orders, and not criticising them when they had learned them".[1] As we shall see, it was his lack of resolution and not of strategical grasp that was Brutus's undoing, for as the battle had shown him, so long as he could check his enemy from operating against his communications with Neapolis, time, because of the Republican command of the sea, was in his favour.

The day following the battle he moved into Cassius's camp, for it commanded his strategic flank, and holding his front strongly he threw out a line of posts facing the marsh to protect his communications. That he adhered to the original plan – namely, to starve his enemy into retreat – is made clear in the address Appian records he delivered to his soldiers. He pointed out that the enemy could obtain nothing from Sicily, Sardinia, Africa, or Spain; that they had exhausted Macedonia and were now dependent on Thessaly alone for supplies. "When, therefore," he said, "you see them eager to fight, bear in mind that they are so pressed by hunger that they prefer death by battle. We will make it part of our plan that hunger shall engage them before we do, so that when it is necessary to fight we shall find them weakened and exhausted. Let no one think that my generalship has become sloth rather than action. . . ."[2] And to win their obedience, for their gallantry on the previous day he promised to pay each soldier 1,000 drachmas.

According to Appian, Antony also addressed his troops, and going one better, he promised to pay each man 5,000 drachmas compensation for losses due to the pillaging of the camp; after which on each succeeding day he offered Brutus battle, but was as often refused. While this was going on, news was received of a Republican victory in the Adriatic.[3]

On the day the first battle of Philippi was fought, Domitius Calvinus set out from Brundisium with two legions and other troops, escorted by a few triremes, to reinforce the Triumvirs, and

[1] Appian, IV, XVI, 123.    [2] Ibid., IV, XVI, 118.
[3] Ibid., IV, XV, 115–116. According to Plutarch ("Brutus", XLVII) Brutus was ignorant of this success, and only learnt of it from a Caesarian deserter the night before the second battle of Philippi, but would not credit the news. "Otherwise", Plutarch adds, "he would not have proceeded to a second battle."

was attacked by Murcus and Ahenobarbus in command of 130
warships, and all but annihilated; many transports were burnt by
fire arrows. When this news was received, as Plutarch tells us, the
autumn rain had set in and the Caesarian tents at Philippi were
filled with mud and with water which froze at once.[1] Added to the

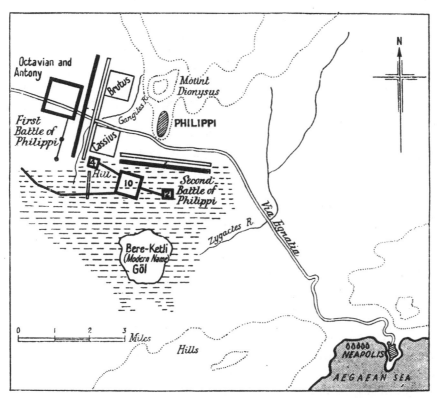

20.   FIRST AND SECOND BATTLES OF PHILIPPI, 42 B.C.

loss of sea communications and scarcity of supplies, this new
difficulty made it imperative that Brutus be brought to battle.
Antony and Octavian decided again to turn their enemy's left
and to compel him to fight for his communications.

The first step taken toward this was to occupy a small hill, so
close to the southern face of Cassius's camp that it was within
bow shot of it; unwisely, Brutus had withdrawn its garrison.
Octavian occupied it at night with four legions and his men
protected themselves with hurdles and hides against the enemy

'Plutarch's "Brutus", XLVII.

archers. Next, under the protection of the hill and the fortified camp built on it, ten legions were pushed out more than five furlongs into the marsh in a south-easterly direction, and four furlongs farther on another camp of two legions was established. Thus in all sixteen legions – that is more than three-quarters of the army – were brought into line facing Brutus's left and the Egnatian Way.

This was a most hazardous manœuvre, and only justified by the precarious position of the two Triumvirs; for with less than four legions and the cavalry to hold the main camp which protected their line of communications with Amphipolis, a wonderful opportunity was offered to Brutus to annihilate them. All he had to do was to hold back his enemy in the marsh and to storm their main camp, when the sixteen legions in the marsh would have been cut off from their supplies.

Instead, he continued to rely on the passive defensive, and built a chain of redoubts parallel to his enemy's new front in the marsh. Meanwhile Thessaly was no longer able to furnish supplies and Octavian and Antony were compelled further to deplete their dangerously extended army by sending a legion to Achaia to collect food. At the same time they ceased offering battle and resorted to a psychological attack.

Their men advanced toward their enemy's entrenchments and "challenged Brutus to fight, reviling and scoffing at him".[1] Further, they "continued to scatter leaflets in the hostile camp, promising to reward deserters",[2] and did everything in their power to belittle Brutus in the eyes of his men.

This attack was eminently successful; for though at first Brutus held to his plan – "to endure a siege, or anything else, rather than come to an engagement with men desperate for hunger" – his soldiers entertained a different opinion. "They took it hard that they should be shut up, idle and cowardly, like women, within their fortifications. Their officers, although they approved of Brutus's design, were vexed, thinking that in the present temper of the army they might overpower the enemy more quickly."[3] At length Brutus gave way and chided his men with these words: "I seem to be carrying on war like Pompey the Great, not so much commanding now as commanded"; and, according to

[1] Appian, IV, XVI, 122.
[2] *The Architect of the Roman Empire*, T. Rice Holmes, vol. II, p. 87. Presumably the leaflets were wrapped round arrows.
[3] Appian, IV, XVI, 123.

Appian, ". . . Brutus restricted himself to these words in order to conceal his greatest fear, lest those of his soldiers who had formerly served under Caesar should become disaffected and desert to the enemy. This both himself and Cassius had apprehended from the beginning, and they had been careful not to give any excuse for such disaffection towards themselves."[1]

About November 16, 42 B.C., Brutus formed his men into line of battle outside his entrenchments and ordered them not to advance far from them. "You have chosen to fight," he said to them, "you have forced me to battle when I am able to conquer otherwise."[2]

At once Antony ordered his men into line. Next, he addressed them, and to rouse their will to win he in no way minimized the danger they were in, for he said: "Let no one prefer hunger, that unmanageable and distressing evil, to the walls and bodies of the enemy, which they will yield to bravery, to the sword, to despair. Our situation at this moment is so pressing that nothing can be postponed till to-morrow, but this very day must decide for us either a complete victory or an honourable death."[3]

At the ninth hour—that is, at 3 p.m.—the battle opened: apparently Antony made the first charge. At once it developed into a hand-to-hand fight, for Appian says: "They had little need of arrows, stones, or javelins, which are customary in war, for they did not resort to the usual manœuvres and tactics of battle, but, coming to close combat with naked swords, they slew and were slain, seeking to break each other's ranks."[4] At length Antony's soldiers pushed back their enemy's front line, which at first retired step by step and then began to disintegrate. Finally it broke and carried back with it in rout the second and third ranks, until ". . . all mingled together in disorder, crowded by each other and by the enemy, who pressed upon them without ceasing until it became plainly a flight".[5] Then Antony's men seized the gates of the enemy's fortifications, and those of the enemy who could not gain entrance fled, "some to the sea, some through the river Zygactes to the mountains".

While Octavian blockaded Brutus's camp, Antony with the

---

[1] Appian, IV, XVI, 124. Commenting on this, Rice Holmes (vol. II, p. 87) writes: "A modern historian may be allowed to conjecture that he had a more cogent reason —the fear that Antony would succeed in his persistent efforts to sever the line of his supply." If this be accepted, he should have attacked Antony's line of communications, as suggested above, and not his front.      [2] *Ibid.*, IV, XVI, 125.
[3] *Ibid.*, IV, XVI, 126.      [4] *Ibid.*, IV, XVI, 128.      [5] *Ibid.*, IV, XVI, 128.

cavalry pursued the fugitives; for he feared lest Brutus should escape and collect another army. Brutus with four legions fled into the mountains "intending to return to his camp by night, or move down to the sea";[1] but, soon surrounded by enemy cavalry, he was unable to do this. On the following day he urged his officers to lead their men against the enemy and to cut their way out, and when they refused, like Cassius, he committed suicide. He was in his forty-fourth year. When he found his body, Antony had it wrapped in his best purple garment and cremated, the ashes he sent to Brutus's mother. But, according to Suetonius, Octavian sent the head of Brutus to be cast at the foot of Caesar's statue in Rome.[2]

Of the casualties suffered in this battle, all Appian records is: ". . . taking both battles into the account, the number of the slain among the victors appeared to be no fewer than among the vanquished,"[3] and that the number of prisoners taken was 14,000.

Thus, as Appian says, the day's work decided what form the Roman government was to take. It was to be autocratic and not democratic.[4] As Plutarch, in one of his moralizing moods, affirms, because Rome could no longer be a democracy, a monarchy was necessary; therefore "Heaven, wishing to remove from the scene the only man who stood in the way of him who was able to govern, cut short the life of Brutus".[5] In future the scheme of government was to take a new channel, and the sole remaining question was whether Antony or Octavian was to control its weirs, sluices, and ferries. If Antony, the future would move in one direction; if Octavian, in another.

Though ten years were to pass before this question was answered, immediately after the battle of Philippi the seed of the pretext which was to bring the rivals into final collision was sown: Octavian returned to Italy to consolidate his position in the West, and Antony went to Egypt to become the lover of Cleopatra, and the East. Thus, accidentally, the Empire moved toward a cultural division.

Immediately after the two rivals separated, relations between them again became strained. First, in 41 B.C., Lucius Antonius, youngest brother of Antony, revolted against Octavian, and was suppressed judiciously. Next, in 40 B.C., Antony entered into an

[1] Appian, IV, XVII, 130.                          [2] Suetonius, *The Deified Augustus*, XIII.
[3] Appian, IV, XVII, 137.      [4] *Ibid.*, IV, XVII, 138.      [5] Plutarch's "Brutus", XLVII.

understanding with Sextus Pompeius, whose powerful fleet, based on Sicily, was still strangling the Roman corn trade. Antony landed at Brundisium in his support and blockaded the town; Octavian marched to its relief. A realist, who always put first things first, his intention was not to fight Antony but, for the time being at least, to detach him from Sextus, for Rome was on the point of starvation. Astutely he turned circumstances at Brundisium to his advantage and patched up the quarrel on the following terms: that Antony should marry his sister Octavia, and that a new division of power should be made: Octavian ruling over Dalmatia, Italy, Sardinia, Spain and Gaul; Antony over all lands east of the Ionian Sea; and Africa was to remain under Lepidus. Further, it was agreed that Antony should carry out Julius Caesar's project of invading Parthia, and recover the standards lost by Crassus at Carrhae, and that together he and Octavian were to settle with Sextus. Regarding the last point, in 39 B.C. the rivals met again at Misenum (near Cumae) and arranged that Sextus was to withdraw the troops he had posted in Italy, refrain from further raids, and supply Rome with grain from Sicily and Sardinia, in return for which he was to be recognized ruler of those islands as well as of the Peloponnese.

Immediately these terms were agreed Octavian and Sextus restarted their quarrel and piracy was renewed, and because Antony was no longer in opposition, Octavian determined once and for all to settle with Sextus. He raised a powerful fleet and placed it under the command of Agrippa, who equipped his ships with a novel engine of war called the *harpax* or *harpago*. It consisted of "a wooden pole about seven feet long, cased with iron, to one end of it was attached an iron hook, to the other a ring, through which passed ropes, controlled by a windlass, so that when the instrument, shot by a catapult, had caught hold of a hostile ship, they could be pulled taut",[1] and the ship hauled in and boarded.

Supported by 120 ships lent by Antony, on July 1, 36 B.C., the campaign against Sextus was opened, and while Lepidus blockaded Lilybaeum, Octavian and Agrippa converged on northern Sicily. Though Octavian's squadron suffered a defeat, on September 3, off the promontory of Naulochus, close to Mylae, Agrippa decisively defeated Sextus and the *harpax* played a leading part in his victory.[2] Sextus escaped and sailed for the East, in the

---

[1] *The Architect of the Roman Empire,* T. Rice Holmes, vol. I, p. 112. See also Appian, v, XII, 118.     [2] Appian, v, XII, 119.

hope of joining Antony in a war against Octavian,[1] while Lepidus, setting out to seize all Sicily for himself, was rapidly brought to heel and expelled from the Triumvirate.

Meanwhile Antony was preparing his Parthian campaign, which he conceived in "the grandiose idea of creating, like Alexander the Great, a vast Oriental kingdom".[2] He assembled ten legions and 10,000 cavalry at Zeugma, and in the early summer of 36 B.C. he marched up the Euphrates, past Karana (Erzerum) and Mount Ararat to Tabriz, and then southward to Phraaspa (Takht-i-Sulieman). Near there he lost his siege train, and with the greatest difficulty, and thanks to his powerful corps of slingers, beat off the Parthian horse-archers. Forced to retire, he withdrew across the Araxes river and eventually got back to Syria, having lost in all 30,000 of his men.

Now that Antony had met his Moscow, Octavian no longer feared an attack from him and in 34 B.C. set out on a campaign in Illyricum, Dalmatia, and Pannonia, to safeguard the north-eastern frontier of Italy. Eminently successful in this undertaking, he added vastly to his prestige, whereas during the same year Antony in no way improved upon his by an inglorious campaign of revenge in which he indulged in Armenia.

The climax was now reached. Antony repudiated Octavia, married Cleopatra, and named her "Queen of Kings", and Caesarion, her son by Julius Caesar, born in 47 B.C., "King of Kings". He declared them joint rulers of Egypt, Coele-Syria, and Cyprus. Further, he appointed Ptolemy, Cleopatra, and Alexander, his own children by Cleopatra, sovereigns of Syria, Asia Minor, Cyrenaica, Armenia, and Parthia, when conquered. This *folie de grandeur* so exasperated the people of Italy that the fast approaching contest between the two remaining Triumvirs assumed in the popular imagination the character of a life-and-death struggle between the East and the West. Thus it came about that on the last day of 33 B.C., the joint rule the rivals had exercised since Philippi terminated.

A pretext for declaring war had now to be found which would not antagonize Antony's adherents in Italy. Opportunely, at this moment L. Munatius Plancus and M. Titius, who detested Cleopatra, came to Rome and informed Octavian that Antony had lodged his will with the Vestal Virgins. Although they

---

[1] In the following year he revolted against Antony and was put to death.
[2] *The Architect of the Roman Empire*, vol. I, p. 124.

refused to hand it over, Octavian seized it and read it first to the Senate and then to the Assembly. When they learnt from the will that Antony had again declared that the father of Caesarion was Julius Caesar, and that he himself had bequeathed "enormous presents to the children of the Egyptian Queen", and had ordered his body to be buried in Alexandria by her side, the people in their indignation were brought to believe "that if Antony should prevail, he would bestow their city upon Cleopatra and transfer the seat of power to Egypt".[1]

Then ". . . . against Cleopatra was launched one of the most terrible outbursts of hatred in history", writes M. P. Charlesworth; "no accusation was too vile to be hurled at her, and the charges then made have echoed through the world ever since, and have sometimes been naïvely taken for facts. This accursed Egyptian was a sorceress who had bewitched Antony with drugs, a wanton who had sold herself to his pleasures for power; this one and that one had been her paramours; Caesar's alleged son was the bastard of an unknown father. She was a worshipper of beast-gods, a queen of eunuchs as foul as herself, a drunkard and a harlot; later she was to be called a poisoner, a traitor and a coward."[2]

This propaganda was extremely effective. The discontent arising out of the war taxes already imposed rapidly subsided, and "in the late autumn [of 32 B.C.] the whole of Italy, town by town, joined in a solemn *coniuratio*, swearing allegiance to Octavian as its general in a crusade against the menace of the East. . . ."[3] Strengthened by public enthusiasm, the Senate deprived Antony of his triumviral power and his right of holding the consulship for 31 B.C. "They did not, to be sure, declare him an enemy in so many words, because they were afraid his adherents would also have to be regarded in the light of enemies, in case they should not abandon him; but by this action they showed their attitude more plainly than by any words. For they voted to the men arrayed on his side pardon and praise if they would abandon him, and declared war outright upon Cleopatra, put on their military cloaks as if he were close at hand, and went to the temple of Bellona, where they performed through Caesar as *fetialis*[4] all the

---

[1] *Dio's Roman History*, trans. E. Cary (1917), L, 4. Some historians consider that the will was a forgery.
[2] *The Cambridge Ancient History*, vol. x, p. 98.          [3] *Ibid.*, vol. x, p. 98.
[4] *Fetiales:* A college of twenty priests whose office was the sanctioning of treaties and declaration of war.

rites preliminary to war in the customary fashion. These proceedings were nominally directed against Cleopatra, but really against Antony . . . knowing full well that he would become an enemy in any event, since he certainly was not going to prove false to her and espouse Caesar's cause; and they wished to have this additional reproach to put upon him, that he had voluntarily taken up war on the side of the Egyptian woman against his native country, though no ill-treatment had been accorded him personally by the people at home."[1]

Meanwhile Antony and Cleopatra wintered (33–32 B.C.) at Ephesus and mobilized their army and fleet. Cleopatra provided her own squadron of warships and half the 300 transports required. Further, she agreed to pay and feed the army and fleet and paid into the war chest 20,000 talents. If Antony did not as yet realize it, she knew that the war was her war more than his, and when some of his officers, notably P. Canidius Crassus, urged him to send her back to Egypt, she resolutely refused to go. Next, in April, 32 B.C., Antony transferred his headquarters to Samos and the army was ferried to Greece. In May, he and Cleopatra crossed over to Athens, where a message was received by him from his supporters in Italy urging him to get rid of Cleopatra; but by now this was clearly impossible, for without her moral and financial support he could no longer hope to wage the war. By September the army and fleet had reached the coast of the Ionian sea, the western boundary of the territories he controlled.

The army consisted of nineteen legions, in all from 60,000 to 63,000 men, excluding the light-armed, which probably numbered 10,000 men, as well as perhaps 12,000 horse; and the fleet totalled eight squadrons, each of sixty ships, including one squadron of Cleopatra's, led by her flagship the *Antonia*. Each squadron was accompanied by a flotilla of scouts. Many of Antony's ships were larger than Octavian's, equipped with four, six, nine, or even ten banks of oars (*i.e.* number of men to the oar), some rising ten feet above the water line. On these larger ships turrets for artillery were built, and their sides were armoured against ramming by belts of squared timber bound with iron; "the crews might number some 125,000–150,000 men."[2]

The army wintered (32–31 B.C.) on the line Corcyra–Methone (Modon a little south of Navarino), the main force occupying

[1] Dio, L, 4 and 6.          [2] *The Cambridge Ancient History*, vol. x, p. 100.

Actium, which lay on the south side of the narrow entrance to the Gulf of Ambracia (Arta) and immediately opposite the modern Turkish town of Prevesa; Antony's headquarters were established at Patrae (Patras). Because Greece could not supply the army and fleet, all corn had to be brought from Egypt by way of Cape Taenarum (Matapan) and thence up the Peloponnesian coast, the route guarded by a string of fortified posts from Methone to Leucas.

If Antony's object was to challenge Octavian for the mastery of the Roman Empire, this distribution was a strange one; for though it was suitable to cover Egypt, it was unsuitable to invade Italy. To carry out the latter task, Antony should have occupied Dyrrhachium and Apollonia, with Thessalonica as his supply base and the Egnatian Way as his overland line of communications. It must never be overlooked that throughout the Classical Age and long after, the greatest danger in an oversea invasion was the weather and usually the shortest sea voyage was sought accordingly. The question then arises, did Antony at the time really intend to invade Italy? Mr. Charlesworth's answer is "no", and it would certainly seem to be the correct one. What he writes is this: "But in fact he had no choice; he could not invade Italy, not because the season was late or the ports guarded, but because he could not go either with or without Cleopatra. . . . As he could not go to Octavian, he must make Octavian come to him; hence the surrender of the Via Egnatia, while in winter he withdrew from Corcyra, leaving free the passage to Dyrrhachium."[1] It seems that Antony was completely paralysed by the situation Octavian had placed him in by his declaration of war on Cleopatra and not on himself. To invade Italy with her would raise the whole country, including his friends, against him; to invade Italy without her was impossible, for to repudiate her would have disrupted his army and fleet. All he could hope for was a miracle, so he left the decision on the lap of the gods.

Antony, through force of circumstances, was compelled to put his trust in chance, but Octavian was so placed that he could mobilize methodically his army and fleet, which he did, at Brundisium and Tarentum. The former consisted of 80,000 foot and 12,000 horse, and the latter of more than 400 ships, the larger of which, like Antony's, were armoured with belts of timber, and also mounted upon them were catapults for firing the *harpax*.

[1] *The Cambridge Ancient History*, vol. x, p. 101.

It was agreed that, while Maecenas was left in charge of Italy, Octavian should command the army and Agrippa the fleet.

Early in the year 31 B.C., and, as it would appear, earlier than Antony expected, the expedition sailed. Agrippa with half the fleet crossed the Ionian Sea, surprised Methone and there captured many enemy grain and munitions ships. While Agrippa struck at Antony's supply line, Octavian carried eight legions and five praetorian cohorts over to the Epirote coast to surprise Actium where most of the enemy's fleet lay at anchor. He disembarked his troops successively at Panormus (Palermo), Toryne (Arpitza) and Glycys (Fanari), and marched rapidly south, but as he had already been descried by Antony's scouting craft, he failed in his aim. Instead he occupied a position five miles to the north of Actium on the high ground of Mikalitzi, a little to the north of Nicopolis,[1] which commanded an extensive view northward as far as Corcyra, and southward and eastward over the bay of Ambracia. About a mile to the west of his camp lay the bay of Comarus, an open roadstead.

Though it is not known whether Antony was surprised by Octavian's appearance, it would appear that he was, for his army was still in winter quarters, and by the time he had collected his troops Octavian had not only strongly fortified his camp, but also had linked it with his sea base in Comarus Bay by two entrenchments, or long walls. Antony, unprepared, was unable to attack his enemy and pitched his camp on the south side of the strait of Prevesa, about two miles south of the promontory of Actium. He also connected his camp by two parallel earthworks with a small haven in which he stationed a squadron of his fleet.

Meanwhile Agrippa "made a sudden dash with his fleet and captured Leucas and the vessels which were there . . . took Patrae . . . and later Corinth also",[2] and thereby cut off Antony from the Peloponnese. This was a most grievous blow, for it severed his supply communications with Egypt. To remain inactive where he was, was to court surrender through starvation; so he transferred part of his army to the north side of the narrow strait and encamped it two miles south of Octavian's. His intention was to hold his enemy in front and to cut him off from his water-supply—the Luro river. Next, he shipped a body of troops, mostly cavalry, up the Ambracian Gulf, landed it at the

---

[1] Nicopolis did not then exist. It was built by Octavian after the battle and in commemoration of it.   [2] Dio, vol. L, 13.

mouth of the Luro and advanced inland; but when Octavian sent out his cavalry to attack the detachment, part of Antony's cavalry deserted, and the whole operation was ruined. He withdrew his detachment to the south side of the strait. Thus it came about that instead of Octavian being besieged, he himself was besieged, and his supply problem became so pressing that he had to arrange for food to be brought over the mountains on the backs of porters, among whom was Nicarchus, the great-grandfather of Plutarch.[1]

So many desertions now took place, including that of Domitius Ahenobarbus,[2] that Canidius suggested to Antony that the fleet should be abandoned and the army withdrawn into Macedonia, where it could fight in the open. This advice was at once rejected by Cleopatra, who held that the war should be decided by a naval battle, and though Antony by now had lost all confidence in the fleet, he agreed with her, perhaps because he realized that even were he to withdraw the army, he still could not feed it. Immediately after this resolve was made he ordered the burning of ships which could not be manned because of desertion or sickness of their crews. All this became known to Octavian through the deserter Quintus Dellius, at one time a lover of Cleopatra.

What was Antony's plan? Dio tells us: "In consequence of these portents [the usual wonders Classical historians delight in, such as 'milk and blood dripping from beeswax'] and of the resulting dejection of the army, and of the sickness prevalent among them, Cleopatra herself became alarmed and filled Antony with fears. They did not wish, however, to sail out secretly, nor yet openly, as if they were in flight, lest they should inspire their allies also with fear, but rather as if they were making preparations for a naval battle, and incidentally in order that they might force their way through in case there should be any resistance."[3] Plutarch says: "However Cleopatra prevailed with her opinion that the war should be decided by the ships, although she was already contemplating flight, and was disposing her own forces, not where they would be helpful in winning the victory, but where they could most easily get away if the cause was lost."[4]

Setting aside the prejudices of Dio and Plutarch against

[1] Plutarch's "Antony", LXVIII.
[2] Plutarch in his "Antony" (LXIII) relates that, though Antony was much annoyed by this particular desertion, he sent Domitius "all his baggage together with his friends and servants". Domitius, a sick man at the time, died immediately after.
[3] Dio, I., 15.                                        [4] Plutarch's "Antony", LXIII.

Cleopatra, Antony's plan would seem to have been a straight-forward one – to prepare for either victory or defeat. Because the odds against the first were high, very naturally he carefully pre-

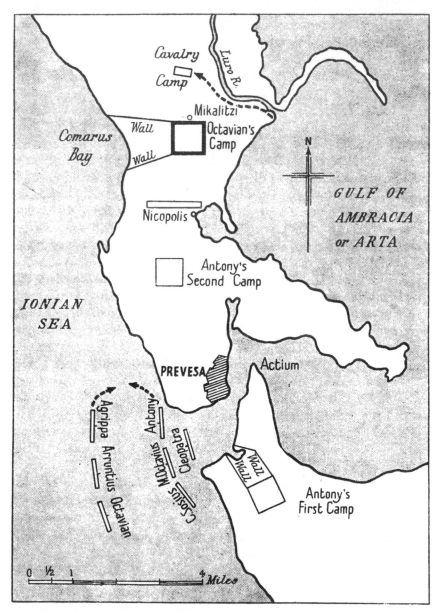

21. BATTLE OF ACTIUM, 31 B.C.

Nicopolis was built by Octavian after the battle (see footnote on p. 222).

pared for the second. Though both he and Ceopatra may have been fools to get into the position they were in, they were not cowards to plan in the way they did to get out of it. After all, they still had eleven legions in Syria, Egypt, and Cyrene. Because the chances of victory were slight, Antony adopted the unusual course of keeping his sails on board his ships, also he shipped the war chests in one of Cleopatra's transports.

Of the two contingencies which faced him, Dr. Tarn writes: "On that coast in summer the wind in the morning normally comes in from the sea, but about mid-day shifts to the north-west and blows with some force. Antony knew that when he came out he would find Octavian's fleet to seaward of him, and he meant to use the wind when it shifted to turn their left and drive them southward (down wind) away from their camp; were they broken or dispersed, he could starve the camp out. . . . But in case the battle miscarried he had a second plan, probably known only to Cleopatra and Canidius (certainly Octavian knew nothing of it): they would break through to Egypt with what ships they could, and Canidius would bring the rest of the army back overland."[1]

Unless this is accepted, the battle of Actium becomes an absurdity. Further, as we shall shortly see, the conduct of Antony during the battle and immediately after his defeat corroborates it.

After deserters informed him that Antony and Cleopatra were preparing to break out, Octavian suggested that they should be encouraged to do so and then attacked in rear ". . . for he hoped that by swift sailing he should speedily capture Antony and Cleopatra", and so "win over the rest without fighting".[2] But Agrippa, an incomparably abler general, disagreed with this suggestion and prepared for battle and not for pursuit, which he saw would be unsuccessful because the enemy "were going to use sails".[3] He drew up the fleet in line of battle facing the strait of Prevesa and "waited for the enemy to sail out".[4]

According to Tarn, Antony shipped some 35,000–40,000 legionaries, and Octavian about the same number. Both sides had over 400 ships.[5]

---

[1] *The Cambridge Ancient History*, vol. x, p. 104.                     [2] Dio, L, 31.
[3] Knowing this, one would have thought that he would have at least ordered some of his ships to carry sails.                                    [4] Dio, L, 31.
[5] According to Plutarch ("Antony", LXIV) Antony shipped 20,000 heavy-armed soldiers and 2,000 bowmen; but Tarn points out that "the 20,000 of tradition, like the 170 ships, refers to the right wing, his own command" (*The Cambridge Ancient History*, vol. x, p. 104). T. Rice Holmes (*The Architect of the Roman Empire*, vol. II, p. 152) gives Antony's fleet at 230 ships – that is, his own 170 plus Cleopatra's

Following Tarn's account:[1] "After stormy weather it fell calm on September 2nd, and Antony's fleet came out and lay on its oars, waiting for the wind to veer. . . ." He had six squadrons in line, divided into right wing, centre, and left wing. The first consisted of 170 ships under his personal command; the second of one squadron under Marcus Octavius; and the third of two squadrons under C. Sosius. In rear of the right and centre Cleopatra drew up her squadron of 60 ships, manned by her own trustworthy mercenaries "to stop any preliminary attempt at desertion". Antony's aim was to turn his enemy's left, and because this manœuvre would cause a gap in the line of battle, his idea would seem to have been that, when he moved outwards, Cleopatra's squadron was to come in on his left to fill the space between his left and the central squadron. Agrippa's fleet was also deployed in three formations; the left wing under his personal command, the centre under Arruntius, and the right wing under Octavian. Like Antony he waited for the wind, and his intention was to turn his enemy's right.

When about noon the wind shifted, both Antony and Agrippa raced to turn each other's outer, or strategic flank. This movement drew both their squadrons away from the centre squadron of the two lines of ships. A fight followed in which Antony lost some ten to fifteen ships and his own flagship was grappled, probably by a *harpax*. The fighting which took place was so stubborn that it does not suggest that Antony was solely concerned to cut his way out, but rather that he was fighting to win. Because Agrippa's ships were on the whole lighter and more mobile than Antony's, it would appear that he resorted to a type of Scythian tactics. According to Dio, if his ships sank an enemy's, well and good, "if not they would backwater before coming to grips, and would either ram the same vessels suddenly again, or would let those go and turn their attention to others". What they dreaded most was "the long range missiles of their enemy no less than the fighting at close quarters. . . . The enemy, on the other hand, tried to hit the approaching ships with dense showers of stones and arrows, and to cast iron grapnels upon their assailants."[2] Further he writes:

---

60. But as Plutarch ("Antony", LXVIII) states that, after the battle, Octavian captured 300 ships, and also well over 100 are reported to have escaped, and 10 to 15 sunk, Antony must have had over 400 ships. According to Florus (II, 21) Octavian had more than 400 ships.

[1] *The Cambridge Ancient History*, vol. X, pp. 104-105.     [2] Dio, L, 32.

"On the one side the pilots and the rowers endured the most hardship and fatigue, and on the other side the marines; and the one side resembled cavalry, now making a charge and now retreating, since it was in their power to attack and back off at will, and the others were like heavy armed troops guarding against the approach of foes and trying their best to hold them. Consequently each gained advantages over the other; the one party would run in upon the lines of oars projecting from the ships and shatter the blades, and the other party, fighting from the higher level, would sink them with stones and engines."[1]

When Antony was thus engaged, the three squadrons of his centre and left suddenly backwatered and returned to harbour, and the two left squadrons of his own wing, which were not able to do likewise because Cleopatra's squadron blocked their retreat, raised their oars in token of surrender. This defection, which all along Antony had dreaded, left him with no alternative but flight. He realized that the battle was irretrievably lost and signalled to Cleopatra to carry out the second plan. She ordered the purple sails of the *Antonia* to be hoisted, and, accompanied by her whole squadron, ran for the open sea between the two still contending wings and their central squadrons, the one now retiring and the other advancing.

This led to a general attempt at flight by such of Antony's ships which as yet had not deserted him. At once the crews began to raise their sails and to jettison their artillery turrets. "While they were occupied in this way their adversaries fell upon them; they had not pursued the fugitives, because they themselves were without sails and were prepared only for a naval battle, and there were many to fight against each ship, both from afar and alongside. Therefore on both sides alike the conflict took on the greatest variety and was waged with the utmost bitterness. For Caesar's men damaged the lower parts of the ships all around, crushed the oars, snapped off the rudders, and climbed on the decks, seized hold of some of the foe and pulled them down, pushed off others, fought with yet others, since they were not equal to them in numbers; and Antony's men pushed their assailants back with boathooks, cut them down with axes, hurled down upon them stones and heavy missiles made ready for just this purpose, drove back those who tried to climb up, and fought with those who came

---

[1] *Dio*, L, 32. Plutarch ("Antony", LXVI) says: "The struggle was therefore like a land battle; or, to speak more truly, like storming of a walled town."

within reach. An eye-witness of what took place might have compared it, likening small things to great, to walled towns or else islands, many in number and close together, being besieged from the sea."[1]

If Dio is to be relied upon, even at this chaotic stage of the battle the resistance was so stubborn that the Caesarians attempted to overcome it by setting fire to their enemy's ships. We read: "And now another kind of battle was entered upon. The assailants would approach their victims from many directions at once, shoot blazing missiles at them, hurl with their hands torches fastened to javelins, and with the aid of engines would throw from a distance pots full of charcoal and pitch."[2]

Though, perhaps, much of this decriptive writing may be discounted as journalism, it tends to show that the battle of Actium was a battle in the accepted meaning of the word and not merely a flight, with Cleopatra, who certainly was no coward, as the villain in the plot.

Meanwhile Antony, who could not extricate his flagship from the grapnels which held her fast, boarded another vessel and with what remained of his squadron, 40 ships in all, he set out after Cleopatra. When he caught up with the *Antonia*, he boarded her and sat down in despair in her prow "by himself in silence, holding his head in both hands".[3] If one accepts this as true, it proves beyond doubt that in spite of the odds against him he, at least, had hoped for victory. Had he from the first planned flight only, and according to Dio and Plutarch, in order to meet the wishes of Cleopatra, surely he would have been overjoyed when he caught up with the *Antonia*? For three days he refused to see Cleopatra, and only when the ship put in at Taenarus, on Cape Matapan, were the Queen's attendants able to persuade him to speak and sup with her. At Taenarus "not a few of the transport ships and some of their friends began to gather about them",[4] and when he learnt from them that, so far as they knew, the army had not yet surrendered, Antony sent messengers to Canidius with orders for him to withdraw his army as quickly as possible through Macedonia into Asia.

When Cleopatra escaped, the confusion would seem to have been so complete that both Octavian and Agrippa failed to realize the fullness of their victory. Instead of pursuing, though this was

[1] Dio, L, 33.
[3] Plutarch's "Antony", LXVII.
[2] *Ibid.*, L, 34.
[4] *Ibid.*, LXVIII.

difficult without sails, they remained at sea all night, and only on the following morning took over the surrender of the squadrons which had deserted – 300 ships in all. Most of these Octavian burnt, but he sent some of their bronze beaks to Rome to adorn the temple of Divus Julius. Meanwhile Canidius attempted to withdraw the army, but his men refused to march and he fled to Egypt. After its surrender the army was incorporated with Octavian's.

Though the catastrophe of Actium broke Antony, Cleopatra sailed into the harbour of Alexandria with her ships "garlanded for victory". As soon as she landed she ordered the execution of all those who might oppose her, and next planned to sail to Spain to seize the silver mines, or to found a new realm in the Indian Seas. But without Antony's cooperation she could do nothing, and he was now so morally crushed that he did not even attempt to collect his eleven legions and to hold the immensely strong line of the Nile.

In the summer of 30 B.C., Octavian landed in Egypt, and on July 31 reached the suburb of Alexandria. Antony, for a moment himself again, fell upon his advanced guard and scattered it; but on the following day his troops and ships deserted to the enemy. He returned to the city where, hearing a rumour that Cleopatra was dead, he stabbed himself, and was carried into the mausoleum in which she had shut herself up. There he died in her arms. Soon after, when she heard that Octavian had decided to take her to Rome, rather than adorn his triumph, Cleopatra had a basket of figs, in which were concealed some asps, smuggled into her, and with her two maids, Iras and Charmion, died from their bites. She was thirty-nine years old and had reigned twenty-two years.

Of her Dr. Tarn writes:

"The ancient world had little pity for the fallen; and it had little for Cleopatra. The hatred which Romans felt for her can be read at large in their literature; but through that literature runs too another feeling, publicly recorded in the Fasti, and if Octavian's propaganda directed the hate, it did not create the fear. Grant all her crimes and her faults; grant that she sometimes fought her warfare with weapons other than those used by men; nevertheless it was the victors themselves who, against their will, raised the monument which still witnesses to the greatness in her. For Rome, who had never condescended to fear any nation or people, did in her time fear two human beings; one was Hannibal, and the other was a woman."[1]

Though Philippi–ironically won for him by Antony–was the copestone of Octavian's power, his defeat of Antony at Actium was the cornerstone of the world empire which had been struggling to come into being since the days of the Diadochi. The one was the climax of a political struggle within a democracy to decide whether autocracy or democracy was to prevail. The other was the climax reached between the contending halves of a divided autocracy to decide whether the split was to be permanent or which half was to dominate the whole. Had Brutus and Cassius won at Philippi, the fruits of their victory could never have matured, because the political roots of the Roman Republic were withering away. Even had Antony and Cleopatra successfully defended Egypt, by preventing Octavian acquiring the treasure of the Ptolemies, without which he could not have paid the rewards he had promised his supporters and soldiers, the division between the East and the West of the Empire might have become permanent, as in a later age it did. But had Antony and Cleopatra won at Actium, there can be little doubt that they would have transferred the capital of the Empire from Rome to Alexandria, which both strategically and commercially was a better site, and that in the stead of the national Roman *Imperium*, established by their conqueror, there would have arisen a cosmopolitan world empire as dreamt of by Alexander. It is because of this probability that Actium was one of the most decisive battles ever fought: it prevented Europe changing its cultural axis.

Its first fruits were plucked immediately. When Octavian had fulfilled Cleopatra's last wish, to be buried beside Antony, he annexed Egypt in the name of the Roman people. He realized the importance of its corn as an instrument of government and took special precautions to bring the country under his personal control; to establish his prestige in the East he assumed the divine honours and titles of its Ptolemaic kings. A little over three years later, on January 17, 27 B.C., outwardly he restored the Republic and was given by the Senate the semi-divine name of Augustus–the Consecrated.

But he never forgot that his adoptive father had perished by,

[1] *The Cambridge Ancient History*, vol. x, p. 111. "Of the manner of her death no doubt should now exist, for it is known why she used an asp; the creature deified whom it struck, for it was the divine minister of the Sun-god, which raised its head on the crown of Egypt to guard the line of Re from harm."

as well as conquered by, the sword, and throughout his reign he sought to disguise the power the sword had won him by introducing new forms under old titles. He grasped at real power and surrendered to the Senate and the people the outward show in which that power was wrapped. According to the letter of his theory of government, sovereignty was vested in the Senate and people; in fact authority over both was vested in himself. Because continuous tenure of the consulship would have been too open a break with tradition, after 23 B.C. he ceased to hold this magistracy, and directly from Rome, through *legati* appointed by himself, governed the provinces where legions were stationed. Elsewhere in the empire, when necessity arose, he could enjoy an authority superior to that of all provincial governors through the *maius imperium* which he was granted. At home he relied on tribunician power, already granted to him for life, and in 23 B.C. strengthened to make good what he had lost when he gave up the consulship. Though he assumed *Imperator* as a first name, *Princeps*–First Citizen–was the title by which, at his wish, men spoke of him. For it was by *auctoritas*–personal prestige–that he governed, as well as in virtue of his cleverly devised constitutional powers.[1]

Augustus realized, as did Thomas Hobbes centuries later, that "Covenants, without the Sword, are but Words, and of no strength to secure a man at all",[2] and he based his rule on military power. Because, in normal times, the legions were quartered in the provinces and not in Italy, when, in 27 B.C., he nominally restored the Senate, he kept all frontier provinces, except that of Africa, under his personal charge; hence all the legions, except one, were under his command.

Under the Republic, in theory at least, the armies had been enrolled for each campaign and disbanded on its conclusion. But during the Civil War this system of raising emergency forces largely had given way to the establishment of professional armies, the main allegiance of which was to their paymasters. One of his first reforms was to abolish this system and to create a standing army on an imperial footing; its men swore fealty to himself alone. He reduced the legions to twenty-eight, and divided the army into two grand divisions–legions and *auxilia*. The former were recruited from Roman citizens; the latter from Roman non-citizen

---

[1] For this complicated constitutional settlement see *The Cambridge Ancient History*, vol. x, chap. v.                    [2] *Leviathan*, pt. II, chap. XVII.

subjects. Service in the legions was for twenty years, recruiting was voluntary, and on discharge each legionary received a bounty or an award of land. In the *auxilia*, service was also voluntary though frequently longer, and on discharge a bounty was paid to the soldier and the Roman franchise granted to him, his wife, and his children. Besides providing many cohorts of foot, the *auxilia* supplied all the archers and nearly all of the cavalry.

Because Augustus's policy was based on security and not on conquest, the legions and the *auxilia* were distributed in groups to hold the frontiers, each groupd based on a defended military centre called a *castellum*, which was linked to the frontier posts by road. This policy of containment, in contradistinction to expansion, had a profound, moral effect on the legions. As their purpose was now to maintain peace and not to make war, their valour, which formerly had been stimulated by patriotism or plunder, gradually deteriorated. First, the growth of pacifism, through loss of fear, led to the recruitment of fewer and fewer citizens and of more and more barbarians in order to keep the legions up to establishment. Secondly, a most pernicious form of militarism crept in–the dependence of the Emperor's political status on the will of the army.

This latter defect was stimulated by yet another reform. Besides the above two bodies of troops, Augustus organized what to-day would be called a "private army" of his own–the Praetorian Guards. During the last year of the Republic many commanders had raised for their personal protection special bodyguards, *cohortes praetoriae*, so named because the general's camp head-quarters was called the *praetorium*. When Augustus restored the Republic, he kept these guards in Italy, organized them into nine cohorts, each of 1,000 men, and placed them under two *praefecti* who commanded them in his name. They were an ever-present sanction of his authority and the symbol of what his government really was, a judiciously organized military tyranny. As we shall see, the danger inherent in this reform was that, because the Praetorians were the instrument of the Imperial authority, in the final issue its existence depended upon their loyalty.

This government, so profoundly undemocratic in practice, was accepted by all Roman citizens and subject peoples because, after a hundred years of civil turmoil and strife, the army of Augustus re-established order and maintained the public peace. For two centuries it secured the Empire against invasion, and for two centuries more it held its own against the Teutonic barbarians in spite of occasional defeat. It was the army which maintained the *Pax Romana*, during which western Europe was latinized and the Christian religion struck root. And it was the battles of Philippi and Actium which enabled Augustus to create it.

# The establishment of the Imperial frontiers

The empire which Octavian won at Actium stretched from the Atlantic to the Euphrates and from the North Sea to the Sahara Desert, including within it all the states which fringed the Mediterranean, now a Roman lake. It had grown by chance and not by design, and to consolidate it and transform its diverse peoples into a single Roman nation demanded two things: first, internal pacification, and secondly, the establishment of secure frontiers. These were the major problems which occupied Augustus during his long reign of forty-one years, and though Suetonius tells us that "the temple of Janus Quirinus, which had been shut twice only, from the era of the building of the city to his own time", Augustus "closed thrice in a much shorter period, having established universal peace both by sea and land", his entire Principate was, nevertheless, one long record of military operations, for the most part conducted by others than himself. These, by the date of his death, had added to the Empire an area even greater than that conquered by his adoptive father, Julius Caesar.

Of the two major problems, the more pressing was the first, which included the pacification of Spain and Africa as well as the reorganization of the provinces generally. Augustus began with the West, set out for Spain in the summer of 27 B.C., and after a series of successful campaigns returned to Rome in 24 B.C. War immediately broke out again, and it was not until 19 B.C. that Agrippa finally broke the spirit of the Cantabrians by a wholesale massacre. This same year witnessed the final subjection of the province of Africa, by Cornelius Balbus.

On his return from Spain, Augustus set out to tackle the problem of the eastern frontier. Six years before, after his occupation of Alexandria and when the whole Orient lay at his feet, popular opinion in Rome had urged the subjection of the East as far as India, and had he been Caesar, undoubtedly he would have set out to conquer Parthia. But he was a diplomatist and not a soldier, and though, in order to restore the prestige of Rome lost by Crassus and Antony in their Parthian campaigns, he understood that action of a kind was necessary, he also realized that, because the Empire was based on the Mediterranean, its proper limits were the Mediterranean lands, and that any considerable extension eastward would result in weakness, not in increased strength. He had made Syria the pivot of the eastern defences and had returned to Rome firmly resolved that Roman interests could better be secured by diplomacy than by war. Now he returned to the problem with this idea in mind. It was a threefold one, for it included the frontiers of Egypt in the south, Syria in the centre, and Asia Minor in the north.

In Egypt he established a line of fortified posts across Upper Egypt, and probably one on the Egyptian north-western frontier, toward Cyrene, though this is not known definitely. These defences proved so successful that no violation of the Egyptian frontiers occurred until the middle of the third century A.D. At the same time he sent an exploratory expedition under Aelius Gallus down the eastern coast of Arabia Felix to Mariaba (Marib), the capital city of the Sabaeans in Yemen (Land of Sheba), to gain control of the Indian trade; but it accomplished nothing.

While Egypt was being secured, he annexed Galatia and extended Roman control over Pontus and Cappadocia, and in 19 B.C. he sent Agrippa to the East to superintend the government of the provinces. Among his tasks was the regulation of affairs in the Bosporan Kingdom, a state north of the Black Sea between the rivers Dniester and Dnieper, inhabited by a Graeco-Iranian people. Its importance was considerable, because it was the main source of wheat for the cities of Asia Minor and the Aegean, and when Roman troops were operat'ng in the northern section of the eastern front their provisioning depended chiefly on south Russia. Later, this kingdom was brought under Roman vassalage.

As he decided on the upper Euphrates and the Syrian desert to the south of it as the natural defensive line to cover the central Mediterranean sector, it would have been as well had Augustus abandoned all claims to Armenia. Not only would its retention establish a salient both difficult to hold and reinforce, but it would create a perpetual source of quarrel with Parthia, which, if left alone, was no great menace; as a feudal country it possessed no standing army, and though its levies of horse archers could win battles, they were so badly supplied that they could not for long be kept together in the field. But prestige was at stake, and, in consequence, Augustus fell back on the old Roman half-measure; instead of annexing Armenia or abandoning it, he decided to convert it into a client state. As this solution annoyed Phraates, king of Parthia, in 23 B.C. he refused to comply with a request to return the Carrhae standards, and in the following year Augustus went to Syria and at the same time instructed his stepson Tiberius to bring a large legionary force out to Armenia. It had the desired effect; on May 12, 20 B.C., Phraates restored the standards lost by Crassus and Antony as well as all surviving prisoners. It was a notable diplomatic success, which Augustus ranked higher than a victory in the field, and Tiberius entered Armenia and placed Tigranes, the Roman monarchial candidate, on the throne. But the settlement was far from a satisfactory one, and toward the end of Augustus's reign Armenia passed out of Roman control.

The northern frontier, as Augustus found it, ran from the mouth of the Rhine and along that river to Bâle, thence over the western slopes of the Jura mountains southward between the Rhône and the Maritime Alps, where it formed a narrow appendix of land west of Cisalpine Gaul with its southern extremity all but touching the Mediterranean. From there it swung northward along the Maritime Alps and thence eastward over the southern slopes of the Alps to north of Aquileia (Aquilega), from where it ran south-eastward to end on the Hellespont.

From a defensive point of view, it was a thoroughly defective frontier, because it did not prevent northern Italy and Macedonia from being raided by the wild tribesmen of the Alps and Danube basin, nor did it allow adequate communications to be established between Italy and Gaul and between Italy and Macedonia. The sole road linking Italy to the former ran along the Mediterranean coast, because the passes of the Little and Great St. Bernard had not yet been secured; and between Italy and Macedonia there was no road at all, all communications with the eastern half of the Empire being by way of the Adriatic and *Via Egnatia*. This, as Augustus had learnt during the Civil War, was a fundamental weakness, because in the age under review storms at sea were incomparably more fatal to the transport of troops and their supply and maintenance in the field than they are to-day. The lack of a road linking Italy with Macedonia had, as we have seen, been the main difficulty Caesar had had to overcome in his 48 B.C. campaign against Pompey. Even in his own Actium campaign, when the command of the sea was his, a sudden storm might have wrecked it at the start.

In 25 B.C. Augustus set out to rectify these strategic defects. He started in Gaul and instructed Terentius Varro and Marcus Vinicius to secure the passes of the Little and Great St. Bernard by reducing the appendix of still unconquered land. This was done successfully by establishing two new lines of approach, one leading by the Little St. Bernard into central Gaul, and the other by the Great St. Bernard toward the upper Rhine. Next, in 17 or 16 B.C., P. Silius Nerva reduced the tribes east of Lake Garda and probably also those in the upper Adige (Val Venosta). Because this advance opened up a road towards the valley of the Inn, in 15 B.C. Augustus decided on a more far-reaching campaign, the aim of which was to bring under Roman subjection the great block of mountainous country which now includes Tirol, eastern Switzerland, western Austria, and southern Bavaria, and to carry the central section of the northern frontier northward to the upper Danube.

This important campaign Augustus entrusted to his two step-sons, Tiberius and Drusus, sons of Tiberius Claudius Nero and Livia, Augustus's second wife. Tiberius was to march eastward from Gaul toward Lake Constance, and Drusus northward from Italy by way of the Val Venosta and over the pass of Resia (the Reschen-scheideck) to the valley of the Inn, and thence into Bavaria where he was to meet his brother. The campaign was a signal triumph, Noricum (Styria, Carinthia and southern Bavaria) was annexed, and Roman control extended down the Danube as far as Vienna. The strategical gain was enormous. Italy no longer required the protection of the army in Illyricum, which could now be set free to win a land route to Macedonia.

Except for the valley of the Save there is no route; therefore Augustus decided to advance from Aquileia to Emona (Ljubljana) and thence down the valley of the Save to Siscia (Sisak), Sirmium (Mitrovitz) and Singidunum (Belgrade), whence the road could be continued eastward by way of Naissus (Nish) and Serdice (near Sophia) to Byzantium. Even to-day this is the only road by which, with some measure of rapidity and comfort, Yugoslavia can be traversed from end to end. Besides this road there was another route down the valley of the Drave to Sirmium by way of Mursa (Osijek). To win these two roads meant carrying the northern frontier of Illyricum to the Danube from Vienna to Belgrade. And when this was done, because of the occupation of Noricum by Tiberius and Drusus, a continuous route could be established from Bâle to Byzantium, which would enable troops to be moved rapidly east and west of the Empire independently of the sea.

In 13 B.C., what the Romans called the *Bellum Pannonicum* was launched by Agrippa and Vinicius against the Pannonian tribes on the Save and Drave. When Agrippa died in the following year, Tiberius took his place, and by 9 B.C., when he had occupied Siscia and Sirmium, he advanced to the Danube, and the extensive area conquered was incorporated into the province of Illyricum. Meanwhile his brother Drusus was warring successfully in Germany.

# CHAPTER 8

# The Battle of the Teutoburger Wald, A.D. 9

The Germans, an Indo-European people, first appear in Roman history towards the close of the second century B.C., and, after they had thrown Rome into a panic as great as previously had the Gauls, were, as we have seen, finally defeated by Marius and Catulus in the great battle of Vercellae in 101 B.C. Some thirty years later the Sequani, a Gaulish tribe inhabiting the country between the Jura and the Vosges, appealed to Ariovistus, the leader of a German host beyond the Rhine, to help them against a neighbouring tribe, the Aedui, west of the river Saône. Ariovistus accepted the invitation, defeated the Aedui, in the battle of Magetobriga and, as a reward, he and his people were allowed to occupy upper Alsace. This battle, writes Mr. C. Hignett, was probably ". . . the decisive factor which produced a chain of consequences leading ultimately to Caesar's intervention in Central Gaul".[1]

Some ten years later, in 59 B.C., two events occurred which brought the north-eastern frontier problem of Gaul into prominence. The first was that Ariovistus formally was recognized by the Senate as "king" and "friend of the Roman people". Friendship was short-lived, for no sooner was he recognized as king than he set out to persuade fresh bands of Germans to cross the Rhine, who, in their turn, demanded fresh grants of land. The second event was that the province of Transalpine Gaul was conferred upon Caesar, and once he had settled with the Helvetii, then moving westward into Gaul to escape hordes of Germans which had entered their country (roughly co-extensive with modern Switzerland), he turned his attention to Ariovistus. In his Commentaries on the Gallic War he writes:

"Next he could see that the Germans were becoming gradually accustomed to cross over the Rhine, and that the arrival of a great host of them in Gaul was dangerous for the Roman people. Nor did he suppose that barbarians so fierce would stop short after seizing the whole of Gaul; but rather, like the Cimbri and Teutoni before them, they would break forth into the Province,

[1] *The Cambridge Ancient History*, vol. IX, p. 546.

and push on thence into Italy. . . . All this, he felt, must be faced without a moment's delay."[1]

In 58 B.C., Caesar ordered Ariovistus to put a stop to further immigration of Germans, and when the order was ignored, he set out by forced marches to Vesontio (Besançon) to enforce it. From there he advanced on the Belfort Gap, where Ariovistus and his army lay encamped awaiting a Swabian horde which was then gathering on the eastern bank of the Rhine, preliminary to crossing. In the middle of September he brought Ariovistus to battle, and after a critical fight routed him. Though Ariovistus himself escaped the slaughter, soon after his crushing defeat he died.

As he realized that, were he now to withdraw, the German migrations would inevitably begin again, Caesar decided to make the Rhine the eastern frontier of central and northern Gaul, and, to establish it as an effective barrier, he next set out to conquer the Belgic tribes, most of which were of German origin.[2] They inhabited the region which is approximately that of present-day Belgium. In 57 B.C. he led eight legions northward from Vesontio and by defeating the Nervii he gained effective control over the left bank of the Rhine below Cologne. Two years later he advanced toward Xanten, and by means of a discreditable trick he inveigled the Germanic chieftains into his power, then he fell upon their leaderless followers and butchered them.[3] When he had thus secured the whole length of the Rhine from Xanten to Belfort, he decided to cross the river, for he writes: ". . . as he saw the Germans so easily induced to enter Gaul, he wished to make them fearful in turn for their own fortunes, by showing them that a Roman army could and durst cross the Rhine," which he now established as the final "limit of the Roman empire".[4] He bridged the Rhine south of Coblenz, carried out a demonstration in force on its eastern bank, and after ravaging the territory of the Sugambri withdrew into Gaul.

Here it is as well, so far as it is possible, to look at the Germans through Roman eyes. Writing of them, Caesar says:

"Their whole life is composed of hunting expeditions and military pursuits; from early boyhood they are zealous for toil and hardship. Those who remain longest in chastity win greatest praise among their kindred. . . .

[1] Caesar, *The Gallic War*, trans. H. J. Edwards (1922), I, 33.
[2] *Ibid.*, II, 4.    [3] *Ibid.*, IV, 13-15.    [4] *Ibid.*, IV, 16.

"For agriculture they have no zeal, and the greater part of their food consists of milk, cheese, and flesh. No man has a definite quantity of land or estate of his own; the magistrates and chiefs every year assign to tribes and clans . . . as much land and in such place as seems good to them, and compel the tenants after a year to pass on elsewhere. They adduce many reasons for that practice – the fear that they may be tempted by continuous association to substitute agriculture for their warrior zeal . . . that some passion for money may arise to be the parent of parties and of quarrels. It is their aim to keep common people in contentment, where each man sees that his own wealth is equal to that of the most powerful.

"Their states account it the highest praise by devastating their borders to have areas of wilderness as wide as possible around them. They think it the true sign of valour when the neighbours are driven to retire from their lands and no man dares to settle near, and at the same time they believe they will be safer thereby, having removed all fear of a sudden inroad. When a state makes or resists aggressive war, officers are chosen to direct the same, with the power of life and death. In time of peace there is no general officer of state, but the chiefs of districts and cantons do justice among their followers and settle disputes. . . . They do not think it right to outrage a guest; men who have come to them for any cause they protect from mischief and regard as sacred; to them the houses of all are open, with them is food shared."[1]

From this full description, it may be gathered that the Germans were a semi-nomadic people, belonging to what in the introduction of this book has been called "wagon-folk'. Though Caesar does not mention that they possessed horses or ox-drawn vehicles, without them they could not have moved in the numbers they did. The Helvetii, we know, did possess carts, for Caesar mentions them; further he informs us that they constructed "ramparts of carts" – that is, wagon laagers – to fight from.[2] It was the restlessness of the German way of life and not over-population which was the urge that moved them.

---

[1] Caesar, VI, 22–23.

[2] *Ibid.*, I, 24 and 26. Of the German peoples, Strabo writes: "All these nations easily change their abode, on account of the scantiness of provisions, and because they neither cultivate the lands nor accumulate wealth, but dwell in miserable huts, and satisfy their wants from day to day, the most part of their food being supplied by the herd, as amongst the nomad races, and in imitation of them they transfer their households in waggons, wandering with their cattle to any place which may appear most advantageous" (VII, i, 4).

Tacitus[1] describes them as being large of body, blue eyed and fair haired, "powerful only spasmodically and impatient at the same time of labour and hard work".[2] Though fierce fighters, their military organization was of the crudest, consisting of squadrons and battalions fortuitously collected by families and clans. "Few have swords or the longer kind of lance: they carry short spears, in their language frameae, with a narrow and small iron head, so sharp and so handy in use that they fight with the same weapon, as circumstances demand, both at close quarters and at a distance. The mounted man is content with a shield and framea: the infantry launch showers of missiles in addition, each man a volley, and hurl these to great distances, for they wear no outer clothing, or at most a light cloak. There is no bravery of apparel among them: their shields only are picked out with choice colours. Few have breast-plates: scarcely one or two at most have metal or hide helmets. The horses are conspicuous neither for beauty nor speed; but then neither are they trained like our horses to run in shifting circles; they ride them forwards only or to the right, but with one turn from the straight, dressing the line so closely as they wheel that no one is left behind. On a broad view there is more strength in their infantry, and accordingly cavalry and infantry fight in one body,[3] the swift-footed infantry-man, whom they pick out of the whole body of warriors and place in front of the line. . . . The battle-line itself is arranged in wedges: to retire, provided you press on again, they treat as a question of tactics, not of cowardice."[4] To this account Strabo adds: "Against these people mistrust was the surest defence; for those who were trusted effected the most mischief."[5]

Their leaders were selected for their valour, and commanded less through force of authority, than by example. Further, Tacitus tells us: "On the field of battle, it is disgraceful for a chief's companions not to equal him, and that to aid, to protect him, and by their own gallant actions add to his glory, were their most sacred engagements." On the other hand, "each companion requires from his chief, the warlike steed, the murderous and conquering

---

[1] Born *c.* A.D. 55 and lived until after A.D. 117.

[2] *Tacitus*, trans. Maurice Hutton (1925), "Germania", 4. The evidence of the *Germania* of Tacitus should not be treated as if it were a modern survey. To praise the German as a "noble savage" was a means of reflecting on what Tacitus considered to be the failings of contemporary civilization in Rome.

[3] See Caesar, *The Gallic War*, I, 48, and VIII, 13.

[4] Tacitus, *Germania*, 6.

[5] *The Geography of Strabo*, trans. W. Falconer (1912), VII, i, 4.

spear and in place of salary, he expects to be supplied with fare homely and plentiful. The cost of which must be met by war and foray."[1]

Such were the people, as known to the Romans, who inhabited the vast unknown area of mountains, forests, and marshes east of the Rhine and north of the Danube, which together had by 12 B.C. become the northern frontier of the Empire.

Strategically it was far from a perfect boundary, because the two rivers formed an extensive salient with its apex at Bâle. Within this the German tribes could work on interior lines, but without the Roman legions were compelled to operate on exterior ones. The former, should they wish to, could attack either the Rhenish or Danubian sectors; but the latter had to defend both, and to reinforce the one from the other meant moving round two sides of a triangle. Further, the Rhine, like the Aegean Sea in the days of Darius I, was not an ethnic frontier. West of it large numbers of the inhabitants were of German stock, and in times of trouble the Germans east of the river were likely to sympathize with them, as the Greeks in Europe sympathized with the Greeks in Ionia. Already in 17 B.C. the Sugambri and other tribes had raided west of the river and had taken Marcus Lollius off his guard.[2] Besides these weaknesses, Augustus looked upon Gaul as the Egypt of the West and, therefore, of vital importance for supplies, especially for the great armies on the Rhine, and though the Rhine was a formidable barrier for barbarians unacquainted with the art of bridging, was it wise, as Gaul was not as yet fully pacified, to leave room in central Europe for the growth of a power hostile to Rome?

Though there was no one solution of these several problems, it was clear to Augustus, now that his legions in Illyricum were freed from conquest, that could the Rhine frontier be pushed first to the Weser and then to the Elbe—eastward of which he did not intend to go[3]—the following improvements in the northern frontier would accrue: The salient would be eliminated and replaced by an approximately straight river frontier running from Hamburg to Vienna; a lateral line of communications could

---

[1] Tacitus, *Germania*, 14.

[2] See Velleius Paterculus, trans. Frederick W. Shipley (1924), II, XCVII, and Dio Cassius, LIV, 20. Suetonius (*Caesar Augustus*, XXIII) says: "In all his wars, Augustus never received any signal or ignominious defeat except twice in Germany, under his lieutenants Lollius and Varus. Of these the former was more humiliating than serious."

[3] Strabo, VII, i, 4.

17

be built from Hamburg by way of Leipzig and Prague to Vienna to supplement the line Cologne–Bâle–Vienna; and though the accretion of territory necessary to effect this would not establish an ethnic frontier, by pushing the existing frontier 200 to 250 miles eastward Gaul would be incomparably better secured against German attack. In fact, what Augustus appears to have had in his mind was not very different from what Napoleon had when, in 1806, he created the Confederation of the Rhine as a buffer state between France and her potential enemies Austria and Prussia– a problem which is still agitating the French.

In 15 and 14 B.C., as we have seen, Drusus was warring with his brother Tiberius in southern Bavaria, after which he was made *legatus* of the Three Gauls. Born in 38 B.C. and cast in the heroic mould, he was a man of immense activity and ambition. He lived for great deeds and vast conquests,[1] and when it was decided that Germany should be invaded, the project he had in mind was not merely to punish the Sugambri for their victory over Lollius, but to cut off the salient between the Rhine and the Danube and so to shorten the line of communications between the armies in Gaul and Illyricum. In this ambitious plan the first step was to reach the upper Elbe and to subdue the tribes *en route*.

First, Drusus established a line of winter camps on the Rhine; the two principal ones were Vetera (? Wesel) facing the valley of the Lippe, and Moguntiacum (Mainz) facing the valley of the Main. Next, in 12 B.C., after he had ravaged Westphalia, he assembled a large flotilla on Lacus Flevo (Zuyder Zee, then a lake); sailed to the mouth of the river Ems; won a considerable naval victory; went on to the mouth of the Weser, and there cemented an alliance with the Frisians. The sea-coast won; next, in 11 B.C., he began his invasion of Germany proper. He marched up the Lippe valley through the territory of the Sugambri, gained the middle Weser, halted there, and then returned to the Rhine. The following year, he left Mainz, invaded the lands of the Chatti (Nassau) and advanced through the Hercynian forest (Harz) from the Main to the Weser, striking at the Marcomanni in Thuringia. Then moving northward he traversed the land of the Cherusci (Brunswick) and reached the Elbe, probably at Magdeburg. On his return journey from there in 9 B.C. he was thrown by his horse and died of his injuries. He was succeeded by his brother Tiberius, six years his senior, and under him the cam-

[1] See *Histoire de la Gaule*, Camille Jullian (1914), vol. IV, pp. 106–113.

paign was brought to a successful issue. On its conclusion, in 7 B.C., Tiberius left Germany to take up an appointment in the East.

Drusus's conquests had been made too rapidly to prove lasting, with the result that in 1 B.C. the Cherusci broke into revolt, and by A.D. 4 the general situation in Germany had grown so serious that Tiberius returned to restore the authority of Augustus.

In his first campaign he marched to the Weser and received the submission of the tribes as far as the shore of the North Sea. He wintered in the valley of the Lippe, and in A.D. 5 he carried out the most distant and extraordinary expedition that had hitherto been undertaken against the northern Germans. He marshalled two armies on the Rhine, embarked one in a large fleet which sailed to the sea, skirted the Frisian coast and entered the mouth of the Elbe. The other army marched eastward from the Rhine, and after defeating the Langobardi (Lombards) united with the seaborne expedition which had meanwhile explored the coast of Jutland as far north as the Skagerrak. When he had subdued the northern tribes, he made ready to turn south and conquer Maroboduus, king of the Marcomanni, who in 9 B.C. had migrated with his tribe from Thuringia to Bohemia.

The plan he decided upon for his A.D. 6 campaign was to pinch out Maroboduus by a simultaneous advance eastward by the army of the Rhine under Saturninus, advancing from the Main toward Nuremberg or Eger, and by the army of Illyricum under his personal command, advancing northward from Carnuntum (near Hainburg) on the Danube. In all, twelve legions were mustered and the campaign which followed has been acclaimed "a master-piece of organization and deserves a proud place in the annals of the military art".[1] But when the two armies were but a few miles distant from their final goal in the centre of Bohemia, news was received of a critical rising in Illyricum. At once Tiberius came to terms with Maroboduus and turned his columns southward.

What had happened was this: the Dalmatians, exasperated by the requisitioning of supplies and men, had revolted, and as the garrisons had been withdrawn, all restraint had been removed. Rapidly the revolt spread until the whole of Illyricum and Pannonia was ablaze; the rebels numbered 200,000 infantry and 9,000 horsemen. Rome was thrown into a frenzy of terror, for no reserves existed; recruits were impossible to find, and in consequence new legions could not be raised. Nevertheless, in spite

[1] *The Cambridge Ancient History*, vol. x, p. 368.

of the extent of the revolt, Tiberius handled it in a masterly way. Instead of seeking pitched battles, he split his army into columns, occupied all points of importance, and by devastating the country methodically reconquered it by famine. In A.D. 8 Pannonia capitulated, followed the next year by Dalmatia. Tiberius left Germanicus[1] to reinstate the reconquered territories and returned to Italy, when five days after the collapse of the revolt a report was received in Rome of a terrible calamity in Germany.

When, in A.D. 6, Tiberius left Germany for his campaign against Maroboduus, Saturninus was succeeded by Publius Quintilius Varus, who had been governor of Syria, where he is reputed to have made a great fortune,[2] in which there is certainly nothing exceptional in this age. He "was a man of mild character and of a quiet disposition, somewhat slow in mind as he was in body, and more accustomed to the leisure of the camp than to actual service in war".[3] He had married the grand-niece of Augustus, in fact he was a "court appointment"; yet because a state of peacefulness had settled on the Rhine frontier, for "the barbarians were adapting themselves to Roman ways, were becoming accustomed to hold markets, and were meeting in peaceful assemblages",[4] there is in this little to find fault, a point which is sometimes overlooked. Gaul was now pacified, and fortunately for Roman rule the German tribes were without a head. Therefore, as so often happens on a quiet frontier, the garrisons had grown soft and indolent.

That Varus should have corrected this is true; but though his faults were many, and were heaped upon him after his defeat, stupidity rather than oppression would seem to have been his main defect. Apparently he was too unimaginative to grasp the difference between virile Germans and effete Syrians. Dio Cassius tells us that "Besides issuing orders to them as if they were actually slaves of the Romans, he exacted money as he would from subject nations".[5] Velleius Paterculus, a hostile critic, says that: "When placed in charge of the army in Germany, he entertained a notion that the Germans were a people who were men only in limbs and voice, and that they, who could not be subdued by the sword, could be soothed by the law."[6] It would appear that he was more

---

[1] The son of Nero Claudius Drusus and Antonia (daughter of Mark Antony and Octavia), born 15 B.C. and adopted by his uncle Tiberius.
[2] Velleius Paterculus, II, CXVII.
[3] *Ibid.*, II, CXVII.
[4] *Dio's Roman History*, trans. E. Cary (1916), LVI, 18.
[5] *Ibid.*, LVI, 18.
[6] Velleius Paterculus, II, CXVII.

of a bureaucrat than a soldier, and his rule was weak rather than calculatedly oppressive.

The real trouble seems to have arisen over the payment of tribute in gold and silver. In the West, as in the East, gold was exacted in payment of taxes; but whereas in the East it returned through the purchase of luxuries, in the West it did not, because few luxuries were produced. The result was a continuous drain of precious metals, which among the Germans were mainly used in the manufacture of ornaments. This caused much discontent among the tribal nobles, for gold was exceedingly scarce.[1]

In all, Varus had under his command five legions, two of which were stationed at Mogontiacum and three, during the winter, at Vetera or at Aliso (? Haltern) on the upper Lippe, and during the summer in the neighbourhood of Minden on the Weser.[2] Because of the prevailing peacefulness, the legions were not kept together, but were engaged upon felling trees, building roads, and bridging. Also, as was usual, the garrisons included many women and children.

The summer of A.D. 9 passed by in profound quiet, when, in September, as Varus was about to move from summer to winter quarters, news was received of a neighbouring tribal rising. He resolved, instead of returning direct to Aliso, to pass through the refractory area, to settle the dispute and then to march back to his winter camp. Before setting out he should have sent the women and children back to Aliso; but possibly he looked upon the rising as a mere local brawl, and therefore did not consider this precaution worth while. As he moved off, little did he dream that what lay in store for him was to be one of the decisive battles in the history of the world.

The revolt of which he had received news was the bait of a skilfully laid plan devised by a young Cheruscan, Arminius, who, under Tiberius, had served with a contingent of Cheruscan troops during the revolt in Pannonia and Illyricum, and who, no doubt, had watched the Romans closely during that campaign. He was son of Sigimer, chief of the Cherusci, had been granted Roman citizenship and held equestrian rank. He was not quite twenty-six years old when he was posted to Varus's headquarters. In character he was impetuous. Tacitus calls him "a frantic spirit" and "the incendiary of Germany". Further, he was

[1] See *The Greatness and Decline of Rome*, Guglielmo Ferrero (1909), vol. v, pp. 124–126.
[2] This distribution is uncertain.

possessed by an inborn hatred for the Romans. Apparently he hoped to effect what the rebellion in the south had failed to accomplish. Also, it would appear, he itched to avenge himself on his uncle, Segestes, a loyal supporter of Varus, who had refused him his daughter, Thusnelda, in marriage, but with whom he had eloped. Lastly, he had the highest contempt for Varus, for he looked upon him as a city praetor and not as a general, and in this he was probably right.

His plot was laid carefully. He made use of Varus's negligence "as an opportunity for treachery, sagaciously seeing that no one could be more quickly overpowered than the man who feared nothing, and that the most common beginning of disaster was a sense of security".[1] When Varus was about to return to Aliso, Arminius engineered the uprising in order to draw him through what appeared to be friendly though difficult country, so that he might be put off his guard, and after he had led him into the depths of the forests he intended to annihilate him.

To keep secret so elaborate a plot was scarcely possible, and Segestes heard of it and informed Varus, whom he advised to place the conspirators in chains. Varus refused to do so, possibly because he considered the accusation of treason an attempt on the part of Segestes to square his quarrel with his nephew. So it came about that, some time in September or October, A.D. 9, at the head of the XVIIth, XVIIIth, and XIXth Legions, some 20,000 men in all, Varus set out followed by a long baggage train and the soldiers' families.

Exactly what happened during the opening stages of the march we do not know, and though several modern writers have given a full description of the disaster, the information provided by the two most reliable authorities – Velleius Paterculus and Dio Cassius – does not warrant it. But what we do know is that Arminius accompanied Varus, his men escorted the column, and that he remained with him until the evening before the insurrection was planned to begin. Again Segestes warned Varus, and again he was brushed aside. Next, as the legions were winding their way through the swamps and forests, Arminius and his followers disappeared, and the first intimation of the revolt was a report that outlying detachments of soldiers had been slaughtered. Then, so it would appear, Varus turned and headed for the road which ran by way of the Dören Pass to Aliso.

[1]Velleius Paterculus, II, CXVIII.

Though, because of his baggage train and followers, his situation was not an enviable one, it was by no means worse than many Julius Caesar or Drusus had faced on former occasions; but then, they were leaders of men and Varus was but a camp attorney. Where the battle proper began is not known; Tacitus mentions the forest of Teutoburgium; it was there, so he relates, that Germanicus discovered the bones of Varus and his legions.[1] The forest lay between the Ems and the Weser, and, in the year A.D. 9, must have covered a vast area. Some authorities place the actual battlefield near Detmold; others, near Münster. Possibly the action began near the former and ended in the vicinity of the latter; because if Minden was Varus's summer camp, in his retirement he would almost certainly make for the Dören Pass, and then, finding Aliso besieged, as it was, his best line of retreat would appear to be along the lower Ems toward Münster. But there is no agreement at all between the experts concerning where the disaster happened.

Once in the forest, Dio tells us that, while the Romans were cutting a track, a violent storm of rain made the ground slippery and walking "very treacherous"; the "tops of the trees kept breaking off and falling down, causing much confusion".[2] It was then, when "the Romans were not proceeding in any regular order, but were mixed in helter-skelter with the wagons and the unarmed",[3] that Arminius suddenly attacked and hurled volleys of javelins into the disordered masses of men. Nevertheless, a halt was made, and a camp fortified.

Next morning, after they had burnt most of their wagons, "in a little better order" the Romans fought their way into open country; then once again they "plunged into the woods" and "suffered their heaviest losses". That night they halted, and when they advanced again on the following morning were caught by a heavy downpour of rain which prevented them "from going forward and even from standing securely, and moreover deprived them of the use of their weapons. For they could not handle their bows or their javelins with any success, nor for that matter, their shields, which were thoroughly soaked."[4] Now came Arminius's opportunity. He closed on his disorganized enemy and broke through his ranks; Vala Numonius, in charge of the cavalry, fled,[5]

---

[1] Tacitus, *Histories and Annals*, trans. C. H. Moore and J. Jackson, I, 60.
[2] *Dio's Roman History*, LVI, 20.          [3] *Ibid.*, LVI, 20.
[4] *Ibid.*, LVI, 21.          [5] Velleius Paterculus, II, CXIX.

and Varus and "all his more prominent officers, fearing that they should either be captured alive or be killed by their bitterest foes (for they had already been wounded), made bold to do a thing that was terrible yet unavoidable; they took their

22.   THE TEUTOBURGER WALD CAMPAIGN, A.D. 9

own lives".[1] At length, Velleius tells us, "Hemmed in by forests and marshes and ambuscades", the Roman army was "extermin-ated almost to a man by the very enemy whom it had always slaughtered like cattle".[2]

Those who were captured were crucified, buried alive, or offered up as sacrifices to the gods. When, a few years later, Germanicus visited the battlefield, he found whitening bones,

[1] *Dio's Roman History*, LVI, 21.          [2] *Velleius Paterculus*, II, CXIX.

fragments of javelins, limbs of horses, and skulls fixed upon the trunks of trees; a grim picture, grimly described by Tacitus.[1]

In spite of this overwhelming defeat, Lucius Caedicius held firmly to Aliso, and by means of his archers beat back every attack made on the camp. Later, when blockaded, he broke out on a dark night, and with the remnants of the army, encumbered with numerous women and children, reached Vetera, where he was met by Lucius Nonius Asprenas and two legions, and Arminius and his hordes then retired. It was a fine ending to a fearful failure.

The extent of the disaster is clearly reflected in the portents of doom which went whispering through the Empire. Dio informs us that the temple of Mars was struck by lightning, that the Alps seemed to collapse upon one another, and that "a statue of Victory that was in the province of Germany and faced the enemy's territory turned about to face Italy".[2] Rationally incredible, morally these portents were true; Roman prestige had received a mortal blow and henceforth the barbarians knew that the legions were not invincible, and that what Arminius had accomplished could be repeated. Further, and worse still, Rome also knew it. This is why "Augustus, when he learned of the disaster . . . rent his garments . . . and mourned greatly . . . because he expected that the enemy would march against Italy and against Rome itself. For there were no citizens of military age left worth mentioning."[3] Nevertheless, he set to work; "and when no men of military age showed a willingness to be enrolled, he made them draw lots, depriving of his property and disfranchising every fifth man of those still under thirty-five and every tenth man amongst those who had passed that age. Finally, as a great many paid no heed to him even then, he put some to death."[4] Yet these drastic punishments effected little; during his lifetime the lost legions were never replaced. This was the most terrifying portent of all. So it came about that "he let the hair of his head and beard grow for several months", and would sometimes thump his head against the door-posts, crying out, "Quintilius Varus, give me back my legions!"[5]

Even should all this be untrue, the fact remains that the three legions were never re-raised, not because Varus had lost them, but because Rome was losing her vigour. It is true that after the

---

[1] *The Annals*, Tacitus, I, 61.          [2] *Dio's Roman History*, LVI, 24.

[3] *Ibid.*, LVI, 23. Concerning this, it should be remembered that Dio is not a very reliable historian.

[4] *Ibid.*, LVI, 23.          [5] Suetonius, "Caesar Augustus," XXIII.

disaster Tiberius again took over the German command, and that in A.D. 13, Germanicus, who succeeded him, in a series of campaigns reached the Elbe and more than once defeated the Germans. Nevertheless, that river was to be the Roman Hyphasis; all these campaigns were little more than an apology for a final retreat to the Rhine, which henceforth was to remain the north-eastern frontier of Latin civilization.

Yet there was a deeper reason still, deeper than the loss of Roman vigour; it must be sought in the character of Augustus himself. In spite of the glamour of his age, he was a splendid rather than an heroic figure. Though not lacking in courage or pertinacity, as a leader of men he cannot compare with Julius Caesar. He was a tolerant opportunist who, by means of his policy of *divide et impera*, became the managing director rather than the monarch of his Empire. He believed in Rome as a great business, a vast monopoly, and looked upon states and frontiers as bonds and securities. He lacked that power to electrify men and to compel them to accomplish the seemingly impossible which distinguishes the man of genius from the merely great. In two words, he was supremely a "bourgeois emperor". So it came about that though his conquests were many, in spirit they were defensive investments, and as the frontiers were closed, simultaneously were closed down with them all intellectual and moral endeavour: adventures of the mind and soul ceased with the cessation of the adventures of the body.

In the end this loss of moral stimulus compelled him to leave the north-eastern frontier where his predecessor had established it, and what were the historical results? In attempting to fathom so hypothetical a question, we must beware of the "might-have-beens"; yet certain and not altogether improbable speculations are permissible. Though Germany was not Gaul, for the Germans were more barbaric than the Gauls, as the Empire was destined to last for another four hundred years, it is not illogical to suppose that, had the north-eastern frontier rested on the Elbe, instead of on the Rhine, the next chapter in this book could not have been written, and because of it every other chapter would have been different. Creasy quite rightly points out that, had the Elbe been held, "This island" of ours "would never have borne the name of England".[1] More important still: we should never have become English. The whole course of our history would have been

---

[1] *The Fifteen Decisive Battles of the World*, Sir Edward S. Creasy (edit. 1931), p. 119.

different. Again, had Germany west of the Elbe been for four centuries Romanized and roaded, one culture and not two in unending conflict would have dominated the western world. There would have been no Franco-German problem, or at least a totally different one. There would have been no Charlemagne, no Louis XIV, no Napoleon, no Kaiser William II, and no Hitler.

Though we are told that, when at Alexandria, Augustus ordered the sarcophagus of Alexander the Great to be opened so that he might place a golden crown upon his head and scatter flowers on his corpse,[1] and though on his ring he had the head of the mighty Macedonian engraved,[2] he set a seal on the limits of his "Great Idea"; for in the mind of Alexander there was no boundary but that of the Great Ocean. Thus, though under succeeding emperors the Empire was still further to expand physically, spiritually it was to stand still, passing from an empire into a limited liability company. This was the "Great Idea" Augustus bequeathed to the Empire when, on August 29, A.D. 14, at the age of seventy-six, he died at Nola and was succeeded by Tiberius.

[1] Suetonius, "Caesar Augustus," XVIII.          [2] *Ibid.*, L.

CHRONICLE 8

# The Pax Romana

The transformation of the Republic into an Empire raised a problem of power which was to plague Rome to the end, and which was not the least of the factors in her fall. Because the power which had been conferred on Augustus by the Senate and people would automatically lapse on his death, provisionally, to solve the difficulty, Augustus secured the association of others with himself, first M. Agrippa and then Tiberius, his stepson. Though on his death in the year 14 his prestige assured Tiberius the succession, no precedent was established, and the inevitable result was that, because the authority of the emperor finally derived from the army, power to nominate first passed into the hands of the Praetorian Guard and then into those of the legions.

In his turn Tiberius nominated his grandson Tiberius Gemellus and his grand-nephew Gaius Caesar (Caligula) not as his successors, which was beyond his powers, but as joint heirs to his personal property, and on his death in 37 Gemellus was set aside because Gaius had the backing of Marco, sole prefect of the praetorians. When Gaius was assassinated in 41, in which act the praetorians were involved, Claudius, a nephew of Tiberius, established the evil precedent of giving a handsome donative to the praetorians and so was hailed *Imperator*. Gaius's nephew, Nero, he advanced in public life before his own son Britannicus, and on Claudius's death in 54, Nero's mother, Agrippina, persuaded the praetorians to proclaim her son emperor on the understanding that they would receive a donative equal to the one given by Claudius. In 68 Nero only escaped assassination at the hands of the praetorians by committing suicide.

Nero's death was followed by an upheaval which probably would have involved the Empire in another long civil war had not Vespasian (69–79), an able general, been proclaimed Emperor by the legionaries in Egypt and the troops on the Danube. When he gained the upper hand over Vitellius he re-established the *Pax Romana*. Nevertheless, the "year of the four emperors"[1] left so

---

[1] Otho, Galba, Vitellius and Vespasian. All were hailed either by the praetorians or legions. The first ousted the second, the third the first, and the fourth the third.

horrible a memory, even in the minds of the soldiers, that when Vespasian's younger son Domitian died in 96 without an heir the praetorians left the choice of his successor to the Senate, and it was not until 193 that the accession of an emperor became again the cause of civil war.

Under Vespasian and his two sons Titus (79–81) and Domitian (81–96), the Empire was brought to a high level of prosperity. Domitian died in 96 and was succeeded by Nerva, who in 98 was followed by Trajan, a Spaniard, and probably the ablest soldier since Caesar. His reign largely was occupied with frontier wars. Between 101 and 106 he warred on the lower Danube, subdued Dacia (Rumania) and colonized it. Next, he turned his attention to the east end of the Black Sea, and in 115–117, he defeated the Parthians and added Armenia, Mesopotamia, and Assyria to the Empire.

He was succeeded by Hadrian (117–138), another able soldier and statesman, in whose reign Rome became the most magnificent city in the world. He held fast to Dacia, but wisely abandoned Trajan's conquests in the East and kept his soldiers busily employed in building great defensive walls between the Danube and the Rhine, and in Britain, and he also built bridges, aqueducts, and other public works. He died in 138 and was succeeded by Antoninus Pius, whose reign was so peaceful that little has been recorded of it. In 161 he was followed by Marcus Aurelius, who had married his daughter, the notorious Faustina.

Under these two emperors the *Pax Romana* attained its zenith. By now there had grown up a Mediterranean nation, and, as foreshadowed by Augustus, Italy had dropped to the level of a province. Of the factors which led to this, the first was the establishment, largely under Stoic influence, of a common law which, as J. H. Robinson writes, "conceived mankind, not as a group of nations or tribes, each with its own lands, but as one people included in one great empire and subject to a single system of law based on fairness and reason". Other factors were the wonderful system of roads, which linked the Empire culturally, commercially, and strategically; a common currency and common weights and measures; the establishment of banks and bank drafts; the freeing of the seas from pirates, and the expansion of trade as far as India and China. West of Sicily the language of civilized intercourse was Latin, east of that island it was Greek. Lastly, the whole Empire was encircled by legions from the borders of Scotland to the

Euphrates and the Province of Africa, "like a dike restraining the stormy sea of barbarians outside".

In the year 175, Aelius Aristides, a Greek sophist, described the conditions of his day in a panegyric addressed to the Emperor Marcus Aurelius, which reads:

"Now the whole world keeps holiday and laying aside its ancient dress of steel has turned in freedom to adornment and all delights. The cities have abandoned their old quarrels, and are occupied by a single rivalry, each ambitious to be more pleasant and beautiful. Everywhere are playgrounds, fountains, arcades, temples, workshops, schools. . . . Cities are ablaze with brightness and beauty and all the earth is adorned like a king's garden. The beacon fires of friendship rise on her plains, and those of war are gone as though a wind had blown them beyond land and sea: in their place has come every beautiful spectacle and an endless number of games. . . . Today Greek or foreigner may travel freely where he will, with full or empty hands, as though he was passing from homeland to homeland. . . . To be safe, it is enough to be a Roman, or rather a subject of yours. You have made into a reality the saying of Homer that earth belongs to all, for you have meted out the whole world, bridled rivers with many a bridge, cut mountains into carriage roads, filled the deserts with outposts, and civilized all things with settled discipline and life."

When Aelius Aristides was penning this somewhat turgid eulogy, little does he seem to have realized that the *Pax Romana* was fast approaching the edge of an abyss. Already, between 162 and 165, Aurelius had been at war with Parthia, and when this war ended he was compelled to march against the Marcomanni, Langobardi, Quadi, and other barbarians who had swept over the northern frontier of the Empire from the source of the Danube to the Illyrian border, and who, in 167, for the first time for two centuries poured down into northern Italy and ravaged the land as far south as Verona. Nor does Aristides mention that, once these wild warriors had been driven back, Aurelius took the dangerous step of allowing many of them to settle inside the frontier.

Besides these external dangers, internal rot was accelerated by the decline in farming, which had been progressive since the days of the Republic. The small estates increasingly were swallowed by the large. Already, in the age of Nero, half the Province of Africa was held by six great landlords, the type of men Petronius Arbiter satirized in the *Satyricon* in his parvenu Trimalchio, who possessed "as much land as a kite can fly over . . . as for slaves, wheugh! by Hercules I do not believe one-tenth of them know their own master".

The great estates, known as "villas", were to be found in all the provinces. At first they were worked mainly by slaves, but when, with the restriction of conquest, this source of labour dried up, the deficit was made good by forcing the free peasants to become *coloni*, virtually serfs tied to the land, and when they proved insufficient, the labour markets were opened to the barbarians, mainly Germans, who also were recruited into the legions to make good the lack of home-bred recruits.

A further cause in the decline of farming was the progressive exhaustion of the soil. The amount of land under cultivation continually decreased, until the Empire no longer could feed its teeming millions. As the economic dry rot spread, all who could drifted to the cities, which became the tombs of the race; for the country-side favoured procreation, the cities recreation. The growing city proletariat became an ever-increasing financial burden. Producing next to nothing, it had to be fed, and when the country communities became too poor to purchase the manufactures of the cities, the dole-fed rabble was multiplied when the city industrial workers were thrown out of work. Lack of agriculture led to the decline of industry.

Coincident with this decline in production, the coinage was debased increasingly in order to keep enough money in circulation for business and trade. In the reign of Augustus the currency was pure silver, in the reign of Aurelius it was a quarter alloy, and two generations later ninety-five per cent. Aurelius had such trouble to find sufficient money for his legionaries' pay that he was compelled to substitute grain for coin. Soldiers were paid also by assignments of land and became known as "frontiersmen" (*limitanei*), who were little more than a peasant militia, a totally inadequate substitute for the magnificent legionaries of Trajan and Hadrian. With the increasing recruitment of barbarian *limitanei*, the legional organization disappeared, and with its disappearance the power of Rome over the barbarians vanished and barbarian soldiery became the highest power in the state.

Another contributory cause of decline was the rapid decay of classical religion and its steady replacement by new creeds. For long the more educated Romans had turned from the old gods to philosophy and the less educated to Oriental cults, such as Isis,

Attis, and Mithras worship, in all of which the central theme was the triumph of the god over death and his attainment of everlasting life. Among these new religions a late comer was Christianity with its conception of a single universal god, as foreshadowed in the days of Ikhnaton. It was communist in origin and, in consequence, appealed to the city proletariat, and because its adherents made a practical distinction between the things which are God's and the things which are Caesar's, they soon developed into a "third race" which stood apart from both Roman and barbarian. In the second century of the peace, Christianity was both rapidly ousting and absorbing all the other new cults, and because its followers persistently undermined the order of things, reviled the pagan deities, shunned the festivals, evinced utter abhorrence for military service, refused to sacrifice to the Emperor as a quasi-divinity and openly prophesied the downfall of the Empire, they were looked upon by the Romans much as to-day western Europeans look upon the Communists. For instance, Suetonius speaks of the "new and impious superstition"; Tacitus of "a foreign and deadly superstition"; and Pliny, in his celebrated letter to Trajan, of "a depraved, wicked and outrageous superstition".

The fatal third century of the *Pax Romana* opened with the death of Marcus Aurelius in 180, and out of the anarchy which followed emerged Septimus Severus, a successful soldier who was in 193 saluted Emperor by the legions and who restored order in 202. His son Caracalla (211–217), by conferring citizenship on all free men in the empire, placed Roman and barbarian on an equal footing, and when, in 235, the line of Severus ended, again the storm broke, and the barbarian troops in one province after another set up and knocked down puppet emperors of their own. The state of affairs reached may be judged from the fact that in the eighty years following the death of the Emperor Commodus in 192, twenty-six emperors came and went. With but one short break during the reign of Aurelian (270–275), anarchy continued until 284, when Diocletian (234–305) established what looked like a lasting peace.

He abolished the Senate, became an absolute monarch, and the state was completely militarized and orientalized. "In these things", writes Breasted, "we recognize a further stage in the commingling of the East and West begun by Alexander the Great over six hundred years before." Worshipped as an oriental sun-god, Diocletian was officially called the "Invincible Sun", and his birthday was fixed on December 25.[1] Compelled throughout his reign to war against the Persians, who had now replaced the Parthians, in order that the West might be administered in his absence and to avert the recurrence of civil war on the death of an emperor, he appointed a co-emperor to rule jointly with himself. He and his fellow emperor each bore the title of Augustus, and each had an assistant, Caesar. Though it was not his intention to divide the Empire, this was, nevertheless, the first step taken towards its division. But, at the moment, what was more important was that, in order to satisfy the two Emperors and two Caesars, the provinces of the Empire, which now numbered over a hundred, were divided into four prefectures: Gaul (Morocco, Spain, Gaul, and Britain); Italy (Africa, Sicily, Sardinia, Corsica, Italy, and present-day Yugoslavia and Austria); Illyricum (Dacia, Macedonia, and Greece); and the Orient (Thrace, Asia Minor, Syria, and Egypt). Because each Augustus and Caesar had his own imperial court, the cost of administering the bankrupt Empire became so great that state Socialism was introduced to solve the financial problem.

The more economic resources dried up, the higher taxation rose and the more the state preyed upon the weak, until the full rigour of the law was let loose on the population and soldiers were employed as bailiffs and secret police. The propertied class was exterminated and the bourgeoisie eliminated. As requisitioning increased, prices rose and the population fell from seventy to fifty millions. To make good this loss in men, all classes not belonging to the privileged governing caste were forced to become state-employed workers tied to their occupations. Thus private economy was replaced by forced labour in the state farms and factories.

A collateral feature of the age was the advance in feudal economy. In the third century there appeared a class of *nouveaux riches* recruited from soldiers, officials, contractors, profiteers and speculators, men who had exploited the state Socialist system for their own benefit, and who, once they had become powerful enough, appeared in the ranks of the state's opponents. These men abandoned the dying cities and took to the country, and in their villas, which became centres of production, the weak sought refuge from state oppression. Thus the bourgeois-city culture of the early Empire passed into the feudal-rural culture of the later.

[1] The worship of the Sun-God was introduced by Aurelian.

18

In 324, after a long struggle which followed the death of Diocletian—and which his arrangements for the succession in no way prevented—the Emperor Constantine the Great (306–337) emerged victorious. He selected Byzantium for his capital and renamed it Constantinople. This change in the imperial seat of government definitely meant the separation of the eastern from the western half of the Empire as soon as Constantine's strong hand was removed. Meanwhile the Christian Church had gained vastly in power. Already in 311, the Emperor Galerius, who realized the dangers threatening Rome from without, and the futility of the struggle against the Christians within, had placed the Church on a footing of equality with the worship of the gods. Though not baptized until on his death-bed, Constantine maintained this decree, and in 325, under his direction, the first great council of the churches of the Empire assembled at Nicaea (Iznik). There "sitting amongst the Christian bishops", writes Mr. N. H. Baynes in the *Cambridge Ancient History*, he "is in his own person the beginning of Europe's Middle Ages".

CHAPTER 9

# The Battle of Adrianople, 378

Constantine the Great died on May 22, 337, and like a burnt-down candle the flame of Empire began to flicker blue. He had again brought imperial unity into being, but division immediately followed his death. The Empire was divided between his three sons Constantine II, Constans, and Constantius, who during his lifetime he had made his Caesars. To the first went Spain, the two Gauls, and Britain; to the second the two Italies, Africa, Illyricum, and Thrace; and to the third the lands south of the Propontis, Asia and the Orient, with Pontus and Egypt. This division inevitably led to civil war, in which Constantine II, in 340, was slain by Constans near Aquileia, and Constans, in 350, was killed by the soldiers of the usurper Magnentius.

Meanwhile, in 338, Constantius was at war with Sapor II, king of Persia, and in 344 or 348, he won a considerable victory over him and his mailed horsemen (*cataphracti*) at Singaral (? Sinjar). Next, he moved against Magnentius, and, on September 28, 351, decisively defeated him at Mursa (Osijek or Esseg) in Pannonia. Magnentius fled to Lugdunum (Lyons) and in 353 committed suicide. Historically this battle is an important one, because the losses suffered in it were so heavy that it is no exaggeration to say that the defence of the Empire in the East was crippled by them. Further, its tactical importance is considerable; it was the first victory won in the West by the newly raised Roman heavy cavalry, armed and armoured by Constantius on the Persian model. It was the impact of its charge which won the battle, and it showed that the day of the legionary was in its twilight.

In 355, Constantius appointed his cousin Julian, surnamed the Apostate, as his Caesar, and sent him to Gaul to repel the hordes of Germans which had swept over the Rhine, occupied Brabant and Alsace, and were then ravaging the centre of Gaul. He checked them in 356 and in the following year Julian defeated the Alemanni at Strasbourg and soon after re-established the Rhine frontier.

When Julian was recovering Gaul, Constantius was warring on

the Danube against the Quadi (a German tribe) and the Sarmatians (related to the Alans). Next, in 359, Constantius again marched against Sapor II, who had laid siege to Amida (Diyarbakir) in Armenia; but, because of his losses at Mursa he did not have sufficient troops and he called upon Julian to send him most of his army. But he omitted to ask Julian himself and as this omission was considered an insult by Julian's barbarian soldiers, much against his own will they proclaimed him "Julianus Augustus". Nevertheless, it was only after considerable delay that the newly hailed emperor set out for Sirmium and Naissus to block Constantius's advance westward up the Danube. Constantius died of fever at Mopsucrene (Mersin) in Cilicia on November 3, 361, while on his way to meet his rival.

Eager to punish Sapor, in 363 Julian established his headquarters at Antioch. He then advanced across the Euphrates, met Sapor at Ctesiphon, and defeated him. He pursued him, but after a useless march he was compelled to withdraw, and during the retreat, on June 26, he was mortally wounded and died that night. At once Jovian, a captain of the Imperial bodyguard, was elected emperor. He made a shameful peace with Persia and surrendered all but one of the five satrapies which Diocletian had won. Seven months later he died.

The next emperor, Valentinian I (364–375), the son of a Pannonian rope-maker, had commanded the legions in Britain and had served under Julian in Gaul. He was an able soldier, and though he at once set to work to strengthen the defences of the Danube, on March 28, 364, by appointing his brother Valens co-emperor, as we shall see, he unwittingly opened the Danubian door to the great Gothic invasion. He died in 375 and was succeeded by his son Gratian, then but a youth of sixteen, who could exert no influence whatsoever on his uncle in Constantinople.

Because Valens is the leading actor in the tragedy to be described in this chapter, it is as well to consider what manner of man he was. The historian Ammianus Marcellinus, our most trustworthy guide, describes him as "a procrastinator and irresolute. His complexion was dark, the pupil of one of his eyes was dimmed, but in such a way as not to be noticed at a distance; his body was well-knit, his height neither above nor below the average; he was knock-kneed, and somewhat pot-bellied";[1] and though Ammianus does not hesitate to inform us that he was cruel, rude, rough and

---

[1] *Ammianus Marcellinus*, trans. John C. Rolfe (1939), XXXI, XIV, 7.

uncultured, he credits him with being a faithful and steady friend, a strict upholder of both military and civil discipline, a very just ruler of the provinces, and an implacable enemy of thievish officials.[1] According to Gibbon, his chief defect was that he considered "the use of dilatory and ambiguous measures as the most admirable efforts of consummate prudence".[2]

Such was the man who was now called upon to meet and beat back the Goths.

Originally it is supposed that the Goths inhabited Scandinavia – the Isle of Scanzia of Jordanes – and then migrated to the upper Vistula. From there they moved south towards the middle Danube, and thence east to occupy the region between the Pruth and the Don. Here, apparently, they split into two groups, one occupying the western half of that area, to become known as Visigoths (West Goths), and the other the eastern, to be called Ostrogoths (East Goths).

In 238, these semi-nomadic people came into contact with the Romans in the province of Lower Moesia (northern Bulgaria), which led, in 250, to the outbreak of the First Gothic War, during which, under their King Cniva (or Kniwa), they laid siege to Philippolis, won a great battle, devastated the entire region, and slaughtered, we are told, more than 100,000 people. Next, in 258, we find them raiding Circassia and Georgia. Four years later they marched on Ephesus and destroyed the Temple of Diana, one of the seven wonders of the world. Five years after this with the Heruli, in 500 boats, they passed through the Bosphorus, occupied Byzantium and laid waste, not only Corinth, Sparta, and Argolis, but Athens. At length, by destroying their boats, the Greeks drove them northward out of Macedonia; but two years later they returned more numerous than ever – 320,000 are mentioned – and were brought to a halt in a great battle at Naissus (Nisch) in which they are said to have lost 50,000 men. Next, shut up in the passes of the Balkans, they were reduced by famine and were compelled to enter the service of the Emperor Claudius II (268–270), surnamed "Gothicus", as *foederati* (allies). Dacia was then abandoned, and, in 270, peace between them and the Romans was established for nearly a hundred years.

Barely had Valentinian and Valens ascended the throne than this long peace began to crumble. On the steppes of Astrakhan,

[1] Ammianus, XXXI, XIV, 2.
[2] *The History of the Decline and Fall of the Roman Empire* (edit. Bury, 1929), vol. III, p. 98.

for some unknown reason vast hordes of Huns began to trek westward. In 370 they fell upon the Alans, a semi-Tartar people who inhabited the country between the Volga and Don, and next upon the Ostrogoths under Hermanric. Though many submitted or were overpowered, thousands moved westward under two chieftains—Alatheus and Saphrax. This trek involved the Visigoths who, under Athanaric, were driven over the Dniester to the Pruth, and soon after the second of these rivers was abandoned. Next, Fridigern, a Christian Gothic chieftain, whose dominions apparently lay southward of Athanaric's, appealed to Valens to allow his tribe to cross the Danube and enter into alliance with the Romans. The situation on the northern bank of the Danube is described by Eunapius, a contemporary historian, as follows:

"The multitude of the Scythians [Goths] who escaped from the murderous savagery of the Huns amounted to not less than 200,000 men of fighting age. These standing upon the river bank in a state of great excitement, stretched out their hands from afar with loud lamentations, and earnestly supplicated that they might be allowed to cross over the river, bewailing the calamity that had befallen them, and promising that they would faithfully adhere to the Imperial alliance if this boon were granted them."[1]

Valens knew Athanaric personally; in 365, when that chieftain, at the head of 10,000 Gothic soldiers, had assisted Count Procopius in his revolt against him he had met him, and, according to Zosimus, the newly appointed Emperor had displayed high ability in quashing the insurrection. He writes:

"For when the Goths did not venture to join in a regular pitched battle, but hid themselves in the swamps and from thence made covert attacks, Valens ordered his soldiers to remain in their regular quarters, but collecting the suttlers and camp followers and those who had charge of baggage, he promised them a certain sum for every barbarian head which they should bring in [to his headquarters]. Stimulated by the hope of such gains these men plunged into the forests and morasses, slew any Goths whom they came across, and received the promised reward. And when a great multitude had been destroyed in this fashion, those who were left began to supplicate the Emperor for peace, which was granted on terms not dishonouring to the Roman name, for it was agreed that the Romans should hold in all

[1] Eunapius (Bonn edit.), p. 48. Quoted from *Italy and Her Invaders*, T. Hodgkin (1880), vol. I, p. 102.

security their former possessions, while the barbarians promised not to cross the river nor attack the Roman frontiers."[1]

After this clever victory it would appear that Valens held the Goths in contempt. Having first strengthened the Danube forts, he returned to Constantinople and shortly afterward set out for Syria to make war on the Persians who, mistakenly, he considered his more dangerous enemy.

It was when he was at Antioch that the gathering of the Goths on the Danube, as described by Eunapius, took place. When informed of it, Ammianus Marcellinus says: ". . . the affair caused more joy than fear", because "by combining the strength of his own troops with these foreign forces, he would have an invincible army".[2] In spite of the obvious danger of allowing the immense horde to cross into Roman territory, there was, nevertheless, something to be said for admitting it, because by now the people were so pacific that the recruiting of Roman subjects had all but ceased. Further, there is no evidence that the Goths would have proved disloyal to the Emperor had they been treated fairly.

The conditions laid down were that all boys not yet of military age should be given up as hostages, and that all arms should be handed over to Lupicinus and Maximus, two Roman officials, before the crossing took place. But such was the corruption and sensuality of these men and their followers that, so long as the Goths were willing to prostitute their wives, daughters, and young sons to them, they were allowed to retain their weapons. Besides, when once the multitudes had crossed the Danube, they were so ill-treated, starved and cheated that the liveliest discontent was aroused. When this was happening, another large horde, this time of Ostrogoths, under Alatheus and Saphrax, who had been refused a crossing, slipped over the river on rafts. Bound by no compact, these two chieftains established an alliance with Fridigern, who by then had moved forward to Marcianoplis (Shumla). "There", writes Ammianus, "another and more atrocious thing was done, which kindled the frightful torches that were to burn for the destruction of the state."[3]

Lupicinus, now thoroughly frightened at the growing unrest among the Goths, invited Fridigern and Alavivus, another Visigothic chieftain, to a banquet; his object was, when in their cups, to have them assassinated. While the feast was in progress, the

[1] *The History of Count Zosimus* (London, 1814), p. 99.
[2] Ammianus Marcellinus, XXXI, IV, 4.          [3] *Ibid.*, XXXI, V, 4.

Gothic bodyguard, which was in another part of the palace, was treacherously attacked. When they heard the cries of their men, the two chieftains leapt to their feet; Alavivus, apparently, was cut down, for nothing more is heard of him, but Fridigern drew his sword, rushed out of the room, and was greeted with shouts of joy by his countrymen. They mounted their horses and rode away determined to revenge their slaughtered comrades.

"Thus these valiant men", writes Jordanes, "gained the chance they had longed for–to be free to die in battle rather than to perish of hunger–and immediately took arms to kill the generals Lupicinus and Maximus."[1] Lupicinus, quite unprepared, met them in the neighbourhood of Marcianopolis, was defeated and fled the field, and his enemies equipped themselves with the arms of the slain legionaries. "Thus that day put an end to the famine of the Goths and the safety of the Romans, for the Goths no longer as strangers and pilgrims, but as citizens and lords, began to rule the inhabitants and to hold in their own right all the northern country as far as the Danube."[2]

Next, Fridigern marched on Adrianople, and joined by another body of Goths under Sueridus and Colias, he set about investing that city; a hopeless task, for he possessed no siege train. Moving on into Thrace, "without distinction of age or sex all places were ablaze with slaughter and great fires, sucklings were torn from the very breasts of their mothers and slain, matrons and widows whose husbands had been killed before their eyes were carried off, boys of tender or adult age were dragged away over the dead bodies of their parents".[3]

When the news of this uprising reached Valens, instead of returning to Constantinople he patched up a peace with Persia, called in his forces operating in Armenia and placing them under Profuturus and Trajan, officers of rank and ambition, but of no great skill in war,[4] he hurried them to Thrace. Simultaneously he sent a message to his nephew, the Emperor Gratian, soliciting his aid. Such was the state of affairs at the end of the year 376. Before relating what followed, for a moment we will turn to the military organization and tactics of the opposing forces.

The main defect in the Roman defensive system, as established by Augustus, was the lack of a central reserve. This was in part

---

[1] *The Gothic History of Jordanes* (or Jordandes), trans. Charles Christopher Mierow 1915), XXVI, p. 89.     [2] *Ibid.*, XXVI, pp. 89–90.
[3] Ammianus Marcellinus, XXXI, VI, 7.     [4] *Ibid.*, XXXI, VII, 1.

remedied during the last decade of the third century by Diocletian. What is so astonishing is that nearly three hundred years
had to elapse before this essential reform was introduced, which
goes to show how conservative soldiers then were–in fact, have
always been. What Diocletian did was to create a regular field
army called the *Comitatenses*, commanded by the Emperor himself. In this the foot-soldiers remained *legiones*, but the cavalry
were called *vexillationes* (banners); and the whole was separated
from the *limitanei* (frontier militia) and *riparienses* (camp garrisons).
Besides these troops, Diocletian created the *palatini*, who replaced
the praetorians. As time went on and disturbances grew more
frequent, large numbers of new bodies were raised, mainly
Moorish, Persian, and German horse. These took the place of the
old legionary cavalry; nevertheless the Roman tactics remained
firmly rooted in the idea that infantry was the decisive arm.

What the strength of Diocletian's army was is not known.
Rough calculations have been made which place the frontier
forces at 250,000 infantry and 110,000 cavalry, supported by a
*Comitatenses* of 150,000 foot and 46,000 horse;[1] a total of well over
half a million men, which seems excessive. Probably it was considerably less, its strength resting more on its increased mobility
than in its numbers; for Diocletian reduced the legion from what
to-day we should call a brigade of some four to six thousand men
to a battalion of one thousand strong, and he fixed the *vexillationes*,
or regiments of horse, at five hundred troopers.

Of tactical ideas and formations, little is discoverable. At the
battle of Mursa, in 351, cavalry proved themselves to be the
decisive arm; but six years later, at Strasbourg, it was the infantry.
But one thing is noticeable, an increasing reliance on the defensive,
due, in all probability, to the trust placed on missile power
(archers, slingers and war engines) instead of on the *arme blanche*.

When the last quarter of the fourth century is reached, the
incursions of plundering hordes of armed men introduced a new
tactical problem, which, as the quotation from Zosimus shows,
Valens was unable to solve by means of his regular army; but
which, nevertheless, was solved to a certain extent by the im-
provisation of bands of light infantry, camp followers, and others
to operate independently. This is to be gathered from Ammianus
when he comments on the reinforcements, under Profuturus and
Trajan, which Valens sent from Armenia to Thrace. He says:

[1] *The Cambridge Medieval History*, vol. 1, p. 45.

When these two generals took the field, and were faced by ambuscades and surprises, instead of dividing their forces into small columns in order "to diminish the enemy's numbers by stealthy and guerilla warfare", they maintained their legionary formations, which "were no match for the countless horde that

23. THE LOWER DANUBE, 378

had taken possession of the mountain heights as well as the plains".[1]

The strength of the Goths lay not only in their numbers and the terror they instilled, but also because thousands of their warriors had served as Roman mercenaries and were far better armed than their ancestors had been in the days of Tacitus. "The rank and file bore iron-bound bucklers, pikes, the short stabbing sword (*sacramasax*), as well as the long cutting sword (*spatha*), and among some races the deadly *francisca*, or battle-axe, which, whether thrown or wielded, would penetrate Roman armour and split the Roman shield."[2] Their method of fighting, like that of

---

[1] Ammianus Marcellinus, xxxi, vii, 2.
[2] *The Art of War in the Middle Ages*, Charles Oman (1924), vol. i, p. 12.

the Huns, and later of Zisca in the fifteenth century and the Boers in the nineteenth, was founded on their wagon-forts, or laagers. Ammianus says that they would form up in circles (masses) with their wagons for a rampart, "as if enclosed in a space between city-walls". From these slow-moving fortresses by a preconcerted signal the predatory bands dispersed for plunder, and on orders from their leaders, "like fire-darts, returned with winged speed to their wagon city (as they themselves called it)."[1] Equally important, the plundering raids were carried out mainly by mounted men; which meant that the Goths had at their disposal a formidable body of cavalry. Their one great tactical weakness lay in their inability to storm walled cities and towns. Fridigern himself once said that "he kept peace with walls",[2] not because he considered their assault to be beneath his dignity, but because he possessed no siege train. Further, so long as the cities remained unconquered, decisive victories were hard to win; it was for this reason that so often an incursion ended in an alliance between friend and foe – the Romans who held the cities and the barbarians who ruled the fields.

When they had cleared the Rhodope country and the line of the Balkans, at length Trajan and Profuturus caught up with the great Gothic laager at a spot named Salices (the "Willows") in the Dobrudja, which shows that the initial phase of their compaign was by no means unsuccessful. There an indecisive battle was fought, which is graphically described by Ammianus Marcellinus. Apparently the Romans were unable to push their attack, because, after some desperate fighting, the Goths fell back behind the rampart formed by their wagons, and for seven days they never once ventured to come forth or show themselves.[3] Next, the Romans attempted to blockade them and starve them out, when the alarming news was received that fresh hordes of barbarians had crossed the Danube. This compelled Saturninus, now in command, to relinquish the siege of the Gothic camp. Thrace was again ravaged and Fridigern was assisted by the Ostrogothic horde of Alatheus and Saphrax as well as by swarms of Huns and Alans, who had been the cause of his exodus. This suggests that, when the year 378 opened, a general agreement had been established between all the nomadic bands. They had sunk their mutual differences, placed themselves under the command of

---

[1] Ammianus Marcellinus, xxxi, vii, 5 and 7.
[2] *Ibid.*, xxxi, vi, 4.                              [3] *Ibid.*, xxxi, viii, 1.

Fridigern and, as a united force, were ready to measure themselves against the might of Eastern Rome.

It would seem that a concentration of the tribes as well as a reported victory of Gratian over the Alemanni, which had aroused the jealousy of Valens, persuaded him to move his court from Antioch to Constantinople, from where he appointed Sebastianus, an Italian general, to succeed Trajan; meanwhile he conciliated his soldiers by distributing a donative, issued extra rations and apparently indulged in a good deal of "courteous talks".

The new Commander-in-Chief was an able general; as Zosimus tells us, "observing the indolence and effeminacy both of the tribunes and soldiers, and that all they had been taught was only how to fly, and to have desire more suitable to women than to men". he picked out 2,000 of the best of them; for "He well knew the difficulty of commanding a multitude of ill-disciplined dissolute men, and that a small number might more easily be reclaimed from their effeminacy".[1] When he had trained them, he set out for Adrianople and occupied it. From there he secretly issued forth at night time, and falling upon a large band of the Goths near the river Maritza, utterly routed it. At once Fridigern took alarm, called in his plundering bands, and made off to gain the open country, where he would not be liable to be straitened for want of provisions, or harassed by secret ambuscades.[2]

This success and the exaggerated reports received from Sebastianus seem to have excited the Emperor to action, for he placed himself at the head of a numerous force "neither unwarlike nor contemptible", and advanced on Adrianople, where he entrenched himself. Next, "Sebastianus sent a request to the Emperor, desiring him to remain where he then was, and not to advance; since it was not easy to bring such a multitude to a regular engagement. He, moreover, observed that it would be better to protract the war in harassing them by ambuscades, until they should be reduced to despair from the want of necessaries, and rather than expose themselves to the misery and destruction of famine, either surrender themselves, or depart from Roman territory and submit to the Huns."[3] But his recent successes in the

---

[1] *The History of Count Zosimus*, p. 106.
[2] Ammianus Marcellinus, XXXI, XI, 5.
[3] *The History of Count Zosimus*, p. 106. Ammianus (XXXI, xii, 6) says that Sebastianus recommended an attack. This seems to run contrary to what we know of the character of that general. Reinforcements under Gratian were on their way, and Richomer, his

field had roused the envy and jealousy of the court eunuchs and those who had lost their command, and it was these men who advised the Emperor to do nothing of the kind, but instead – attack.

Fridigern, either because he feared a pitched battle or wished to delay such action until he had gathered in his bands, sent an embassy to the Emperor suggesting that if he would grant him Thrace, he would agree to a perpetual peace with the Romans. Valens would not consider this proposal, and parking his baggage wagons under the walls of Adrianople, on August 9, 378, he set out, and when he had marched some eight miles, toward noon came in sight of the Gothic laager.

The day was a sweltering one, and it would appear from the somewhat confused account given by Ammianus (Zosimus says practically nothing) that the Romans were already exhausted and straggling badly. The right wing cavalry seems to have been in the van with the bulk of the infantry following, the left wing cavalry in the rear. Apparently, in order to cover the deployment of the legionaries, Valens drew up his right wing cavalry in front. Had Fridigern been ready, obviously now was the time to attack; but he was far from being so, because his main force of cavalry, the Ostrogothic horse, under Alatheus and Saphrax, was away, presumably foraging. Therefore, to gain time for their return, he did two things; first, he resorted to his former ruse and sent ambassadors to Valens "to ask peace"; and secondly, he set fire to the crops "by burning faggots and fuel" in order still further to delay the deployment of the Romans. In any case we are told "that both men and cattle were suffering from extreme hunger" which must also have meant thirst. Unfortunately for him, Valens fell into the trap; in fact conditions forced him into it. Tactically it was no easy task to storm the laager, not only because innumerable missiles would be hurled from it, but because such an operation meant the breaking up of the rigid infantry lines, and once in disorder they would be at the mercy of the Gothic cavalry. Further, Sozomen tells us that the laager was drawn up "in a very advantageous position",[1] which obviously means on a hill or a rise. Therefore, when the ambassadors appeared, Valens did

ambassador, implored Valens to wait a little while for him, and not rashly to face the danger before him single-handed. But this he refused to do, "in order that Gratian might not have a share in the victory" which, his eunuchs, and others, fancied was already all but won.

[1] Sozomen's *Ecclesiastical History*, trans. E. Walford (1855), VI, 40.

not reject their overtures, but hoping to gain time to complete his deployment–assuming that he was not a complete fool–he pretended to be offended at the lowness of their rank, and informed them that if Fridigern wished to make a lasting peace he must send him nobles of sufficient dignity.[1]

Nothing could have better suited the Gothic chieftain, when suddenly the unexpected happened. As Valens's ambassador, on his way to parley with Fridigern, approached the laager, his undisciplined escort of Iberian archers opened fire on it and then beat a hasty retreat. Most unfortunately for Valens, at that very moment Alatheus and Saphrax returned and with them a battalion of Alans. Infuriated at what had taken place and seeing the still straggling columns in the plain below them in the process of forming up, the Alans descended from the mountains "like a thunderbolt. . . ."[2] "Then the lines of battle [the Ostrogothic horse and the Roman right wing cavalry] dashed together like beaked ships, pushing each other back and forth in turn, and tossed about by alternate movements like waves at sea." Meanwhile the Roman left wing cavalry had advanced up to the wagons, with the intent to push on still farther, were they adequately supported. But as the right wing had been pushed back in rout, the left flank of the left wing was uncovered, and its men were so pressed upon by the superior numbers of the enemy that they were overwhelmed and beaten down, "like the ruin of a vast rampart".[3]

The whole of the Roman cavalry had now been driven from the field and the infantry were left unsupported. Apparently they were still forming up, because, when the Gothic cavalry turned on them, "the different companies became so huddled together that hardly anyone could pull out his sword, or draw back his arm, and because of clouds of dust the heavens could no longer be seen, and echoed with frightful cries. Hence the arrows whirling death from every side always found their mark with fatal effect, since they could not be seen beforehand nor guarded against."[4]

It was now, so it would appear, that Fridigern launched his infantry horde from the laager, which, as Ammianus says, trampled down horse and man, and left no spot to which the Romans could fall back to deploy. Further, the latter were so closely packed that it was impossible for them to escape by forcing

[1] Ammianus Marcellinus, XXXI, xii, 13.  [2] Ibid., XXXI, xii, 17.
[3] Ibid., XXXI, xiii, 2.  [4] Ibid., XXXI, xiii, 2.

a way through their enemy. Thus the battle became a frenzied slaughter. . . . "Then you might see the barbarian towering in his fierceness, hissing or shouting, fall with legs pierced through, or his right hand cut off, sword and all, or his side transfixed, and still, in the last gasp of life, casting round him defiant glances." At length the ground was covered with streams of blood; men slipped this way and that and were even killed by their own weapons, until "the whole scene was discoloured with the hue of dark blood, and wherever men turned their eyes heaps of slain met them, they trod upon the bodies of the dead without mercy".[1]

When the rout of the main force of his infantry was complete, Valens withdrew to some reserve battalions not yet engaged, which stood firm until the superior numbers of the enemy became wholly irresistible, and as night fell, among a crowd of common soldiers, he was mortally wounded. How he died is uncertain, but the most probable story is that he was carried to a peasant's cottage in the neighbourhood, which was strongly built, and that, because its garrison of desperate men refused to surrender, the Goths, quite unaware that it sheltered the Emperor, fired it, and all but one man, who leapt from a window, perished in the flames.[2]

Besides the Emperor, many illustrious men fell in this disastrous defeat: Trajan, Sebastianus, thirty-five tribunes, many captains of battalions, the Master of the Horse, the High Steward, a former Commander-in-Chief, and two-thirds of the entire army, about 40,000 men.

On several occasions in her history Rome had suffered as overwhelming a disaster, yet never so decisive a one; for the battle of Adrianople, like that of Gaugamela, was an epoch-making conflict. It was far more than a second Cannae. "The Empire rocked to its foundations", writes Professor Martin Bang. "Sheer panic fell upon all that bore the name of Rome. The power and glory of the Empire seemed stamped into the dust by the barbarian hordes. The struggle between Rome and the Teutons which we have followed through five centuries was drawing to a close. The battle

[1] Ammianus, xxxi, xiii, 3–6.
[2] *Ibid.*, xxxi, xiii, 14–15. Zosimus (p. 107) gives a similar ending, and so do Sozomen (vi, 40) and Theodoret (*History of the Church*, Bonn edit., 1854, iv, 36). The last mentioned writer, a Christian and Bishop of Cyrus, says that Valens did not take part in the battle, but instead "remained in a village waiting the issue" and there "perished in the flames". This of course is a piece of anti-Arian propaganda—Valens was an Arian.

of Adrianople introduces the last act of the great drama, the most pregnant with consequences which the history of the world has ever seen."[1]

This great battle clearly showed: (1) that valour remained the first requisite in shock warfare, and that a return to barbaric vigour was inevitable unless a new moral inspiration could be discovered; and (2) that the old tactics of phalanx and legion had exhausted their virility, therefore a new technique was required. It introduced a new cycle in the art of war. Hitherto infantry normally had been the decisive arm, and when they relied upon shock weapons, they had little to fear from cavalry as long as they maintained their order. But the increasing use of missiles carried with it an unavoidable loosening and disordering of the ranks. The old shield-wall began to be replaced by a firing-line, and because archers and slingers cannot easily combine shield with bow or sling, and as the range of these weapons is strictly limited, and, further still, because they are all but useless in wet weather, opportunity for the cavalry charge steadily increased. The problem was how to combine missile-power with security against cavalry, a problem which was only partially solved by the introduction of the socket-bayonet in the late seventeenth century, and not finally until the percussion cap was invented during the early nineteenth, for it permitted the musket to be fired irrespective of the weather.

In order to appreciate what this battle accomplished, it is necessary briefly to review the events of the next thirty years. Directly the slaughter was ended, the Gothic horde moved upon Adrianople and blockaded the city. But their cavalry proved useless, for they were met by missiles fired from behind walls, which even when thrown at random among so vast a crowd, could not fall without effect.[2] Therefore they abandoned the siege and marched to Perinthus (Heraclea in Thrace) and a little later invested Constantinople. As it was quite impossible for them to storm the capital of the East, they moved through Thrace, Moesia, and Illyricum, devastated and plundered the country, and finally halted at the foot of the Julian Alps. What next happened is unknown—no more battles are recorded. Fridigern died in 380 and Athanaric the next year; after which the Emperor Theodosius (378–395) offered the devastated districts of Thrace

[1] *The Cambridge Medieval History*, vol. I, p. 217.
[2] Ammianus Marcellinus, xxxi, xv, 10.

to their followers on condition that they furnished soldiers for the imperial army.

All seems to have run smoothly until 390, when Alaric, a prince of the Visigoths, then about twenty years of age, broke the peace by again ravaging Thrace. Apparently his rebellion was a brief one; for no further trouble seems to have occurred until 395, when, on the death of Theodosius, a general rising took place, not so much of the Gothic tribes but of the Roman army, which was now, from man to officer, almost entirely composed of Goths. Alaric marched along the coast of Macedonia and Thessaly, entered Boeotia and Attica, seized the Piraeus, forced the capitulation of Athens, and then "broke like a torrent" upon Corinth, Argolis, and Sparta. Thus the final years of the fourth century found the Eastern Empire in complete chaos and definitely separated from the Western.

With the opening of the new century there began for the West what had been suffered in the East. In 401, Alaric left Epirus and marched on Aquileia, and Honorius (395–423), the Western Emperor, sent Stilicho[1] to beat him back. Forced to abandon the siege of Milan, on April 6, 402, Alaric was brought to battle at Pollentia (Pollenza). The engagement was indecisive, and Alaric withdrew unmolested.

In 405, yet another invader, Radagaisus, far the most savage of all past or present enemies of Rome,[2] appeared at the head of an immense horde of Ostrogoths, Vandals, Alans, and Quadi; but they seem to have been rapidly disposed of by Stilicho, for he surrounded them in the valleys of the Apennines about Faesulae (Fiesole) and starved many to death. Next year hordes of Vandals crossed the Rhine at Mainz, swept over Gaul, where they occupied Trèves, Rheims, Tournai, Arras, Amiens, Paris, Orleans, Tours, Bordeaux, and Toulouse, but were unable to break through the fortified passes of the Pyrenees. Simultaneously the Alemanni conquered Worms, Speyer, and Strasbourg, while revolution swept Britain. In the midst of all this anarchy, Stilicho, the only man who might have saved the Western Empire for a time, was put to death by Honorius on August 23, 408. "So died", says Zosimus, "the man who was more moderate than any other who bore rule in that time."[3]

---

[1] Stilicho was the son of a Vandal captain and, under Honorius, was the real ruler of the West.

[2] Orosius, *Seven Books of History against the Pagans* (trans. I. W. Raymond, 1936), VII, 37.          [3] *The History of Count Zosimus*, p. 160.

At length Alaric's opportunity came. He marched to Aquileia, pushed on to Cremona where he crossed the river Po, passed Ravennæ, now the residence of Honorius, and proceeded to Rome. He blockaded the Tiber, cut off the supplies of African corn, and finally was bought off by the Senate with 5,000 pounds weight of gold, 30,000 of silver, 4,000 silken tunics, 3,000 hides dyed scarlet and 3,000 pounds of pepper. Thus ended the First Gothic siege of The City, "a siege in which no swords were crossed, no blood drawn. Famine was the only weapon used by Alaric."[1]

Two years later he again besieged Rome, withdrew and then lay siege to it for a third time. Again a terrible famine swept away thousands, when, on August 24, 410, the Salarian Gate, half a mile from the Baths of Diocletian, was treacherously opened, and Rome was sacked. Thus, in the unheroic and simple words of Orosius, the dream of Alexander faded away into the twilight of the Dark Ages: *Adest Alaricus, trepidam Romam obsidet, turbat, irrumpit* ("Alaric appeared before trembling Rome, laid siege, spread confusion and broke into the city").[2]

Of what happened little has been recorded other than that, before he entered the city, Alaric gave orders that all Christian edifices should be left uninjured, and that right of asylum in the basilicas of St. Peter and St. Paul should be respected. These orders would appear to have been obeyed. At the time, St. Jerome was in his cell at Bethlehem, when "a terrible rumour from the west was brought to him", and as he heard it he exclaimed: "To quote a common proverb, I well nigh forgot my own name." Also, at this time, St. Augustine was at Hippo (Bona) in Numidia, and the news of the fall stimulated him to write his greatest work, for he says in his "Retractations": "Rome, meanwhile, by the invasion of the Goths, under their King Alaric, was overthrown with the crash of a mighty slaughter. . . . Wherefore, I, inflamed with zeal for the Lord's house, determined to write a treatise on The City of God."

---

[1] *Italy and Her Invaders*, Thomas Hodgkin (1880), vol. i, p. 347.
[2] Orosius, vii, 39.

# The wandering of the nations

The Wandering of the Nations, or what the Germans call the *Völkerwanderung*, began, as we have seen, with the crossing of the Danube by the Goths in 376, an incursion definitely caused by the westerly advance of the Huns from the region of the Volga. But whether the Huns were also responsible for setting in motion the second wave of Teutonic peoples which swept over the Rhine in 406, though not known, seems highly probable. Yet even had they nothing to do with it, it was an inevitable event, for since the days of Tacitus the Germans had not only increased in numbers, but the small tribes, which had existed in his day, had been replaced by large groupings of tribes under recognized leaders. Added to this "the Roman population", writes Sir Ernest Barker, "had decayed for century after century, and the land had gone steadily out of cultivation, until nature herself seemed to have created the vacuum into which, in time, she inevitably attracted the Germans", and ". . . when the barrier finally broke, the flood came as no cataclysm but as something which was almost in the nature of things". Further, the invaders did not come as actual enemies, but, nominally, as *foederati* to defend the Empire against their like, and, once enlisted as such they were able to establish a legal claim to remain within the Empire. Next, when they had been armed and equipped, they gained the power to elect their own puppet emperors, and, lastly, to establish kingdoms of their own.

Thus it came about that in the hundred years of the Wandering (376–476) the Western Empire was digested into a number of independent kingdoms. It did not so much collapse as vanish in them, bit by bit as each was established. Why the Eastern Empire did not suffer a similar transformation was because its emperors discovered in the virile and warlike Isaurians a substitute for barbaric auxiliaries. Thanks to these people, who inhabited the country north of the Taurus, between Pisidia and Cilicia, the existence of the Eastern Empire was prolonged for centuries after the Western had disappeared.

In 407, Constantine, a common soldier in Britain, was proclaimed emperor and crossed to Gaul. Two years later Gerontius, his general in Spain, revolted against him, and, in order to strengthen himself against Constantine, he invited the Vandals and their allies to cross the Pyrenees. Shortly after they had entered Spain, yet another wave of barbarians, this time of Franks, Alemanni, and Burgundians, occupied the region west of the Rhine. The Franks were divided into two groups, the Salians who seized the lands between the Scheldt and Meuse, and the Ripuarians between the Moselle and Rhine.

At the time of this third incursion, Constantius, the new Master of the Troops, arrived in Gaul to defend the cause of Honorius. In 411 he overwhelmed both Constantine and Gerontius, after which he turned against the Franks, Alemanni, and Burgundians, who meanwhile had elected a puppet emperor named Jovinus to give legal colour to their position in Gaul. But no sooner had Constantius done so, than he learnt that Ataulf (Adolphus), who had succeeded Alaric in 410, had left Italy for Gaul and had carried away with him Placidia, the sister of Honorius. Infuriated at this, for his intention long had been to marry Placidia so that he might secure the succession on the death of Honorius, who was childless, he set out after Ataulf, who had seized Toulouse and occupied Narbonne. When he failed to take Marseilles, which was held by Boniface (the future Count of Africa), Ataulf withdrew and in 414 married Placidia. In retaliation Constantius blockaded the Gallic ports with his fleet to bring Ataulf to submission by cutting off his African supplies. To escape starvation, Ataulf crossed into Spain, and at Barcelona Placidia gave birth to a son, who was named Theodosius. Soon after the child died, and in 415 Ataulf was assassinated and succeeded by a chieftain called Wallia.

In order to feed his men, Wallia decided to cross to Africa; but when it put to sea his fleet was wrecked in a storm, his people were reduced to starvation, and in 416 he was compelled to seek peace with Constantius. The terms were agreed: for 600,000 measures of corn he surrendered Placidia, became Rome's ally and promised to recover Spain from the Vandals, Alans, and Sueves.

In 417 Constantius at length achieved his aim, and, much against her will, married Placidia, and was raised to the status of an Augustus. She bore to him two children, Honoria and Valentinian. Meanwhile Wallia defeated the Vandals and their allies and drove them into the north-west corner of Spain, the present-day Galicia. For this he was rewarded by permission to establish his people in Aquitania and to occupy Toulouse. This was the first time the Imperial Government, of its own accord, gave a settlement to a Teutonic people within the Empire under their own king.

In 421 Constantius died and was succeeded by Castinus as Master of the Troops. Soon after, Honorius and Placidia quarrelled and two parties were formed in Italy, one under Boniface which supported Placidia and the barbarians, and the other under Castinus which favoured Honorius and the Romans.

This year or in the following, Theodoric I, who had succeeded Wallia in 418, fulfilled the agreement he had made with Constantius to send a contingent to the Roman army which was operating under Castinus against the Vandals. But in the middle of the battle which followed it suddenly changed sides, fell upon the Roman rear and routed the Romans. About the same time, Boniface, who was now in Africa, revolted from Honorius and Placidia and her two children were banished to the court of Theodosius II (408–450), at Constantinople, and were there when, in 423, Honorius died. As her son was then only four years old, she became virtual regent. She returned with him to Italy in 424, and in the following year the boy was proclaimed emperor and became Valentinian III (425–455).

The death of Honorius gave rise to a new personality, Aetius, who was to dominate events during the next thirty years. He was a Roman from Silistria, born about 390, and had been a hostage once with Alaric and once with the Huns, who by 423 formed the bulk of the armies of the Empire, for the German recruiting grounds were now largely closed. On Valentinian's accession he was made *comes* (count) and given the command of Gaul. In 425 he marched against Theodoric, who was then besieging Arles, the key city of the Rhône valley. He forced him to raise the siege, made peace with him, and granted him full sovereignty over the provinces originally assigned to Wallia.

Three years later the Vandals, under Gaiseric, born about 400 and one of the most famous figures in the Wandering of the Nations, began to move from Spain to Africa; the immediate occasion was furnished by a revolt of the Moors. In May, 429, the main body, some 80,000 people, crossed from Julia Traducta, now Tarifa, to find the final home of their wandering.

Because this new invasion threatened the main Italian corn

supply, the Romans came to terms with Count Boniface; yet in spite of the resistance he put up against the Vandals, he was beaten back and in 437 Hippo was occupied by them. Again defeated, Boniface was summoned to Italy by Placidia to act as a counterpoise to Aetius, who meanwhile had recovered Gaul from the Franks and had become, like Caesar before him, the leading man in the West.

At once a struggle began between the two, in which Aetius was defeated near Ravenna, now the Imperial capital of the West. He sought refuge with his old friends the Huns and was well received by their king Rua or Rugila. Shortly after his victory Boniface died and his son-in-law Sebastian took his place.

Boniface now out of the way, in 433 Aetius returned with an army of Huns and compelled Placidia to dismiss Sebastian and to admit himself to the dignity of *Patricius* (Patrician), a title introduced by Constantine the Great.[1] Hence onward until his death in 454 he ruled the West. His first action was to come to terms with the Vandals by ceding Mauretania and part of Numidia to Gaiseric; his second was to march against the Burgundians, who were attacking the lands round Metz and Trèves; and his third, to repress a jacquerie of revolted peasants and slaves (the Baguadae) which then raged in many districts, and to drive back the Visigoths who were attacking Narbonne. In all three operations he was successful, and ended his campaign in 442 by making peace with the Goths and planting a colony of Alans near Orléans in order to guard the valley of the Loire against them.

In spite of the peace, the Vandals paid little attention to it and continued their piratical operations in the western and central Mediterranean. On October 19, 439, they unexpectedly captured Carthage, which they at once adopted as their main naval base. Next, in 440, they ravaged Sicily, and Theodosius sent a fleet against them. As he did not wish to be involved with the Eastern Empire while raiding the Western, Gaiseric, the outstanding diplomatist of his age, fell back on his now considerable wealth and by its judicious use induced the Huns on the Danube to attack the Eastern Empire. Once threatened in the north, Theodosius recalled his fleet. At this juncture the state of the Western Empire was as follows.

---

[1] At first, the holder ranked next after the emperor and the consul. Later the title became synonymous with "vice-regent", and in the days of Ammianus Marcellinus, a *patricius* was regarded as "father of the emperor" or "paternal guardian of the state" (xxix, ii, 2).

Gaul had been recovered, but was sown with barbaric settlements: the Franks in the north; the Visigoths in the south-west; the Burgundians in Savoy; the Alemanni on the upper Rhine; the Alans at Valence and Orléans; and the Bretons in the north-west. Africa had been lost completely and so had Britain which, since the great raid of 406 and 407 across the Rhine, virtually had been severed from the Empire. Lastly, in Spain the Sueves had found a leader in a chieftain called Rechiar, who in 439 took Merida and in 441 Seville, and then conquered the provinces of Baetica (Andalusia) and Cartagena. All that was left to the Romans in Spain was its north-eastern corner, the present Catalonia. Besides these many losses, the diocese of Illyricum had been partly ceded to the Eastern Empire and partly occupied by the Huns.

CHAPTER 10

# The Battle of Châlons or of the Mauriac Plain, 451

The Huns with whom, in or about the year 440, Gaiseric opened negotiations, were a nomadic people of Turanian stock, and in their conflicts with the Romans and German tribes is again introduced the clash between the wagon folk and the city dwellers. Though, so far as war is concerned, the Huns at first carried all before them, in the end they were overwhelmed, not so much by the arms of the western peoples as by their lack of civilization. In at least one respect their story is that of the Hyksos over again, for in both incursions—as in centuries to come was to be repeated in the Arab, Seljuk, and Mongol invasions—the dominant factor which led to their initial successes was the horse.

Who the Huns were and where they originated have not yet been determined. In the middle of the eighteenth century M. Deguignes,[1] a French Chinese scholar, conceived that they might be identified with the Hiong-nu (or Hsiung-nu),[2] who at the time of their supremacy inhabited the region between the Altai, Kuen-lun and Khingan mountains, and to limit whose depredations, in 258 B.C., the Emperor Hwang-te built the Great Wall of China. But whether this is so is of little consequence here, for what matters in this chapter is their coming and its influence on western history. Further, what caused their westerly advance against the Alans, another people of Turanian stock, which precipitated the Gothic invasions of 376, is also unknown. Some think that it may have been due to the epoch of increasing aridity which set in in central Asia during the first few centuries of the Christian era and which culminated in about A.D. 500.[3] Others believe that it was caused by the destruction of irrigation canals by nomadic raiders, for as Mr. T. Peisker points out: In order to make a whole oasis liable to tribute "they need only seize the

---

[1] In his *Histoire Générale des Huns, des Turcs, des Mongols, et des autres Tartares Occitentaux, avant et depuis Jésus Christ jusqu à present* (1756–8), 4 vols. See also appendix 6 of Bury's edition of Gibbon's *Decline and Fall*.
[2] The word means "common slaves".
[3] See *The Pulse of Asia*, E. Huntington (1907), p. 359.

main canal; and the nomads often blindly plundered and destroyed everything. A single raid was enough to transform hundred of oases into ashes and desert. The nomads moreover not only ruined countless cities and villages of Central Asia, but also denuded the steppe land itself, and promoted drift-sand by senseless uprooting of trees and bushes for the sake of firewood."[1] Judging from subsequent nomadic inundations, this second reason would seem the more probable. Gibbon thinks likewise, and when considering the violence of the Mongols, he writes: "... from the Caspian to the Indus they ruined a tract of many hundred miles which was adorned with the habitations and labour of mankind, and five centuries have not been sufficient to repair the ravages of four years."[2] As we shall see, when the Huns came into contact with Latin civilization, because they could give it nothing, they could only take from it, and, in fact, *had* to in order to survive alongside it. Had this process of a lower civilization living on a higher endured long enough, the latter would have perished utterly, and Roman Europe would have become a second Khorasan.

Like all wagon folk the Huns were wanderers, and in consequence civilization was all but unknown to them. For unnumbered generations they had driven their herds and flocks – cattle, horses, goats, and sheep – over the steppes of central and southern Siberia; yet so primitive were their handicrafts that it would appear they were unable to weave, and, therefore, make woollen garments. Ammianus Marcellinus, who lived and wrote in the days of the Emperor Valens, has left us the following contemporary description of them:

"They all have compact, strong limbs and thick necks and are so monstrously ugly and misshapen, that one might take them for two-legged beasts or for the stumps, rough-hewn into images, that are used in putting sides [adorning] to bridges. . . . Roaming at large amid the mountains and woods, they learn from the cradle to endure cold, hunger and thirst. . . . They dress in linen cloth or in the skins of field-mice sewn together. . . . They are not at all adapted to battles on foot, but they are almost glued to their horses, which are hardy, it is true, but ugly. . . . They are all without fixed abode, without hearth, or law, or settled mode of life, and keep roaming from place to place, like fugitives, accompanied

[1] *The Cambridge Medieval History*, vol. I, p. 327.
[2] *The Decline and Fall of the Roman Empire*, vol. VII, p. 10.

by the wagons in which they live. . . . In truces they are faithless and unreliable, strongly inclined to sway to the motion of every breeze of new hope that presents itself, and sacrificing every feeling to the mad impulse of the moment. Like unreasoning beasts, they are utterly ignorant of the difference between right and wrong.''[1]

Like all true nomads, agriculture was unknown to the Huns; therefore the linen garments, mentioned by Marcellinus, must, like many other things they possessed, have been obtained through barter. Of internal trade there can have been practically none, because the standard of living was so low that each family group could supply its own needs. Their external trade consisted in bartering horses, meat, furs, and slaves for the produce, arms, and manufactures of the settled agricultural peoples with whom they came into contact.

In order to subsist, it is clearly impossible that they can have wandered about in enormous hordes, if only because as they had to live upon their herds and flocks, these demanded extensive grazing grounds. Probably, like many other nomadic people, they were split into patriarchal groups of from fifty to a hundred persons, each group moving over a comparatively wide front from grazing ground to grazing ground. Their society was communistic and, according to Marcellinus, though the groups were under paternal leaders, whom he calls "important men", the whole had no king.[2] The high figures, so frequently quoted by classical and ecclesiastical historians, were undoubtedly exaggerated by the rapidity with which the Huns moved and the terror their uncouthness and lack of resemblance to Europeans instilled. According to Jordanes, the Goths believed that the Huns were the offspring of sorceresses and "the unclean spirits, who beheld them as they wandered through the wilderness, bestowing their embraces upon them and begat this savage race, which dwelt at first in the swamps, a stunted, foul and puny tribe, scarcely human and having no language save one which bore but slight resemblance to human speech". He adds:

"For by the terror of their features they inspired great fear in those whom perhaps they did not really surpass in war. They made their foes flee in horror because their swarthy aspect was fearful, and they had, if I may call it so, a sort of shapeless lump, not a head, with pin-holes rather than eyes. Their hardihood is

---

[1] Ammianus Marcellinus, xxxi, ii, 2–11.        [2] *Ibid.*, xxxi, ii, 7.

evident in their wild appearance, and they are beings who are cruel to their children on the very day they are born. For they cut the cheeks of the males with a sword, so that before they receive the nourishment of milk they must learn to endure wounds. Hence they grow old beardless and their young men are without comeliness, because a face furrowed by the sword spoils by its scars the natural beauty of a beard. They are short in stature, quick in bodily movement, alert horsemen, broad shouldered, ready in the use of bow and arrow, and their firm-set necks are ever erect in pride. Though they live in the form of men, they have the cruelty of wild beasts."[1]

Two generations after their first appearance, though the terror they instilled continued to paralyse the Romans, the ease with which they were able to extract tribute from their neighbours brought them to a standstill in the Danubian lands; when their social order rapidly began to change. In or about 430 they were no longer an amorphous mass of family groups, but instead a confederacy under a single ruler, Rua—the friend and protector of Aetius—who was sufficiently powerful to force a treaty on the Eastern Romans, by the terms of which Theodosius II (408–450) undertook to pay him a yearly tribute of 350 pounds of gold. When he died in 433, Rua was succeeded by his two nephews Attila and Bleda. Of the latter nothing is known other than that, in 445, he was murdered by his brother, of whom Jordanes and Priscus have left the following vivid description. He was of short stature, his eyes were small and bead-like, his nose snub and his skin swarthy. His head was large, his beard scanty, and his hair was already sprinkled with white. He was covetous, vain, superstitious, cunning, excessively arrogant, and cruel. Yet in his way of living he was markedly simple. As Priscus informs us, while "the guests drank from cups of gold and silver, Attila had only a wooden cup; his clothes . . . were only distinguished from the other barbarians because they were of one colour, and were without ornaments; his sword, the cords of his shoes, the reins of his horse, were not like those of the other Scythians, decorated with plates of gold or precious stones".[2]

---

[1] *The Gothic History of Jordanes*, trans. Charles Christopher Mierow (1915), xxiv, pp. 85–87. Jordanes wrote his history about 100 years after the events recorded in this chapter and many of his statements are epic tales.

[2] "Priscus' Narrative of the Embassy sent in 449 to Attila, by Theodosius the Younger, Emperor of the East", quoted from *The History of Civilization* by F. Guizot (1856), vol. II, p. 430. See also J. B. Bury, *History of the Later Roman Empire* (1923), vol. I, pp. 279–288.

Attila's rule over the Confederacy he inherited was absolute, and though when he appeared among his people they received him with shouts of applause, their respect for him was based solely upon fear, for all stood in terror of him. "He realized more clearly than any of his predecessors", writes Mr. Thompson, "that if all the tribes could be united under an unquestioned and absolute leader, the Huns would form an unparalleled instrument for the exploitation of the peoples of central Europe. . . . Instead of relying on the unruly and divided tribal chiefs, he based his power on vassals . . . who were bound to him personally by an inviolable allegiance without the handicap of tribal obligations."[1]

When, in 499, Theodosius sent his famous embassy under Priscus to Attila, the Huns had ceased to be a wholly nomadic people and had become "a parasitic community of marauders. . . . Instead of herding cattle they had now learned the more profitable business of herding men. Sharp differences of wealth have appeared among them, though not perhaps differences of class. Their society could only be maintained as long as Attila was able to supply the mass of his men with the necessities of life and a few luxuries. . . ."[2] This change may be gathered from Priscus's narrative, for he informs us that Attila no longer lived in a tent or a wagon, but in a log-hut of considerable size, surrounded by a palisade. In this hut he received the Roman ambassador Maximin, and welcomed him with the appellation of "shameless beast". A feast next followed which is minutely described. Further, Priscus tells us that Attila married his daughter Esca–"the laws of the Scythians allow this"–and that when the embassy put up at a certain village "one of the wives of Bleda, sent us nourishment and beautiful women. This among the Scythians is looked upon as an honour." In fact, the Hunnish customs were not far removed from those which are still to be met with in certain regions of central Asia.

As a soldier, Attila was no more than a plunderer. Hodgkin says of him: "He made war on civilization and on human nature, not on religion, for he did not understand it enough to hate it."[3] Of constructive genius he shows none, in spite of the fact that Priscus tells us that he believed himself destined to be lord of the whole world. The extent of his empire is but vaguely known. Its

[1] *A History of Attila and the Huns*, E. A. Thompson (1948), pp. 208–209.
[2] *Ibid.*, p. 177.
[3] *Italy and Her Invaders*, Thomas Hodgkin (1880), vol. II, p. 130.

central grazing ground appears to have covered modern Hungary and Transylvania, and the rest stretched from Gaul eastward into the unknown.

Though the mode of life of the nomad was primitive in the extreme, as Ellis H. Minns points out, it possessed certain military advantages over that of the village or city dweller, and so fitted him better for war. "His life is laborious and dangerous", writes Minns; "it requires skill, courage, endurance, but he is exempt from that continuous back-breaking toil which bends the hoeman to mother earth. He has change of scene, wide spaces, and a sense of freedom. His leaders are used to problems of transport and the management of large bodies of men. The whole people is a ready-made army, easily marshalled, self-supporting, capable of sudden attacks, of long-distance raids. In the steppe the nomad is always on a war footing, prepared to extend his pastures at another tribe's expense, or to defend his own. . . . But whether for attack or defence the tribe must be well led; and the leader must have absolute authority."[1]

The Huns' conquests were not due to superiority of numbers, but to the high mobility of small bands of horse-archers who could concentrate rapidly at any given point, quickly disperse and re-concentrate at another. Though, on their first appearance, their ponies were no match for the Roman horses, they soon acquired the latter and the disadvantage rapidly disappeared.

When on the war path, the bands of mounted men, moving on a wide front, were followed by their families and wagons–travelling fortresses–which could quickly be drawn up into a defensive laager. Though the bands were extremely mobile, the wagon columns were slow-moving and frequently must have been immobile, expecially in the hilly and wooded country of western Europe. Therefore it must often have happened that the fighting horde–the bands in total–was separated from its base, and when this occurred the horde had to keep moving in order to live, and as movement depended on forage, not only had the horde to split into groups, but campaigning during the winter months was normally not attempted. It was for this reason that Emperor Leo the Wise laid it down that Scythians and Huns should be attacked during February and March, when their horses are weakened by the hardships of winter.

[1] "The Art of the Northern Nomads", Ellis H. Minns, *Proceedings of the British Academy*, 1942, pp. 51–52.

To overcome the difficulties of rationing, the Huns, like the Mongols in the twelfth and thirteenth centuries, lived on their horses. In Genghis Khan's army, Marco Polo informs us that each Mongol was obliged to take with him eighteen horses and mares, so that he might have mare's milk and horse's blood for food and drink.[1] Their steeds were not only mounts and remounts, but self-replenishing canned food.[2] With this may be compared a remark made by T. E. Lawrence on operations in Arabia: "Our cards were speed and time, not hitting power. The invention of bully-beef had profited us more than the invention of gunpowder, but gave us strategical rather than tactical strength. . . ."[3]

From this self-supplying base a cyclonic strategy was developed; operations took the form of whirlwind advances and retirements. Whole districts were laid waste and entire populations annihilated, not only in order to establish a heat of terror which would evaporate opposition, but also to leave the rear clear of all hostile manpower and so to facilitate withdrawals. The tactics adopted may be defined as "ferocity under authority". Fury, surprise, elusiveness, cunning and mobility, and not planning, method, drill and discipline were its elements. "Try twice, turn back the third time" is as much a Hunnish as a Turkoman proverb; and as Amédée Thierry points out: "The nomads, unlike ourselves, do not consider flight a dishonour. Considering booty of more worth than glory, they fight only when they are certain of success. When they find their enemy in force they evade him to return when the occasion is more opportune." Their master weapon was the bow, mainly made of horn as the steppes were treeless. Its value largely lay in the noiselessness of the arrows, which were tipped with bone. But in close-quarter fighting they relied on the sword "regardless of their own lives; and while the enemy are guarding against wounds from the sabre-thrusts, they throw strips of cloth plaited into nooses [lassos] over their opponents and so entangle

---

[1] See the *Book of Ser Marco Polo*, trans. Colonel Sir Henry Yule (3rd edit., 1903), vol. I, p. 254.

[2] "The principal food consists of milk-products—not of the fresh milk itself, which is only taken by children and the sick. A special Turko-Tartar food is *yogurt*, prepared with leaven from curdled milk. The Mongols also ate butter—the more rancid the more palatable—dripping with dirt, and carried without wrapping in their heavy greasy coat-pockets. From mare's milk, which yields no cream, *kumiz* (Kirghiz), *tshegan* (Mongolish) is fermented, an extremely nutritious drink which is good for consumption, and from which by itself life can be sustained" (*The Cambridge Medieval History*, vol. I, p. 339).

[3] *Seven Pillars of Wisdom*, T. E. Lawrence (1935), p. 196.

them that they fetter their limbs and take from them the power of riding or walking".[1]

The weakness in their tactics lay in that they could seldom halt in any one place for long, because forage was rapidly exhausted. This and their inability to storm fortresses and walled cities rendered their occupation of any given area impermanent. At Asemus (Osma), twenty miles south of Sistova, in 443, Attila was easily repulsed, and when he started plundering the neighbouring country sallies against him were made from that fortress. In brief, the Hunnish method of fighting, though admirably suited for the steppes of Asia, in the end failed in more civilized and topographically difficult Europe.

The first great incursion of the Huns came in 395. They crossed the frozen Danube and their hordes devasted Dalmatia and Thrace, but their greatest effort was made far away to the east. They passed through the defiles of the Caucasus overran Armenia, devastated Cappadocia and parts of Syria and Cicilia, and laid siege to Antioch and many other cities on the Halys, Cyndus, Orontes, and Euphrates. The terror caused by this extensive raid is vividly described by St. Jerome. "Lo," he writes, "suddenly messengers ran to and fro and the whole East trembled, for swarms of Huns had broken forth from the far distant Maeotis (Sea of Azov) between the icy Tanais (Don) and the monstrous peoples of the Massagetae, where the Gates of Alexander pen in the wild nations behind the rocks of Caucasus. They filled the whole earth with slaughter and panic alike as they flitted hither and thither on their swift horses. . . . They were at hand everywhere before they were expected: by their speed they outstripped rumour, and they took pity neither upon religion nor rank nor age nor wailing childhood."[2]

The next incursion of importance came in 441, immediately after Gaiseric's negotiations with Attila. Again the Huns crossed the Danube and destroyed Viminacium (Kostolacz),[3] Margus, at the mouth of the Morava, Singidunum (Belgrade), Sirmium (Mitrovitz), and many lesser places. This lightning campaign compelled Theodosius to recall his fleet from Sicily and to abandon his projected attack on Gaiseric.

[1] Ammianus Marcellinus, xxxi, ii, 9. See also Sozomen's *Ecclesiastical History*, trans. E. Walford (1855), vii, 26, 8.
[2] Quoted from *A History of Attila and the Huns*, p. 27.
[3] In recent times 100,000 coins, buried at the time of this raid, have been dug out of the site of this city (*ibid.*, p. 80).

In 442 a truce was agreed upon, but as Theodosius refused to hand over to Attila the fugitives demanded by him, in the following year the war was renewed. By occupying Ratiaria (Anzar Palanka), capital of the province of Dacia Ripensis and the base of the Roman fleet on the Danube, Attila secured his rear and then advanced up the valley of the Margus (Morava) and destroyed Naissus. Next he moved up the river Nischava and razed Sardica (Sofia) and Philippopolis to the ground. By-passing Adrianople and Heraclea because they were too strong for him to storm, in the neighbourhood of Constantinople he defeated Theodosius's army under Aspar, an Alan, in a series of battles, and finally exterminated it on the shores of the Dardanelles. These defeats compelled Theodosius to seek peace, which was granted by Attila. The main terms were that all fugitives should be handed over to him, that arrears of tribute, calculated at 6,000 lb. of gold (£280,000), should be paid, and that the annual tribute should be fixed at 2,100 lb. This peace was agreed upon in August, 443.

In 447 Attila again invaded the Eastern Empire, but on what pretext is unknown. When he was about to advance, a series of terrible earthquakes threw down the walls of many Greek cities, and did such extensive damage to the fortifications of Constantinople that at first it appeared that the city was doomed. To protect it, the army of Theodosius advanced to the river Utus (Vid), and though it met with defeat, it would seem to have inflicted such heavy losses on the Huns that, after they had plundered and devastated the land as far south as Thermopylae, Attila thought it better to withdraw.

His rear secured by these incursions, Italy and Gaul lay at his mercy; but as Gaiseric looked upon the former as his private preserves, some time before the spring of 450 he pointed out to Attila how profitable it would be for him to raid the lands of the Visigoths. This suggestion, it would seem, decided the question Attila had for some time been turning over in his mind—namely, how best to attack Gaul? He fell in with Gaiseric's idea, and as he knew that the Visigoths were the inveterate enemies of the Romans, he decided to march against them in the guise of Valentinian's ally, hoping thereby to neutralize Roman opposition. Further, Theodoric and Gaiseric were at loggerheads because Hunneric, Gaiseric's son, had recently repudiated his wife, Theodoric's daughter, and had returned her to her father minus her nose and ears. Therefore, with the Romans neutralized and Gaiseric hostile, Theodoric would be completely isolated.

While this scheming was in progress, on July 26, 450, Theodosius was thrown by his horse, and two days later died of his injuries. He was succeeded by Marcian (450–457) who had married Theodosius's sister Pulcheria, and one of the first acts of the new emperor was to stop paying tribute to the Huns. Enraged by this, Attila sent two embassies, one to Constantinople to demand the resumption of tribute, which was emphatically refused, and the other to Ravenna to make a request relative to an incident which had occurred sixteen years earlier.

In 434, Honoria, Valentinian's sister, when in her seventeenth year, had been seduced by one of her chamberlains and was sent by her mother Placidia in disgrace to Constantinople. She bitterly resented this and in a passion sent a ring to Attila begging him to accept her as his wife. Now that she had returned to Ravenna, the mission of the second embassy was not only to claim her as Attila's bride, but also to demand half the Western Empire as her dowry. No sooner was this demand refused than an event occurred which further widened the breach between Attila and Valentinian. The king of the Ripuarian Franks died and a succession quarrel broke out between his two sons; the elder appealed to Attila for aid and the younger to Aetius. As the latter was well received and adopted by Aetius as his son, it must have become apparent to Attila that he could no longer rely on Aetius's former friendship to maintain Roman neutrality during his projected attack on Gaul; therefore that, before he could deal with Marcian, he must first settle his account with the Western Empire, where he had many supporters among the Bagaudae–again in revolt–where the Visigoths were still hostile to the Romans and Vandals, and where the Ripuarian Franks were in the throes of a civil war. To Attila, Ravenna seemed impotent; but, as so often happens, the unexpected lurked round the corner. Again a single man was destined to change the course of the apparently inevitable: this man was Aetius, called "The last of the Romans".

Renatus Frigeridus has left us the following brief description of him:

"Of middle height, he was manly in appearance and well made, neither too frail nor too heavy; he was quick of wit and agile of limb, a very practised horseman and skilful archer; he was indefatigable with the spear. A born warrior, he was renowned for the arts of peace, without avarice and little swayed by desire, endowed with gifts of the mind, not swerving from his purpose for any kind of evil instigation. He bore wrongs with the utmost patience, and loved labour. Undaunted in danger, he was excelled by none in the endurance of hunger, thirst, and vigil. From his early youth he seemed forewarned of the great power to which he was destined by the fates."[1]

Early in 451, when war between Attila and Aetius became certain, the problem the latter had to consider was: would the kingdoms and tribes of Gaul set aside their quarrels and unite against the invader? Above all, would Theodoric, the most powerful of the kings, join hands with him—his old and persistent enemy? Attila's aim clearly was to prevent this, and being "a subtle man", and one who "fought with craft before he made war",[2] he sent an embassy to both Valentinian and Theodoric. To the former he proclaimed that his invasion was but a continuation of the former campaign of Roman and Hun against the Visigoths, and to the latter he pointed out the danger of an alliance with Rome. Valentinian guessed what Attila had in mind and sent ambassadors to Theodoric to warn him against Attila. Among other things these ambassadors said: "Since you are mighty in arms, give heed to your own dangers and join hands with us in common. Bear aid also to the Empire, of which you hold a part. If you would learn how such an alliance should be sought and welcomed by us, look into the plans of the foe."[3]

While Theodoric hesitated, Attila struck, and, early in 451, he set out from beyond the Rhine and marched westward. His army is reputed to have numbered 500,000 men, a figure obviously exaggerated by panic. It was a conglomerate force, for besides the Huns there were in it Ostrogoths and Gepids, who formed its kernel, as well as Sciri from Riga, Rugi from Pomerania, Franks from the Neckar, Thuringi from Bavaria, and Burgundians from east of the Rhine. His first objective was probably the lands of the Ripuarian Franks, and his next Orléans, for located as it is at the apex of the great bend in the river Loire, once in his hands he could sweep into Gothia (Aquitania).[4]

His army poured through Belgic Gaul in three columns of fighting groups and advanced on a wide front, its right moving

---

[1] *The History of the Franks*, by Gregory of Tours, trans. O. M. Dalton (1927), II, 7 (8), vol. II, pp. 48–49.
[2] Jordanes, XXXVI, p. 103.     [3] *Ibid.*, XXXVI, p. 104.     [4] See map on p. 343.

on Nemetacum (Arras), its left up the Moselle to Mettis (Metz) and its centre on Lutetia Parisiorum (Paris) and Aureliani (Orléans). The devastation was appalling; fire, smoke, murder and rapine swept through the lands. Rheims, Metz, Cambrai, Trèves, Arras, Tongres, Tournai, Thérouanne, Cologne, Amiens, Beauvais, Worms, Maintz and Strasbourg were sacked and burnt. Paris, then but a small town built on an island in the Seine, was saved, so the story goes, by a young girl of the neighbouring village of Nanterre, Genovefa by name, better known to posterity as Saint Geneviève. When its inhabitants in panic were about to flee, she urged them to place their trust in God, and through her simple prayers held them to the city walls.

Meanwhile Valentinian's embassy had failed to win Theodoric over, and the vital question remained – could a coalescence of the tribes be effected? As usual, there was no reserve army in Italy, which the year before had been devastated by a terrible famine. For twenty-five years Aetius had relied upon the Huns to fill his ranks; now they were his enemy, and nothing but blank files met his anxious gaze. He hurried to Gaul and collected together such *feoderati* as were to be found there; apparently checked the impulse of the Alans at Valence to open the gates of that city to Attila; and then went to Arverni (Clermont in Auvergne) and sent to the Gothic court at Tolosa (Toulouse) a Roman Senator named Avitus (the future Emperor of the West, 554–456), who won Theodoric's support.

Meanwhile the hordes of Huns swarmed toward Orléans, in the neighbourhood of which Sangiban, king of the Alans, who had been settled there by Aetius in 442, promised to betray the city to Attila. When a report of this came to the ears of Aetius and Theodoric they set out at top speed to occupy the city before Attila could seize it, but the Huns arrived first and at once besieged the city. According to Gregory of Tours, it was saved through the intercessions of the blessed bishop Anianus (St. Aignan).[1] In the *Vita Aniani*, as quoted by Amédée Thierry, the story is as follows: He visited Aetius and impressed upon him the fact that Orléans could not hold out beyond June 14. Early in May, Attila appeared and for five weeks pounded at the walls with his rams and poured an unceasing hail of arrows into the city. As the walls crumbled, the worthy bishop restored them by perambulating certain holy relics round and round the battle-

[1] Gregory of Tours, ii, 5 (6), vol. ii, p. 46.

ments. Toward the middle of June all seemed lost, when one morning a soldier ascended the highest turret and spied in the distance a tiny cloud of dust—it hid Aetius and Theodoric. As it grew bigger, out of it gleamed the eagles of the legions and the embroidered banners of the Goths. Lastly, the armies met in a fierce fight in the suburbs. "Driven from street to street, beaten down by the stones hurled at them by the inhabitants from the roofs of the houses, the Huns no longer knew what was to become of them, when Attila sounded the retreat. The patrician, Aetius, had not failed in his word; it was the 14th of June. Such was that famous day which in the West saved civilization from total destruction."[1]

Whatever happened, it would appear that Attila experienced a disastrous defeat; for instead of pressing the attack, he and his horde slipped away during the night, passed by Sens and made for the valleys of the Seine and the Aube where the country was open and called "Campania"—Champagne. On the former river, probably in the vicinity of, or at Méry-sur-Seine, he established his rearguard, a horde of Gepids, and retired his main body a little east of it on to "the Catalaunian Plains, which are also called Mauriacian".[2] Against the rearguard Aetius launched a night attack, which must have crushed it out of existence, for, according to Jordanes,[3] his enemy lost in killed and wounded 15,000 men, which though an impossible number, suggests heavy fighting.

Presumably on the next day, June 20,[4] the battle opened.

It would appear from Jordanes that Attila was in no way confident of success, and to shorten the engagement so that he might

[1] *Histoire d'Attila*, Amédée Thierry (1856), vol. I, p. 178.
[2] Jordanes, XXXVI, p. 105. I have adopted the locality as given by Hodgkin (vol. II, pp. 160–162). Professor Bury (*History of the Later Roman Empire*, vol. I, p. 293) places the battlefield near Troyes, 20 miles south of Méry-sur-Seine, and *The Cambridge Medieval History*, vol. I, pp. 280 and 416, says a few miles "in front" (i.e. west) of that city. That the battle was fought in the vicinity of Troyes is quite possible, because from Sens the topographical line of retreat would be up the Vanne valley and then presumably north on Arcis-sur-Aube. But that the battle was fought west of Troyes is unlikely, for Attila would scarcely have halted with his back to the Seine. Really all that can be said is that the battle was fought in the triangle Troyes–Méry–Arcis, because the Mauriac Plain, according to Jordanes, was "in length one hundred *leuva*, as the Gauls express it, and seventy in width". As the *leuva* measured a distance of 1,500 paces, the Mauriac Plain is a district and not a locality, and because Jordanes also calls it the Catalaunian Plain, this has led to the battle being known as "The Battle of Châlons".
[3] Jordanes, XLI, p. 112.
[4] This date is a conjecture. (See Bury, vol. I, pp. 292–293.) As Troyes or Méry-sur-Seine is a little over 100 miles from Orléans, if Attila's retreat was a rapid one, it is possible that the battle was fought on this day. Hodgkin (vol. II, p. 139) says "early in July", and Clinton (*Fasti Romani*, vol. I, p. 642) on September 27.

continue his retreat under cover of night, he did not issue out of his wagon laager until the early afternoon, when he formed up his horde in the following order. He took command of the centre with his bravest troops, with Walamir and the Ostrogoths on the left and Ardaric and the Gepids, etc., on the right. Apparently his idea was to charge his enemy's centre, to drive it back in confusion and then to withdraw to his camp and await nightfall. In his turn Aetius, who presumably realized what was in his opponent's mind, decided upon two outflanking attacks, the aim of which was to cut off the Huns from their laager. He drew up his most unreliable troops, the Alans, under Sangiban, in the centre; placed Theodoric and his Visigoths on his right to oppose the Ostrogoths; and himself took command of the left wing with his Romans.

When the armies were being marshalled, a skirmish for a rising piece of ground took place in which Thorismund, son of Theodoric, threw the Huns' advanced guard back in confusion. Disconcerted by this attack, Attila, according to Jordanes, addressed his troops. He pointed to the Alans and said: "Seek swift victory in that spot. . . . For when the sinews are cut the limbs soon relax, nor can a body stand when you have taken away the bones. . . . No spear shall harm those who are seen to live; and those who are sure to die Fate overtakes even in peace."[1] Their hearts being warmed by these words, "they all dashed into battle".

Next Jordanes writes: "Hand to hand they clashed in battle, and the fight grew fierce, confused, monstrous, unrelenting – a fight whose like no ancient time has ever recorded. There such deeds were done that a brave man who missed this marvellous spectacle could not hope to see anything so wonderful all his life long." A terrific struggle took place along a brook: "Here King Theodorid [Theodoric], while riding by to encourage his army, was thrown from his horse and trampled under foot by his own men, thus ending his days at a ripe old age. . . . Then the Visigoths, separating from the Alani, fell upon the horde of the Huns and nearly slew Attila. But he prudently took flight and strait way shut himself and his companions within the barriers of the camp, which he had fortified with wagons."[2]

Darkness now set in, and with it complete confusion; for Thorismund, we are told, lost his way in the blind night, and thinking that he was rejoining his own men came upon the

[1] Jordanes, xxxix, p. 108.          [2] Ibid., xl, p. 109.

wagons of the enemy; while "Aetius also became separated from his men in the confusion of night and wandered about in the midst of the enemy. Fearing disaster had happened, he went about in search of the Goths. At last he reached the camp of his allies and passed the remainder of the night in the protection of their shields."[1]

"At dawn on the following day, when the Romans saw the fields were piled high with bodies and that the Huns did not venture forth, they thought the victory was theirs, but knew that Attila would not flee from the battle unless overwhelmed by a great disaster. Yet he did nothing cowardly, like one that is overcome, but with clash of arms sounded the trumpets and threatened an attack. He was like a lion pierced by hunting spears, who paces to and fro before the mouth of his den and dares not spring, but ceases not to terrify the neighbourhood by his roaring. Even so this warlike king at bay terrified his conquerors. Therefore the Goths and Romans assembled and considered what to do with the vanquished Attila. They determined to wear him out by a siege, because he had no supply of provisions and was hindered from approaching by a shower of arrows from the bowmen placed within the confines of the Roman camp."[2]

In spite of his roarings and ravings, Attila's situation was a desperate one, and further still he knew it, for in the semi-legendary history of Jordanes, we are told that he considered his position so critical that he constructed a funeral pyre of horses' saddles in the flames of which he determined to hurl himself should the enemy break through. Curious as it may seem, Aetius's situation was almost as perturbing; for shortly after the sun rose Theodoric's body was found and Thorismund was proclaimed king of the Goths.[3]

Apparently it was only then Aetius decided that though he had Attila cornered, it would be wiser to let him escape. Seemingly he did not trust Thorismund, and he feared that, were Attila and his horde annihilated, the Visigoths would at once replace the Huns as the enemies of Rome. This is Jordanes's opinion, for he says:

"But Aetius feared that if the Huns were totally destroyed by the Goths, the Roman Empire would be overwhelmed, and

---

[1] Jordanes, XL, p. 110.  [2] *Ibid.*, XL, p. 110.
[3] In 1842 near the village of Pouan, on the south bank of the Aube and about ten miles from Méry-sur-Seine, the grave of a Gothic warrior was discovered, and from the ornaments found in it M. Peigne Delacourt considered it to be that of Theodoric. See *Italy and Her Invaders*, Thomas Hodgkin, vol. II, 155–159.

urgently advised him (Thorismund) to return to his own dominions to take up the rule which his father had left him. Otherwise his brothers might seize their father's possessions and obtain
the power over the Visigoths."[1] Further, the conditions at
Ravenna were such that Aetius could feel safe only as long as he
was indispensable, and to remain so it was necessary that Attila
should not be crushed completely.[2]

The upshot was that, once Thorismund had marched away,
Attila noticed his empty bivouac, harnessed his wagons and
trekked back to beyond the Rhine. What his losses were is not
known. Jordanes says that 165,000 men were slain on both sides,
not including the 15,000 killed and wounded in the night before
the battle. Idatius puts the number of killed at 300,000. All these
figures are fantastic.

No sooner had Attila returned to his timber palace than again
he claimed Honoria as his bride, and, in the spring of 452, he set
out to invade Italy. He crossed the Julian Alps–from which the
garrisons had been withdrawn–descended upon Aquileia, and
after a long and desperate siege stormed the city and so annihilated
it that even a century later scarcely the vestiges of it remained.
Next he marched into Venetia and he wiped out Julia Concordia,
the luxurious Altinum and Patavium (Padua). As he marched on,
Vicenza, Verona, Brescia, Bergamo, Milan, and Pavia, struck by
the terror of Aquileia, opened their gates, and though their
buildings were not destroyed their inhabitants were either massacred or carried away into captivity. At length, Attila halted on
the Mincio.

Aetius had been caught so completely unaware by this bold
campaign that, unhinged by the prevailing panic, his first thought
was to take Valentinian with him and to abandon Italy. Then,
when he recovered his nerve, he decided to beg peace of Attila.
Once this decision was agreed upon, an embassy consisting of
Pope Leo, Trygetius, an ex-prefect, and Gennadius Avienus,
consul for 450, was sent to the Mincio, and, according to ecclesiastical legend, the dreaded king of kings was vanquished "before
the unarmed successor of St. Peter. . . . The awe of Rome was

[1] Jordanes, XLI, p. 111.
[2] The whole story of Attila's escape is so strange that it may be that Aetius never
lost his way on the night of June 20–21; but instead paid a secret visit to Attila and
arranged the whole incident with him. Otherwise, why did not Attila attack him
after Thorismund left: or why did not Aetius follow up Attila's retirement and cut
off his foragers?

upon him . . . and he was forced incessantly to ponder the question 'What if I conquer like Alaric, to die like him?' "[1] But as Bury points out: "It is unreasonable to suppose that this heathen king would have cared for the thunders or persuasions of the Church."[2]

The true reasons are probably those given by Thompson:[3] that Italy was still suffering from the famine of the previous year, which meant its inseparable companion, pestilence. Further, when Attila entered Italy, Marcian seized the opportunity to send an army under a general, also named Aetius, over the Danube. His enterprise was successful, for he routed the Huns left behind by Attila to protect his base. It was this bold counter-stroke, coupled with lack of supplies and the dread of pestilence, which in all probability compelled Attila to come to terms. His losses at Châlons had been so heavy that he dared not risk a further loss of men.

The next year he took to himself another wife, a girl Ildico (Hilda); drank copiously at the wedding feast and retired to his marriage bed. During the night he was attacked by a violent fit of bleeding at the nose, and lay on his back when the blood poured down his throat and drowned him.

Attila dead, his empire flew to pieces. As soon as he was secretly buried his tribe of sons divided his realm between them, then quarrelled over the divisions and fought each other. While thus engaged, the Ostrogoths, who had been herded by Attila into the valley of the Theiss (Tisza), revolted. A general rising of the German tribes followed, and finding a leader in Ardaric, king of the Gepids, in 454, on the unknown river Nedao, in Pannonia, they routed the Huns so completely that within two or three generations they virtually disappeared.

The sequel to these events – Attila's death and the collapse of his empire – is a strange one. Two daughters and no son had been born to Valentinian and the empress Eudoxia, daughter of Theodosius II, and Aetius, to secure the succession for his own family, in 454 sought to gain the hand of one of the daughters for his son. In a passion Valentinian stabbed Aetius to death, and in

---

[1] *Italy and Her Invaders*, Thomas Hodgkin, vol. II, pp 174–179. The whole story is dramatic in the extreme. Regarding it, see also Milman's *History of Latin Christianity*, vol. I, pp. 200–203; Bury's *History of the Later Roman Empire*, vol. I, pp. 295–296, and Gibbon's *The Decline and Fall of the Roman Empire*, vol. III, pp. 500–501.

[2] *Later Roman Empire*, vol. I, p. 295.

[3] *A History of Attila and the Huns*, pp. 147–148.

the following year was himself assassinated and succeeded by Petronius Maximus. He forced Eudoxia to marry him, and it is said that in revenge she appealed to Gaiseric to aid her. In June, 455, he sailed up the Tiber, was met by Eudoxia, whom he stripped of her robes and jewels, and for fourteen days sacked Rome, but the lives of its inhabitants were spared by the intercession of Pope Leo. Before the looting Maximus was assassinated, and when Gaiseric withdrew, power passed into the hands of Ricimer, the barbarian Master of the Troops and grandson of Wallia the Visigoth. In rapid succession emperor followed emperor until 475, when Orestes, a Roman who had served as secretary to Attila, won the support of the barbarian mercenaries, had his young son Romulus, surnamed Augustulus, proclaimed emperor at Ravenna, and marched on Rome. But no sooner had he set out than his troops demanded one-third of Italy as their reward, and because this preposterous claim was refused, on August 23, 476, they raised their leader, Odovacar—who appears to have been the son of one of Attila's lieutenants, the Hun Edeco[1] —upon a shield and proclaimed him king of Italy. From then until Christmas Day of the year 800, when Pope Leo III crowned Charlemagne in St. Peter's and inaugurated what was to become the Holy Roman Empire, there was no Emperor of the West. Romulus opened the great cycle in the legendary year 753 B.C., and twelve hundred and twenty-nine years later his effete namesake closed it. Henceforth for long centuries the twilight of legend returned in the West.

It will be seen from these events that the victory Aetius and Theodoric won at Châlons in no way saved the Western Empire from obliteration. Also it will be seen that, even had they suffered defeat, Attila's empire would have collapsed on his death; it had no political bottom—it was built wholly on terror and was devoid of creative force. Nevertheless, when we look back on the making rather than the winning of the Battle of Châlons, its importance becomes apparent.

It was not a Roman victory or a Teutonic victory, but a victory of both peoples combined over Asiatics, as Salamis had been a victory of both Athenians and Spartans over Persians. Once again West and East—Europe and Asia—were in clinch, and once again Europeans set aside their private quarrels in order to face a common foe.

[1] Edeco was probably king of the Scirs.

More important still, the ecclesiastical organization in the Frankish territories remained unbroken, with the result that the Church became the chief international authority during the Middle Ages, and the only authority which could trace unbroken descent from Roman times. Frankland was, therefore, more fortunate than England, where ecclesiastical organization was destroyed completely by the Saxons, with the result that its inhabitants had to be reconverted by missionaries from Ireland and Rome. Had the same happened in what to-day is France, the whole course of medieval history would have been changed.

Further, the prestige of the papacy was vastly enhanced, for though the probability is that, when Pope Leo met Attila on the Mincio, he came as a humble suppliant, the sudden death of the ferocious Hun following so closely on the meeting appeared to a superstitious age to be the judgement of God. The devil had been subdued by God's vicar, and the legend which sprouted from this victory of righteousness over evil went far to set the papal chair firmly on the floor of the miraculous, and as Thomas Hodgkin writes: ". . . thus it is no paradox to say that indirectly the King of the Huns contributed more perhaps than any other historical personage, towards the creation of that mighty factor in the politics of medieval Italy, the Pope-King of Rome."[1] What Attila began Gaiseric added to. "From now on", writes Dean Milman, "Rome ceased altogether to be a pagan city."[2] And as the old Roman nobility went down, the papal power went up; yet the horror of these invasions lived on and the very features of Attila were transmogrified into the countenance of Satan – the Black Magician. Even to-day, when we seek to insult our enemies, we call them Huns.

As religious outlook changed, so did the outlook on war, which so often is the physical expression of mystical beliefs. Horror was so complete, impotence so deep-founded, and fear so universal that the miraculous alone could be relied upon. Though the generals created hell on earth, the priests could at least promise heaven in the world to come. Had not a girl saved Paris by her prayers? Had not 11,000 virgins been martyred in Cologne, and did not their dusty bones stir forth miracles? Was it not a bishop who had saved Orléans? Had not Heraclea in Macedonia been defended by a saint? Therefore, would not the innumerable cities

[1] *Italy and Her Invaders*, Thomas Hodgkin, vol. ii, p. 189.
[2] *History of Latin Christianity*, Henry Hart Milman (1857), vol. i, p. 204.

wasted by the Huns have beaten back their onslaught had there been more saints, even if less soldiers? Thus it came about that relics became spiritual ammunition and papal authority the engine which detonated their power.

As the greatness of Alexander may be judged from his legend, so may the horror of Attila be translated from his. He was the *Flagellum Dei*, the Grandson of Nimrod, the Anti-Christ of the Scriptures, and the Etzel of the Nibelungenlied. It was he who married Kriemhild (Ildico); the Nibelungs visited him in Hunland, and "reaping the due of hoarded vengeance" Kriemhild murders him for love of her girlhood husband Siegfried. The great epic sprouts out of the blood-soaked fields of Europe, cropping forth a common heritage. It is found in Byzantium, in Germany, France, Italy, Scandinavia, and Iceland; it is one of the great legends of the western world. Taken together, these things made the Battle of Châlons one of the decisive moments in western history.

# The conquest of Italy by the Ostrogoths

After the collapse of the Hun Empire in 454, the Ostrogoths, freed from subjection, under three brothers of the royal house of Amal, Walamir, Theodemir, and Widemir, occupied northern Pannonia as *foederati* of the Emperor Marcian, and for their services were granted an annual payment of 100 pounds of gold. About the same time many of them, under a leader named Theodoric Strabo ("the squinter"), enlisted in the army of Aspar, the Emperor's Master of the Troops. A few years later, when Marcian's successor Leo I (457–474) refused to continue the grant of gold, the Ostrogoths set out to ravage the Illyrian provinces and continued to do so until it was reaffirmed, when, according to the terms of the agreement, Theodemir's son Theodoric, then a child of eight–born in 454–was sent as a hostage to the court at Constantinople. There he remained for ten years, during which Theodemir, now sole ruler of the Ostrogoths, had so firmly established himself on the middle Danube that Leo, to cultivate his friendship, sent his son back to him. On Theodemir's death in 474, Theodoric was elected king, and apparently without the Emperor's consent he moved his people into Lower Moesia (northern Bulgaria). Meanwhile Theodoric Strabo–by marriage related to Theodemir–had been proclaimed king by his troops on the death of Aspar in 471, and he compelled Leo to recognize him king of the Goths.

Leo died in 474 and was succeeded by Zeno (474–491) who found two turbulent and antagonistic Gothic kings on his hands and set about playing the one off against the other. This continued until 481, when Strabo met with a fatal accident and was succeeded by his son Rekitack, who at once killed his two uncles. Becoming intolerable to Zeno, in 484, at the latter's instigation Theodoric invited Rekitack to a banquet, assassinated him and took over his followers. This accretion of strength put Theodoric in so powerful a position that, when two years later a quarrel arose between him and the Emperor, he devastated Thrace and marched on Constantinople; but on the intervention of his sister, then at Zeno's court, desisted from further action and retired to Moesia.

Zeno, it would appear, now decided to kill two troublesome birds with one stone. Having an old score to square with Odovacar and being eager to rid himself of Theodoric, he suggested to the latter that he should proceed to Italy and conquer the former, and to give legal sanction to this conquest, he made Theodoric a patrician, the same rank which Odovacar held.

In the late autumn of 488 Theodoric set out from Novae (Sistova) on the lower Danube, and with him went the people of the Goths, with their wives and children in wagons, and driving their flocks and herds. What their numbers were is not known: Bury suggests 100,000 and Dahn 250,000. Without incident the horde passed through Singidunum, but on approaching Sermium it found its road barred by the Gepids. As there could now be no turning back, a battle was fought in which the Ostrogoths were victorious. Other engagements followed, after which the horde, moving slowly westward, crossed the Julian Alps in August, 489, descended into Italy and reached the river Sontius (Isonzo) a few miles to the north of the site of Aquileia. There Theodoric found Odovacar ready to meet him, and on August 28 a battle was fought in which the latter was beaten severely. Another battle, near Verona, followed on September 30, and again defeated, Odovacar sought refuge in Ravenna.

Leaving him there, for Ravenna was one of the most difficult cities in Italy to attack, Theodoric moved westward and occupied Mediolanum (Milan), where Tufa, Odovacar's Master of the Troops, deserted to him. He trusted Tufa and sent him and his followers to lay siege to Ravenna; but instead of doing so Tufa rejoined his old master. Thus reinforced, Odovacar set out from Ravenna and blockaded Ticino (Pavia) where Theodoric had moved. This unexpected change placed Theodoric in so critical a position that it might well have led to his ruin had not the Visigoths and Burgundians seized the opportunity to cross the Maritime Alps and invade Liguria. Under cover of this diversion Theodoric advanced against Odovacar, and on August 11, 490, defeated him on the river Adda, after which he drove him back into Ravenna and besieged him.

The siege dragged on until the summer of 492, when at length Theodoric took a step he should have taken from the first. He occupied Ariminum, either built or collected a fleet of ships, and by blockading the port of Ravenna, reduced his enemy to such straits that, on February 25, 493, Odovacar opened negotiations. Two days later, through the mediation of John, Archbishop of Ravenna, a peace was agreed, according to which Theodoric and Odovacar were to be joint rulers of Italy. Such an unstable arrangement could not last long, and it did not. On March 5, Theodoric entered Ravenna, and ten days later he invited his rival to a banquet at which he slew him with his own sword. Next, the whole of Odovacar's family was exterminated.

Free from all rivals, Theodoric sent a mission to Constantinople to seek the Emperor's recognition of his kingship over Italy; but as Zeno had no intention of parting with his purely nominal suzerainty, Theodoric decided the question by assuming the royal mantle in the capacity of "Governor of the Goths and Romans". Under his rule as king, the Goths retained their own rights, and under his rule as *de facto Imperator*, the Italians continued to be governed as they had been in the past. There was no drastic political change, and for the simple reason that as he had no substitute for the existing machinery of government, had Theodoric failed to maintain it, law and order would have become impossible, because he would have been unable to collect the taxes, and to pay his troops and civil servants. More so than any other barbaric conqueror, he realized the value of the traditional Roman system; therefore his aim was to restore the old power of Italy and to build his own administration on the model of the Roman *civilitas*. He respected the Senate, and though an Arian by faith, in his dealings with the Church he played the part of an impartial arbiter in its constant disputes.

Throughout his reign he compelled his Goths to submit to taxation; secured the food supply of the people; repaired the Italian seaports; restored works of art in Rome and Ravenna; and though illiterate encouraged a revival of learning. His foreign policy was conducted in the same manner as his home policy, and its aim may be judged from the alliances he established through the marriages of his daughters and sisters. His eldest daughter, Arevagni, he married to Alaric II, king of the Visigoths; his second daughter, Theudegotha, became the wife of the son of the king of the Burgundians; and his third, Amalasuntha, became the wife of Eutharic, an Amal noble and a direct descendant of Hermanaric. The last alliance was made to secure a successor, for Theodoric had no son. One of his sisters, Amalafrida, he married to Thrasamund, king of the Vandals, and another, Amalaberga, to the king of the Thuringians, and he himself wedded Audefleda, sister of Clovis, king of the Franks.

He imposed his will on the barbarian tribes along his frontiers and carried out many wars against them. Pannonia he took from the Gepids; he secured the passes of the Graian Alps and occupied Provence; settled the Alemanni in Rhaetia; took the Visigoths in Gaul under his protection; established Amalaric, son of Alaric II, in Spain; and became so renowned as the arbiter of the West that even a deposed Scandinavian prince found refuge at his court and the Estonians on the distant Baltic paid to him a tribute of amber. To-day he is still remembered under the name of Dietrich of Bern in the Nibelungenlied.

At the time of his death, his rule extended over Italy, Sicily, Dalmatia, Noricum, Pannonia, the two Rhaetias (Tyrol and Grisons), Lower Germany as far north as Ulm, and Provence. "Indeed", writes Professor Maurice Dumoulin, ". . . if his supremacy over the Goths in Spain be also taken into account . . . he had succeeded in re-establishing the ancient Western Empire . . . with the exceptions of Africa, Britain and two-thirds of Gaul."

Thus, under Theodoric, we see the makings of a true revival of the West through the fusion of barbaric vigour with what remained of Roman civilization. Nevertheless, this profitable union, which had it endured would have gone far to change the whole course of western history, was destined barely to outlive its creator; for in 523 the Emperor Justin I (518–527) took the fatal step of proscribing the Arian faith throughout the Empire. This was a direct attack on the Goths, and Theodoric saw it as such. He saw that his whole life-work was threatened with ruin; for it meant nothing less than the sowing of a religious war within his realm.

Theodoric died in 526 and was succeeded by his grandson Athalaric, and as he was but ten years old, his mother Amalasuntha–now a widow–became regent. More Roman in her sentiments than Gothic, friction arose between her and her subjects, and rapidly grew so acute that, fearing a court revolution, she entered into communication with the Emperor Justinian (527–565), who had succeeded his uncle Justin in 527, and secretly informed his ambassadors that in return for a promise of personal safety she was willing to surrender her kingdom to the emperor. Thus matters stood when on October 2, 534, Athalaric died. Amalasuntha, to maintain her supremacy and so to prevent her secret negotiations becoming known, then determined to share the throne with Theodahad, son of her sister Amalafrida and now heir presumptive of the Gothic crown, and trusted that as he was of weak character the sovereignty would remain in her hands. She invited him to ascend the throne with her and bound him by an oath to be no more than nominally king, and as he was already married, the association agreed upon was that they should rule as sister and brother. No sooner had this agreement been made than Theodahad allied himself with her enemies, had her seized and imprisoned on an island in the lake of Bolsena, and there, a few weeks later, she was strangled. Once knowledge of this came to the ears of Justinian's ambassador, Peter of Thessalonica—then on his way to Ravenna—he at once sought an audience with Theodahad and protested to him and his followers "that because this base deed had been committed by them, there would be war without truce between the emperor and themselves". A war which, as we shall see, may be compared with the Thirty Years War, for it left Italy, as Germany was left eleven hundred years later, a desert.

# CHAPTER II

# The Battles of Tricameron, 533, and Taginae, 552

Justinian, named the Great, and one of the most remarkable of the Eastern Roman emperors, was by birth a barbarian peasant. Born in 483 in the district of Dardania, a region of Illyricum, in 523 he married the notorious Theodora, daughter of a bear-feeder of the amphitheatre at Constantinople, and at one time a courtesan and dancer in Alexandria. A woman of remarkable resolution and courage, her influence over her husband was so pronounced that on their marriage he raised her to the patriciate, and once emperor he appointed her co-regent.

An insatiable worker and centralizer, Justinian was called "the emperor who never sleeps". He looked upon himself not only as heir of the Caesars, but also as the supreme head of the Church, and throughout his reign he held two fixed ideas: the one was the restoration of the Western Empire, and the other the suppression of the Arian heresy. Hence all his western wars took on the character of crusades, for he felt that his mission was to lead the heathen peoples into the Christian fold. But before he could set out on this task, he had to find a pretext for intervention; besides, on his accession, he had a war with Persia on his hands.

A good judge of men, he selected Belisarius, a young officer of his body-guard, who was born in Macedonia about 505, to command the Eastern Army. In 530 he won a signal victory over the Persians at Daras, soon after which he was recalled to Constantinople and peace was hastily patched up. The reason for this was that a revolution had occurred in Carthage in which Gelimer, a great grandson of Gaiseric, had dethroned Hilderic the Vandal king, and the latter, as the Emperor's vassal, had appealed to Constantinople for aid. At once Justinian seized upon this appeal as the pretext to launch the first of his crusades.

While Belisarius prepared for the reconquest of Africa, a rising known as the Nika ("Victory") insurrection nearly brought, not only his preparations, but the reign of Justinian to an end. On January 11, 532, the Emperor was hissed in the Hippodrome, and the disturbance rapidly spread; the Blues and the Greens–the two hostile factions in Constantinople[1]–for once made common cause. They stormed round the imperial palace, fired the city and proclaimed Hypatius, nephew of Anastasius, who had preceded Justin, emperor. The situation grew so critical that Justinian would have saved himself by flight had not Theodora risen in the council and proclaimed: "If now it is your wish to save yourself, O Emperor, there is no difficulty. For we have much money, and there is the sea, here the boats. However consider whether it will not come about after you have been saved that you would gladly exchange that safety for death. For as for myself, I approve a certain ancient saying that royalty is a good burial-shroud."[2]

These stirring words brought courage to the Emperor and his councillors, who so far had given way to the insurgents. At once Belisarius and a middle-aged Armenian eunuch named Narses, who had attained the rank of Grand Chamberlain, were instructed to suppress the rebellion. While the former put himself at the head of a body of armed men, the latter stole out of the palace with a heavy bag of gold to bribe the leaders of the Blues back to their old allegiance to the Emperor. When he heard that the rebels were mainly congregated in the Hippodrome, Belisarius forced his way into it, and helped by another general, Mundus, fell upon them and slaughtered 35,000. Thus ended the Nika insurrection, and its chief interest to us is that in it we are brought face to face with the two men who were to reconquer Italy–Belisarius and Narses.

Two more different men it would be hard to find, as different as were Gustavus Adolphus and Wallenstein in the Thirty Years War. In 532 Belisarius was twenty-seven years of age, and Narses was fifty-four; the one had been a soldier since boyhood, the other only became one in late middle life. Belisarius was tall, well-built, and of handsome appearance. Narses was small in stature, lean and wizen. One possessed a most winning character, was bold to the verge of rashness, resourceful and of an inventive mind, a general always ready to make the most of the inadequate means allotted him by his parsimonious master. The other was a sinister

---

[1] The Blues (Veneti) and the Greens (Prasini) were factions (Demes) of the hippodrome, the guilds of the contending parties in the chariot races. The Blues were orthodox and were supported by Justinian and the Greens monophysite, encouraged by Theodora. Thus, normally, the Emperor and Empress were able to control the rabble of the capital.

[2] Procopius, Evans, H. B. Dewing (1916), "The Persian War", I, xxiv, 36–37.

intriguer, a flatterer and dissembler, astute, calculating and cunning, who never consented to risk his own glory should he consider his means inadequate. Both were able tacticians, and in different ways staunch disciplinarians, but as a strategist Narses was probably the superior, as he certainly was in statecraft.

Belisarius was a merciful conqueror who normally attempted to mitigate the horrors of war, and sometimes to his strategical disadvantage, but Narses looked upon war as an instrument of policy which on no account must be blunted by other considerations. He had the ear of the Emperor, Belisarius had not, and because of Belisarius's successful generalship, he was eyed with suspicion by Justinian. There can be little doubt that, coupled with his great abilities, the influence Narses wielded over his master was largely because he was a eunuch, for as such he could not replace him on the throne. Compared with him, Belisarius's one great disadvantage lay in his wife Antonia, whose origin was similar to that of the Empress Theodora; she was the daughter of a charioteer and a theatrical prostitute. Unlike her royal mistress, who was twenty years younger than Justinian, according to Procopius, Antonia was twenty-two years older than Belisarius; nevertheless, throughout their married life he was abjectly devoted to her. She accompanied him on nearly all his campaigns, exerted as much influence over him as Theodora did over Justinian, and frequently to his detriment and discredit. It is strange that so great a man could have been both the dupe and slave of so domineering, intriguing, and in her old age so licentious a woman. As Gibbon remarks of him, his "unconquerable patience and loyalty" to her "appear either *below* or *above* the character of a MAN".[1]

Though many innocent people perished in the Nika massacre, the blood-letting was politically a salutary one, for the quarrelsome rabble of Constantinople was so reduced by it that Justinian's authority was never again challenged. Therefore, he could devote his entire attention to his imperial plans, the immediate one being the recovery of Africa from the Vandals and the extermination of Arianism throughout their realm.

Militarily his means were very different from those of Diocletian and Constantine, for since their days the army had fallen into decay. The great peripheral bulwark of the *limitanei* had all but disappeared on the Illyrian front, and in other regions it was represented by insignificant bodies of troops. The *palatini* and

[1] *The Decline and Fall of the Roman Empire* (edit. Bury, 1925), vol. IV, p. 363.

*comitatensis* had been reduced to a purely nominal existence, and the name of legion had become obsolete. Under Anastasius, Justin and Justinian, officially the army comprised three categories of troops, the *numeri, foederati* and *bucellarii*. The first were the regular soldiers of the Empire, both foot and horse, and had fallen into such disrepute that even slaves were recruited. The second now consisted wholly of mercenaries raised mainly by soldiers of fortune and recruited from many nations, more particularly the Huns. The third were the armed retainers of the Byzantine magnates, and though belonging to private armies, they were obliged to take an oath of allegiance to the emperor as well as to their immediate chiefs. It was with this highly denationalized and mercenary force that Justinian set out to regain Africa.

When one considers the extent of the area to be conquered and the uncertainty of Gelimer's strength, the army Justinian allotted to Belisarius was hazardously small. It consisted of 10,000 infantry and 5,000 cavalry, practically all of whom were barbarians recruited from every quarter of the Empire. Like most wholly mercenary forces, though its men were highly trained, they were uncertain in their allegiance, brutal in victory and treacherous in defeat.

In preparing the invasion, Belisarius's first problem was where to establish an advanced base? To concentrate the army in Egypt and approach through Libya and Tripolis was out of the question because of the difficulties of supply. To establish the base in the Peloponnese and to cross the Mediterranean was too risky because of the danger of storms, and besides, the Vandals commanded a powerful fleet. Therefore Belisarius decided to advance by way of Sicily, and as Amalasuntha was well disposed towards the Empire and was still quarrelling with the Vandals because in 527 Hilderic had put her aunt Amalafrida to death, she agreed to grant the expedition a friendly reception in Sicily. This acquiescence was eventually to prove the ruin of her people, for without the advantage which Sicily offered it may be doubted whether the expedition could have succeeded, and had it failed, the likelihood is that Italy would never have been invaded and, in consequence, that to the benefit of the West the Ostrogothic empire would have endured.

On June 22, 533, the army embarked at Constantinople in 500 ships[1] manned by 20,000 sailors and escorted by ninety-two

[1] The largest was 750 tons burden and the smallest 45 tons.

dromons (small fast warships) rowed by 2,000 Byzantine slaves. At Methone in the Peloponnese a long delay because of unfavourable wind occurred, and due to bad food 500 soldiers died of pestilence. At length Zante was reached, and from there, again because the winds were contrary, the armada took sixteen days to reach Catania in Sicily, where, thanks to Amalasuntha, it was well received.

Belisarius's problem now became one of information, and strange to say he was totally ignorant of the strength and position of the Vandal army and of the best landing points in Africa. All he knew was that the Vandals possessed a powerful fleet and, therefore, were his transports caught in mid-passage they would probably be sunk. Consulting Procopius – the historian – whom in his Persian campaign he had selected as his legal adviser, he sent him to Syracuse, ostensibly to buy stores, but actually to gather all the information he could. On his return he reported that Gelimer was not as yet aware that the expedition had left Constantinople, and that his best soldiers, under command of his brother Tzazon, were in Sardinia putting down a revolt fomented by Justinian.

Without the loss of a moment, Belisarius embarked his army, hoisted sail and stood out to sea. He called at Malta and Gozo on his way, and early in September, nearly three months after leaving Constantinople, the coast of Africa was sighted. He made for Caputvada (Ras Kapudia), 130 miles south of Cape Bon; disembarked his army; was well received by the provincials; built a fortified camp; circulated Justinian's proclamation that the invading army came to make war not on the people, but solely on Gelimer; and then set out northward for Carthage. He was preceded by an advanced guard of 300 horse under John the Armenian, 600 Huns covered his left flank, and the whole fleet steered along the coast on his right. On September 13 the advanced guard reached the defile of Ad Decimum – the tenth milestone from Carthage.

When he heard of the enemy landing, Gelimer's first intention was to protract the war until Tzazon could be recalled, and he lamented the policy of his ancestors who, by destroying the fortifications of the African cities, had left Carthage uncovered. He heard next how small Belisarius's army was and instructed his brother Ammatus, in command at Carthage, to prepare to attack the invaders; meanwhile he had Hilderic and all his relatives and friends put to death.

Gelimer's plan of operations was an over-complicated one: he decided, once his enemy had entered the Ad Decimum defile, to launch a combined attack on him from three directions. While Ammatus sallied forth from Carthage and engaged the Byzantine van, he himself with the main body was to fall upon the rear of the enemy's main body, and at the same time his nephew, Gibamund, was to move over the hills from the west and to attack the enemy's left flank. Procopius expresses his astonishment that Belisarius's army should have escaped destruction. But, because correct timing was the prerequisite of success, in a clockless age it would have been a fluke had the three columns engaged simultaneously.

Ammatus moved out of Carthage on September 13, struck before the other two columns had got into position, and was mortally wounded; at once his troops took panic and fled. Next, Gibamund attacked and was routed by the Hun flank guard. And it was only after these two attacks had failed that Gelimer, ignorant of what had happened, misguided by the windings of the hills, inadvertently missed the rear of the enemy's main body and when he reached the scene of action where Ammatus had fallen, came up with its leading division, then far ahead of those in rear, and routed it. The fugitives galloped back in panic and carried with them an unengaged detachment of 800 guardsmen. Victory was Gelimer's had he known how to seize it. "For if, on the one hand", writes Procopius, "he had made the pursuit immediately I do not think that even Belisarius would have withstood him . . . or if, on the other hand, he had even ridden straight for Carthage, he would easily have killed all John's men, who heedless of everything were wandering about the plain one by one or by twos and stripping the dead. And he would have preserved the city with its treasures, and captured our ships, which had come rather near, and he would have withdrawn from us all hope both of sailing away and of victory."[1] Instead he fell back and, when he came upon the mutilated body of his brother, he was so overwhelmed with grief that he abandoned further attack until he had given it befitting burial. Meanwhile Belisarius had rallied his broken troops, and a little before nightfall he counter-attacked and dispersed the Vandals.

Next day the Byzantine army moved up to the walls of Carthage to find that most of the Vandal troops had withdrawn from the

[1] Procopius, trans. H. B. Dewing (1916), "The Vandalic War", III, XIX, 26–29.

city. On September 15 its gates were opened, Belisarius entered and was received with shouts of welcome by its inhabitants. Still fearful of his enemy, his first act was to repair its fortifications, which for a century had been in ruins. Meanwhile Gelimer had retired to a spot called Bulla Regia (Hamman Daradji), 100 miles west of Carthage. From there, while collecting the fragments of his army, still a formidable force, he sent a message to Tzazon in Sardinia to speed to his aid. On his arrival, Gelimer's strength was so considerable that, according to Procopius, he found himself at the head of an army ten times as numerous as his enemy's.[1] He then marched on Carthage, broke down the aqueduct which supplied the city, and next, when he learnt that Belisarius's Huns were discontented with their terms of service, so worked upon them that they promised to turn on the Romans in the next battle. Gelimer then retired to a place called Tricameron, which lay about eighteen miles from Carthage, and there built a stockaded camp.

Belisarius heard of the defection of his Huns and courted them "with gifts and banquets and every other manner of flattering attention",[2] with the result that among themselves they decided, instead of falling on the rear of the Byzantines in the next battle, to wait until they saw toward which side victory inclined. This incident clearly illustrates the outstanding danger in mercenary armies; loot was their one aim and victory but a means of obtaining it.

With his Huns provisionally neutralized, Belisarius gambled on the probability that boldness of action would prevent their defection and, in spite of his own numerical inferiority, decided to attack Gelimer. In the circumstances it was a bold decision; but he had judged his enemy rightly, as may be gauged from a sentence in his address to his troops—namely: "Now as for the host of the Vandals, let no one of you consider them. For not by numbers of men, nor by measure of body, but by valour of soul is war wont to be decided."[3]

He sent forward, under John the Armenian, the whole of his horse, less 500, and on the following day, about the middle of December, 533, Belisarius set out with his infantry and 500 horsemen for Tricameron, and that night bivouacked at a considerable

---

[1] Procopius, IV, ii, 18. This is a gross exaggeration. Tzazon's army when sent to Sardinia was 5,000 strong (ibid., III, xi, 23).

[2] Ibid., IV, i, 9.                                        [3] Ibid., IV, i, 15–16.

distance from his enemy's camp. When Gelimer learnt of his approach he exhorted his troops to court death rather than bring shame on the fame of Gaiseric. Then, about noon, he led out his army and came unexpectedly on John's cavalry corps as its men were preparing their midday meal.[1] Instead of at once exploiting this stroke of luck by attacking his enemy before he could form up, he halted and awaited attack. Such complete lack of generalship brought with it its deserts. John rapidly mounted his men, deployed them in three divisions and took command of the central one. Belisarius, who presumably had been informed of Gelimer's approach, "leaving the infantry behind advancing at a walk",[2] at once joined him with his 500 horse. Meanwhile Gelimer had also deployed his horsemen in three divisions, the central one commanded by his brother Tzazon. The order given to the Vandals was to use the sword only.

The battle, Procopius tells us, did not begin for a considerable time, and when it did it was opened by John at the head of a small body of selected horsemen. He crossed a brook which flowed between the two armies and charged the Vandal centre, but was speedily "crowded back" by Tzazon, who chased him to his camp. Next, John led out the guardsmen and made a dash for the forces of Tzazon, but again he was driven back to his camp. For a third time John advanced, this time with all the guards and spearmen, yelling at the tops of their voices, and a desperate encounter followed in which Tzazon was cut down. This was the signal for the whole of the Byzantine cavalry to be unleashed, "and crossing the river they advanced upon the enemy, and the rout, beginning at the centre, became complete; for each of the Roman divisions turned to flight those before them with no trouble. And the Massagetae [Huns] seeing this, according to their agreement among themselves, joined the Roman army in making the pursuit. . . ."[3] The whole of the Vandal cavalry was driven back to its stockaded camp, and at once the Byzantines started pillaging the dead.

The cavalry battle cannot have lasted for much more than an hour, and the main battle yet remained to be fought, for Belisarius's horsemen could not storm the Vandal camp. Further, thus far casualties had not been heavy, for the Roman losses were less than fifty and those of the Vandals about 800.

Late in the afternoon, when the Byzantine infantry came up,

[1] Procopius, IV, ii, 1.      [2] *Ibid.*, IV, iii, 5.      [3] *Ibid.*, IV, iii, 18.

Belisarius moved them against the Vandal camp. When he saw them the miserable Gelimer, who that morning had exhorted his troops not to sully the fame of Gaiseric, "without saying a word or giving a command leaped upon his horse and was off in flight on the road leading to Numidia".[1] Such was the decisive event which won for Belisarius the battle; for once the king's desertion became known, a general panic swept through the camp, "and leaving all behind them, every man fled in complete disorder just as he could".[2]

This extraordinary flight of a headless army was followed by an equally extraordinary incident. When the deserted Vandal camp was entered and the wealth contained in it discovered, the whole of Belisarius's army broke its ranks and began to plunder it, ". . . drenched as they were by their present good fortune . . . and . . . going about, not in companies but alone or by twos, wherever hope led them. Searching out everything round about among the valleys and the rough country and wherever there chanced to be a cave or anything such as might bring them into danger or ambush. For neither did fear of the enemy nor their respect for Belisarius occur to them, nor indeed anything else at all except the desire for spoils. . . ."[3] Had Gelimer possessed but an ounce of courage—and he must have realized the insatiable lust for plunder which governs mercenary soldiers—instead of deserting his army he would have withdrawn it and left his camp a bait for his enemy's troops. Once they had fallen upon it he would have fallen upon them and regained his camp and his kingdom. This is what Belisarius feared he might do, "being fearful throughout the whole night lest the enemy, uniting by mutual agreement against him, should do him irreparable harm". "And if this thing had happened at any time in any way at all", writes Procopius, "I believe that not one of the Romans would have escaped and enjoyed his booty."[4]

On the following morning, when he had established some semblance of order, Belisarius sent out John the Armenian and his cavalry in pursuit of Gelimer, but it was not until March, 534, that the Vandal king, by then reduced to beggary, surrendered, and shortly after adorned Belisarius's triumph at Constantinople.

No sooner had Belisarius left Africa than, like vultures, the Emperor's tax gatherers arrived, and such were their extortions

[1] Procopius, IV, iii, 20.          [2] Ibid., IV, iii, 23.
[3] Ibid., IV, iv, 3–5.             [4] Ibid., IV, iv, 1–2.

that the Byzantine soldiers, many of whom had married Vandal women, mutinied. At the same time, the Arian population, because it was prohibited from baptizing its children and from exercising all religious worship, rose, and the Moors took advantage of the general turmoil and raided and devastated the reconquered province for more than ten years. ". . . such was the desolation of Africa", writes Gibbon, "that in many parts a stranger might wander whole days without meeting the face of a friend or an enemy. . . . When Procopius first landed, he admired the populousness of the cities and country, strenuously exercised in commerce and agriculture. In fewer than twenty years, that busy scene was converted into silent solitude; the wealthy citizens escaped to Sicily and Constantinople; and the secret historian has confidently affirmed that five millions of Africans were consumed by the wars and government of the emperor Justinian."[1]

The conquest of Africa furnished Justinian with an admirable supply base for operations against Italy, and the murder of Amalasuntha by Theodahad in 534, which came on the heels of the collapse of the Vandal kingdom, was at once seized upon by the emperor as his next *casus belli*. Two armies were marshalled forthwith, the one under Mundus to invade the Gothic province of Dalmatia, and the other under Belisarius to conquer Sicily. Both, because of the emperor's parsimony, were absurdly small: the one probably numbered no more than 3,000 to 4,000 men, and the other, as Procopius tells us, consisted of 7,500.

When one looks back on the first years of the war, that Belisarius was able to accomplish what he did with so small an army is seen to be because of his superior generalship and armament, and because in Italy, as in Africa, the Roman population favoured his cause. He realized that with so minute an army he could not successfully meet the Goths in the field, knew them to be inept in siegecraft, avoided pitched battles, and made the utmost use of walled cities, not only to multiply his strength but to force his enemy to wear down his own by besieging them. But his tactics were by no means static, for he made frequent sallies and raids from the cities he held, and this he was able to do because of his superior missile power, which he explains as follows:

"And the difference was this, that practically all the Romans and their allies, the Huns, are good mounted bowmen, but not

---

[1] *The Decline and Fall of the Roman Empire*, Edward Gibbon, vol. IV, p. 421; ref. to Procopius's *Anecdota* or *Secret History*, XVIII, 8–9. The figure is clearly an exaggerated one.

a man among the Goths has had practice in this branch, for their horsemen are accustomed to use only spears and swords, while their bowmen enter battle on foot and under cover of the heavy-armed men. So the horsemen, unless the engagement is at close quarters, have no means of defending themselves against opponents who use the bow, and therefore can easily be reached by the arrows and destroyed; and as for the foot-soldiers, they can never be strong enough to make sallies against men on horseback."[1]

Toward the close of 535 Belisarius landed in Sicily, and was so well received that, except for Palermo, all the cities opened their gates to him. Once Palermo fell, Theodahad was so terrified that he tendered his submission to Justinian and offered to cede Italy to him for a sum of money. But while these negotiations were in progress, Belisarius was called away to Africa to suppress a rebellion, and Mundus was defeated and killed at Salona (near Spalato) in Dalmatia. These unexpected events so influenced the cowardly and changeable Gothic king that he revoked his submission and impounded the imperial ambassadors. Belisarius was then recalled, and in May, 536, he carried his army over the strait of Messina, laid siege to Naples and took it by entering the city through an aqueduct. Meanwhile Byzantine diplomacy had secured an alliance with the Franks,[2] just as before the opening of the Vandal War it had secured one with the Ostrogoths. Thus a two-front war was opened on Theodahad.

On the fall of Naples, Theodahad was deposed and a warrior named Vittigis was elected in his stead. To stabilize his position, Vittigis divorced his wife and married Matasuentha, sister of Athalric and granddaughter of Theodoric. His first act was to buy off the Franks by ceding to them the Gothic possessions in Gaul (Provence and part of Dauphiné). As disastrous as this act was wise, his second was to withdraw from Rome, where he left but a small garrison and entrusted the care of the city to Pope Silverius. On December 10, 536, and in spite of his oath of fealty to Vittigis, Pope Silverius opened the city gates to Belisarius. Vittigis realized his mistake and in March the following year, at the head of 150,000 warriors,[3] he laid the Eternal City under a siege which, if not the longest, was the most disastrous it ever experienced.

---

[1] Procopius, "The Gothic War", v, xxvii, 27–28.
[2] Procopius (ibid., v, xi, 29) says that "These Franks were called 'Germani' in ancient times".
[3] Ibid., v, xvi, 11. A gross exaggeration.

His first act was to destroy the aqueducts, which provided more than one million Romans with some 350,000,000 gallons of water a day.[1] This great wealth of water supplied the *thermae* (baths), fountains, gardens, and private dwellings, and hundreds of water mills used for milling flour and other industries. Though in later days some of the aqueducts were repaired, the full system was never again restored and the social life of Rome was changed.

About March 21 Vittigis attempted a full-scale assault on the walls between the Pincian and Salarian Gates, but was beaten back by the projectiles shot by Belisarius's *ballistae*, catapults, and archers, after which he resorted to blockade. Next, in April, Belisarius, who had been reinforced by 1,600 cavalry, ordered a sally which might have ended the war at a single stroke had not his men at the crucial moment begun to plunder the Gothic camp instead of pressing on and securing the Milvian bridge (Ponte Molle) which carries the Via Flaminia over the Tiber.

In December reinforcements numbering 5,600 men reached Italy, and with them came an able though headstrong general, John, nicknamed *Sanguinarius*. Belisarius now felt strong enough to operate against his enemy's rear and he ordered John and 2,000 horse to move into Picenum (Marches) to lay waste the country round the Adriatic end of the Via Flaminia. John disobeyed his orders by failing first to reduce the fortresses of Urbino and Osimo, and pressed on to Rimini. Such was the terror of his name that he carried the city at the first assault. This bold advance to within thirty-three miles of Ravenna, the Gothic capital, so completely upset Vittigis's calculations that, about March 12, 538, he raised the siege of Rome and departed northward. What in years to come the retreat from Moscow was to be to Napoleon, the siege of Rome was to Vittigis: it was "the grave of the Gothic monarchy in Italy", dug by "the deadly dews of the Campagna".[2]

Though John's disobedience was flagrant, there can be little doubt that, once he had occupied Rimini, Belisarius's correct course was to try to exploit the event. Instead, he ordered John to withdraw from the city, and when John refused to do so, the tension between the two was exploited by Vittigis, who moved on Rimini and invested John. At the same time Justinian, fearful that the prestige Belisarius had gained by his defence of Rome

---

[1] See *Italy and Her Invaders* Thomas Hodgkin (1880–1885), vol. I, pp. 394–396, and vol. IV, pp. 171–174.          [2] *Ibid.*, vol. IV, p. 285.

might make him a dangerous rival, sent to Italy strong reinforcements under the eunuch Narses, of Nika insurrection fame, and known as "Count of the Sacred Largesses", who, though he was to help Belisarius to finish the war, was also to keep him under close surveillance.

Narses landed his army in Picenum, and if at Ancona, then less than sixty miles south of Rimini, and no sooner had he done so than a dispute arose over the relief of John. Narses favoured it, Belisarius did not; but as the former had the ears of the emperor, the latter had to give way, and the relief was carried out by an extremely able combined land and sea operation. Because John thanked Narses and not Belisarius for his deliverance, the antagonism between the two commanders-in-chief became one of undisguised hostility. Compromise and half-measures followed, with the result that, early in 539, Milan, which since the raising of the siege of Rome had been recovered by the Imperialist troops, was retaken by the Goths under Urais, nephew of Vittigis, and its occupation was followed by an appalling massacre in which, according to Procopius, 300,000 people perished.[1] Coupled with this disaster, Tuscany, Emilia, and Liguria were now in the grip of famine, and in Picenum alone 50,000 peasants are said to have died of starvation "and a great many more north of the Ionian Gulf (Adriatic)".[2] Soon the dual command[3] of Belisarius and Narses proved so disastrous that the former wrote a strongly worded letter to Justinian which led to the recall of the latter. Freed from Narses, Belisarius laid siege to Fiesole and Osimo, the sole remaining Gothic fortresses which held out south of Ravenna. As he was thus engaged, 100,000 Franks under king Theudibert invaded Italy, ravaged far and wide and defeated both Goths and Romans,[4] but because of the pestilence throughout the land they were forced to withdraw.

By the end of 539, when he had reduced and occupied Fiesole and Osimo, Belisarius marched on Ravenna, Vittigis's last stronghold, and laid siege to it. But a threatened invasion of Illyria, Macedonia, and Thrace by Huns, coupled with the discovery that Vittigis had been corresponding with Chosröes,

---

[1] Procopius, "The Gothic War", VI, xxi, 39.

[2] *Ibid.*, VI, xx, 21.

[3] Compare Napoleon's saying: "*Un mauvais général . . . vaut mieux que deux bons*" (*Corresp.*, vol. XXIX, 107).

[4] The Franks were armed with sword, short-handled, double-bladed axe and shield. Their method of attack was to advance to within close range, hurl their axes, smashing their enemy's shields, and then charge home with the sword.

king of Persia, urging him to attack the Empire in the East, so agitated Justinian that, early in 540, he sent an embassy to Ravenna and offered Vittigis unexpectedly favourable terms of peace: all Italy north of the Po was to be recognized as Gothic, and all south of it, including Sicily, as Roman. It was a statesman-like proposal; for with the ferocious Lombards in the north and the equally ferocious Franks on the west of Italy, it was clearly to the advantage of the Empire to establish the Gothic kingdom as a buffer state north of the Po. But Belisarius, who had set his heart on ending the war unconditionally and on leading Vittigis, as he had led Gelimer, a captive to the feet of the Justinian, refused to become party to the proposed peace, forbade the imperial ambassadors' entrance into Ravenna, and pressed on with the siege.

Though now sorely stricken by famine, Vittigis, who presumably had learnt of Belisarius's non-compliance, resorted to an exceptionally astute move and also a most unselfish one: he offered Belisarius the Empire of the West; in other words, the Gothic crown. Though there can be little doubt that Belisarius had no intention of breaking the oath he had taken,[1] never during the lifetime of Justinian "to organize revolution", in none too honourable a way he turned this offer to his advantage by accepting it, if the Goths would first open the gates of Ravenna. He sent envoys to Vittigis, offered to meet all his wishes, except for a reservation that he would not take the coronation oath until *after* his entry, and in the spring of 540 Ravenna was surrendered to him. Once established there he dropped his mask, and though he did not plunder the city, he seized Vittigis, his leading nobles, and the immense Gothic treasure, and sent all three to Constantinople.

Crafty and discreditable though this action was, it was decisive; for the occupation of Ravenna was immediately followed by the surrender of all the north-eastern Italian cities, except Verona and Pavia. The former was held by Ildibad, nephew of the king of the Visigoths, and the latter by Urais. To these two cities fled the bravest of the Goths still free, and after they had first offered the crown to Urais, who refused it, they elected Ildibad their king.

So far as he was concerned, Belisarius's dishonourable trick soon proved to be double-edged. Justinian, afraid to leave his ambitious general in the palace at Ravenna, recalled him to Constantinople, and after having refused him a regular triumph, in the spring of

[1] Procopius, VI, xxix, 20.

541 he sent him to the Euphrates to try conclusions with Chosröes, with whom the Empire was again at war.

When Belisarius left Italy, the empire of Theodoric had been reduced to the single city of Pavia, held by Ildibad and one thousand Gothic soldiers. Yet before the year was out, with an army largely recruited from Byzantine deserters, he routed the Imperialists in a great battle near Treviso and reconquered the whole of Italy north of the Po. He was able to do this because when Belisarius left the conduct of the war had been put in the hands of eleven squabbling generals, all bent on plunder, and with no one of them in supreme command. Also, no sooner had Italy been rewon than it was invaded by a swarm of Imperial *logothetes* (imperial accountants) under Alexander, nicknamed *"Psalidion"* (the "Scissors") because of his predilection for clipping the coinage, and such were their extortions that the whole country, already suffering from appalling devastation, was reduced to anarchy.

In the spring of 541 Ildibad was assassinated and succeeded by Eraric, who, after a reign of eight months, was slain by Ildibad's nephew Totila, also called Baduila, a remarkable soldier who, because of his generous spirit, chivalrous conduct, and valour, is described by Hodgkin as "quite the noblest flower that bloomed upon the Ostrogothic stem".[1] Early in 542, when he had been elected king, he defeated the Imperialists at Faenza, crossed the Apennines and defeated John of Thessalonica at Mugello, a battle which won for him the whole of central and southern Italy, except for Rome and a few fortresses. Practically all Belisarius had won was lost, and in May, 543, when he had taken Naples, Totila resolved to lay siege to Rome. At length these events roused Justinian, and in the spring of 544 he decided to send Belisarius back to Italy.

Belisarius raised a number of troops in Thrace, and with no more than 4,000 men he first relieved Otranto, and next proceeded up the coast to Pola and thence crossed the Adriatic to Ravenna, from where he wrote to Justinian for men, horses, arms, and money. Soon after this appeal and in the autumn of 545, Totila laid siege to Rome, then held by an Imperial garrison under Bessas, who cornered the wheat and sold it at an inflated price to the soldiers and citizens. The siege brought Belisarius to Porto and Ostia, the ports of Rome, where he established his base; but he accomplished next to nothing, and on December 17, 546, the city was betrayed

[1] *Italy and Her Invaders*, vol. IV, p. 439.

to Totila. At the time, according to Procopius, its once 1,500,000 inhabitants had been reduced to not more than 500 males.[1]

Again the Goths sought peace; but as Justinian left the decision in the hands of Belisarius, the war continued, and because at the time John was devastating Lucania, after evacuating from Rome all its remaining citizens,[2] and leaving a small garrison in occupation, Totila moved against him. Thereupon Belisarius out-manœuvred the garrison and occupied the city. On learning of this Totila speedily returned and, after two abortive attempts to carry Rome by assault, withdrew his army to Tivoli.

Two years of desultory fighting and pillaging followed, and early in 549, at his own request Belisarius was recalled to Constantinople "with wealth much increased but glory somewhat tarnished".[3] Meanwhile Totila had laid siege to Rome for a third time and again the city was betrayed to him, and again he sought peace, but Justinian did not deign to receive his ambassadors. Soon after the Imperialist hold on Italy was reduced to four cities – Ravenna, Otranto, Ancona, and Crotona.

Meanwhile Justinian had selected his nephew Germanus[4] to command in Italy; but before he could set out he died of disease when repelling a Sclavonian incursion, and about the same time Totila occupied Reggio, crossed into Sicily and re-conquered the island as well as Sardinia and Corsica.

On the death of Germanus, John, his son-in-law and nephew of Vitalian, then commanding an army at Salona, was expected by the generals in Italy to come to their relief. But, seemingly, because his rank was the same as theirs, Justinian feared that they would not obey him and offered the command to his Grand Chamberlain Narses, who, in spite of his age, for he was seventy-five,[5] eagerly accepted it. The appointment was a popular one; for Narses was noted for his free-handed generosity, and in consequence the Byzantine condottieri flocked to his standard. But more important still, because he was in the innermost council of the Empire, he was in a far stronger position than Belisarius had ever been to get what he required: in the words of

---

[1] Procopius, "The Gothic War", vII, xx, 19.　　　　[2] *Ibid.*, vII, xxii, 19.

[3] *Italy and Her Invaders*, vol. IV, p. 591. In 558 Belisarius was employed in a war against the Huns, and in 562 was accused of conspiring against Justinian and disgraced. He was restored to favour in 563, and two years later, about eight months before Justinian's death, he died.

[4] Immediately after he married Matasuentha, widow of king Vittigis, because he thought that her influence on the Goths would assist him to become Caesar of the West.　　　　[5] He died in 573 at the age of ninety-five.

Procopius—"a notable army and great sums of money from the emperor".[1]

While Narses marshalled his troops, Totila manned 300 ships and set out to win command of the Adriatic. First he plundered Corfu, then he sailed up the coast of Epirus and Dalmatia and destroyed the ships "which were carrying provisions from Greece for the army of Narses".[2] At the same time he pressed on with the siege of Ancona, and Valerian, commanding at Ravenna, appealed to John at Salona for aid. Though John had been forbidden to move until Narses arrived, on his own initiative he put to sea with 38 sail, linked up with 12 of Valerian's ships, and won a naval battle which led to the siege being raised. "This engagement", writes Procopius, "especially broke the spirit and weakened the power of Totila and the Goths."[3]

Again Totila sought peace, and again Justinian dismissed his envoys, "hating as he did the Gothic name and intending to drive it out absolutely from the Roman domain".[4] To strengthen his position, Totila negotiated an alliance with Theudibald, king of the Franks, whose army had occupied most of Venetia. The arrangement was that neither would wage war on the other until the Romans had been defeated.

At length, in the spring of 552, Narses, having mobilized his forces at Salona, set out by road to Italy. What the strength of his army was is unknown, Procopius merely says that it was "an extraordinarily large one", and, therefore, probably in the neighbourhood of 20,000 men. Like all Byzantine armies it was mainly composed of barbarian contingents—Huns, Lombards, Gepids, Herulians, and a body of Persians—but its main assets were Narses himself and the "exceedingly large sum of money"[5] he carried with him, an essential for a leader of condottieri. On reaching the head of the Adriatic, he found his passage barred by the Franks, supported by a Gothic army under Teias at Verona, and as he did not have sufficient ships to transport his men from the mouth of the Isonzo to Classis, the port of Ravenna, he ordered his soldiers to march close to the coast and in touch with the fleet, the ships of which ferried them across the estuaries of the numerous Venetian rivers and lagoons.

He reached Ravenna safely, linked up with whatever Roman army was there, and after a halt of nine days marched on to

---

[1] Procopius, "The Gothic War", VIII, xxiii, 42.          [2] *Ibid.*, VIII, xxii, 32.
[3] *Ibid.*, VIII, xxiii, 42.          [4] *Ibid.*, VIII, xxiv, 5.          [5] *Ibid.*, VIII, xxvi, 4.

Rimini, then held by a Goth named Usdrilas. He defeated and killed him in a skirmish, advanced down the Flaminian Way to Fano. There he learnt that the all but impregnable fortress of Petra Pertusa (Passio di Furlo) was held, and passed on southward to Sinigallia, from which he turned westward and debouched on the Flaminian Way at Cagli. From Cagli a fourteen mile march brought his army to the posting house of Ad Ensem (Scheggia) on the crest of the pass over the Apennines, from where a valley spreads southward. When he heard that Totila was advancing toward him, Narses encamped and prepared for battle.

Totila, who was in the vicinity of Rome when he heard that Narses had reached Ravenna, at once recalled Teias, and with the whole of his army,[1] less 2,000 horsemen who were to follow, crossed Tuscany and established his camp at the village of Taginae[2] (Gualdo Tadino near Gubbio), about thirteen miles south of his enemy. There, or on his way, he received an embassy from Narses which urged him to submit as his cause was a hopeless one; but if he were intent on fighting it out, to name a day of battle. The reply Narses received was that "At the end of eight days let us match our strength".[3] He suspected treachery and decided to fight on the following day. Nor was his judgement in error, for the next morning Totila advanced to within two bowshots of his line of battle.

The two armies, facing each other, were stretched across a narrow plain somewhere between Scheggia and Tadino, high up in the Apennines, flanked on its eastern side by the foothills of the main Apennine ridge and on its western by a range of hills – the Mountains of Gubbio. In front of the extreme left of the Imperialist line was a small detached hill, which commanded a path leading toward the Roman rear. Narses recognized its tactical importance, and late on the night before the battle he sent forward 50 bowmen to occupy it, and though the next morning they were again and again attacked by squadrons of Gothic horse, they held it.

During this engagement both sides drew out their lines of battle. As was customary among the Goths, Totila ranged his cavalry in front with the whole of his infantry, mostly archers, in rear; his idea was to win the battle by a single charge which would break

---

[1] The strength is unknown, except that it was considerably smaller than the Roman.
[2] More properly spelt Tadinum.
[3] Procopius, "The Gothic War", viii, xxix, 8.

his enemy's centre. According to Procopius, he ordered his entire
army "to use neither bow nor any other weapon . . . except the
spear".[1] Should this be true, it may well be asked what purpose he
hoped to achieve with his infantry?

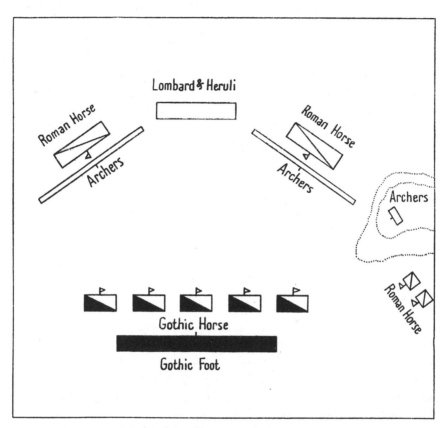

24.  BATTLE OF TAGINAE, 552

To meet this frontal attack, Narses adopted a novel order of
battle, which, as Sir Charles Oman points out, "recalls Edward
III's device at Crécy" and "seems to have been his own invention".[2] He dismounted 8,000 Lombards, Heruli, and other
*feoderati*, formed them up in a solid phalanx in the centre across
the Flaminian Way, and on each of its flanks drew up 4,000 Roman
foot-archers, both wings thrown forward "so that an enemy
advancing against the centre would find himself in an empty space,
half encircled by the bowmen and exposed to a rain of arrows

[1] Procopius, VIII, xxxii, 6.      [2] *A History of the Art of War*, vol. I, pp. 33-34.

from both sides".[1] The left wing was held by Narses and John, nephew of Vitalian, and the right by Valerian and John the Glutton. To protect the archers, Narses drew up behind them his mounted Roman cavalry, apparently 500 to each wing; also, on the extreme left of the left wing and just beyond the detached hill, he posted 1,000 horsemen who "at the moment when the enemy infantry began action" were "to get behind them immediately . . . and place them between two forces".[2]

Narses left the initiative to Totila and awaited the attack, which was long delayed because the Gothic king waited for the arrival of the 2,000 horsemen he had ordered to join the army. To occupy the time, in gilt armour he gave a solo display of horsemanship between the two lines, and at length, about noon, when the 2,000 came up, he commanded all to take their meal, while he changed his parade armour and equipped himself like a private soldier. Apparently his aim was to persuade the Imperialists to break their ranks for dinner, and then to fall upon them unexpectedly. In this he was disappointed, because Narses had already "given orders that not a single man should either sit down to lunch or go off to sleep or even remove his cuirass, nor yet his bridle off his horse. However, he did not allow them to be altogether without food, but commanded them to eat a small meal in ranks and with their equipment on."[3]

Some time after the midday meal had been taken, the battle was opened by the Gothic cavalry, to be continued until nightfall, and though the account given by Procopius is sketchy—he was not an eye-witness—it is not difficult to picture what actually happened. The Goths took no notice of the bow-wings of their enemy's line and charged straight forward against the phalanx of dismounted barbarian *feoderati*, with the inevitable result that, while the central squadrons failed to break through its bristling hedge of spears, those on the flanks were raked by the Roman archers. Hundreds of Goths must have fallen immediately and scores of riderless horses have galloped away, plunging and careering over the battlefield to add confusion to the central squadrons which, presumably, were out of bow-shot. It would appear that the initial charge was the only organized one, and that those which followed were improvised by individual leaders, for no mention is made of the Gothic horse retiring behind their infantry to reorganize. Toward

---

[1] Oman. *A History of the Art of War*, vol. I, p. 34.
[2] Procopius, "The Gothic War", VIII, xxxi, 7.　　　[3] *Ibid.*, VIII, xxxii, 3–5.

evening the Romans began to advance, and the Gothic cavalry, no longer able to offer resistance, gave ground and finally broke back on their infantry, not, as Procopius writes, "with the purpose of recovering their breath and renewing the fight with their assistance, as is customary . . ." but to escape. "Consequently the infantry did not open intervals to receive them nor stand fast to rescue them, but they all began to flee precipitately with the cavalry, and in the rout they kept killing each other just as in a battle at night."[1] "So ended in complete success the first experiment in the combination of pike and bow which modern history shows."[2]

Six thousand Goths perished in the battle and all those captured were massacred, including "great numbers of the old Roman soldiers who had earlier detached themselves from the Roman army and deserted. . . ."[3] Among those who fell was Totila, who either early or late in the battle was mortally wounded. He was carried off the battlefield and died in the village of Caprae (probably Caprara).

The battle won, Narses first paid off his Lombard *feoderati* and sent them home. He was glad to see the last of them, for their savagery was such that it impeded his operations. Next, he set out to exterminate the surviving Goths, who after their defeat had crowned Teias their king. After he had occupied Rome, Narses cornered Teias and his small band at Sarno, not far from Vesuvius. There he blockaded him for two months, but eventually the Goths retired to Monte Lettere where a battle was fought in which Teias was slain. A capitulation was then agreed upon, according to which the remnants of the once powerful Gothic people were to collect such money as was still stored in their various fortresses and to leave Italy to live as free men in any barbarian kingdom they chose.

The Franks alone had now to be dealt with; for while Narses blockaded Sarno, a great horde of them, under command of the brothers Lothar and Buccelin, advanced down the peninsula and, in 554, at Casilinum, now the modern town of Capua on the Volturno, was annihilated by Narses, who used much the same tactics he had employed at Taginae.

Thus, in the year 554, Justinian accomplished the task he had

---

[1] Procopius, VIII, xxxii, 17–19.
[2] *A History of the Art of War*, Charles Oman, vol. I, p. 35.
[3] Procopius, "The Gothic War", VIII, xxxii, 20.

set his mind upon in 532. By annihilating the Vandals in Africa and the Ostrogoths in Italy, he extirpated Arianism within the bounds of the greater part of the old Western Empire, and brought under his dominion the whole of North Africa, Dalmatia, Italy, southern Spain, Sicily, Sardinia, Corsica and the Balearic Islands. Except for the Visigoths in Spain and Septimania (the region between the eastern Pyrenees and the Rhône) and the Franks in Provence, the Mediterranean was again a Roman lake. It was indeed a remarkable achievement; but what did it cost and what were its repercussions on history? It is in these things that must be sought the importance of the battles of Tricameron and Taginae.

Like Africa, Italy emerged out of twenty years of war ruined by long sieges, famines, massacres, devastations, plunderings, and pestilences. "The largest towns, such as Naples, Milan, and specially Rome", writes Professor Charles Diehl, "were almost devoid of inhabitants, the depopulated country was uncultivated and the large Italian proprietors were repaid for their devotion to Byzantium and their hostility to Totila by total ruin."[1]

Gibbon is even more scathing. He writes: "But the wars, the conquests, and the triumphs of Justinian are the feeble, and pernicious efforts of old age, which exhaust the remains of strength, and accelerate the decay of the power of life. He exulted in the glorious act of restoring Africa and Italy to the republic; but the calamities which followed . . . betrayed the impotence of the conqueror and accomplished the ruin of those unfortunate countries."[2] And again: "The triple scourge of war, pestilence, and famine, afflicted the subjects of Justinian, and his reign is disgraced by a visible decrease of the human species, which has never been repaired in some of the fairest countries of the globe."[3]

And what was the outcome of Justinian's victories? From the Euphrates to the Pillars of Hercules, war, fiscal oppression[4] and religious persecutions prepared ". . . the provinces of the East, pale, emaciated, and miserable, for the advent of the Moslem con-

---

[1] *The Cambridge Medieval History*, vol. II, p. 23.
[2] *The Decline and Fall of the Roman Empire*, vol. IV, p. 415.
[3] *Ibid.*, vol. IV, p. 469.
[4] "The imperial *logothetae* applied the burdensome system of Roman taxes to the ruined countries without making any allowance for the prevailing distress. They mercilessly demanded arrears dating from the time of the Goths, falsified the registers in order to increase the returns, and enriched themselves at the expense of the taxpayer to such an extent that, according to a contemporary writer, 'nothing remained for the inhabitants but to die, since they were bereft of all necessities of life' " (*The Cambridge Medieval History*, vol. II, p. 23).

querors, who", within a century of Justinian's death, "were to win the fairest of them and were to hold them even to our own day".[1] Africa under the Moors, who had been kept in check by the Vandals, returned to her primitive barbarism, and in consequence could in no way withstand the Saracens of the following century. And Italy, once the Goths had been exterminated and the *logothetes* under Narses had for twelve years sucked dry whatever wealth was left from war, was in 568 invaded by the ferocious Lombards under Alboin, the last of the German peoples to establish themselves within the bounds of the former Western Empire. They rapidly occupied the region north of the Po—still called Lombardy—more gradually extended southward, pillaging and massacring as they went, and eventually, except for Ravenna and Rome, overran the northern two-thirds of the peninsula. In 589, under Zotto, they stormed and destroyed St. Benedict's monastery on Monte Cassino, and in 774 were conquered by Charles the Great and absorbed into his empire.

Had Italy never been invaded; had the battle of Taginae never been fought; and had the Ostrogoths continued to rule in Italy, medieval history would have been different. Instead of reduction to a ruined, second-rate city of no political importance, Rome would have remained the active centre of western culture and civilization, and the blending of Gothic vigour with Latin culture would have gone far to dispel the gloom which since the battle of Adrianople had steadily crept over the West. Although for Justinian, Taginae was his greatest victory, for the Christian world of his day and for many years to come it was an immeasurable disaster.

---

[1] *Italy and Her Invaders*, vol. IV, p. 427.

# The rise and expansion of Islam

Justinian was the last of the great Roman emperors, for under his successor, Justin II (565–578), the Eastern Empire ceased to be Roman even in theory, and became wholly Byzantine. From then on all thought of reconquering the West was set aside, imperial policy became purely defensive, and threatened on the lower Danube by the Avars and Slavs, and on the upper Euphrates by the Persians, Justin was faced by the impossible strategical problem of holding two widely separated defensive fronts with forces inadequate to hold one securely. The outcome was an unceasing shuttling of armies from one front to the other, a condition his enemies were not slow to exploit.

The first shift of forces came in 572, when war again broke out with Persia, and by 591, when Maurice (582–602) was emperor, the garrisons in Europe had been so heavily drawn upon that peace was patched up with Chosröes II (590–628), in order to repel the Avars and Slavs. The former were a Tartar people who had been pushed westward by the Turks,[1] and the latter a non-German group of Indo-European peoples who in 577 began to sow the seeds of the future Slav kingdoms in the Balkans. In 591 the Avars swarmed southward, plundering and ravaging until in 604 they were bought off by the emperor Phocas (602–610) in order that he might meet Chosröes, who had broken the peace.

In 610, Phocas–"a hideous nightmare brooding over an exhausted and weary realm"–was hewn to pieces by Heraclius (610–642), who succeeded him. The war continued, and in 613 the Persians invaded Syria and took Damascus and Jerusalem. With the latter was lost "The Wood", as the True Cross, discovered by Helena the mother of Constantine the Great, was called; a loss which seemed to portend the ruin of the Empire. Next, in 617, when the Slavs raged at will over the European provinces and the Avars surged up to the Golden Gate, Chalcedon (Kadikeui) on the Propontis was lost, and two years later Egypt was invaded

---

[1] The name Turk (Tou-Kiue) is first mentioned in Chinese history in 545. Between 546 and 582 the Turks established themselves as a great power between China and Persia, and in 565 sent a mission to Justin to open up the silk trade and to seek his cooperation against the Persians.

and its corn supply cut off; meanwhile Armenia was overrun and the Empire deprived of its main recruiting ground. These disasters so overwhelmed Heraclius that he resolved to transfer the capital to Carthage, and was only prevented from doing so by the patriarch, who exacted from him an oath that he would never abandon Constantinople. The relief caused by this was so great that a sudden outburst of religious enthusiasm seized the people and a crusade was preached to rescue the Holy City and the Holy Cross.

Thus it came about that in 623 Heraclius took the field to fight six campaigns, during the fifth of which, in 626, hordes of Avars, Slavs, Bulgars, and Gepids, acting in concert with the Persian forces at Chalcedon, laid siege to Constantinople. Because of Byzantine command of the sea the city was saved. The following year Heraclius invaded Persia by way of Azerbaijan, marched southward, and on December 1 reached the Great Zab; eleven days later he decisively defeated the Persians in the neighbourhood of Nineveh. He then marched on Ctesiphon, but was compelled to retire before he reached the Persian capital. But no further campaign was necessary, for in the spring of 628 Chosröes was assassinated and peace followed. Its terms are unknown, except that they included the restoration of the Cross and the evacuation of the Empire's territory by the armies of Persia.

Thus, at the very moment when a new invader mobilized in the south, the two great empires in the East lay exhausted; their territories ravaged, their man-power wasted, their wealth gone; they were vacuums ready to be filled by the followers of the Prophet.

A few months after the True Cross had been restored to the Holy City on March 21, 630, a struggle began which, with scarcely an intermission, was to last for a thousand years. In the autumn of that year Mahomet who, at the important battle of Bahr, in 624, had finally established his authority over the Arabs, sent northward a raiding force, which at Muta, east of the Dead Sea, clashed with a Byzantine outpost and was defeated. Three years later, on June 7, he died, and as he left no son a minority of his followers recognized Abu Bakr (632–634) as Caliph ("Successor"). Because many Arabs objected to paying tribute to Medina, which since the year of the *hegira* (622) had become the centre of the Islamic faith, a rebellion, known as the *Ridda*, followed, which was finally suppressed by Khalid ibn al-Walid in his victory over the Meccans at Akraba. After this battle, to keep his victorious troops employed, Abu Bakr sent Khalid and 500 men to raid Irak, and three small forces to help the Christian Arabs of the border districts of Syria who, because the yearly subsidies paid to them by the Byzantines had been suspended, had sought his aid.

At the time these raiders set out, Heraclius was at Emesa (Homs), and because he trusted the Christian Arabs of the desert to prove a sufficient barrier against a Moslem advance, he had made no preparation to oppose one. But when he heard that southern Palestine had been raided, he assembled a considerable army south of Damascus under his brother Theodorus and ordered him to repel the invaders. When Khalid heard this, with lightning speed he passed from Hirah on the Euphrates through Palmyra and suddenly appeared before the walls of Damascus. From there, with great difficulty, he joined the three raiding columns, met Theodorus at Ajnadain, between Jerusalem and Gaza, and on July 30, 634, won a brilliant victory.

Soon afterward Abu Bakr died and was succeeded by Omar (634-644), and as he decided not merely to raid but to conquer Syria, an inundation of Moslem tribes under Khalid moved north. Damascus was betrayed to him, and toward the end of 635 he occupied Emesa.

In the spring of 636, Heraclius sent a new army, about 50,000 strong, under Theodorus Trithurius to oppose Khalid. At once the latter fell back, and relinquishing Damascus concentrated his forces, 25,000 in all, south-east of the Yarmuk valley, where, after much manœuvring and several engagements, on August 20, 636, he cut Trithurius's communications and annihilated his army. The battle was decisive; for so hated was Byzantine rule that everywhere in Syria the Moslems were welcomed as deliverers: the whole country fell to them, and in the north for centuries to come the Amanus range became the northern boundary of the Caliph's dominions.

The collapse of Persia was as swift and complete as that of Syria, and the main reason for it was the same; for, like the Syrians, the Aramaic peasants greeted their conquerors as deliverers. In the autumn of 635, Mutanna, a local chieftain, helped by troops from Medina, defeated a Persian army at Buwaib (south of Kufa) and in June, 637, Rustam, at the head of a numerically superior Persian army, was routed and slain by Sad ibn Wakkas at Khadisiya (west of Buwaib). The king of Persia and his court then fled before Sad's advance up the Tigris to the Iranian mountains. Next, Ctesiphon opened its gates, and lastly the whole of Irak passed into Arab hands. From now on, Islam ceased to be dependent on Medina, and instead represented the Arabs as a common empire. In consequence systematic conquest took the place of desultory raids, and during it whole tribes usually participated. Syria and Irak were linked by the conquest of Mesopotamia; Ecbatana fell in 641; the Persian Gulf passed under Arab dominion; and by 652 Khorasan was overrun.

Astonishing as it may seem, the conquest of Egypt falls in the same period, and again this can only be explained by reaction to Byzantine rule, which had imposed extortionary taxes on the Egyptians and had prohibited the Coptic faith.

The conqueror of Egypt was Amr ibn al-As. In January, 640, he took Pelusium and in July defeated the Byzantines at Heliopolis. Babylon, near modern Cairo, was occupied in April 641, and Alexandria surrendered on terms on September 17, 642. Next, to cover his western flank, Amr overran Cyrenaica.

This last advance was followed by decades of plundering raids, and though the Moslems penetrated to Kairouan in present-day Tunisia, and more than once held the town, it was not until they substituted a policy of occupation for that of plunder and gained naval command of the Mediterranean that they were able to seize and hold the Byzantine coastal towns, which were the keys to the hinterland. When, at the close of the century, this was done, Hassan ibn an Numan, basing himself on Kairouan, took Carthage in 695, and in a remarkably short time Latin civilization was extinguished in northern Africa.

Throughout the expansion, the conquest of Constantinople remained the ultimate Moslem goal, and the first attempt to attain it was made by the Caliph Othman (644–656) as early as 655. That year he sent out a naval expedition to effect it; but though the Byzantine fleet was decisively defeated, the assassination of Othman in the following year and the succession war which immediately broke out between Muawiya (660–680) and Ali, the son-in-law of the Prophet, forced its abandonment. In 659, occupied with Ali, Muawiya made peace with Byzantium. He was the founder of the Omayad line of Caliphs, with his capital at Damascus.

When he had consolidated his position, Muawiya returned to the project in 668. That year he sent an expedition into Asia

Minor—called by the Byzantines "Romania"—which occupied Chalcedon, from where, in the spring of 669, it crossed into Thrace and attacked Constantinople, though no serious siege was undertaken. In 672 Muawiya followed up this expedition by sending a fleet to win command of the Bosphorus, and from then until 677 Constantinople was attacked intermittently, each attack being frustrated by the fleet of Emperor Constantine IV (668–685). Loss of men and ships compelled the Moslems to withdraw, and during their return most of their fleet was lost in a storm and its remnants destroyed by the Byzantines. This disaster caused Muawiya for a second time to make peace.

On Muawiya's death, in 680, another war of succession occupied the greater part of the stormy reign of the Caliph Abd-al-Malik (685–705), and under his successor Walid (705–715) the Arabian Empire attained its greatest expansion. In the west the Atlantic coast was reached in 710, and Spain was overrun the following year. In the east the Arabs penetrated into the Punjab, and in central Asia reached the borders of China. In the last years of his reign Walid returned to the project of capturing Constantinople, and on his death in 715 it became an inheritance of his successor, the Caliph Suleiman.

# CHAPTER 12

# The siege of Constantinople, 717–718, and the Battle of Tours, 732

When, in 711, the Emperor Justinian II, who succeeded Constantine IV in 685, died, the Empire sank to the lowest level of impotence it had yet reached. Distracted, depopulated, plundered by Bulgars and Slavs in Europe and ravaged by the Saracens in Asia Minor, its army and fleet in constant mutiny, it appeared that its last days were at hand, when suddenly, in 717, out of the débris of twenty years of anarchy, a man created a new empire which was destined to become the bulwark of Europe against Asia for 700 years. A soldier by profession, this man is known to history as Leo the Isaurian.

Of his origin we know next to nothing. Probably he was a Syrian and not an Isaurian,[1] for he was born about the year 687 at Germanicea (Marash) in the province of Commagene, the north-easterly district of Syria. His true name was Conon, and we first hear of him and his family in 705 in Thrace, when his father made a gift of 500 sheep to Justinian, who in return made his son Leo a *spatharius* or aide-de-camp. Later, apparently to get rid of him, the Emperor sent him on a mission to Alania, a country north of the Caucasian mountains, and, after his return, the Emperor Anastasius (713–716), who was seeking out able soldiers, gave him command of the Anatolic theme. When in 716 Anastasius was deposed, all eyes were fixed upon Leo as the man best qualified to succeed him.

Meanwhile the Caliph Suleiman (715–717), as a first step toward carrying out Walid's projected expedition against Constantinople, sent two armies from Taurus into Romania, one under his brother Maslama and the other under a general named Suleiman. The latter advanced through the Anatolic theme and approached Amorium, which lay to the north of Lake Aksehir. Though it had no garrison, he was forced to blockade the city, and as he thought Leo destined to be the next emperor, he resorted to a ruse in order to capture him. In this he was unsuccessful, and

[1] Isauria, a district of Asia Minor on the north side of the Taurus, modern Konia.

when the siege of Amorium was raised, Leo, after having removed its women and children, garrisoned the city with 800 soldiers. Next, Maslama, who was advancing through Cappadocia, set out to trap Leo; but, like Suleiman, he was outwitted by the crafty Isaurian.

While this strange campaign of wits was being fought, Theodosius III (716–717) invested his son with the purple and posted him on the Asiatic side of the Sea of Marmara. First Leo assured himself that Maslama had evacuated Romania, then he advanced to Nicomedia (Ismid) and routed the young prince, whose name is unknown; after which he probably wintered at Nicaea or Nicomedia, and early in 717 crossed to Constantinople. This persuaded Theodosius to exchange the throne for a monastery, and on March 25 Leo was crowned by the Patriarch in St. Sophia and became Leo III (717–740).

Leo had not a moment to lose. The granaries and arsenals of Constantinople were replenished, its walls repaired and numerous engines of war mounted upon them. Strategically the city was immensely strong, virtually impregnable, as long as its sea communications were kept open. It was built on a promontory flanked on the north by the Golden Horn and on the south by the Sea of Marmara. On its western or landward side ran an inner and an outer wall; the former built by Constantine the Great and the latter by Theodosius II, which was some four miles in length. At this period the normal population numbered about half a million, but it must now have been swollen considerably with refugees. If strongly held, to take the city by storm was not, until the invention of gunpowder, a practical operation of war; therefore the only certain method was blockade. This meant closing the Bosphorus as well as the Dardanelles, and to close the former was difficult, because the city flanked its approach from the south. Therefore, for Leo, everything depended on his fleet, which numerically was vastly inferior to his enemy's.

Maslama's plan was a twofold one: to advance by land and sea and to surround the city. The army, some 80,000 strong, he kept under his own command, and the fleet he handed over to Suleiman the General; it is said to have numbered 1,800 vessels and to have had on board 80,000 infantry. Besides these, other forces were in preparation: 800 ships, probably mostly supply vessels, were being made ready in the ports of Africa and Egypt, and at Tarsus a reserve army was being formed under the Caliph.[1]

[1] All these figures are probably much exaggerated.

First, Maslama marched to Pergamum, and once he had taken it he next advanced to the Hellespont, crossed it at Abydus, probably in July, and appeared before the outer, landward wall of Constantinople on August 15, 717. There he entrenched his army and sent a detachment to watch Adrianople and Tervel, king of the Bulgars, with whom Leo was in communication.

A land attack was at once attempted; but when it was beaten back by the engines and the skill of the Byzantine engineers, Maslama surrounded his camp with a deep ditch and decided to reduce the city by blockade. To do this, he instructed Suleiman the General to divide his fleet into two squadrons, one to be stationed at Eutropius (Mundi Burnou) and Anthemius on the Asiatic coast, to cut off supplies from the Aegean, and the other to move through the Bosphorus to above Galata and to cut off the city from the Black Sea and, more particularly, from the cities of Cherson (near Sevastopool) and Trebizond.

The second squadron arrived on September 1, and on September 3 got under way to sail north of the Golden Horn, where Leo lay with his fleet. The entrance to the harbour was protected by a great chain suspended between two towers, from which it could be raised or lowered.

While the blockading squadron approached, the strong current which sweeps round Seraglio Point threw its advanced ships into confusion. At once Leo ordered the chain to be lowered, stood out with his galleys, and before his enemy could form a line of battle, poured Greek fire[1] upon his ships, destroyed twenty and captured others. Immediately after, when he saw the main body of Suleiman's fleet approaching, he returned to the inner waters of the Golden Horn.

This rapid and well-directed attack was so successful and terrifying that though, in order to entice his enemy on, Leo kept the boom lowered throughout the rest of that day and the following night, no further attempt was made to force the strait. A victory

[1] An inflammable composition. According to the *Chronography of Theophanes*, during the reign of Constantine Pogonatus (684–685) an architect named Callinicus, who fled from Heliopolis in Syria to Constantinople, prepared a "wet fire" which was projected by means of siphons. Lieut.-Colonel Hime (see his *Gunpowder and Ammunition, their Origin and Progress*, 1904) considers that it was composed of sulphur, naphtha and quicklime which took fire spontaneously when wetted, and that portions of it were "projected and at the same time ignited by applying the hose of a water engine to the breech of the siphon". Somewhat similar substances had long been in use, see Thucydides II, 77, and IV, 100: Siege of Delium, 424 B.C. Vegetius (*c.* A.D. 350) gives as a receipt naphtha or petroleum. (See also Gibbon's *The Decline and Fall of the Roman Empire*, vol. VI, pp. 9–12.)

had been won at practically no loss, so complete that Leo was able to pour supplies into Constantinople and prevent its reduction through famine. To add to Maslama's difficulties, his brother the Caliph, who was then on his way to reinforce him, suddenly died of indigestion.[1] He was succeeded by Omar II (717–730), a religious bigot and no soldier.

A partial investment had now to be resorted to, and during it winter set in with unwonted severity. For a hundred days snow lay on the ground, and unaccustomed to the rigours of a European winter, thousands of Moslems died, among them Suleiman the General. In spring the following year the Egyptian squadron from Alexandria, 400 ships in all, commanded by Sofiam, arrived, passed Constantinople under cover of darkness, took station at Kalos Argos (Buyuk-Deré), and closed the passage of the Bosphorus. Shortly after it was followed by the African squadron, 360 ships under Yezid, which cast anchor on the Bithynian shore. Finally, the reserve army, now under Merdasan, arrived to reinforce the garrisons of the trenches, which were so decimated by famine that many men were reduced to feed upon human flesh.

Though the closing of the Bosphorus would in time have compelled capitulation, fortunately for Leo large numbers of the Egyptian crews were impressed Christians, and many of these men deserted and provided him with exact information concerning the Moslems. He lowered the boom, again put to sea, fell upon his enemy and caught him completely unprepared. It was a rout rather than a battle; for the Christian crews deserted by thousands, and their unmanned vessels were rammed or burned with Greek fire. This decisive naval victory was, astonishing as it may seem, followed by a land pursuit; for immediately after Leo had destroyed the African squadron, he ferried over to the Asiatic shore a considerable force of soldiers, which trapped Merdasan in an ambush, cut many of his men to pieces and routed the rest.

Meanwhile, through his diplomacy, Leo had persuaded Tervel and his Bulgars to march against Maslama and they won a battle somewhere south of Adrianople in which 22,000 Moslems are said to have been killed. To add to the terror the Moslems now

---

[1] According to Gibbon (*The Decline and Fall of the Roman Empire*, vol. VI, p. 7), "The Caliph had emptied two baskets of eggs and figs, which he swallowed alternately, and the repast was concluded with marrow and sugar." In one of his pilgrimages to Mecca, Suleiman ate, at a single meal, seventy pomegranates, a kid, six fowls, and a huge quantity of the grapes of Tayeff . . . (Abulfeda, *Annal. Moslem*, p. 126, quoted by Gibbon).

were in, "A report was dexterously scattered that Franks, the unknown nations of the Latin world, were arming by sea and land in the defence of the Christian cause, and their formidable aid was expected. . . ."[1]

This last disaster persuaded the Caliph to recall Maslama, and on August 15, 718, he raised the siege, which had now lasted exactly twelve months. He embarked the remnants of his army and landed them at Cyzicus (Bal-Kis) on the Asiatic coast of the Sea of Marmara. His fleet stood out for the Hellespont and was lost in a storm. We are told that only five galleys of the 2,560 vessels employed in the siege returned to Syria and Alexandria. Of the land forces, which, according to Arab reckoning, must have totalled well over 200,000 men, no more than 30,000 regained Tarsus.

Thus Leo's victory was decisive, and further added to by his defeat of the Arabs at Acroinon (Afyon Karahisar) in Phrygia in 739, which compelled them to withdraw from western Asia Minor. It was his generalship which had won it, and every historian of his reign has dwelt upon its importance. Vasiliev writes: "It is justly claimed that by his successful resistance Leo saved not only the Byzantine Empire and the eastern Christian world, but also all of Western European civilization";[2] Bury calls 718 "an ecumenical date";[3] Foord considers that it was "the greatest success in Roman history";[4] Finlay, "that it was one of the most brilliant exploits of a warlike age";[5] and Gibbon calls the Moslem defeat an "almost incredible disaster".[6] This was not because of the ships lost and the men who perished, both of which could be replaced; but because the fall of Constantinople would have remodelled the entire history of the East, as seven centuries later it did. Beyond question, the Moslem repulse was one of the great decisive events in western history, for it saved Europe from invasion at the moment when a new power within its as yet undefined frontiers was struggling into being. This power was the Frankish kingdom, which was now about to take the first step toward creating a new universal empire.

In 710-possibly a few years earlier-the Arab invasion of

---

[1] *The Decline and Fall of the Roman Empire*, vol. VI, p. 9.
[2] *History of the Byzantine Empire* (1928), vol. I, p. 289.
[3] *History of the Later Roman Empire* (1889), vol. II, p. 405.
[4] *The Byzantine Empire* (1911), p. 171.
[5] *History of Greece from its Conquest to Present Times* (1877), vol. II, p. 18.
[6] *The Decline and Fall of the Roman Empire*, vol. VI, p. 9.

Africa, as mentioned in Chronicle 11, had reached the shores of the Atlantic. It was only made possible because the Berbers or Moors – the Numidians of Hannibal's day – were able to supply the necessary men. Plunderers by nature, once the western sea was reached, in order to keep them employed, Musa ibn Nusair, governor of northern Africa, turned his gaze toward Spain. To conquer that country does not seem to have been his intention, instead, merely to raid it, and as he had no ships he approached a certain Julian,[1] the Byzantine governor of Ceuta. This man readily agreed to assist him, for he bore a grudge against Roderic, the Visigothic king in Toledo, who had dishonoured his daughter. Promised four vessels by Julian, Musa sought permission of the Caliph, then established at Damascus, to invade Spain. Grudgingly he agreed, for he replied: Do not for the present expose a large army to the dangers of an expedition beyond the seas. The issue was that, during the summer of 710, Abu Zora Tarif and 400 men crossed the strait, pillaged the neighbourhood of Algeciras and returned with plunder.

Encouraged by this reconnaissance, and having heard that Roderic was engaged in a war with the Franks and Vascons in the north of Spain, in 711 Musa decided upon an extensive expedition, and in batches of 400 men at the time, for he still had no more than Julian's four ships, he sent over 7,000 under Tarik ibn Ziyad. Tarik landed at Gibraltar, did not wait for Musa and the main body, but pushed westward along the coast, met Roderic in the Valley of the Wadi Bekka (Salado), between Lake Janda and the town of Medina Sidonia, and thanks to treachery in Roderic's army, on July 19 he routed him. Tarik won another battle at Ecija and occupied Toledo, the Visigothic capital. Next year Musa took over the supreme command, and by showing leniency to all who submitted and by using violence against all who opposed him,[2] he conquered nearly the whole of Spain before the close of the year, when he was recalled by the Caliph.

No sooner was Spain overrun than the Moorish-Moslem horde flowed over the Pyrenees into Aquitaine, then ruled by Duke Eudo; according to M. Mercier, this invasion began in 712.[3] In 717–718, Musa's successor, Hurr, set out on a full-scale plundering expedition, which in idea seems to have become more and more

---

[1] Also called Urban and Olban, probably a Christian Berber.
[2] See *Invasions des Sarrazins en France*, Reinaud (1836), p. 8.
[3] *Revue Historique* (May, 1878), "La Bataille de Poitiers", E. Mercier, p. 3. Part of the Visigothic kingdom lay north of the Pyrenees.

an invasion of conquest as the siege of Constantinople lagged and ultimately failed; for we are told that the Moslem intention was to push through France and to return to Damascus by way of Germany, taking Constantinople on the way, and thus to make the Mediterranean a Moslem sea.[1] In 719 Narbonne was occupied, and two years later, when Samh laid siege to Toulouse, he was defeated by Eudo and routed. In spite of this defeat, the Moslem flood returned; in 725 Carcassonne and Nîmes were occupied and, the following year, Anbaca advanced up the Rhône valley, ravaged Burgundy and penetrated as far north as the Vosges.[2]

When this incursion took place, the future conqueror of the Moors was warring on the Danube; he was Charles, son of Pepin II, and the sworn enemy of Eudo of Aquitania.

To appreciate the relationship between these two men, who soon were to act in unison, it is necessary to go back into history. At the battle of Châlons legend affirms that the Salian Frankish *feoderati* who joined Aetius were led by a chieftain called Merovech (Merovaeus) who founded the Merovingian dynasty, which in power reached its zenith under Clovis his grandson, who by his victory at Vouillé, in 507, finally drove the Visigoths out of France into Spain. But since 639 this dynasty had fallen into decay and had produced a succession of *rois fainéants*.[3] Under these effete kings all power passed into the hands of the Mayor of the Palace,[4] the old Master of the Trooops, of whom the most able came from Austrasia, the region roughly lying between the Meuse and the Main. Of this line, Pepin II established himself as mayor in 687, and made himself master of Austrasia, Neustria (between the Loire and Meuse) and Aquitania (between the Garonne and Loire). When in 714 he died, his natural son Charles was in prison accused of the murder of Pepin's legitimate son Grimoald and the mayoralty passed to his son, a minor. In the circumstances, as was all but inevitable, anarchy swept Gaul, and in the turmoil Charles escaped from prison and Eudo proclaimed his independence. Charles collected a band of adherents, first established himself in Austrasia, and next, in 719, he marched against Eudo,

---

[1] See *Invasions des Sarrazins*, Reinaud, p. 9, and *Cambridge Medieval History*, vol. II, p. 373.

[2] *Revue Historique* (May 1878), "La Bataille de Poitiers", E. Mercier, p. 4.

[3] "It was a dynasty of children; they died at the age of 23, 24 or 25, worn out by precocious debauchery. They were fathers at sixteen, fifteen and even fourteen years, and their children were miserable weaklings" (*Cambridge Medieval History*, vol. II, 125–126).

[4] For his functions see *Histoire de France*, edit. Ernest Lavisse, vol. II, pt. I, pp. 176–177.

defeated him near Soissons and subdued Neustria. With Eudo brought to terms, he set out to war against the Germans, Saxons, and Swabians, in order to secure his north-eastern frontier before he subjected Aquitania, and in 725 he was warring on the Danube when he learnt of Anbaca's advance up the Rhône.

Meanwhile Eudo, though he knew nothing of Charles's intention to establish his authority over the whole of Gaul, nevertheless realized the precariousness of his position, wedged between the Franks in Neustria and the Moslems in Spain. Therefore, to secure his southern frontiers, he entered into relations with a Berber potentate named Othman ben abi Neza, whose realm lay on the northern side of the Pyrenees, and cemented an alliance with him by marrying his daughter Lampagie, a girl of remarkable beauty. Realizing that Eudo could not at the same time defend both his southern and northern frontiers, Abd-ar-Rahman, Governor of Spain, set out to punish the rebellious Othman, and in 731 he chased him into the mountains, when, to escape capture, the latter leapt over a precipice, and Lampagie, because of her beauty, was sent to Damascus to adorn the Caliph's harem.

Eudo's Moslem ally overcome, Abd-ar-Rahman decided to invade Aquitaine. His object was undoubtedly plunder and not the conquest of France; yet again it would seem that in his head there lurked the possibility of "uniting Italy, Germany and the empire of the Greeks to the already vast domains of the champions of the Koran".[1] He concentrated his main army along the upper reaches of the Ebro, took the road to Pamplona, crossed the Bidassoa at Irun and advanced into Gascony. His army cannot have been large, because we are told that it marched in a single column, and when it was moving north an independent force was detached to strike at Arles, in order to distract the enemy and spread terror throughout Aquitaine.

Directing his course on Bordeaux, Eudo met him there and was defeated decisively, and the city was stormed, plundered and burnt. The valley of the Garonne left behind him, Abd-ar-Rahman moved north and crossed the Dordogne, pillaging and massacring as he advanced. In order to plunder more freely, he split his army into several columns and moved on Tours; for he had heard that its abbey possessed untold treasures. At Poitiers, some sixty miles south of Tours, he found its gates closed to him, invested the city, and then continued his advance.

[1] *Invasions des Sarrazins en France*, Reinaud, p. 35.

Meanwhile Charles, his Saxon and Danubean conquests finished, had arrived in Neustria, from where, in 731, he crossed the Loire and ravaged Berri. Placed thus between two fronts,

25. HUNNISH AND MOSLEM INVASIONS OF FRANCE,
451 AND 732

Eudo had no option but to turn to Charles, hurried to Paris and won his support on the condition that he submitted to Frankish control. Then, at the head of a horde of fighting men, Charles crossed the Loire, probably at Orléans. Abd-ar-Rahman, whose army was now loaded with loot, then fell back upon Poitiers.

Of Abd-ar-Rahman's military organization little is known, except that the bulk of his men were Moors and that most of them were mounted. The bow seems to have been little used by them, instead the lance and sword, and armour was seldom worn. It is known that many mules followed the fighting troops; but it would seem that these animals were used mainly for carrying plunder and not supplies. The army lived on the country, was followed by a rabble of cut-throats, and its tactics were wasteful of men, for they consisted entirely in wild, headlong charges.

Of the Frankish army we have a more detailed account. Unlike the Gothic, the infantry arm solely was relied upon. It was divided into two classes of men, the General's private host, which had to be constantly employed, for plunder was the only remuneration it received, and local levies, a militia of ill-armed men. The host had been trained in many wars, and the levies were little more than foragers. The whole organization was primitive in the extreme and could only be kept together as long as food was obtainable. When it was not, it dissolved.[1] Of discipline there was virtually none; things were much the same as they had been in the days of Gregory of Tours when he wrote: "What were we to do? no one fears his king, no one fears his duke, no one respects his count; and if perchance any of us tries to improve his state of affairs, and to assert his authority, forthwith sedition breaks out in the army, and mutiny swells up."[2]

It would seem that in the Frankish army horses were seldom used, except by the nobles, and then only on the line of march. Armour rapidly was coming into vogue again; for, in 574, we find Bishop Saggettarius blamed for going to war "armed not with the sign of the heavenly cross, but with the secular cuirass and helmet", and, in 585, Gundovald Ballomer was saved by his body armour from a javelin.[3] The shield was universal, and arms consisted of swords, daggers, javelins, and two kinds of axes, one for wielding and the other for throwing—the *francisca*.

Though tactics were crude, Charles, a good general, understood his enemy's weakness. According to Gibbon, he wrote to Eudo: "If you follow my advice you will not interrupt their

---

[1] For further particulars see *Histoire de France*, edit. Ernest Lavisse, vol. II, pt. I, pp. 191–194.
[2] *Gregory of Tours*, IX, 31.      [3] *Ibid.*, IV, 18, and VII, 38.

march nor precipitate your attack. They are like a torrent, which it is dangerous to stem in its career. The thirst of riches and the consciousness of success, redouble their valour, and valour is of more avail than arm or numbers. Be patient till they have loaded themselves with the encumbrance of wealth. The possession of wealth will divide their counsels and assure your victory."[1]

The sudden appearance of Charles caused consternation among the Moslems, for by now they were so weighed down with loot that they had lost all mobility; so encumbered that Abd-ar-Rahman contemplated abandoning his plunder, but did not do so, possibly because his men would have refused to obey him, and possibly also because Charles did not press him; for we are told that the two armies faced each other for seven days. What occurred during this pause is obvious: Abd-ar-Rahman withdrew his plunder southward, and Charles awaited the arrival of his levies.

Of the battle itself we have few details, nor do we even know where it was actually fought, but the date given is October, 732. Probably the armies came into contact somewhere near Tours and skirmished for a while. Next, that Abd-ar-Rahman fell back towards Poitiers,[2] and when he found that his loot had got no farther south, decided to accept battle in order to cover its withdrawal.

As the Moslems were solely an offensive force and lacked defensive power, this meant that, whatever the circumstances, Abd-ar-Rahman was forced to attack. Clearly realizing this, Charles drew up his army in solid phalanx, the kernel of which consisted of his Frankish followers. Isidore de Béja calls it an army of Europeans (*Europenses*) because it was composed of men speaking many languages.

As was usual with the Moslems, the battle was opened with a furious cavalry charge, which was repeated again and again; nevertheless, the Frankish phalanx remained unshaken. "The men of the North", says one chronicler, "stood as motionless as a wall; they were like a belt of ice frozen together, and not to be dissolved, as they slew the Arab with the sword. The Austrasians, vast of limb, and iron of hand, hewed on bravely in the thick of the

---

[1] *The Decline and Fall of the Roman Empire*, Edward Gibbon, vol. VI, p. 15, and *Histoire de la Gaule Méridionale, etc.*, Fauriel, vol. III, p. 127.

[2] In all there were three famous battles fought at or near Poitiers: the first in 507, that of Clovis and his Franks against the Visigoths, in which he slew Alaric II with his own hand and added Aquitaine to his dominions; the second, the one here described; and the third fought by the Black Prince on September 19, 1356.

fight; it was they who found and cut down the Saracen King."[1] Seemingly, toward evening Eudo and his Aquitanians turned one of the Moslem flanks, and launched an attack on Abd-ar-Rahman's camp, in which the bulk of his loot was still stacked. Upon this the Moslems fell back, and only then discovered that Abd-ar-Rahman had been killed. Night set in and the battle ended.

On the following morning, Charles again drew up his army to meet a second attack, when his scouts reported to him that the Moslem camp had been abandoned. Apparently, seized by panic at the loss of their leader, the Moslems and Moors had fled south and left the bulk of their plunder behind them.

There was no pursuit and the reasons for this are apparent. First, Charles could not pursue a retiring mounted force; secondly, the capture of the plunder prohibited such an operation; and thirdly, it was not Charles's policy entirely to relieve Eudo of Moslem pressure; for it was solely the threat from the south which enabled the Franks to keep some hold over Aquitaine. So he collected the loot and recrossed the Loire, to become known to posterity as Charles Martel–"The Hammer". "*Comme le martiaus debrise et froisse le fer et l'acier, et tous les autres metaux, aussi froissait-il et brisait-il par la bataille tous ses ennemis et toutes autres nations.*"[2]

Of the casualties, fantastic figures are given, mounting to 360,000 Moslems killed; and Charles's losses are stated to have been 1,500. Probably the forces engaged were not large, and for the simple reason that, as neither side possessed a supply train, it would have been impossible for hundreds of thousands of men to face each other for even seven days without starving. Of the results of this famous battle Gibbon writes:

"A victorious line of march had been prolonged above a thousand miles from the rock of Gibraltar to the banks of the Loire; the repetition of an equal space would have carried the Saracens to the confines of Poland and the Highlands of Scotland: The Rhine is not more impassable than the Nile or Euphrates, and the Arabian fleet might have sailed without a naval combat into the mouth of the Thames. Perhaps the interpetation of the Koran would now be taught in the schools of Oxford, and her pupils might demon-

[1] Quoted from Oman's *The Art of War in the Middle Ages*, vol. I, p. 58; also *L'art militaire et les armées au moyen age*, Ferdinand Lot (1946), vol. I, p. 113.
[2] "Chronicle of Saint-Denis", quoted in *Recueil des Historiens des Gaules*, Bouquet, vol. III, p. 310 (compiled *c.* 1270).

strate to a circumcised people the sanctity and truth of the revelation of Mahomet."[1]

This apocalyptic picture has long been discounted; yet, as frequently happens, the pendulum of criticism has swung too far in the opposite direction. Though, in effect, Charles's victory cannot be compared with Leo's, it was nevertheless one of the decisive victories in the history of Europe, if only because it was the epilogue of Leo's masterpiece. Had Constantinople fallen in 717, there can be little doubt that Moslem pressure in the east would have stimulated Moslem conquest in the west; and, if this probability is accepted, then it follows that it was Leo as much as Charles Martel who saved France. Nevertheless the immediate factor which halted further Moslem expansion in the west was the Berber revolt in Morocco, the cause of which briefly was as follows:

About the time of the battle of Tours, internal dissensions broke out within the Arabian Empire, for though the Arabs were united by the bond of Islam they continued to maintain their tribal institutions and with them their old feuds and factions. Of the latter the two most important were the Maadites and the Yemenites, the one representing the original northern tribes and the other the original southern tribes of Arabia. The Meccans belonged to the former and the Medinians to the latter. When the Maadites gained the upper hand, the Berbers in Africa refused to obey them, rose in revolt and the whole territory of what now is Morocco seceded. The final result was that out of the turmoil most of Spain became an independent Moorish state, the Christian kingdoms of Leon, Castile, and Navarre, as well as the County of Barcelona took form, and in Africa a series of independent states was gradually precipitated. But the important point to note is that, because of the revolt immediately after Abd-ar-Rahman's defeat at Tours, the Arab leaders in Spain were cut off from the Caliph in Damascus, and because of the revolution in Morocco they were no longer able to recruit their Berber armies. Added to this, it is highly probably that, because plunder was the main incentive which kept the Berbers in the field, Charles's victory added much to the general confusion.

But the real importance of the battle of Tours lies in quite another direction. It was not that Charles's victory saved western Europe from Arab rule, and, therefore, prevented the Koran

[1] *The Decline and Fall of the Roman Empire*, vol. VI, p. 15.

from being taught at Oxford, but that it made Charles supreme in Gaul and enabled him to establish his dynasty. As H. Pirenne writes: "Without Islam the Frankish Empire would probably never have existed and Charlemagne, without Mahomet, would be inconceivable."[1]

In 735 Eudo died at the age of sixty-six, and Charles overran Aquitaine and compelled his two sons to do homage to him, after which for four years he undertook several campaigns against the Moslems in the Rhône valley, and so completely undermined their power that a few years later they withdrew south of the Pyrenees for good.

Throughout these many wars his supreme difficulty was always the payment of his army. Money was scarce, and as the Roman system of taxation had vanished in the general chaos, two alternatives remained: plunder or the sequestration of lands and estates. Because many of the latter were in the hands of the Church, frequently it happened that Charles seized them in order to reward his turbulent vassals. This brought him into conflict with the Papacy, and how violently may be judged by the stories which accumulated round his name. After his death in 741 Gibbon writes: "His merits were forgotten", and "His sacrilege alone was remembered".[2] Thus it came about that as the years passed, not a few of his successes were credited by ecclesiastical writers to his grandson, Charles the Great–Charlemagne.

Six years before the battle of Poitiers was fought and for many years after it, a still more violent dispute had arisen between the Papacy and Leo III; a quarrel which caused Pope Gregory III, in 739, to appeal to Charles and to offer him the significant, yet undefined title of Roman consul. This quarrel was the first fruit of the siege of Constantinople.

The siege had vastly increased Leo's prestige, and he at once began to invest it in a series of reforms, out of which a new Eastern Empire emerged. Not only was he the ablest general of his age, but also its greatest statesman; for besides knowing how to win a war, he knew how to win the peace ensuing. The reforms which he introduced fall under three main headings: military, civil, and religious; they were all-embracing. The army was overhauled and a police force created; the judicial system was entirely reformed, and order and justice were established; the whole of the financial

[1] "Mahomet et Charlemagne", in *Revue belge de philologie et d'histoire* (1922), I, p. 86.
[2] *The Decline and Fall*, vol. VI, p. 18.

system was reorganized, and industry, agriculture and trade encouraged. He realized that it would be impossible to enforce these reforms in his Italian provinces and he decided to let Italy fend for itself. The effect of this was threefold: it opened Rome to the incursions of the Lombards; it eased his path in carrying out his religious reforms; and the two together brought upon his head the anathemas of the Papacy and widened the gap between the Eastern (Orthodox) Church and the Western (Catholic).[1]

Strange as it may seem, it was his contact with Islam which precipitated and shaped his religious reforms. A man of inquiring mind who was not beneath learning from his enemies, he saw that the Moslem successes were founded upon a high morality, a firm discipline, and above all a fanatical belief in the unity of God, a God who had no rivals or collaborators. Yet, when he looked at his own people, what did he see? As Iorga says, that "What was lacking in a society for long accustomed to an autocratic govern-ment was the autocrat himself".[2] This deficiency he determined to make good by reducing the immense powers and privileges of the Church, and the means he decided to employ were, by prohibiting the worship of images, icons, and relics, to liberate the people from the thralls of the clergy and monks who relied on image-worship as their strongest tool in securing the allegiance of the masses and in extracting money from them.

Thus opened the great inconoclastic controversy, an extremely complex problem, for its political implications were as involved as its theological. To appreciate this, it is only necessary to realize that at this date the monasteries and their vast estates were exempt from taxation; that education was in their hands; that the number of their monks has been estimated at 100,000,[3] and that this vast segregation of unproductive man-power seriously influenced industry and agriculture, and deprived the army of thousands of recruits. Further, the Asiatic provinces of the Empire were strongly iconoclastic, and in consequence religious friction with the European was endemic.

The first edict against image-worship was not promulgated until the year 726, and if it did not accomplish its end, it came as a

---

[1] Though final separation did not come until 1054 when Pope Leo IX smote Michael Cerularius and the whole of the Eastern Church with an excommunication; from the middle of the eighth century onward separation was nominal if not actual, and was inevitable from the day Constantine the Great transferred his capital to Byzantium.

[2] *Histoire de la vie Byzantine* (1934), vol. II, p. 17.

[3] *History of the Byzantine Empire*, A. A. Vasiliev, vol. I, p. 314.

salutary shock to the sorcery which was replacing religion. At once the Papacy thundered forth its disapproval, and the result was that, by the time Leo died, on June 18, 740, in the orthodox histories he was represented as little better than a Saracen. Nevertheless the influences of this quarrel, both on peace and war, were profound. A new life was breathed into the Byzantine Empire, which kept it virile for over three hundred years, and during them it became the reservoir of culture, which in time was destined to be drawn upon by western Europe.

Leo and Charles were, therefore, the parents of vital historical changes which would not have occurred had the one lost Constantinople or had the other been defeated at Tours. Separated by fifteen hundred miles of barbaric ignorance, their influences upon history were as complementary as their lives. Both emerged out of chaos; both won great victories over a common enemy; the one saved the East and the other heralded a new imperialism in the West.

# The rebirth of imperialism in western Europe

In the year 751, Pepin the Short, who ten years before had succeeded his father Charles Martel as Mayor of the Palace, with the sanction of Pope Zacharias set aside the effete Childeric III and was crowned by St. Boniface *"Gratia Dei Rex Francorum"*. Soon after he was re-crowned by Pope Stephen II and the title "Patrician of the Romans" was conferred upon him. Thus the Merovingian dynasty gave way to the Carolingian, and out of gratitude for the extraordinary powers granted him, Pepin marched against the Lombards, wrested the exarchate of Ravenna from them, and presented it to the Pope, and thereby created the Papal States, which endured until 1870.

Pepin died on September 24, 768, and was succeeded by his two sons, Charles and Carloman. On the death of the latter, in 771, the former was left sole ruler of Frankland, and was to become known to history as Charlemagne, or Charles the Great.

Great both in body and mind, his master idea was to bring all western peoples into one vast Christian empire, and in the realization of this mission, by the end of his reign he had established his rule from the Baltic to the Tiber and from the Elbe and Böhmerwald to the Atlantic and the Pyrenees.

In order to maintain his authority over the turbulent peoples of this vast area, Charles made systematic use of fortified posts. Each district was, so to say, picketed by a number of palisaded "burgs", which could be used as pivots of manœuvre by his mobile forces. The emphasis was on quality rather than quantity, and as these forces consisted mainly of armoured cavalry, the poorer classes were relieved from the burden of war. Such foot soldiers that he raised were not as they had been hitherto, a rabble carrying clubs and agricultural implements, but a well-equipped force armed with sword, spear, and bow. Further, each count was compelled to provide his horsemen with shield, lance, sword, bow, and dagger. Charles realized that no army could be really mobile as long as it relied on foraging and was unable to storm walled cities, and he organized two separate trains, one for siege and the other for supply.

In these changes we see the first blossoming of a new military order, the feudal, which provided the security necessary for Christendom to take root and to grow. But as the Church was the ministry of the eternal, and the feudal state represented no more than the temporal, it followed that complete religious dominance could only become possible when war, as much as peace, was conducted according to the rulings of the Church. Out of this struggle for dominance emerged the medieval conception of war as a trial by battle, in which the Church refereed for God. War was not prohibited, nor were attempts made to abolish it, because it was recognized as part of man's very nature, the fruit of original sin, which was the fulcrum of the Church's power. Therefore, war could only be restricted and mitigated by Christianizing – ennobling – the warrior and by limiting its duration.

As war teaches men how to die bravely, war is the school of heroism: such was the pagan ideal. But as death is the portal of the life eternal, war must also be the school of righteousness, or death can lead only to eternal damnation: such is the Christian outlook. Thus the classical soldier is transformed into the idealized Christian knight of chivalry, "uniting", as Lecky writes, "all the force and fire of the ancient warrior with something of the tenderness and humility of the Christian saint . . . and although this ideal, like all others, was a creation of the imagination not often perfectly realized in life, yet it remained the type and model of warlike excellence to which many generations aspired".

The fighter ennobled, the next task was to restrict his activities by sanctions and rules. The first step taken toward this end was the establishment of "The Peace of God" (*Pax Dei*), which is first heard of in the year 990. Its aim was to protect ecclesiastical buildings, clerics, pilgrims, women and peasants from the ravages of war; also cattle and agricultural instruments. The means to enforce this peace were religious sanctions – excommunication and interdict – and though the results were meagre, these sanctions did effect something, for in the eyes of Christendom they branded the aggressor the culprit.

The ennoblement of war carried with it two further restrictions. The first was, that as only men of wealth and position could afford armour, war was placed on an aristocratic footing. And as the wearing of armour led to in-fighting, missile warfare was restricted, and in consequence, casualties were reduced. Many of the battles of this period were no more than shock skirmishes between small bodies of armoured knights, in which individual combats were sought, rather to prove the worth of the fighter than his destructive capabilities. The object was to unhorse his opponent rather than to slay him, and then to put him to ransom. In brief, battles were frequent–little more than sharp-weapon tourneys in which ransom was the prize.

The second was an attempt by the Church to limit the use of missile weapons which were likely to proletarianize war, such as the arbalest or crossbow. Though the origins of this weapon are unknown, it would appear to have come into use at the beginning of the eleventh century. It was the most deadly missile thrower before the introduction of the longbow. In 1139 the Second Lateran Council forbade its use–except against infidels–under penalty of anathema "as a weapon hateful to God and unfit for Christians". Yet, in spite of this, its adoption was fairly general, except in England.

It is important to bear these restrictions in mind when we consider the warcraft of this period, for though, as Sir Charles Oman points out, the accession of Charles the Great marks the birth of a new epoch in the art of war, that epoch was essentially romantic. "The hero of the imagination of Europe", as Lecky remarks, "was no longer a hermit, but a King, a warrior, a knight. . . ." The age of the ascetic and of martyrdom was fast withering and the age of chivalry blossoming.

This romanticism was thrilled into life by Charles's conquests, which had raised him above the narrow limits of a national king, and his self-imposed mission to convert the entire German world into a Christian empire demanded that his authority should assume a theocratic and universal form. "If the Christian teaching", points out Professor G. L. Burr, "was to conquer the world, political power must be aimed at along with the spread of the faith." Therefore two forces were required–a spiritual and a secular. The one existed, the other had to be created, and as frequently happens when times demand a radical change, an accident brought it about.

In April, 799, Pope Leo III, accused of adultery and perjury, fled to Charles's court at Paderborn, and was sent back by Charles to Rome and reinstated. As this annoyed the anti-papal party, in the autumn of 800 Charles went to Italy and settled the dispute. On Christmas Day, clothed in the robe of a patrician, he entered St. Peter's, kneeled before the altar, and Leo took from it a crown and placed it upon his head. Then the multitude shouted: "Hail to Charles the Augustus, crowned of God, the great and peace-bringing Emperor of the Romans." After this cry of homage, Leo offered him the adoration due to the Byzantine Emperors and proclaimed him Emperor and Augustus. Thus the birthday of Christ was the birthday of the new Western Roman Empire.[1]

This sudden crowning took Charles completely by surprise, and though the Frankish Annals give no reason for it, it may be conjectured that it was Leo's reward for the services Charles had rendered him. Be this as it may, it raised Charles from the position of a Frankish king to that of the consecrated lord of Christendom, and since for long past the faith represented by the Pope had been one, from now onward the temporal authority over the realm of that faith became one also in the Emperor. The consequences of the coronation were vast: it was, as Bryce says, "the central event of the Middle Ages".

Charles's empire did not survive his death, and its disintegration and eventual resurrection were vastly influenced by two great ethnic upheavals: the coming of the Vikings[2] in the ninth century and of the Magyars in the tenth. The latter were a Ural-Altaic people who in 895 occupied the region of the upper Theiss, and by doing so divided the northern from the southern and the western from the eastern Slavs, and in consequence altered the course of European history. Between 907 and 955 they were the scourge and terror of central Europe.

The anarchy following these incursions, coupled with that created by the Vikings and Slavs, resulted in West Frankland reverting to its tribal divisions of Saxony, Bavaria, Franconia, Swabia, and Thuringia, each under its own duke. Although these duchies tended toward becoming separate kingdoms, they could not altogether afford to dispense with a central government. Nevertheless, anarchy continued until 918, when Conrad I (911–918)–then nominal King of Germany–offered the crown to Henry the Fowler (919–936), son of Otto the Illustrious, Duke

[1] Since in 800 the theory still held that there was but one Roman Empire, not until 812, when the Byzantine Emperor Michael I Rangabé (811–813) saluted Charles as Emperor Basileus, was his imperial election legalized. Thence, theoretically, two emperors ruled the single empire, as they had done in the days of Honorius and Arcadius, the Byzantine Empire becoming the eastern half and the Frankish the western.

[2] A generic term for the Scandinavian sea rovers of the ninth and tenth centuries; called also Northmen or Norsemen, Danes and Varangians, according to the localities of their operations. The word is derived from "vik", an inlet, creek, or bay, and as "wick" is to be found in many English place-names.

of Saxony, as the only man able to cope with the prevailing disorder.

A born soldier and able statesman, Henry subdued Swabia and Bavaria, annexed Lorraine, drove back the Slavs and Magyars, and finally reunited all Germany. On his death in 936, he was succeeded by his son Otto I (936–973), known as the Great, a brother-in-law of King Athelstan of England. He overthrew the Magyars at Lechfeld, near Augsburg, in 955, and next forced the Bohemians, then the strongest Slav state, to pay tribute to him. In 961 he was called to Rome by Pope John XII, who needed his aid. There, on February 2, 962, he was crowned by John, and after the customary courtesies and promises had been exchanged between them, John owned himself his subject, and the citizens of Rome swore that in the future no pontiff would be elected without the Emperor's consent. Thus, by vesting the sovereignty of Germany and Italy in a German prince, the Holy Roman Empire, as it was known in later centuries, came into being. It was a prolongation of the empire of Charles, and as Bryce says, "not a mere successor after an interregnum, but rather a second foundation of the imperial throne of the West".

Before these changes, the Vikings – the wagon-folk of the seas – had swept up the creeks and rivers of western Europe, and though the first of their raids came early in the reign of Charles the Great, it was not until after his death that they grew more and more formidable. In 850 the whole manhood of Scandinavia took to the sea, and the half-century which followed was one of the darkest in European history.

These incursions, which were carried as far as Novgorod, Sicily, Iceland, Greenland, and America, vastly stimulated the military organization initiated by Charles. As ill-armed levies were useless, professional soldiers became essential, and because mounted men alone could keep pace with the raiders, more and more did military power pass into the hands of the nobility. Thus, out of these troubled times, emerged a completely feudalized society based on the stronghold and the mounted knight. In England alone were other means adopted by King Alfred (871–900); for although he also relied on fortifications, instead of raising cavalry he built a fleet and beat the Vikings on their own element. This led to the English continuing to rely upon infantry, while on the Continent cavalry became the dominant arm.

Of these many incursions, the two most pregnant with future

events were those made against England and northern France. Both began with plundering raids, were succeeded by settlements and finally developed into conquests. The former, which began at the end of the ninth century, ended when England was annexed to Denmark under King Cnut (995–1035) to become part of his Scandinavian empire. The latter dates from 896, when a Viking named Rollo or Rolf came to France. For a time he struggled against Charles the Simple (893–929), and in 911, Charles, unable to overcome him, by the treaty of Saint Clair-sur-Epte, agreed to cede to him and his followers the region of the lower Seine on condition that they were baptized, and he himself did homage to him for his lands. Thus was created the Duchy of Normandy, which by 933 extended to the Breton border. Thus also was the stage set for the struggle between Normandy and England.

In brief, the events which led to this climax were as follows:

In the year 1002, as some historians suppose, in order to deny the harbours of Normandy as refuges to the Danish invaders, Aethelred II, the Unraed (of No-Counsel) or Unready, married Emma, sister of Rollo's great-grandson, Richard II of Normandy. Next, in 1013, during the invasion of England by Swein Forkbeard, King of Denmark, Aethelred, his wife and two sons, Alfred and Edward, fled to Normandy and were kindly received by Richard. A few weeks later Swein died, and when Aethelred returned to England, Cnut, the younger of Swein's two sons, found himself unready to meet him and carried the Danish fleet back to Denmark to recruit fresh forces. In 1015 he returned and within four months of his landing established himself firmly in Wessex. On Aethelred's death, in the following year, the war against the Danes was continued by Edmund Ironside, son of Aethelred by his first wife Aelfgifu. After fighting six battles, in 1016 Edmund was defeated decisively at Ashingdon (Assandun), and came to an agreement with Cnut. By its terms Edmund was to keep Wessex, and the whole of England north of the Thames was to go to Cnut. This settlement was short-lived, for on November 30 Edmund died, and in order to avert a renewal of the war, the West Saxons accepted Cnut as king of all England. Edmund's two young sons, Edmund and Edward, were then banished by Cnut, and to avert assassination they sought refuge in Hungary. The next year, to forestall any action by Richard of Normandy on behalf of his nephews–Aethelred's and Emma's two sons–Cnut entered into treaty with Richard and married Emma.

Cnut's empire included the kingdoms of England, Denmark, and Norway, and on his death in 1035, like Charles the Great's, it was divided between his three sons. Swein took Norway, Harthacnut Denmark, and Harold, surnamed Harefoot, claimed England. The first and third were Cnut's alleged sons by Aelfgifu of Northampton, and the second his legitimate son by Emma; therefore, so far as succession was concerned Harthacnut had a better claim than Harold to the English throne. But there were other candidates in the field who had as good, if not a better claim than either— namely, the sons of Edmund Ironside and those of Aethelred and Emma. The former were out of reach in Hungary, and the latter were no longer under the care of the friendly Robert I who had succeeded Richard II in 1028 and who had died in 1035. He had left his duchy in the hands of his son William, later to become known as the Conqueror, but as he was not yet eight years of age, and his duchy was distracted, he was not capable of intervening on behalf of the Aetheling Alfred and his brother.

In order to settle the question of succession, a national Witanagemot was convened at Oxford, and there, after much contention, Harold was elected but not crowned. Taking advantage of the broil, the Aetheling Alfred, supported by Baldwin V of Flanders, landed in England, and when on his way to London was met by Godwine, Earl of Wessex, who had been Cnut's chief lieutenant. Godwine greeted him in a friendly way and trapped him and his party during the night. He seized the Aetheling and sent him to London, and Harold had him blinded in so brutal a way that shortly after he died. Harold was then re-elected and acknowledged king, and Emma was expelled and found refuge with Baldwin of Flanders.

In 1040 Harold died, and the Witan, with general approval, elected Harthacnut, who so far had not pressed his claim to the English throne because Denmark was threatened by Magnus the Good of Norway, who had succeeded Swein in 1036. Not until a treaty between the two was arranged which provided that should either die without heir, his kingdom would pass to the survivor, was Harthacnut free to turn his attention to England. He landed at Sandwich about June 17, 1040, and was well received and hallowed king.

Because Harthacnut was childless and unmarried, in 1041 he invited his half-brother Edward, still in Normandy, to return to England, a request which implied a tacit recognition of Edward as heir presumptive to the throne. A year later, on June 8, Harthacnut died, and, according to the *Anglo-Saxon Chronicle*, "before he was buried all the people chose Edward as king in London"; yet it was not until Easter Sunday, April 3, 1043, that at Winchester he was consecrated king by Archbishop Eadsige.

Edward, later surnamed the Confessor, was not only half Norman by blood but fully Norman by upbringing, for he had resided in the duchy since 1013. His following was Norman and he was surrounded by Norman priests and clergy. The upshot was that England was soon divided between two parties, a pro-English, led by Godwine of Wessex, and a pro-Norman, supported by Leofric of Mercia and Siward of Northumbria, and to strengthen his position Godwine married his third son, Tostig, to Judith, sister of Baldwin V of Flanders. In 1051 a crisis was reached, and Godwine and his sons Swein, Harold, Tostig, Leofwine, and Gyrth were outlawed and fled oversea.

No sooner had the dominance of the Norman party been established than an event occurred which was destined to change the axis of English history. Duke William of Normandy, Edward's cousin, now about twenty-four years old, came to England, and all we are told of his visit is that he arrived with a great force of Frenchmen, that Edward received him, loaded him with presents and sent him home. Yet, considering the situation in England at the time, and that Edward was childless and vowed to perpetual chastity, it is all but inconceivable that the visit was a mere act of courtesy. Far more probable is it that the question of succession was discussed, and that William left for home with a claim of some sort to the English crown in his pocket.

Be this as it may, in the following year the entire situation was reversed. Godwine returned, was supported by the people, and Edward was compelled to restore to him his earldom. Further, we are told that "all the Frenchmen who had promoted in-justices and passed unjust judgments and given bad counsel in the country" were outlawed. It was a complete triumph for the English party, and again the question of succession arose; but Godwine was fated not to take part in the answer, for in 1053 he died, and the earldom of Wessex went to his son Harold, as that of Northumbria had gone to Tostig two years before.

There was only one claimant who fitted the policy and aspira-tions of the English party, the Aetheling Edward, son of Edmund Ironside, as his elder brother was now dead. In 1054 his recall to England was resolved upon, and Bishop Ealdred of Winchester was sent to the Emperor Henry III to effect it. Delays followed, and it was not until 1057 that the Aetheling landed with his wife and infant son Edgar in England. Thus it must have appeared to all that the succession was now secured; but fate decided against it. Within a few days of his landing, and before he could be presented to the king, the Aetheling died, and "to the misfortune of this poor realm", as the Chronicle records.

# CHAPTER 13

# The Battle of Hastings, 1066

William, named the Bastard, and later the Conqueror and the Great, was the natural son of Robert I of Normandy by Arlette,[1] the daughter of a tanner of Falaise. Born, probably, in September, 1027, when he was seven years old his father went on a pilgrimage to the Holy Land, and on his way back died at Nicaea in July, 1035. From then on William's youth was surrounded by dangers, but when he attained manhood he rapidly showed his worth. When twenty, with the help of King Henry I of France, he defeated his rebel barons at Val-ès-Dunes, near Caen. He then demolished their castles and until 1064 was at constant war with either Anjou, the Bretons, his vassals, or the King of France.

That he was ever able to establish his authority was due to his masterful character, his indomitable will, and his unalterable purpose. A man of steel, he could be brutal or lenient as it paid him to be so, but never merciful when it did not. He would tolerate no opposition; his will was law, and he would not be thwarted, whether by overlord, vassal, or pope. He was a great administrator and an able soldier, who based his strategy on striking at the towns and castles of his enemy and on winning possession of them by intimidation rather than by assault. In his hands devastation was the decisive weapon, and he used it with annihilative effect; he showed no feeling for the wretched peasantry he exterminated.

In the *Anglo-Saxon Chronicle* we read that "He was gentle to the good men who loved God, and stern beyond measure to those people who resisted his will. . . . Also, he was a very stern and violent man, so that no one dared to do anything contrary to his will. He expelled bishops from their sees, and abbots from their abbacies, and put thegns in prison, and finally did not spare his own brother [Odo]. . . . Amongst other things the good security he made in this country is not to be forgotten—so that any honest man could travel over his Kingdom without injury

---

[1] After Robert's death she married Herlouin Viscount of Conteville and bore him William's half-brothers Odo Bishop of Bayeux and Robert Count of Mortain.

with his bosom full of gold: and no one dared strike another, however much wrong he had done him."[1]

Another contemporary account of him reads:

"This king excelled in wisdom all the princes of his generation, and among them all he was outstanding in the largeness of his soul. He never allowed himself to be deterred from prosecuting any enterprise because of the labour it entailed, and he was ever undaunted by danger. So skilled was he in his appraisal of the true significance of any event, that he was able to cope with adversity, and to take full advantage in prosperous times of the false promises of fortune."[2]

In order to strengthen his position, he determined on an alliance with Baldwin V of Flanders, and in 1048 proposed for the hand of his daughter Matilda. Although in the following year the marriage was objected to by Pope Leo IX on the ground of affinity–which remains obscure–in spite of this prohibition, in 1053 he married her, and six years later a formal recognition of the marriage was granted by Pope Nicholas II on the understanding that he and Matilda built two monasteries at Caen, which they agreed to do and did.

The year after this recognition, William's strategic position was greatly strengthened by the death of Henry I, who was succeeded by his infant son Philip I, under the guardianship of Baldwin of Flanders. This most fortunate event raised William to the position of potential master of France, with her king in the pocket of his father-in-law.

In 1064, shortly after William had ruthlessly devastated Maine and annexed that county to Normandy, an unlooked for event occurred which was to furnish him with his strongest claim to the crown of England. It was a visit to France from Harold Earl of Wessex, now Edward the Confessor's chief lieutenant. There are two main versions of this strange episode, the one given by William of Poitiers and the other by William of Malmesbury. The first reads:

Edward, "who loved William as a brother or a son", feeling "the hour of his death approaching", in order to establish William "as his heir with a stronger pledge than ever before . . . dispatched Harold to William in order that he might confirm his promise

---

[1] "The Anglo-Saxon Chronicle (1042–1154) E", in *English Historical Documents,* edit. by David Douglas (1953), vol. II, pp. 163–164.

[2] "An account of the death and character of William the Conqueror written by a monk of Caen", in *English Historical Documents,* edit. by David Douglas, vol. II, p. 280.

[? of 1051] by an oath". On his way across the Channel Harold ran into a storm and was forced to land on the coast of Ponthieu, where he fell into the hands of Count Guy, who cast him into prison. When he learnt of his misfortune, William brought about his release, and at Bonneville Harold "swore fealty to the duke employing the sacred ritual recognized among Christian men". He swore: "firstly that he would be the representative (*Vicarius*) of Duke William at the court of his lord, King Edward, as long as the king lived; secondly that he would employ all his influence and wealth to ensure that after the death of King Edward the kingdom of England should be confirmed in the possession of the duke; thirdly that he would place a garrison of the duke's knights in the castle of Dover and maintain these at his own care and cost; fourthly that in other parts of England at the pleasure of the duke he would maintain garrisons in other castles and make complete provision for their sustenance."[1]

William of Malmesbury's version is as follows:

From Bosham, then an important seaport in Wessex, Harold went on a fishing cruise, and caught in a storm was driven on to the coast of Ponthieu. There he was at once seized "and bound hand and foot". To effect his release he persuaded "a person, whom he had allured by very great promises", to go to William and inform him of his predicament, and "that he had been sent into Normandy by the king, for the purpose of expressly confirming, in person, the message which had been imperfectly delivered by people of less authority". William at once compelled Guy–his vassal–to release Harold, and William took Harold with him on an expedition against Brittany. Next we read: "There, Harold, well proved both in ability and courage, won the heart of the Norman; and, still more to ingratiate himself, he of his own accord, confirmed to him by oath the castle of Dover, which was under his jurisdiction, and the Kingdom of England, after the death of Edward. Wherefore, he was honoured both by having his daughter, then a child, betrothed to him, and by the confirmation of his ample patrimony. . . ."[2]

Both accounts are suspect. Regarding the former, would Harold,

---

[1] "William of Poitiers: 'The Deeds of William, duke of the Normans and king of the English' ", in *English Historical Documents*, edit. by David Douglas, vol. II, pp. 217–218. William of Poitiers was William the Conqueror's chaplain.

[2] *William of Malmesbury's Chronicle of the Kings of England*, trans. J. A. Giles (1904), pp. 254–255. At the time William's daughter Adela or Agatha was about eleven years old.

who at the time was virtually under-king of England, have agreed to carry out such a mission? Further, as Sir James Ramsay points out, even if he did, surely on so important an embassy he would have travelled under safe-conduct, which would have made it unlawful for Guy to arrest him.[1] And for the latter it would appear far more probable that when he learnt of Harold's misfortune, William looked upon it as an act of God, and once he had Harold in his power, he refused to release him unless he did homage to him and swore that on his return to England he would recognize William's claim to the English throne.

Be this as it may, there can be no doubt that the oath was taken. Not only does the episode figure conspicuously in the Bayeux Tapestry, but, as we shall see, when William presented his claim to the pope, the Emperor, and the world in general, Harold did nothing to refute it, and the most probable reason why he did not is that he could not because the evidence against him was overwhelming.

Soon after Harold's return to England he was faced by a national crisis, which was to prove as detrimental to him as his oath. The appointment of his brother Tostig to the earldom of Northumbria had never been popular, and when, in early October, 1065, Tostig was absent with the King at Brentford, the thegns of Yorkshire rose against him, deposed him and offered his earldom to Morcar, grandson of Leofric and brother of Edwin Earl of Mercia. Morcar accepted the offer and marched on Northampton, where he was joined by Edwin. At Oxford, Harold met the rebels, and when he failed to establish concord between them and Tostig, much against his will Edward was compelled to outlaw Tostig and to accept Morcar. Tostig and his wife sought refuge with her brother, Baldwin of Flanders.

This was a grievous blow for Harold; it split the house of Godwine and exalted that of its rival Leofric, and it drove Tostig into the arms of William's father-in-law and ally.

The exertions which Edward underwent during the rebellion would appear to have hastened his end. In December, he held his usual Christmas court in London, but on the 28th was too ill to attend the consecration of his new abbey at Westminster. On January 5th, 1066, just before he died, he held out his hand to Harold and commended to his care his wife, his foreign retainers, and all his kingdom. The next day he was buried hastily in his

[1] *The Foundations of England* (1898), vol. I, pp. 496–497.

abbey, and immediately afterward the members of the Witan[1] present in London held a council to consider his successor. Although nothing is known of their deliberations, their decision was to elect[2] Harold. The times demanded a strong king, for the kingdom was beset with dangers: by Normandy, under William; by Norway, now ruled by Harold Hardrada, who had succeeded Swein; by Tostig in Flanders; and by Malcolm Canmore of Scotland, his sworn brother. If the council ever considered the Aetheling Edgar, grandson of Ironside, its members must immediately have banished him from their minds, for he was still a minor, and Harold was a man of mature age who in the recent wars against the Welsh had proved himself an able general. When to this is added Edward's commendation, there was really no choice other than Harold.[3] The decision made, Harold was taken to Westminster Abbey and crowned by Ealdred, Archbishop of York.

The news of Edward's death and Harold's election was rapidly conveyed to William at Rouen, and at once, as William of Poitiers informs us, he "resolved to avenge the insult by force of arms and to regain his inheritance by war".[4] But before doing so, to justify a declaration of war in the eyes of the world, he sent an embassy to Harold formally demanding the fulfilment of his oath.[5] It is as well here to assess the strategical positions of the contending parties.

William was well placed, as he deserved to be, for ever since his victory at Val-ès-Dunes, his policy consistently had been to strengthen his duchy internally and to secure it externally, and in this, as we have seen, he had been greatly assisted by good fortune. From the Scheldt to the Loire every harbour was either in his hands or those of an ally.

In the east he was secured by his alliance with Flanders; in the west by his subjugation of Brittany; and in the south by his occupation of Maine, a friendly regency in Paris, and by another stroke of good fortune. In 1060–the year Henry I died–William's most formidable enemy, Geoffrey Martel of Anjou, also died, and since

---

[1] The Witanagemot was partly an assembly of Notables (earls, bishops, abbots and nominated thegns) and partly a royal Privy Council. It had a voice in all public matters of importance and also performed the duties of a Supreme Court of Justice.

[2] For the "elective" and "hereditary" principles in the Anglo-Saxon monarchy see F. M. Stenton's *Anglo-Saxon England* (1947), p. 544, and *William the Conqueror and the Rule of the Normans* (1908), pp. 149–152.

[3] The Witan, had it knowledge of it, was in no way bound by Harold's oath, for not being of royal blood, it was not in his power, even morally, to pledge the English crown.

[4] William of Poitiers, p. 218.　　　　　[5] William of Malmesbury, p. 271.

his death his county had been distracted by a civil war between his two nephews. This meant that William had nothing to fear from Anjou during his projected conquest of England. Lastly, his position internationally was considerably strengthened by Harold's accession, for the Continent in general looked upon Harold as a usurper and on William as the aggrieved party.

Compared with William, Harold could hardly have been in a worse position. England was disunited, and Harold, not of royal blood, could not even evoke its mystical support. The two great northern earls, Edwin and Morcar, could not possibly have welcomed his accession. Indeed, the latter refused to recognize it, and while William mobilized his forces, Harold was compelled to journey to York to win over Morcar. This he did in a nominal way by marrying his sister Ealdgyth. On his return to London at Easter, April 16, Harold was acknowledged king of all England.

Tactically, his position was almost as bad, as a comparison between the English and Norman military systems will show. The former consisted of two forces, the fyrd, or national militia, and the housecarles. Apparently, the former was recruited on the basis of one man from each five hides—a hide being 120 acres—"each hide giving the soldier four shillings for pay and rations for two months, or twenty shillings in all".[1] The latter, originally the personal body-guards of king, earls, and thegns, in Harold's time had developed into a small force or forces of paid, professional men-at-arms, whose main purpose in war was to stiffen the ranks of the fyrd. Though in numerical strength the two forces were sufficient to meet normal emergencies, because the fyrd was scattered all over England it was difficult to concentrate it at short notice, and once its two months' pay and rations were exhausted, it would seem that no system of maintenance other than a fresh levy of money (Danegeld) existed, and this was highly unpopular. Though the housecarles and most of the fyrd were mounted, fighting was on foot. The one recorded instance of a mounted action, in Norman fashion, made by Ralph, Earl of Hereford in 1055, ended disastrously,[2] and, it seems, was not repeated. Of weapons, the more important were the spear, javelin,

---

[1] *The Foundations of England*, Sir James H. Ramsay, vol. I, p. 520.

[2] Of it we read: "But before any spear had been thrown the English army fled because they were on horseback" (*Anglo-Saxon Chronicle C*, p. 133). This should be substantiated by the fact that Ralph's mounted men were received by such volleys of missiles from the Welsh javelin and bowmen that they experienced a foretaste of Crécy. Cavalry, unsupported by archers, could not face archers: it took nearly 300 years to learn this lesson.

two-edged sword, and cumbersome long-handled Danish axe—clearly, in origin, a boarding weapon. Archery, though practised as a sport, was little used in war. Shields were both round and kite-shaped, and the helmet and coat of mail (*byrne*) were worn by all who could afford them.

A further difficulty Harold had to face was that Edward had disbanded the small fleet he inherited, and in consequence there was neither a fleet in being, nor the means of raising one in 1066, other than by requisitioning commercial and fishing craft and impressing their crews. As Professor Stenton points out, the mobilization of such a fleet was a slow business, "and the period for which it could remain at sea was narrowed by the absence of any organization for the replacement of the provisions with which it had sailed".[1] On the other hand, at the opening of 1066, William would appear to have had no ships suitable for carrying horses, and therefore had to build them. The only serious difficulty he had to face—a really terrifying one—was the crossing of the Channel.

The Norman military system was very different. Each baron or bishop held his land from the duke on the understanding that he maintained and equipped for his immediate service a number of mounted knights determined on by the duke. It was on this armoured and mounted cavalry that Norman military power was based, and during William's numerous wars it had become highly skilled and disciplined. The main arms were lance, sword, and mace, and its armour, as may be judged from the Bayeux Tapestry, was similar to that of the English. Of the Normans in general William of Malmesbury says: "They are a race inured to war, and can hardly live without it, fierce in rushing against the enemy, and when strength fails of success, ready to use stratagem, or to corrupt by bribery . . . they are faithful to their lords, though slight offence renders them perfidious."[2]

The Norman infantry consisted of men-at-arms and archers, the latter armed with either the short Norman bow or the crossbow. William was a highly skilled general, familiar with every device of continental war, and knew not only how to enforce discipline but how to supply his army in the field.

The English made practically no use of castles[3] for internal

---

[1] *Anglo-Saxon England*, p. 574.    [2] William of Malmesbury, p. 280.
[3] Most castles in the eleventh century were stockades built on mounds. Not until after the conquest of England did stone castles appear in numbers.

defence, but William held his dukedom and his subjugated lands by means of them. This enabled him to hold extensive areas with a minimum of troops, and, comparatively speaking, to concentrate large forces in the field. Nevertheless, in his day, two to three thousand men would be a considerable army.

Once he decided to challenge Harold, William recognized that his project was no feudal affair of overlord against vassal or vassal against overlord, but an international undertaking, and that, in consequence, it had to be placed on an international footing. And because in his day the two great international authorities were the Pope and the Emperor, it was essential to gain their sanction and, if possible, their support. His first step was, therefore, to open negotiations with both, as well as to send envoys to the principal courts of Europe, to set forth his claim to the English crown. Through the diplomatic skill of his confidant and adviser, the learned Lanfranc, Prior of Bec, he won the support of Arch-deacon Hildebrand (later Pope Gregory VII), who in his turn persuaded Pope Alexander II to bless the Norman cause and to send William a consecrated banner. From the Emperor Henry IV William obtained a promise of German help, should he need it, and Swein Estrithson, king of the Danes, also pledged his support, but did not keep his word.[1] Though Harold must have heard of these many negotiations, he nevertheless allowed William's case before the papal court to go against him by default.

William realized that the army he would need could not be recruited from Normandy alone, and as by feudal law he did not possess the power to call out his vassals for service oversea, William assembled a great council of his barons at Lillebonne to ascertain their sentiments on his venture and "to prepare shipping in proportion to the extent of their possessions".[2] Later, he appointed Matilda regent during his absence, and supported her with a council presided over by Roger of Beaumont.

With the papal sanction behind it, William's cause attracted many followers, for the conquest of so extensive and wealthy a country as England offered all but unlimited plunder and estates to soldiers of fortune and land-hungry younger sons of the nobility. From every quarter of France and from places beyond its borders volunteers flocked to William's standard: from Brittany, Maine, Flanders, central France, Poitou, Burgundy, Aquitaine, and southern Italy. Among the men of his own allegiance, the more

[1] William of Poitiers, pp. 219–220.          [2] William of Malmesbury, p. 273.

important were his two half-brothers, Odo Bishop of Bayeux and Robert Count of Mortain. Others were: Geoffrey Bishop of Coutances; Ivo, son of Guy of Ponthieu; William, son of Richard Count of Evreux; Geoffrey, son of Robert Count of Mortagne; Robert of Meulan, son of Roger of Beaumont; Roger of Poitou, son of Roger of Montgomery; William fitz Osbern; Walter Giffard; Ralph of Tosny; Hugh of Grantmesnil; William of Warenne; Hugh of Montfort; William Malet; and Humphrey of Tilleul. And from those who came from beyond his domains, the most noted were: Eustace of Boulogne; Alan of Brittany; Gilbert of Ghent; Walter of Flanders; Gerbod, son of Matilda by her first husband; Amaury Viscount of Thouars; and Geoffrey of Chaumont. Such a gathering of notables had never been seen before, and it presaged the approaching days of the crusades.

About the time when the Norman barons were assembled at Lillebonne, Tostig, who had nothing to gain from Harold's election, left Flanders for Normandy, and, according to Ordericus Vitalis, obtained William's permission "to return to England".[1] What is actually meant by this is not clear, because the duke's preparations were only in their initial stage, and not until they were well advanced could Tostig effect anything of predictable importance. What seems more probable is that Tostig was unable to pay his followers, and as he had estates in the Isle of Wight he decided on his own to go there to collect what money he could. In May he sailed from the Continent with sixty ships, landed in the Isle of Wight, obtained money and provisions,[2] and then set out to harry the coast of Sussex and Kent. At Sandwich he impressed a number of men, but he heard there that Harold was marching from London against him and rapidly re-embarked his force and sailed for the Humber. There he landed and, it seems, was caught unawares while ravaging by the northern fyrd, under Edwin, and so heavily defeated that he was left with only twelve small ships. In them he effected his escape to Scotland, where he sought refuge with Malcolm Canmore.[3]

Unsuspected by either William or Harold, this fiasco would appear to have had an important bearing on the approaching Hastings campaign; for it would seem to have persuaded Harold to assume that William's invasion was imminent. The result was

[1] *The Ecclesiastical History of England and Normandy*, trans. Thomas Forester (1853), vol. I, p. 463.
[2] *Anglo-Saxon Chronicle C*, p. 142.
[3] *The Chronicle of Florence of Worcester*, trans. Thomas Forester (1854), p. 168.

that Harold prematurely ordered the mobilization of his sea and land forces, for we are told that when he heard that Tostig was at Sandwich, "he assembled a naval force and a land force larger than had ever been assembled before".[1] In other words, he ordered a general and not a partial mobilization,[2] and on its completion, which must have taken a considerable time, he posted the fyrd along the coast of Sussex and Kent and assembled his fleet off the Isle of Wight. Thus things stood until about September 8 when the legal term of service expired and the provisions and money were exhausted, and he was compelled to disband the fyrd and order the fleet to London to be dispersed.[3] Thus, as we shall see, at the very moment when William was ready to embark, the Channel was opened to him. It may, therefore, be asked, had it not been for Tostig's raid, would Harold have called out a general mobilization when he did? Also, it may be asked, had he delayed doing so for, say, a month, would England have been conquered? Again fortune favoured William.

No sooner had demobilization begun than Harold received the startling news that Harold Hardrada (1015–1066), King of Norway,[4] accompanied by Tostig, had invaded the North. Apparently what had happened was that Tostig, soon after he had sought refuge in Scotland, had visited Norway and urged Hardrada to invade England and to claim its crown on the strength of the treaty between Harthacnut and Magnus.[5] Yet it would seem even more probable that William's threat to England was itself sufficient reason for Hardrada to go on a plundering expedition while the going was good.

Hardrada sailed from the Sogne Fiord, near Bergen, with 300 ships[6] to the Shetlands and the Orkneys, and next, turning south, he picked up Tostig and his followers off the Tyne. He plundered and burnt Scarborough, rounded Spurn Head, entered the Humber, and thence rowed up the Ouse to Riccall, ten miles south of York. There he disembarked his army, set out for York, and at Gate Fulford, two miles from the city, met the Yorkshire fyrd, under Edwin and Morcar. On September 20 a fierce battle

---

[1] *Anglo-Saxon Chronicle C*, p. 142.
[2] Seeing that the fyrd could only be called out for 40 days, the sole possible way to keep a force in the field for longer was to call it out in relays.
[3] Florence of Worcester, p. 169, and *Anglo-Saxon Chronicle C*, p. 144.
[4] One of the most noted soldiers of his day, who had served in the Eastern Roman Empire and visited Jerusalem.
[5] See *The Heimskringla Saga*, trans. Samuel Laing (1889), vol. IV, pp. 31–32.
[6] *Anglo-Saxon Chronicle E*, p. 142.

was fought, which is poetically described in the saga.[1] Its outcome was the rout of the two northern earls. The Chronicle mentions "heavy casualties and many of the English host were killed and drowned",[2] and the saga informs us that so many English were slain that "they paved a way across the fen for the brave Norsemen".[3]

When he learnt of Harold Hardrada's invasion, Harold took his housecarles and such men of the fyrd who had not yet been disbanded–almost certainly a mounted force[4]–and "went northwards day and night".[5] On the 24th he rode into Tadcaster, and on the following day, when Hardrada was negotiating over hostages with the two earls, he surprised the invaders, forced a passage over the Derwent, and after a prolonged and desperate struggle at Stamfordbridge all but annihilated them. Not only did Hardrada and Tostig perish in the fray, but when the battle was over, we are told that no more than twenty shiploads of the enemy were left. These Harold allowed Olaf, Hardrada's son, to take back with him to Norway.[6] That Harold's losses were heavy is recorded in the Chronicle, and Ordericus Vitalis, writing between 1123 and 1141, informs us that in his day great heaps of bones still lay on the battlefield, "memorials to the prodigious number which fell on both sides".[7]

The importance of these two actions cannot be overestimated, coming as they did less than a month before the Battle of Hastings, for they seriously reduced the strength of Harold's army. In Professor Stenton's opinion, the losses suffered by Edwin and Morcar were so severe that they "deprived them of any chance of effective action during the critical weeks of early October". Further, he writes of the two earls:

"They have often been regarded as unpatriotic because they held aloof from the campaign of Hastings. It can at least be urged on their behalf that they had recently stood for the defence of the realm against the greatest northern warrior of the age, and that the battle of Hastings had been fought long before either of them could have replaced the men whom he had lost at Fulford."[8] This may be true, yet against it may be urged: Was it for the defence of the realm that they faced up to Harold of Norway; was not

---

[1] See *Heimskringla Saga*, vol. IV, pp. 37–38.
[2] *Anglo-Saxon Chronicle C*, p. 144.  [3] *Heimskringla Saga*, vol. IV, p. 39.
[4] See *ibid.*, vol. IV, pp. 40 and 41.  [5] *Anglo-Saxon Chronicle C*, p. 144.
[6] See *ibid.*, pp. 145–146; *Heimskringla Saga*, vol. IV, pp. 40–50, and Florence of Worcester, p. 169.
[7] Vol. I, p. 480.  [8] *Anglo-Saxon England*, p. 582.

it rather for the defence of their earldoms? After all, Tostig was Harold Hardrada's ally and also their bitterest enemy, and his brother Harold was no *persona grata* of theirs.

What seems more important than either their loyalty or treachery is that Harold's housecarles almost certainly were mounted, and that probably most of Edwin's and Morcar's fyrd-men were not, and that when Harold heard of William's landing, as we shall see, he moved south with such speed that it was quite impossible for an unmounted force to keep pace with him along the Ermine Street, which probably had not been repaired for 600 years. Though rather obscurely, this is corroborated by William of Malmesbury, who says: "Edwin and Morcar, by Harold's command, then [*i.e.* after the battle of Stamfordbridge] conveyed the spoils of war to London, for he himself was *proceeding rapidly* to the battle of Hastings; where, falsely presaging, he looked upon the victory as already gained."[1] Therefore, what would appear to be more important than Edwin's and Morcar's losses at Fulford, are the losses suffered by Harold's housecarles – his *élite* troops – at Stamfordbridge.

When Tostig was sheltering in Scotland and Hardrada was preparing his invasion, William was busily engaged upon building a fleet and recruiting an army, and such was his energy that towards the middle of August everything was ready, most of the armament having by then been gathered together along the banks and in the mouth of the river Dives. What it actually consisted in is impossible to determine with any exactness. William of Poitiers states that the army numbered 50,000 men, and William of Jumièges that the ships built totalled 3,000. These are impossible figures, and Sir James Ramsay suggests that they should be divided by ten.[2]

The only reliable standard of measurement we have, is that we are told that both the embarkation at St. Valéry and the disembarkation at Pevensey occupied one day – that is, about twelve hours.[3] From this it follows that William's army could not have

---

[1] William of Malmesbury, p. 285. Italics ours.

[2] *The Foundations of England*, vol. II, p. 17. Other estimates are: J. H. Round, *Feudal England* (1895), pp. 289–293, 5,000; *The Cambridge Medieval History*, vol. V, p. 498, 5,000; Ferdinand Lot, *L'Art Militaire et les Armées au Moyen Age* (1946), vol. I, p. 285, below rather than above 7,000; and Wilhelm Spatz, *Die Schlacht von Hastings* (1896), p. 30, not more than 6,000 to 7,000.

[3] Sir James Ramsay points out that "At Harfleur, in 1415, three August days were required for the landing of Henry's 8,000–10,000 men" (*The Foundations of England*, vol. II, p. 17).

much exceeded 5,000 men, though when boatmen and non-combatants are added, the grand total may have been between 7,000 and 8,000. Accepting Mr. Corbett's estimate of 2,000 knights and 3,000 foot, and that of the former, 1,200 came from Normandy,[1] even then, how the knights in so short a time embarked and disembarked their horses from the type of boat depicted in the Bayeux Tapestry is a puzzle, unless portable ramps were carried, and none is shown in the one example of horses disembarking.[2]

Concerning the number of boats required for these conjectural figures, we know that the average crew of the Viking ships of this period was forty men. Also, if it can in any way be relied upon, the Bayeux Tapestry shows in one case ten horses in a single boat. Assuming, then, that each boat had a crew of five men, and accepting that thirty-five soldiers or ten horses was a boat-load, the number of boats required for the combatants would be 343. If to these we add, say, 100 for food, wine, munitions, tools, possibly also some tents, extra horses and non-combatants, we obtain a grand total of nearly 450. This figure is probably not far out, for William of Malmesbury informs us that, in 1142, Robert Earl of Gloucester embarked "more than three, but less than four hundred horsemen [say 350 knights and horses] on board fifty-two vessels".[3]

For a whole month from August 12 bad weather and a northerly wind detained the fleet in the Dives. On September 12, the wind veered west. William took advantage of the change and promptly moved his ships to St. Valéry in the estuary of the Somme, from where the crossing of the Channel would be shorter. But the wind changed north, and a further delay followed, which caused so much discontent that William was hard put to it to maintain discipline.[4]

At last, on September 27, the wind changed to the south. William embarked his army, and so energetically was the task carried out that everything was on board by nightfall. He instructed each boat to bear a light and on the mast of his own ship, the *Mora*, presented to him by Matilda, he had a great lantern lashed, which the fleet was ordered to follow. About midnight the expedition sailed, and at nine o'clock on the following day—Thursday, September 28, 1066—the duke set foot on the English shore at

---

[1] *The Cambridge Medieval History*, vol. v, p. 498. For the 1,200 knights see pp. 488–489.
[2] Inscribed "EXEVNT CABALLI DENAVIBUS".
[3] P. 533.
[4] See William of Poitiers, p. 221.

Pevensey, the Anderida of the Romans. There the army disembarked, and on the next day William marched it to Hastings, the coastal terminus of the great north road to London. At Hastings he pitched his camp, built a timber castle to secure his base, and set about ravaging the country-side and gathering supplies.

When William landed, Harold was at York, resting his men and celebrating his victory. There, on October 1, he received the unwelcome news, and even if he forthwith issued summons for the reassembly of the fyrd, he must have realized that, unless the country south of London was to be abandoned, it would be possible only for the men of the shires along his march southward to reach London in time to join him in a campaign in Sussex.

Presumably, he set out on October 2 to cover the 200 miles to London, and pushing on at top speed he reached the capital on October 5 or 6. There he remained until the 11th, collecting such forces as came in. According to William of Poitiers, he planned a surprise or night attack on his enemy, and to prevent his escape, he "sent out a fleet of seven hundred armed vessels to block their passage home".[1] Ordericus Vitalis sensibly reduces this number to seventy.[2]

Probably Harold's best course would have been–and had William been in his shoes he would most certainly have taken it–to remain in London until his whole army had been assembled, and meanwhile to harry the country to the south, in order to starve William out. But in temperament Harold was too impatient and impulsive to pause. Besides, the bulk of his supporters inhabited the south, and to have begun devastating part of his own estates would most certainly not have added to their loyalty. Further, it would seem that he held his enemy in contempt.

He assembled his army in London. Its core consisted of his own housecarles, now considerably depleted, and those of his brothers Gyrth and Leofwine. The remainder was composed of such men of the fyrd–mounted and unmounted thegns and their retainers– who were able to reach London during his five or six days' halt. It was, therefore, a quality army, and the stories that at Hastings Harold's fyrd-men were a rabble of ill-armed peasantry is quite untrue. What the strength of his army was is unknown. W. Spatz suggests 6,000–7,000 men,[3] but when one considers the losses suffered at Stamfordbridge, the absence of Edwin and Morcar,

[1] P. 224.  [2] P. 483.  [3] *Die Schlacht von Hastings* (1896), pp. 33–34.

and the shortness of the period of mobilization, this seems a high figure. It may be wiser to reduce it to 5,000, or even 4,000. Florence of Worcester says that when Harold led his army out of London "he was very sensible that some of the bravest men in England had fallen in the two battles [Fulford and Stamford-bridge], and that one half of his troops was not yet assembled". Further, that at Hastings he met William "before a third of his army was in fighting order",[1] which suggests that the rapidity of his advance had been too much for many of his unmounted men. Also, William of Malmesbury says that he went to Hastings "accompanied by very few forces",[2] yet even 4,000 men was a large army in the eleventh century.

On October 11, Harold set out from London to cover the sixty miles to Hastings, and on the night of October 13–14 he arrived at the site of the present town of Battle, and encamped his men on or near a rise in the downs marked by a "hoary apple-tree".[3] William of Poitiers says, "they [the English] took up their position on . . . a hill abutting the forest [of Anderid] through which they had come. There, at once dismounting from their horses . . ."[4] And William of Jumièges writes: "after riding all night, he [Harold] appeared on the field of battle early in the morning."[5] If surprise was Harold's aim, then, in all probability he encamped in the forest, and only occupied the "hoary apple-tree" position early on the following day.

According to Malmesbury and Wace, Harold's men passed the night of October 13–14 in drinking and singing and the Normans in confessing their sins and receiving the sacrament.[6] Though, no doubt, after a forced march the English were thirsty, and before an impending battle many Normans offered up fervent prayers, common sense dictates that Harold's men—certainly his foot—slept like logs, and that, as William had learnt through his scouts of his enemy's approach,[7] his men spent most of the night in preparing for battle.

[1] P. 170. It is a point of interest to note that in his march from York to London (October 2–6) Harold averaged 40 miles a day, and in his march from London to Battle (October 11–13) only 19 miles. This points to his having been encumbered with unmounted men on the latter. Had he left them behind, he could have reached Hastings on the 12th, and, possibly, have surprised William, but whether he would have been numerically strong enough to defeat him is another question.

[2] P. 274.        [3] *Anglo-Saxon Chronicle D*, p. 144.        [4] P. 225.

[5] William of Jumièges: description of the invasion of England by William the Conqueror", in *English Historical Documents*, edit. by David Douglas, vol. ii, p. 216.

[6] P. 276 and *Roman de Rou* (edit. Pluquet, 1827), p. 184.

[7] William of Poitiers, p. 224.

What was Harold's plan? Was it to surprise William, as has already been mentioned, or was it to assume a passive defensive – that is, to block the London Road and await attack? That Harold did fight a purely defensive battle is true, but he may have been compelled to do so because he had not reached the Battle position as early as he had hoped. To have pushed on the remaining seven miles to Hastings after dark, and then to have attempted a night attack, unpreceded by a daylight reconnaissance, would have been madness. In the circumstances, the only chance to surprise William was to attack him at dawn, which would have demanded an advance soon after midnight. Even if considered, the weariness of Harold's men must have prohibited this. That surprise based on speed was in his mind is supported by his previous generalship. In his Welsh campaign of 1063[1] and in his Stamfordbridge campaign he had moved like lightning in order to surprise; therefore, probably Mr. Round is right in surmising that this was also his intention in the present campaign.[2] Simply to hold the "hoary apple-tree" position was not sufficient to rid England of her invaders, because it did not prevent William from re-embarking his army under the cover of his archers and moving it to some other spot along the coast. Therefore, its occupation did not pin William down, nor did it compel him to attack Harold. Yet, as we shall see, William did attack, and he moved so rapidly against his enemy that it was Harold and not he who was surprised. This is supported by the Chronicle, which states that "William came against him by surprise before his army was drawn up in battle array".[3] In other words, Harold and his men would appear to have overslept themselves.

Harold's position must next be considered.

The high ground (Wealden Hills) north of Battle is connected with a rise or ridge – now in part occupied by the abbey buildings – by a neck or isthmus along which the present High Street of Battle runs. The highest point on this ridge is the site of the Abbey House, and from it the ground falls gently east and west. On its southern side the slope drops about a hundred feet in 400 yards to the head of the Asten brook, now dammed to form a series of fishponds. From the Asten it rolls southward, gradually rising to Telham Hill one and a half miles south-east of the abbey. To the

---

[1] See Florence of Worcester, p. 164.
[2] *Revue Historique*, September, 1897, vol. LXV, p. 61 *et seq.*
[3] *Anglo-Saxon Chronicle D*, p. 144.

north of the ridge the flanks of the isthmus are sufficiently steep to form serious military obstacles, and, in 1066, the drainage from the high ground had cut them into ravines, which were covered with brushwood. Further, on the northern side of the ridge, and in each case 300 yards from the Abbey House–on the western along a little brook, and on the eastern at the junction of the Hastings and Sedlescombe roads–the ridge drops so sharply that its slope forms an effective obstacle to cavalry.

In all probability, it was on the summit of the ridge that Harold first planted his two standards, the Dragon of Wessex and his personal banner, the Fighting Man, which at the close of the battle fell at a spot seventy yards to the east of the Abbey House, and marked later by the high altar of the Abbey Church. Rightly, Harold drew up his housecarles on their flanks, because–assuming he occupied the crest of the ridge–his centre was more open to cavalry assault than his wings, which must have been composed mainly of fyrd-men. Although we have few details of Harold's formation, the normal Saxon one was that of the shield-wall–a phalanx: "shield to shield and shoulder to shoulder" as Asser describes it at Ashdown in 871. It was an admirable formation against infantry armed with sword, spear and axe, and an essential one for infantry against cavalry relying on shock.

Tactically, Harold's problem was both to maintain an unbroken front and to prevent the flanks of his shield-wall from being overlapped; therefore, as Mr. Baring suggests, it is highly probable that he occupied the 600 yards between the little brook west of the Abbey House and the junction of the Hastings and Sedlescombe roads in order that his flanks might rest on the two steep depressions.[1] If Harold drew up his army in a phalanx of ten ranks deep, allowing two feet frontage for each man in the first rank–the shield-wall–and three feet frontage for those in the nine rear ranks, then, on a 600 yards front, his total strength would be 6,300 men, and, if in twelve ranks–7,500. These figures tally closely with those suggested by Spatz–6,000 to 7,000.[2]

Because we are told that the battle of Hastings opened at nine o'clock on the morning of October 14, William must have set out at an early hour. He had nearly six miles to cover before reaching Telham Hill, somewhere north of which he deployed.

[1] See his *Domesday Tables for the Counties of Surrey, etc.* (1909), appendix B, pp. 217–232. There is an excellent plan of the battle in this book showing contours at ten feet intervals.
[2] *Die Schlacht von Hastings*, p. 33.

Therefore, after reckoning the time taken for assembly, march and deployment, he must have started at between 4.30 a.m. and 5 a.m. His order of battle was in three divisions, left, centre, and right. The left consisted mainly of Bretons, under Count Alan of Brittany; the right of William's French and other mercenaries, under Eustace of Boulogne; and the centre of Normans, under

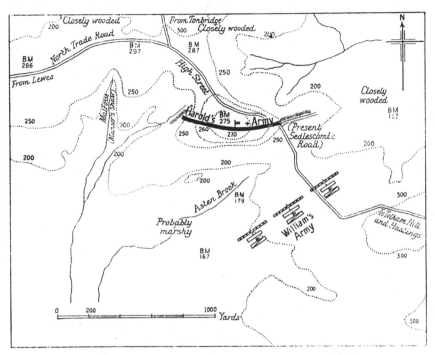

26.   THE BATTLE OF HASTINGS, 1066

his personal command: before him was carried the papal banner. Each division was divided into three *échelons* or lines: the first, archers and crossbow men in front; the next, the more heavily armed infantry; and lastly the mounted knights.[1] Therefore, tactically, the order of battle closely resembled that of the early Roman legion, the *triarii* now being mounted.

At nine o'clock, to the blast of trumpets, the battle opened when the Normans slowly advanced up the rise toward the wall of English shields crowning its crest. The lay of the ground suggests that, when William's central division, which must have advanced on the western side of the Hastings Road, moved directly on

[1] William of Poitiers, p. 225.

Harold's standards, the right and left divisions moved outwardly in order to prolong his front. Further, that the left wing, before mounting the slope on the English right, must have crossed the Asten brook, which runs into a stream coming from the ravines on the western side of the isthmus.

As William's centre closed on Harold's, the Norman archers began to discharge their arrows, but as they had to shoot uphill, most of them must either have struck their enemies' shields or passed over their heads. Following William of Poitiers' description of the battle,[1] the English resisted valiantly and met the assault with showers of "spears and javelins and weapons of all kinds together with axes and stones fastened to pieces of wood". Then "the shouts both of the Normans and of the barbarians were drowned in the clash of arms and by the cries of the dying, and for a long time the battle raged with the utmost fury".

Harold's men had the advantage of ground, and, as William of Poitiers points out, "profited by remaining within their position in close order", and maintained an impregnable front. Further, he informs us that the attackers suffered severely because of "the easy passage" of the defenders' weapons through their shields and armour, which does not speak much for them. The English, he continues, "bravely withstood and successfully repulsed those who were engaging them at close quarters, and inflicted loss upon the men who were shooting missiles at them from a distance" – namely, the Norman archers. Should this be correct, it points to a failure on the part of the Norman archers and infantry to make any real impression on the shield-wall.

The next recorded event supports this contention, for without further introduction William of Poitiers tells us that "the foot-soldiers and the Breton knights, panic-stricken by the violence of the assault, broke in flight before the English", and that soon "the whole army of the duke was in danger of retreat". This suggests that when it mounted the slope the Norman left wing got into difficulties, and that the English right, or part of it, suddenly counter-attacked, and swept the Breton archers and infantry down the slope so that they carried away with them in their flight the knights in rear. Next, William's central division found its left flank uncovered and began to fall back, as did his right division.

Now was Harold's chance, and he failed to seize it. He has often

[1] Pp. 226–229.

been blamed for not having rigidly maintained his shield-wall throughout the battle. Though to have done so might have saved him from defeat, it could not have gained a victory. Had he now seized his chance, he would have ordered a general advance, and pouring down the slope on both sides of the Hastings road would, almost certainly, have annihilated the Norman archers and infantry. True, the Norman cavalry would have got away, but bereft of their infantry, in all probability they would not have drawn rein until they had found security behind their stockade at Hastings. The victory would have been Harold's, and it might well have been decisive enough to have compelled William to re-embark and abandon the campaign.

As it happened, as soon as the panic on the Norman left wing began to affect the morale of the centre, a fortuitous event occurred which would have gone far to crown a general counter-attack on Harold's part with success.

During the initial attack William was in rear and, it seems, when the front of his central division broke back, in the resulting confusion he was unhorsed, and a cry went up that he had fallen. For him, this must have been the most critical moment in the battle; for in classical and medieval warfare the loss of the general-in-chief, which carried with it the loss of the entire command, as often as not led to immediate defeat. It was as if in a modern battle the whole of an army's general staff were suddenly eliminated. In the present case, the danger though critical was momentary, for William mounted another horse, pushed back his helmet so that he might be recognized by all, and stayed the panic in the centre by shouting out: "Look at me well. I am still alive and by the grace of God I shall yet prove victor." Meanwhile, on the left, presumably around the Asten brook, the English counter-attackers had got into difficulty, and when the Norman centre turned about a general rally followed, and some of the pursuers were cut off and slaughtered. William of Poitiers mentions "several thousands", but immediately qualifies this estimate by informing us that, even after this loss, the English "scarcely seemed diminished in number".

As soon as the Normans had re-formed their ranks, the attack was renewed, but this time under William's personal leadership, which means that the knights were brought forward and the infantry withdrawn from the immediate front. From now on for several hours the struggle raged along the whole line, individual bodies of knights riding forward at the charge to hurl or thrust their spears at the shield-wall. Nevertheless, all attempts to force a gap proved ineffectual.

Unable to break the shield-wall, William now made use of a *ruse de guerre* common in Byzantine and Oriental warfare. He determined to lure his enemy down from the hoary apple-tree hill by means of a feint retreat.

The most suitable part of the field for this somewhat risky operation, for we may assume that the Normans were not exercised in it, was probably on the right, for there a withdrawal would bring William's men down to the valley and next up to high ground where they could face about as their pursuers moved uphill. Also a withdrawal in this direction would enable his centre to take the pursuers in flank. Clearly this was a purely cavalry operation; therefore we may assume that, while the fighting was in progress, the Norman infantry was withdrawn out of harm's way.

All this is, of course, conjecture, for all William of Poitiers tells us is the following:

"Realizing that they could not without severe loss overcome an army massed so strongly in close formation, the Normans and their allies feigned flight and simulated a retreat, for they recalled that only a short while ago their flight had given them an advantage. The barbarians thinking victory within their grasp shouted with triumph, and heaping insults upon our men, threatened utterly to destroy them. Several thousand of them, as before, gave rapid pursuit to those whom they thought to be in flight; but the Normans suddenly wheeling their horses surrounded them and cut down their pursuers so that not one was left alive. Twice was this ruse employed with the utmost success."

Harold has been blamed for falling into the trap, but probably the discipline of his troops was such that they acted on their own initiative, and wrongly, because the tactical situation was very different from the one which led to the initial counter-attack.[1] Then they were faced by foot, but now by horse, therefore they could not possibly hope to outpace them.

Though, after the second feigned flight and slaughter of the pursuers, William of Poitiers tells us that Harold's army "was

[1] With reference to these advances, it should not be overlooked that in all early warfare in which javelins and arrows were the missiles, the normal way of replenishing their stock was to drive the enemy back and gather them from the ground he abandoned.

still formidable and very difficult to overwhelm", it is certain that its left wing must have been seriously weakened, and it may have been now, in order to strengthen it morally, that Harold moved his standards from the summit of the hill nearer to his left. Also it may have been at this time that to prepare the way for what was to be the final assault, William instructed his archers to use high-angle fire[1]–that is, to shoot their arrows into the air so that they would pass over the heads of his knights and, falling vertically on the enemy, induce the men of the shield-wall to raise their shields.

Night was closing in when the final phase of the battle opened, and by then we may assume that the English missiles had been spent and that Harold's men were exhausted. What happened is largely conjectural, but the most probable sequence of events would appear to be as follows: When twilight was setting in, Harold was hit in the eye by an arrow,[2] and a moment after was cut down.[3] As his brothers Gyrth and Leofwine had already fallen there was no one to replace him. Next, the weakened English left gave way before Eustace of Boulogne. The whole shield-wall then began to disintegrate, and Harold's men, some on horseback and some on foot, fled the field to the west and north-west to escape from Eustace, who would appear to have led the pursuit. Nevertheless, in spite of the panic, a number of Harold's men–probably housecarles–remained unaffected, fell back on the isthmus, and showed so bold a front that Eustace signalled his men to fall back. A moment later, William came up, counter-ordered the signal and urged his men forward. They scattered the housecarles, and a group, in the twilight, following the fugitives through the undergrowth, fell headlong into a ravine on the west of the isthmus, at a spot to become known as the Malfosse–probably the present Manser's Shaw.[4]

It must have been nearly dark when William returned to the main battlefield, to find Harold's body stripped and so hacked that it was barely recognizable. He had it brought to his camp, and later it was buried by the seashore.

Of William, William of Poitiers writes: "He dominated this battle, checking his own men in flight, strengthening their spirit,

---

[1] This incident is mentioned by Henry of Huntingdon, see *The Chronicle of Henry of Huntingdon*, trans. Thomas Forester (1853), p. 212.
[2] Florence of Worcester (p. 170) says that Harold fell at twilight.
[3] For both see the Bayeux Tapestry.
[4] See *Domesday Tables, etc.*, p. 229. Mr. Baring writes: "The original name being Malfosset, corruption was easy to Manfussé (? Manfsey), Mansey and finally Manser's."

and sharing their dangers. He bade them come with him, more often than he ordered them to go in front of him. Thus it may be understood how he led them by his valour and gave them courage. . . . Thrice his horse fell under him." Unfortunately, no friendly pen has depicted the part played by his valiant antagonist.

Two days after the battle William returned to Hastings, and five days later he occupied Dover. When he had strengthened its castle, he set out for Canterbury. Thence, following Mr. Baring's account,[1] he advanced by way of Lenham, Seal, and Westerham to Godstone, where he gained the London–Hastings road. From Godstone he sent a party of horsemen north, who burnt Southwark, while the main body marched on westward through Guildford and Micheldever to Basing. From Alresford he appears to have been reinforced from either Chichester or Portsmouth, where his fleet had moved at some time after the battle. Next, he swept northward by way of Lambourn to Wallingford, where his army crossed the Thames, circled round the Chilterns and came southward to Little Berkhampstead. There William was met by the magnates of London, who tended to him the submission of the city and offered to him the crown.

From the ravagings deduced from Domesday Book, Baring's conclusion is that William's army cannot have been more than from 8,000 to 10,000 strong. "Nor", he writes, "can he have had much time for mere devastation; he could hardly have covered some 350 miles between Canterbury and Little Berkhampstead within seven weeks, if he had allowed his troops to be scattered for wide-spread ravage. . . . Outside the line of march the immediate effect of the conquest on the value of land in the south-east seems to have been very slight."[2]

When he was offered the crown, William at first feigned hesitation, then he accepted it, sent forward a picked body of men to build what was to become the Tower of London, and on Christmas Day, 1066, he was crowned by Ealdred of York in Westminster Abbey. Thus his claim to England was vindicated.

The next three years were spent by William in putting down rebellions, more particularly in Northumbria, and in each case he did so by methodical devastation, until, in 1069, a third of his

[1] Who traces the march by the ravages deduced from Domesday Book. See *ibid.*, appendix A, pp. 208–216.
[2] *Ibid.*, pp. 14 and 16. *Anglo-Saxon Chronicle D* (p. 145) says: ". . . and ravaged all the region that he overran until he reached Berkhamsted."

kingdom had been reduced to little more than a wilderness. Meanwhile, in order to police and hold the land, he built a castle in every important borough. In 1070, he felt himself sufficiently secure to disband his mercenary troops, and two years later he invaded Scotland, and at Abernethy compelled Malcolm Canmore to do homage to him. When, on September 9, 1087, he died from an injury sustained during the siege of Mantes, he was the most powerful potentate in western Europe.

For England, Hastings was not only the most decisive battle ever fought on her soil, but also the most decisive in her history, in fact, there is no other battle which compares with it in importance. In the place of a loosely-knit and undisciplined country was substituted a unified and compact kingdom under a firm and hereditary central authority, a king who knew how to combine feudalism with personal government. William left local institutions as they were and appropriated to himself the entire land, the fiscal value of which he had assessed in his great Domesday Book survey.

Himself a feudal vassal, who had rebelled against his overlord, he understood well the inherent weakness of the Frankish feudal system, and would have none of it in England. As his kingdom was to be indivisible, no man should be to him what he was to the King of France. Although he gave his vassals vast estates on military tenure, they were scattered over different parts of his kingdom, except for the great border earldoms of Chester, Shrewsbury, Durham, Kent, and Cornwall. No man was to swear fealty to anyone but himself, and it was with this object in mind that, in 1086, he held a great assembly at Salisbury, "and there", as we read, "his councillors came to him, and all the people occupying land who were of any account over all England, whosoever's vassals they might be; and they all submitted to him, that they would be loyal to him against all other men".[1]

His external policy was as masterful as his internal. Though a respecter of the institutions of the Church, he refused to admit that the papacy was entitled to impose its policy upon secular rulers. He repudiated Gregory VII's claim to universal dominion and forbade that any pope should be recognized in England without his own consent. When, in 1080, Gregory demanded that he take an oath of fealty to him as his vassal, William repudiated the demand outright.

[1] *Anglo-Saxon Chronicle E*, pp. 161–162.

Second only to the crowning of Charles the Great, William's victory at Hastings, which led to his own crowning – also on Christmas Day – was the greatest event of the Middle Ages. As the former drew the distracted peoples of western and central Europe toward a common secular authority, the latter, as Professor Stenton points out, "drew England from its Scandinavian connection, and united it to the richer world of Western Europe".[1] Therefore it not only put an end to Viking dominance in the West, but by giving the West a new partner, it tended toward consolidating the West at the very moment when eastern Europe was on the point of collapsing before Islam.

[1] *William the Conqueror and the Rule of the Normans*, p. 4.

# The decline of the Caliphate and the revival of the Byzantine Empire

At the time when in the West the conception of a Roman empire coextensive with Christendom was fostering a political growth which more than anything else was to enable Europe to withstand the onslaught of Islam, in the East Omayad rule was brought to an end by the Abbasids, whose claim to the caliphate was based on their descent from Abbas, the eldest uncle of Mahomet. In the reign of Caliph Merwan II (744–750) their opposition culminated in the rebellion of the Iman Ibrahim, fourth in descent from Abbas, who raised an army in Khorasan. On his death, in 747, his brother Abul-Abbas as-Saffah took command of the revolt, and, in 750, in an eleven-day battle fought on the Greater Zab, he routed Merwan's army and was proclaimed caliph. His victory was followed by a general massacre of the Omayads, of whom only one of note escaped – Abd-ar-Rahman – who sought refuge in Spain, where, in 756, he founded the Omayad dynasty of Cordova.

With the fall of the Omayads the hegemony of the Moslem world passed from Syria to Irak, and with this change the supremacy of the Arabs ended. Thenceforth, the army, which had been recruited from Arab tribes, for the greater part was replaced by a mercenary force of non-Arab soldiers, and, in consequence, the barrier which had separated the Arabs from the peoples they had conquered began to crumble. Nevertheless, the Arab religion, language, and civilization continued to dominate the new caliphate.

Under the Omayads the unity of Islam had been precariously maintained, but under the Abbasids it disintegrated rapidly; each provincial governor became potentially and often actually an independent ruler. Mansur, the second Abbasid caliph, moved the seat of government to Baghdad, and from then on Persian influence predominated. The chief offices were filled by Persians, and notably by members of the family of Barmecides, which, in 803, was exterminated by the fifth Abbasid caliph, the great

Harun-al-Rashid (788–809). In spite of the loss of north-west Africa and Transoxiana, his reign was the most brilliant in the annals of the caliphate. He is pictured as the hero of many of the stories of the *Arabian Nights*; innumerable anecdotes are told of him, and he corresponded with his great contemporary Charlemagne and agreed to place the Holy Sepulchre at Jerusalem under his authority.

In spite of the glory of his reign, it would seem that Harun realized that the break-up of the Arab empire was inevitable, for in 802 he arranged to divide it between his two sons. Nevertheless, on his death, in 809, civil war immediately followed. Khorasan became virtually independent; Egypt broke away; and during the reign of Caliph Mutasin (833–842) the fatal step was taken to recruit the army almost entirely from Turks, who, like the Roman praetorians, made and unmade caliphs as they pleased. Deliverance came from Persia, when the Buwaihids, who claimed descent from one of the Sassanid kings, entered Baghdad in 945, and having delivered the caliph from his Turkish palace guard, for nearly a century they established their own authority; the caliphs became puppets under their emirs and remained so until the coming of the Ghaznevids and Seljuks.

While these changes reshaped the Moslem world, the Byzantine empire was beset with many troubles: internally, because there was no recognized principle of imperial succession; externally, because it was constantly faced by war on two far-spaced fronts – the European and the Asiatic. In 867, the anarchy which had prevailed since the death of the Empress Irene in 802 was brought to an end by Basil I (867–886), one of those unexpected deliverers from chaos which chaos so frequently throws up.

Born in 812, the son of a Macedonian peasant, because of his handsome appearance and herculean strength, in 856 he attracted the notice of the Emperor Michael III (842–867), who took him into his service as chief groom. He rose in favour and so that he might have no rival, in 866 he assassinated Caesar Bardas, Michael's uncle, and next prevailed upon his master to associate him with the imperial authority. Shortly after this the emperor took a fancy to a boatman and Basil, out of favour, had Michael assassinated and proclaimed himself emperor. Thus was the Macedonian dynasty founded, which was to give the empire one hundred years of prosperity and splendour and to last for nearly two hundred years.

Once stability of succession had been established, a progressive foreign policy became possible, and the outcome was that internal security led to external expansion. A crusade was developed against Islam and it was greatly helped by the anarchy which then prevailed in the Moslem lands.

Basil died in 886, and between then and the accession of Romanus II in 959, the Bulgarian empire reached its zenith under Simeon (893–927). In 923 he besieged Constantinople, and as by then his dominions stretched from the Adriatic to the Black Sea and from the Carpathians to Thessaly, he laid aside the title of khan and proclaimed himself tsar of the Bulgarians and Greeks.

Menaced by this formidable power, Basil's successors, Leo VI (886–912) and Constantine VII (912–959), were at constant war with the Bulgarians, and to this threat was added that of the Northmen from Russia. In 941, Igor, the Varangian prince of Kiev,[1] laid siege to Constantinople, but when his fleet was partly destroyed by Greek fire, he withdrew. Yet, in spite of these distractions in Europe, the eastern frontier was pushed to the Euphrates, and the foundations were laid for the brilliant triumph of Nicephorus Phocas, the able general of Romanus II (959–963). In 961 he retook Crete, which had been lost in 826.

Romanus died in 963 and left his two infant sons, Basil and Constantine, under the regency of their mother Theophano; but because of their youth Nicephorus Phocas was proclaimed emperor, and to consolidate his position he married Theophano. He continued his victorious career and in 965 took Tarsus and recovered Cyprus. Next, in 968, he set out to invade Syria, and occupied Homs, Tripoli, Jiblah (Byblus) and other towns, before he besieged Antioch, which fell to him on October 28, 969. Shortly after this important success, Theophano hired one of his captains, John Tzimisces, to assassinate him. Tzimisces murderd Phocas on the night of December 10–11, 969, but immediately afterward he incarcerated Theophano in a convent and assumed the diadem as John I (969–976).

---

[1] In the middle of the ninth century the Slav and Finnish tribes around lake Ilmen paid tribute to the Northmen of the land of Rus (Sweden, or part of it) and in 859 expelled them. Soon after they quarrelled among themselves and invited the Northmen to return. Three princes of Rus—Rurik, Sineus, and Truvor—accepted the invitation and founded what was to become the Russian Empire. Rurik established his capital at Novgorod on the great waterway the Neva–Volkhov–Lovat–Dnieper, which linked the Baltic to the Black Sea. It was by this route that came the Varangian (men of Rus) bodyguard of the Byzantine emperors. Later the capital was moved to Kiev.

In the first years of his reign Tzimisces was engaged in suppressing a revolt at home and with wars against the Bulgarians and the Russians. The former he defeated in two great battles, then, in 947, he concluded an alliance with Armenia and set out to free Jerusalem. He marched south from Antioch and occupied Damascus, Tiberias, Nazareth, and Caesarea. At Tripoli his army suffered a reverse, in September, 975; he withdrew to Antioch, and on January 10, 976, he died in Constantinople.

He was succeeded by Romanus II's two sons, Basil II (976–1025) and Constantine VIII (976–1028), who had been crowned respectively in 960 and 961. The latter took no part in the government, and the former, now in his nineteenth year, left the administration of the empire in the hands of the eunuch Basileios, who, so it would appear, hoped to make Basil his puppet. Internal revolts followed, the more serious of which was that of Bardas Phocas, who, in 987, was proclaimed emperor by his troops; but with the aid of a body of Varangian mercenaries, lent him by his brother-in-law, Vladimir Prince of Kiev, Basil advanced upon the would-be usurper and defeated him at Abydus.

Freed from internal danger, Basil first got rid of Basileios, and next waged a ruthless war on the great feudal landlords in Asia Minor, who threatened his authority and also the unity of the empire by dividing its peoples into two antagonistic classes, the *Dunatoi* (rich) and the *Penates* (poor). Basil championed the latter, won over the lower and middle classes, and by so doing greatly strengthened his position. In 995 he gained some success against the Saracens, but his most important work in the east was the annexation of large portions of Armenia, which he converted into a strongly fortified frontier. Throughout the remainder of his reign his main activities were concentrated against Samuel (976–1014), tsar of the Bulgarians.

In 996 he set out on his campaign of conquest, and by the year 1000 rewon eastern Bulgaria. The war dragged on until 1014, when in the great battle of Bêlasitza the Bulgarian army was annihilated. This victory earned for Basil the surname of Bulgaroktonos ("Slayer of Bulgarians"). In 1018 the war ended, and for more than a century and a half (1018–1186) Bulgaria remained subject to the Byzantine emperors. In December, 1025, Basil died when preparing a naval expedition to recover Sicily from the Saracens.

# CHAPTER 14

# The Battle of Manzikert, 1071

The reign of Basil II was the culmination of Byzantine greatness. Never since the days of Justinian I had the empire
risen to such glittering heights; yet, like the empire left by
Justinian, fifty years later it was encompassed with rack and
ruin.

The weakness in Basil's conquests was that they were purely
military: he ravaged, fought and won, and left behind him vast
depopulated areas – mere vacuums of victory.

Nevertheless, had he been succeeded by a soldier-statesman of
the calibre of Leo III, the empire might have received a new
lease of life; instead, it passed into the hands of a series of dotards,
sensualists and courtesans – female rule once again predominated.
During this period must be sought the reasons why a total collapse
rushed in upon a single defeat: a collapse as dramatic and ruinous
as that which followed the Battle of Adrianople.

It was a period in which, as Bussell says, "the noiseless dissolution of the Roman system"[1] took place. It was mostly a period
of peace, misdirected by a court of eunuchs and favourites, whose
sole object was to guard against revolution and rebellion; a court
of sycophants and servile hangers-on, of corrupt priests, of palace
domestics and even of slaves. Constantine VIII (1025–1028), who
assumed sole rule on Basil's death, was both a pacifist and a despot,
and no worse extremes can meet in combination. Surrounded by
parasites, he blinded all possible opponents and also any man who
showed a modicum of ability. The army and the state services he
placed in the hands of eunuchs; for, though such men could
intrigue and rebel, they could not succeed him on the throne.
Where Basil had attempted to limit the power of the nobles, he
pandered to them, and when he felt his end was approaching, he
married his daughter Zoe, a middle-aged harlot, to one of them,
who on his death succeeded him as Romanus III (1028–1039).
His accession was followed by twenty-nine years of female rule,
during the initial period of which the new emperor set out to win
God and man by lavish donations to the Church, the court

[1] *The Roman Empire from A.D. 81 to A.D. 1081* (1910), vol. 1, p. 340.

officials, and the people. Scandal and licentiousness prevailed. First, Zoe locked up her elder sister, Theodora, in a convent; next she adopted a certain Michael, a money-changer, as her son, and made him her paramour; and lastly, she poisoned her husband and on the day he died married Michael, who became Michael IV. On his death, in 1041, she adopted his nephew, Michael the Caulker, who became fifth of that name. After a reign of four months he was dethroned, blinded, and locked up in a monastery. At the age of sixty-two, Zoe married an old lover who became Constantine IX Monomachus (1042–1054), and as he refused to part from his mistress Scleraina, the people of Constantinople were treated to the novel spectacle of an emperor seated between two empresses – a wife and a paramour.

From this brief summary it will be appreciated what the court rule of this period was like. Bussell calls it a "brilliant unreality . . . sovereigns who are play-actors, ministers who are the viziers of 'Hamlet' or a pantomime, a well trained stage-mob who come in opportunely with loyal cries just in time to save innocence, injured if not conspicuously youthful".[1]

During this moral decline the empire was beset by the Normans in southern Italy. They had appeared there in 1017, when a band of them, returning from a pilgrimage to Jerusalem, had settled in Calabria. First they hired themselves out as mercenaries to the Byzantine emperor and the pope, then they assumed the role of conquerors. In 1042, one of their chiefs, William of the Iron Arm, proclaimed himself count of Apulia, and about the same time another installed himself at Aversa. Simultaneously a new race of invaders appeared in the East, the Seljuk Turks, who poured into the Empire. Why they so easily overran its Asiatic themes was due as much to Byzantine foreign policy as to internal decay and pre-occupation with the Normans in Italy and the Patzinaks on the Danube.

For centuries wars had raged between the empire and the caliphate, which, during the eleventh century, was almost as decrepit as the empire. But the Seljuk invasion soon began to revitalize Islam, and in consequence the eastern frontier of the empire was again threatened. As it abutted upon Armenia, and stretched from the Caucasian mountains to the upper waters of the Euphrates, the empire should have sought to support that Christian kingdom as a buffer state. Instead, it set out to destroy it, not

[1] Bussell, *The Roman Empire from A.D. 81 to A.D. 1081* (1910), vol. I, p. 344.

because there was any likelihood of an alliance between the Armenians and the Seljuks, but because it was a rich country which offered vast plunder.

The first and fatal step was taken by Basil II in 1022, when he forced King John of Armenia to agree to the cession of his domains after his death, which, in 1045, Constantine IX with the greatest treachery compelled King Gaghik to do and also to disband the Armenian national militia, still 50,000 men strong, and to surrender to him his capital Ani.[1] Though Matthew of Edessa was an Armenian, it would seem that he does not greatly exaggerate the plight his country was in, when he informs us that "it was delivered up to the Turks by that sterile, effeminate and ignoble nation the Greeks. It was they who scattered the more courageous of our nobles, who destroyed our national throne and who deprived us of all means of self-defence. And having done so, what did they do? As guardians of our country they placed over it generals who were eunuchs. . . ." Further, he writes: "When they discovered an illustrious warrior they either blinded him or drowned him in the sea. . . . They made eunuchs of our sons, and instead of furnishing them with armour, they dressed them like women. . . ."[2] Worse still, when he had overrun Armenia, plundered it, and deprived it of all power of self-defence, Constantine, to help to fill his treasury, which he had drained by his lavish expenditure, withdrew the Byzantine garrisons from Armenia and so left it open to attack. Nor was it long in coming, for the year 1049 saw the beginning of the Seljuk invasions, which in a few years were destined to extend Turkish rule, or rather misrule, from Kashgar to the neighbourhood of Constantinople.

In the year 1034 these ferocious and destructive people, under Tughril Bey and Chaghri Bey, grandsons of Seljuk, crossed the Oxus into Khorasan. The former then moved westward and overran Irak, Kirmanshah, Hamadan, and Azerbaijan, and in 1049 reached Armenia, now almost deprived of all power of self-defence. He moved against the unwalled city of Ardzen, west of Lake Van, carried it by assault, burnt it to the ground, and is said to have massacred 150,000 people—men, women, and children.[3]

---

[1] See Matthew of Edessa: *Chronique de Matthieu d'Édesse (962–1136)*, pt. I, LXV–LXVI and LXXVI, trans. E. Dulaurier (*Bibliotheque Historique Arménienne*, Paris, 1858). See also René Grousset's *Histoire de l'Arménie des Origines à 1071* (1947), pp. 574–583.

[2] *Ibid.*, pt. II, LXXXIV.

[3] Though this figure may be exaggerated, Ardzen was a wealthy city containing, according to Matthew of Edessa, 800 churches (pt. I, LXXXIII).

After an indecisive action with the Byzantine forces at Kape-tron, Tughril defeated the Armenians at Kars, and next moved against the city of Manzikert,[1] which he besieged. Unable to take it by assault, he brought up an immense engine, formerly used by Basil II, which required 400 men to drag into position. The governor of the city was terrified when he saw it and offered a liberal reward to anyone who would destroy it. A Frankish mercenary volunteered to do so. He tied a letter to the point of his lance, hid in his dress three glass pots of naphtha, and galloped out of the town toward the *ballista*. The Seljuks took him for a messenger and imagined that he was drawn toward the engine through curiosity. They let him ride up to it, when to their consternation he threw the bottles at the machine, which burst into flames, and galloped back to Manzikert.[2] Tughril had to abandon the siege, mainly because of the murderous fire of the innumerable engines with which the besieged defended their walls. One of them was used to hurl the carcass of a pig into the Seljuk camp and the citizens shouted: "O Sultan, take this sow to wife and we will present you with Manzikert as her dowry."[3]

In 1050 the Empress Zoe died, and four years later Constantine IX died. He was succeeded by the Empress Theodora, a timid old woman, and she, in 1056, by Michael VI, who the following year was dethroned by Isaac I (Comnenus). The latter reigned until 1059, and was followed by Constantine X (Ducas), who died in 1067.

Throughout this period of degeneracy there would seem to have been not the slightest realization that the empire was approaching a precipice. By now the Court had assumed complete control, and the result was that the well-trained civil service which had for centuries held the empire together became extinct. Pageants yearly grew more splendid; communications and frontier defences fell into decay; and the depopulation of the country-side continued until it was found impossible to recruit the army. The result was that units were either reduced in strength or mercenaries were enlisted in large groups. Hitherto the wealth of the emperors had enabled them to buy the services of the best soldiers in Europe;[4] but to save money, under Constantine X there was a

---

[1] Manzikert is the first city of importance on the Arsonas river. It was a strong fortress and surrounded by many gardens. It is also called Malazkird, Minazjird, Manzikart, Milasgird, and Minazkird.

[2] Matthew of Edessa, Pt. II, LXXVIII.

[3] *Ibid.*, pt. II, LXXVIII.     [4] One of these was Harold Hardrada.

considerable falling off in quality; indifferent foreigners were enlisted, arms, artillery and warlike stores neglected, and castles and fortresses allowed to fall into ruin. In spite of these military "economies", the imperial finances were in deplorable condition. The extravagances of Constantine IX and the vast sums of money monopolized by the monasteries had emptied the treasury. Lastly, justice was so persistently ill-administered that the people in the provinces increasingly sought protection of the great landed aristocrats, who in consequence became more and more powerful and unruly.

While the western provinces were being ravaged by the Seljuks and the eastern by the Hungarians, who stormed and took Belgrade; while the Guzes (or Uzes) and Patzinaks, both Turanian tribes, crossed the Danube and wasted the country as far south as Salonica, Constantine X remained an inactive spectator of the ruin. At length he condescended to lead an army into Thrace, dispersed the Guzes, and to make good his lack of men recruited many of these semi-savages, who were to prove the most treacherous of soldiers.

When this new deluge of destruction flooded the western themes of the empire, even more terrible incursions burst upon the east; for there Tughril Bey, who had stormed Baghdad in 1055, and subdued Mosul and Diarbekir, was, in 1065, succeeded by his nephew Alp Arslan (1065–1072), the son of Chaghri Bey. Born in 1029, he was a man of marked ability, and thanks to his vizier, the great Nizam-al-Mulk, the foundations of a new and more virile caliphate were laid, which later were to support the empire of the Ottoman Turks.

Alp Arslan wasted the kingdom of Iberia (Georgia), then marched against Ani, the Armenian capital, and laid siege to it, "surrounding it like a serpent in his toils".[1] We are told that the city possessed a thousand churches and was crowded with thousands of refugees. Apparently it was taken either through treachery or by ruse on June 6, 1064, when the usual massacre followed: "its inhabitants being mown down like the grass of the fields".[2] Finlay writes of these campaigns in Georgia and Armenia:

"The plan by which they [the Seljuks] expected to render themselves masters of the provinces they invaded, was to exterminate the cultivators of the soil in the extensive plains, in order to leave the country in a fit state to be occupied by their own

---

[1] Matthew of Edessa, pt. II, LXXXVIII.        [2] *Ibid.* ,pt. II, LXXXVIII.

nomadic tribes. The villages, farmhouses, and plantations were everywhere burned down, and the wells were often filled, in order that all cultivation might be confined to the immediate vicinity of fortified towns. By this policy they soon rendered agricultural property in many extensive districts of Asia Minor so insecure, that whole provinces were left vacant for their occupation before the Seljouk power was able to conquer the cities. So boldly did they pursue these ravages, that Scylitzes records incursions of Seljouk bands even into Galatia, Honorias, and Phrygia during the reign of Constantine X."[1]

Such was the position when, in 1067, Constantine X, near death, appointed the Empress Eudocia guardian of his three sons, Michael VII (1067–1078), Adronicus I (1067–1185), and Constantine XI (1067–1071). He extracted a promise from the Empress, then in her forty-eighth year, not to marry a second husband. Like most Byzantine promises it was not kept. According to Matthew of Edessa, as soon as Constantine was dead she took as paramour[2] and then as husband Romanus IV, Diogenes (1068–1071), who had been convicted of treason against her sons. The choice was an unfortunate one, for though Romanus was a courageous soldier, he was impetuous. Further, he was not trusted by the army–then in the worst possible state of discipline– and more particularly so by the Varangian Guard because he favoured the native-born troops. Romanus came from a distinguished family in Cappadocia, a province overrun by the Turks, and he at once decided to hurry his cosmopolitan army of Varangians, Macedonians, Sclavonians, Patzinaks, Guzes, Armenians, Bulgarians, and Franks into the field. To make matters worse, no sooner had he set out than the empress and her miserable son Michael VII, who spent his time writing iambics and anapaests, started an intrigue against him, seemingly because his dictatorial behaviour had become irksome. It would appear that the empress plotted Romanus's defeat.[3]

Whatever may have been the defects of the empire, and it had many, it would have been impossible for it to have endured the centuries it did, had it not possessed a military organization incomparably superior to that of any of its neighbours. The first point to note is that, between the age of Leo III and the sack of

---

[1] *A History of Greece from the Conquest by the Romans to the Present Times*, George Finlay (1877), vol. III, pp. 19–20.
[2] Matthew of Edessa, pt. II, xcviii.
[3] *Histoire de la Vie Byzantine*, N. Iorga (1934), vol. II, p. 222.

Constantinople by the Crusaders in 1204, organically it remained static, where those of other European kingdoms and Oriental, also, were in a continuous state of flux and in consequence lacked stability. There were several reasons for this: the wealth of the empire; the incomparable strength of Constantinople as a fortress; and, not least, the codification of the art of war by the Emperors Maurice and Leo VI (the Wise) in their manuals the *Strategicon* of 579 and the *Tactica* of 900. It is no exaggeration to say that not until well into the nineteenth century were military manuals of such excellence produced in western Europe.[1]

Military stability sprang naturally from the ultra-conservative policy of the empire. From the days of Justinian onward, the strategy and tactics of the Byzantine army remained fundamentally defensive. The entire realm was divided into themes, or army corps districts, each protected by a number of well-sited fortresses, connected by good roads, and supported by a highly organized and mobile corps of troops. It was this system, rather than the valour of the soldiers or the skill of their generals, which enabled the empire to withstand for centuries the shock of invasion. The invading armies or hordes could seldom storm the fortresses, and as they possessed no adequate supply system they were compelled to live by foraging and when so occupied were at the mercy of any organized force. Byzantine strategy, therefore, was very similar to that of Marshal Saxe in the eighteenth century. A general did not seek battle, usually he avoided it and retired to a fortress when threatened. There he remained in complete safety while the enemy besieged it, and when, through lack of supplies, the besiegers were forced to raise the siege to seek a new "feeding-ground", he would catch them when foraging and annihilate them. Though, generally speaking, the Byzantine armies were small when compared with those of their enemies, because they were self-contained and based on fortresses (protected supply depôts), time and again they were able to concentrate superiority of force at the point of attack.

The army was organized and trained according to this strategy. Like a modern army it was divided into two categories of troops – administrative and combatant. The first were highly organized, and consisted of a baggage train, a supply column, field engineers,

[1] For a full account of the organization of the Byzantine army under Maurice (582–602) see *L'art Militaire et les Armées au Moyen Age*, Ferdinand Lot (1946), vol. I, pp. 43–56, and for the period 963–1025 see *Histoire du Moyen Age* (edit. Gustave Glotz, 1936), vol. III, pp. 463–467.

and an ambulance corps.[1] "For every sixteen men there was . . . provided a cart to carry biscuit, etc., and a supply of arrows, as well as a second cart carrying a hand-mill, an axe, a saw, a chopper, a sieve, a mallet, two spades, two pickaxes, a large wicker basket, a cooking-pot, and other tools and utensils for camp use. In addition to the carts there was . . . a pack-horse, so that when the infantry were forced to leave the waggon-train behind . . . the horses might . . . carry eight or ten days' biscuit with them for immediate use."[2]

The combatant forces were divided into cavalry, infantry, and artillery. The first wore steel caps and mail shirts, carried circular shields, and were armed with bow, lance, sword, axe or mace. The infantry were organized in sections of sixteen men, called a "decury"; ten of these formed a "century"; and three centuries a "band" or battalion. Bands were divided into heavy and light; men of the former were clothed in mail and carried a shield, lance, sword, and axe, and the latter consisted almost entirely of archers, equipped with a bow, a quiver of forty arrows, and an axe.

The artillery worked the mangonels, a generic name for any engine which projected stones, arrows, or fire-balls. There were three definite types, the catapult, *ballista*, and trebuchet.[3]

In spite of this thorough organization, recruiting of native-born men was always a difficulty; consequently the ranks were filled with foreign mercenaries and many Turks enlisted during the ninth, tenth, and eleventh centuries.[4] Generalship usually was conventional, the leaders working almost entirely by book. This was far from being detrimental because Leo had laid down in his *Tactica* a series of alternative instructions, not only for each type of country to be fought in, but also for each type of enemy, and as the Moslem or Turkish methods of fighting, because of lack of organization, remained unchanged, a sealed-pattern tactics could be followed safely.

Usually the cavalry were divided into three lines: a fighting line, a supporting line and reserves, and detachments on the wings to protect the flanks or threaten the enemy's. Behind them came

[1] To each "band" or battalion (480 men) was attached a surgeon and six or eight bearers (Oman's *The Art of War in the Middle Ages*, 1924, vol. i, p. 190).
[2] *Ibid.*, vol. i, p. 189.
[3] For a full description of these engines and various types of bows, see *The Projectile-Throwing Engines of the Ancients*, Sir Ralph Payne-Gallway (1907). Also *Mathematicail Veteres*, Melchisedich Thévenot (1693).
[4] See *Byzace et les Turcs Seldjoucides dans L'Asie Occidentale jusqu'en 1081*, L. Laurent (1913), p. 15.

the heavy infantry in columns of sixteen ranks; the first advanced with shields locked while the remainder held theirs aloft after the manner of the Roman *testudo*. Behind the heavy infantry were ranged the bowmen, who kept up a discharge of arrows over the heads of those in front of them. Once the enemy had been broken, disordered, or distracted by the cavalry charge, the heavy infantry assaulted in column, hurled their spears, and then set to with sword and axe while a barrage of arrows was poured over their heads. There was, therefore, a close combination between cavalry and infantry and also between shock and missile. Cavalry pursuits were seldom attempted, and more especially so against the Turks who, though they lacked stability, were exceedingly mobile.

There can be little doubt that in the year 1071 this organization was nearly as perfect as it had been under Basil II; but the army, though still virile, was rotten, for forty years of court mismanagement and parsimony had undermined it morally. It was not courage, organization, and tactical skill which were lacking, but discipline, morale, and confidence. The army was a highly organized vacuum – the shell of a blown egg.

Could this internal decay have been averted, there would have been little chance of Turkish success; for organization was non-existent in the fighting bands of the Seljuks. They consisted mainly of cavalry bowmen, each under a chief who often fought a neighbouring chief and sometimes even the Sultan, whose position was always a precarious one. As Laurent writes: "The free-minded Turkoman served the strongest, the bravest, the most daring, the most fanatical and above all the most fortunate leader. An abortive surprisal or less abundant booty than usual would cause him without a scruple to change from one band to another."[1] Finlay says: "Their policy was . . . directed . . . to two objects: in the first place, to enrich their followers, increase their own fame, and augment the numbers of their troops by rapid inroads for the collection of plunder; in the second, to reduce the open country as quickly as possible to such a state of depopulation as would admit the establishment of permanent nomade encampments . . . the great Sultan Alp Arslan was well aware that this war of incursions and devastation offered greater prospects of ultimate success than a series of pitched battles with the disciplined mercenaries of the empire."[2]

[1] *Byzance et les Turcs Seldjoucides, etc.*, L. Laurent, p. 100.
[2] *A History of Greece, etc.*, vol. III, p. 27.

This was the position when Romanus Diogenes hastily assembled his army in Phrygia, where Alp Arslan lay in winter quarters. Romanus set out for the province of Lycandus (north of Marash) and Alp Arslan broke camp, sending half his forces south and half north.[1] When he heard that the northern horde had invaded Pontus and was pillaging Neocaesarea (Niksar), Romanus left his heavy baggage at Sebaste (Sivas), crossed the mountains, and fell so suddenly upon the Turks that he compelled them to abandon their plunder and prisoners. Next, he turned southward, crossed the Taurus mountains and invaded the territory of Aleppo, then returned by way of Alexandretta to Podandus (Bazanti Han). There he learnt that fresh hordes had penetrated between the fortresses and were ravaging the country round Armorium (Karapuna) and turned against them, but they retreated so rapidly that he was unable to intercept them and he continued his march westward. He returned to Constantinople in January, 1069.

His next campaign soon followed, but was at once interrupted by a rebellion of his Frankish mercenaries in the Armeniac theme (around Amasia). He put down the revolt, then marched into Cappadocia where the Turks were plundering the country round Caesarea (Kaiserie). He delivered this province, then crossed the Euphrates with the intention of marching to Khilat (Ahlat) on Lake Van. When laying siege to that town, his field army, which he had sent forward, was defeated, and the victorious Turks poured towards Iconium (Konia). First returning to Sebaste, next Romanus marched south and hemmed in his enemy at Heraclea (Kybistra), but though he compelled him to abandon his plunder, he broke through his forces and escaped to Aleppo.

The following year, to save Barium (Bari), in Apulia, from falling into Norman hands, he entrusted his eastern army to Manuel Comnenus, nephew of Isaac I, who established his headquarters at Sebaste. Manuel advanced against a Turkish horde under the sultan's brother-in-law Arisiaghi, but was defeated and taken prisoner. Arisiaghi, who was contemplating a rebellion against Alp Arslan, then admitted Manuel to his counsels, and the latter persuaded his captor to visit Constantinople and to enter into alliance with Romanus. When he did so Alp Arslan demanded his extradition, and when it was refused he again took

[1] For Alp Arslan's campaign see Claude Cahen, "La campagne de Manzikert d'après les sources musulmanes", in *Byzantion* (1934), vol. IX, no. 2, p. 621.

the field, besieged and captured Manzikert, invested Edessa (Urfa), and when he failed to take it retired into Persia.

Then came the emperor's fourth and fatal campaign. Thus far, though his successes had not been spectacular, they had more than cancelled out his defeats, and above all they had shown that as long as his generals and soldiers remained loyal the Byzantine military organization was so superior to the Turkish that he had little to fear as long as he acted with caution. This he did not do, and though he was a fearless leader and his troops were well equipped and trained, it was above all things their lack of loyalty which caused his disaster.

Infuriated by the fall of Manzikert, early in 1071 Romanus advanced to Sebaste, "like a cloud growling with thunder and munitioned with hail".[1] There he collected a considerable army,[2] and had it been disciplined, probably all would have gone well. But it was far from being so, and trouble at once occurred when his men pillaged the inhabitants. His first attempt to enforce discipline led to the mutiny of his German mercenaries, who only condescended to follow him after much argument. From Sebaste he advanced on Theodosiopolis (Erzerum) where he considered his plan of campaign. As he believed that the sultan was in Persia and would be delayed there while he made ready, he decided to take Khilat, on the north-west shore of Lake Van, and Manzikert, some thirty miles to the north of it, in order to establish a base of operations against Persia. To do so he divided his army into two main columns: one, consisting of his Frankish mercenaries under Roussel de Bailleul, was to secure Khilat, and the other, under his personal command, was to occupy Manzikert; both were held by Turkish garrisons.

Romanus has been blamed by Sir Charles Oman for having violated all the precepts set down by Leo VI in his *Tactica*,[3] but faulty tactics was not the main cause of his ruin, it was the gross disloyalty of some of his subordinates and troops, coupled with faulty information.

When Romanus decided on his plan, the sultan was not in Persia but in Syria, and when he learnt that the emperor was in Armenia, in spite of the fewness of his own troops, he decided to advance north-eastward by way of Mosul and Khoi against

---

[1] Matthew of Edessa, pt. II, ciii.
[2] Cahen (*op. cit.*, p. 629), quoting Moslem authorities, mentions 200,000, 300,000, and 400,000, all obvious exaggerations.
[3] *The Art of War in the Middle Ages*, vol. I, p. 217.

him.[1] At Mosul he was joined by the cadi of Manzikert and other fugitives, and after he had collected some 14,000 Turks and Kurds he continued his march on Khoi. Meanwhile Romanus had reinforced Roussel de Bailleul with a strong contingent of Byzantine infantry under George Trakhaniotes, and had further weakened his main body by sending out other detachments, including one, said to be 12,000 strong, to gather supplies in Georgia.[2] Further, he had laid siege to Manzikert and had taken it.

At Khoi, 125 miles east of Lake Van, the sultan halted to await reinforcements from Azerbaijan, and once they had come, he set out westward, presumably along the southern side of Lake Van, to relieve Khilat. His advanced guard would appear to have taken Roussel and Trakhaniotes completely by surprise, for on its arrival before Khilat on August 16 they hurriedly withdrew their detachments toward Malatya instead of falling back on the main Byzantine army. Whether they did so from military reasons or treasonable motives has not been determined. Yet such was their haste, or craft, that they failed to inform Romanus of their withdrawal.

Once Khilat was his, Alp Arslan pushed on toward Manzikert, and at the same time Romanus left Manzikert for Khilat. But the former was well aware of his enemy's approach and the latter was ignorant that the main Turkish army was in Armenia. The result was that the Byzantine advanced guard suddenly found itself confronted by a vastly superior force by which it was roughly handled and forced back in rout on the main body. Romanus realized now that the whole Turkish army[3] was in the vicinity and hurriedly sent orders to Roussel and Trachaniotes to rejoin him, which they could not or would not do, for they were moving westward and away from him.

In spite of this reduction in strength, Romanus did not lose heart, and was so confident of victory that when the sultan suggested a peaceful settlement of their dispute, for the Seljuks never much liked meeting the Byzantines in a pitched battle, he scornfully brushed the proposal aside and informed his envoy that he would not consider peace unless the sultan surrendered his camp and agreed to make no further invasions of the empire. As these terms were refused, battle became inevitable.

[1] Cahen, *Byzantion*, p. 629.   [2] *Histoire de l'Arménie*, René Grousset, p. 627.
[3] Oman (vol. I, p. 217) says "more than a hundred thousand", and Gibbon (vol. VI, p. 239) gives 40,000, but also quotes 300,000, 15,000, and 12,000. As the Sultan's march must have been rapid, his army was probably of moderate size, under 40,000.

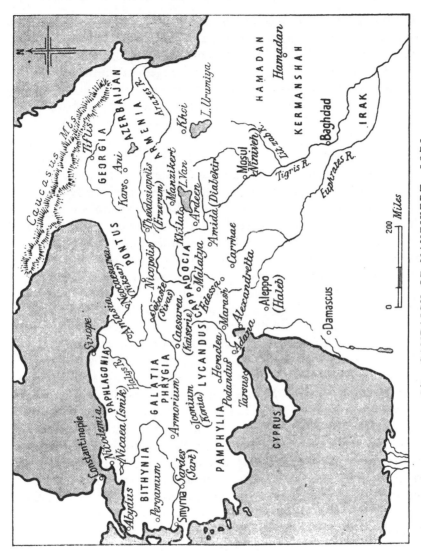

N

Caucasus Mts.

GEORGIA

Tiflis

AZERBAIJAN

ARMENIA

Araxes R.

Ani

Kars

Theodosiopolis
(Erzerum)

Manzikert

Khoi

L. Urumiya

HAMADAN

Hamadan

KERMANSHAH

Baghdad

IRAK

L. Van

Akhlat

Ardeeh

Amida (Diabekir)

Mosul

Ninweh

Tigris R.

Litzab R.

Euphrates R.

PONTUS

Sinope

Neocaesarea
(Niksar)

Amasia

Halys R.

Nicopolis

Sebaste
(Sivas)

Caesarea
(Kaiserie)

CAPPADOCIA

Carrhae

Edessa

Malatya

Marash

Alexandretta

Aleppo
(Haleb)

Damascus

0        200   Miles

PAPHLAGONIA

Nicomedia

Nicaea (Isnik)

Constantinople

Abydus

BITHYNIA

Pergamum

Smyrna

Sardes
(Sart)

GALATIA

PHRYGIA

Armorium

Iconium
(Konia)

LYCANDUS

Heraclea

Podandus

PAMPHYLIA

Tarsus

Adana

CYPRUS

27. CAMPAIGN OF MANZIKERT, 1071

It was either on August 19 or 25, more probably the former date,[1] that the emperor marched out of his camp and drew up his army in order of battle. He took command of the centre, which consisted of his Guard and metropolitan regiments, and placed the Cappadocian general Alyattes in command of his right wing, and Nicephorus Bryennius in command of his left. The former consisted of mounted Guze and Kipchak mercenaries and the latter of mounted Patzinaks. In rear he drew up a strong reserve line of mercenary cavalry, which included a regiment of Germans and some Normans from Italy as well as the levies of the nobles of the eastern frontier, and placed them under Andronicus Ducas, the son of Caesar John Ducas, one of his bitterest enemies.

The sultan handed the marshalling of his forces to his eunuch general Taraug and gave him the brief and precise order – "win or be beheaded". Then Alp Arslan "set aside his bow and arrows, armed himself with a sword and mace; had the tail of his horse platted . . . donned a white robe and having perfumed himself said: 'Should I be defeated this spot shall be my tomb' ".[2] The strength of the Byzantine army lay in its heavy infantry and cavalry; of the Turkish, in its light horsemen.

The battle opened in the usual way: the Turkish horse-archers galloped forward, showered arrows on their enemy, but made no attempt to close, and as they did so a considerable body of Romanus's Kipchaks and Patzinaks deserted.[3] The Byzantine cavalry charged when they could; but because many horses were killed and wounded, Romanus gave orders to his line to advance. This it did in good order and successfully, for it drove back the Turks to their camp and even beyond. Nevertheless, it was an unwise move, not only because the day was far spent, but because the Turks had unlimited ground in which to fall back, and unless Romanus could reach some spot where water was to be found for his men and horses, he would be compelled to retire and then most certainly would be counter-attacked.

This is what happened: as twilight began to close in, Romanus ordered the retreat, but was so furiously attacked that he was forced to turn about to drive back his enemy. As the front rank faced round to confront the Turks, Andronicus, out of malice, refused to obey the order, and instead of advancing in support he

[1] See Cahen, *op. cit.*, pp. 632–634, and Laurent, *Byzance et les Turcs Seldjoucides*, p. 43, note (10).
[2] *Histoire Général des Huns, etc.*, M. D. Deguignes (1756–1758), vol. ii, p. 209.
[3] Cahen, *op. cit.*, p. 633.

retired to the camp, and by doing so uncovered the rear of the army. At once the Turkish light horse swept round the emperor's flanks, concentrated on the right and rear of their enemy's right wing, and drove it in rout from the field. Next they fell upon the exposed right flank and rear of the centre and forced it away from the left wing, or possibly held it while the left wing, for some reason, fell back. The centre became isolated. Nevertheless, it held out gallantly until nightfall and Romanus displayed the highest courage; but his horse was killed under him and he was wounded and taken prisoner. The centre then broke back and was cut down almost to a man.

Romanus's defeat was as overwhelming as that of Crassus at Carrhae, in 53 B.C., but tactically it cannot be compared with it; for though the emperor's pursuit had been foolhardy, there is little doubt that, in spite of heavy casualties, he would have regained his camp had it not been for the treason of Andronicus. It was he who was responsible for a defeat which was destined to change the course of history; yet so little was this realized at the time that Gibbon says: "The Byzantine writers deplore the loss of an inestimable pearl: they forget to mention that, in this fatal day, the Asiatic provinces of Rome were irretrievably sacrificed."[1]

On August 20, 1071, the day after this disastrous battle was fought, Romanus was brought before Alp Arslan, who treated him with the highest courtesy and respect, and concluded a treaty with him, according to the terms of which a ransom of 1,500,000 byzants[2] was to be paid as well as a yearly tribute of 360,000 byzants to extend over fifty years. Then he released him, but his misfortunes were not at an end; for during his short captivity Caesar John Ducas had seized power in Constantinople; had forced the Empress Eudocia into a nunnery, and had proclaimed himself guardian of his nephew, the effete Michael VII. Directly he had collected a few troops, Romanus marched against him, but was defeated at Doceia, pursued by the traitor Andronicus to Adana and there captured, dethroned, and blinded in so cruel a manner that a little later he died of his injuries. But before he died he remembered the chivalrous conduct of the sultan, and in proof of his good faith he collected such money as he could and sent it to him.

---

[1] *The Decline and Fall of the Roman Empire*, Edward Gibbon, vol. VI, p. 240.
[2] The value of a gold byzant varied from ten to twenty English shillings.

27

When he learnt that his peace terms had been repudiated, Alp Arslan forthwith invaded Asia Minor; but in 1072 he was assassinated and succeeded by his son Malik Shah. The devastation then carried out beggars description. Laurent writes, quoting contemporary authorities in evidence: "It is difficult even to imagine the complete ruin the Turks left behind them. Whatever they could reach, men or crops, nothing remained alive; and a week was sufficient under dread of famine to force them to abandon the most prosperous areas. On their departure all that was left were devastated fields, trees cut down, mutilated corpses and towns driven mad by fear or in flames." At Armorium, it is said, 100,000 people perished, and at Touch 120,000 were massacred and 150,000 sold into slavery—thus the destruction went on. Whole districts were depopulated. "When the Turks had passed by, such as were left alive feared to return . . . trusting in neither the walls of their cities, nor the crags of the mountains, they crowded into Constantinople where they were decimated by plague. In a few years Cappadocia, Phrygia, Bithynia, and Paphlagonia lost the greater part of their Greek population." Further, Laurent writes:

"In brief, the population of Asia Minor vanished before the Turks. The people fled far away, or shut themselves up in their cities, or sought refuge in the mountains which border the central plateau of the peninsula. The valleys and the plains which stretch from Caesarea and Sebaste to Nicaea and Sardes remained all but empty. And as they fell fallow, the Turks with their tents and their flocks wandered over them contentedly, as they had done in the deserts out of which they had come."[1]

The loss of the Asiatic themes deprived the empire of its best recruiting ground; henceforth mercenaries were alone employed –Franks, Turks, Patzinaks, Russians, and Lombards, men who could be bought and sold. The result was a series of mutinies and civil wars. In 1078 Michael VII was dethroned and Nicephorus III (1078–1081) replaced him; next Alexius Comnenus rose against Nicephorus and marched on Constantinople, which was betrayed to him by a body of German mercenaries. On April 1, 1081, it was sacked and the following day Alexius was crowned.

An able and astute diplomatist, Alexius might have righted the situation had it not been for the Normans. In 1071, Robert Guiscard, Duke of Apulia, captured Bari and so ended Byzantine rule

---

[1] *Byzance et les Turcs Seldjoucides, etc.*, L. Laurent, pp. 106–109.

in southern Italy. Now, ten years later, he conceived the idea of assuming the imperial crown, and in the spring of 1081 reduced Corfu and in October occupied Durazzo. He handed over his army to his son Bohemond and the latter defeated Alexius and pushed on into Thessaly as far as Larissa. Beset on all sides, for shortly afterward the Patzinaks broke over the Balkans and spread havoc up to the walls of Philippolis and Adrianople, the empire was no longer capable of self-defence, and from 1081 onward it gradually yielded its political importance to the states of the West. Thus it came about that, twenty-four years after the fateful battle of Manzikert, the great counter-attack of medieval Europe on Moslem Asia was launched.

# The counter-attack of Christendom on Islam

In the crisis which followed the disaster of Manzikert, the Emperor Michael VII appealed to Pope Gregory VII (1073–1087), as the supreme head of Christendom, for assistance. He wanted western mercenaries to defend Constantinople, and not to win back the Holy Land. But Gregory saw in his appeal a heaven-sent opportunity to attain his three great aspirations: the restoration of the Eastern Church to Roman obedience; the acknowledgement of the kings of Christendom as liege servants of the Church; and the initiation of a crusade against Islam. At the time, Gregory, the complete autocrat and supreme product of the Cluniac movement, was shackled by his quarrel over lay investitures with the Emperor Henry IV (1056–1106), and was unable to do more than to propagate the idea of a crusade. Nevertheless it caught on, and in the rising enthusiasm the modest request for mercenaries was lost to sight in the development of a mass movement.

In 1076 Gregory excommunicated Henry and proclaimed that it was the right of the pope, should he see fit, to depose emperors; that as vicar of Christ, he could be judged by no one, and that he held the power to absolve from their allegiance the subjects of the wicked. Thirty years earlier, Henry III had sat in judgment over Gregory VI, now Gregory VII sat in judgement over Henry IV, and, in 1077, he brought him a sinner seeking absolution to Canossa. But his triumph was ephemeral, for, in 1084, Henry retaliated, and on May 25, 1085, Gregory died in exile. He was succeeded by Victor III, who, in 1088, was succeeded by Urban II (1088–1099).

Meanwhile in the East, the Emperor Alexius I Comnenus (1081–1118), beset by wars with the Normans and Patzinaks, had come to terms with the Turks, and when, in 1094, these wars were ended and the recovery of his provinces in Asia again became feasible, he appealed to Urban for help. Like Michael, he appealed for mercenaries to aid him against the Turks and not to regain the Holy Land. This time, it not only fell on willing ears, but on those of a man whose hands were unshackled at a time when

Christendom was eager to meet the challenge of Islam. Thus, for the first time in history, as Professor Bury points out, "two universal religions stood face to face, each aspiring to win the universe": the psychological hour had struck.

Ever since the days of Gregory IV (827–844), one pope after the other had taken an active interest in the Moslem wars, and now that, in large measure, all secular power had become subject to papal control, the pope had by divine right become the accepted military leader of Christendom. Thus it came about that, on November 27, 1095, at the Council of Clermont, Urban II launched the First Crusade. "All Christendom", he declared, "is disgraced by the triumphs and supremacy of the Muslims in the East. The Eastern Churches have asked repeatedly for help. The Holy Land, which is dear to all Christian hearts and rightfully a Christian possession, is profaned and enslaved by infidel rulers. Christian kings should therefore turn their weapons against these enemies of God, in place of warring with one another as they do. They ought to rescue the Holy Land and the Holy City, they ought to roll away the reproach of Christendom and destroy for ever the power of Muslim attack. The war to which they are called is a Holy War and *Deus volt* is the fitting battle-cry. Those who lose their lives in such an enterprise will gain Paradise and the remission of their sins."[1]

The news of this decision came as a shock to Alexius, because the last thing he wanted was a crusade. Western Christendom looked upon the schismatic East as more abominable than Islam, and he looked upon the crusaders as barbarians and no better than Turks and Patzinaks. "To the Western eye", writes the Greek historian D. Bikélas, "the Crusaders present themselves in all the noble proportions of a great movement based upon motives purely religious, when Europe . . . appears the self-sacrificing champion of Christianity and of civilization. . . . But when the Easterners beheld swarms of illiterate barbarians looting and plundering the provinces of the Christian and Roman Empire, and the very men who called themselves the champions of the Faith murdering the priests of Christ on the ground that they were schismatics, it was equally natural that they should forget that such a movement had originally been inspired by a religious

---

[1] There are various versions of this appeal: the original version has not come down to us. On this question see D. Munro's "Speech of Pope Urban II at Clermont, 1095", in *The American Historical Review* (1906), XI, pp. 231–242.

aim. . . ." Thus, at the very opening of the greatest adventure in western history, occurred that fault which was destined to split, and ultimately to wreck it. To Alexius the problem was a strategical one, to secure the Byzantine empire as a bulwark against the Turks; to Urban it was ideological, to effect the union of the Churches and to secure the Holy Land for pilgrims. Yet behind Urban's religious aims there were strategical reasons which were even more compelling.

Though the counter-attack of western Christendom on Islam had been opened by Charles Martel, it was not until the eleventh century that it began seriously to be developed, and then by the Pisans and Genoese, who drove the Moslems out of Sardinia and won the mastery of the Tyrrhenian Sea. About the same time, the Normans began to gain a footing in southern Italy, and, by 1060, when they had established themselves there, they set out to conquer Sicily, a task they accomplished in 1091. During the same period two other successful operations were undertaken; in 1085, Alphonso VI of Castile mastered Toledo, the fall of which resounded throughout Islam, and, in 1087, the Genoese and Pisans made a joint expedition against Mahdiyah (Mahdia), the Moslem capital in Tunis. They captured the town and burnt the Moslem fleet in its harbour and so won command of the western Mediterranean. This was the most important gain of all, because the supremacy of the fleets of the Italian republics was the prerequisite of a counter-attack on the East, not so much to move armies as to keep them supplied. This possibility appealed largely to the commercial appetites of Pisa, Genoa, and Venice, which for years past had been trading actively with Syria, Egypt, and the Byzantine empire, and clearly Italian commerce had everything to gain from Christian settlements in the East.

A further incentive was that the pilgrimages *en masse* to Jerusalem, stimulated by the Cluniac revival, had, during and after the Seljuk invasions, led to the West being flooded with anti-Turk propaganda which generated a violent war psychosis. So it came about that when Alexius made his appeal, the times were strategically, commercially, and psychologically ripe for the counter-attack. Also were they demographically, for since about the year 1000 the populations of France and Flanders had increased, and during the eleventh century frequent famines, droughts, and violent epidemics made people think "of far distant lands full of abundance and prosperity".

Urban's summons met with immediate and enthusiastic reception, and in the following six months hosts of preachers, including Peter the Hermit, carried the pope's appeal into every part of France. Urban travelled from place to place and offered something to every man: to kings, cheaply bought land from their vassals; to the nobles, new lands in the East for those they sold; to the merchants, the wealth coincident in equipment and supply of the crusading forces; to the people, freedom from serfdom as a reward for enrolment; to the monks, release from their discipline; and to all, alliance with the supernatural and eternal life under the invincible banner of their general--Jesus.

This persuasive propaganda, which offered to each crusader the best of two worlds, led to contingents being raised in every western land, but more particularly in France, where the crusade grew into a great national movement. No supreme leader was appointed, and when the crusaders assembled at Constantinople they did so not as a united army but as a confederation of forces, the rivalries between the leaders of which went far to determine the failure of the whole enterprise. The more important of these men were: Hugh Count of Vermandois, brother of Philip I of France; Raymond Count of Toulouse, who raised the largest contingent; Robert of Normandy, son of William the Conqueror; Robert II of Flanders; Godfrey of Bouillon, Duke of Lorraine, and his brothers Baldwin and Eustace; and Bohemond of Taranto, the ablest of the leaders, who was accompanied by his nephew Tancred.

The incredible numbers ascribed to the crusade by medieval chroniclers are to be discounted as propaganda aimed at the glorification of the movement. The contingents must have been moderate in size or they could not have been supplied *en route*, and a rough guess of the forces which passed into Asia Minor has been made by Professor Stevenson, who places them at between 25,000 and 30,000.[1]

At Constantinople, Alexius rightly demanded of each crusading leader an oath of allegiance, but it was only grudgingly given by Godfrey of Bouillon. The other crusaders held the Greeks in contempt. At length all was ready, and on May 14, 1097, the crusade was opened with the siege of Nicaea. It surrendered on June 19 and the crusaders set out for Antioch on the Orontes. On

[1] See *A History of the Crusades*, Steven Runciman (1951), vol. I, appendix II, for calculations.

July 1 they won their first battle at Dorylaeum (Eskischir), and then, because the Moslems were too weak to risk another battle, the scramble for territories was begun by Baldwin, who established a Latin state in Euphratesia (region of Marash) and became count of Edessa. On June 3, 1098, Antioch was taken by treachery; but immediately after its occupation the crusaders were besieged by Karbogha, and their position became so critical that in spite of their rivalries they appointed Bohemond to the supreme command. Providentially, on June 14 the discovery of the Holy Lance led to such unbounded enthusiasm that Bohemond decided to put all to the hazard of a single battle. In this Karbogha was defeated, and after it Bohemond became prince of Antioch.

A six-month halt was made at Antioch, and it was not until January 13, 1099, that Raymond, Tancred, and Robert of Normandy set out for Jerusalem. At Tripoli they were joined by Godfrey and Robert of Flanders, and from there the five together pushed southward, possibly accompanied by some 12,000 followers, and on June 7 they encamped outside the walls of Jerusalem. On July 15 the Holy City was carried by storm and its inhabitants were mercilessly slaughtered. The victory was celebrated in the Church of the Holy Sepulchre, after which Godfrey of Bouillon was proclaimed its Defender (*Advocatus Sancti Sepulcri*).

Thus, though the crusaders gained the end they had set their hearts upon, which was mainly because of the confusion and civil war which had engulfed the Moslem world after the death of the great Seljuk sultan, Malik Shah, in 1092, their victory was not followed by a conquest of the land, but merely by the military occupation of certain of its districts. Further, Baldwin I (1100–1118), though acknowledged as *dux* or *princeps*, was no more than nominal overlord of the prince of Antioch and the counts of Edessa and Tripoli. Damascus, Emesa, Hama, Aleppo, and other towns remained in Moslem hands; but so long as civil strife separated their emirs, the Moslems could do no more than raid the Christian territories. But two important events followed the fall of Jerusalem: the occupation of Jaffa, which won for the Italian merchants a port, without which the crusaders could not have been supplied, and the establishment of the military Orders.

Since the early years of the eleventh century, the Hospital of St. John had been established in Jerusalem to help sick and poor pilgrims. This foundation suggested to Hugh de Payen the idea of raising a body of knights to protect pilgrims on their way to the Holy City, and in the reign of Baldwin II (1118–1131) these knights were given a dwelling near the Temple of Solomon and became known as Knights of the Temple. Soon after, a similar organization was adopted for the knights of St. John, and the two Orders–the Templars and Hospitallers–rapidly grew into the most important element in the military strength of the kingdom. Other Orders were created later, the most notable of which was that of the Teutonic Knights in 1191.

Division between the Moslem emirs continued until 1127, when Imad ed-Din Zangi, Atabeg of Mosul, set out to establish his rule over Syria. Within three years he mastered Hamah and Aleppo, and on Christmas Day, 1144, conquered Edessa, then ruled by Joscelin II. Two years later Zangi was assassinated and succeeded by his son Nur ed-Din.

In western Europe the fall of Edessa was recognized as a disaster of the first magnitude, and its immediate consequence was the preaching of the Second Crusade by St. Bernard of Clairvaux. At his bidding, Conrad III of Germany and Louis VII of France took the cross in the spring of 1147. Both met with disasters on their way through Asia Minor, but Louis, by a circuitous route, and Conrad, by sea, carried the remnants of their armies to the Holy Land. There they united with Baldwin III (1143–1162) and decided to lay siege to Damascus, then held by Mujir ed-Din Abaq, who sowed dissension between the western and Syrian Franks, and by bribes persuaded the latter to abandon the siege. The Second Crusade collapsed, Conrad returned home in 1148, and Louis in 1149. This failure led to the renewal of attacks by Nur ed-Din. In 1149 he defeated Raymond of Antioch; in the following year he conquered the districts of Edessa that still remained in Christian hands, and in 1154 he occupied Damascus, the key of Syria. With him was a boy some sixteen years old; his name was Saladin (1138–1193)–the hero of the next decisive battle.

# CHAPTER 15

# The Battle of Hattin, 1187

The failure of the Crusaders to take Damascus in 1148, or even to comtemplate taking Emesa, Hama, and Aleppo to the north of it, must be attributed as much to their ignorance of strategy and siegecraft as to their jealousies and quarrellings. Yet to the Emperor Julian, Damascus was "The Eye of the East" and to the Arabs "The Bride of the Earth", and to understand these qualifications it is necessary to examine the strategical values of Syria.

Syria and Palestine may be divided into four topographical zones: (1) the shallow coastal plains; (2) the mountainous uplands to the east of them; (3) the deep valleys of the Orontes, Litany, and Jordan; and (4) the western margin of the great desert to the east of these rivers. North of Aleppo the country is mountainous and south of the Dead Sea it is desert; therefore, should all four zones be occupied from the Amanus Mountains to the Gulf of Akaba, Syria and Palestine become easily defensible. Further, so long as they are firmly held, they separate the entire country north of the line Alexandretta–Basra (valley of the Euphrates) from Egypt. The four zones may be compared with a natural fortress, with one flank open to the sea, standing between northern and southern Islam.

From north to south run three lines of communication: (1) along the coast; (2) up the Orontes and down the Litany and Jordan; and (3) the desert road, Aleppo–Damascus–Amman–Akaba. The ultimate failure of the crusading Franks largely lay in their neglect to gain control of the third which, by linking Syria and Egypt, united Moslem power in the north with that in the south. Had the crusaders held it, the battle of Hattin would never have been fought, and in consequence the whole course of crusading history would have been changed.

As mentioned in the preceding Chronicle, the crusaders never conquered the land, all they did was to occupy parts of it, which on one flank were supplied by the sea, and on the other protected by a chain of magnificent castles. From south to north the more famous were: Aila (Akaba) on the gulf of Akaba; Montreal (Esh

Shobek) and Kerak of Moab (Petra Deserti). Next, a long chain blocked the defiles leading to the Jordan: Beaufort (Qalat ash Shaqif), Château-Neuf (Hunin), Beauvoir (Kawabel Hawa), Saphet (Safed), and Castillet (Qasrel Atra). Then a gap, and lastly the castles of Akkar (El Kaa), Krak des Chevaliers (west of Homs), and Montferrand (Barin) watching the chain of the Lebanon.

Supply by sea and defence by castles, these were the abutments of the crusaders' strategy, and so long as the castles held out and the Venetians and Genoese commanded the Mediterranean, all that was required were reserves of men, not only to hold the castles and to provide mobile field forces to manœuvre between them, but above all to re-blood the crusaders as they became mongrel-ized; for it was lack of European women which ruined them morally. But this is exactly what did not happen; because the new-comers came to fight in order to save their souls, and as all avail-able land had by now been occupied, the best of them returned home and the worst remained to quarrel with the settlers who, having become more economically than religiously minded, wanted peace and not war. Be it remembered that St. Bernard looked upon the second crusade largely as the vehicle for a miracle. He had pointed out in an appeal to the criminal classes, that God should summon to his service, as though they were innocent, murderers, ravishers, adulterers, perjurers, and those guilty of every crime, offered to even the most evil of men an exquisite and priceless chance of attaining salvation. As was to happen in the days of Wellington, the gaols were emptied, but this time no discipline was enforced.

Lack of numbers, control, and discipline were in part made good by armour, that of the Franks was vastly superior to their opponents', also their courage was fanatical. These assets enabled them repeatedly to defeat vastly superior Moslem forces. Thus, on one occasion, in 1177, 370 knights met, charged and routed 26,000 of Saladin's Mamaluks, and even should the true number be 2,600, it was a remarkable performance. Their tactical failing was that they did not appreciate the need for cooperation between infantry and cavalry. When they did, success was generally theirs; when not, frequently, unless the first charge succeeded, they were beaten.

This was the general strategical picture for the operations which followed the occupation of Damascus by Nur ed-Din in 1154.

Damascus lay on the desert road, and from it direct communication could be established with Egypt; the sole point of interference was Kerak of Moab, in Oultrejourdain. Therefore it followed that, should Egypt be occupied by the Syrian Moslems or enter into alliance with them, the latter would be able to bring pressure to bear on the kingdom of Jerusalem from both north and south. This Nur ed-Din understood well, and during the next fifteen years, the winning of Egypt became his all-absorbing task. His main difficulty was a religious one: the Moslems of Egypt were Shias headed by the Fatimid caliph. They abhorred the Sunnis of Syria and the caliph of Baghdad as much as they did the Christians, and the crusaders were well aware of this.

The first step taken toward the solution of the problem was the stabilization of the Moslem position around Damascus, and once accomplished, Nur ed-Din and Amalric I (Amaury) (1163–1174), king of Jerusalem, stood face to face. Both were able generals. The latter received a yearly subsidy from the Fatimid caliph in Cairo, where, in 1163, Shawar, the Egyptian vizier, was deposed by a rival called Dirgham, and fled to Nur ed-Din. Because Dirgham refused to continue the subsidy, Amalric marched into Egypt and defeated him, but was compelled to withdraw when Dirgham flooded the country. Nur ed-Din sent Shawar back to Egypt with an army under Shirkuh, the uncle of Saladin, and Saladin accompanied him on his staff. Shawar found the tutelage of Shirkuh irksome and fled to Amalric, who, in 1167, forced Shirkuh to withdraw. A series of campaigns then followed, in which, by degrees, Shirkuh firmly established himself in Egypt. On March 23, 1169, he died, and three days later the Fatimid caliph chose his nephew, Saladin, as his successor, who from then until the death of his master, Nur ed-Din, played a somewhat self-interested game.[1]

Saladin was one of the really great characters in medieval history, so great that when Dante made his visionary descent into hell, he wrote "*Solo in parte vide 'l Saladino*" ("Alone and apart I beheld Saladin").[2] By birth he was a Kurd, son of Nasir ed-Din Ayyub (Job), brother of Asad ed-Din Shirkuh, Nur ed-Din's general, and he was born at Tekrit on the Tigris in 1137–1138. His brother was Saif ed-Din el-Adil, the "Saphadin" of the crusading chroniclers, and his own name also was similarly

---

[1] For these exceedingly involved operations see *A History of the Crusades*, Steven Runciman (1952), vol. II, book IV, chap. IV.
[2] *Inferno*, Dante, IV, 129.

abbreviated, for in full it read "el-Melik en Nasir Salah ed-Din Yusuf ibn Ayyub": Salah ed-Din meaning "The prosperity of the world and of the faith". By nature he was studious, and by predilection a scholar rather than a soldier—a lover of chess and of poetry. As a youth he was loth to accompany his uncle on his first Egyptian campaign, for he loved peace more than war, and spent most of the years 1154–1164 in Damascus among his cultured friends. A devout Moslem, he was fanatically anti-Christian, and when greatness was thrust upon him he accepted it grandly yet calmly. As a general he was cautious, a strategist rather than a tactician; careful of his men, generous and kindly. As an administrator he was far in advance of his age; yet it is as a man that he stands supreme, his chivalry toward his opponents surrounded him with a glamour which created a romantic literature still read in the East. This was all the more remarkable when it is remembered that the Franks frequently did not consider it dishonourable to break their pledged word to the infidel.

In spite of the incessant intrigues of the Fatimids and the rising jealousy of Nur ed-Din, Saladin established himself in Egypt. But it was not until 1169 that he secured his position there by repulsing a concerted attack by Amalric and the Emperor Manuel I Comnenus (1143–1180) on Damietta. Next, he took his first decisive step toward achieving his policy of reuniting Islam. In 1171 he abolished the Fatimid caliphate and brought Egypt under the spiritual authority of the caliph of Baghdad. Thus, writes Lane-Poole, the kingdom of Jerusalem was placed "as it were, in a cleft-stick, squeezed on both sides by armies controlled by the same power".[1] This is confirmed by Beha ed-Din,[2] a contemporary writer, who says of the Damietta expedition: "When the Franks heard what had happened to the true believers and to their own armies, and saw the Sultan (Salah ed-Din) establishing his authority in Egypt upon a firm basis, they were convinced that he would obtain possession of their dominions, would lay waste their dwelling-places, and wipe away all traces of their rule. . . ."[3] It was only too true, for when in 1173 Nur ed-Din instructed Saladin to lay siege to Kerak, "The Crow's Castle", as well as Esh-Shobek, Beha ed-Din tells us why, ". . . because they were

---

[1] *Saladin*, Stanley Lane-Poole (1898), p. 103.

[2] Beha ed-Din (Bohadin) was one of Saladin's secretaries. He was born at Mosul in 1145 and died in 1234. His life of Saladin is a standard authority. The translation quoted is that of the "Palestine Pilgrims' Text Society", 1897.

[3] Beha ed-Din, pp. 56–57.

nearest to Egypt, and lay on the road to that country. They thus prevented travellers from resorting thither. No caravan could pass through that district unless the Sultan marched out and escorted it in person. His object, therefore, was to make the road freer and more easy, to put the two countries [Syria and Egypt] into communication, so that travellers might come and go without hindrance."[1] Kerak was for years a thorn in Saladin's side, because it was the one point at which the crusaders could always cut the desert road.

In 1174 two events took place which radically changed the political situation. First, on May 15, Nur ed-Din died at Damascus, and because his son and heir, Malik as-Salih Ismail, was but eleven years old, a regent had to be found, and though Saladin had the better claim, the Emir Ibn al-Muqqaddam seized the regency. Amalric saw in this an opportunity to weaken Saladin and set out for Banias to win the regent to his side. Then came the second event. Amalric fell ill on the way with dysentery and was compelled to return to Jerusalem, where he died on July 11. For the Franks his death was a paralysing loss, because the sole remaining prince of the royal house was Baldwin, son of Amalric and his first wife Agnes of Courtenay, a boy eleven years old and afflicted with leprosy. His sister Sibylla was one year older and unmarried, and his stepmother, Maria Comnena, had one daughter, Isabella, aged two. Baldwin was the only possible choice. He was accepted by the barons and on July 15 was crowned fourth of his name by the Patriarch. The inevitable regency dispute then followed and it was not until several months later that the barons chose Raymond III of Tripoli to be guardian of the kingdom.

In the meantime Saladin was busy in Egypt, and once his affairs there were settled, he set out for Damascus, where he arrived on November 26. There he found that his approach had so terrified as-Salih and his mother that they had abandoned al-Muqqaddam and fled to Aleppo. He bore in mind the importance of making himself master of Syria before turning against the Franks, and Saladin next set out to subdue Aleppo.

At the time of his appointment as regent, Raymond, a man of outstanding ability, was in the prime of life. He was supported by the native barons and the Hospitallers and opposed by the newcomers and the Templars who, in 1175, found their leader in

[1] Beha ed-Din, p. 63.

Reynald of Châtillon. Raymond and his followers were against risky adventures, their opponents were aggressively military. So began a tussle between the two factions which was to divide the kingdom and hasten its ruin.

Since Egypt had been lost, Raymond's first problem was to prevent Saladin from gaining Aleppo and thereby consolidating his rule over the whole of Syria. Early in 1175, he set out against Homs, in order to cut off Saladin from Damascus. The movement had its desired effect, for directly the latter found his line of communications threatened he raised the siege of Aleppo and marched southward to secure his base. This compelled Raymond to fall back, and once he had done so, in September Saladin returned to Egypt to reorganize its defences.

Although 1176 saw a respite from fighting, it gave birth to an event which was so disastrous to the Christian cause that, whatever might subsequently have happened, it doomed the whole crusading movement to ultimate failure. Hitherto and in spite of the frequent friction between the Franks and Constantinople, it had been largely because of the growing power of the Emperor Manuel in Anatolia, as well as to his occasional assistance, that the crusaders had been able to maintain their hold on Palestine. The Byzantines in Anatolia threatened Syria from the north, and as long as this threat held it prevented the Syrian Moslems from concentrating their whole strength against the Franks.

This situation was complicated by the Seljuk sultanate of Rum, now under the rule of Kilij Arslan II. During Nur ed-Din's lifetime the sultanate had been threatened both by him and by the emperor, but after Nur ed-Din's death Kilij Arslan's hands were free and he grew restive. Manuel decided to crush him, and thereby to simplify his own strategical situation. He directed his march on Kilij Arslan's capital Konia, but on September 17 Manuel was surrounded in a mountain pass near the fortress of Myriocephalum and his army all but annihilated.[1] The disaster was catastrophic both for the Byzantines and the Franks. For the former it was a second Manzikert, and for the latter it predicted final ruin; for without Byzantine help the Franks had not sufficient men to hold Palestine. Manuel's defeat meant the triumph of Islam.

---

[1] B. Kugler says that "The battle of Myriocephalum decided for ever the destiny of the whole east" (*Studien zur Geschichte des Zweiten Kreuzzuges*, 1866, p. 222). If so, then it must be numbered among the decisive battles of the western world.

When Manuel made his fatal decision to march against Kilij Arslan, Baldwin's leprosy was growing steadily worse, and because in 1177 he would come of age and Raymond's regency would cease, in order to secure the succession, in October his sister Sibylla was married to William of Montferrat, who as her husband became heir apparent. Soon after he fell ill and died in June, 1177. Sibylla gave birth to a son in the late summer. The high probability therefore was that on Baldwin's death his successor would be a minor – the one thing the barons had tried to avert.

In November, Saladin crossed the Egyptian frontier, and after masking Ascalon he headed for Jerusalem. But barely had he done so than, on November 25, his army was caught dispersed in a defile near Ramleh and routed. Saladin escaped capture on a swift camel and hurried back to Cairo. Though tactically his defeat was complete, strategically it was of little account, because the resources of Egypt were so great that he soon recruited another army, and in 1178 he returned to Syria to renew the war. No decision was reached, and in the spring of 1180, both sides grew weary of the struggle and on Baldwn's suggestion a two-year truce was cemented by treaty. About the same time, against the wishes of his barons, Baldwin reluctantly consented to the marriage of his sister Sibylla to Guy of Lusignan, a young knight who had arrived recently from France. He was a weak and foolish youth without character and power of decision, and the result was increased friction between the two factions.

To add to the crisis which now gripped the kingdom, the Franks lost their most powerful ally. On September 24 the Emperor Manuel died and was succeeded by his son Alexius, a boy of eleven, with his mother as regent. Disliked by the people because she was a Latin by birth, in 1182 Andronicus Comnenus led a popular rising against the empress, and in a fit of frenzy all the Latins in Constantinople were massacred by the populace. Soon after the empress and her son were murdered and Andronicus was proclaimed emperor. Once installed, he feared that because of the massacre he would be attacked by the Sicilians, and to safeguard his eastern frontier before the attack could be made, Andronicus came to terms with Saladin, on the understanding that for his alliance with him against the Seljuks he would allow him a free hand against the Franks.

As Saladin was freed by Manuel's death from immediate danger from the north it was imperative for the Franks in no way to disturb the truce. That Saladin, a man of punctilious honour, would do so was highly unlikely, but unfortunately among the Franks there was one to whom honour was unknown. He was Reynald of Châtillon, who for sixteen years had been Nur ed-Din's prisoner, and who, in 1175, had been released and given the seigniory of Oultrejourdain and its immensely strong castle of Kerak, which stood at no great distance from the Damascus-Mecca road. Although, by the terms of the truce, it had been agreed that both Moslem and Christian merchants could freely use this road, in the summer of 1181, Reynald suddenly pounced upon a caravan bound for Mecca and pillaged it. At once Saladin claimed that the truce had been broken and that it could not be renewed unless compensation was paid. Baldwin admitted the justice of this and ordered Reynald to give up the pillaged merchandise. This he refused to do and was supported by the faction of the newcomers and Templars, of which he was now the leader. A renewal of the war became inevitable.

In May, 1182, Saladin set out from Egypt and fought his way back to Damascus, from where he advanced against Mosul. When he failed to take it, he consolidated his position in Jezireh (Al Hammar), and in May, 1183, returned to Aleppo. In August he was back in Damascus. He was now at the height of his power and the most potent prince between Carthage and Baghdad. So powerful did he consider himself that, in a letter to the pope, he styled himself "*Rex omnium regnum orientalium*".

When, in 1182, Saladin was campaigning around Mosul, Baldwin, now fingerless, toeless, and nearly blind, under pressure from his mother and sister, reluctantly agreed to the appointment of Guy of Lusignan as regent. Were this not sufficiently unfortunate for the kingdom, at the same time Reynald of Châtillon seized the opportunity offered by Saladin's absence to carry out a project he had for long had in mind. It was to raid the Moslem Red Sea merchantmen plying between Egypt, India, and Arabia. Further, and what was sheer madness on his part, his aim was also to destroy the Prophet's tomb at Medina and the Kaaba at Mecca. To carry out this audacious adventure he built a squadron of galleys on the shore of the Dead Sea, and had the vessels transported in sections across the desert to the Gulf of Akaba, where they were assembled. Next, while he laid siege to Aila, which had been occupied by the Moslems in 1170, he sent his galleys raiding down the Red Sea. First Aidab on the Nubian coast opposite Mecca was sacked, and then the ports of Medina and Mecca were pillaged. The suddenness and audacity of this unexpected incursion sent a shudder of horror throughout the Moslem world. But the raid was short-lived, for when he heard of it, Saladin's brother, Malik al-Adil, then governor of Egypt, at once put to sea and soon after retook Aila and destroyed the raiding squadron. Most unfortunately for the Franks, Reynald escaped.

Saladin vowed that Reynald should not escape his vengeance and in September he invaded Palestine. On September 29 he crossed the Jordan, advanced up the valley of Jezreel, and found himself faced by Guy and his army. Fortunately for Guy, though much against his will, he was dissuaded from attacking his numerically superior antagonist who, presumably short of supplies, recrossed the Jordan on October 8.

At length Baldwin realized the ineptitude of Guy, and supported by Raymond of Tripoli and others of his barons, he deprived him of the regency and proclaimed his nephew, Baldwin–Sibylla's son by her first marriage–then a child of six, his heir. Meanwhile Saladin, more than ever bent upon wreaking vengeance on Reynald, set out to surprise Kerak, and on November 20 suddenly appeared before its walls.

The surprise was complete, for on that same day Isabella, the younger daughter of Amalric I, was being married to Humphrey of Toron. Taken unawares, Reynald and his knights withdrew over the fosse into the castle and a single knight held the bridge while it was sawn through behind him. Then an event took place which well illustrates the curious nature of war at this date. Reynald sent Saladin a piece of the bridecake, so that he might share in the feast. In the old French of Ernoul we read: "*Si envoia à Salehadin des noces de son fil pain et vin et bues et moutons; et si li manda salut, qu'il l'avoit maintes fois portée entre ses bras quant il estoit esclave et castiel, et elle estoit enfes.*" Always the punctilious knight, Saladin "gave strict orders . . . that the nuptial tower of the bride and bridegroom should be scrupulously respected by his archers and artillery".[1] The siege failed and, on December 4, Saladin was back in Damascus.

Still eager to settle his account with Reynald, in the autumn of 1184 Saladin again appeared before Kerak. But he could make no impression on its immensely strong fortifications, and on the approach of an army from Jerusalem he was again compelled to withdraw.

[1] *Chronique d'Ernoul*, Librarire de la société de l'histoire de France (1871), p. 103.

For the Franks, the year 1185 opened in profound gloom. Throughout Syria and Palestine drought and famine prevailed, and Baldwin knew his end was near and prepared for death. Early in the year he assembled his barons, and with their concurrence he appointed Raymond regent, who, in the event of the early death of Baldwin's nephew, was to continue as such until the pope, the emperor and the kings of France and England had decided on a successor. Then, to make certain of his nephew's succession, he had the child crowned by the Patriarch Heraclius. In March Baldwin IV died and Raymond took over the regency.

As he saw that because of the famine he could not with any hope of success carry on the war, Raymond wisely opened negotiations with Saladin and proposed a four-year truce. This suited the latter well enough, because it would enable him to sell corn to the Franks,[1] to reopen his trade with the Mediterranean ports, and to gain time to strengthen his hold over his feudatory princes. Nevertheless he saw that it could not be a permanent peace and that sooner or later a trial of strength would have to be made, but he also saw the longer he delayed it the weaker would his enemies become through their internal squabbles, which were now so violent that civil war between them seemed probable.

Thus far, these quarrels had been prevented from reaching flash-point by the statesmanship of the leper king; but now he was dead everything depended upon loyalty to the regent whose authority was derived from the boy king. This situation was not destined long to endure. Toward the end of August, 1186, Baldwin V died at Acre, and at once the Seneschal, Joscelin of Courtenay, with the connivance of the Patriarch Heraclius, Reynald of Châtillon and Gerard of Ridfort, Grand Master of the Temple, decided on a *coup d'état*. To get Raymond out of the way, Joscelin persuaded him to go to Tiberias to assemble a council of barons to carry out the terms of Baldwin IV's will, while he brought the king's body to Jerusalem. Next, Guy and Sibylla were summoned to Jerusalem, ostensibly to attend the funeral, but actually so that, while Raymond was away, Sibylla might be crowned, for in accordance with feudal law this would automatically raise Guy to the throne.

They hastily assembled their supporters, and on the arrival of Sibylla and Guy the four conspirators, among whom Gerard would appear to have been the master-mind, had the gates of

[1] See Beha ed-Din, pp. 104-105.

Jerusalem shut and the walls manned, and in the Church of the Holy Sepulchre Sibylla was crowned by Heraclius. The patriarch said to her: "Lady, you are but a woman, wherefore it behoves that you have a man to stay you in your rule; take the crown you see before you [two had been brought to the Church], and give it to him who can best help you to govern your realm." Beckoning to her husband, she said: "*Sire, venés avant, et si recevés ceste couronne; car je ne sai ou je le puisse miex emploÿlier que à vous.*"[1] He then knelt before her and was crowned.

When he found that he had been tricked, Raymond, as lawful regent, summoned his supporters to Nablus (Shechem) to decide upon the course to be followed. The decision arrived at was to crown Isabella and to set up a rival king in the person of her husband, Humphrey of Toron. But Humphrey, who feared the greatness which was to be thrust upon him, fled to Jerusalem and did homage to Guy. Raymond then released his followers from their oath of allegiance to him, and one by one they went to Jerusalem and, like Humphrey, tended their submission. Raymond refused to do so.

Torn as the kingdom now was between the contentious factions, it was essential that nothing should disturb the truce, and Guy undoubtedly did not intend to do so. Nevertheless, at this critical moment it was once again treacherously broken by Reynald of Châtillon. Toward the close of 1186, he fell upon an unusually rich caravan on its way from Cairo to Damascus, slew its escort and pillaged it.

At once Saladin appealed to Guy, who ordered Reynald to release the caravan. The latter answered that as he was lord of his own castle he could do as he liked, and that it was not he but Raymond, Count of Tripoli, who had agreed upon the truce. To Saladin's envoy he replied: "Ask your Muhammad to deliver it to you", and "The Sultan, to whom these words were reported, took an oath to slay the infidel with his own hand, if God should ever place him in his power",[2] and proclaimed a *Jihad*, or Holy War, against the Christians. Next, at the beginning of the month of Moharrem (March, 1187), he marched against Kerak to lay Reynald's lands waste and also to protect another caravan then on its way from Egypt.

The truce thus broken, Bohemond of Antioch at once renewed it with Saladin and so did Raymond for his territory, which in-

[1] *Chronique d'Ernoul*, p. 134.          [2] Beha ed-Din, p. 43.

cluded his wife's principality of Galilee, the main fortress of which was at Tiberias. Further, because Raymond considered that under Guy the kingdom would be utterly ruined, he decided to oust him and to make himself king, and to do this he took the exceedingly dangerous course of entering into correspondence with Saladin to win his support.

Bad as the situation was, it was rendered worse by Gerard of Ridfort–Raymond's bitterest enemy–who persuaded Guy to call out a *levée en masse*, not to march against Saladin, but against Raymond, then sheltering in his castle at Tiberias. When he heard of this Saladin sent a body of troops to support Raymond, and next assembled his forces at Paneas, some thirty miles north of the Sea of Galilee. Meanwhile Guy concentrated his army at Nazareth, where Balian of Ibelin strongly advised him to abandon his proposed attack on Tiberias; for, if he besieged it, of a certainty Saladin would come to its support. Instead, he suggested that an embassy should be sent to Raymond to win him over. To this Guy agreed.

While this proposal was discussed, an extraordinary arrangement was arrived at between Raymond and Saladin. The latter, who wished to send a force toward Acre to pillage the land, asked Raymond's permission for it to pass through Galilee. This request placed Raymond between the horns of a dilemma: should he refuse, he would lose Saladin's support; should he consent, he would be banned as a Christian. Eventually he proposed that, if Saladin would carry out no more than a twelve-hour demonstration and would undertake to do no harm to the Christian lands and people, he would agree to the "raid". Saladin accepted this half-measure, and, on May 1, 7,000 of his mounted men filed past Tiberias and rode due west, did no damage whatever to the Christians, and in the evening turned about to return. Simultaneously Guy's embassy set out;[1] it consisted of 90 knights reinforced on the way by 40 others, under Gerard of Ridfort and the Master of the Hospital. Near Sephoria (Kitron), it fell in with the returning demonstrators, and Gerard boastfully sent a message back to Nazareth announcing that he had defeated the Moslems and that all the townsfolk need do was to come out and collect the booty. Then he charged his enemy and was defeated. Many of his small party were killed, including the Master of the Hospital, though he himself, most unfortunately for the Christian cause,

[1] A full account of this expedition is given by Ernoul (pp. 148–152) who took part in it.

escaped. Shortly after the booty-hunters from Nazareth appeared and were at once cut down by Saladin's men.

Raymond was now thoroughly frightened, and as, no doubt, he had felt all along that he was prejudicing himself as a Christian, he seized upon this accidental encounter as an excuse to sever his relationship with Saladin and to make peace with Guy. He left his wife, the Princess Eschiva, to defend his castle, and rejoined the Christian army.[1]

Guy's army consisted of 1,200 knights, some 2,000 native light cavalry and nearly 10,000 infantry, many of whom were Turco-poles—bastards or renegade Moslems. To raise so great a force he had been compelled to sweep clean of their garrisons practically every castle in the land. Saladin's army was now encamped near Tiberias; his strength is uncertain, though it was probably greater than Guy's, and nearly all his men were mounted. His position, tactically, was a dangerous one, because to his back lay the Sea of Galilee. If he were beaten he had no avenue of escape; but if he defeated the Christians they had only a void to fall back upon— their empty castles and towers.

Directly Saladin laid siege to Tiberias, Eschiva appealed to her husband to come to her rescue. This led to a council of war being assembled at Acre, where Guy and Raymond met and made peace with each other. Gerard of Ridfort and Reynald of Châtillon urged Guy to advance against Saladin; but Raymond, although he was the more interested party—his wife was in danger—urged that this was to play Saladin's game and to risk falling into a trap; numerically they were inferior to the enemy, it was the hottest time of the year and water was scarce. "Let Saladin waste him-self before Tiberias", he said, while we "remain on the defensive and await an opportunity to counter-attack him".

Common sense though his words were, Reynald and Gerard accused Raymond of being a traitor, and his advice was set aside. Thus it came about that Guy ordered a general concentration at Sephoria, which caused great elation, for the knights, swept off their feet by a wave of chivalrous enthusiasm at the idea of succouring the countess of Tripoli, had lost all balance. "*Alonz rescorre les dames et les damoiseles de Tabarié*",[2] they cried as they set out on the road to Sephoria, which was reached on July 2.

---

[1] See Beha ed-Din, pp. 110–111, for a full account.
[2] Quoted from *Histoire des Croisades et du Royaume France de Jerusalem*, René Grousset (1935), vol. II, p. 790.

Once encamped there, Raymond went again to the king and said: "Sire, I beg you to abandon Tiberias, in spite of the fact that my wife and children are besieged there. . . . Because it is better that it should fall with all those who are dear to me, than that we should lose the kingdom. . . . Between here and there there is but one small spring and nothing an army can live upon, and no sooner shall you have set out than the Saracens will harass you and will compel you to halt. Again, should you attack them, they will seek refuge in the hills, where you will not be able to follow them. And if you are halted and forced to bivouac, what will your men and horses do for water? Without water many will die of thirst, and the next day the Saracens will round you up!"[1]

It was, therefore, agreed to cancel the advance, but at midnight Gerard secretly went to the king's tent and said to him: "Sire, do not believe what the Count has told you, for he is a traitor and wishes you to be dishonoured." Next, he urged him to change his mind, and succeeded because Guy did not "dare to contradict the man who had made him king".[2] Gerard of Ridfort had won, and grimly was he to suffer for his slippery victory.

Had the crusaders possessed any strategic sense whatsoever, it is not possible that they would have agreed to advance on Tiberias, for the salvation of their realms lay, as it had done for nearly a century, in the maintenance of an active defensive on the lines laid down by the Byzantine emperors Maurice and Leo the Wise – castles and counter-attacks. But the castles were now unmanned and the strategy of the attack was not primarily concerned with beating the enemy, but with reaching water – the Sea of Galilee – before nightfall. Water was the controlling factor, and possibly 20,000 men stood between them and their next drink.

At dawn, on July 3, 1187, they set out eastward from Sephoria, heavily laden with fears and doubts. They left the sweet wells behind then and entered the stony, barren and parched hills of Jebel Turan, some twenty miles from Tiberias, the land of their suicide.

When Saladin heard that they were advancing, joyfully he exclaimed: "This, indeed, is what we wished most for!"[3] and at once sent forward certain light divisions to pin his enemy down

---

[1] A free and condensed translation from Ernoul, pp. 159–160. For corroborative account, see Grousset's *Histoire des Croisades*, vol. II, pp. 790–792.

[2] *Chronique D'Ernoul*, p. 162.

[3] *Histoire des Croisades*, René Grousset, vol. II, p. 794.

in the desert. They fell in with the van of Guy's army, commanded by Raymond of Tripoli,[1] and attacked it while others swarmed past it toward the main body. The heat was intense and the dust suffocating. Soon all the water was drunk and the exhausted men began to straggle; the situation grew so critical that Raymond galloped up to Guy and urged that unless they pressed on and gained the Jordan or the Sea of Tiberias the army was lost. In spite of his suspicions that Raymond was acting treasonably, the king urged his soldiers to advance more rapidly, when a messenger galloped up and reported that the rear guard, consisting of the Templars, Hospitallers, and Turcopoles, had been forced to halt by swarms of bowmen. At once he also halted, near the deserted village of Marescalcia, and Raymond, in agony, cried out: "Alas! alas, Lord God! The war is over; we are dead men; the Kingdom is undone!"[2]

Though the van pushed on several miles further, the main body, now completely exhausted, bivouacked on the slopes of a hill, the two low hummocks on the crest of which earned for it the name of the Horns of Hattin.[3] The village of Hattin lay below the hill and a few miles north of Marescalcia. No sleep was possible, for all night long the crusaders were tortured with thirst and harassed by constant attack; arrows were poured upon them incessantly, and out of the darkness came the cries of *"Allah Akbar!"* ("God is most Great") and *"la ilala il Allah!"* ("There is no other god but God"). Worse still, the Saracens had set fire to the scrub and suffocating clouds of smoke swept the doomed army.

The next morning, Saladin, having reinforced his horse archers and still refusing to clinch, brought up seventy camels laden with arrows and continued without ceasing his missile attack. Beha ed-Din writes: "Terrible encounters took place that day; never in the history of the generations that have gone have such feats of arms been told."[4] Meanwhile Raymond with his advanced guard pushed on, and became separated from the main body under the king who, in order to protect his infantry, drew them inward,

[1] With him was Balian of Ibelin, and with Balian was Ernoul the Chronicler, who gives a vivid description of this march; see pp. 166–168.
[2] *Saladin*, Stanley Lane-Poole, p. 209, and *A History of the Crusades*, Steven Runciman, vol. II, p. 457.
[3] For a description of the ground see Lane-Poole's *Saladin*, pp. 205–207, and Oman's *Art of War in the Middle Ages*, vol. I, p. 325. The northern Horn is 1,191 feet high, east of it the ground falls towards the Sea of Galilee; Tiberias is 653 feet below the level of the Mediterranean. The Horn was believed to be the Mount of Beatitudes where Christ taught the people the blessedness of peace.
[4] Beha ed-Din, p. 112.

while the knights charged the enemy's archers. This led to a loss of formation, and in the confusion a foot soldier scrambled up the hill and started a panic by shouting: *"Sauvons-nous, sauvons-nous!"*

28. CAMPAIGN OF HATTIN, 1187

Then all order disappeared, and in terror the men climbed up the slope after him.

In vain Guy appealed to them to come down; all they could do was to groan for water. At length, with a body of his knights, he took up a position near them, in the centre of which he raised the True Cross. At once their morale revived and they ran down in crowds. All became mixed up, foot, archers, and knights, huddled together in a confused mass around the sacred emblem.[1] Simultaneously the rear guard began to come in, but only to make the confusion worse. Nevertheless, many of the knights, though suffering even greater hardships than the foot soldiers, were by no means demoralized, and concerning one of their gallant charges Saladin's young son al-Afdal, who was at his father's side, says: "I looked at my father and saw that he was much agitated, that he had blanched and that he held his beard in his hand." Charge followed charge, and when at length the knights retired, the boy cried out: "We have scattered them!" Saladin replied: "Silence, we shall not have defeated them until the King's tent falls."[2] And at that moment it fell!

Guy was lost; for now it would appear that Raymond and the remnants of his advanced guard were driven in, and that the entire army was surrounded; thousands of its men with uplifted arms supplicated the Cross and frenziedly called for a miracle. Then Guy turned to Raymond and besought him to save him. The Count of Tripoli gathered in such of his knights who were still mounted, including the young prince presumptive of Antioch, Balian of Ibelin, and Reynald of Sidon, charged the encircling Moslems and cut his way out. A Moslem account reads:

"The Count of Tripoli and his followers judging the situation lost, adopted the desperate solution of charging the Moslems who surrounded them. Their leader was Taki-el-Din Omar, the nephew of Saladin, and he, realizing that the charge was made in desperation, felt that he could not withstand it. Therefore he ordered his followers to open out a passage, which was done."[3]

The end came. In the words of Beha ed-Din:

"The upholders of Islam surrounded the upholders of infidelity and impiety on every side, overwhelming them with arrows and

---

[1] See *Histoire de Saladin*, F. L. C. Marin (1758), vol. II, p. 17.
[2] Quoted from *Histoire des Croisades*, René Grousset, vol. II, p. 796.
[3] Ibn-el-Athir, quoted by Grousset, vol. II, p. 796. Raymond retired to Tripoli, where shortly after he died of grief and shame, or, as some say, was murdered by the Assassins.

harassing them with their swords. One body of the enemy took to flight, but they were pursued by the Moslem warriors, and not one of the fugitives escaped. Another band climbed Hattin hill ... near which is the tomb of the holy patriarch Shuaib (Jethro). The Moslems hemmed them in, and lighted fires all round them, so that, tortured by thirst and reduced to the last extremity, they gave themselves up to escape death."[1]

So utterly exhausted were these men that a single Saracen was seen dragging some thirty Christians he had taken himself, tied together with a tent rope.[2]

Among the captured were King Guy, Amalric the king's brother, Reynald of Châtillon, the stepson of Humphrey of Toron, the son of Raymond of Tripoli, Gerard of Ridfort, Hugh of Embriaco, the aged Marquis of Montferrat, the Grand Master of the Hospitallers and many lesser barons. But of all the losses, whether killed or captured, the one which was overwhelming was the loss of the True Cross. Emad ed-Din, an Arabian historian, says:

"The great cross was taken before the King, and many of the impious sought death about it. When it was held aloft the infidels bent the knee and bowed the head. They had enriched it with gold and jewels; they carried it on days of great solemnity, and looked upon it as their first duty to defend in battle. The capture of this cross was more grievous to them than the capture of their King."[3]

After the battle Saladin had the most noble captives brought to his tent, and as Guy of Lusignan was tortured by thirst, Saladin chivalrously invited him to sit by his side, calmed his fears and offered him a bowl of iced sherbet. The king drank, then handed it to Reynald of Châtillon; at which Saladin rose in anger and exclaimed: "You have not asked my leave to pass the cup to him; therefore I am in no way bound to respect his life." He upbraided Reynald for his many perjuries and brigandages, but the lord of Kerak replied insolently, for he was a man without fear. Then Saladin struck him with his scimitar and the guard dispatched him by cutting off his head. The King trembled with fear, but Saladin turned to him and said: "A king slays not a king; but the perfidy and insolence of that man passed all bounds."[4]

Of this decisive battle, Mr. Runciman writes: "The Christians

[1] Beha ed-Din, p. 113.                  [2] *Ibid.*, p. 114.
[3] See also *Chronique d'Ernoul*, chap. XIV.
[4] Quoted from *Histoire des Croisades*, René Grousset, vol. II, p. 798. See also chap. XV, *Chronique d'Ernoul*, and Beha ed-Din, p. 115.

of the East had suffered disasters before. Their Kings and Princes had been captured before; but their captors then had been petty lordlings, out for some petty advantage. On the Horns of Hattin the greatest army that the Kingdom had ever assembled was annihilated. The Holy Cross was lost. And the victor was lord of the whole Moslem world."[1]

Tiberias was surrendered on July 5 and the heroic Countess of Tripoli was allowed to depart in safety. Virtually no resistance to Saladin was offered; the great castles were now but piles of un-defended stone and worse still, the people of the land welcomed the conqueror. On July 10 Acre was occupied and Tyre was only saved by the providential arrival from France of Conrad of Mont-ferrat[2] and three shiploads of knights. Ascalon opened its gates on September 4, when a total eclipse of the sun paralysed the burgesses of Jerusalem with terror.

Saladin wished to spare Jerusalem, for it was sacred to Moslem and Christian alike, and offered the burgesses autonomy if they would open its gates. But though the city was inadequately garrisoned, they nobly replied: "*Se Diu plaist, la cité ne renderoient il ja où Diex recut mort et passion.*"[3]

Shortly before this happened, Balian of Ibelin, who es-caped from Hattin with Raymond, had petitioned Saladin for a safe-conduct to go to Jerusalem to bring back his wife and children to Tyre. It was granted on the condition that he would remain but one day in the Holy City and promise never again to bear arms against the sultan. Nevertheless, when Balian arrived, the patriarch absolved him from his oath, and forthwith he took charge of the city, now crammed with fugitives, shut its gates and prepared to hold it. This brought Saladin before Jeru-salem on September 20; yet, in spite of Balian's broken word, when the city was faced with starvation and the patriarch treated for terms, Saladin's demands were moderate in the extreme. For their liberty each man was to pay ten pieces of gold, "and two women or ten children could be reckoned as one man"; of the poor, who possessed no gold, 7,000 would be set free for the sum of 30,000 byzants. These terms were accepted and signed on October 2, on which day Saladin entered Jerusalem.

It was now that Saladin, the man, displayed the full greatness of his soul. In contrast with what took place when the crusaders

[1] *A History of the Crusades*, vol. II, p. 460.
[2] Brother of Sibylla's first husband.        [3] *Chronique d'Ernoul*, p. 186.

stormed the city in 1099,[1] he opened markets in and around Jerusalem in order that the citizens might raise the price of their freedom. Yet there remained thousands who could not pay their ransom, and Saif-ed Din, Saladin's brother, asked the sultan to allow him to take a thousand slaves from these people; and when his request was granted he at once set them free. "Then came the Patriarch and Balian, and begged likewise, and Saladin gave them another thousand slaves, and they were set free. Then said Saladin to his officers: " 'My brother has made his alms, and the Patriarch and Balian have made theirs; now I would fain make mine'. And he ordered his guards to proclaim throughout the streets of Jerusalem that all the old people who could not pay were free to go forth. And they came forth from the postern St. Lazarus, and their going lasted from the rising of the sun until nightfall."[2] "*Ce fu l'aumosne que Salehadins fist sans nombre des povres gens.*"[3]

The battle of Hattin was a catastrophe from which the crusades never recovered. Fought as it was under the shadow of the True Cross–the supreme emblem of Christendom–had Guy won it would have been God's victory; as it was, it was Allah's, and in this many Christians must have sensed the triumph of temporal power over spiritual. Thus it was that Saladin's victory struck at the foundations of the whole crusading movement and at those of the papacy itself, which hence onward became increasingly secularized because the secular powers would not accept the papal doctrine that they were subject to the divine law as interpreted by the popes. The result was that the secular powers increasingly used the crusades as instruments of their own aggrandizement, and in its turn this reacted on the prestige of the papacy and the popes had to juggle with the different secular powers and to play one off against the other.

As described, from the very opening of the first crusade there had been a confusion of aims. To Urban II and the peoples of western Europe generally the intention was to regain the Holy Land for Christendom; to many of the knights it was to win lands

---

[1] Gibbon gives the following lurid description: "A bloody sacrifice was offered by his mistaken votaries to the God of the Christians; resistance might provoke, but neither sex nor age could mollify their implacable rage; they indulged themselves three days in a promiscuous massacre; and the infection of the dead bodies produced an epidemic disease. After seventy thousand Moslems had been put to the sword, and the harmless Jews had been burnt in their synagogue, they could still reserve a multitude of captives whom interest or lassitude persuaded them to spare" (*The Decline and Fall*, 1898, vol. VI, p. 311).

[2] Quoted from *Saladin*, Stanley Lane-Poole, p. 232.

[3] *Chronique D'Ernoul*, p. 228.

for themselves in the East; and for the Byzantine emperor it was to secure Constantinople and to liberate his Asiatic themes from Turkish subjection. The second of these aims pinched out the first, and the third so completely wrecked the second that "When the news of Saladin's victory [at Hattin] reached Constantinople the Emperor Isaac Angelus sent an embassy to Saladin to congratulate him and to ask that the Christian Holy Places should revert to the Orthodox Church".[1]

The differences between the Byzantines and the Franks were so profound that they ended by wrecking the whole crusading movement, and led not to the liberation of the Holy Land, but instead to the political, though temporary, extinction of the Byzantine empire. In the same month (June, 1185) that Guy of Lusignan was marshalling his forces at Acre before advancing on Hattin, William II of Sicily seized Durazzo, then marched on Thessalonica, took it and massacred its inhabitants. He next advanced on Constantinople and was defeated near Musinopolis. The effect of this invasion was that the Emperor Andronicus I was deposed, tortured to death, and succeeded by Isaac II Angelus, who, in 1195, was blinded, dethroned and imprisoned by his brother Alexius, who became Alexius III (1195–1203).

Meanwhile the third crusade (1189–1192) had come and gone – a fiasco of self-seeking kings – to be followed, after the election of Pope Innocent III in 1198, by the calling of the fourth. As none of the principal sovereigns of western Europe responded to Innocent's appeal, the conduct of the crusade passed into the hands of Enrico Dandolo (1193–1205), the blind or semi-blind doge of Venice, then over eighty years of age. He was a man without scruples about the means he employed, and had been commissioned to provide the ships which were to transport the crusaders to Egypt, then the heart of Moslem power. But when the crusaders had assembled at Venice, it was found that the sum they had agreed to pay for the hire of the transports was not forthcoming, and the doge acceded to their demands on condition that before they sailed to Egypt they would reconquer for him the city of Zara on the Dalmatian coast, which had recently seceded from Venice and passed over to Hungary. The crusaders agreed in spite of a threat by Innocent to excommunicate them and the Venetians. Zara was besieged and stormed, and the excommunication was pronounced, but lifted soon after.

[1] *A History of the Crusades*, Steven Runciman, vol. II, pp. 467–468.

During the siege a new personality appeared; the Byzantine prince Alexius Angelus, son of the dethroned Isaac II. Seeking refuge with his brother-in-law, Philip of Swabia, he begged his assistance, but as Philip could do nothing directly to aid him, he sent an embassy to Zara to urge the doge and the crusaders to reinstate Isaac, and Alexius promised that were this done he would subject the eastern to the western Church and pay 200,000 marks toward the cost of the expedition to Egypt.

Aware of the advantages Venice would reap from this proposal, Dandolo won from the crusaders its acceptance on the understanding that, once Isaac was reinstated, the crusade against Egypt would proceed. Thus a treaty of the conquest of Constantinople was concluded, and on April 7, 1203, the crusaders set out. They appeared in the Bosphorus on June 23. They seized Galata, on the northern shore of the Golden Horn, won possession of the iron chain which secured its entrance, sailed into the harbour and stormed the city on July 17. Alexius III abandoned his capital and the blind Isaac was freed from his dungeon and restored to his throne, with his son Alexius (IV) as co-regent.

Dandolo and the crusaders then camped outside the city walls, awaiting the payment of the 200,000 marks Alexius had promised them. Prolonged negotiations followed, during which, early in 1204, Alexius Ducas Mourtzouphlos, son-in-law of Alexius III, fomented an insurrection, deposed and imprisoned Isaac II, had Alexius IV strangled, and assumed the diadem as Alexius V.

The crusaders now considered themselves freed from all obligations toward the empire and in March they concluded with the doge a treaty for its partition. Preparations were then set in hand to storm Constantinople by land and sea. For some days the city resisted stubbornly, but on April 13, 1204, it was stormed. Alexius V fled and for three days the city was sacked in scenes of hideous carnage. "The booty gained was so great", writes Villehardouin, "that none could tell you the end of it . . . never, since the world was created, had so much booty been won in any city."[1] Thus, after nearly 1,000 years of existence, the Byzantine empire became a Frankish feudal empire (1204–1261), and the colonial empire of Venice was created.

In this act of sanctified robbery Pope Innocent III (1198–1216) not unwillingly acquiesced; for though he had vehemently

[1] *La conquête de Constantinople*, Geoffroy de Villehardouin (edit. N. de Wailly, 1872), par. 147. Villehardouin was an eye-witness of the sack.

opposed the conquest of the Eastern Empire, once it became a *fait accompli*, he saw in it the subjection of a schismatic people and the union of the eastern and western Churches. Nevertheless, in every way the fourth crusade was disastrous to the papacy and to the whole crusading movement. Worse still, instead of securing Europe against Asia, the destruction of the Eastern Empire smashed the great eastern bastion which for centuries had held Asia back. The empire never recovered from this fatal blow, politically it ceased to exist.

Yet, in spite of this, for over a century the crusades inspired western Europe with a unity it has never seen since, and has never quite forgotten. They combined its many peoples and stimulated the sense of national unity and of national hostility between them which speeded their growth into nations. Peoples became race-conscious. France emerged as a great power, as England had already done after the conquest. Spain and Portugal won greatness out of their Moorish turmoils and the foundations of Prussia were laid by the crusading enterprises of the Teutonic Knights. Before the coming of the crusades, all the Holy Roman Empire could offer to its distracted subjects was the shadow of unity, during them this shadow was all but dissipated by the substantial glory of the medieval papacy.

Under Innocent III, the papacy reached the zenith of its power; to the western world he was "king of kings". To the ambassadors of Philip Augustus he said: "To princes power is given on earth, but to priests it is attributed also over souls. Whence it follows that by so much as the soul is superior to the body, the priesthood is superior to the kingship. . . . Single rulers have single provinces, and single kings single kingdoms; but Peter, as in the plenitude, so in the extent of his power is pre-eminent over all, since he is the Vicar of Him whose is the earth and the fullness thereof, the whole wide world and all that dwell therein."[1]

The establishment of this spiritual autocracy, as it could not fail to do, led to a conflict over fiscal control; and so we find that out of the first crusade there emerged two financial instruments, indulgences and tithes. Urban II applied the first "to the whole of Christendom by his assurance that 'those who die there in true penitence will without doubt receive indulgence of their sins and the fruits of the reward hereafter' ".[2] Indulgences thus became a

---

[1] *Encyclopaedia Britannica* (eleventh edit.), article Innocent III.
[2] *The Cambridge Medieval History*, vol. v, p. 323.

source of revenue. In 1184 service was commuted for payment, and, in 1215, a plenary indulgence was promised to all who contributed to the crusade funds. Even more profitable were the clerical tithes: in 1146 Louis VII of France imposed one on all clerics under his jurisdiction, and immediately after the battle of Hattin, Richard I and Philip Augustus established the "Saladin Tithe". Boniface VIII proclaimed that "The Apostolic See" had "absolute power" over ecclesiastical property. "It can exact, as it sees fit, the hundredth, the tenth, or any part of this property."[1]

Thus began to sprout the second great revolution since the decline of Rome, out of which was to emerge the economic and financial civilization of the present day. Demands for money led to the establishment of banks by Jews, Italian merchants, and the military Orders. And because money was kept on the move, and the turbulent spirits went east to leave the burgher classes in peace at home, prosperity was stimulated until many former luxuries became necessities. The Tyrians taught the Sicilians how to refine sugar and weave silk. Damascus steel rose in demand and Damascus potters became the masters of the potters in France. Windmills were introduced, also maize, lemons, apricots, melons, cotton, muslin, damask, brocades, perfumes, carpets–and hot baths.

Prosperity created leisure, and with leisure the intellect reawoke. Many chroniclers appear; Aristotle was brought to the West through Spain and later from Constantinople; the knowledge of medicine and mathematics was advanced, and the astrolabe, gnomon, sextant, and mariner's compass were adopted.

Increased knowledge led to doubt. Thus the crusades witness the beginnings of the age of heresies such as the Waldensian, Paulician, and Albigensian. At Hattin the miracle was exploded; if the True Cross could not conjure forth victory, what could?

Rapidly the social changes, either created or stimulated by the crusades, began to outstep religious conviction and brought the Church into conflict with temporal power, for "the attempt to free the members of the Church from secular control, ended in a more subtle secularization of its very heart–the Papacy itself".[2] In the thirteenth century a steady decline set in, violently hastened by the instrument of the crusade being used to extirpate not the infidel, but the Christian heretic. When, in 1255, Pope Alexander IV preached a crusade against Manfred, son of the emperor,

[1] *The Cambridge Medieval History*, vol. v, pp. 324–325.    [2] *Ibid.*, p. 321.

Matthew Paris wrote: "When true Christians heard this announcement, they were astonished that they were promised the same [rewards] for shedding the blood of Christians as they were formerly that of infidels, and the versatility of the preachers excited laughter and derision."[1]

Yet another influence must be mentioned, and possibly the most remarkable of all. The spirit of adventure, released by the crusades, began to trace out the filaments of travel and discovery. Because the sword failed in the Holy Land, greater trust was placed in the word. In 1252 St. Louis sent the Franciscan William of Rubruquis to the Great Khan in central Asia, in the hope that the Mongolian empire, when once converted to Christianity, might descend upon the rear of the Turks and help the Christians in Palestine. Fantastic though the idea may seem,[2] it stimulated the missionary work of the Franciscans and Dominicans and led to traders, notably the Venetian Polos, penetrating as far east as the Great Wall of China. These men, by discovering Asia, fired that economic imagination which eventually led to the discovery of the New World.

[1] *Matthew Paris's English History*, trans. J. A. Giles (1854), vol. III, p. 143.
[2] Yet there may have been something in the idea, for in 1256 Hulagu and his Mongols invaded Caucasia and on February 15, 1258, entered and sacked Baghdad and brought to an end the Abbasid caliphate. In 1260 Aleppo was stormed and Damascus surrendered, after which Hulagu meditated the capture of Jerusalem with the intention of restoring it to the Christians, but on hearing of the death of the Khakan Mangu he abandoned the project and returned to Mongolia.

# The disruption of the Western Empire and the rise of France and England

The crusades released forces no pope could control and the spiritual impulse of the first of these great adventures was lost in the mercenary impulse of the fourth. This was not due to chance or accident, but largely because the crusades turned war from a private affair of aristocracy into a commercial undertaking, with the consequence that, as internal strife declined, the western peoples were able to devote more of their energies to peaceful occupations—that is, to secular affairs. The result was the growth of commercial cities and towns; of municipal liberties and citizen militias; of commerce and trade; of crafts and guilds and markets; and the introduction of a fixed coinage and common weights and measures. Also, of a host of universities; speculative philosophy (*e.g.* Peter Abelard, 1079–1142, Thomas Aquinas, 1227–1274); empirical sciences (*e.g.* Albertus Magnus, 1206–1280, Roger Bacon 1214–1294); and of heresies, as already mentioned.

Out of these changes and many others the idea of the national state began to oust the conception of the papal satrapy; the end which Gregory VII had set out to gain and Innocent III had all but attained ultimately was defeated by the very means they championed and a new course was set which carried the majestic vessel of the Universal Empire of western Christendom on to the rocks of the Reformation. Nevertheless, three centuries were to separate the death, in 1216, of Innocent III and the nailing of Luther's ninety-five theses on the church door at Wittenberg in 1517, and they were to be centuries of war, during which the theocratic-feudal order passed into the nationalist-monarchical system.

The first of these wars arose out of the position of the Papal States, which were wedged between the two Sicilies and the northern dominions of the empire, and it was the threat to their security which led to a quarrel between Innocent III and the Emperor Otto IV (1198–1218). The former was supported by Philip II (Augustus) of France, and the latter by John (Lackland) of England (1199–1216), and when, in 1208, England was placed under interdict and John excommunicated (1209), Philip prepared to lead a crusade against John. But in 1213, because of John's surrender to the pope, the invasion was not attempted. In the following year John joined Otto against Philip, and on July 27 the Emperor was defeated decisively at Bouvines. For John, now totally discredited, the outcome was that, in 1215, the English barons compelled him to issue the *Magna Carta*, and though Innocent declared it null and void and excommunicated the barons, fortunately for England his and John's death in 1216 ended what might have developed into a devastating civil war.

Two years after Otto's death in 1218, Innocent's ward, Frederick king of Sicily, born in 1194 and son of the Hohenstaufen Emperor Henry VI, was crowned emperor and became Frederick II (1220–1250). A man of unique character and remarkable abilities, he has been called both "The last of the Medieval Emperors" and "The first European". Alone among the Roman emperors he holds the distinction of being consigned by Dante to the pit of Hell (Canto X). Though he had promised Innocent never to unite Sicily and the empire, soon after his guardian's death his activities were directed toward bringing northern and southern Italy completely under his control. In 1227 this brought him into conflict with Gregory IX (1227–1241), who excommunicated him for not starting out on a crusade, as he had promised to do, and in 1228 he excommunicated him again for daring to do so unabsolved. Unsupported by the pope and the Military Orders, Frederick sailed with a small band of knights for the Holy Land, and through astute diplomacy gained possession of Jerusalem, Bethlehem, and Nazareth, and on March 18, 1229, sealed this remarkable achievement by crowning himself king of Jerusalem. Thus, and practically without bloodshed, he accomplished more than any crusader had done since the first crusade.

On his return in 1229 he found that the pope's troops were overrunning his southern kingdom, drove them out, and then came to terms with Gregory at San Germano in 1230. He established his imperial court at Palermo and it soon became the most brilliant in Europe and the greatest cosmopolitan centre of learning in the medieval world.

Peace between the papacy and the empire did not last, and when Frederick set out to subdue Lombardy he was again excommunicated by Gregory. Frederick then proclaimed that his cause was that of all other rulers. "If the pope succeeded in undermining him by aiding rebels", he declared, "it would only be a matter of time before all other rulers would be treated in the same way by the pope." Next, Gregory denounced him as "Antichrist" and "the King of Pestilence" who had openly maintained "that the whole world had been deceived by three imposters, namely Jesus Christ, Moses and Mohammed", and that "all are fools who believe that God, who created all things, could be born of a virgin". These accusations, even if exaggerated, show how times were changing.

Soon after this denunciation Gregory died, and his successor Innocent IV (1243–1254) declared Frederick deposed. Frederick retaliated by urging the rulers to prevent the raising of money on behalf of the papacy, because his battle was equally theirs. Again h's appeal was to Europe more than to Christendom.

Frederick died in 1250 and his son Conrad IV in 1254. The latter was succeeded as king of Sicily by his son Conradin (1254–1268); and Pope Alexander IV (1254–1261), who determined never to permit the hated Hohenstaufens to reign again, kept Germany in a furore of civil war unparalleled since the days of the Carolingian *débâcle*. And when, in 1265, Conradin set out to regain his Italian inheritance, Clement IV (1265–1268) called in Charles of Anjou, brother of the king of France, to help him and offered him as a reward both Sicily and Naples. Charles accepted the call, and on August 23, 1268, Conradin was defeated decisively at Tagliacozzo. Eight weeks later he was beheaded at Naples.

Thus perished the last of the Hohenstaufens; nevertheless, the struggle continued until 1273, when Rudolph of Habsburg was recognized as king of Germany and elected emperor of the Holy Roman Empire on condition that he would not interfere in Italy. In 1278, at the battle of the Marchfeld, he wrested Austria from Ottokar of Bohemia and established the power of the house of Habsburg in the Danube valley; it was to last until 1918.

The effects of this long struggle were disastrous. The papacy was discredited by using its spiritual power to gain purely political ends; Italy was lost to the empire and for generations was distracted by the discords of Guelfs and Ghibellines; the splendid civilization of Norman Sicily was largely destroyed by the ruthless rule of Charles of Anjou; and unity in Germany was rendered impossible by her division into a vast congeries of principalities and towns: hence onward for centuries to come she became little more than a geographical expression. The sole beneficiary was France.

When, in 1152, Henry of Anjou married Eleanor of Aquitaine the royal domains of Louis VII of France (1137–1180) covered no more than the middle waters of the Seine and Loire. And when two years later Henry became Henry II of England and Duke of Normandy (1154–1189), Louis was on the one side faced by the Angevin empire stretching from the Cheviots to the Pyrenees, and on the other by the Holy Roman Empire under Barbarossa, and France was at the mercy of both.

Louis's son and successor Philip II (1180–1223)–called "Augustus"–who first secured his home position by adding a number of cities and districts to his domain, set out to rectify his intolerable position. He won Vermandois by diplomacy, then wrested Normandy from King John, and the siege of Château Gaillard, in 1204, decided the fate of that duchy. The conquest of Maine, Touraine, Anjou, and Poitou followed, and in 1206 he occupied Brittany and gave it to Peter of Dreux, as warden of the children of his wife (Constance of Brittany). In 1213 he invaded Flanders, and, as already stated, in the following year defeated the Emperor Otto at Bouvines–the copestone of his many conquests. Languedoc fell to his son Louis VIII in 1226 as the fruit of the Albigensian crusade, and later Champagne, La Marche, and Angoulême were added to the royal domain. The only province left to the English was Gascony.

Because this growth was piecemeal, it followed that in the middle ages France was never so unified as England. Even when annexed to the French crown the great fiefs retained much of their former independence. Nevertheless, under Philip IV, the Fair (1285–1314), in contradistinction to a feudal sovereign, the king became a popular ruler, and again a contest with the papacy was precipitated. Neither he nor Edward I of England (1272–1307) would accept the doctrine that a king was not entitled to tax his own clergy or that it was essential for his salvation to be subject to the pope. The upshot was that when Boniface VIII (1294–1303) set out, like Gregory VII, to enforce "the lordship of the papacy over all the kingdoms of the world", Philip had him arrested, and shortly after he died. Further, to make certain that his successor should not emulate him, in 1305 Philip induced the College of Cardinals to elect a Gascon, Bertrand de Got, pope, who became

Clement V (1305–1314), and who took up his residence at Avignon. Thus began the seventy-year "Babylonian captivity of the Church".

During the above wars, and largely because of the crusades, profound military changes were taking root. On the one hand, the contact of western chivalry with the superb castles and fortified towns of the Eastern Empire and the building of great castles, such as Kerak-in-Moab and Krak des Chevaliers in Palestine, led to castle building throughout western and central Europe, until in the fourteenth century the feudal castle dominated every district and county. On the other hand, the increasing wealth of the towns, due in no small measure to the loans raised by them to finance the crusades, led to the recruitment of city militias, such as fought at Bouvines and Courtrai (1302) and also to the introduction of specialist mercenary soldiers, notably crossbow-men to defend the castle walls. Further, as the feudal knight would neither dig, hew, mine, nor batter, paid specialists to work the siege and other engines came more and more into demand. Another reason for the increasing employment of mercenaries was the introduction of plate armour toward the end of the twelfth century and its full development in the fourteenth. This added enormously to cost, and because the real fighters were the armoured men-at-arms, all who could afford to purchase armour so gained an international commercial value and could auction their services. In contrast with these salaried specialists and superbly armoured mercenaries, war to the rank and file of the feudal levies must have seemed a very unremunerative business.

Another change arose from this. Mercenary soldiers, as long as they were paid, could be maintained indefinitely in the field, but the feudal baron and landed knight could be mustered only for forty days. During the reigns of Philip III (1279–1285) of France and Edward I of England, in order to carry out a prolonged campaign the payment of soldiers became general and whole armies, whatever the source of their recruitment, whether feudal or mercenary, became paid forces. This led to the replacement of feudal by regular service and to the appearance of a class of soldiers, such as the *routiers* in France and the *condottieri* in Italy. These professional fighters raised bands of followers and sold their services to the highest bidder, and as they served only for payment they were anti-feudal, for no code of honour bound them to their masters. A forerunner of this type of soldier was the German mercenary Roger de Flor (de Blum) who, in 1303, with his band of desperadoes, known as the Catalan Grand Company, was hired by the Emperor Andronicus II, to his regret as well as his successor's.

Although at the opening of the Hundred Years War, except for Genoese crossbow-men and galley fighters, the French and English armies and fleets were recruited from the subjects of their respective kings, the employment of hired mercenaries soon became general. When, after the battle of Poitiers, Edward III carried his national forces back to England, many *routiers* were thrown out of employment and as they refused to disband themselves they became brigands in order to live. It was these discharged mercenaries who rendered the Hundred Years War so terrible, for a peace or a truce substituted pillage and massacre for regular warfare. Hence the long, drawn-out struggle, and hence also the paradox that at a time when war was fast becoming national, the soldiers were international: men of all nations, under leaders of every social class, ready to sell their services to whoever paid them best.

Besides these military changes, a political one of fundamental importance also was taking shape. In England, under Edward I, parliament became an established institution, and, because of the development of trade, the merchant class rose in importance, for Edward depended on the merchant community to raise his national revenue, which in its turn demanded the establishment of a less feudal type of government. In the English House of Commons there was close cooperation between the knights of the shires and the representatives of the boroughs, but in France the nobility despised the burgesses, neglected to act with them, and it was only in 1343 that, in the form of local assemblies, the first Estates began to appear to consider grants in aid. Not until 1484 is the name "States General" mentioned.

Thus, by the opening of the fourteenth century, the empire was little more than a name; the papacy was in eclipse; England was becoming a nation in the modern sense of the word, and France a nation in the medieval sense. Throughout western Europe the intellectual awakenment, so largely caused by the study of Aristotle, increasingly was leading to the belief in the self-sufficiency of individual intellect and faith. This struck hard at papal policy. For instance, Dante (1265–1321) in his *De Monarchia*, yearns for a universal monarchy with its title held directly from God and in no way subject to the papacy. What would have been the outcome of these changes had they not been interrupted it is impossible to say, for their progress in the most advanced countries of the West was in part arrested and in part accelerated by the Hundred Years War waged between England and France from 1337 to 1453.

# CHAPTER 16

# The Battles of Sluys, 1340, and Crécy, 1346

Edward III was born at Windsor on November 13, 1312. Son of Edward II, his mother, Isabella of France, was the daughter of Philip IV and sister of Charles IV, who, in 1322, succeeded his brother Philip V as king of France; therefore Edward was Charles's nephew. In 1325, at Isabella's wish, Edward II relinquished the duchy of Aquitaine to his son and Charles IV willingly agreed to the transfer against a conveyance fee of 60,000 *livres*.

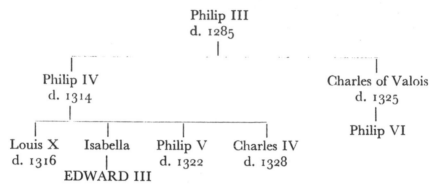

On September 10 that year the young prince performed the same homage to Charles as his father, grandfather, and great-grandfather had in their days done to the king of France. Fifteen months later Edward II was compelled to abdicate, and on January 13, 1327, his son, then in his fifteenth year, was proclaimed Edward III of England and was crowned on January 29.

Almost a year later, Charles IV died and left a daughter and a widow with child. But when, on April 1, 1328, the latter gave birth to a daughter, Philip of Valois, nephew of Philip IV and, therefore, first cousin of Charles IV, on the ground that the succession could only be transmitted through the male line, was recognized by an assembly of the French barons and peers as king of France, and on May 29, at Rheims, was crowned Philip VI.

The news of his election was most unwelcome to his cousin Isabella, who held that, because her son was of the senior branch of the Capetian line, he had the better claim, and to champion it, immediately after Philip's coronation, an embassy was sent from

London to Paris to set forth Edward's claim to the crown of France and to protest against Philip's usurpation. The English court was then in no position to enforce its demands, the protest was not taken seriously, and shortly after Philip took advantage of England's weakness and in retaliation sent an embassy to London to tell Edward that, as he alone of all Philip's vassals had failed to pay homage to him, he must do so. Because the English court temporized and sent back an evasive answer, Philip sent a second embassy to Edward with a thinly disguised ultimatum that, unless he took the oath of fealty due to the king of France, Aquitaine would be confiscated. This threat brought Edward to heel, for he could not defend his duchy by force of arms at the time. On April 14, 1329, he wrote to Philip to say that, as soon as the difficult conditions in his kingdom permitted, he would cross to France and pay homage. On June 6 he fulfilled his promise, and in the cathedral at Amiens became Philip's man.

In this exchange of claims and demands, we touch upon the main cause of the Hundred Years War. It had nothing directly to do with the French royal succession; instead it was based on the fact that Edward, as duke of Aquitaine, was an abnormal type of vassal. Normal French vassals could, at the risk of a brawl, be bullied into submission by their liege lord, the king of France; but to do so with Edward, as king of England, was to risk a full-scale foreign war. In other words, though *de jure*, kings could be vassals of kings, *de facto* they remained kings and therefore equals. Further, as long as Edward was duke of Aquitaine, he held his duchy not merely in fief to the French king, but also as an English bridgehead in France, and unless he was bound in vassalage to the king of France, tied by no moral obligation he could exploit his bridgehead with impunity. Clearly, then, if Philip could not force the English out of Aquitaine, it was to his advantage to insist on Edward's vassalage being as binding as possible; and, as clearly, if Edward could not abrogate it altogether, it was to his advantage to maintain it in its most limited form. When eventually Philip ordered the confiscation of Guienne, which, as Professor Edouard Perroy points out, was his way of declaring war on Edward, the latter forthwith "assumed the position of claimant to the throne of the Capetians" in order to transform "the feudal conflict, in which he was an inferior, into a dynastic struggle, which would make him his adversary's equal".[1]

[1] *The Hundred Years War* (English edit. 1951), pp. 92–93.

Besides this wholly feudal matter, there were others which, by impinging upon it, made a conflict nearly certain. The more important of these were the collapse of the empire in the thirteenth century and the degradation of the papacy by its transference to Avignon, because England and France were left without a counterpoise, either temporal or spiritual, to balance their claims and to distract their quarrels. Another was the question of Scotland. Since 1295, when an alliance between Scotland and France was agreed, it had been exploited by the latter to distract and weaken England. Equally true was this of Flanders, which, after the battle of Cassel, in 1328, had become wholly bound to the French king. Though Edward could not break the alliance, to weaken it he cleverly exploited the dependence of the Flemish weavers on English wool.

Seen in focus, the causes of the Hundred Years War were by no means rooted solely either in the dynastic or in the feudal questions, but rather in the multiple conditions of the age which gave it birth. The authority of the papacy was on the wane; the influence of the empire was all but spent; kingdoms were rising into power; trade was becoming increasingly a cause of contention between kingdoms; the command of the sea was looming over the horizon; the spirit of chivalry, begotten during the crusades, had become blatantly bellicose; and, above all, there was not sufficient room for two would-be dominant powers in western Europe. All these things, under the cloak of Edward's feudal claim to the crown of France, precipitated the Hundred Years War, the greatest tourney of the middle ages, which, in spite of its follies and disasters, sowed the seeds which were to sprout into a greater England and a greater France.

In this long struggle, strictly speaking there were no great decisive battles such as those which so far have been described; yet tactical decisions were not wanting, and more especially at the beginning and toward the end of the war.

With Edward having been compelled to pay homage to Philip at Amiens, the court of France had won the first round and encouraged by England's weakness it set out to win the second. It raised the question of the validity of the oath of fealty Edward had taken, which though not so precise as the one sworn by the great French vassals, was in no important respect different from the oaths of Edward II, Edward I, and Henry III. It was proclaimed "simple" and not "liege" homage, and without further discussion Edward was summoned to appear before Philip's court on July 28, 1330, to declare that his homage implied the latter.

The barons in England were in rebellion against Isabella and her paramour Roger Mortimer at the time, and Edward, tired of his mother's tutelage, sided with the malcontents, banished Isabella and had Mortimer executed at Tyburn. He was, therefore, badly placed to refuse the summons, and on March 30, 1331, he addressed a latter to Philip saying: "We recognize that the homage which we did at Amiens to the King of France was, is, and ought to be accounted liege homage, and promise him faith and loyalty, as Duke of Aquitaine and Peer of France, and Count of Ponthieu and Montreuil."[1] Four days later Edward crossed to France, and during his short visit, as Philip deemed the written engagement sufficient, amicable relations between the two countries were established. The question appeared settled and Philip began preparations for a crusade which was then being preached throughout Europe. Nevertheless, in a little over a year the first spark of the great conflagration was to gleam, not across the Channel, but north of the Tweed.

On the death of Robert Bruce—victor of Bannockburn in 1314— on June 7, 1329, the crown of Scotland passed to his son David, then a child of five years old, who, in accordance with the treaty of Northampton of May, 1328, was recognized by Edward as king. The treaty also provided that former owners of forfeited lands in Scotland, with three exceptions, were to be reinstated.

In November, 1331, David was crowned at Scone and Edward Baliol,[2] one of the "Disinherited" and *protégé* of Edward, set out to regain his inheritance. On July 31, 1332, at the head of a small body of men-at-arms and archers, he invaded Scotland and, on August 11, at Dupplin Muir, won an astonishing victory over the Regent. Meanwhile Edward learnt that David had been subsidized by Philip, set aside the treaty of Northampton, which he disliked, marched north, laid siege to Berwick and, on July 19, 1333, decisively defeated the Scots at Halidon Hill. David fled to France and was well received by Philip, who refused to discontinue his support of the Scots unless Edward withdrew his troops from Scotland.

[1] Froissart's *Chronicles*, trans. Thomas Jones (1854), vol. I, p. 45.
[2] He was the son of John Baliol who, in 1292, had been forced upon the Scots as their king by Edward I.

As the situation worsened Pope Benedict XII came forward as mediator and, in November, 1335, persuaded Edward and David to agree to a short truce as a preliminary step toward the settlement of their quarrel. Shortly after he informed Philip that until a general peace was established the crusade would have to be postponed. Annoyed by this, Philip, who had set his heart upon leading the venture, in order to bring pressure to bear on Edward, peremptorily ordered his fleet, then assembled at Marseilles, to convey the crusaders to the Holy Land, to move to the Normandy ports, as if he were about to intervene in support of Scotland.

The effect of this on England was immediate. Parliament saw in it a threat of invasion and in September, 1336, voted the subsidies necessary to place the country on a war footing and at the same time ordered the fleet to concentrate in the English Channel. In reply to this counter-challenge Philip sent troops to the borders of Guienne, and on May 24, 1337, he took the decisive plunge and declared Guienne forfeited.

Meanwhile a subsidiary incident had occurred which helped to precipitate hostilities. In 1332, Robert of Artois, Philip's brother-in-law, accused of poisoning his wife, was stripped of his estates and banished. At first he sought refuge in Hainault, but when Philip let it be known that he would take up arms against anyone who harboured him, late in 1336 Robert crossed to England. Royally received by Edward, he incited him against Philip and urged him to reassert his claim to the French crown. Though, as duke of Aquitaine, Edward could not support Robert against his legal sovereign without breaking his oath to Philip, were Philip's accession declared to be illegal he could do so with impunity. The means was at hand – his dynastic claim. Therefore, on November 1, 1337, he sent the Bishop of Lincoln to Paris with an ultimatum in which he addressed Philip as *soi-disant* king of France. Though he did not as yet claim the crown of France, what this form of address conveyed was that his homage at Amiens had been paid to a usurper and so had no binding value. Thus, in the autumn of 1337, Edward won the third round, and the conflict which had been simmering since 1328 reached boiling point.

To conquer France in the present-day sense of the word – that is, by occupation – was out of the question; for not only was the kingdom of France in the fourteenth century a large and prosperous country, but it had a population of some 20,000,000,[1] and in 1377, after the Black Death of 1348–1349, that of England has been reckoned at about 3,700,000.[2] Against this superiority it must be remembered that the feudal system of war, still maintained in France, was based on selected men and not on mass man-power, and though the French chivalry was superior numerically to the English, it was less disciplined, and it still regarded the appearance of infantry on the battlefield as an insult to its class pride.

Compared with France, England was a more united kingdom, and Edward had at his disposal for the recruitment and maintenance of his military forces an incomparably better financial system. To win his battles, all he had to do was to beat the French knights, and whereas French feudal tactics were to dismount one's opponent and to hold him to ransom, Edward's were more definitely out to kill. His tactics were "modern" more than feudal in idea, and the longbow, adopted by his grandfather from the Welsh, enabled him to base them on missile power as well as shock. Therefore, when all is considered, the tactical disparity lay with the French. Nevertheless the size of France prohibited lengthy, let alone permanent, occupation.

Following the plan of his grandfather Edward I in 1297, Edward decided to distract any attempt on the part of Philip to wrest Aquitaine from him by attacking France through the Low Countries – that is, to draw the war northward. And though an alliance with Louis Count of Flanders was out of the question, by grants of money, totalling 300,000 florins, he won over John III Duke of Brittany; Reginald Count Palatine of the Rhine; the Emperor Ludwig of Bavaria; and others. Also he signed conventions with Hainault, Guelders, Limburg, Juliers, and Brabant.

In the meantime Louis of Flanders – French by birth – to give proof of his loyalty to Philip, had posted a strong garrison on the island of Cadsand – below Sluys – expressly to harry English sea communications with the Low Countries. Edward seized upon this as a *casus belli* and sent out an expedition to capture the island, and on November 11, 1337, under cover of a rain of arrows,[3] the

---

[1] *The Cambridge Medieval History*, vol. VII, p. 342. Professor Perroy (*The Hundred Years War*, p. 36) estimates it at "a minimum of 10 to 12 million souls".

[2] *British Medieval Population*, J. C. Russell (1948), pp. 246–260.

[3] Froissart says: "The archers were ordered to draw their bows stiff and strong, and to set up their shouts; upon which those that guarded the haven were forced to retire, whether they would or not, for the first discharge did great mischief, and many were maimed and hurt" (vol. I, p. 44).

Earl of Derby and Walter Manny landed their men on it and destroyed the post. The Hundred Years War had begun and it was to last 116 years.

Next, to disrupt Flanders from within, Edward prohibited the export of English wool. Because of this the Flemings placed themselves under the authority of the celebrated Jacques van Artevelde, a leading member of the Weavers' Guild of Ghent. Artevelde broke away from Count Louis and made a commercial alliance with England. After this success the Emperor Ludwig denounced Philip for withholding homage for certain fiefs held by the empire and demanded that he restore the kingdom of France to its rightful owner–Edward of England. Lastly, the emperor appointed Edward Imperial Vicar for all the provinces west of the Rhine, and homage was rendered to him as such.

While Edward accumulated a heavy debt in his endeavours to enlarge the circle of his allies, Philip waged war in earnest on the English coasts. Squadrons manned by Normans, Spaniards, Bretons, and Genoese swept the Channel, and as early as 1336 English ships trading with Gascony had been ordered to sail in convoy.[1] In 1337 the Channel Islands and the Isle of Wight were ravaged, and in the following year Portsmouth, Portsea, and Southampton were burnt. In May, 1339, most of Hastings was burnt, and late in July a combined fleet of French and Genoese ships not only did great damage at Dover, Sandwich, Winchelsea, and Rye, but so firmly held the Channel "that no vessel could leave England without being plundered, and the crew taken or slain".[2] The most notable of these losses were the *Christopher* and *Edward*, both large ships laden with wool for Flanders. Meanwhile in Guienne, La Penne in the Agenais, which had been besieged since April, 1338, fell in January, 1339.

As a set-off to these mishaps and also to give some assurance for his heavy borrowings, on July 16, 1339, Edward, in a declaration addressed to the pope and cardinals, set out at great length his claim to the crown of France. Next, he met his half-hearted allies, in all 15,000 strong, at Vilvoordun and at Brussels, and in order to reassure them, he renounced his homage to Philip and thereby transformed the feudal conflict into a dynastic war. Then, in true spirit of chivalry, he set out at top speed with forty lances to surprise the castle of Mortagne at the junction of the

---

[1] *A History of the Royal Navy*, Sir Nicholas Harris Nicolas (1857), vol. II, pp. 21–22.
[2] *Ibid.*, vol. II, p. 36.

rivers Scarpe and Scheldt, and when he failed to take it, pressed on and surprised Thun-l'Évêque, near Cambrai.

Unprepared for an autumn campaign, Philip called for a muster of his barons at St. Quentin and Edward advanced into Cambrésis, ravaging as he went. By the time he had reached Marcoing on September 25, Philip had moved his army to Péronne, from where, on October 18, he challenged Edward to meet him in a pitched battle on any "fair field" of his own choice. But Edward fell back to La Flamengerie, near La Capelle, and Philip advanced to Buironfosse. On October 23 both armies prepared for battle. Edward, set upon fighting a defensive action on the lines he had adopted at Halidon Hill, had no intention of attacking, and Philip, counselled by his advisers that the stars were unfavourable, awaited the advance of his rival. The result was that neither side moved, and at vespers Edward retired to Avesnes, and on November 1 was back in Brussels. Thus Edward's first campaign for the crown of France ended in a bloodless and costly fiasco. He had incurred a debt of £300,000 and had forfeited the good will of the pope. Meanwhile in Gascony the French had captured Bourg and Blaye and Bordeaux was threatened directly.

Nevertheless Edward was far from despondent and on January 25, 1340, in order to "legalize" his position with the Flemings, who were still bound by homage to the crown of France, he publicly assumed the double title of king of England and France and quartered the lilies with the lions on the royal coat of arms.[1] The Flemings, relieved of their oath of allegiance to Philip, recognized Edward as king of France, and on February 21 he returned to England.

Once back, Edward's most pressing problem was to raise money to continue the war, and it was not until Parliament had made new grants that he made ready to return to Flanders, where Philip had assumed the offensive against Edward's allies; the armies confronted each other on the Scheldt. Nor had the pope been idle, for at Philip's instigation he had launched a Bull of excommunication against the rebellious Flemings, to appease whom Edward wrote that "the first time he should cross the sea, he would bring priests from his own country, who should say mass for them, whether the pope would or not. . . ."[2]

In order to frustrate his rival's return, Philip assembled a

---

[1] There the lilies remained until 1801.          [2] Froissart, vol. 1, p. 63.

powerful fleet under Admiral Hue Quieret, Admiral Pierre Béhuchet, and the Genoese sea rover Barbanero, to watch the English coasts, to prevent Edward from recrossing the Channel, and should he attempt to do so, to capture him. When reports of this reached England, Edward was persuaded much against his will to postpone the crossing until an equally powerful fleet had been collected in the Orwell (Harwich).

When all was ready and the west wind blew, at about one o'clock on Thursday, June 22, 1340, Edward embarked in the cog[1] *Thomas* and the fleet got under way. It probably consisted of 147 vessels,[2] and was divided into three squadrons, respectively commanded by Sir Robert Morley, the Earl of Huntingdon, and the Earl of Arundel; Edward held supreme command. With it sailed a convoy of "fair dames and damsels" to reinforce the court of Queen Philippa, who had remained at Ghent.

Toward midday, on Friday, when they neared the Flemish coast, the French fleet was seen in the harbour of Sluys, resembling, according to Froissart, "a forest of masts".[3] In a letter addressed to his son Edward Duke of Cornwall, dated June 28,[4] Edward placed its strength at 190 vessels manned by 35,000 men-at-arms and others. But though the day was still young, because of the tide, instead of sailing to Sluys,[5] which lay some ten miles to the east, the fleet cast anchor off Blankenberg, and a mounted party was sent ashore to reconnoitre the enemy. On its return it reported that nineteen of the enemy vessels were abnormally large and that among them was the *Christopher*.

At daybreak on Saturday, June 24, both fleets prepared for action. Barbanero, a professional sailor, urged attack; but the two French admirals insisted upon passive defence within the harbour. A compromise was agreed upon, by which the French were to move out to the mouth of the harbour by the island of Cadsand,[6] while Barbanero and his squadron of galleys took to the open sea. Once at the harbour mouth, the French admirals, who completely lacked sea-sense, drew up their ships in three divisions or lines with the largest in the van, and as their flanks were secure, in order to make certain that their front would not

---

[1] A broad ship with bluff bow and stern. The word still survives in "cockboat".
[2] *Genesis of Lancaster*, Sir James Ramsay (1913), vol. I, p. 277.
[3] Froissart, vol. I, p. 72.
[4] For the letter in French and English see Nicolas, vol. I, pp. 502 and 61.
[5] The harbour of Sluys has since been silted up, and Sluis today is an inland town.
[6] Kadzand is now part of the mainland.

be stove in, they linked the ships of the van together with iron chains and cables. In their top castles they placed soldiers provided with stones and other missiles. With the van was the *Christopher*, full of Genoese crossbow-men, and near her were the *Edward, Katherine*, and *Rose*, all three recently captured from the English.

Edward's fleet was also ranged in three divisions, with the largest ships, under Sir Robert Morley, in the van. Men-at-arms were posted in every third ship, archers in the two intervening ones, and some ships would appear to have carried primitive cannon[1] as well as catapults. In rear was a reserve squadron, also manned by archers, and 300 men-at-arms were ordered to protect the ships carrying the women.

As the initiative was Edward's, he could afford to wait for wind, tide, and sun, and it was not until after midday[2] that the tide was suitable and the battle of Sluys opened.

To the sound of trumpets, nakers (kettle-drums), viols, tabors, and other instruments, Sir Robert Morley, with the sun to his back, sailed straight for the French van, one side shouting "St. George, Guienne!" and the other "France!" As his ships crashed into the French at their moorings, the English archers poured in volley after volley of arrows to cover the ships bearing the men-at-arms who, when they had grappled an enemy ship, boarded her and cleared her in hand-to-hand fight. Showers of stones, hurled from the fighting tops, crashed on the combatants below. The great cog *Chistopher* and her two sister cogs the *Edward* and *Rose* were speedily captured; their flags were hauled down and the lions and lilies run up. The *Christopher* was manned immediately with archers and sent to attack the Genoese galleys. The French fought with their customary valour and it is said that the entire crew of one English ship was stoned to death; but the decisive weapon was the arrow: it would seem in many cases to have cleared the French decks.

It would appear that some time before the battle Edward had summoned his supporters from Bruges and neighbouring towns to his aid, and, according to Froissart and other chroniclers but not all, they readily answered his call. They crowded out of Sluys in boats and attacked the French in rear. Barbanero considered

[1] See Kervyn de Lettenhove's *Froissart* (1863–1877), vol. III, p. 492.
[2] "*Post horam nonam*", see *Chronicon Galfridi le Baker de Swynbroke*, edit. Edward Maude Thompson (1889), p. 68.

the battle lost and with his twenty-four galleys headed for the open sea and escaped the slaughter.

On the defeat of their van, the French abandoned all hope and the crews of their second and third divisions in panic took to their boats, many of which capsized through overcrowding. Nevertheless the struggle lasted until sunset, and according to Edward, late into the night, and ended in the complete annihilation of the three French divisions, 166 ships in all. Admiral Quieret was killed in fair fight; but it would seem that Béhuchet was taken alive, and because he had burnt Portsmouth, in reprisal was hanged from a yard-arm.

Edward remained in the *Thomas* for several days of high carousal, with trumpets blowing and tambours beating in honour of the victory. When he landed he went in procession with the 300 priests he had brought with him to fulfil his promise to the Flemings to the chapel of My Lady of Ardenburg to attend high Mass. Next, he rode on to Ghent to greet Queen Philippa and her newly born son, named after his birthplace John of Gaunt.

Strange as it may seem, the victory, and tactically it was one of the most complete ever won by an English fleet, gave no impulse to the campaign on the Scheldt. Instead of exploiting it strategically, as he could have done, Edward decided to lay siege to Tournai, apparently because it was one of the places he had promised the Flemings as the price for their recognition of him as king of France. On July 23 he established his headquarters between Courtrai and Tournai and invested the latter, while Philip entrenched his army between Aire and Armentières. Philip had no urgency to intervene, for events were moving in his favour: in Gascony his cause was making rapid progress, and in Scotland the Scots had recovered Perth. For nearly two months the siege of Tournai was pressed and cannon were used in its bombardment. Lack of money to keep his motley army together compelled Edward to raise the siege, and on September 25 he agreed reluctantly to the Truce of Esplechin, which was to last until June 22, 1341.

The importance of the Battle of Sluys does not lie in the influence it had on Edward's second Flanders campaign, which ended in as great a fiasco as his first, but on the war as a whole. It was so complete that for the space of a generation it gave to England the command of the Channel, without which it is highly improbable that the war would have continued for long or that the psychologically decisive battle of Crécy would ever have been fought.

Edward returned to England on November 30, and in 1341, when his affairs in Scotland were going badly, an event on the Continent again compelled him to look south. In April, John III, Duke of Brittany and Earl of Richmond in England, died without an heir and a dispute over his succession followed. The claimants were Charles of Blois, a nephew of Philip VI, who married John's niece, and John Count of Montfort, John's half-brother. Philip supported the former, and Edward, who saw in the quarrel the means to counter the Franco-Scottish alliance by an Anglo-Breton one, championed the latter, with the result that a deplorable war began which gave new life to the struggle between England and France and lasted for twenty years. According to Sir James Ramsay it "made the Hundred Years War possible".[1]

Though Philip took no official part in this war, his son, the Duke of Normandy, and his brother, the Count of Alençon, joined de Blois, and on November 21 they forced the surrender of Nantes and were fortunate enough to capture de Montfort. But they had not reckoned with the countess, his wife, who, in the words of Froissart, "possessed the courage of a man, and the heart of a lion".[2] A true forerunner of Joan of Arc,[3] her heroic defence of the castle of Hennebont (north of Lorient) was one of the most remarkable incidents of the Hundred Years War. It roused Edward's chivalrous spirit, and in May, 1342, when the countess was reduced to the last extremity, he sent Sir Walter Manny with 300 lances and 2,000 archers to her relief. Manny raised the siege, but was not strong enough to venture inland, so another army, under the Earl of Northampton and Robert of Artois, was sent out. Robert was mortally wounded at Vannes, and on September 30 Northampton won a desperately fought battle at Morlaix. This success so encouraged Edward that on October 23 he sailed to Brest, resolved that his third campaign should be fought in Brittany. Like his first and second, it proved an all but unqualified fiasco and ended on January 19, 1343, in a three-year truce signed at Malestroit, which included Scotland, Hainault, and Flanders.

Soon after both sides took advantage of the truce to push their respective interests, and Pope Clement VI, who saw that the prospects of a final settlement were rapidly evaporating, persuaded the contending parties to meet in conference at Avignon in October–December, 1344. There Edward first set forth his

[1] *Genesis of Lancaster*, vol. I, p. 297.    [2] Froissart, vol. I, p. 96.
[3] See for her exploits Froissart, vol. I, pp. 105–107.

claim to the French crown, then came down to business. He demanded an enlarged Guienne in full sovereignty–that is, freed from all vassalage. In their turn Philip's councillors contended that although Aquitaine was well and truly confiscated, Philip would nevertheless agree to restore the fief–incidentally Edward was still in occupation–and even to enlarge its frontiers, as long as it was held in vassalage from him.[1]

As neither party would give way, the war was renewed and Edward resolved simultaneously to attack France from Brittany and Guienne. In June, 1345, de Montfort, who by then had escaped from France, and the Earl of Northampton, were sent to Brittany, and a little later the Earl of Derby took ship for Bordeaux. Edward heard that van Artevelde's régime was tottering and on July 5 he sailed for Sluys. There, on July 7, he met van Artevelde, who was assassinated on his return to Ghent. On July 26 Edward was back in England.

In September, de Montfort died in Brittany, and Northampton, who had accomplished little, went into winter quarters. Derby, in the south, was more successful, and in a skilfully fought campaign, the success of which was largely due to his moderation,[2] he took Bergerac, and in a brilliant operation relieved Auberoche. After these successes, Angoulême and many other cities opened their gates to him and he returned to Bordeaux for the winter of 1345–1346.

These many losses roused Philip to action, and toward the end of 1345 he summoned the levies of Normandy, Picardy, Burgundy, Lorraine, Provence, and Languedoc to gather at Toulouse under command of the Duke of Normandy. Early in the spring of 1346 the duke set out, and in April laid siege to the castle of Aiguillon (on the junction of the Garonne and the Lot) then held by Ralph Lord Stafford, Sir Walter Manny, and others. The castle was immensely strong and the siege soon developed into one of the most famous of the whole war. It was pressed until August 20, when the duke suddenly raised it; for that day the alarming news came from the north that Edward had invaded France. Derby–now Earl of Lancaster–had also heard of the king's landing, and now that Aiguillon was safe he set out for Saintonge and Poitou as a diversion in Edward's favour.

---

[1] See *The Hundred Years War*, Edouard Perroy, p. 116.

[2] Froissart (vol. 1, p. 130) records that to the inhabitants of Bergerac Derby said: "He who begs for mercy should have mercy shown him: tell them to open their gates, and let us enter, when we will assure them of safety from us and from our people."

On his return from Sluys, Edward at once began to raise an army to push the war in Gascony, and as he had learnt through experience that feudal levies were unfitted for continental warfare, he decided to recruit a picked force of men by Commissions of Array, a system which on occasions had been used by his father and grandfather.[1] In accordance with this, the sheriffs and commissioners of array first compiled a list of all landlords, next each man who owned land or rents to the value of £5 was ordered by them to find one archer; those rated at £10, one hobeler;[2] and those with holdings worth £25, one man-at arms; and so on upward to the great feudal lords who, according to their means, raised well-organized retinues. Thus, Richard Lord Talbot recruited 14 knights, 60 esquires, and 82 archers, and John de Vere Earl of Oxford, 23 knights, 44 esquires, and 63 archers.[3] Landowners not able to serve in person were allowed to find substitutes, and if they failed to do so were fined at the rate of £1 an archer, £3 6s. 8d. a hobeler, and £6 13s. 4d. a man-at-arms. The archers were recruited from the yeomen,[4] a class completely above villeinage. The French had to resort to hiring Genoese and other crossbow-men to make good their lack of home-trained archers.

Here, a few words must be said on the longbow, a weapon which was to dominate the battlefields of France until Agincourt, after which its decline was rapid. As we have seen, it was adopted from the south Welsh by Edward I. It was made of a six-foot length of elm, from which a three-foot arrow was shot. It was a far more powerful weapon than the short Norman bow and less cumbersome than the crossbow, and its arrows could penetrate two layers of mail armour.[5]

In 1298, Edward I put this weapon to the test against the Scots under Wallace at Falkirk with terrible effect, and because Edward II failed to do so against Bruce at Bannockburn he was

[1] See Stubbs's *Constitutional History of England* (1887), vol. II, pp. 284–285.

[2] Hobelers, or hobilars, were mounted infantry, spearmen or archers, first raised in Scotland to operate with cavalry in the Scottish raids.

[3] *A History of the Art of War in the Middle Ages*, Sir Charles Oman, vol. II, p. 128.

[4] As a national sport, archery was encouraged after the conquest. In 1252, according to Henry III's Assize of Arms, all forty-shillings freeholders were required to possess a bow and arrows. The yeomen were, in fact, a standing archer militia.

[5] In a trial made before Edward VI, in 1550, arrows were shot through a one-inch board of well-seasoned timber (*Archery*, Badmington Library, 1894, p. 431). Its range was about 250 yards. Shakespeare mentions as a notable feat 280 to 290 yards (*King Henry IV*, part II, act III, scene 2). In 1798, 1856, 1881, and 1897, ranges of 340, 308, 286, 290, and 310 were attained with the longbow.

defeated decisively and the lesson of the longbow had to be relearned in 1332 at Dupplin Muir.

As already mentioned, this battle was fought between the "Disinherited"–Edward Baliol, Henry Beaumont, and others– and Donald Earl of Mar, the Scottish regent. The former had 500 knights and men-at-arms and between 1,000 and 2,000 archers. The latter commanded, it is said, 2,000 men-at-arms and 20,000 foot–an exaggeration.

Fully aware of the desperate odds against them, the "Disinherited" first attacked Mar by night. But when dawn broke and they discovered their enemy advancing in battle array, they took up position on the slope of a hill. They dismounted all but forty of their cavalry and formed them up in phalangial order, with archers thrown forward on their flanks. Thus their order of battle assumed a crescent formation. Mar paid no attention to the archers, charged down on Baliol's centre and drove it in. At once the flanking archers wheeled inward and opened so devastating a fire that the Scots were driven into a confused mass and all but exterminated. Henry de Beaumont and some of his followers then mounted their horses and chased the fugitives off the field. In 1333, Edward may be said to have patented these tactics at the battle of Halidon Hill, for thence onward for a hundred years they remained the norm of English fighting.

Edward's army mustered at Portsmouth. According to Sir James Ramsay, the forces raised were 3,580 archers from the counties of the Trent, with 100 from the county Palatine of Chester; 3,500 Welshmen, half archers and half spearmen; 2,743 hobelers; and 1,141 men-at-arms, who with miners and supernumeraries, made a total of approximately 10,000 men.[1]

This army d'élite was organized, disciplined, and paid by the king. Tactically, it was superior to the French: in the one missile and shock were combined; in the other shock was all but entirely relied upon. Edward's tactics were defensive, Philip's were offensive; in the former the arrow disorganized and demoralized before the shock set out to annihilate; in the latter, as among the Goths, shock action dominated from start to finish and each subsequent charge became more chaotic than the one before. Because mounted men could seldom play a decisive part during the act

---

[1] *Genesis of Lancaster*, vol. I, p. 319. Oman in *A History of the Art of War*, vol. II, p. 130, says 2,400 horse and 12,000 foot. Ferdinand Lot in *L'art Militaire et les Armées au Moyen Age* (1946), vol. I, p. 346, accepts Ramsay's figures.

of disorganization and demoralization, Edward normally dismounted the bulk of his men-at-arms and formed them up in phalanx, both to withstand the enemy's mounted attack and to protect his own archers. His normal formation was in three battles or divisions, two dismounted in front with an interval between them, and one in rear, either mounted or ready to mount, and held in reserve. The archers were formed up on the flanks of the two forward battles *en herse*[1]–that is, at an angle thrown forward (see diagram), the two inner flanking bodies meeting at an angle,

and the two outer, when possible, resting on an obstacle, such as a wood, stream or village. To protect themselves the archers almost invariably dug *trous de loup* and drove ironshod stakes into the ground in front of their position. Because of these obstacles and the arrows, the French chivalry usually avoided the archers and instead charged the dismounted men-at-arms; when they did so the archers raked their flanks, as we have seen happened at Taginae in 552. There was another reason for attacking the dismounted men-at-arms: according to the code of chivalry it was beneath a knight's dignity to attack infantry because infantry had little or no ransom value. Usually they were indiscriminately slaughtered after a victory to prevent them from turning into brigands, for prisoners' cages were unknown in the fourteenth century.

Simultaneously with his military preparations Edward launched a propaganda campaign against the French in which he denounced "Philip as threatening 'to root out the English tongue'. This document was addressed to the Provincial of the Friars Preachers for circulation through the pulpit."[2] Further, he rejected all interventions on the part of Pope Clement VI to preserve the peace, which made it clear to Philip that a full-scale invasion of France was in prospect. Therefore Philip wrote to King David of Scotland to beg him not to miss an opportunity to strike at England.

On July 11, 1346, when all was ready, the expedition put to sea.

[1] See *Battles of English History*, Hereford B. George (1895), p. 62. Though *herse* means "harrow", Mr. George points out that it also means "the stands used in church for seven candles, the centre one forming the apex and those on the sides gradually lower".

[2] *Genesis of Lancaster*, Sir James H. Ramsay, vol. 1, p. 320.

According to Froissart its destination was Gascony;[1] but on the way across the Channel, a Norman refugee, Godfrey of Harcourt, convinced Edward "that it would be more for his interest to land in Normandy", because that province was "one of the most fertile in the world" and that "the Normans have not been accustomed to the use of arms; and all the knighthood, that otherwise would have been there", was "with the duke before Aiguillon".[2] Edward changed his mind and ordered the fleet to make for St. Vaast-la-Hogue on the Cotentin Peninsula. What his strategic aim was it is impossible to fathom; but as Sir Charles Oman points out, as Edward's conduct of the campaign of Crécy shows no proof of any rational scheme one can only conclude that the expedition was nothing more than "a chivalrous adventure" or "a great raid of defiance pushed deep into France to provoke its king".[3]

The next day, July 12, Edward put in at La Hogue, and remained there six days to disembark his army. On July 18 he set out for Valognes, advanced by way of Carentan, St. Lô, and Fontenay--le-Pesnel (near Tilly), and arrived at Caen on July 26. Edward left the castle to defend itself, but the city, which was unwalled, was sacked indiscriminately. Edward then ordered that all wounded and booty should be embarked in the fleet, which had put into the mouth of the river Orne, but in the meantime the crews had mutinied and had set sail for England.[4] It would seem that it was this act of indiscipline which settled for Edward his strategic problem. Without a line of communications he could not remain where he was, and because to turn south and to join the Earl of Lancaster would bring him into head-on collision with the superior army of the Duke of Normandy, then moving north, Edward's sole remaining course was to move eastward to establish a base in Flanders.

From Caen he set out on July 31, passed by way of Lisieux and Brionne and reached Elboeuf on August 7. He found the bridge at Rouen broken and ascended the left bank of the Seine to seek

---

[1] Froissart writes: "The King of England, having heard how pressed his people were in the castle of Aiguillon, determined to lead a great army into Gascony" (vol. I, p. 150).
[2] *Ibid.*, vol. I, pp. 151–152.
[3] *A History of the Art of War in the Middle Ages*, vol. II, p. 131.
[4] *Welsh Wars*, John Morris (1901), p. 108. He writes: "In 1346 it is an undoubted fact . . . that Edward III and his army were left stranded in Normandy simply because the fleet disappeared in complete defiance of orders . . . so that the army had to proceed as best it could, and Crécy was as it were an accident."

a crossing. On August 13 he neared Paris. Along the whole of his line of march he devastated the country in a savage way while the French watched him from the right bank of the river. He reached Poissy, repaired the bridge there, forced a crossing on August 16 and pushed on to Grisy. Meanwhile Philip had done nothing to dispute his crossing, and to the consternation of the citizens of Paris had fallen back to St. Denis.

From Grisy Edward set out by forced marches northward, and on the 21st reached Airaines, ten miles south of the river Somme, where his scouts reported to him that all the bridges and fords above Abbeville were either broken or held. Philip was then at Amiens and his army grew stronger day by day.

Unable to cross at Abbeville, Edward pressed on to Acheux and reached it on August 23. There he offered a large reward to any man who could point out to him a ford. A native of the village of Mons-en-Vimeu, Gobin Agache, claimed the reward and offered to guide the king to the ford of Blanque Taque ("The White Spot") ten miles below Abbeville, which could be crossed at low tide. As Philip was now on his enemy's heels, not a moment was to be lost, and at midnight Edward set out and reached the ford early on August 24. There he halted for an hour or two until the tide was out, when, under cover of his archers, he forced a crossing and carried the whole of his army over as Philip came up, but only to be cut off by the rise of the tide. That night Edward rested at Noyelles, where the Countess of Aumale, sister of the late Robert of Artois, was living, and the next morning he resumed his retreat toward the forest and village of Crécy-en-Ponthieu. Meanwhile Philip returned to Abbeville to cross the Somme by its bridge.

When he arrived at Crécy Edward decided to accept battle. The reason given by Froissart is a sufficient one in the age of chivalry – namely, that having reached the inheritance of his grandmother he resolved to defend it; besides he found there a position which fitted his tactics. But to suggest, as some writers have done, that he was compelled to make a stand because further retreat would have demoralized his army, is highly unlikely, for at Crécy he was within three marches of Flanders, and Philip was a day's march in rear of him.

As he suspected that Philip would advance by the Abbeville-Hesdin road – which he did – and as he knew that unless he were to manœuvre round his enemy's left flank, which would have been contrary to chivalrous etiquette, he would be compelled to attack frontally, Edward selected a position which would meet this contingency and fit his tactics and strength. It was a gentle rise of ground between the villages of Crécy and Wadicourt, which still remains much as it was in his day.[1] To the east of them–that is, on Edward's prospective front–lay a dip in the downland called the *Vallée des Clercs*, on the far side of which stood the village of Estrées-les-Crécy, south of which was the village of Fontaine-sur-Maye, a little to the west of the Abbeville–Hesdin road. From Fontaine-sur-Maye, a small stream, the Maye, originates and runs westward through Crécy, south of which the great Forest of Crécy extends. The distance between Crécy and Wadicourt is a little more than 3,000 yards.

Edward's army was marshalled in the usual three battles or divisions, two on the forward slope of the rise east of the Crécy–Wadicourt road with a gap between them, and one in rear, presumably on the road. The right forward battle–the one nearest Crécy–was under the nominal command of the Prince of Wales, then a boy of seventeen; the actual commanders were Warwick the Earl Marshal and the Earls of Oxford and Harcourt. The left battle was commanded by Northampton the Constable and the Earl of Arundel, and was deployed south of Wadicourt. The rearward battle was commanded by Edward, who established his battle headquarters at a windmill on the Crécy end of the rise; the mound upon which it stood can still be seen. To protect his right flank Edward had a series of shallow ditches dug, *trous de loup* were also dug in front of the Prince's battle.

The archers were drawn up *en herse*–as already described–on the flanks of each of the forward battles, the outer detachments at an angle which linked the outer flanks of the battles with the villages of Crécy and Wadicourt, and the inner covered the gap between the battles, forming a V pointing eastward.

According to Froissart, the right battle consisted of about 800 men-at-arms, 2,000 archers and 1,000 Welshmen; the left, 800 men-at-arms and 1,200 archers; and the rearward one, 700 men-at-arms and 2,000 archers; a total of 8,500 men.[2] Though the categories of soldiers may be incorrect, the total number would

---

[1] I visited the battlefield in 1917, and comparing the locality with a copy of a map alleged to have been made in the fifteenth century, I found very little difference in the lay-out of the villages.

[2] Froissart, vol. 1, p. 163. Lot in *L'Art Militaire*, etc., vol. 1, p. 347, says 9,000.

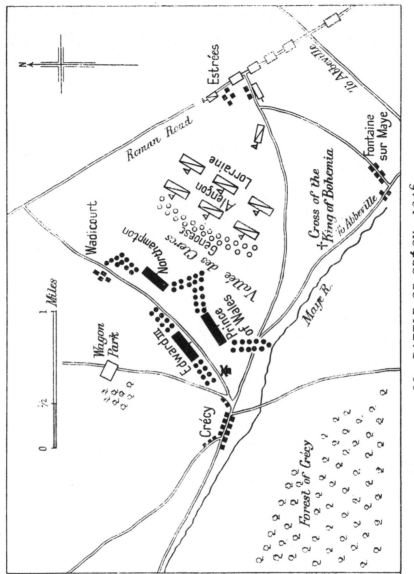

Estrées

To Abbeville

Roman Road

Fontaine
sur Maye

Lorraine

Alençon

Cross of the
✝ King of Bohemia

To Abbeville

Wadicourt

Northampton

Genoese

Vallée des Clercs

Maye R.

Prince
of Wales

Wagon
Park

Edward III

Crécy

Forest of Crécy

1 Miles

½

0

seem reasonable as Edward's fighting strength on landing at La
Hogue was about 10,000.

In the rear of the battle front Edward "enclosed a large park
near a wood" and in it marshalled "all his baggage-wagons and
horses".[1] According to Villani in his *History of Florence* and the
*Grandes Chroniques de France*, Edward had with him three cannon,[2]
which were posted with the archers.

Once deployment was ended, Edward, attended by his two
marshals, rode at a foot pace down the ranks encouraging his men.
They were then ordered to eat their midday meal and when they
had refreshed themselves they again formed battle order and sat
on the ground "placing their helmets and bows before them, that
they might be the fresher when their enemies should arrive".[3]

Meanwhile Philip had gathered in his army at Abbeville. With
him were the blind, or half-blind, King John of Bohemia and his
son Charles, King of the Romans; James III King of Majorca;
Philip's brother Charles of Alençon; Philip's nephew Louis of
Blois; Louis of Flanders; John of Hainault; Rudolf Duke of Lorraine; and most of the chivalry of France. Never before during
the middle ages had such a galaxy of knights been seen on one
battlefield. According to Lot's estimate, the French men-at-arms
numbered 8,000 supported by 4,000 foot,[4] including a body of
Genoese crossbow-men under command of Odone Doria and
Carlo Grimaldi. The French men-at-arms were also marshalled
in three battles, the first commanded by the King of Bohemia and
the Counts of Alençon and Flanders; the second by the Duke of
Lorraine and the Count of Blois; and the third by King Philip and
the King of the Romans.

Not certain where the English were, early on August 26 Philip
set out on the Abbeville–Hesdin road and sent forward the Lord
Moyne of Bastleberg and three knights to seek them. On their
return, Moyne informed the king that Edward was in position at
Crécy, and he suggested that the king should halt his army and
bivouac for the night, so that the rear might catch up with the
van and the whole army attack on the following morning.

---

[1] Froissart, vol. i, p. 163.
[2] See Ramsay's *Genesis of Lancaster*, vol. i, p. 331. Oman, vol. ii, p. 142, suggests
that they were probably *ribauldequins*, weapons "consisting of several small tubes
clamped together and with their touch-holes so arranged that one sweep of the
linstock would discharge them simultaneously" (*ibid.*, p. 216).
[3] Froissart, vol. i, p. 163.
[4] *L'Art Militaire et les Armées au Moyen Age*, vol. i, p. 347. But it also suggests that the
French army may have been numerically inferior to the English (p. 348).

Philip ordered that this should be done. Then, writes Froissart: "Those that were in front halted; but those behind said they would not halt, until they were as forward as the front. When the front perceived the rear pressing on, they pushed forward; and neither the king nor the marshals could stop them, but they marched on without any order until they came in sight of their enemies. As soon as the foremost rank saw them, they fell back at once in great disorder, which alarmed those in the rear, who thought they had been fighting. . . . All the roads between Abbeville and Crécy were covered with common people, who, when they were come within three leagues of their enemies, drew their swords, bawling out, 'Kill, Kill'. . . . There is no man, unless he had been present, that can imagine, or describe truly, the confusion of that day. . . ."[1]

The hour of vespers (6 p.m.) had passed, when the sky suddenly darkened and "a heavy rain fell, accompanied by thunder and a very terrible eclipse of the sun; and before this rain a great flight of crows hovered in the air over the battalions, making a loud noise". As rapidly as it had come the storm cleared, "and the sun shone very bright, but the Frenchmen had it in their faces, and the English in their backs".[2] Meanwhile the Genoese, who had regained some order, were brought forward, with the Counts of Alençon and of Flanders in their rear, and began descending into the *Vallée des Clercs*. As they approached the English they raised a loud shout "in order to frighten them"; but their enemy remained still. They shouted again, but "the English never moved". A third time they shouted, and began to shoot their quarrels. "The English archers then advanced one step forward, and shot their arrows with such force and quickness, that it seemed as if it snowed. When the Genoese felt these arrows, which pierced their arms, heads, and through their armour, some of them cut the strings of their crossbows, others flung them to the ground and turned about and retreated quite discomfited." Seeing this the King of France cried out: "Kill me those scoundrels; for they stop our road. . . ."[3]

The English archers continued to shoot, and soon their arrows fell among the horsemen and sent their horses plunging among and trampling down the crowds of flying Genoese. Vying with each other to get to the front, the French chivalry pushed their way through the fugitives, hacking at them with their swords.

[1] Froissart, vol. I, p. 164.    [2] *Ibid.*, vol. I, pp. 164–165.
[3] *Ibid.*, vol. I, pp. 165–166.

The English archers next turned their arrows on the French men-at-arms, and this is what we read: "For the bowmen let fly among them at large, and did not lose a single shaft, for every arrow told on horse or man, piercing head, or arm, or leg among the riders and sending the horses mad. For some stood stock still, and others rushed side-ways, and most of all began backing in spite of their masters, and some were rearing and tossing their heads at the arrows, and others when they felt the bit threw themselves down. So the knights in the first French battle fell, slain or sore stricken, almost without seeing the men who slew them."[1]

Once it had been repulsed, no attempt was made by the first French battle to clear the field for the second battle behind it, with the result that before the latter could charge it was thrown into complete confusion, and in its scramble forward the blind king of Bohemia was killed. At times, when the French men-at-arms fell back, the Welshmen in Edward's army, who carried long knives, rushed forward and "falling upon earls, barons, knights and squires, slew many, at which the King of England was afterwards much exasperated";[2] and no wonder, for a dead man brought in no ransom.

It is interesting to read in Froissart that in the assaults made by the Counts of Alençon and Flanders, the French men-at-arms "coasted, as it were, the archers";[3] that is to say, their horses shied away from the enemy arrows, and whether their riders despised the archers or not, they were willy nilly carried toward the dismounted English battles. This happened more particularly on the English right, and the Prince of Wales's battle was so roughly handled that Warwick sent back to the King at the windmill to ask for aid. When he heard that the Prince was unharmed, Edward said to the messenger: ". . . return back to those that sent you, and tell them from me, not to send again for me this day, or expect that I shall come, let what will happen, as long as my son has life: and say, that I command them to let the boy win his spurs. . . ."[4] Nevertheless he sent the Bishop of Durham and thirty knights to strengthen his son's battle.

Probably the reason why he sent no more was that he saw at the time that the left battle, under Northampton, was wheeling to its right to take in flank the French charging the right battle.

[1] Quoted by Oman, *A History of the Art of War*, etc., vol. I, p. 143.
[2] Froissart, vol. I, p. 166.   [3] *Ibid.*, vol. I, p. 166.   [4] *Ibid.*, vol. I, p. 167.

And as the French were repulsed, Philip came up with the third French battle, but only to add to the confusion.

From first to last the English counted fifteen separate and successive assaults made against them, the last ones taking place in the night. Throughout the battle the French had no concerted plan; for each band of knights had but one idea, to close with its enemy; hence, from first to last, the inextricable confusion.

There was no question of a pursuit. Edward kept his men under arms on the battlefield and at dawn next day, when the levies of Beauvais and Rouen, unaware that the battle had been lost, came up, he easily routed them. Meanwhile Philip, who had been wounded in the neck by an arrow and had had a horse shot under him, was persuaded by John Count of Hainault to leave the field. He rode to the castle of Broye, where he halted until midnight to refresh himself, and then remounted and rode on to Amiens, where he arrived about daybreak.

When, on the morning of August 27, the last of the French had been driven away, Edward allowed his men to break their ranks and strip the dead. It was then found that among the slain were the King of Bohemia, the Duke of Lorraine and the Counts of Flanders, Alençon, Auxerre, Harcourt, Sancerre, Blois, Grandpré, Salm, Blamont, and Forez, as well as 1,542 knights and esquires. Of the French common soldiery the number of killed varies from 10,000 upwards. The English casualties, as reported, were minute: two knights, one esquire, some forty men-at-arms and archers, and a few dozen Welsh.[1]

On Monday, August 28, Edward advanced from Crécy to Montreuil, and from there by easy stages he moved on Calais, outside the walls of which he arrived on September 4.

Enclosed as the fortress was by a double wall with wet ditches, it could not be stormed; therefore Edward set about to invest it on its landward side, and, as he was master of the Channel, to blockade it on its seaward: hence, unless it could be relieved, its doom was sealed. But Philip, it would appear, was so stunned by his defeat that for six months he did nothing, and to add to his moral collapse, on October 17, 1346, King David of Scotland, who to support him had invaded England and had advanced to Durham, was defeated decisively and captured at Neville's Cross. Not until June, 1347, did the Duke of Normandy appear on the field, and on July 27 he approached Calais. But he found Edward's position

---

[1] These figures are quite unreliable.

too strong to attack; six days later he retired, and on August 4, Jean de Vienne surrendered the fortress. On September 28 a truce between all the allies of both sides was signed to last until July 9, 1348, and on October 12 Edward returned to England.

Calais was the sole strategic gain of the campaign, and as events were to prove, the sole English gain of the whole of the Hundred Years War. It was certainly an important one, as much so as Gibraltar was to be to England in years to come. Edward converted it into an all but impregnable *place d'armes* as well as into a highly profitable commercial centre; for he ordered that no merchandise was to be exported from England to the Continent except by way of Calais. Not only did the fortress provide him and his successors with a bridgehead in France, but as General Wrottesley points out, as long as it was firmly held no invasion of England was possible before the invention of the steamship.[1] For over two hundred years it remained in English hands, and not until it was lost to the Duke of Guise on January 8, 1558, did a serious threat of invasion arise, to materialize thirty years later in the coming of the Spanish Armada.

But the most pronounced influence of Crécy on the war was that it made the English a military nation. Henceforth England's fighting prestige was held so high that it had to be maintained by the English. As Sir Charles Oman says, the English victories over the Welsh and Scots had hardly been noticed on the Continent, and their French wars under Henry III and Edward I "had brought them little glory".[2] But Crécy was a revelation, not only to the French, but to the English also: the former were stunned and the latter inebriated by it. Thus its importance in history is that it morally founded the Hundred Years War, a conflict which was to endure until another moral *débâcle* was to precipitate its close.

[1] "Crecy and Calais", Major-General the Hon. George Wrottesley (*Collections for a History of Staffordshire*, 1897), vol. XVIII, p. 57.
[2] *A History of the Art of War*, etc., vol. II, p. 146.

# The dissolution of the Middle Ages

The hundred years which followed the battle of Crécy witnessed the dissolution of the Middle Ages and the emergence of the Renaissance, and of the several causes two of the most important were the Black Death and the discovery of gunpowder.

The former, which was probably bubonic plague, came out of the East in 1347 and recurred at intervals throughout the second half of the fourteenth century. According to Hecker it carried off a quarter of the population of Europe. Its influences on society were catastrophic. Not only were people disorganized and demoralized by death, but barbarized. Witchcraft and sorcery were stimulated; waves of mysticism and doubt swept Europe, and the medieval system of tillage was disrupted by the dearth of labour. This led to an increased demand for hired service and the rapid extinction of the villeinage: the bondage of money replaced the bondage of the soil.

According to Colonel Hime (*The Origin of Artillery*, 1915), the first receipt for the manufacture of gunpowder is to be discovered in Roger Bacon's (1214–1292) *Epistolae de Secretis Operibus Artus et Naturae et de Nullitate Magiae*, written before 1249. But there is nothing in his writings to suggest that he ever contemplated its use in firearms, and who first thought of propelling a ball through a metal tube by exploding gunpowder is unknown.

Apparently the earliest extant document that mentions cannon is one in Arabic, dated 1304. Of others, two belong to the city of Ghent, dated 1313 and 1314 respectively; also in an illuminated MS. of 1326, now in Christ Church, Oxford, there is a picture of the earliest form of cannon, a "dart-throwing vase", also called a "*pot-de-fer*". This primitive weapon appears to have been used in the siege of Metz in 1324, and by Edward III in Scotland in 1327.

According to Sir Charles Oman, in 1339 the first mention is made of another firearm, called *ribauldequin*, a primitive mitrailleuse of several small iron tubes so arranged that they could be fired simultaneously. This weapon was used by Edward III in his war with France, and in 1387 one of 144 barrels was made, the barrels grouped in batteries of twelve apiece, allowing twelve salvoes of twelve balls each.

When one considers the crudeness of fourteenth-century mechanics and the religious restrictions of the age, progress in firearms was rapid. In 1340 we hear of powder mills in Augsburg, and if, in 1346, Edward III did not make use of cannon at Crécy –as some doubt–that year they are known to have been used at the siege of Calais.

By 1391 iron shot are met with, for mention is made of 928 stored in the arsenal of Bologna. Before the century was out progress had so far advanced that it was possible to build bombards of a calibre of twenty-five inches, such as the still existing *Dulle Griete* of Ghent. About this time the hand-gun, first heard of in 1364, was adopted more generally. It resembled a small cannon on a straight stock, which could be carried and fired by a single man. It weighed about ten pounds, was fired by applying a match to a touch-hole, and its bullet was of lead. Usually it was fired from behind defences, and indifferent infantry were armed with it.

Toward the end of the fifteenth century the hand-gun gave way to the match-lock, an iron barrel mounted on a stock which fitted against the chest. It was provided with a cock to hold the match and a trigger to bring it down on to a pan containing the priming. This weapon appears to have been a German invention. It was called *hakenbüsche*, in France *arquebuse*, and in England sometimes "caliver". It was the first true infantry firearm.

With the discovery of gunpowder war passed into its techno-logical phase. Valour gave way to mechanical art: he who could wield the superior weapon was the more formidable foe, irrespec-tive of his social status or his courage. For as Carlyle has said, the genuine use of gunpowder is "that it makes all men alike tall". In short, it democratizes fighting.

Thus, by changing the character of war, gunpowder changed the medieval (Christian) way of life. The search for the perfection of firearms and of defence against them gave birth to a spirit of inquiry which soon embraced all things. It was gunpowder more than contact with Islam during the crusades which gave life to the Renaissance, because it shattered the medieval order physic-ally and morally. War as a trial of moral values by battle, in which the Church refereed for God, gradually gave way to a new certainty: that war is a means toward a political end in which the deciding factor is power. As war was secularized, peace followed suit, idealism gave way to realism, and by the end of the fifteenth century we find such noted soldiers as the condottieri Gian Paolo Vitelli and Prospero Colonna declaring that "wars are won rather by industry and cunning than by the actual clash of arms". Gunpowder blasted the feudal strongholds and the ideals of their owners. As portable firearms multiplied, the medieval contempt for unmounted troops was undermined, until in tactical importance foot soldiers were raised to the level of the mounted men-at-arms.

Though these changes did not begin to take visible shape until the close of the Hundred Years War, those that resulted from the Black Death and its recurrences in no way sobered the rivalries of England and France, and in spite of the efforts of the pope to convert the successive truces which followed the occupation of Calais into a permanent peace, war broke out again in 1355. That year, Edward Prince of Wales, later to be known as the "Black Prince", set out to ravage Languedoc. Meanwhile Philip VI had died on August 22, 1350, and his son and heir, John Duke of Normandy, now John II of France, set out to oppose the Black Prince. On September 17, 1356, at the head of a superior army, he met him near Maupertuis in present-day Vienne, and on the field of Poitiers was defeated decisively and captured, and the Truce of Bordeaux was agreed. Bereft of its king, France was paralysed, and a peasants' revolt, known as the Jacquerie, followed in 1358. Retribution was swift, for within a few weeks of its outbreak the rising was suppressed brutally by the French nobility.

In March, 1359, John, in order to regain his liberty, agreed to abandon to Edward all the west of France from Guienne to Calais, but when nothing came of this war broke out again, and in the spring of 1360 Edward appeared before Paris. As he did not know what next to do, he decided to listen to the papal legate, who was urging him to make peace. The outcome was the Convention of Brétigny and the Treaty of Calais; the latter was signed on October 24. According to its terms Normandy was assigned to France and a vastly enlarged Aquitaine to England, as well as Calais and Ponthieu; John agreed to purchase his liberty at a ransom of 3,000,000 gold crowns, and Edward agreed to renounce the title of king of France.

The relief of the French was immense, but no sooner were the armies disbanded than France became prey to bands of unemployed soldiers, known as "Companies". To rid himself of them, Charles V, who in April, 1364, succeeded John II, gave the task to Bertrand du Guesclin, a rough and stubborn soldier who had gained great renown in Brittany. He collected the Companies and crossed the Pyrenees to support Don Henry of Castile against Don Peter the Cruel, who was being aided by the Black Prince, and in the warring which followed the Companies were largely exterminated.

Once rid of this internal pest, Charles prepared to reverse the Treaty of Calais. First, he established law and order within his kingdom; next he reformed the army, extending the use of the bow, raising artillery, and partly re-walling Paris and other towns. Also he reorganized the royal navy under Jean de Vienne. In diplomacy he took a step which was to have prodigious consequences. In 1369 he arranged the marriage of his brother Philip the Bold, Duke of Burgundy, with Margaret, daughter and heiress of Louis de Male, Count of Flanders, which brought Flanders under the influence of France.

In 1368 tension again grew acute, and when Charles V supported a revolt against the English in Gascony, Edward III resumed the title of king of France. To meet this challenge Charles made du Guesclin Constable of France. He refused to fight pitched battles, relied on attrition to exhaust his enemy, and reconquered Poitou and Brittany. These conquests led to yet another truce in 1375, which was soon followed by the death of the main participants in the war. The Black Prince died in June, 1376, Edward in June, 1377, du Guesclin in July, 1380, and Charles in the September following, by which date the English territories in France had in the north shrunk to Calais, Cherbourg, and Brest, and in the south to Aquitaine, but barely as extensive as it had been in 1336. France, though ravaged, was centrally stronger, and in the struggle national sentiment had become self-conscious.

Nevertheless, largely because of the minorities of Richard II (1377–1400), son of the Black Prince, and of Charles VI (1380–1422), son of Charles V – the one was thirteen and the other twelve years old and of unbalanced mind – both countries became prey to factions and revolts. In June, 1381, in England the peasants revolted under Wat Tyler, and in the following year disturbances occurred in Paris and Flanders. In the latter, Louis de Male called in Philip the Bold of Burgundy, who ruthlessly suppressed the Flemings at Roosebeke on November 27, 1382.

In 1384, Louis de Male died, and Philip the Bold, through his wife, became count of Flanders. At the time, because Charles VI had become insane, Burgundy was the leading power in France, and to put a stop to English intervention in Flanders, in 1395 Philip arranged the marriage of Richard II with Charles VI's daughter Isabella, a child of seven. At the betrothal on March 12, 1396, the truce was prolonged for twenty-eight years. With the end of war in France, regular armies of French knights left for the East to fight the Turks, and John the Fearless, son of the Duke of Burgundy, at the head of one of these armies, was disastrously defeated on September 28, 1395, at Nicopolis (Nicopoli) on the Danube.

Meanwhile the growing rivalry between Philip the Bold and Louis Duke of Orléans, Charles VI's youngest brother, was further stimulated by the Great Schism (1378–1417), which divided the Church into two hostile camps. In 1367, Urban V, to avoid the bands of brigands then roaming southern France, returned to Rome. He died in 1370 and was succeeded by Gregory XI, who, in 1376, abandoned Avignon altogether for Rome. When, in 1378, he was succeeded by Urban VI, under French influence the cardinals objected to him and elected Robert of Geneva as anti-pope, who assumed the style of Clement VII.[1] France, Scotland, Savoy, Castile, and Aragon were Clementine, and England, Bohemia, Hungary, and Portugal Urbanist. Thus each side had its own pope, which rendered a renewal of the conflict all the more certain.

In 1389, Urban VI died and was succeeded by Boniface IX, and Clement VII, who died in 1394, was followed by a Spaniard under the title of Benedict XIII. Because no means could be found to end the schism, which shocked all Europe, in 1398 the University of Paris and the Burgundian party in France withdrew their obedience from both popes. The Duke of Orléans then championed Benedict and, in 1403, effected the restoration to him of the obedience of the French crown.

During this same period violent changes were occurring in England, where Lollardy, established by John Wycliffe (1324–1384), was ploughing the ground for the Reformation. From England his teaching spread to Bohemia, a country noted for its puritan heresies. Influencing John Huss (1369–1415), it helped to stimulate the ferocious Hussite Wars (1419–1436) in which, under

[1] Not to be confused with Clement VII (Giulio de' Medici), 1523–1534.

Ziska, the *Wagenburg*, or wagon fortress equipped with artillery, played a decisive part in his victory at Deutschbrod in 1422, and after his death, at Aussig in 1426 and Taus in 1431. These wars carried fire and sword into the heart of the empire, already weakened by the wars of emancipation of the Swiss which had started in 1307 with the League of the three Forest Cantons, and which gave rise to the growth of a new and formidable democratic infantry mainly composed of pikemen, who defeated the Habsburg feudal levies at Morgarten in 1315, Sempach in 1385, and Näfels in 1388. "After this achievement", remarks Colonel Lloyd in his *A Review of the History of Infantry*, ". . . it was idle to say that the wearing of armour and the use of weapons was reserved by God and nature for persons of quality."

When in April, 1404, John the Fearless succeeded his father Philip the Bold, France, sunk in corruption, was in the hands of the Duke of Orléans. John denounced the Orleanist government, seized Paris, and though a public reconciliation between the two dukes followed it in no way damped the antagonism of their adherents, and on the night of November 24, 1407, the Duke of Orléans was assassinated. For France it was a fatal blow; it split the French into two violent factions—the Burgundians and the Orleanists, or Armagnacs as they were called. Though fearful excesses at once followed, it was not until 1411 that civil war began in earnest, when, to reinforce their respective sides, each party called in the English to its aid; the Armagnacs in 1412 offered Henry IV, son of John of Gaunt, who had ousted Richard II in 1399, the whole of ancient Aquitaine for his support. Nothing came of this offer because on March 20, 1413, Henry IV died and the crown passed to his son Henry V, born in August, 1387.

Henry V was a man of unlimited ambition, and instead of realizing that peace abroad was needed in order firmly to establish the Lancaster dynasty at home, he forthwith decided to take advantage of the division in France and to revive Edward III's claim to the French throne. In order to accomplish this end, in May, 1413, he entered into an alliance with the Duke of Burgundy, the terms being that, while John remained neutral, he would set out to conquer France and if successful would recompense John with territories for which he would do liege homage to him as king of France.

Henry assembled an army some 6,000 strong at Southampton, and on August 13, 1415, landed it near the mouth of the Seine and

besieged Harfleur, which capitulated on September 22. Next he
set out for Calais, crossed the Somme, and at Agincourt came
face to face with a French army recruited almost exclusively from
the Armagnac faction. It was commanded by the Constable
Charles d'Albret, the Dukes of Orléans, Bourbon, Alençon and
Bar and Marshal Boucicaut. On October 24 the battle of Agincourt was fought, to end, like Crécy and Poitiers, in a total
French defeat. Many notable Frenchmen were killed, including
the Constable, three dukes, and seven counts, also many, among
whom was the Duke of Orléans, were taken prisoner. From Agincourt Henry marched to Calais and from there returned to
England.

Though, at the time, the Emperor Sigismund was anxious to
unite all Europe against the Turks, and attempted to mediate
between Henry and Charles, the former would accept nothing less
than the full terms of the treaty of Calais, and when this was refused, in August, 1417, he landed at Trouville. Henry's intention
was to make a systematic conquest of the whole of Normandy, and
by the end of 1419 he accomplished it with the exception of the
island fortress of Mount St. Michael.

Meanwhile Paris was betrayed to the Burgundians, and John
began to play fast and loose between Henry and Charles. Negotiations with the latter led to a meeting between John and the
dauphin on the bridge of Montereau on September 10, 1419, and
in a heated argument, during which the dauphin withdrew, some
of his followers fell upon John and assassinated him.

In the ourburst of fury which followed the murder, Philip, the
new Duke of Burgundy, opened negotiations with Henry, and on
May 21, 1420, a treaty was agreed and signed at Troyes, according
to which Henry was to marry Charles VI's daughter Catherine;
Charles VI was to disown his son the dauphin (presumably as a
bastard) and to declare Henry his heir to the French crown. Meanwhile, during Charles's life, Henry was to retain Normandy and
his other conquests and to share the government of France with
the Duke of Burgundy.

On June 2, 1420, Henry married Catherine, but her disinherited
brother had still to be reckoned with. He rallied Languedoc and
in May, 1421, Charles won a success at Beaugé which brought the
Duke of Brittany to his side. This brought Henry back to France,
but in the spring of the following year he fell seriously ill and died
at Bois Vincennes on August 31, leaving as heir a son nine

months old – Henry VI. When he was dying, he begged his brother and uncle never to make peace without at least ensuring the retention of Normandy. Charles VI was also approaching his end. In September he came to Paris, fell sick and died there on October 21. The Duke of Bedford, brother of Henry V and regent for Henry VI, was the only prince who accompanied his body to Saint-Denis. There, under the vaulted roof of the old abbey, rang out the cry of the King of Arms: "God grant long life to Henry, by the Grace of God King of France and England, our Sovereign Lord."

# CHAPTER 17

# The raising of the siege of Orléans, 1429

The iniquity of the Treaty of Troyes roused French patriotism, and when, ten days after his father's death, the dauphin had himself proclaimed Charles VII, King of France, had he possessed but a modicum of courage his court at Bourges would at once have become the centre of a great movement of liberation. Throughout the provinces occupied by the English insecurity reigned, and in Normandy, which was inadequately garrisoned by them, resistance dropped social distinctions and many nobles, monks, townsmen, and peasants merged with the partisans. All that was lacking to detonate a national revolt was the spark of leadership.

But Charles was both a weak king and a degenerate, and unable to count upon the support of anyone except his Armagnac captains, who were little better than brigand chiefs, for his more extended campaigns he had to rely on foreign mercenaries–men equally brutal–notably the Scots under Archibald, Earl of Douglas, and John Stuart, Earl of Buchan who, in 1421, became Constable of France. Incapable of giving a lead, instead of supporting the partisans, Charles allowed military operations to meander on, and with disastrous results. On July 30, 1423, the English and Burgundians, who had joined forces at Auxerre, beat his Scottish and Armagnac supporters at Cravant. Worse was to follow, for on August 17, 1424, the Duke of Bedford inflicted a terrible defeat, as disastrous as Agincourt, on another of his armies, commanded by the Duke of Alençon, Marshal de la Fayette, the Constable Buchan, the Duke of Touraine (Earl of Douglas) and others, at Verneuil, in which the first two leaders were captured. Nevertheless the English losses were heavy, and with his hands full in Normandy, Bedford could ill afford them.

Because of the disaster of Verneuil the Duchess of Anjou, Charles VII's mother-in-law, sought an alliance with John V, Duke of Brittany, which, in 1425, led to the duke's brother Arthur, Earl of Richemont (or Richmond), coming to Bourges, where he was appointed Constable of France. Richemont's aim was to secure Brittany by compelling Charles to come to terms with the

Duke of Burgundy, and as a step in this direction he caused the assassination of two of Charles's favourites and imposed upon Charles one of his own choice, an adventurer named George de la Trémoille, who rapidly set out to usurp his benefactor's powers.

In consequence of the changed attitude of Brittany, in January, 1426, Bedford declared war on John V, and de Richemont hastened to his brother's assistance; but on March 6 he was routed at Saint James (south of Avranches), a defeat which compelled John to come to heel, which he did on July 3 by promising to abide by the Treaty of Troyes. Meanwhile the Earls of Suffolk and Warwick had laid siege to Montargis (east of Orléans), and when they got into difficulties the Earl of Salisbury was sent to England to press for reinforcements. At the same time the quarrel between de Richemont and la Trémoille paralysed the national party in France, and Lord Talbot (later the Earl of Shrewsbury), took Laval in Maine.

Toward the end of 1427 de Richemont was dismissed, and as this made Charles weaker than ever, Salisbury was given 450 men-at-arms and 2,200 archers, and late in January, 1428, he returned to France. After he had recruited further forces he was ordered to lay siege to Angers, because Bedford had decided to conquer Anjou as an appanage for himself. He set out from west of Paris, and when in the neighbourhood of Chartres, much to the annoyance of Bedford, the Anglo-Burgundian Council instructed Salisbury to gain the crossing of the Loire at Orléans, in order to strike at Berry, the heart of Charles's kingdom.

Salisbury, now at the head of between 4,000 and 5,000 men, pressed on from Chartres, first occupied Meung, Beaugency, and Jargeau on the Loire, and, on October 12, took up a position on its left bank immediately south of Orléans. Among his subordinates were the Earl of Suffolk and his brother, Lord de Ros and Lord Scales, Sir Lancelot de Lisle, and Sir William Glasdale.

Orléans was a populous city and one of the strongest fortresses in France. In shape it was a quadrilateral; its western, northern, and eastern sides were strongly walled and moated, and its southern rested on the Loire, which was spanned by a bridge that connected the city with the suburb of Portereau. At the far end of the bridge stood a twin-towered masonry work called the "Bastille des Tourelles", beyond which lay the Monastery of the Augustins, also fortified, and, at the time, between the two the

Orleanists were engaged upon building a work *"faict de fagotz et de terre"*,[1] called the "Boulevard (or Boulevart) des Tourelles". This work was linked to the bastille by a drawbridge across a water moat.

The city walls were well defended by numerous catapults and seventy-one large cannon, without counting some small culverins,[2] and before the siege opened all food had been collected to be shared in common. Whoever in the surrounding country was willing to help in the defence was promised free rations, an inducement which made many partisans tender their services. The governor of Orléans was the Sire Raoul de Goncourt, and its defence was entrusted to the Bastard of Orléans, later Count of Dunois, a natural son of Louis the assassinated Duke of Orléans, whose legitimate son, the reigning duke, was at this time a captive in England.

Salisbury's plan was first to gain the Tourelles, in order to cut Orléans off from the south, and next to transfer his army to the right bank of the Loire and to invest the city. On his approach, the Orleanists abandoned the Augustins, set fire to Pontereau and withdrew into the unfinished boulevard which, on October 21, Salisbury attempted to storm, but failed. Next day an arch of the bridge was broken, and the boulevard having been mined, on October 23 the pit props were fired and its defenders withdrew to the bastille. On the following day this was stormed by the English, who at once established a battery in the Tourelles. That same evening Salisbury looked out of one of its windows and was mortally wounded by a splinter of a stone cannon shot, and died on October 27.

The Earl of Suffolk succeeded to the vacant command, and a pause in operations followed, during which the bulk of the army went into winter quarters at Jargeau, Meung, Beaugency, and Paris. On Christmas Day a six-hour truce was agreed,[3] and on December 30 the army returned. On the following day, in order to celebrate the event a tourney was held between two French and two English champions, *"Pour lesquelz regarder avoit assez prez d'eulx plusiers seigneurs, tant de France comme d'Angleterre".*[4]

With the opening of the new year – 1429 – Suffolk carried the

[1] *Journal du Siège d'Orléans, 1428–1429*, edit. Paul Charpentier et Charles Cuissard (1896), p. 5.
[2] Throughout the siege cannon played a dominant part, moral more than material, which may be learnt from the *Journal*, see in particular pp. 4, 5, 26, and 29.
[3] *Journal du Siège d'Orléans*, p. 17.                    [4] *Ibid.*, p. 21.

bulk of his army over the Loire, and, in order to blockade the city, he built seven forts, or bastilles, on its main northern approaches, four already having been built south of Orléans.[1] But through lack of men, the blockade on the eastern side of the city was never completed, with the result that a trickle of supplies reached Orléans,[2] but it was not sufficient to guarantee its citizens against starvation.

Early in February the defenders became so pinched for food that their sole chance of deliverance lay in Charles's army intercepting Suffolk's supply convoys, and thereby forcing him to raise the siege. An attempt to do so was made on February 12, when a convoy of 300 wagons carrying "herying and lenten stuffe", under command of Sir John Fastolf, was attacked at Rouvray, a few miles north of Orléans. Forthwith Fastolf drew up his wagons in laager, fought a typical Hussite action, and routed the French in what is known as the "Battle of the Herrings".[3]

By now Orléans had become the symbol of French resistance, the one hope of all true Frenchmen; nevertheless, at the time la Trémoille and de Richemont were engaged in a private war of their own, and the situation in the city grew so desperate that an appeal was made to the Duke of Burgundy to take the city over as neutral territory on behalf of its captive duke. But Bedford would not listen to this, and Charles, when he learnt of the failure of the negotiations, was advised by his courtiers to abandon France and to seek refuge in Dauphiné, Castile, or Scotland.[4] But the situation was not as dark as it looked. Everywhere the peasants were rising against the English, whose strength was due almost entirely to the inertia of the French. All that was lacking was a leader, and at this moment, unexpectedly, one was making ready to appear, a girl of seventeen, Jeanne d'Arc.[5]

The story of Joan of Arc is one of the most extraordinary in all history and one of the best documented. Though she did not

---

[1] In *L'Armée Anglaise Vancue par Jeanne D'Arc sous les Murs D'Orléans*, Boucher de Molandon (1892), p. 149, sixty bastilles in all are mentioned, but many were very small works.

[2] See *Journal du Siège d'Orléans*, in particular pp. 22, 25, 27, 53, and 56.

[3] See *L'Art Militaire et les Armées au Moyen Age*, Ferdinand Lot (1946), vol. II, pp. 47–53.

[4] Lavisse's *Histoire de France* (1902), vol. IV, pt. II, p. 47.

[5] D'Arc seems to have been a *soubriquet* personal to her father; for at the time of her trial she could give no surname (*Procès*, Quicherat, vol. I, p. 46). "To the world of her own time, English as well as French, she was essentially a mysterious nameless being, La Pucelle de Dieu, *The Maid of God*" (*Lancaster and York*, Sir James H. Ramsay, 1892, vol. I, p. 388).

know her age,[1] the probability is that she was born early in 1412 at Domrémy in the duchy of Bar on the border of Lorraine, near the town of Vaucouleurs, an Armagnac outpost which in 1429 was commanded by Robert of Baudricourt. Her parents were peasant folk.

When Joan was thirteen years old, voices,[2] unheard by others and accompanied by a cloud of brilliant light, bade her go to de Baudricourt, who would provide her with the means to travel to the king's court at Chinon. She was to inform Charles that she had been sent by God to raise the siege of Orléans and to lead him to Rheims to be consecrated king of France. She paid three visits to Vaucouleurs, and on the third de Baudricourt agreed to provide her with a horse and an escort of six soldiers. So she cut her hair short, changed her peasant's gown for male attire,[3] and, on February 13, 1429, set out on a 300 mile ride to Chinon, where she arrived on February 23.

On her arrival, la Trémoille was hostile to her; but in spite of his influence, in a secret conversation she convinced Charles (always to her "*gentil dauphin*" until his consecration) of his legitimacy and of her divine mission.[4] Next, after she had been examined at Poitiers by theologians and the Queen of Sicily, who vouched for her orthodoxy and virginity, she was given the style of *Chef de Guerre*, and on April 27, dressed in full armour and carrying a banner on which was blazoned "*Jhesus Maria*", she set out for Orléans at the head of three to four thousand men and a convoy of supplies. With her rode the Duke of Alençon, recently returned from captivity and to her always "*mon beau duc*"; Etienne de Vignolles (La Hire); Marshal de Sainte-Sévère and Marshal Gilles de Rais; Louis de Culen, Admiral of France; and Ambroise de Loré.

Meanwhile her fame had spread far and wide, her faith in her divine mission inspired the French with faith in victory. Equally important for France, her fame had already begun to terrify the English, to whom, before setting out from Blois, she had addressed a letter saying:

[1] *Procès de Condamnation et de Réhabilitation de Jeanne D'Arc dite La Pucelle*, Jules Quicherat (1849), vol. I, p. 51. (For French translation of the Latin sections, see *Procès de Condamnation de Jeanne d'Arc: Traduction avec Eclaircissements*, Joseph Fabre.)

[2] Soon after, the Archangel Michael, St. Margaret, and St. Catherine appeared to her in bodily form in a cloud of heavenly light and addressed her as "*Jehanne la Pucelle, fille de Dieu*". Clouds, wheels, and flames of light are common phenomena with mystics, and with Yogis are experienced in the state of *Dhyâna*.

[3] This played an important part in her trial. For her reasons for assuming man's attire see "Chronique de la Pucelle", *Procès*, Quicherat, vol. IV, p. 211.

[4] See *Histoire de Charles VII*, G. de Fresne de Beaucourt (1882), vol. II, pp. 208–210.

*"Roy d'Angleterre, et vous duc de Bethfort (Bedford) . . . rendés a la Pucelle cy envoiee de par Dieu le roy du ciel, les clefs de toutes les bonnes villes que vous avés prises et violées en France . . . alés vous an, de par Dieu, en vous païs; et se ainssi ne le faictes, attendés lez nouvelles de la Pucelle qui vous ira veoir briefment a vostre bien grant domaige. Roy d'Angleterre, se ainssi ne le faites, je suis chief de guerre, et en quelque lieu que je attaindré vous gens en France, je lez en feray aller, veulhent ou non veulhent, et se ilz ne veullent obéir, je lez prandray à mercy. Je suis cy venue de par Dieu, le roy du ciel, corps pour corps pour vous bouter hors de toute France. . . ."*[1]

When, on April 27, the convoy and its escort set out from Blois, Joan's "voices" had directed that Orléans was to be entered from the north through the district of la Beauce; therefore it in no way concerned her that an advance in this direction would bring her up against the strongest section of the English defences. But her companions thought differently, and with the concurrence of the Bastard of Orléans, quietly they led the army south of the Loire through the district of Sologne,[2] and seemingly, at the time, Joan was in far too ecstatic a state to notice the change.

That night the army bivouacked in the fields, and when it moved on next morning it encamped opposite the Grande île aux Bœufs. It was only then that Joan became aware that she was on the south bank of the Loire, and growing very angry she accused her companions of having tricked her. Meanwhile the Bastard of Orléans had heard of her approach and had crossed the river to greet her. When he met Joan, who was no respecter of persons (he was first cousin of the king), the following conversation took place:

" 'Are you the Bastard of Orléans?' asked Joan. 'Yes, I replied, and I rejoice at your arrival.' – 'Is it you who advised that I should come here, on this side of the river, and that I was not to go straight on to where Talbot and the other English are?' – 'I told her that I and the wisest among us advised what had been done, believing it to be the best.' – '*En nom Dieu*,' replied Jeanne, 'the advice of the Lord is more certain and wise than yours. You thought to deceive me, but you have deceived yourselves; for I bring you the greatest help that has ever been brought to knight or city, seeing that it is the help of the King of Heaven. . . .' "[3]

Next, Joan demanded that an attack should be made forthwith

---

[1] *Procès*, Quicherat, vol. v, pp. 96–97.
[2] *Journal du Siège d'Orléans*, p. 74.
[3] *Procès*, Quicherat, vol. III, pp. 5–6. In "Chronique de la Pucelle" (*Procès*, Quicherat, vol. IV, p. 218) a slightly differently worded version is given.

on Saint Jean le Blanc, the nearest English bastille on the south side of the river; but her companions protested and the convoy was directed to Pont de Saint Loup, where the Bastard had assembled a flotilla of river craft. With 200 lances Joan boarded the boats while the army stood by. But the wind was blowing from the north-east and it was found impossible to sail. This caused great anxiety, for night was closing in; nevertheless, all Joan said was: "*Attendez un petit, car, en nom Dieu, tout entrera en la ville.*"[1] Immediately the wind veered round, the sails filled and the boats stood out up the Loire. This "miracle" sent her followers' confidence in her bounding into the infinite. The attention of the English in the Bastille de Saint Loup had been distracted by a French attack and its garrison prevented from obstructing the unloading of the flotilla on the north bank of the Loire. From there Joan rode on to Reuilly, near Crécy, where she spent the night.

On April 29 the bulk of Joan's army set out on its return march to Blois. It had previously been arranged with her – apparently in order that her divine instructions might be obeyed to the letter – that at Blois the army should cross the river and by moving through la Beauce advance on Orléans from the north, as Joan had intended originally. At eight o'clock that evening, armed *cap à pie*, riding a white horse and with her banner borne before her, Joan entered Orléans and was met by the Bastard and a great gathering of notables, soldiers, and citizens carrying torches "*et faisans autel joye comme se ilz veissent Dieu descentre entre eulx*".[2] They led her through the city to near the Porte Regnart, where lived Jacquet Boucher, treasurer of the Duke of Orléans, in whose house she lodged.

Though no battle had yet been fought, and the English still held their defences in force, the deliverer of France had arrived. She was there in their midst, and morally everything was changed.

On April 30, when la Hire was engaged in a skirmish outside the Bastille Saint Pouair, Joan, ever eager to avoid bloodshed, addressed a letter to Talbot in which she said: "*Messire (the Lord) vous mande que vous en aliez en vostre pays, car c'est son plaisir, ou sinon je vous feray ung tel hahay. . . .*"[3] She received an insulting reply,

---

[1] "Chronique de la Pucelle", *Procès*, Quicherat, vol. IV, p. 218. Joan, it would seem, possessed second sight; there are so many well-authenticated instances of her power to foresee and foretell coming events that they are unlikely all to be apocryphal.

[2] *Journal du Siège d'Orléans*, p. 77.

[3] *Procès*, Quicherat, vol. III, p. 126. *Hahé* in modern French is a hunting cry meaning "ware there!"—halo!

but that evening, *"fort yrée"*, she made another attempt to end hostilities. She went down to the Boulevard de la Belle Croix on the bridge and shouted to William Glasdale, commander of the Tourelles, in the name of God to surrender; to which his men shouted back *"vachère!"* ("cow-girl") and worse, and that they would burn her when they caught her.[1]

The next day the Bastard left Orléans for Blois and Joan and an escort accompanied him part of the way. That these comings and goings were so seldom interfered with was because the English were shut up in their bastilles, which made if difficult for them rapidly to concentrate. So completely were they pinned down in their earth-works that on the following day Joan rode out and reconnoitred them, apparently without any molestation whatever, and, on May 3, the garrisons of Gien and Montargis marched into Orléans. Much the same happened the following day when Joan, at the head of 500 men, rode out, *"à estendart desployé"*, to meet the army and the Bastard on their way back from Blois through la Beauce. Triumphantly, at prime (between 6 and 7 a.m.) she rode with him into Orléans under the noses of the English.

Joan had been up early that day, and on her return she lay down to rest; but while she was asleep, the excitement caused by the return of the army would seem to have been too much for the Orleanists, for at noon a party of them issued from the town and attacked the Bastille de Saint Loup, held by Talbot. Suddenly awakening, she sprang from her bed crying out: *"En nom Dé, mon conseil m'a dit que je voise conotre les Anglois."* Running downstairs, she met her page, Louis de Contes. *"Ha sanglant garson"*, she cried, *"vous ne me dysiez pas que le sanc de France feust repandu."*[2] She ordered him to fetch her horse, was helped into her armour, seized her standard, and mounted and galloped for the Porte de Bourgogne, her horse's hooves striking sparks from the pavement.[3] When near Saint Loup she found that the English had made a sortie from the Bastille Saint Pouair and were attacking in rear the French assaulting Saint Loup. A bloody battle ensued and the Bastille of Saint Loup was stormed and carried; but Talbot effected his escape.

It was an important victory; the capture of Saint Loup opened the road to Jargeau. That evening the bells of Orléans were rung

---

[1] *Journal du Siège d'Orléans*, p. 79.   [2] *Ibid.*, vol. III, p. 68.
[3] *Ibid.*, vol. III, p. 124.

in celebration of the first success gained over the English since the siege began, a carillon "*que Anglois pouvoient bien ouyr (hear); lesquels furent fort abaissez de puissance par ceste partye, et aussi de courage*".[1]

May 5 was Ascension Day and Joan decreed that there should be no fighting; but the day was not wasted, for a council of war[2] was held at which the leaders of the army decided, under cover of a feint attack on the Bastille de Saint Laurent, to assault the bastilles on the southern side of the Loire. When this had been arranged, Joan was called in, and, apparently, as they did not trust her to keep a secret, she was told only of the proposed feint attack. To this, angrily she exclaimed: "*Dites ce que vous avez conclut et appointié. Je celeroie bien plus grant chose que cestre-cy*" ("I shall know how to keep a far greater secret than that").[3] The Bastard then told her everything, after which, still wishing to avert bloodshed, Joan dictated another letter to the English, saying: "The King of Heaven commands and orders you, through me the Pucelle, to abandon your bastilles and return to your own country. Should you fail to do so, I will make such a *hahu* that it will eternally be remembered. This is what I write to you for the third and last time. . . ."[4] Wrapping the message round an arrow, she went down to the bridge, and there picked up a crossbow and shot the arrow into the Tourelles. The English derisively shouted back: "Here comes news from the Armagnac harlot", which reduced Joan to a flood of tears.

On the following morning, a boat bridge was thrown over the Loire from the island of Saint Aignan; but when the French approached the Bastille of Saint Jean le Blanc its garrison withdrew to the Bastille des Augustins. The French judged it too strong to assault and began to retire. Joan and la Hire then came up and to stop the withdrawal couched their lances and charged the English, who meanwhile had sallied out of the Augustins to pursue their enemy. This bold action put new heart into the retiring French, they again advanced and after a stiff fight drove the English out of the Augustins into the Tourelles.

The Augustins was then occupied and Joan returned to Orléans. There, when at supper, a "noble and valliant captain" came to her room and informed her that the council of war had decided

---

[1] "Chronique de le Pucelle", *Procès*, Quicherat, vol. IV, p. 224.

[2] Joan did not and could not attend a council of war, her council was—through her "voices"—with God alone. All directions came from Him, and what the tactical leaders of the army decided was no concern of hers.

[3] *Procès*, Quicherat, vol. IV, p. 59.  [4] *Ibid.*, vol. III, p. 107.

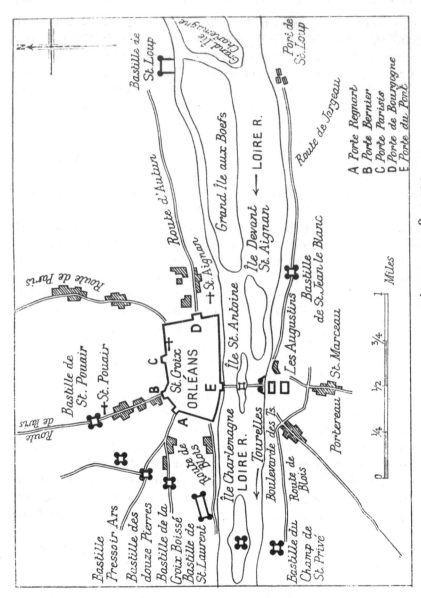

30. SIEGE OF ORLÉANS, 1428–1429

A Porte Regnart
B Porte Bernier
C Porte Parisis
D Porte de Bourgogne
E Porte du Pont

not to renew the attack until further reinforcements had arrived, She said to him: "You have been at your council and I have been at mine. Believe me that the council of the Lord will hold good and be accomplished, and that yours will come to nothing." Next, addressing her confessor, Jean Pasquerel, she said to him: "Rise tomorrow at a very early hour . . . and keep near me throughout the day, for I shall have much to do, more than ever before. Blood will flow from my body above my breast."[1]

For the English, May 7 was the most fatal day of the war; for the French it was the *"Journée des Tourelles"*, still celebrated yearly.

The *tête de pont*, comprising the Bastille and Boulevard des Tourelles, was held by Sir William Glasdale and some 500 soldiers. To the north of it the bridge was still broken and on its south side the Bastille des Augustins was now in French hands, as also were the bastilles Saint Jean le Blanc and Saint Privée, the latter abandoned by the English the previous night. Completely isolated as the *tête de pont* now was, the Bastard, Marshal de Rais, and other commanders were opposed to a direct attack on it. They preferred a siege, but Joan would have none of this, for rightly she sensed that the psychological moment had come: enthusiasm was at its height and the populace ecstatically supported her: she was not to be gainsaid, and it was she who dominated the situation.

Early on May 7 she left Orléans by the Porte de Bourgogne, crossed the Loire and joined the troops at the Augustins. Meanwhile the Tourelles was bombarded from the island of Saint Antoine, and men were set at work to repair the bridge so that access to the *tête de pont* might be gained from the north.

At seven o'clock, according to Percival de Cagny, Joan ordered her trumpets to be sounded as a signal to make ready to assault, and as the cannon began to thunder, with standard in hand she advanced to the edge of the fosse, or ditch, of the boulevard.[2] From all accounts most of the fighting took place in the ditch itself, which was deep, and each attempt made to storm its far side by means of scaling ladders was beaten back: the struggle is epically described in the *Journal*.[3] In one of the assaults Joan was hit between the neck and shoulder by an arrow, which, according to the Bastard, penetrated her flesh to a depth of six inches.[4] Joan pulled the arrow out and went back to have the wound dressed.[5]

---

[1] *Procès*, Quicherat, vol. IV, p. 109.     [2] *Ibid.*, vol. IV, p. 8.
[3] *Journal du Siège d'Orléans*, p. 85.     [4] *Procès*, Quicherat, vol. III, p. 8.
[5] "Chronique de la Pucelle", *Procès*, Quicherat, vol. IV, p. 228.

At once the energy went out of the attack and the Bastard and others suggested to her that it would be as well to abandon further assault until the morrow. She cried out at this: " '*En nom de Dieu*, you will enter the boulevard very soon; have no doubt of it, for the English have less strength than you. Why not rest a little and drink and eat?' *Ce qui'ilz firent, car à merveilles lui obeissoyent.*"[1] Then, says the Bastard, she mounted her horse, and "alone and apart retired to a vineyard to pray for half a quarter of an hour".[2] On her return she found that the soldiers had eaten their hasty meal and ordered them in the name of God to renew the assault; the English, she said, had no longer strength to resist them. This was true, for when they saw her again they "shivered and were seized by a great terror".[3] Rushing forward, the ladders were planted in the fosse, and the boulevard was stormed. When Glasdale and his men sought refuge in the Bastille des Tourelles, Louis le Contes relates, Joan shouted to her companions: "Be of good heart; do not fall back, the bastille will be yours . . . when you see the wind blow the banner toward it."[4] The writer of the *Journal* gives a slightly different version. He says: "Be ready, when the flag-end of my banner touches the boulevard (? bastille)." Soon after a cry arose from the soldiery: "Jehanne, it touches it!" Whereupon she shouted back to them: "All is yours, enter!"[5]

At the same time, the gap in the bridge now repaired, Nicolas de Giresmes, a valiant knight of Rhodes, followed by his men, attacked the Tourelles on its northern side. But the action was brief, for caught between two attacks the English garrison was seized by panic and rushed wildly for the drawbridge connecting the Tourelles with the boulevard. Joan saw Glasdale among the fugitives and cried out: "*Clasdas!* (Glasdale) *Clasdas! rent-ti au Roi des Cieux!* You called me a harlot, but I have pity on your soul and the souls of your men."[6] The bridge gave way at that moment and Glasdale and those following him were precipitated into the river and drowned, "which was a great loss for the valiant French who from their ransoms would have received *grant finance*".[7]

Thus, as night closed, the Tourelles, now on fire, was won, and as the flames shot up, Joan recrossed the Loire to have her wound dressed and to sup on a few slices of bread dipped in wine and

[1] *Journal du Siège d'Orléans*, p. 86.
[3] *Ibid.*, vol. III, p. 8.
[5] *Journal du Siège d'Orléans* , p. 86.
[7] *Journal du Siège d'Orléans*, p. 87.
[2] *Procès*, Quicherat, vol. III, p. 8.
[4] *Ibid.*, vol. III, pp. 70–71.
[6] *Procès*, Quicherat, vol. III, p. 110.

water. The bells of Orléans were ringing out and the people were singing the *Te Deum Laudamus.*

Next morning, Sunday, May 8, the English fired their cantonments on the north side of the Loire, abandoned most of their artillery, and marched away to Meung, Beaugency, and Jargeau.

The news that the siege had been raised thundered through France and across her borders. The English were paralysed; the Duke of Bedford in a letter written some years later to Henry VI, expresses in it the feeling which then prevailed. ". . . there felle, by the hand of God, as it seemeth", he wrote, "a grete strook upon your peuple that was assembled there (at Orléans) in grete numbre, caused in grete partie, as Y trowe, of lakke of sadde beleve (sound faith), and unlevefulle (unbelieving) doubte that thei hadde of a disciple and lyme (limb) of the Feende, called the Pucelle; that used fals enchauntements and sorcerie; the whiche strooke and discomfiture, nought oonly lessed in grete partie the nombre of youre peuple there, but as well withdrowe the courage of the remenant in merveillous wyse; and couraiged youre adverse partie and ennemys to assemble them forthwith in grete nombre".[1]

In spite of this, Charles VII did nothing to exploit Joan's victory; he did not even honour Orléans with a visit, and those around him, especially la Trémoille, feared that the enthusiasm which had stormed the English bastilles might also storm their own positions.

On May 13, Joan met Charles at Tours. Of the two promises she had made to him, the first had now been fulfilled; but as her second had not, she urged Charles at once to proceed to Rheims. But the military leaders rightly saw the danger of plunging into Champagne until the English had been driven from the Loire, and directly the troops had been concentrated, siege was laid to Jargeau and Beaugency. On June 12 the former was taken by Joan and the Duke of Alençon and the Earl of Suffolk and his brother were captured. Immediately after, Joan and her companions marched on Beaugency, which capitulated on June 18.

Meanwhile Lord Talbot and Sir John Fastolf were hurrying south with reinforcements from Paris. When they heard that Jargeau had fallen the latter urged retreat, but Talbot would not, and the army pressed on for Beaugency. When they neared Beaugency and learnt that it was under attack, Talbot marched to Meung to link

---

[1] Quoted from *Lancaster and York,* Sir James H. Ramsay, vol. I, p. 398. See also *Procès,* Quicherat, vol. v, pp. 136-137.

490 THE DECISIVE BATTLES OF THE WESTERN WORLD

up with its garrison. When he arrived he was told that Beaugency had surrendered and he ordered a retreat to Patay.

The prestige of the English in the field was still so high that when, on July 19, the French caught up with Talbot, they hesitated to attack, and the Duke of Alençon asked Joan—who was not on the battlefield—what he should do. In a loud voice she answered: "Make use of your spurs!" Those around her were perplexed. "What say you?" they asked. "Are we to turn our backs on the English?" "No!" replied Joan, "it is the English who are going to turn their backs on us. They will be unable to defend themselves, and you will have need of your good spurs to catch them up."[1]

It was as she said. The English were routed, many were killed, and among the captured were Talbot and Lord Scales.[2]

Coming on the heels of the raising of the siege of Orléans, the moral effect of the victory of Patay was electric. Nothing now could stop Joan from realizing her second call—that Charles should be anointed at Rheims.

On June 29, the king and the army set out from Gien. Joan had gone on in advance and town after town opened its gates to her. Troyes alone offered resistance, and though la Trémoille advised retreat, Joan's prestige was irresistible. Threatened with assault, on July 10 the city capitulated. Then Châlons and Rheims submitted and Charles entered the latter on July 16. Two days later he was anointed, while Joan, in full armour and banner in hand, stood by the altar. She had kept her word; her heavenly voices had been obeyed; the anointment of an unworthy king rather than her martyrdom was her apotheosis.

The moral effect of this coronation cannot be exaggerated. It was the decisive moment, not only in Charles's reign, but in the second half of the Hundred Years War. Of it Professor Perroy says: "Now Charles, whom Joan had hitherto persisted in calling only the Dauphin, was King of France, a new Melchisedec sanctified by the sacrament which bestowed upon him the power of a thaumaturge. Henceforth no believer could doubt who was the legitimate sovereign, since there was now a king crowned in circumstances so incredible that they seemed miraculous. . . . So the coronation annulled the deposition illegally pronounced by

[1] *Procès*, Quicherat, vol. III, pp. 10–11.
[2] For a contemporary account of the battle of Patay see "Prise de Meung et de Beaugency. Battaile de Patay", included in Charpentier's edit. of *Journal du Siège d'Orléans*, pp. 137–140.

the Treaty of Troyes and restored to the Valois the legitimacy which had been questioned for the past nine years. . . . How, moreover, could the Burgundians . . . continue their obedience to Bedford without obvious treason?"[1]

To the people, Joan was now *l'Angelique*; of her, chansons, *"moult merveilleuses"*, were sung throughout the land; many held her to be a saint, some even a magician who could command the winds, and to the English she was a sorceress: to all, she belonged to the supernatural. Bona Visconti asked for her help to regain the duchy of Milan, and the Count of Armagnac sent to ask her whether it was Clement VIII (Aegidius Muñoz) or Martin V who was the true pope.[2] All the Soissonnais, Valois, Senlisien, Beauvaisis, and part of Parisis submitted to Charles as their rightful king. Paris was at his mercy, and the political importance of Paris was so great that to ring in victory from Notre Dame might, then and there, have decided the war. Joan must have sensed this in a mystical way, for she urged an immediate advance on the capital. But Charles remained inert, his only wish was to get back to the quietude of the Loire, and la Trémoille encouraged him, for at the time he was intriguing with the duke of Burgundy over a paltry truce.

Meanwhile Bedford, who feared the defection of Paris, was reinforced, and on August 7 he advanced to Montereau, from where he sent a challenge to Charles, and on August 15 both armies came face to face at Montépilloy. But Bedford dared not attack; for he feared that his army would be demoralized at the sight of Joan's banner.[3] Neither would Charles, the creature of la Trémoille, whose one aim was a reconciliation with Burgundy.

While la Trémoille negotiated at Arras, national feeling swept on; yet, in the words of Sir James Ramsay – a most sober historian –"It was admitted on all hands that a bold, prompt advance into the basin of the Somme would have raised all Picardy and brought the English dominion to a speedy close".[4] Without awaiting the issue of the Arras negotiations Joan left Compiègne on August 23 and occupied Saint Denis. There, reluctantly, Charles followed her on September 7, and two days later, though siege material was lacking, she made an impetuous assault on Paris. When engaged in battle in the fosse outside the Porte Saint Honoré she

---

[1] *The Hundred Years War*, pp. 284–285.
[2] *Procès*, Quicherat, vol. I, p. 245.
[3] *A History of the Art of War in the Middle Ages*, Sir Charles Oman, vol. II, p. 395.
[4] *Lancaster and York*, vol. I, p. 404.

was struck down by a crossbow bolt and borne off the field by the Sire de Goncourt.

Wounded though she was, she ordered a renewal of the assault on the following day; but Charles forbade it, and instead signed a four-month truce with the Duke of Burgundy. Next, she was ordered by Charles to follow him to Berry. So she hung up her armour at Saint Denis, and, on September 21, set out with the army on its return to Gien, "*Et ainssi*", writes Perceval de Cagny, "*fut le vouloir de la Pucelle et l'armée du roy rompue*".[1] At Gien the army was disbanded.

In spite of the truce fighting continued, and Bedford's position became increasingly precarious because his reinforcements shirked service against the *Pucelle de Dieu*. Then, suddenly, the joyous news was received that "the fals wych" had fallen into the hands of the Burgundians.

Unable to bear the inactivity in which la Trémoille sought to keep her, and believing that the only peace possible was one gained at the point of the lance,[2] Joan slipped away from the court of Sully to Melun, and when there, during Easter week 1431, the voices of Saint Catherine and Saint Margaret told her again and again that soon she would be captured; but on what day they did not divulge.[3] In spite of this warning she left Melun for Crépy-en-Valois, and learning that the Duke of Burgundy and the Earl of Arundel were on the north side of the Oise and were about to lay siege to Compiègne, at midnight on May 22–23 she rode to Compiègne, where she arrived at dawn. She rested, then, at about five o'clock in the afternoon of May 23, she rode out to reconnoitre the enemy and in a rearguard action which followed was cut off, unhorsed and captured by soldiers of John of Luxembourg.[4]

Bedford at once saw in her capture a means whereby the moral significance of Charles's coronation could be politically annulled. In order to gain the political initiative—that is, to re-establish the full legality of the boy king Henry VI as king of France—not only was it necessary to crown him king of France, but at the same time to invalidate Charles's crowning. And, as among all Charles's followers, Joan was immeasurably the one responsible for his anointment at Rheims, were she to be condemned by the Inquisition as a heretic and sorceress, in the public eye Charles's corona-

[1] *Procès*, Quicherat, vol. IV, p. 29.       [2] *Ibid.*, vol. I, p. 108.
[3] *Ibid.*, vol. I, p. 115.                    [4] *Ibid.*, vol. I, pp. 116-117.

tion would be utterly discredited. It was an astute plan, and in its accomplishment the first step taken was to buy Joan from the Duke of Burgundy for 10,000 francs, and the second to bring her to Rouen for trial and there to have her condemned as a harlot, a witch and an envoy of the devil. Then, as Edouard Perroy says, Charles would not only be overwhelmed with ridicule, but "his fleeting successes would be put down to an odious liaison between a criminal bastard and a shameless sorceress".[1]

The preliminaries of the trial opened on January 9, 1431; but it was not until February 21 that for the first time Joan was brought before her judges—Pierre Cauchon, Bishop of Beauvais, and Jean Lemaistre, Inquisitor of France—when every available fact in her life was raked up. "I saw well enough", writes Guillaume Manchon, the court recorder, "that they acted more by hate than by any other sentiment. They intended that Jeanne should die."[2] He should have said, "should be convicted".

The main charges were those of heresy and sorcery, and her chief crime was that she had set her revelations above the judgements of the Church. Thus we read: "If the prelates of the Church do not see to it, subversion of the whole authority of the Church may ensue; men and women may rise on every side, pretending to revelations from God and His angels, sowing lies and errors. . . ."[3] And the University of Paris came to the decision that she had so disseminated her poison that it had infected almost the whole of western Christianity.[4]

On May 24 she was broken down by incessant questioning and induced to place her mark on a recantation, which four days later she revoked; her "voices" had by then renewed her strength of mind. At nine o'clock, on the morning of May 29, she was taken to the Old Market Place at Rouen and burnt, and as the flames and smoke smothered her, John Tressart, secretary to the king of England, cried out: "We are lost, for we have burnt a saint."[5] After the burning, her remains were gathered and thrown into the Seine.[6]

Throughout her trial Charles VII made no attempt to save

[1] *The Hundred Years War*, pp. 287–288.
[2] *Procès*, Quicherat, vol. III, p. 138. On the trial Prof. Perroy writes: "These men felt only horror and hatred of the accused. . . . The cruelty of the procedure . . . was simply that of the Inquisition, which was daily applied. . . . There was no vice of form or substance in the trial itself; but, once it had begun, it could end only in conviction" (pp. 288–289).
[3] *Ibid.*, vol. I, p. 317.
[4] *Ibid.*, vol. I, p. 409.
[5] *Ibid.*, vol. II, p. 347.
[6] *Ibid.*, vol. III, p. 182.

her; not even de Beaucourt, his most favourable historian, can find a trace of any such action.[1] Talbot was still in French hands, and had the Duke of Bedford been told that whatever Joan suffered Talbot should suffer, there can be little doubt that she would never have been sent to the stake. For a brief while Joan's death checked the uprising of French nationality and, on December 13, this enabled the English to crown the infant King Henry VI king of France in Notre Dame at Paris.

In 1433 la Trémoille was overthrown, and on September 21, 1435, the twenty-five year feud between the Burgundians and Armagnacs was brought to an end by the Peace of Arras, which caused an explosion of fury in England, for without the support of a continental ally the English dominion in France was doomed. Nevertheless the peace brought few benefits to the French, for when the war with Burgundy ended the country-side was infested with demobilized soldiers, known as *écorcheurs* (flayers), because they stripped their victims to their shirts. The anarchy which now swept France beggars description: murder, pestilence and famine became the order of the day; whole districts were depopulated and the situation grew so desperate that mass migrations from the provinces began to take place.[2] Eventually the exhaustion of both the English and French became such that on April 16, 1444, a truce was agreed at Tours which was to last until 1449.

This breathing space of five years was spent by the French, under the guidance of the Constable de Richemont, in reorganizing the French army with the aim of producing a police force capable of suppressing the *écorcheurs* and *routiers* as well as to provide a standing army ready to engage the English should the truce be broken. It was effected in stages by a series of ordinances, the first of importance being promulgated in 1445. According to this, a general amnesty was granted to all soldiers who had turned brigands, and after the more undesirable had been eliminated,[3] the remainder was formed into fifteen (later twenty) *Compagnies de l'Ordonnance du Roi*, each commanded by a noble chosen for his skill and trustworthiness. The Companies were organized and paid feudal levies, consisting of 100 lances each, each lance comprising one man-at-arms, one *coutilier* to act as squire and,

[1] *Histoire de Charles VII*, vol. ii, pp. 240-255.
[2] See Lavisse's *Histoire de France*, vol. iv, pt. ii, chap. iv.
[3] A considerable number had already been sent under the Dauphin Louis to war in Alsace and Switzerland, where many were exterminated, 2,000 perishing in the battle of St. Jacob on the Birs.

normally, three archers, all mounted. The Companies formed the king's cavalry and were lodged in selected towns, paid for by the provinces and kept under strict discipline.

Under the ordinance of 1448, the *Francs-Archers*, so called because they were exempt from taxation, were instituted as an infantry militia; each group of fifty hearths furnished one archer or cross-bow-man. In all 8,000 were raised, the men selected for their fitness and good characters. Simultaneously, the artillery was reorganized by the brothers Gaspard and Jean Bureau, and thanks to them it soon became the most efficient in Europe.[1]

These reforms not only put an end to the terrible anarchy which had hitherto followed each truce, but it placed a powerful instrument in the hands of the king, by means of which he could both control his barons and meet his foreign enemies. They established the foundations of the standing army system, which was the essential ingredient of a national monarchy.

With this reformed army Charles VII brought the long war to an end, for though Henry VI wanted peace, Charles's advisers wanted war, and an infringement of the truce by one of the English captains presented them with the pretext to set it aside on July 17, 1449.

The English still held Normandy and Guienne, and in the former, because of the hostility of the people, precariously held their own in the walled towns. These the French rapidly reduced by cannon. On April 15, 1450, a decision was reached. At Formigny, near Bayeux, an English army under Sir Thomas Kyriel and Sir Matthew Gough, after it had been disordered by two French culverins (long guns of small calibre) was virtually exterminated by the Count of Clermont and the Constable de Richemont.[2] This disaster was followed by the siege of Bayeux and the occupation of Avranches and Caen, the latter entered by Charles VII on July 6. Siege was next laid to Cherbourg, and after a determined defence it fell to the cannon of the brothers Bureau on August 12. English rule in Normandy was at an end – "And we have not now a foote of londe in Normandy".[3]

The conquest of Guienne was more difficult, for it had been

---

[1] For a full account of these reforms see de Beaucourt's *Histoire de Charles VII*, vol. IV, pp. 387–400.

[2] This disaster was immediately followed by the rising of Jack Cade in England. In vol. VII, pt. I of *Histoire du Moyen Age* (*Histoire Générale*, edit. Gustave Glotz), p. 450, M. Déprez calls Formigny *"un véritable Waterloo"*.

[3] *Paston Letters*, edit. J. Gardner (1872), vol. I, p. 139; August 17.

occupied by the English for 300 years; their rule had been more tolerant there and commercial ties with England were strong. In the spring of 1451 the Count of Dunois (the Bastard of Orléans) led an army of 6,000 men into the duchy. On June 30 he occupied Bordeaux, and on August 20 took Bayonne. In October, 1452, Talbot, Earl of Shrewsbury, then over seventy years of age yet still full of fire, was sent out to retrieve the situation. He disembarked his 3,000 men at a sandy cove, still known as *l'anse à l'Anglot*, in the mouth of the Garonne, the country rose in his favour, and Bordeaux opened its gates to him. In the summer of 1453, at the head of 8,000 Gascons and English, he set out to raise the siege of Castillon. Confronted by entrenchments and the batteries of Jean Bureau, for a full hour on July 17 he assaulted the French, but only to suffer heavy losses from their cannon fire. Finally, he was attacked in flank, and in the rout which followed was wounded, unhorsed and trampled to death. With him perished the last hope of English dominion in France. Bordeaux fell to the French on October 19.

With the fall of Bordeaux, the struggle between France and England, which opened with the battle of Hastings, ended; France became truly French and England truly English. In France, Louis XI (1461–1483) in his wars with Charles the Bold of Burgundy, which were concluded by the death of the latter at the battle of Nancy on January 5, 1477, established the royal control. In England, the Wars of the Roses (1455–1485) killed many of the English feudal nobility, and with the death of Richard III on Bosworth Field on August 22, 1485, the rule of England passed to the first of the Tudors, Henry VII (1485–1509).

Both Louis and Henry were "bourgeois" kings: the feudal age was at an end, the age of business began, and with its advent western history stepped on to the threshold of the modern epoch. Henceforth, though England and France were to remain antagonistic nations, their jousting days were over.

In the long struggle between the battles of Sluys and Castillon the raising of the siege of Orléans was the grand climacteric. Though in the final lap of the war gunpowder played an increasingly important part in bringing English dominion in France to an end, had it not been for the spiritual enthusiasm of Joan of Arc, the course of history would have been different. Her real achievement was not that she freed Orléans and carried war through Champagne to the gates of Paris; but that she freed the

French from their obsession of inevitable defeat. By making Charles VII the idealized champion of France, she gave voice to the soul of France herself. Miserable creature though he was, through her inspiration the monarchy in France became the symbol of victory around which the people mustered. And had she not been handicapped by his invincible inertia and the self-interest of his councillors, "she might", as Sir Charles Oman has said, "have swept the English out of France in her first impetus".[1] But this was not to be. Nevertheless, though taken and martyred, her spirit lived on unconquerable.

"The heroic peasant girl of Lorraine", writes John Payne, ". . . created the French people. Until her time France had been inhabited by Bretons, Angevins, Bourbonnais, Burgundians, Poitevins, Armagnacs; at last the baptism of fire through which the land had passed and the breath of heroism that emanated from the Maid of Orleans had welded together the conflicting sections and had informed them with that breath of patriotism which is the beginning of national life. France had at length become a nation."[2]

That this passing from medieval manhood into early modern adolescence was realized at the time is improbable; for so many of the great changes in world affairs, like seeds buried in the soil, germinate in darkness, and the flowers which blossom from them are more commonly to be plucked in the light of after events. Nevertheless, no sooner did Charles VII feel that victory was within his grasp than he remembered Joan, not in order to see that justice was done to her memory, but because he did not wish to go down to history as the accomplice of a sorceress. In 1450, when he had regained Rouen and with it come into possession of the documents of her trial, he ordered an investigation into the legality of her condemnation. But Pope Nicolas V would have nothing to do with it, because his aim was to bring about a reconciliation between Henry VI and Charles in order to promote a crusade against the Turks, who were then closing in on Constantinople. In 1455, his successor, Calixtus III, who hoped to persuade Charles to march against the Turks, consented to a revision of the trial, and on July 7, 1456, the proceedings of 1431 were declared irregular in constitution and in procedure. Thus Joan was rehabilitated as the *"Pucelle de Dieu"*, a fitting epilogue to the war in which she sacrificed her young life for France.

[1] *A History of the Art of War in the Middle Ages*, vol. II, p. 397.
[2] In his Introduction to *The Poems of Master François Villon of Paris* (1892), p. viii.

# The rise of the Ottoman Empire

The Latin kingdom, wedged between the Bulgars and Serbs in the west and the Greeks of Nicaea and Seljuks of Rum in the east, distracted within by the quarrellings of the Venetians and Genoese and the contentions of the Latin and Greek Churches, could not be other than impermanent. In 1261 its end came; that year Michael Palaeologus, the Greek emperor of Nicaea, won the support of the Genoese against the Venetians and after slight resistance occupied Constantinople on July 25. Immediately following, he was crowned in St. Sophia as Michael VIII (1261–1282), and in greater part Latin rule ceased in Greece. To secure his position, in 1274 he agreed to a union of the Churches, but this did not last long.

Nevertheless the damage done by the Latin occupation was irreparable, and had it not been that the great Mongol invasion of 1256–1260 under Hugalu, grandson of Genghis Khan, had ruined the Seljuk power in Rum, it is highly improbable that the resuscitated Byzantine empire would have lasted even as long as the Latin kingdom. It was during Hugalu's invasion that a tribe of Turks, recently settled in Mesopotamia under a chieftain named Ertughril, trekked into Anatolia, and for services rendered to the Seljuk sultan, was granted a tract of pasture land in the neighbourhood of Eski-Shehr, under a hundred miles east of the Sea of Marmara. In 1281 Ertughril died, and his son Osman or Othman–after whom his tribe became known as the Osmanli or Ottoman Turks–set out to extend his territory. In this his way was eased by anarchy in the empire, where Andronicus III (1320–1341) struggled against the inroads of Bulgars, Serbs, and Tartars, while his Grand Catalan Company tried to dethrone him. Under cover of this anarchy, in 1326 Osman took Brusa, which became the centre of Ottoman operations against Europe. A few months later he died, and was succeeded by his son Orkhan (1326-1359).

Soon Orkhan decided to occupy Nicaea (Iznik) and Nicomedia (Ismid). The former he captured in 1329 and the latter in 1337. after which he reorganized his army and, at the suggestion of the dervish Hajji Bektash, recruited a regiment of Christians, known as janissaries or "new troops". Meanwhile Thrace had again been overrun by the Tartars, and in 1344 the position of the empire was so desperate that, in order to win the neutrality of Orkhan, the Emperor John V, Cantacuzene (1341–1383), gave him his daughter Theodora in marriage. Three years later, when the Serbs, under Stephen Dushan, threatened the existence of the empire, Orkhan sent 6,000 Ottomans into Europe to assist his father-in-law. The Ottomans defeated the Serbs and withdrew, but only to return in 1349, when 20,000 crossed into Europe to drive the Serbs from before Salonica. In 1352, Suleiman, Orkhan's eldest son, led another expedition into Europe and defeated the Serbs in the vicinity of Demotika.

It would seem that the utter inability of the Greeks to defend themselves roused Orkhan's ambitions. Thus far the Turks had crossed into Europe as plunderers, allies or mercenaries, either to pillage or defend the empire or to make profit out of its frequent civil wars. But in 1356 Orkhan decided to send an army under Suleiman to conquer and occupy European territory. Suleiman ferried 30,000 troops from Sestus and in the following year took Adrianople and Demotika. The former was held permanently, and the date of its occupation marks the beginning of the conquest of European territory by the Ottoman Turks.

On the death of Suleiman in 1359, his brother Murad took possession of Adrianople, and two months later, on Orkhan's death, he succeeded to the sultanate as Murad I (1359–1389). He continued his father's policy of conquest, in 1363 came to an agreement with the Genoese to transport 60,000 troops into Thrace, and three years later defeated an army of 50,000 south Serbs which had set out to capture Adrianople. This victory woke Europe to her danger; but though the pope pressed for a crusade, France and England were too occupied in the Hundred Years War to take an active part against the common enemy of Christendom. Murad continued his conquests and on September 26, 1371, he annihilated an army of 70,000 south Serbs under King Vulkasin, at Harmanli, on the Maritza; a defeat which placed the Greeks in so hopeless a position that soon after the Emperor John V was reduced to recognize the sultan as his suzerain.

Many Ottoman successes followed, but when, in 1386, Murad took Nish from the north Serbs, King Lazar Hrebeljanovich, son of Stephen Dushan, formed a Pan-Serbian league, and in 1387 won a great victory over the Turks on the banks of the river Toplica. This success at once decided the waverers, and Croats, Albanians, Poles, and Hungarians flocked to his standard. To crush the revolt, Murad first turned on the Bulgarians, and once they were subjected he marched on Old Serbia by way of Kustendil and came up with the army of the league on the plain of Kossovo (Plain of the Blackbirds), some 50 miles north of Uskub. There, while arraying himself for battle, he was mortally wounded by a Serb noble named Milos Kobilic who gained access to him by posing as a deserter. Murad's brother Bayazid immediately took over command, and after a fierce battle, the most famous in Serbian history, he routed the allies. Lazar was taken prisoner and slain in the tent in which Murad lay dying. The Ottoman victory was complete; it was the Waterloo of the Serbian empire, and was to remain unavenged until the Battle of Kumanovo in 1912.

Bayazid (1389–1403), known as *Yilderim* ("The Thunderbolt"), who succeeded Murad, was a ferocious warrior who lacked the statecraft of his brother. Between 1392 and 1393 he waged a war of extermination in Thrace, and in 1394 was called to Asia. During his absence the Emperor Manuel II (1391–1425) appealed to the western princes for aid. He was successful, for Pope Boniface IX preached a crusade and a vast army, numbering, it is said, between 50,000 and 100,000 men – mostly Hungarians – was assembled at Nicopolis under Sigismund King of Hungary and the Dukes of Burgundy and Nevers. There they were routed by Bayazid on September 28, 1396, to the dismay of the West.

After this victory Bayazid's one idea was to master Constantinople, where, in 1400, Manuel was reinforced by Marshal Boucicault, who sailed into the Golden Horn with 1,400 men-at-arms in the nick of time to save Galata from the Turks; after which Manuel sailed for France and England to seek aid, and in 1402 set out on his return.

During his absence Constantinople was all but completely isolated by Bayazid. At length, in 1402, he decided to carry it by assault; but no sooner had he invested it than he received a message from the Mongol chieftain Timur the Lame (Tamerlane) – a ferocious monster of destruction – ordering him forthwith to return to the Greeks all cities and territories he had taken from them.

In 1386, Timur, having conquered Persia, had appeared before Tiflis at the head of an immense army of Mongols and Turks, and in 1394, thoroughly alarmed by his western advance, Bayazid had gone to Erzinjan to resist him; but when he found that Timur had no intention to proceed farther west, he returned to Europe. In 1398 Timur conquered northern India and occupied Delhi, and in the following year returned to his capital Samarkand, from where he set out for Aleppo, slaughtering every man, woman, and child on his way. Once Aleppo had been sacked, he headed for Jerusalem *en route* for Egypt, but was forced to turn back by a plague of locusts which deprived his horses of their grazing. Next, he took Damascus and then Baghdad; the heads of the inhabitants of each captured city were piled in pyramids before its gates.

It was when he was at Damascus that Timur sent his message to Bayazid, who forthwith raised the siege of Constantinople and carried his army into Asia. At Angora he was met by Timur who cut him off from his drinking water and so forced him to battle on July 20, 1402. Bayazid's army was routed and he was taken prisoner, to die at Samarkand in the following year. After his victory, Timur moved westward, sacking towns and cities and slaughtering their inhabitants. Brusa, the Ottoman capital, was burnt, Nicaea, Gemlik, and many other towns were sacked, and Smyrna, after a fourteen-day siege, was stormed: its inhabitants as usual were butchered. From Smyrna Timur set out on his return to Samarkand contemplating the invasion of China, and in the midst of his preparations he died in 1405 at the age of sixty-nine.

The advance of the Asiatic hordes had thrown Christendom into consternation, and when the news of Timur's victory was received in the West, it seemed as if Europe were about to be submerged by Asia. But when it was learnt that he had withdrawn eastward, hope revived, and to some, at least, it appeared possible that were the Christian kingdoms to lay aside their quarrels and to form common front against the defeated Ottomans, they might easily be driven out of Europe.

The opportunity was immense and it lingered for ten years; for it was not until 1413 that the war of succession between Bayazid's three elder sons, Suleiman, Musa, and Mahomet, ended when the third re-established the sultanate, by which date its European possessions had shrunk to little more than Adrianople itself. Had the Christians been capable of uniting, as the Greeks had done in the days of Xerxes and Darius, they might have crowned the battle of Angora by taking Adrianople, and had they done so, the power of the Ottomans in Europe would have been annihilated, for Adrianople was its centre of gravity.

Instead of exploiting this heaven-sent opportunity, in the self-same year that Mahomet brought the war of succession to an end, Henry V lay claim to the crown of France and entered into alliance with the Duke of Burgundy to win it. As detrimental, the Hussite Wars were about to deluge central Europe with blood, and worst of all, from 1402 to 1454 the wars of the Milanese, Venetians, and Florentines in Italy paralysed any concerted effort against the Turks. Had Agincourt been fought in the East instead of in the West, the battle of Angora, though it concerned two Moslem powers, would have taken its place in the annals of history as the most decisive battle ever fought for the preservation of Christendom.

The reign of Mahomet I, called Chelebi "the Gentleman" (1413–1421), was spent in establishing order out of chaos. He was a rebuilder and restorer and not a conqueror, as was his successor Murad II (1421–1451) who, because of the ceaseless flood of Turks moving westward, set in motion by Timur's gigantic raids, never lacked recruits, and before his reign ended he was able to carry the Ottoman banner throughout the length of the Balkans.

In 1422, he laid siege to Constantinople, but was compelled to abandon it because of a revolt in Karamania (the region round Konia), and soon after the Emperor John VI (1425–1448)[1] agreed to pay tribute to him. In 1430, Murad regained Salonica, took Uskub, invaded Transylvania, and in 1435 besieged Belgrade. Four years later, in order to gain western aid, at the Council of Florence John agreed to the union of the Churches, which in the following year led the pope to call upon all Christian princes to march against the Turks. Vladislav, King of Hungary, responded to the call, and in 1441 Hunyadi (John Corvinus), the Voivode of Transylvania, drove the Turks out of Serbia. This success was followed, in 1443, by a disastrous Turkish defeat near Kustenitza (45 miles south-east of Sofia), which in 1444 led to a truce between Murad and the king of Hungary. But no sooner

---

[1] John VI was the son of Manuel II, and in 1420 he became associated with his father, after which Manuel became a purely nominal ruler.

had it been agreed than on the suggestion of Cardinal Julian Cesarini—who held that an oath with the infidel might be set aside—it was broken by the Christian allies. Infuriated by this treachery, Murad marched against them and routed them at Varna. In 1446, he destroyed the fortifications of the Isthmus of Corinth, ravaged the Morea, and two years later prepared to invade Albania, then held by the famous George Castriotes, better known as Scanderbeg.

Meanwhile, under the directions of Pope Nicholas V, Hunyadi assembled an army of 24,000 Hungarians, Poles, Wallachs, and Germans on the plains of Kossovo. Murad dropped his Albanian project and, at the head of 100,000 men, marched against him. On October 18, 1448, a battle began, which ended on October 20 in a complete victory for Murad; 8,000 of the flower of the Hungarian nobility were left dead on the field. For Hungary and western Europe the effect of this defeat was catastrophic. For years onward the Turks had nothing to fear from their enemies north of the Danube. Except by sea, Constantinople was isolated and ripe to fall. In 1451 Murad died in Adrianople, and was succeeded by his son Mahomet II (1451–1481), surnamed "the Conqueror".

# CHAPTER 18

# The siege and fall of Constantinople, 1453

When, on July 6, 1449, the Emperor John VI died and his brother, Constantine XI, surnamed Dragases, succeeded to the imperial throne, the Eastern Empire, which in the days of Constantine I had extended over the whole of the Balkan peninsula (less Illyria), Asia Minor, Syria, Palestine, Egypt, and Cyrenaica, had shrunk to little more than the walls of Constantinople. John had done nothing during his reign except to maintain an abject *status quo*, and to appease his enemy he had even congratulated the sultan on his victory at Varna. Nor were the clergy and nobles less servile, and of the people, Chedomil Mijatovich writes: "The nation became an inert mass, without initiative and without will. Before the Emperor and the Church prelates it grovelled in the dust; behind them it rose up to spit at them and shake its fist. Tyranny and exploitation above, hatred and cowardice beneath; cruelty often, hypocrisy always and everywhere, in the upper and lower strata. Outward polish and dexterity replaced true culture; phraseology hid lack of ideas. Both political and social bodies were alike rotten; the spirit of the nation was languid, devoid of all elasticity. Selfishness placed itself on the throne of public interest, and tried to cover its hideousness with the mantle of false patriotism."[1]

This ignoble state of affairs was largely the product of the centuries old attempt by Rome to unite the Latin and Greek Churches, a question of theology which occupied the critical mind of the Byzantines to the exclusion of nearly everything else, and because in the Age of Faith theology was politics, religious union was the political question which prevented strategic union, the lack of which unbarred the eastern gate of Europe to the Turks.

Though the estrangement between the two Churches dated from the fifth century, it was not until the eleventh that it became acute. In 1073 Pope Gregory VII declared to Ebouly de Rossi: "It is far better for a country to remain under the rule of Islam, than be governed by Christians who refuse to acknowledge the

---

[1] *Constantine the Last Emperor of the Greeks*, Chedomil Mijatovich (1892), pp. 5-6.

rights of the Catholic Church.''[1] To such an extent was hatred carried that when, on December 12, 1452, the union which had been agreed at the Council of Florence in 1439 was reaffirmed in Constantinople by Cardinal Isidore, the Grand Duke Lucas Notaras declared that "It is better to see in the city the power of the Turkish turban than that of the Latin tiara".[2] Even during the siege itself, when the situation was desperate, the historian Ducas says: "That even if an angel from heaven descended, and declared that he would save the city from the Turks, if only the people would unite with the Church of Rome, the Greeks would have refused.''[3]

In spite of the reaffirmation of the union the assistance given to the Greeks by the western powers was negligible. The Genoese settlement of Galata (Pera), the suburb of Constantinople on the northern side of the Golden Horn, remained neutral throughout the contest, while such help that was offered by others was bargained for material gains. The Emperor Frederick III talked, but did nothing; and Alphonso, king of Aragon, Naples, and Sicily did likewise. Hunyadi demanded for his support Silivria (Silivri) or Mesembria (Misivria), and the king of Catalonia haggled for Lesbos. Only the Venetians, Genoese, and the pope offered some assistance; the first two because their trade was in jeopardy, and the latter because the union had been reaffirmed: this was considered to be worth Cardinal Isidore and 200 soldiers!

Among the Christians we find only disunity and weakness, but among the Turks we see the strength of a young people united under the direction of one of the most remarkable men in Oriental history, the Sultan Mahomet II (1451–1481), son of Murad II and a beautiful Albanian slave. When, early in February, 1451, his father died, he was twenty-one years old, and as soon as the news reached him in Magnesia (western Anatolia), he set out at top speed, crossed the Dardanelles into Gallipoli and thence rode to Adrianople, where he arrived on February 9 and was proclaimed sultan. Typical of the man, his first act was to drown his infant brother;[4] his second to execute the assassin he had hired; and the third to marry the child's mother to a slave.

In appearance he was handsome, of middle height, with a

[1] *Byzantinische Geschichten*, August Friederich Gfrörer (1872–1874), vol. ii, p. 459.
[2] *History of the Byzantine Empire*, A. A. Vasilier (1929), vol. ii, p. 349, citing Ducas's *Historia Byzantina*, chap. xxxvii, p. 264.
[3] Cited by J. von Hammer, *Histoire de l'Empire Ottoman* (1835), vol. ii, p. 426.
[4] Later he legitimized the slaughter of younger brothers by the sultan.

long aquiline nose which seemed to overhang his thick red lips, partly hidden by long drooping moustaches. Highly strung and nervous, he was too suspicious to make friends and too cruel to make enduring enemies. He loved the grim and the brutal and was known to his followers as "Hunkar", the "Drinker of Blood", a name not undeserved, for after the capture of Constantinople he had the heads of his executed enemies placed on a table before him. He seldom smiled; one of the few occasions would seem to have been when he heard that Drakul, Prince of Wallachia, had nailed the turbans of his envoys on to their heads because they had refused to uncover themselves in his presence. It so tickled his fancy that he at once adopted this form of torture. Again, perhaps, he smiled when Drakul impaled several thousands of his Turkish prisoners; when he heard of it he exclaimed in admiration: "It is impossible to drive out of his country a prince who does such grand things as that."[1] Nevertheless he was a man of high intelligence, which had been sharpened by his stepmother, the cultured Mara Brankovich. Unusual for a Turk, he could speak, write and read five foreign languages—Greek, Latin, Arabic, Chaldean, and Persian, probably also Slavonic. Throughout his life he was a seeker after knowledge and ever anxious to learn. He was a student of philosophy, theology, and astrology and a patron of Persian poetry and the arts. "He united", says Finlay, "the enterprise and valour of youth with the prudence and wisdom of old age",[2] a combination providing an intellectual basis for his generalship and statesmanship which, if not of the highest order, were remarkable. The great men of history were his models, and he greedily studied the lives of Cyrus, Alexander, Julius Caesar, Octavian, Constantine, and Theodosius. " 'He wished', says Tetaldi, 'to conquer the whole world, to see more than Alexander and Caesar or any other valiant man who has ever lived'."[3]

As a general he relied on the force of numbers rather than upon skill. Though time and again he was checked by John Hunyadi and Scanderbeg, and was triumphantly repelled by the Knights of Rhodes and the Persians, his generalship was of no mean order. Unlike many of the sultans, he always commanded his own army; lived and dreamed of war; decided everything for

[1] *Les Sultans Ottomans*, Halil Ganem (1902), vol. I, p. 147.
[2] *A History of Greece, etc.*, George Finlay (1877), vol. III, p. 498.
[3] Quoted by Edwin Pears in *The Destruction of the Greek Empire and the Story of the Capture of Constantinople by the Turks* (1903), pp. 292–293.

himself; brooked no interference and demanded the strictest discipline. As Gibbon writes: "Of a master who never forgives, the orders are seldom disobeyed."[1] He was energetic, painstaking and secretive. Disguised, he would mix with his men and listen to their conversations, and woe to anyone who gave a sign that he recognised him; even a welcome meant instant death. Once he said of his secret preparations: "If a hair of my beard knew, I would pluck it out and burn it."[2] His plans were thorough and meticulously prepared; his movements rapid; he was never discouraged by defeat; and he never let his enemy recoup. He invaded the European provinces twenty times and reduced them to his will. But, above all, as an artillerist he stands supreme: he was the first really great gunner in history.

As a statesman he kept himself in complete isolation and appeared to his subjects as a supernatural power—a god. He was an administrator of the first order, a politic and even a tolerant ruler, also one who knew how to organize his conquests by leaving to his subjects things which were of secondary importance while he held fast to those which were of first.

From early youth his overmastering idea was the capture of Constantinople and from the day of his accession he set out to realize it. First he confirmed the treaty Murad had made with Constantine, and professed to him his peaceful intentions. Next, to obviate an attack in rear by the emir of Karamania, such as had compelled his father to raise the siege of Constantinople in 1422, he brought him to heel. Then he pacified the Venetians, concluded a three-year truce with Hunyadi, and made peace with Hungary, Wallachia, and Bosnia. As Gibbon says: "Peace was on his lips, while war was in his heart."[3] Lastly, remembering that his father in his Varna campaign had to pay the enormous toll of one ducat (about nine shillings) for each soldier ferried across to Gallipoli, he decided to free himself of this inconvenience. Already master of the Asiatic shore of the Bosphorus, where Bayazid had built the castle of Anatolia-Hisar, he determined to become master of the European shore as well and in March, 1452, he landed a force of soldiers and 5,000 workmen a little to the north of Constantinople and began to build the strong fortress of Roumelia-Hisar (Boghasi-Kesen), also called by the Greeks *Laemocopia*

---

[1] *The Decline and Fall*, Edward Gibbon, vol. VII, p. 172.
[2] *Histoire de l'Empire Ottoman*, J. von Hammer, vol. III, p. 68.
[3] *The Decline and Fall*, vol. VII, p. 170.

"Cut-Throat Castle". Nicolò Barbaro writes in his *Journal of the Siege*: "This fortification is exceedingly strong from the sea, so that it is absolutely impossible to capture it, for on the shore and walls are standing bombards in very great numbers; on the land side the fortification is also strong, though less so than from the sea."[1] Six months later, when the work was finished, all communication between Constantinople and the ports of the Black Sea was severed, which meant that the capital was cut off from its main corn supply in the Ukraine. Mahomet then appeared before the land wall at the head of a force, reputed to be 50,000 men strong, reconnoitred it, and on September 6, 1452, he withdrew to Adrianople to complete his preparations.

The Turkish army comprised three bodies of troops, janissaries, bashi-bazouks, and provincial levies. The first was now a standing regular army, between 12,000 and 15,000 strong, of the most formidable soldiers of the fifteenth century: no Christian kingdom, not even France under Charles VII's ordinances, had a body of troops comparable with them. Since the reign of Murad I they had been recruited by means of a blood tax levied on the Christian provinces, each of which was yearly compelled to surrender a quota of boys between the ages of seven and twelve, distinguished for their strength and intelligence. These unfortunates were forcibly converted to Mahommedanism and subjected to the severest discipline and self-denials. They were forbidden to marry, allowed no luxuries, and not permitted to trade or accumulate wealth: they were military monks, and when too old to serve were pensioned.[2] Unlike the janissaries, the bashi-bazouks were little more than an undisciplined rabble of poorly armed Turks and renegade Christians, and the provincial levies, largely recruited in Anatolia, were little better.

The Turkish army and tactics of this period are described by Bertrandon de la Brocquière in his *Travels* of 1432–1433. He informs us that the Ottomans wore coats of mail descending almost half-way down their thighs, and carried on their heads a round white peaked cap ornamented with plates of iron. Their arms were the bow, sword, and mace. The obedience of the Turkish soldier to superiors was boundless, "and it is chiefly owing to this steady

---

[1] Cited by Vasiliev (*History of the Byzantine Empire*, vol. II, p. 348) from Barbaro's *Giornale dell' assedio di Constantinopli* (1856), p. 2.

[2] For a summary of the rules prescribed for them by Murad I see *Constantine the Last Emperor of the Greeks*, Chedomil Mijatovich, pp. 27–32, and *État Militaire Ottoman depuis la Fondation de l'Empire*, Ahmed Djevad Bey (1882), p. 66.

submission that such great exploits have been performed, and such vast conquests gained". They were adepts at discovering their enemy, keeping him under observation, and then suddenly by a forced march surprising him, as they did at Nicopolis. "Their manner of fighting", he writes, "varies according to circumstances. When they find a favourable opportunity they divide themselves into different detachments, and thus attack many parts of an army at once ... it is in their flight that thay are formidable, and it has been almost always then that they have defeated the Christians. .... When the chief, or any one of his officers, perceives the enemy who pursues to be in disorder, he gives three strokes on this instrument [a tabalcan–drum]; the others on hearing it, do the same, and they are instantly formed round their chief like so many hogs round the old one; and then according to circumstances, they either receive the charge of the assailants, or fall on them by troops, and attack them in different places at the same time. In pitched battles they employ another stratagem which consists of throwing fireworks among the cavalry to frighten the horses. They often post in their front a great body of dromedaries and camels, which are bold and vicious; these they drive before them on the enemy's line of horse, and throw it into confusion."[1]

More important even than his janissaries was Mahomet's artillery, the men of which were also mainly Christian: Critobulus says, "it was the canon which did everything".[2] In all, Mahomet had twelve or thirteen great bombards (cannon) and fourteen batteries of lesser pieces; each battery consisted of four guns. His largest bombard was cast in Adrianople by a Hungarian or Wallachian named Urban. Its barrel was twelve *palma* in circumference – that is, twelve span of eight inches each, giving ninety-six inches in all – and it has been calculated that the weight of its stone shot must have been 1,456 lb. avoirdupois.[3] This monstrous weapon required 60 oxen to drag it, 200 men to march alongside to keep it in position, and 200 more to level the ground it passed over.[4] It took two hours to load, and, therefore, could

---

[1] *Early Travels in Palestine*, edit. Thomas Wright (1855), pp. 363–366.
[2] *The Cambridge Medieval History*, vol. IV, p. 698.
[3] Machines throwing larger balls than Mahomet used were in use just before the general adoption of cannon. At the siege of Zara, in 1346, shot of 3,000 lb. were hurled by the Venetians, and, in 1373, the Genoese used some nearly as large at the siege of Cyprus. Mons Meg at Edinburgh was cast in 1455; its granite balls are twenty-one inches in diameter.
[4] See *Le Siège, la Prise et le Sac de Constantinople par les Turcs en 1453*, Gustave Schlumberger (1922), pp. 58–60.

fire only six to eight times a day. According to Phrantzes, eventually it blew up and killed Urban.[1]

When the siege opened, Nicolò Barbaro, who took part in it, states that there were 150,000 men in the besieging army between the Golden Horn and the Sea of Marmara, and Tedaldi, a Florentine soldier, says 200,000, of whom 140,000 were effective soldiers and the rest "thieves, plunderers, hawkers, and others following the army for gain and booty'.[2] Mahomet's fleet was not an efficient one; it is said to have numbered between 145 and 350 warships of various types, mostly small vessels.

To meet this formidable array, outside the walls of Constantinople Constantine had nothing, and within them and in the harbour of the Golden Horn he had only a handful of mercenaries and a few galleys in lamentable condition. Though the city contained some 100,000 inhabitants, when he ordered a census of its fighting men to be made only 4,973 answered the call. In spite of this cowardice Constantine heroically began preparations for the now inevitable death-struggle.

Constantine's first task was to repair the walls, which were in a state of decay. They surrounded the city and, omitting Galata which was in neutral hands, their circumference was about thirteen miles. Topographically they may be divided into three sections:

(1) The land wall of Theodosius II, built in the fifth century, four miles long, stretching from the Sea of Marmara and the Golden Gate in the south to the Xylo Porta (Gate of Wood) and the Blanchern Palace on the Golden Horn in the north.

(2) The sea wall along the Golden Horn from the Xylo Porta to the Acropolis (Seraglio Point), about three and a half miles long.

(3) The continuation of this wall along the Sea of Marmara to the Golden Gate–five and a half miles long.

Though the second and third of these walls were single in construction, the first was triple, consisting of (a) an inner wall forty feet high with 112 towers, each about sixty feet high; (b) an outer wall, twenty-five feet high, also furnished with towers; and (c) a breastwork in front of it, formed by a continuation in height of the inner wall of the water ditch, or fosse, which was some sixty

---

[1] *Histoire de l'Empire Ottoman*, vol. ii, p. 398.
[2] *The Cambridge Medieval History*, vol. iv, pp. 695–696. See also Bury's edit. of Gibbon, vol. vii, p. 180. All these figures are suspect.

feet broad and fifteen deep. Between each of the walls was an enclosure about twenty yards broad; the one between the inner and outer walls was called the *Peribolos*, and that between the outer and the breastwork, the *Parateichion*.

For convenience, the land wall may be divided into three tactical sections: (1) From the Golden Gate to the Gate of St. Romanus (Top Capou–Cannon Gate); (2) from the St. Romanus Gate to the Adrianople Gate; and (3) from the Adrianople Gate to the Xylo Porta. Through the second section runs the Lycus stream, and the area immediately west of it was called the *Mesoteichion*.

The main harbour, as to-day, was the Golden Horn, protected on its southern side by the northern sea wall of the city, and on its northern by the sea wall of Galata. Its entrance into the Bosphorus was secured by a great chain–already described in Chapter 12– which was reinforced by immense baulks of wood. Behind it was gathered the imperial fleet which, when the siege began, numbered about twenty-six ships, ten Greek and sixteen Venetian, Genoese, etc.; fifteen of which were allotted to its defence under the command of the Venetian, Gabriel Trevisano, who had offered his services *"per honor de Dio et per honor de tuta la Christianitade"*.

Though Constantine could raise no more than 5,000 fighting men out of the 25,000 males of military age in the city, he received small but highly valuable assistance from certain condottieri and others, which brought his total forces to about 8,000. The first reinforcements to arrive were 200 soldiers under the papal legate, Cardinal Isidore, former metropolitan of Kiev and participator in the Council of Florence, who in November, 1452, sailed into the Golden Horn. But his coming only accentuated the ineradicable hatred between the East and the West; for when, on December 12, according to the terms of the Council of Florence, he celebrated a service commemorating the union between the Churches in St. Sophia, the infuriated people, roused by Gennadius (later patriarch), broke into open riot and shouted, "Death to the Azymites (the excommunicated)." Thus, from the very opening of the siege, the Greeks resolutely sacrificed their political independence to their hatred of Rome.[1] Next, in January

---

[1] A factor working strongly in favour of the Turks was that in the provinces they had already occupied, the bishops, nominated by the patriarchs, were fully recognized as the civil and religious heads of the Christian community.

the following year, the Genoese soldier John Giustiniani (Giovanni) arrived with 700 men in two large ships, and with him was Johann Grant, an experienced German artillerist and military engineer.

Giustiniani's arrival was an event of the greatest importance, not only because he brought with him two powerful warships and 700 soldiers, of whom 400 were fully armoured; but because he was one of the most noted soldiers of his age: a skilful leader and a man of outstanding energy, audacity, and courage. When he offered his sword to the emperor, Constantine made him commander-in-chief of the defence forces of the city, and endowed him with all but dictatorial powers. From his arrival a spirit of hope swept Constantinople.

Mahomet, who had reduced two small Byzantine posts at Therapia and Studium on the Bosphorus and impaled their garrisons, and who had used burning sulphur to gas-out the garrison of the castle on the island of Prinkipo, on April 5, 1453, again appeared before the land wall and deployed his army into four corps. They were: (1) Zagan Pasha's to watch Galata and to build a bridge over the western end of the Golden Horn preparatory to an attack on the Xylo Porta. (2) Caraja Pasha's corps to attack the wall between the Xylo Porta and the Adrianople Gate, while (3) Isaac Pasha's neutralized the wall from the St. Romanus Gate and the Sea of Marmara. (4) In the Lycus valley, between the two gates last mentioned, Mahomet drew up his staunchest troops and janissaries under his grand vizier, Halil Pasha, for it was here that he intended to deliver his main attack. To supervise it, he had his red and golden headquarters tent pitched immediately in rear of this corps.

Constantine saw where the main blow was to fall and moved his headquarters behind the land wall in the Lycus valley. He allotted the defence of the central section of the land wall to Giustiniani. North of it he posted the brothers Antony, Paul, and Troilus Bocchiardi, Theodore of Karystos, and Johann Grant; and south of it Catarin Contarini, Andronicus Cantacuzene, and other leaders. The remainder of the walls and the harbours was held by minute bodies of men, many of the towers garrisoned by squads only three or four strong.

On April 12, when the Turkish fleet, under the Bulgarian renegade Baltoglu, was at anchor in the roadstead of Prinkipo, the great cannon, opposite the land wall in the Lycus valley, were advanced to the edge of the fosse, and the first great organized bombardment in history was opened to the beating of drums, accompanied by the shoutings of thousands of excited men. Mijatovitch says: "Since the creation of the world nothing like it had been heard on the shores of the Bosphorus." Nevertheless it was a slow affair; it took two hours to load the great cannon and they could fire only seven to eight times a day.

Though the artillery assault was maintained day in and day out, its effect was slight until an envoy from Hunyadi instructed Mahomet's gunners that they should not disperse their shot, as they were doing, but should concentrate in volleys upon triangular sections of the wall. Phrantzes says that the Hungarians desired Constantinople to fall, because a Serbian hermit had foretold that Christendom would never be rid of the Turks until that seat of heresy was obliterated.[1] Though this Christian aid greatly assisted the Turks, as the wall crumbled it was as rapidly patched up, and, on April 18, Mahomet, impatient, ordered a general assault on the wall and the boom.

The attack was launched to the shouts of *Yagma! Yagma!* ("To the sack! To the sack!"), and with terrifying howls and yells the Turks rushed the ditch. Then, writes the Slavonic Chronicler: "The reports of muskets, the ringing of bells, the clashing of arms, the cries of fighting men, the shrieks of women and the wailing of children, produced such a noise, that it seemed as if the earth trembled. Clouds of smoke fell upon the city and the camp, and the combatants at last could not see each other."[2] But Giustiniani was ready; he opened a terrific fire from hand guns, wall guns,[3] bows, crossbows and catapults and swept the leading ranks of the attackers back into the ditch. Meanwhile the Grand Duke Notaras beat off the naval assault on the boom. So furious was Mahomet at his ill-success that his generals had the greatest difficulty in persuading him not to load his trebuchets with his own dead and to hurl them over the walls of the city.[4]

Two days after this repulse there occurred an incident which led to an astonishing naval battle. In March, three large Genoese

[1] *Chronicle of Constantinople*, George Phrantzes (1838), p. 239. (See Mijatovich, p. 155.)
[2] *The Slavonic Chronicler*, p. 27. (See Mijatovich, p. 156.)
[3] These guns were loaded with five to ten lead balls. See E. A. Vlasto, *1453 Les Derniers Jours de Constantinople* (1883), p. 84.
[4] Not a new idea, for at the siege of Carolstein in 1422, 'Coribut caused the bodies of his soldiers whom the besieged had killed to be thrown into the town in addition to 2,000 cartloads of manure." See *The Projectile-Throwing Engines of the Ancients*, Sir Ralph Payne-Gallwey (1907), p. 39.

warships, carrying troops and munitions on their way to Constantinople, had been delayed by contrary winds at the island of Chios. There they remained until March 15, when the wind veered to the south and they set sail again. They fell in with a large imperial grain ship, continued their course with her, and sighted the dome of St. Sophia at ten o'clock on the norning of March 20.[1]

When he heard of their approach, Mahomet at once sent orders to his fleet to put to sea and destroy or capture them, after which with his staff and a large body of troops he hurried to the Bosphorus shore of Galata to watch. He saw 145 Turkish galleys row out, and it seemed to him inevitable that the four Christian ships would be sunk, as it also did to the thousands of spectators who crowded the sea walls of Constantinople and the roofs of its houses.

Howling with joy, Baltoglu rowed straight for his enemy; but the wind was strong and the great Genoese warships and the transport crashed through his fleet, stove in his galleys or carried away their oars. Next, as they rounded Seraglio Point, the wind dropped and they were at once surrounded. A desperate action began. When the Turks attempted to grapple and swarm up their sides, they were cut down with axes. Rocks, pots of Greek fire, darts, and javelins were hurled upon them, and hand-guns and swivel-pieces swept their decks with ball. For two hours the contest continued. Mahomet yelled and threatened and at times galloped his horse into the sea to urge on his admiral. Suddenly a puff of wind returned, the harbour chain was lowered, and the four ships again crashed through their enemy and entered the Golden Horn.[2]

Mahomet, in his rage, ordered Baltoglu to be impaled forthwith, and when his generals prevented this, while four slaves held him stretched upon the ground, he thrashed him with a heavy stick.

Though again checked, Mahomet was far from checkmated. He realized all along how vitally important it was to win control of the Golden Horn, for once in his hands he could threaten the northern sea wall and so compel Constantine still further to disperse his minute garrison. So he decided, probably on the

[1] According to Schlumberger (p. 126) the names of the Genoese sea captains were Leonardo of Chios, Maurice Cattaneo, and Domenico of Navarra, with Baptisto of Felliciano. The captain of the transport was Phlantanelas. Their bravery deserves that their names should be remembered.

[2] J. von Hammer quoting Ducas; see *Histoire de l'Empire Ottoman*, vol. II, p. 405.

suggestion of a Genoese in Galata, to transport part of his fleet across the mile of land[1] which separates the Bosphorus from the stream called The Springs, which flows into the Golden Horn west of Galata. With his usual impetuosity he collected thousands of workmen to level the ground, to build a wooden runway and to grease it. Over it some seventy ships with sails unfurled and flags flying were hauled, and under cover of artillery they slid into the Golden Horn. This unexpected manœuvre produced consternation among the Greeks, but when they found that these ships did not attack the boom, they plucked up courage and attempted a night assault on them. This was severely repulsed because it was betrayed to the Turks by the Galata Genoese. Meanwhile, in order to unite the two wings of his army, Mahomet ordered a barrel-bridge 2,000 feet long with a roadway eight feet broad to be built across the Horn: this was done immediately.

The Greeks were now so thoroughly disheartened that a proposal was made to Constantine that he should save himself by escaping from the city. He listened quietly to the suggestion, then replied: "I thank all for the advice which you have given me. . . . How could I leave the churches of our Lord, and His servants the clergy, and the throne, and my people in such a plight? What would the world say about me? I pray you, my friends, in future do not say to me anything else but, 'Nay, Sire, do not leave us!' Never, never will I leave you! I am resolved to die here with you! And saying this the Emperor turned his head aside, because tears filled his eyes; and with him wept the Patriarch and all who were there!"[2]

Constantine's determination infused new life into the defence; nevertheless the situation remained a desperate one, for, unless succour came soon, it was only a matter of time before the city would, if not be stormed, be starved out. Therefore, on May 3, a small, fast brigantine, disguised as a Turkish vessel and manned with a crew of twelve men, slipped out to seek the promised papal fleet, which was supposed to be on its way north. All these days the bombardment continued, and on May 7 and again on May 12 determined assaults of 30,000 and 50,000 Turks were made on the walls about the St. Romanus Gate; in each case they were beaten back by Giustiniani with great slaughter.

---

[1] Again this idea was not an original one. J. von Hammer, vol. II, pp. 405–408, gives a number of past examples.
[2] *The Slavonic Chronicler*, p. 116. (See Mijatovich, p. 174.)

The numerical strength of the Turks, which was steadily increased by the arrival of fresh contingents, now began to tell in favour of the besieged, for Mahomet's problem of supply became so difficult that, unless he could gain the city by the end of the month, he would be forced – as had happened so often on previous occasions – to abandon the siege. When he found that he could not command the shattered walls and so prevent his enemy from repairing them, his next attempt to storm them, on May 18, was

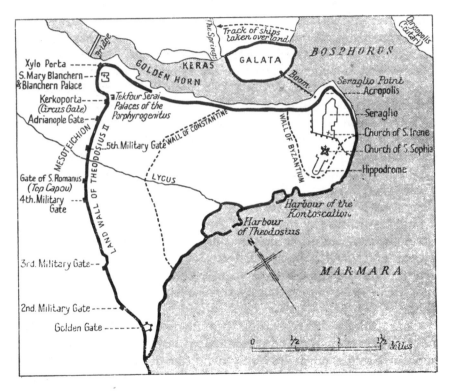

31.   SIEGE OF CONSTANTINOPLE, 1453

made under the protection of an immense wooden tower, a *Helepolis* or "city-taker", which was dragged up to the fosse, and from it a deadly fire was poured upon the besieged. Giustiniani blew it up by rolling barrels of powder into the fosse, and the sultan exclaimed: "What would I not give to win that man over to my side!"[1] He attempted to bribe him; but to no avail.

Assault and tower-attack having failed, resort was made to

[1] *Histoire de l'Empire Ottoman*, J. von Hammer, vol. II, p. 417.

mining, more particularly in the neighbourhood of the Adrianople and Kaligaria Gates; the latter was situated close to the Blanchern Palace, where the wall was single. The work was first put in hand on May 15, and from then on to May 25 various attempts were made to undermine the walls;[1] but each was frustrated by Johann Grant, who counter-mined. Either he blew up[2] the Turkish miners or smoked them out, suffocated them by stink-pots or drowned them by letting in water, or else met them underground and fought them with knife, axe and spear.

These repeated failures and the constant rumours that an Hungarian army was approaching Constantinople from the north and the papal fleet from the south, made the Turks lose heart. Even their indomitable leader grew doubtful, and when he failed to induce the emperor to surrender the city on terms, on May 26 or 27 he summoned a council of war to ascertain the opinions of his generals. Halil Pasha, the grand vizier, who throughout had been against the siege, strongly recommended abandoning it. But Zagan Pasha, his rival, scoffed at the idea, reminded the sultan that Alexander the Great had conquered the world with a far smaller army than the one now besieging the city, and said:

"Thou, O Padishah, knowest well the great dissensions that are raging in Italy especially, and in all Frankistan generally. In consequence of these dissensions the Giaours (infidels) are incapable of united action against us. The Christian potentates never will unite together. When after protracted efforts they conclude something like a peace amongst themselves, it never lasts long. Even when they are bound by treaties of alliance, they are not prevented seizing territories from each other. They always stand in fear of each other. No doubt they think much, speak much, and explain much, but after all they do very little. When they decide to do anything, they waste much time before they begin to act. Suppose they have even commenced something, they cannot progress very far with it because they are sure to disagree

---

[1] At this period the art of mining had little advanced since the days of Philip of Macedon, who made use of this means of attack in his siege of Byzantium in 340 B.C. It consisted in digging out a chamber under the wall, propping up its roof with baulks and then setting fire to them.

[2] *The Slavonic Chronicler*, p. 12 (see Mijatovich, p. 186), says: "It was as if the lightning had struck the place, for the earth shook and with a great crash a greenish whirlwind carried the Turks into the air. Fragments of men and timber fell into the city and into the camp. The besieged ran away from the walls and the besiegers fled back from the ditch." If this is correct, then it is the first recorded case of the use of gunpowder in mining.

amongst themselves how to proceed. . . . Therefore, O Padishah, do not lose hope, but give us the order at once to storm the city!"[1]

The Sultan was overjoyed with this oration and forthwith determined upon a simultaneous assault on the land and sea walls on May 29.

While the bombardment was continued steadily, he decided upon his plan of attack, which was to be a combined one of army and fleet; the object of the latter was, as on the previous occasion, by fire to pin down the defenders of the sea walls and so to prevent them from reinforcing the land wall. He selected three main objectives: (1) the wall between the Tekfour Serai and the Adrianople Gate; (2) the wall in the Lycus valley about the St. Romanus Gate; and (3) the third military gate, half-way between St. Romanus and the Golden Gates. The second of these three objectives was to be the point of decision.

The attack was to be carried out without let or pause, night and day, until the defenders were so exhausted that the final assault would meet with little opposition. Mahomet is reported to have said: "I have decided to engage successively and without halt one body of fresh troops after the other, until harassed and worn out the enemy will be unable further to resist."[2] The plan settled, he issued orders to his fleet to keep the sea walls under fire, and he instructed Zagan Pasha to cross to the south side of the Golden Horn and to engage the northernmost objective. Lastly he arranged for the collection of a vast amount of material: 2,000 scaling ladders, iron hooks to pull down the barricades Giustiniani had built to block the breaches, and a mass of fascines with which to fill in the ditch.

Electrified by his energy, his army at once set to work, and, on the nights of May 27–28 and 28–29, its vast camp was illuminated, a foreboding crescent of fire encircled the city. On the morning of May 28 the sultan inspected his fleet, now commanded by Hamoud (Chamouza), and rode round his entire army, to find all in readiness.

When enthusiasm swept the Turkish ranks, dejection and dissension gripped the life of the doomed city. On May 23 the valiant little brigantine returned, having found no succouring fleet. The news extinguished the last spark of hope in the hearts of the

---

[1] *Phrantzes*, p. 269 (quoted by Mijatovich, pp. 201–202).
[2] See Schlumberger, *op cit.*, p. 259, quoting Critobulus.

inhabitants. Portents of disaster were whispered from mouth to ear: an icon had been seen to sweat; rumbling noises had been heard, and a light had glowed strangely upon the dome of the great cathedral. The garrison now numbered barely 4,000 fighting men, and the rest of the inhabitants, incapable of bearing arms, could do nothing except pray for a miracle. Yet in this pall of gloom one man maintained his dignity and courage: it was Constantine, he who bore the name of the first and the last of the eastern emperors. On the night of May 28–29 he addressed his followers – Greeks, Venetians, and Genoese – saying: "Let us work together, my companions and my brethren, to gain for ourselves liberty, glory and eternal memory! Into your hands I commit now my sceptre. Here it is! Save it! Crowns await you in heaven, and on earth your names will be remembered honourably until the end of time." Thereupon all cried out: "Let us die for faith and father-land! Let us die for the Church of God and for thee, our Emperor!"[1]

Next, all gathered in St. Sophia, and amid sobs and wailings and cries of *Kyrie eleison* the last Christian service was celebrated in the church of the Holy Wisdom. Based on Byzantine sources, Edwin Pears gives us a striking picture of the ceremony. "The emperor", he writes, "and such of the leaders as could be spared were present and the building was once more and for the last time crowded with Christian worshippers. It requires no great effort of imagination to picture the scene. The interior of the church was the most beautiful which Christian art had produced, and its beauty was enhanced by its still gorgeous and brave Byzantine aristocracy; priests and soldiers intermingled, Constantino-politans, Venetians and Genoese, all were present, all realizing the peril before them, and feeling that in view of the impending danger the rivalries which had occupied them for years were too small to be worthy of thought. The emperor and his followers partook together of the 'the undefiled and divine mysteries', and said farewell to the patriarch. The ceremony was in reality a liturgy of death. The empire was in its agony and it was fitting that the service for its departing spirit should be thus publicly said in its most beautiful church and before its last brave emperor. If the scene so vividly described by Mr. Bryce of the coronation of Charles the Great and the birth of an empire is among the most

---

[1] The whole address is given by Phrantzes, pp. 271–278, who was present at the time.

picturesque in history, that of the last Christian service in St. Sophia is surely among the most tragic."[1]

After the service Constantine rode out westward toward the setting sun, and with Giustiniani and Don Francis of Toledo he took up his position in rear of the St. Romanus Gate as twilight crept over the city.

Because of the weakness of the garrison, the emperor decided that, because numbers were insufficient to man both the walls, and as the outer wall was not yet completely destroyed, he would hold the *Peribolos*, and, in order to assure that no one should leave it, he ordered that all the military gates leading into it were to be closed and locked. This was done directly the defenders had taken up their posts. Thus it was to be a fight to the finish; either the Turks would be repulsed or the defenders annihilated.

Toward midnight the emperor went the rounds of the walls in the Lycus valley. The night was dark and misty, a few large drops of rain began to fall, when suddenly all the fires in the Turkish camps were extinguished. Until about half-past one in the morning of May 29 all was still, when with equal suddenness there broke forth a cacophony of trumpets, drums and voices: it was the signal for the general assault.

In the Lycus sector, where the principal attack was made, Mahomet had drawn up his troops in three echelons: the bashi-bazouks, the Anatolians, and the janissaries – the worst first and the best last. The first had as their object the exhaustion of the defenders and their ammunition. In wild confusion thousands of them rushed the now half-filled ditch and threw their ladders against the stockade which had replaced the outer wall, but they were met by such discharges of projectiles, Greek fire, and boiling oil that they were driven back in confusion, only to be urged on again by a line of *Chaoushes* (sergeants) armed with iron maces and chain-whips.

At length Mahomet withdrew them and sent forward the Anatolians, and the struggle became fiercer than ever. Some broke into the *Peribolos*, but were driven out by Giustiniani, whose men, being fully armoured, suffered little injury. The attack failed, and lastly 10,000 janissaries, "grand masters and valiant men", says Barbaro, "ran to the walls, not like Turks, but like lions".[2] As they tore at the stockade, "Giustiniani and his

---

[1] *The Destruction of the Greek Empire*, pp. 330–331.
[2] *Ibid.*, p. 340.

little band met the attack with lances, axes, pikes, and swords, and cut down the foremost of their assailants. For a short time the fight became a hand-to-hand encounter, neither party gaining any advantage over the other."[1]

Meanwhile, half a mile to the north of where Giustiniani held his own against the most formidable troops in Europe, a minor incident occurred which led to the fall of the city. At the angle between the triple wall of Theodosius and the single wall which surrounded the palaces of the Porphyrogenitus (Tekfour Serai) and the Blanchern, was a small postern known as the Kerkoporta or Circus Gate.[2] In 1204 it had been blocked up by the Emperor Isaac II, the Angel, but had recently been reopened, and in the attack now made, the Turks having crowded into the ditch and gained possession of the outer enclosure, a party of janissaries, some fifty strong, noticed that the gate was undefended, rushed it and were rapidly followed by others. They entered the inner enclosure, took its defenders in flank, and so enabled their comrades to storm the wall and enter the city, where at once they hauled down the flag of St. Mark and ran up the Turkish standard. Next, they began to plunder the palaces, and the brothers Bocchiardi regained the enclosure; the incident seemed to be at an end.

But fate decided against the defenders; though the third assault in the Lycus valley was beaten back and the emperor shouted to his followers: "Bear yourselves bravely for God's sake! I see the enemy retires in disorder! If God wills, ours shall be the victory!"[3] suddenly, as he spoke, a projectile struck down Giustiniani.[4] He was hit either in the hand, foot, neck, or breast, and bleeding profusely, in great pain he retired for medical aid. Though the emperor implored him to remain, the agony was so great that he refused, and one of the military gates of the inner wall was opened to allow him to be carried out.[5]

According to the Venetian historians, the fall of the city is

---

[1] *The Destruction of the Greek Empire*, p. 341.

[2] According to Alexander van Millingen (*Byzantine Constantinople, the Walls of the City and the adjoining Historical Sites*, pp. 89–94) its full name was the "*Porta Xylokerkou*". Mr. Pears doubts this, see *op. cit.*, p. 342.

[3] Phrantzes, p. 283. (See Majatovich, p. 215.)

[4] He had already been wounded by a splinter on May 27.

[5] He was carried to his ship and taken to Chios where he died a few days later or on the way there. In the Church of St. Domenico, where he lies buried, may be read the following epitaph on his monument: "Here lies John Giustiniani of illustrious fame, Genoese patrician and Master-Merchant of Chios, who, in the war of Constantinople against Mahomet the Turk, as Generalissimo of his Serene Highness Constantine, last Emperor of the Eastern Christians, died of a mortal wound."

attributed to this incident. They say that panic followed, the wall was stormed and the city entered, and because of their intense hatred for the Genoese it would seem that they threw the blame on Giustiniani. That his withdrawal caused confusion is probably true, a confusion which the experienced eye of Mahomet did not miss; for the janissaries returned to the assault led by a gigantic Turk named Hassan. Nevertheless he was killed and his followers beaten back, which certainly shows that the defenders fought as staunchly as ever. What now apparently happened was this, and here we will follow M. Vlasto.[1] The Turks, who had broken in by the Kerkoporta, found their retreat cut off by the Bocchiardi brothers, worked their way south to the Adrianople Gate, and thence toward the St. Romanus, then took their defenders in flank and so enabled the sultan to launch his fifth and final assault, which carried the *Peribolos*.

When this attack was made, shouts rose in rear that the city was taken, which seemed to be confirmed by a Turkish flag seen flying over a tower near the Adrianople Gate. Though it was not true, a panic resulted and thousands of the enemy rushed the *Peribolos*. At this moment the emperor returned from another part of the wall, and when he discovered what had happened he galloped down the enclosure calling upon his men to follow him. With Don Francis of Toledo on his right and Theophilus Palaeologus on his left, he rushed upon the Turks crying out "God forbid that I should live an Emperor without an Empire! As my city falls, I will fall with it!"[2] A moment later he was cut down.

With his fall fell the city, which was soon entered on all sides. Panic then swept it from end to end. Though the slaughter was terrible, it was less so than it had been in 1204. It would seem that some 4,000 persons of both sexes and all ages were massacred when, at about midday, Mahomet regained control over his men and put a stop to the orgy. The houses were systematically plundered, the churches ransacked, some 50,000 men, women, and children seized as slaves, and innumerable books destroyed or sold.[3]

Once some semblance of order had been restored, the sultan entered St. Sophia, in which the thousands of people who had sought refuge there were herded as captives. He ordered an *Imaum*

[1] *1453. Les Derniers Jours de Constantinople*, E. V. Vlasto, p. 126.
[2] *Constantine the Last Emperor of the Greeks*, Chedomil Mijatovich, p. 220.
[3] The public library is supposed to have contained 600,000 volumes (Lebeau, *op. cit.*, p. 294). Gibbon, quoting Cardinal Isodore, says 120,000 books were destroyed.

(priest) to mount the pulpit to dedicate the church to Allah, and then, looking around on the scene of desolation he muttered the words of Firdusi:

> The spider's curtain hangs before the portal of Caesar's palace;
> And the owl stands sentinel on the watch-tower of Afrasiab.

Later, he amused himself by buying from his followers those of the Greek nobles who had not escaped and having them executed before him. Among these were the Grand Duke Notaras and his two young sons.

The desolation of the city was complete, and so few people were left in it that for years after Mahomet sent contingents from other places to repopulate it. Wisely he showed toleration towards the Orthodox Church by appointing Gennadius (George Scholarius) patriarch, and though he uprooted the feudal system he did not interfere with the customs of the people. There was astuteness in this policy; for by supporting the Orthodox Church he irrevocably divided the east from the west of Europe.

The shock which followed the catastrophe was stunning. Hallam says: "A sentiment of consternation, perhaps of self-reproach, thrilled to the heart of Christendom";[1] and there was good reason for this, for the fall of Constantinople opened wide the eastern door of Europe. Overrunning the Illyrian peninsula and the Peloponnese,[2] Mahomet turned upon Serbia, and though defeated by Hunyadi, the death of that hero was full compensation for this misfortune. Next, he retook Simendra and established himself in Bosnia; was defeated by Etienne IV of Moldavia; occupied Croatia; and on Scanderbeg's death, decided to invade Italy and march on Rome. But this was not to be. He failed to take Rhodes in 1480 and died the next year, leaving behind him an empire that stretched from the Danube to the Taurus and from the Black Sea to the Adriatic. These were his material gains, but his moral gains were greater still, because for nearly two centuries and a half, that is, from 1453 to 1683, when John Sobieski relieved Vienna, the one topic of European politics was the Turk. When, as described in Chapter 20, Don John of Austria destroyed the Turkish fleet at Lepanto, in 1571, the Venetians proclaimed that the devil was dead.

---

[1] *View of the State of Europe during the Middle Ages*, Henry Hallam (1858), vol. II, p. 136.
[2] He converted the Parthenon at Athens, then the Church of the Holy Virgin, into a mosque.

The reason for this fear was not only that the Turk had been victorious, but that, after a thousand years of a hectic unity, Christendom was segmented – physically broken and spiritually divided. This is how Aeneas Silvius Piccolomini (later Pope Pius II), at the time secretary of the Emperor Frederick III, looked upon Christendom:

"I do not hope for what I want. Christianity has no longer a head: neither Pope nor Emperor is adequately esteemed or obeyed; they are treated as fictitious names and painted figures. Each city has a king of its own; there are as many princes as houses. How might one persuade the numberless Christian rulers to take up arms? Look upon Christianity! Italy, you say, is pacified. I do not know to what extent. The remains of war still exist between the King of Aragon and the Genoese. The Genoese will not fight the Turks: they are said to pay tribute to them! The Venetians have made a treaty with the Turks. If the Italians do not take part, we cannot hope for maritime war. In Spain, as you know, there are many kings of different power, different policy, different will, and different ideas; but these sovereigns who live in the far West cannot be attracted to the East, especially when they are fighting with the Moors of Granada. The King of France has expelled his enemy from his kingdom; but he is still in trouble, and will not dare to send his knights beyond the borders of his kingdom for fear of sudden landing of the English. As far as the English are concerned, they think only of taking revenge for their expulsion from France. Scots, Danes, Swedes, and Norwegians, who live at the end of the world, seek nothing beyond their countries. The Germans are greatly divided and have nothing to unify them."[1]

First of all Mahomet created Turkey in Europe, and so bequeathed to Europe the Ottoman problem. Secondly, the fall of Constantinople, in 1453, rendered irrevocable the schism between the two Churches; henceforth division and not unity was to be a Christian principle. And thirdly, the Turkish conquest not only destroyed all traces of civilization in the cradle of its birth, but deprived that part of Europe of the benefits of Christian autonomy. The lands of the Eastern Empire were utterly degraded: art, literature and commerce foundered under the dead weight of Turkish ignorance and brutality. Fields were uncultivated, industries lost, family life undermined, the people reduced to cattle, and morality emasculated.

[1] Quoted by G. Voigt in *Enea Silvio Piccolomini* (1862), vol. II, pp. 118–119.

But, as the East sank, the West rose. The Greek dispersion, which both preceded and followed the fall of Constantinople, was as prolific in its intellectual conquests as the Hebrew dispersion, which preceded and followed the fall of Jerusalem in the year 70, had been prolific in its spiritual conquests: and in both commercial greed played its part.

Greek scholars percolated through the West, and while science was resuscitated among the thinking, the old Homeric myths again fascinated the common people. Architecture became classical, Cicero and Virgil the masters of the schoolmen, and Alexander and Caesar the instructors of soldiers, and these changes coincided with the discovery of printing—"the money of the mind". Thus it came about that the profoundest influence in this humanist revival, which is called "The Renaissance",[1] was the increasing substitution of pagan for Christian morality. John Addington Symonds once suggested that Faust is the great symbol of this age, Faust who is "content to sell his soul to the devil, but in return he sees Homer and Alexander and obtains Helen as his bride".[2]

This rational (Greek) light brought into flaming day the deadlock between the papal and feudal systems, and before it both were shrivelled up; for the spiritual rampart of Rome had fallen with the storming of the land wall of Constantinople, and the feudal system could save neither. Again, their fall threw a dust of doubt over the entire West: hence the Reformation, that economic crisis which, masquerading under a monk's cowl, ended by exalting Mammon above God.

[1] Though, as Vasiliev points out, the fall of Constantinople did not call forth the Renaissance, which had embraced all Italy during the first half of the fifteenth century, "by transmitting classical works to the West and thereby saving them from destruction at the hands of the Turks, Byzantium performed great service for the future destinies of mankind" (*History of the Byzantine Empire*, vol. II, pp. 433 and 444).
[2] *The Destruction of the Greek Empire*, Edwin Pears, p. 409.

# The reconquest and unification of Spain

Cut off from the rest of Europe by the Pyrenees, and dominated by the Moors, it was not until 1037, when Ferdinand I, surnamed "El Magno" (1028–1065), established the kingdom of Castile, that Spain began to creep back into European history. Assuming the title of "King of the Spains", Ferdinand set out to foster unity between the Christian peoples, and was so far successful that, by marrying the daughter of Alphonso V of Leon, he brought Leon and Galicia under his rule. Next, he initiated what in Spanish history is called the *Reconquista*–the reconquest of the Moorish lands.

His success was considerable, for he advanced to the gates of Seville, and had the other Christian kingdoms supported him, the whole of Spain might well have been rewon. Nevertheless, in spite of their chronic dissensions, his son Alphonso VI (1065–1109) in 1082 carried war as far south as Tarifa, and in 1085 conquered Toledo, a victory of decisive importance. Believing themselves faced by total ruin, the Moors in Andalusia called upon Yusuf ibn Tashfin, emir of the Almoravides (a Berber people) in Morocco, to come to their assistance. Yusuf decided to come as master rather than as ally. He swept into Spain, where he assumed complete ascendancy over the Moors, and on October 23, 1086, routed Alphonso VI's army at Zallaca, in the neighbourhood of Badajoz, but failed to take Toledo.

In the luxurious surroundings of southern Spain, the deterioration of the Almoravides was so rapid that Alphonso I of Aragon, surnamed "the Battler" (1104–1134), who had in 1118 occupied Saragossa, in 1120 marched against them and routed them at Cutanda and again at Arinsol in 1126. Immediately following his death in 1134, Aragon and Catalonia were permanently united, and in 1135 his stepson Alphonso VII (1135–1157) was crowned king of Castile at Leon, and "Emperor in Spain and King of the men of the two religions". In 1144 he captured Cordova and advanced as far south as Almeria in 1147, compelling the Moorish princes to become his vassals. On his death in 1157, Castile and Leon again separated.

Meanwhile, in 1147, French and German knights on their way to the second crusade stormed Lisbon and presented it to Alfonso Henriques, son of Henry Duke of Burgundy, who became the first king of Portugal. Next, in 1148, the Almohades, tribesmen of the Atlas Mountains, who in 1125 had conquered the Almoravides's empire in Africa, burst into Spain, and during the latter part of the twelfth century, after subduing the Almoravides, they rolled back the Christian advance, and on July 18, 1196, routed at enormous loss Alphonso VIII of Castile (1158-1214) at Alarcos, west of Ciudad Réal. Again and again, Pope Innocent III urged the Christian kingdoms of Spain to unite against their common enemy, and his endeavours were so far successful in that a confederacy of Aragon, Navarre, Portugal, and Castile, supported by many foreign knights, under Alphonso VIII, was formed, which on July 16, 1212, routed the Almohades in the battle of Las Nevas de Tolosa. The victory was complete, and the predominance of the Christian cause was secured in Spain.

In 1214, Alphonso VIII died, and, in 1217, the crown of Castile passed to the son of his daughter Berangaria, who became Ferdinand III (1217–1252). He permanently united Castile and Leon and continued the crusade. In 1236 he conquered Cordova, and in 1248, with the help of his vassal the Moorish king of Granada, took Seville. Meanwhile James I of Aragon, the Conqueror (1213–1276), gained possession of the Balearic Islands in 1229; overran Valencia in 1238 and Murcia in 1265. This last conquest brought the *Reconquista* to a close: except for the Moorish kingdom of Granada and a chain of ports stretching westward to Cadiz, the whole of Spain was rewon for the Catholic Church.

The extreme slowness of the Reconquest was due not only to the disunity of Spain, but also to the character of the war waged. It consisted almost entirely of sporadic forays and skirmishes, in which organization, discipline, and any recognizable system of supply were conspicuously lacking. Battles were few and far between and raids constant; their main incentive was not to bring the enemy to battle but to obtain booty and plunder. Because both belligerents were mounted, the inhabitants of the field-lands increasingly sought safety within the walls of the towns and in the innumerable castles, the ruins of which are now dotted over the length and breadth of Spain. The result was a return to city states, each more or less self-sufficient and governed by a primitive democracy.

No attempt at unity, nor even at the formation of a loose confederation of Christian states, followed the great victory of Las Nevas de Tolosa. In fact, under Peter III of Aragon (1276–1286), son of James the Conqueror, division became further stressed. Through his marriage with Constance, daughter of Manfred of Beneventum, he came forward as representative of the claims of the Hohenstaufens in Naples and Sicily against Charles of Anjou, who, as we have seen, in 1268 overwhelmed Conradin at Tagliacozzo. In 1282, taking advantage of the Sicilian Vespers—a popular rising which doomed Charles's hold on Sicily—Peter III was offered the Sicilian crown by the pope, landed in Sicily, raised the siege of Messina and drove the remnants of Charles's army into Calabria. Thus was started the long struggle between the Aragonese and Angevin parties in southern Italy.

The position within Spain at the time was as follows: Castile was assimilating its conquests and was torn by civil wars; Aragon was more concerned with Sicily, Sardinia, and Naples than with Spain; Navarre had its heart in France; and Portugal was beginning hopefully to gaze out over the Atlantic. Castile and Leon had been united, and so had Aragon and Catalonia: such was the sum of the gains towards unity won in 200 years of war.

From now on for nearly a century, no attempt toward a consolidation of Castile and Aragon was made. The former was crippled by a succession of short-lived kings and many long minorities, and the latter was distracted by its Italian ambitions. In Castile, up to the end of the reign of Peter the Cruel (1349–1369) there were constant turmoils and civil wars; order was not restored until the accession of Henry II of Trastamara (1369–1379).

The next event of outstanding importance occurred in 1406; that year John II (1406–1454) succeeded to the throne of Castile, and, as he was still a child, his uncle Ferdinand of Antequera, son of John I of Castile by his wife Eleanor, daughter of Peter IV of Aragon, was appointed regent. The importance of his appointment lay in that, in 1410, Martin I of Aragon (1395–1410) died without issue, and a lengthy dispute over his successor followed, which, in 1412, was decided by the Cortes of Caspe, which offered the crown of Aragon to Ferdinand. By right the Cortes should have offered it to his nephew John II of Castile, for he was the son of Ferdinand's elder brother; but Aragon and Castile were not yet ripe for union. Nevertheless the choice of

Ferdinand, who now became Ferdinand I of Aragon (1412–1416), was a definite step toward its accomplishment.

On the death of John II of Castile the crown passed to his son Henry IV, the Impotent (1454–1474), and when he died in 1474 the legitimacy of his alleged daughter Joanna (La Beltraneja) was disputed by his sister Isabella, who claimed the succession, and who in 1469 had married her cousin Ferdinand, son of John II of Aragon (1458–1479) and grandson of Ferdinand of Antequera. On his death, in 1479, John transmitted his kingdom to his son Ferdinand, whose wife Isabella had been proclaimed queen of Castile and Leon on December 13, 1474.

Thus were the kingdoms of Castile and Aragon united under a dual monarchy, and, except for Navarre and Granada, the whole of Spain was unified. But it is improbable that the union would have proved permanent had not Isabella been compelled to revive the *Reconquista*. Strictly speaking, it had never lapsed completely, but had smouldered on since the days of James the Conqueror. In 1410 Antequera had been wrested from the Moors by Ferdinand I when regent; in 1431 Granada had been invaded and the battle of Higueruela won, and in 1462, after numerous sieges, the rock of Gibraltar was ceded to Castile. From then to 1476 disorders within Castile had halted further progress; but when, during that year, Isabella demanded of Ali Abul Hassan, who had succeeded to the throne of Granada in 1466, the payment of the annual tribute exacted from his father Ismail III, his reply was that "the mints of Granda coined no longer gold, but steel". This meant war, a war which was destined to introduce the Atlantic period of western history. The whole outlook of Europe was about to be changed.

CHAPTER 19

# The siege of Málaga, 1487, and the
# conquest of Granada, 1492

When, in 1479, Ferdinand and Isabella assumed their joint rule of Aragon and Castile, the union of the two kingdoms was wholly nominal, and although, in accordance with their marriage contract, all royal charters were signed by both and the heads of both appeared on the coinage, the administration of Castile was reserved to Isabella in her own right and that of Aragon to Ferdinand in his. Therefore Castile and Aragon remained politically apart, and in order to consummate their union some great adventure was required, which in its singleness of purpose would draw away the attention of both Castilians and Aragonese from their internal interests as well as from their mutual jealousies and focus it on a goal of outstanding importance to all Spaniards.

Though in the accomplishment of this quest religion was to play a dominant part, of itself it was insufficient. Other things were needed: a leader, a unifying instrument, and a cause based on a common fear, for fear, like a magnet, brings men together. The first was found in Queen Isabella herself, a fervent Catholic and a practical woman; the second in the establishment of the Spanish Inquisition by Pope Sextus IV in 1478,[1] and the third in the dread of another great Moslem invasion; for Africa was never lacking in fighting men.

The personality of Isabella not only dominated Spain, but was its oriflamme, its *étendard vivant* which, synchronizing with a chivalrous age, gave *élan* to a quixotically minded people in a way which no male leadership could have done.[2] Of the many and

---

[1] The Inquisition was the sole common instrument to both kingdoms, and there was but a single Inquisitor General for all Spain. Unlike in other countries, the Inquisition was completely under royal control; its officers were paid servants of the Crown. As far as it was concerned, internal political divisions ceased to exist. "It tended to reduce all men—irrespective of their wealth and rank—to a common level before the law, as well as to a common subjection to the Crown" (*The Golden Century of Spain, 1501–1621,* T. Trevor Davies (1937), p. 13).

[2] Walsh calls her "a woman crusader who changed the course of civilization and the aspect of the entire world" (*Isabella of Spain* (1931), p. 15).

frequently exaggerated panegyrics which have been pronounced on her, one which rings true is that of de Maulde la Clavière:

"She was a wonderful mixture of different kinds of heroism", he writes. "She was brave and resolute without a touch of the virago. After a night spent in dictating orders, she would tranquilly resume a piece of church embroidery, or, like Anne of France, the practical education of her daughters. In her own private affairs she was plain and simple, in public she was all ostentation. She was a conversationalist of the first order and loved to attack high philosophical questions, here and there dropping into a discussion some original phrase, some bold and clear-cut thought, while her deep blue eyes lit up and darted upon her company a certain glance of warmth and loyalty the renown of which still clings to her name. A strange woman! ardent like Anne of France, guileless, straightforward, somewhat starched perhaps, but all heart for her friends, so fond a mother that she died of the loss of her children, so thorough a woman that she declared she knew only four fine sights in the world: 'a soldier in the field, a priest at the altar, a beautiful woman in bed, a thief on the gibbet'."[1]

As regards the second, though eventually the Inquisition became an instrument of persecution, "It was", writes Mr. R. Trevor Davies, "the offspring of that fierce desire for racial purity that bursts out from time to time like a devouring flame in many parts ot the world"; for in Spain "racial purity and religious orthodoxy had become mutually dependent". Further, he says: "The value of the Inquisition as a royal instrument for strengthening the monarchy and unifying the country would be difficult to exaggerate."[2] This is easily understandable when it is recognized that, generally speaking, the greatness of a nation is in direct proportion to the intolerance of its rulers, as long as intolerance has a mystical origin and an heroic goal. These two requirements were to be found in Spain: the former produced St. Ignatius Loyola (1491–1556), founder of the Society of Jesus, and the latter that spirit of knight-errantry which is parodied in *Don Quixote*.

The third—the copestone—fitted the moment, not for Spain alone, but for the whole of western Christendom, because the expansion of the Ottoman empire had awakened the distant memories

[1] *The Woman of the Renaissance* (English edit., 1901), p. 323.
[2] *The Golden Century of Spain, 1501–1621*, pp. 11–12.

of 711 and the many invasions since. Checked for the time being on the Danube and in the Adriatic, there was no saying that Islam would not again flow westward through Africa, and Málaga was but a day's sail from Morocco. This possibility had for centuries terrified Christian Spain, and because Spain was as much the bridgehead of western Europe as Byzantium was of eastern, it now terrified Europe as a whole. Then, suddenly, on December 26, 1481, the unexpected happened, and all these ingredients of Spanish unification crystallized. That day Abul Hassan, king of Granada, misreading the internal conditions of Castile, under cover of night and of a howling gale surprised the fortified town of Zahara, north-west of Ronda, slaughtered its Castilian garrison and swept its inhabitants into slavery. Many such raids had occurred during the last 700 years, but this was to be the last one the Moors were destined to make, and it was to lead, not only to their final ruin, but to the unification of Spain and the outburst of yet another imperialism.

Although, at the time, Ferdinand and Isabella were far from ready to face up to the affront, on his own initiative–so it would seem–Don Rodrigo Ponce de Leon, Marquis of Cadiz, did so, and in retaliation, on February 28, 1482, he surprised and captured the town of Alhama, which lies twenty-five miles southwest of Granada. When they heard of this success, the king and queen, then at Medina del Campo, not far from Valladolid, realized that the whole strength of Granada would be turned against the marquis and forthwith determined to support him.

It was well that they did so, for on March 5 Abul Hassan, at the head of a powerful army, appeared before the town, but such was his haste to take the field that he had left his siege train in Granada. Once before Alhama, he found it so strongly defended that it could only be starved out. Next, while he invested it he heard that a relieving force was on its way and on March 29 he raised the siege and returned to Granada to fetch up his train. Barely had he returned to Alhama and planted his batteries than Ferdinand approached, and fearing to be caught between him and the Marquis of Cadiz, he raised the siege and withdrew. On May 14 Ferdinand entered the town.

Ferdinand mustered his army there and on July 1, at the head of 4,000 horse and 12,000 foot, he set out to seize Loja, on the Antequera–Granada road. He ran into an ambush and was so severely routed that the war might there and then have ended, had it not been for a harem intrigue within Granada which led to a *coup d'état*. Abul Hassan was dethroned by his son Boabdil, known as "el Chico" ("the Little"), and to save his life he sought refuge at the court of his brother Abdullah, surnamed "el Zagal" ("the Valiant"), at Málaga.[1]

Meanwhile the war, as on former occasions, had degenerated into a series of fitful forays and skirmishes, when suddenly another disaster befell the dual monarchy. In the spring of 1483, the Marquis of Cadiz, accompanied by the Grand Master of Santiago, set out from Antequera to raid the environs of Málaga, and as they traversed a sierra, called the Axarquia, they were caught in its defiles by el Zagal and routed even more completely than Ferdinand had been at Loja. Nevertheless the ultimate result of this victory was so unfavourable for the Moorish cause that, had it not occurred, the probability is the war would have meandered on indefinitely as so often had happened in the past. The result was that Boabdil in Granada, envious and fearful of his uncle's renown, decided to emulate him. He assembled 9,000 foot and 700 horse and set out to seize the town of Lucena, north-west of Loja, but when about to invest it, was fallen upon by the Count of Cabra and defeated and captured.

When the count discovered who his prisoner was, he sent an urgent message to the king and queen, then at Vitoria. Ferdinand hurried south and assembled a council of war at Cordova. After a hot debate it was decided to release Boabdil and to send him back to Granada on terms which would bind him to the Spanish cause and simultaneously ensure a continuance of the internal Moorish quarrels. The more important of the terms were that: a truce of two years would be granted to Boabdil on the stipulation that he paid 12,000 gold doubloons yearly to the Spanish sovereigns; suffered their troops to pass freely through his territories for the purpose of carrying on the war against his father and uncle; attended the Cortes when summoned to do so; and surrendered his son as hostage. These ignominious terms were accepted. They meant that hence onward the kingdom of Granada would be split in two and, therefore, that each half could be destroyed in turn.

Strategically, this division of their enemy's power presented

[1] Abul Hassan reigned between 1462–1482 and 1483–1485; el Zagal (as Mohammed XII) between 1485–1487, and Boabdil (as Mohammed XI) between 1482–1483 and 1487–1492. These changes of dates are illustrative of the chaotic conditions the Moors were in.

Ferdinand and Isabella with so propitious an opportunity to eliminate Moorish dominion in Spain that it could not well be missed. All now depended on the tactical means at their disposal, and as they stood they were far from adequate. Their fighting forces were little more than a gathering of feudal bands – brave, chivalrous, undisciplined, and quixotic. Orders were communicated by the ringing of bells, as monks were wont to be called to prayer in their churches, and before fighting the opposing generals would, as in their tourneys, settle the day of battle in advance, and when it took place it was a mêlée in which luck or courage was the deciding factor.[1] If Admiral Jurien de la Gravière is righ when he says *"L'histoire des nations, c'est l'histoire de leurs armées"*,[2] then, as we shall see, the changes wrought in the Spanish army during the Moorish war are a measure of the national changes effected by Ferdinand and Isabella during this period. When it ended, the Spanish soldier had become the most noted in the world, and he remained so until the day of Rocroi (1643), in which battle, the army which had been created by men like the "Great Captain", Gonsalvo of Cordova (1453–1515), went down before the Great Condé (1621–1686).

Isabella's first problem was to find some common factor which would enable her to weld her forces into a single instrument, and there being as yet no true political unity, there was no national spirit to build on. Therefore, a magnetic idea had to be created before the local patriotisms could be united. This she and Ferdinand achieved by basing the war on a religious motive – that is, by substituting the idea of a crusade for that of a war of political liberation. In this they were helped by the recent Ottoman successes in eastern Europe. Only the year before the Alhama was stormed, to the consternation of all Christendom, Mahomet II had occupied Otranto, and when in the following year Pope Sextus VI learnt of the fall of Alhama, so overjoyed was he that he sent to the Spanish king and queen, by way of a standard, a massive silver cross, which was borne by Ferdinand in each of his campaigns. It was invariably raised on the topmost pinnacle of each conquered town and adored by the assembled host. Further, during the war unity was stimulated by the constant presence of Ferdinand and Isabella in the midst of their advancing armies.

---

[1] See *Histoire d'Espagne*, Rosseeuw St. Hilaire (1844), vol. v, p. 438.
[2] *La guerre de Chypre et la bataille de Lépante*, Vice-Admiral Jurien de la Gravière (1888), vol. i, p. xlii.

As Merriman points out: "It was the surest possible way of keeping the factious nobles from deserting, of maintaining order and discipline in the ranks, of convincing the soldiers that there was no duty they were called upon to perform in which their sovereigns were too proud to bear a part."[1]

Correctly it may be said that, from 1483 onward, Isabella became the soul of the entire enterprise, until from a crusade it evolved into a vast pan-Spanish movement, which under her grandson, the Emperor Charles V, led to the establishment of an empire unequalled since the days of Charlemagne. While she prepared, Ferdinand fought, and during the long war she proved herself to be one of the ablest quartermaster-generals in history.

Though in extent the kingdom of Granada was not large—two hundred miles from east to west and sixty from north to south—because of its mountainous nature, which rendered supply in the field most difficult, the task of conquest was formidable. Roads were few and castles many, and as for the most part they were built on hill-tops or the brinks of precipices, they were virtually impregnable until the advent of the cannon which, at this early stage in their development, were so heavy and cumbersome that they demanded good roads. It was castles and supply difficulties which in the past had forced field operations into the groove of the *cavalgada*, or cavalry foray, which seldom led to permanent gain: hence the excessive slowness of the Reconquest. Therefore, because cavalry was of little use in siege warfare, which was the essence of the problem, Isabella turned her attention to artillery, engineers, and infantry.

She made use of three means of recruitment: first, feudal levies; but as their independence and lack of discipline rendered them unreliable, secondly she turned to the recently created *hermandad* (constabulary), and converted it into the beginnings of a national army; thirdly, she hired Swiss mercenaries who, at the time, were the most noted infantry in western Europe.[2] Besides these troops, many volunteers flocked from Germany, England, and France to join her crusade, and prominent among them was Sir Edward Woodville, brother-in-law of Edward IV, who assumed the title of his elder brother Lord Scales.

---

[1] *The Rise of the Spanish Empire in the Old World and in the New* (1918), vol. II, p. 66.
[2] In Prescott's opinion (*History of the Reign of Ferdinand and Isabella* (1842), vol. I, p. 452): "Their example no doubt contributed to the formation of that invincible Spanish infantry, which, under the Great Captain and his successors, may be said to have decided the fate of Christendom for more than half a century."

Her three main problems were: (1) the reduction of castles; (2) the supply of the besieging forces; and (3) the devastation of the land adjacent to the town or castle attacked. The first demanded an artillery train, the second a supply train, and the third a body of devastators. In order to raise the first, she invited into Spain gunfounders from France, Germany, and Italy. Forges were built, powder manufactured, and cannon balls made as well as imported from Sicily, Flanders, and Portugal. Don Francisco Ramirez was placed in command of the artillery, and under him was assembled a train "such as was probably not possessed at that time by any other European potentate".[1]

The largest lombards (or bombards) were twelve feet long and of fourteen inch calibre. They were built of iron bars two inches in breadth, held together by rings and bolts, and they threw iron and marble cannon balls, and at times also fired balls "which", says an eye-witness, "scattering long trains of light in their passage through the air, filled the beholders with dismay, and descending on the roofs of the edifices, frequently occasioned extensive conflagration".[2] These large pieces could neither be elevated nor traversed; they were bedded in wooden carriages without wheels,[3] and as they had to be dragged by oxen over the roughest country, special roads had to be built for them. For this work immense bodies of pioneers were employed, and we are told that at the siege of Cambil 6,000 were needed to build a single causeway.

The supply train consisted mainly of pack mules, of which the enormous number of 80,000 is said to have been collected. The work carried out by the corps of devastators was appalling. According to Prescott: "From the second year of the war, thirty thousand foragers were reserved for this service, which they effected by demolishing farm-houses, granaries, and mills (which last were exceedingly numerous in a land watered by many small streams), by eradicating the vines, and laying waste the olive-gardens and plantations of oranges, almonds, mulberries, and all the rich varieties that grew luxuriant in this highly favoured region."[4]

Besides these preparations, Isabella introduced two novel organizations, a corps of field messengers and a medical service. Many tents were equipped for the wounded, and as Merriman

[1] *History of the reign of Ferdinand and Isabella*, vol. 1, p. 442.
[2] *Ibid.*, vol. 1, pp. 433–444.
[3] For light pieces, the wheeled gun-carriage began to appear about 1470.
[4] *Ibid.*, vol. 1, p. 440.

notes, "It is the earliest recorded case of anything resembling a modern field hospital."[1]

The army was assembled at Cordova, and in all it is said to have numbered 80,000 troops and as many pack animals. The former were made up of from ten to twelve thousand horse, between twenty and forty thousand infantry, and an unknown number of gunners, miners, pioneers and foragers. When one considers the difficulties of the terrain and the thoroughness of the projected operation, even if the total of 80,000 men is an exaggerated one, the forces required must have been large.

Besides the army, the Castilian fleet played an important part in the war; its main task was to cut off the Moors in Africa from their blood relations in Granada. On the fall of Alhama, Abdul Hassan's first action was to solicit aid from the Merinites in Morocco. In answer to this call Isabella had ordered the Castilian fleet south, but as yet it lacked a suitable naval base from which to operate.

Taken as a whole, the Spanish strategy was one of increasing attrition based on: (1) establishing naval bases on the southern coast of Granada; (2) on blockading that coast line and cutting it off from contact with Morocco; and (3) meanwhile devastating Granada itself.[2] Under cover of this attrition a methodical series of sieges was to be carried out, in which Ferdinand, who was commander-in-chief of the army, resorted to the policy of treating each town or castle which surrendered at call with moderation, and each which did not, when taken, with rigour. In the case of Benemaquez, which first surrendered and subsequently revolted, when he retook it he had one hundred and ten of the principal inhabitants hanged above its walls; the remainder he sold as slaves, and the town itself he razed to the ground. Commenting on this piece of frightfulness, Prescott writes: "The humane policy usually pursued by Ferdinand seems to have had more favourable effect on his enemies, who were exasperated, rather than intimidated, by this ferocious act of vengeance."[3]

When, in 1485, all was ready, Ferdinand set out on his initial campaign of conquest. Adhering to his strategy of attrition, his first two aims were to occupy Málaga and Almeria, in order to cut off Granada from Africa. The occupation of Málaga demanded

[1] *The Rise of the Spanish Empire*, vol. II, p. 69.
[2] See *Isabella the Catholic*, Baron de Nervo (English edit., 1897), p. 155.
[3] *Ferdinand and Isabella*, vol. I, p. 446.

two distinct operations, the occupation of Marbella, to gain a base for his fleet, and the occupation of Loja and Velez-Málaga, so that, should he be compelled to lay siege to Málaga, his rear and left flank would be secure; for Loja commanded the Málaga–Granada road and Velez the coastal road linking Málaga with Almeria.

To gain Marbella, in May, 1485, he laid siege to Ronda, and reduced it by his cannon. Next, in 1486, he occupied Alora, and from there he advanced by way of Cartarma and Coin, pinched out Marbella and forced its surrender. He based his fleet on that town and next laid siege to Loja. After he took it, on April 7, 1487, he set out from Antequera, advanced through most difficult country and appeared before the walls of Velez-Málaga on April 17.

El Zagal, then at Guadix, fully realized the strategical importance of that town and made a desperate effort to relieve it, but he was repulsed by the Marquis of Cadiz and fell back on Granada. He found its gates closed to him by Boabadil and withdrew to Guadix, which with Almeria and Baza still remained faithful to his cause. On April 27, Velez-Málaga capitulated to Ferdinand, and following its fall Málaga was encircled by land and sea.

Both in size and importance, Málaga was second only to Granada, and with the exception of Almeria it was the only port left to the Moors from which contact could precariously be maintained with Africa. It was inhabited by eleven to fifteen thousand people, without counting its garrison which numbered several thousands, mostly staunch African troops. It was surrounded by strong walls which were commanded by a citadel, known as the Castle of the Genoese, which by a fortified way was connected with the Castle of Gebelfaro. The town was prepared to stand a siege and was commanded by Hamet Ez Zegri, a faithful follower of el Zagal.

Ferdinand learnt that the inhabitants of Málaga were eager to capitulate and instructed the Marquis of Cadiz to open negotiations with Ez Zegri. But when the latter refused to consider a surrender, on May 7 Ferdinand ordered the camp at Velez to be struck, and after a successful advanced guard action on the coastal road, he arrived before Málaga.

He enclosed Málaga and its suburb with works of contravallation and completed the investment by blockading its harbour with his fleet, then he stormed the suburbs, and next ordered up his heavy siege pieces which were still at Antequera. While roads were built to facilitate their approach, he sent to Algeciras to bring forward supplies of marble cannon shot which had lain there ever since its capture by Alphonso XI in the preceding century. More important still, he sent for the queen, whose presence, much like that of Joan of Arc, inspired the soldiers with the highest heroism. At this time, St. Hilaire writes that "An unbelievable spirit of courage and devotion was shown throughout the land. The whole of Spain was exalted, as Europe had been in the age of the Crusades. From every pulpit the cry of the holy war went forth, and from every corner of the realm reinforcements marched towards the scene of action."[1]

When the siege pieces arrived, wishing to spare the town, Ferdinand again summoned its citizens to surrender and offered liberal terms in the event of immediate compliance. If they refused, then when he captured the town he would reduce the whole of its inhabitants to slavery. Though the people were willing enough to comply, Ez Zegri's answer was a series of vigorous sallies which kept the Spanish camp in constant alarm. Meanwhile el Zagal was not idle. He knew the importance of Málaga and sent two relieving forces from Guadix. On its way, the first was cut to pieces by Boabdil, who at the same time sent an embassy with a present of Arab horses and costly silks to Ferdinand and Isabella, as tokens of his friendship. The second, in part succeeded in penetrating the Spanish lines and in gaining Málaga, but in the attempt many of its men were cut down, and among the prisoners taken there was one who informed the Marquis of Cadiz that he could make important disclosures to the king. Cadiz believed him and had him taken to the royal tent, where, mistaking Don Alvaro, son of the Duke of Braganza, for the king, and Dona Beatrice of Bobadilla for the queen, he suddenly drew a dagger from beneath the folds of his mantle and wounded both. Before he could repeat his attack he was cut down. His remains were shot by a trebuchet over the walls of Málaga.[2]

The position within Málaga rapidly worsened and the city became straitened for supplies, largely because of the numbers of refugees who had flocked into it. Meanwhile the bombardment continued, and when the supply of cannon shot – a crucial problem

[1] *Histoire d'Espagne*, Rosseeuw St. Hilaire, vol. v, p. 483.
[2] A similar incident, but with a live instead of a dead man, is recorded to have taken place, in 1345, at the siege of Auberoche (*Chroniques de J. Froissart*, edit. Simeon Luce, 1872, vol. III, p. 65).

in sieges of this period—grew short, Ferdinand resolved to storm the city. To assist in this he had a number of large wooden towers, moved on rollers, built and equipped with swing-bridges and ladders. Mining was also resorted to under the supervision of Francisco Ramirez. Anticipating what was in progress, in desperation the Moors countermined, attacked the Spanish fleet and continued their sorties, but to no avail. At length a mine was sprung[1] under one of the towers and a possible entrance into the city was gained.

Terrified by this disaster, the citizens of Málaga, many dying of starvation and not a few of whom deserted to the Spaniards, urged Ez Zegri to capitulate, and so critical grew the situation that he withdrew the garrison to Gebelfaro, leaving it to the Malagueños to make the best terms they could with the enemy. At once they sent a deputation of the leading citizens to Ferdinand. But he refused to receive it, saying that because his offer of surrender on terms had twice been rejected, nothing would now satisfy him except an unconditional capitulation. Two further deputations failed to change his decision and on August 18, 1487, the gates of Málaga were opened and the besiegers entered the city.

Pillage was strictly prohibited and Ferdinand's first act was to cleanse the city by the removal of all dead bodies and filth. Next, he had the principal mosque consecrated to the service of Santa Maria de la Encarnacion, and in it mass was held and a *Te Deum* sung. Lastly, he pronounced its doom. It was that all Christian renegades should be executed, all relapsed Jews burnt, and that the rest of the population should be sold as slaves. One third was transported to Africa in exchange for an equal number of Christian captives; one third was sold to pay toward the cost of the war; and the rest distributed as presents—100 picked Moorish soldiers went to the pope, 50 of the best-looking Moorish girls to the Queen of Naples, and 30 to the queen of Portugal.

On the day following the occupation of Málaga the fortress of Gebelfaro surrendered, and well pleased with his success, shortly after Ferdinand led his army back to Cordova and dispersed it for the winter.

Although the fall of Málaga rendered the conquest of Granada inevitable, because it was the port from which the latter received

---

[1] Prescott (vol. ii, p. 29) considers that this is the first authenticated employment of gunpowder in mining. As we have seen, if correctly reported, the first is to be credited to the siege of Constantinople in 1453.

the bulk of its reinforcements and supplies, in order completely to cut off the Moorish kingdom from its potential base – Africa – in June, 1488, Ferdinand advanced against Almeria. He failed to carry it by a *coup de main*, and withdrew to Jaén, from where, toward the end of May, 1489, at the head of 15,000 horse and 80,000 foot,[1] he laid siege to Baza. Six thousand men were employed for two months encircling the town with continuous line of contravallation. The siege proved a long one,[2] and when autumn set in, instead of withdrawing into winter quarters, Ferdinand ordered a hutted camp to be built in which his troops were so well supplied by Isabella that, though plague raged throughout Andalusia, they remained unaffected. Reduced to extremities, Baza capitulated on December 4 and Ferdinand showed great moderation. The terms agreed were that all mercenaries were allowed to march out with the honours of war and that the inhabitants could either remain in the suburbs of the town, or, should they wish, freely go elsewhere.

The fall of Baza was at once followed by the submission of el Zagal, who agreed to surrender the whole of his domains, including Almeria and Guadix. The former of these cities was immediately occupied by Ferdinand, and el Zagal, who some years before is supposed to have assassinated his brother Abul Hassan, was offered the puppet kingship of Andaraz in fief to the Castilian crown. He refused to accept it, withdrew to Africa, and is reported to have ended his days there in indigence.

With the disappearance of Abul Hassan and the submission of el Zagal, all that remained for Ferdinand to do was to occupy Granada. From Almeria, therefore, he sent an embassy to Boabdil to demand its surrender in accordance with the terms of the treaty of Loja, which stipulated that this should be done on the capitulation of Baza, Guadix, and Almeria. But either Boabdil was unwilling, or what would seem more probable, he was now no longer a free agent but the prisoner of the ruined and desperate men of the *routier* class who now thronged Granada.[3] They, it would appear, decided to hold fast to the city, for war was their sole means of livelihood and the city was strongly fortified.

[1] There is something stereotyped about the figures 15,000 and 80,000, which constantly are quoted during this war. They would appear to represent the total establishments rather than the actual field forces. Circourt, *Histoire des Mores, etc.* (1846), vol. I, p. 321, gives Ferdinand's strength as "12,000 horse and 50,000 foot".
[2] Circourt, (*op. cit.* vol. I, p. 323) states that el Zagal had accumulated fifteen months' supplies in Baza.
[3] See Circourt's *Histoire des Mores, etc.*, vol. I, pp. 328–329.

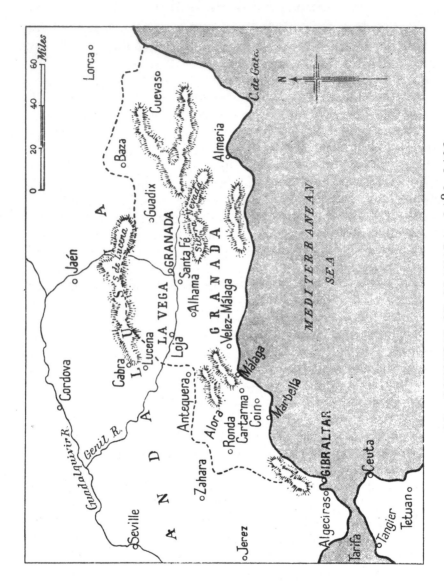

32. CONQUEST OF GRANADA, 1481–1492

It was built at the foot of the Sierra Nevada upon two hills, below which flowed the small rivers Genil and Darro. On the summits of the hills rose two fortresses, the Alhambra and the Albaycin. The town was surrounded by a brick wall, strengthened by a vast number of towers, and at the foot of the Alhambra and beyond the city wall stretched an extensive *vega* (plain) covered with vineyards, gardens, orchards, and fields of wheat, which were irrigated from the Genil. The population of the city is said to have numbered 200,000 at the time, though this figure is probably exaggerated.

Ferdinand's summons rejected, while Isabella prepared for the siege of Granada, in the spring of 1490 he began to devastate the fertile *vega* west of the city. He continued this in the autumn, when he destroyed twenty-four towns and castles, burnt many villages, and swept the country-side clear of all food stocks and cattle. With Granada thus deprived of its sources of supply, in April, 1491, he appeared before its walls at the head of 80,000 men, determined that however long the siege might last, he would carry on with it until the city capitulated. He had learnt during the siege of Baza the economy of sheltering his troops, and he built a new town for them six miles west of Granada, which, symbolically, he named Santa Fé. It was laid out in the form of a Roman camp, and was to be, in the words of a Castilian writer, "the only city in Spain that has never been contaminated by the Moslem heresy".[1] Its building profoundly discouraged the Moors in Granada; it was proof that the king would never cease his efforts until their city was his.

From then on, in spite of its formidable fortifications, its innumerable towers and its two great castles of the Albaycin and the Alhambra, Granada was doomed either by starvation or assault. Again the appearance of Isabella raised the enthusiasm of the besiegers to the highest pitch of devotion, and "with her order and abundance reigned in the Castilian camp. Night and day on horseback she inspected the works, saw everything, not a detail escaping her eye. She distributed the rations, allotted the billets, arranged the routes of the convoys, and by her wit stimulated the good will and courage of her men."[2]

In September the town of Santa Fé was finished, and its building so terrified Boabdil, who by now it would appear had

[1] Quoted by Prescott in *Ferdinand and Isabella*, vol. II, p. 83.
[2] *Histoire d'Espagne*, Rosseeuw St. Hilaire, vol. v, p. 502.

regained some of his former authority, that he asked for a suspension of arms in order to treat for peace. Nothing could have suited Ferdinand and Isabella better, and on October 5 they agreed upon a truce of seventy days, during which the royal secretary, Hernando de Zafra, and Gonsalvo de Cordova were entrusted by Ferdinand to negotiate. On November 25 a final settlement was reached, the terms of which were exceedingly liberal. The city was to be surrendered within sixty days; all artillery and fortifications were to be handed over; the Moors were permitted to retain their property, dress, customs, laws and religion, and to be ruled by their own magistrates under a governor appointed by the Spanish king, and those who wished to migrate to Africa were to be given free transport. The surrender took place on January 2, 1492, when Boabdil handed the keys of Alhambra to Ferdinand saying: "They are thine, O King, since Allah so Decrees it; use thy success with clemency and moderation."[1] Then the gates were thrown open, and to the chanting of the *Te Deum* the great silver cross, borne by Ferdinand throughout his crusade, was carried into the city.[2]

Thus, after seven hundred years of conflict, was the Reconquest finally accomplished, and, with the exception of Navarre, Spain was united into one great Christian kingdom ideally placed to establish a new order. Not only was she wedged between the Mediterranean and the Atlantic, and, therefore, could exploit both; but she was protected against invasion in the north by the long rampart of the Pyrenees, and in the south was linked to Africa by the narrow Strait of Gibraltar. Therefore she stood sentinel between the two western continents of the Old World. Potentially she was the strategic hub of a new world system, ready to replace the hub of the old which had been lost in 1453. No other kingdom in Europe was so well placed at the time to expand into a great empire, and expansion now coursed through the veins of her people, and its outburst was immediate.

Because, in the idealistic sense, Spain was now a nation, the tolerance which Ferdinand and Isabella had shown to the conquered Moors acted as an irritant to the rising spirit of nationalism. This may be judged from an event which immediately followed the fall of Granada: the Jews in Spain were offered the alternative

[1] *Ferdinand and Isabella*, William H. Prescott, vol. II, p. 87.
[2] Like his uncle, el Zagal, Boabdil was given a puppet kingdom; but he soon abandoned it and passing over to Africa fell in battle in service of an African prince, his kinsman.

of Christian baptism or exile, and many thousands quitted Spain.[1]

Nothing now could divert the spirit of intolerance, begotten by victorious nationalism, from its course. It demanded not only one God and one monarchy, but also one race. Had it not been for the Ottoman threat, which haunted all Christendom, and that after the conquest many Moors withdrew to Morocco to stimulate the Barbaresque pirates, persecution might have been kept within bounds. But this was not to be; the increasing Algerian slave raids and plunderings kept intolerance alive. The Moors in Spain, conquered or unconquered, were, as Louis Bertrand points out, a standing danger. Had they remained, he writes, "The Peninsula, with its unassimilable Moors and Jews, would have been nothing more than a transit territory, as the countries of the Levant still are to-day; a hybrid country, without unity, without character. Europe would have had its 'Levantines' like Asia. Spain would have become one of those bastard countries which live only by letting themselves be shared and exploited by foreigners, and have no art, or thought or civilisation proper to themselves."[2] However cruel the final expulsion of the Moors may have been, it was inevitable; it was a cry of the blood, of the race, of the soul of the Spanish peoples—an all-compelling urge.

Machiavelli (1467–1527), a contemporary of these events, calls Ferdinand "a new prince", adding that "in the beginning of his reign he attacked Granada, and this enterprise was the foundation of his dominions".[3] Yet far greater things than the consolidation of his power emanated from the war. It did not mark the ending of an epoch, rather, as Mr. Merriman says, "it was not so much an end as a beginning".[4] Militarily and politically it ushered in a new age. Militarily, in that it was a school of war in which was trained the finest army in Europe. Politically, in that, "since the conquest of the Holy City, Europe had not experienced a joy equal to what she experienced on the news of the taking of Granada".[5] "The fall of Granada", writes Prescott, "excited general sensation throughout Christendom, where it was received as counterbalancing, in a manner, the loss of Constantinople, nearly half a century before."[6] But what made it so overwhelmingly impor-

---

[1] On this question see *Isabella of Spain*, William Thomas Walsh, chap. xxv.
[2] *The History of Spain*, Louis Bertrand and Sir Charles Petrie (1934), p. 228.
[3] *The Prince* (Everyman's Library, 1914), p. 177.
[4] *The Rise of the Spanish Empire*, vol. ii, p. 74.
[5] *Histoire d'Espagne*, Rosseeuw St. Hilaire, vol. v, p. 507.
[6] *Ferdinand and Isabella*, William H. Prescott, vol. ii, p. 91.

tant was that in the same year – 1492 – in which Spain became a united country and took her place among the great nations of Europe, under the auspices of and with the assistance of Isabella, Christopher Columbus (1451–1506) discovered for Spain a new world.

This was the most fruitful event in western history since in 334 B.C. Alexander crossed the Hellespont, and both were no accident, but part and parcel of the urge to expand which throughout history has sprung to life in every virile people on attaining nationhood. Therefore the key to the understanding of the world's greatest drama – the discovery of the New World – is to be sought in the extension of the idea behind the Conquest of Granada – the coming of age of Spain. It was the ultimate crusade against Islam.

The times were ripe for this, the greatest of all geographical discoveries, and the two things which assured it were both related to the crusades. The one was the restriction of trade between Asia and Europe through the interposition of the Turks, and the other was the old belief of St. Louis that were the Great Khan of the Indies reached he might be persuaded to attack Islam in rear. The two dovetailed, and no sooner had a solution of the former been ushered in by the Portuguese voyages of discovery, initiated by Dom Henry of Portugal, the Navigator (1433–1460),[1] than Pope Nicholas V (1447–1455) suggested to him that, if he could only render the Oceanic Sea – that is, the Atlantic – navigable as far as the Indies, which were said to be subject to Christ, then by entering into relations with their inhabitants he might be able to persuade them to come to the help of Christendom against the Turks. Thus, in idea, the strategic problem was shifted from the eastern Mediterranean to the Atlantic, in order to continue the crusades as well as to reopen the Asiatic trade routes.

The idea of reaching the Indies by sailing westward instead of eastward had for long intrigued the geographers, for as yet no one imagined that between the western shores of Europe and the eastern shores of Asia there lay a vast continent. Further, Roger Bacon's assumption that the distance between Spain and Asia could not be very great,[2] had been adopted by Cardinal Pierre d'Ailly in his *Imago Mundi*, published in 1410,[3] and also

---

[1] Henry's first ventures down the African coast were in pursuance of a vague plan to unite with the legendary Christian monarch Prester John, whose realm was supposed to be located in Abyssinia, in a campaign against the Turks.

[2] In his *Opus Majus* of 1267 (edit. Jebb, 1733), p. 183, quoted by Fiske in his *The Discovery of America*, vol. 1, pp. 371–372 and 378–379.

[3] Probably printed in 1486 or 1487; see Vignaud's *Études critiques sur la vie de Colomb* (1905), p. 298.

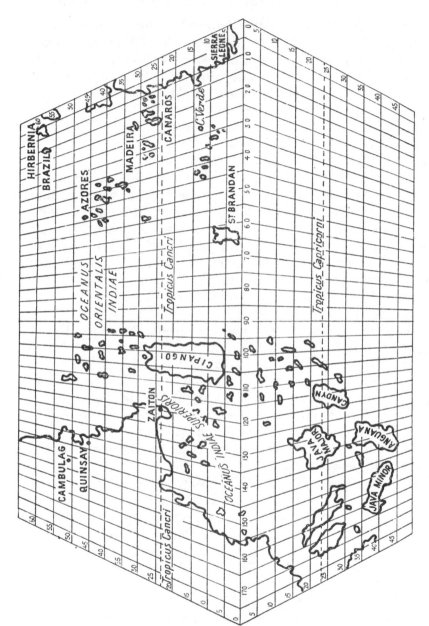

33. TOSCANELLI'S MAP OF THE ATLANTIC OCEAN, 1474

by Paul Toscanelli, the noted astonomer and cosmographer of Florence, who, in 1474 sent to Alfonso V of Portugal a map illustrating the possibilities of the western sea route.[1] Although Toscanelli correctly estimated the equatorial distance round the globe, he so exaggerated the extent of Asia and Europe as to reduce the distance between them by an Atlantic voyage to about 6,500 geographical miles. This put the eastern coast of China in the longitude of Oregon, and Japan, the Cipango of Marco Polo, at about 3,250 miles due west of the Canaries.

Such was the background of the great discovery, which owed its accomplishment to the vision, pertinacity and overwhelming presumption of Christopher Columbus, one of the most enigmatic personalities in history, and whose character and achievements have been as much confused as clarified by modern scholarship.

Until the last quarter of the nineteenth century, when Henry Harisse searched through the archives of Genoa, Savona, Seville and other places,[2] the traditional view held of Columbus was that he was one of the greatest heroes of history. Since then, by several of his biographers, notably Justin Winsor,[3] Henry Vignaud,[4] and Marius André,[5] because of the fantastic stories he invented about his family and his early life, he has been written down as one of the greatest of charlatans. Because these stories have been proved to be pure fabrications, Vignaud goes so far as to hold suspect practically everything he said or wrote. Yet there would appear to be a very sound reason for these fictions – namely, to impress his personal importance upon those he hoped to interest in his grand idea.

Instead of coming from a noble family, as he asserted, he was son of a weaver of Quinto al Mare, near Genoa, and was born in 1451.[6] He followed his father's trade, and in 1476 sailed from Genoa with four merchantmen for England, which, when off St. Vincent, were attacked by a French squadron. Two of the ships were sunk, but Columbus, although wounded, reached the

[1] Vignaud, *op. cit.*, p. 23, doubts whether this letter was ever sent. The copy of the map is taken from Fiske (*op. cit.*, vol. 1, p. 357). It was used by Columbus in his first voyage across the Atlantic. Each longitudinal space represents 250 geographical miles. This map was the source of the western part of Martin Behaim's globe of 1492.
[2] See his *Christophe Colomb*, 1884.
[3] *Christopher Columbus*, 1891.
[4] *Op. cit.* and *Histoire critique de la grande entreprise de Christophe Colomb*, 1911.
[5] *La véridique adventure de Christophe Colomb*, 1927.
[6] This date is favoured by Vignaud; see his *A Critical Study of the Various Dates Assigned to the Birth of Christopher Columbus* (1903). Other dates vary between 1430 and 1456. That he was a Galician of Jewish parentage, as some suggest, is unlikely.

shore and proceeded to Lisbon. From there, in one of the remaining ships, he journeyed to England, and in 1477 returned to Lisbon, where he remained for seven years.

It would seem probable that during his stay in Lisbon the idea of exploring the far side of the Atlantic took definite form in his mind, and of all places Lisbon was the most likely to foster it, for it was the port of departure and return of the Portuguese expeditions of discovery. Lisbon, accordingly, was the centre of maritime gossip and of sailors' yarns about enchanted islands and the wonders of rumoured lands. These stories must have appealed to Columbus's vivid, romantic and uncritical imagination, which must have been further stimulated and exaggerated by his readings of the *Travels* of Marco Polo, the *Marvellous Adventures* of Sir John Mandeville, and the *Imago Mundi* of Pierre d'Ailly, all of which he accepted at face value.

From these books he cannot have failed to have become acquainted with the prevailing idea of the comparative proximity of eastern Asia to western Europe, and to have been fascinated by the stories of Prester John, the Great Khan, and the amazing wealth of Cipango,[1] until the idea of navigating the Atlantic became so overwhelming an obsession that it shaped itself into a divine destiny.

When at Lisbon, probably in 1483, he placed his proposal before King John II, and when it was rejected, in 1484 he left Portugal for Spain. Two years later we find him at Cordova, where the Spanish court was then assembled. There he submitted his scheme to Queen Isabella, but with no result. In 1488 he revisited Lisbon to meet his brother Bartholomew who, in the previous December, had returned with the Diaz expedition which had discovered the Cape of Good Hope. Fired by this remarkable voyage of 13,000 miles, he persuaded his brother to journey to England to interest King Henry VII in his project, and should he fail to do so, to place it before Charles VIII of France.

Nothing came of this mission, and in May, 1489, Columbus returned to Spain; was present at the siege of Baza, and when, in 1491, he was at Santa Fé, he convinced the duke of Medina-Celi that his scheme was practical. Queen Isabella promised to consider it once Granada had surrendered. That she did so shows that she must have had considerable belief in it, because Columbus's demands were extravagant in the extreme. They were, that

[1] See *The Travels of Marco Polo,* bk. III, chap. II.

he should be appointed Admiral of the Ocean and viceroy of all heathen lands he might discover, and that he should receive one eighth of all revenue and profits which might accrue from the expedition.

It would appear that it was now that the crusading idea took precedence in his mind; for, according to his *Journal*, soon after the fall of Granada he wrote to Ferdinand and Isabella as follows:

"And immediately afterwards, in this same month (January, 1492), in consequence of information which I had given Your Highnesses on the subject of India and of the Prince who is called the 'Great Khan', which, in our Roman, means 'the King of Kings' – namely, that many times he and his predecessors had sent ambassadors to Rome to seek doctors of our holy faith, to the end that they should teach it in India. . . . Your Highnesses, as good Christian and Catholic princes, devout and propagators of the Christian faith, as well as enemies of the sect of Mahomet and of all idolatries and heresies, conceived the plan of sending me, Christopher Columbus, to this country of the Indies, there to see the princes, the peoples, the territory, their disposition and all things else, and the way in which one might proceed to convert these regions to our holy faith."[1]

Success crowned his endeavours. His terms were accepted and an agreement signed on April 17, 1492, and a letter in Latin (the universal language) given to him to hand to the Great Khan, which reads:

"To the Most Serene Prince, our very dear friend. . . . According to reports which have been made to us by many of our subjects, and also other travellers come from your kingdom and the neighbouring regions, we have had the satisfaction of learning of your good disposition and your excellent intentions towards us and towards our State, and at the same time of your keen desire to be informed of our recent success (the conquest of Granada). . . . In consequence whereof we have decided to send you as ambassador our Captain, the noble Christopher Columbus, bearer of these presents, from whom you may learn of our good health and our fortunate estate, as of other matters which we have ordered him to report to you on our behalf."[2]

Thus it came about that, on the morning of Friday, August 3,

[1] Quoted from *The History of Spain*, Louis Bertrand and Sir Charles Petrie, p. 238.
[2] Quoted *ibid.*, p. 247.

1492, Columbus set sail from Palos in three small caravels: the *Santa Maria*, 100 tons; the *Pinta*, 50 tons; and the *Niña*, 40 tons. Their crews numbered ninety men, besides whom there were thirty others, including the brothers Martin Alonzo and Vicente Yañez Pinzon, both noted navigators, and Louis de Torres, a Jew who could speak Hebrew, Greek, Latin, Arabic, Coptic, and Armenian, to act as interpreter should Cipango or the realm of the Great Khan be discovered. On August 9 the Canaries were reached, and a halt was made until September 9, when the little fleet stood out again, this time into the unknown. At two o'clock on the morning of Friday October 12 (new style, October 21) land was sighted, and at dawn a landing was made, probably on Watling Island, which Columbus named San Salvador, and significantly he called the natives who greeted him "Indians".

He sailed on, and on October 28 he struck Cuba, which he thought part of the mainland of China and, therefore, in the realm of the Great Khan. Forthwith he sent two of his followers to seek out the court of that potentate and to present to him the compliments of Queen Isabella and King Ferdinand. Thence he sailed south-east to Haiti, which he imagined was Cipango, and he christened it Hispaniola.

On January 4, 1493, he set out on his return, and on March 15 was back at Palos. From Seville he was summoned to the court at Barcelona, where he was received with triumphal honours. There, without question, it was assumed that his theory had been proved correct; that Cuba was the eastern extremity of China and Haiti the northern extremity of Cipango–therefore, a far shorter sea route to Asia than the one the Portuguese were seeking had been discovered to those lands of illimitable wealth described by Marco Polo. "The sovereigns", writes Fiske, "wept for joy as they thought that such untold riches were vouchsafed them by the special decree of Heaven as a reward for having overcome the Moor at Granada. . . ."[1]

Whether Columbus was a hero or a charlatan, a seer or a driveller, matters little, for the fact remains, as Fiske says, that his discovery was "a unique event in the history of mankind", and that "nothing like it was ever done before, and nothing like it can ever be done again".[2] The old Mediterranean world collapsed. "Millenary barriers", writes Louis Bertrand, "were broken. That world was no longer blockaded by Islam at the two outlets

[1] *The Discovery of America*, vol. 1, p. 445.          [2] *Ibid.*, vol. 1, p. 446.

from the Mediterranean. The horizon expanded, and new ways were opened to human activity, and to human thought. The world escaped at last from that little inland sea where there had been so much scuffling and struggling among European peoples for centuries. Men felt themselves liberated and, at the same time, increased in strength. The power of man had grown, coincidently with the extension of his dominion over new seas and lands. It was, in short, a New Man who was born."[1]

From that moment imperialism began to assume its modern colonial complexion. Trade, rather than pillage and exaction, grew to be its governing principle, and in order to enrich Castile, Queen Isabella restricted the trade of the newly discovered lands to one port – Seville – which became the Alexandria of the Atlantic. On May 4, 1493, Pope Alexander VI traced his famous line of demarcation on a map of the world, a straight line running a hundred leagues west of the Azores from north to south. East of it was to be Portuguese, west of it Castilian, the Indies were given to the one, the Americas to the other – surely the most remarkable gifts in history.

Though for long now the reconnaissances of the navigators had been in progress, the moment had arrived when the Age of Discovery was to engulf the Old World. On March 5, 1496, John Cabot, a citizen of Venice, received letters patent from King Henry VII of England to seek Vineland (the land discovered by the Vikings). So it came about that, early in May, he and eighteen men stood out from Bristol in the *Mathew*, and on June 24 struck the shore of Cape Breton Island,[2] where was laid the foundation stone of the British Empire. Twenty-eight years later, Francis I commissioned Giovanni da Verrazano to reconnoitre the Atlantic shore from Florida to Newfoundland, and when he did so he called that stretch of land "New France". Meanwhile the eastern route was yearly explored, and, in 1498, conquered by Vasco da Gama. He left the Tagus on July 9, 1497, sailed round the Cape of Good Hope, past the Island of the Moon (Madagascar), and in ten months and twelve days arrived at Calicut in India. Thence he and his men returned to Lisbon with a sixty-fold profit, and "with pumps in their hands and the Virgin Mary in their mouths". Twelve years later, on March 4, 1510, Albuquerque entered the

---

[1] *The History of Spain*, p. 306.
[2] Significantly, it was thought to be the Chinese coast "in the territory of the Grand Cham".

roadstead of Goa, received the keys of the fortress and initiated the European conquest of India and incidentally of the greater part of the Moslem world. The counter-attack had begun.

But of all these great navigators the Portuguese sailor Fernão da Magalhães (Magellan) was the most daring. On September 20, 1519, he set out from San Lucar in five ships manned by 280 men, rounded South America, lost four of his ships, and was killed at Zebu in the Philippine Islands. Nevertheless, his will accomplished its end; for, on September 6, 1522, the sole ship surviving, the *Victoria*, limped home to Portugal "with tackle worn and weather-beaten yards". Eighteen men were left to tell the tale that the world had been circumnavigated.

Meanwhile the Conquistadores were at work. They came mainly from Andalusia and Estremadura, where their ancestors had for centuries struggled with the Moors, and they embarked upon their conquests with a fanatical zeal. Cortés (1485–1547) with 508 soldiers, 109 mariners, and 16 horses set out to conquer Mexico, and Pizarro (1475–1541) with a single shipload of followers, horses and war-dogs, set out to conquer Peru. A religious frenzy seems to have possessed these men and to have driven them through and athwart the most unimaginable difficulties. Cruel though they were, they civilized as they conquered; they brought with them the horse, gunpowder, and steel; also wheat, the vine and the olive. They created a new world and in doing so they transformed the old.

"What a strange thing it is!" writes Louis Bertrand, "– the American enterprise, the last Crusade against Islam, thus presents itself to us as the final flowering of the thought of the Middle Ages, as the liquidation of the whole, long past. It was out of this religious idea that was born the modern world, sceptical and rational."[1] And all this came suddenly to life, like a gale of wind, out of the *Mirabilis Navigatio* of Columbus. The silent thoughts of illimitable ocean awaking in the mind of man the thunderous thoughts of illimitable power. And this would not have happened in the way in which it did happen had it not been for the Conquest of Granada.

[1] *The History of Spain*, Louis Bertrand and Sir Charles Petrie, p. 308.

# The supremacy of the Spanish and Ottoman Empires

O n February 23, 1516, Ferdinand of Spain died, and was succeeded by his grandson Charles, son of his daughter Joanna and Philip Duke of Burgundy. Already on his father's death in 1506, Charles had inherited the Netherlands and Franche Comté; now, as Charles I, he added to them Spain, which again was in turmoil, more especially in Valencia and Castile, where the Germania and Comunero Movements reduced those provinces to anarchy. Once order had been reinstated, as it was in 1521–1522, Charles, who with the assistance of the Fuggers –the great bankers of Augsburg–had been elected emperor (Charles V) in 1520, set out to found a world-wide Catholic monarchy. This brought him into conflict with France, the hereditary enemy of Spain; the quarrel arose over the duchies of Milan and Genoa–"the keys and the door", as they have been called, to the domination of Italy.[1]

It was this question which had led to the defeat of Louis XII (1499–1515) at Novarra, in 1513, and the loss of all his Italian conquests. He died in 1515 and was succeeded by Francis I (1515–1547), who at once crossed the Alps and defeated an army of Swiss mercenaries at Marignano and rewon Lombardy. Now, under Charles, the war continued, and on February 25, 1525, Francis I was routed and captured by the Imperialists under Lannoy at the decisive battle of Pavia. Soon after he threw in his lot with the Turks, sent secret help to Barbarossa the Barbaresque pirate and suggested to the sultan that he should invade Hungary. Such was the start of French oriental policy.

Charles's victory at Pavia alarmed all Italy–whose people wanted to be free from both France and Spain–and Pope Clement VII (1523–1534) persuaded France and a number of Italian

---

[1] The marriage of the duke of Orléans, brother of Charles VI, in 1389, with Valentina Visconti, daughter of the duke of Milan, later became the root claim of the French upon Milan and Naples, which in 1494 led to the French invasion of Italy by Charles VIII. This brought France into clash with the Spanish claims, which, as we have seen, dated from the marriage of Peter III of Aragon with Constance, daughter of Manfred of Beneventum, more than two hundred years earlier.

princes to unite in the Holy League of Cognac against Charles. In reply, he marched on Rome, and on May 6, 1527, in an orgy of pillage and massacre the Eternal City was again sacked. Next, he bought off the Genoese admiral, Andrea Doria, wrested the command of the western Mediterranean from France, and, on February 24, 1530, received from the hands of the pope the imperial crown and the crown of Italy. At length he was free to turn against the Turks.

While the Christian kings quarrelled, the Turks advanced; but this time eastward. In 1502 they invaded Persia, and the modern history of that country opens with Ismail, its first Shah (1499–1524). In 1514 he was decisively defeated by Selim I (1512–1521) on the plain of Chaldiran, and northern Mesopotamia was added to the Ottoman empire. Next Selim advanced into Syria, defeated the Mamaluks at Aleppo, carried the war into Egypt, when the whole of Arabia submitted to him and the caliphate was absorbed in the sultanate.

Again, as on so many previous occasions, distracted Christendom was thrown into panic; yet, in spite of the endeavours of Pope Leo X (1513–1521) to unite the empire, France, and Spain against the Turks, nothing came of his efforts. Selim laid siege to Rhodes, and on his death in 1521 he was succeeded by Suleiman I, the Magnificent (1520–1566), under whom the Ottoman empire reached its zenith. In 1521 he took Belgrade and pressed on with the siege of Rhodes. When it fell on Christmas Day, 1522, the knights of St. John of Jerusalem sought refuge in Crete and later in Malta. On the heels of these victories came the defeat of Francis I at Pavia, which wrecked any possibility of Christian unity. Suleiman fell in with the French king's suggestion, and at the head of 100,000 men and 300 cannon he invaded Hungary, and, on August 29, 1526, defeated King Louis II on the field of Mohacs. This battle sealed the doom of Hungary as an independent kingdom until the battle of Vittorio Veneto in 1918. Next, he occupied Buda and, in 1529, advanced on Vienna. He failed to storm it and retired to Constantinople.

The extent of the Ottoman empire was now vast indeed; it stretched from Baghdad in the east to the Atlas mountains in the west, and from Aden in the south to Buda in the north; and "from the headlands of Istria to the cliffs of Kent", writes Sir William Stirling-Maxwell, the Turkish cruisers "levied a tax on the coasts of Christendom and the commerce of the world".

The Ottoman empire now circumscribed two-thirds of the shores of the Mediterranean, sea-power was even more vital than land power in the maintenance of Turkish integrity, and realizing this, in 1535, Charles V sacked and occupied Tunis, the headquarters of the Algerian pirate and Turkish admiral Barbarossa. In retaliation, Barbarossa raided Calabria in 1538, and met the Genoese admiral Andrea Doria off Previsa, near the scene of the battle of Actium. But as Doria declined to do more than skirmish, the sea war continued, until, in 1541, Charles was compelled to abandon it again to turn against France in order to safeguard Milan. In 1556 he abdicated in favour of his son Philip, who had recently married Mary Tudor, daughter of Henry VIII of England; the empire passed to Charles's younger brother Ferdinand, and therefore, in fact, remained an extension of Spain.

On the accession of Philip II (1556–1598) his rule extended over Spain, the Netherlands, Franche Comté, Sardinia, Sicily, the Balearic Islands, the greater part of Italy, and most of the then discovered New World. Later, after the battle of Alcantara (1581), he added Portugal and the Portuguese colonies to his empire, and also, all but in name, controlled the Holy Roman empire. To hold together so vast a conglomeration of lands, nations and peoples demanded a common factor, and this he found in religion. Therefore, as Defender of the Faith, he set out to establish his hegemony, and as an absolute sovereign became the example of a new system of rule, which was copied by other European monarchs and which only ended with the French Revolution.

Because this hegemony ran counter to the spirit of the Reformation, war was inevitable, and as wars are costly undertakings, more especially those that aim at religious compulsion instead of material gains, war meant money–gold, silver, and credit. It is now that, suddenly, the wealth of the New World impinged upon the poverty of the Old and set up a violent fermentation. In 1493 the stock of gold and silver in Europe has been estimated at £33,400,000, but from the opening of the sixteenth century bullion began to trickle in from Africa and the Americas until, in 1536, it developed into a steady stream, next into a torrent, and lastly into an inundation, so mighty that between then and 1636, Mr. Trevor Davies calculates that well over £250,000,000 of bullion entered Europe.

Because of the Reformation, which challenged Philip's principle of religious unity and, therefore, his hegemony, this vast increase of bullion was spent mainly on war. It flowed through Spain, and instead of fertilizing it laid it waste and left sharper dearth behind. Not only did it destroy the Spanish export trade, but it demoralised the Spanish people. Further, it stimulated the growth of a new civilization, the modern capitalist way of life, much as the release of Persian gold by Alexander the Great had paved the way for Hellenistic and Roman capitalism. Because of war, this stream of bullion flowed into the hands of the money-lenders of Genoa, Antwerp and Augsburg. Gold and silver spent in the Netherlands financed the Baltic States and became the magnetic centre of the reformed religion which, by equating God and Mammon, ripened into a comfortable creed for bankers, traders and merchants—the props of bourgeois civilization.

Strategically, the axis of Philip's hegemony lay between Milan and Flanders. The former enabled him to grip the south of western Europe, the latter allowed him to grip the north—France, England and the Baltic; and only by threatening France from the north could he be sure to keep France distant from Milan.

The Spanish Netherlands were the most prosperous regions in Europe at the time, and though Charles V's attempts to stamp out heresy had led to religious grievances, it is unlikely that they would have led to open rebellion had not the bankrupt Dutch nobility seen in the Protestant cause the means to despoil the monasteries and other ecclesiastical foundations. In 1559 trouble began when the regent, Margaret of Parma, a natural daughter of Charles V, proposed to reorganize these foundations; for at once the nobles under William of Nassau, Prince of Orange—who also was hopelessly in debt—saw in her reforms the loss of patronage and preferment—the means to pay their debts. They bound themselves together by a document known as the *Compromise*, and in derision were called by the Spaniards *"les gueux"* ("the beggars").

Next, under cover of the disturbances fomented by "the beggars", bands of Calvinists from France, Germany, England, and Geneva swarmed into the Netherlands and sacked 400 churches, including the cathedral at Antwerp. As Mr. Trevor Davies says, "Calvinism . . . was the Third International of the sixteenth century", and Philip II, who saw in it a rabble-rouser and feared that were the rebels to unite with those already warring in France, Spain might be exposed to the contagion, in 1567, when the Dutch Catholics rose in their own defence, sent the Duke of Alva and 10,000 picked Spanish troops to their support. From then the rebellion took the form of a religious war, a war which was to last intermittently until 1609, when a twelve-year truce was patched up between Spain and the United Provinces.

This revolt, or rather, war of pillage and of retaliation, at once had its repercussion on Spain; not because the Protestant cause flourished there, but because ever since the fall of Granada the Moorish problem had agitated that country. In 1499 the restrictions then impossd caused a serious revolt, and a campaign of repression followed which ended in the whole kingdom of Granada being declared Christian; the Moors were given the alternative of exile or baptism. Many adopted the latter course and became known as Moriscos, men and women who though outwardly Christian were still inwardly Mahommedan. As such they persistently intrigued with the Barbaresque pirates and the Ottoman empire, and in this they were supported, if only indirectly, by French Oriental policy.

Because the House of Austria was the sultan's natural enemy, and because the Ottoman and Barbaresque fleets commanded the Mediterranean, the Turks supported the Moriscos. The result was that when Philip was engaged in the Netherlands, in December, 1568, a formidable rebellion broke out in Spain in which thousands of Christians, amid scenes of fiendish cruelty, were massacred, and thousands of others were seized and sold as slaves to the Berbers in exchange for arms. When, in the following year, the Moriscos again appealed to the sultan, Philip II sent his half-brother Don John of Austria (1545–1578), son of Charles V and a German lady – Barbara Blomberg – to suppress the rebellion. In this Philip showed considerable magnanimity. The Moriscos were scattered over northern Spain, their welfare cared for and, among other things, free education provided for their children.[1] Then, suddenly, Don John was called upon to undertake a more formidable task: it was to regain the Christian command of the Mediterranean.

---

[1] It was not until 1609–1613 that the expulsion of the Moriscos took place.

CHAPTER 20

# The Battle of Lepanto, 1571

Disunity within Christendom, more than their prowess, had facilitated the Turks' expansion westward. Before the fall of Constantinople in 1453, theological differences between the Catholic and Orthodox Churches had made union impossible; now, a hundred years later, it was the Reformation which did so, splitting western Christendom into two violently hostile religious camps. Added to this division of power, the speedy growth of nationalism, and the influx of wealth from the New World, stimulated the rise of self-interested states, whose commercial prosperity appeared to them more important than the security of Europe as a whole. Among these, the two which more immediately concern us were Venice and Spain.

The former, to secure its trade, had entered into treaty with the Turks immediately after the fall of Constantinople, and so blinded were the Venetians by their commercial hegemony that they could not see that their possessions in the Levant – the main source of their prosperity – must inevitably bring them into collision with the expanding energy of the Turks, and that single-handed they could not hold them. The latter state, since the Spanish disaster at Jerba (in the Gulf of Gabes) in 1560, followed by the Turkish attempt to seize Oran in 1563 and Malta in 1565, stood in terror of a Moslem invasion, not only of Sicily and Naples, but of its homeland, a fear which was only in part allayed by the repression of the Morisco rebellion. In short, the eastern half of the Mediterranean was vital to the commercial interests of Venice, and the western half was vital to the strategical security of Spain, hence the divergent outlooks.

Three years before the Moriscos rebelled, Suleiman the Magnificent died and was succeeded by his son Selim II (1566–1574), probably the vilest of the many vile occupants of the Ottoman throne. In 1568, so that he might be free to seize Cyprus, which had been acquired by Venice in 1488,[1] he came

[1] In 1488, on the extinction of the Lusignan dynasty—founded by Guy of Lusignan in 1192, when he purchased Cyprus from Richard I of England—Caterina Conaro, a Venetian lady and widow of James II, king of Cyprus, ceded the island to Venice because she could no longer hope to hold it against the Turks.

to terms with the Emperor Maximillian II (1564–1576). This project was urged upon him by his favourite Miquez Nasi,[1] who held Naxos in fief and hoped to gain the investiture of Cyprus. Also Selim's admiral Piali Pasha–a Hungarian renegade–and his general Mustafa Pasha favoured the enterprise, for in it they saw an opportunity to efface the stigma of their repulse before Malta by La Valette in 1565. On the other hand, the Grand Vizier Mohammed Sokolli, a far-sighted statesman, favoured peace with both the empire and Venice. He saw that the Turks had nothing to fear from either, and that their enemy was Spain. Further, it was apparent to him that the moment to strike at her was opportune, because Philip II was distracted by the Moriscos, was deeply involved in the Netherlands, and was without an ally in Europe. Besides, France was friendly to the sultan; the empire impotent without Spanish support; Poland at war with Russia; Italy torn by internal feuds; and England had more to gain than to lose from a Turco-Spanish war. Therefore, Sokolli opposed the venture and in its stead urged that, as Venice was in alliance with the sultan, a more profitable course would be to attack Spain by helping the Morisco revolt. Possibly his plan would have been accepted had not an unlooked-for disaster suddenly smitten Venice. On September 13, 1569, an explosion in one of the powder factories at the arsenal[2] was followed by a vast conflagration, and though the damage done was considerable, by the time it was reported in Constantinople it was so exaggerated that it was believed the whole Venetian fleet had perished (actually only four galleys were lost) and that, therefore, Cyprus could not be reinforced. Because of this false report the war party carried the day.

Preparations were at once put in hand, and in April, 1570, a Turkish envoy was sent to Venice to demand the surrender of Cyprus on the plea that, as formerly it had belonged to the kingdom of Jerusalem, it was now by right a Turkish possession. Although there were few Venetian troops in Cyprus, the doge and Senate refused to consider the proposal, and knowing that their refusal meant war, they appealed to the Christian powers for aid. But Venice was so hated by all kings because she was a republic; by all maritime powers, because she was a rival; and by one and

[1] For him see *Histoire de l'Empire Ottoman*, J. Von Hammer (1836), vol. vi, pp. 383–386.
[2] The arsenal was the finest in Europe and the heart of Venetian power. It comprised docks, gun foundries, gunpowder factories, and it provided all war equipment, whether for sea or land. For a full account of it see *La vie d'un Patricien de Venise au seizième siècle*, Charles Yriarte (1874), chap. XII.

all because of her alliance with the Turks; that no one would listen to her except Pope Pius V (1566–1572), who saw in her appeal a possible means to realize his fondest hope–to place himself at the head of a maritime league and to wage a new crusade against the infidels. He offered twelve galleys at his own expense as the nucleus of a fleet and persuaded Philip II of Spain–at first very reluctant –to order his viceroys in Sicily and Naples to supply the Venetian fleet, and to add his own Sicilian fleet to the papal and Venetian squadrons.

Meanwhile Selim assembled a fleet of 150 galleys and 50 troop-carrying transports at Rhodes under Piali Pasha and Mustafa Pasha. They landed at Limasol in Cyprus, on July 22, 1570, and laid siege to Nicosia which, with the exception of Famagusta, was the only defensible town in the island. On September 9 it was stormed and its garrison put to the sword. Next, siege was laid to Famagusta, held by 7,000 Venetian troops. But so determined was the resistance made by its governor, Antonio Bragadino, and its military commander, Astor Baglione, that every assault was beaten back, and Ali Pasha sailed home for the winter. During these sieges a powerful allied Christian fleet of more than 200 sail, under a Venetian noble, Girolomo Zani, assembled at Candia in Crete, but because of dissensions between its contingents it accomplished nothing.

The only man in Christendom who was determined that some-thing should be done and that quickly was Pius V, who in July, 1570, had assembled a conference to frame the charter of a Christian League. He fully grasped the danger that faced Christendom, and was a man of commanding character who possessed no little strategical insight. What he saw was, that could the command of the Mediterranean be regained, the Ottoman empire would strategically be cut in two, for its African provinces would then be severed from its Asiatic and European. This, he hoped, would prevent the Turks from spreading farther westward into Europe.

Next came the fall of Nicosia, which affected him deeply, for Pius realized that unless Venice were strongly supported, should Famagusta also fall, the Venetians would be compelled to make peace with the Turks. Meanwhile the conference meandered on: each party in turn raised some new difficulty. At length Philip, who by now had been fully won over to the support of the League, determined to have the principal voice in its control. His representatives at the conference insisted accordingly that his half-brother, Don John of Austria, should be appointed Captain-General of the forces of the League, with Marco Antonio Colonna, the papal admiral, as his second-in-command. As this did not suit the Venetians, who feared Spanish control, in order to reach a general agreement, a half-measure was adopted. Though Don John was to be in supreme command he was to be debarred from taking any decisive act without the consent of the leaders of each of the allied contingents. How, in part at least, he overcame this anomalous position will be told later.

In 1571 he was twenty-six years of age, the same age as Alexander at Arbela, Hannibal when made commander-in-chief in Spain and Bonaparte at Lodi. Brantôme says of him: "*Il estoit fort beau . . . et de bonne grâce, gentil en toutes ses actions, et courtois, affable d'un grand esprit, et sur tout très brave et vaillant . . .*"[1] But he was more than this; in spite of his youth he was an astute and electrifying leader. "He seemed to personify", writes Merriman, "the crusading ardour of the Pope. His inspiring presence swept men off their feet, and made them temporarily forget their own selfish aims in an over-whelming enthusiasm for the common cause. He seemed the incarnation of 1095."[2]

At length, on March 7, 1571, when the conference was on the brink of a final decision, Cardinal Granvelle,the leading Spanish representative, raised further difficulties. This so exacerbated the doge and Senate that they sent an envoy, Jacopo Ragazzoni, to Constantinople to try to come to terms with the Turks. He arrived there on April 26, and saw the grand vizier, who would listen to no compromises and demanded the unconditional sur-render of Cyprus. "Peace is better for you", he said, "than war. You cannot cope with the Sultan, who will take from you not Cyprus alone, but other dependencies. As for your Christian League, we know full well how little love the Christian Princes bear you. Put no trust in them. If you would but hold by the Sultan's robe you might do what you please in Europe, and enjoy perpetual peace."[3] With these persuasive words ringing in his ears, Ragazzoni set out on his return, but before he arrived in Italy the Holy League had been formed and proclaimed. The announcement had been made on May 25, and there was now no turning back.

[1] *Œuvres Complètes de Brantôme*, edit. Prosper Mérimée (1858), vol. II, p. 122.
[2] *The Rise of the Spanish Empire* (1934), vol. IV, pp. 134–135.
[3] Quoted in *Don John of Austria*, Sir William Stirling-Maxwell (1883), vol. I, p. 339.

The leading clauses of the famous treaty, the parent of so many in after years, were as follows: The League was to be perpetual, and directed not only against the Turks, but also against Algiers, Tunis, and Tripoli. The forces of the League were to consist of 200 galleys and 100 other vessels of war, 50,000 infantry, 4,500 light cavalry, and a large number of cannon, and were to be ready each March to proceed to the Levant or on any other expedition decided upon. The Confederates were bound reciprocally to defend each other against the Turks, and the expenses of the war were to be met one-half by Spain, two-thirds of the remaining half by Venice, and the other third by the pope. In the conduct of the war the three commanders-in-chief were each to have a voice, but the execution of the plans decided upon was to be left to the Captain-General. The emperor and the kings of France and Poland were to be given the option of joining the League; but no mention was made of the queen of England (Elizabeth), because she was not a Catholic sovereign. All territories conquered were to be divided in accordance with the rules laid down, except acquisitions in Algiers, Tunis, and Tripoli, which were to go to Spain. The pope was to act as arbiter in the event of differences between the Confederates, and no Confederate was to make a truce, peace or alliance with the Turks without the consent of the others.

In spite of these terms, intentions clashed with decisions. Venice wanted to use the League to regain Cyprus and to cripple Ottoman power in the eastern Mediterranean; Philip II wanted to cripple that power, and the Barbaresque pirates, in the western. Both had entered the League suspiciously, and each detested the other. The pope alone was single-minded and full-hearted. He had a universal outlook and saw that Christendom as a whole was in peril, and not merely Spain and Venice. Such success which was to follow the formation of the League was due to Pius V, for he was its heart and soul.

On June 6, Don John of Austria set out from Madrid and arrived at Barcelona on June 16. He found the squadron of Don Gil de Andrade assembled there and he ordered the Marquis of Santa Cruz, then at Cartagena, to join it. Don John sailed from Barcelona on June 20, arrived at Genoa on June 26, and there linked with the squadron of Giovanni Andrea Doria. He put into Spezia on August 2 to pick up troops, then sailed on and cast anchor at Naples on August 9. There he was met by Cardinal

Granvelle, who handed to him the banner of the League. Already, when at Genoa, he had received a letter from the pope urging him to risk a battle against any odds.

At Naples ten days were spent in discussing plans and embarking troops, and on August 20 sail was set for Messina, the appointed *rendezvous*. When Don John arrived there on the evening of August 23 he was met by Marco Antonio Colonna, commander of the papal contingent, and Sebastian Veniero, then seventy-five years old, commander of the Venetian; the former had arrived on July 21, and the other on July 23.

Meanwhile Selim at Constantinople, intoxicated by the capture of Nicosia, believed that the ancient prophecies, cherished by the house of Ottoman, were about to be fulfilled: that the Turk was to rule all the islands of the Mediterranean and that St. Peter's was to be as St. Sophia. More determined than ever to push the siege of Famagusta, in April he reassembled the fleet under Ali Pasha at Negropont in order to intercept any naval forces of the League which might attempt to sail to Cyprus. At the same time he strongly reinforced Mustafa's investing army.

Toward the end of May, the bombardment of Famagusta was reopened and an entrance gained to the fosse. Mining was next resorted to as well as smoking-out the defenders "by the noxious fumes of a wood, grown in the island, called *tezza*".[1] Late in July, when half the garrison had fallen and powder was exhausted, in order to save the town from the horrors of sack, Baglione and Bragadino proposed capitulation on terms. It was at once agreed to by Mustafa, and on August 1 the surrender was made. Four days later Mustafa demanded hostages, and when this was refused as contrary to the terms of the capitulation, he had Baglione and the leading Venetian officers slaughtered, but Bragadino he reserved for torture. First he had his nose and ears cut off; then he had him flayed alive and ordered that his skin should be stuffed with straw and paraded through the town. Later it was swung from a yardarm, and sent to Constantinople to decorate the slave market. Men of the surrendered garrison were reduced to galley slaves; the Cathedral of St. Nicholas was sacked, and the contents of the Christian tombs scattered to the winds. But for the Turks the siege was costly; during it, it is said, Mustafa lost 50,000 men.

As no attempt to relieve Famagusta was made, Ali Pasha sailed

[1] *Don John of Austria*, Stirling-Maxwell, vol. 1, p. 367.

from Negropont, ravaged the Venetian possessions in the Morea as well as the island of Zante and Cephalonia, landed on Corfu, but was repulsed, and from there he sailed up the Dalmatian coast and appeared off the Venetian lagoon. There was not a single galley left to oppose him; but shortly after, when he learnt that the allied fleet was at Messina, he feared that he might be bottled-up in the Adriatic and turned about and made for Corfu, satisfied that he had done the maximum damage to his enemy.

When all the Confederate forces had assembled at Messina, Don John found himself at the head of upward of 300 sail and 80,000 men, of whom 30,000 were soldiers and 50,000 mariners and galley slaves. The naval contingents were as follows: the fleet of the king of Spain, 90 galleys, 24 galleons and great ships, and 50 frigates and brigantines; the Venetian fleet, 106 galleys, six galleasses, two galleons and 20 frigates; and the papal fleet, 12 galleys and six frigates. In all, there were 208 galleys (later reinforced by 17 others), six galleasses, 26 galleons and 76 brigantines and frigates; a grand total of 316 sail. When he found that the Venetian fleet lacked men, Don John transferred to it 2,500 Italian and 1,500 Spanish soldiers. Veniero accepted them reluctantly, because it might lead to quarrellings.

Because quarrels were frequent and disputes endless, Don John, in face of much opposition, cut the Gordian knot by a drastic reshuffle of his command; nationalities were distributed throughout the fleet in every squadron. This not only lessened the likelihood of individual leaders withdrawing their ships, but by weakening their authority it considerably strengthened his own, and, in consequence, went far to overcome the handicap with which he had been encumbered because of the half-measure adopted at the conference.

Appointing Ascanio de la Corgnia to command the land forces, he pooled his three naval contingents and, like an army in three battles, formed them into three tactical divisions – a centre, a right, and a left wing – with a vanguard and a rearguard. The first consisted of 64 galleys under himself, with Veniero and Colonna to help him; the second, of 54 galleys, he placed under the command of Doria; and the third, of 53 galleys, under the Venetian admiral Augustino Barbarigo. The vanguard of eight galleys he handed over to Don Juan de Cardona, general of the Sicilian squadron, and the rearguard, of 30 galleys, he placed under the command of the Marquis of Santa Cruz. The six galleasses, in pairs, were allotted to each division, and the galleons and great ships carrying supplies were formed into a separate squadron; dependent upon sail alone, they were less mobile than the galleys. The frigates and brigantines were divided between the above forces and ordered to sail astern of them.

On September 10, a council of war was held. Colonna and Veniero there declared themselves for immediate attack, and Doria and la Corgnia for further delay. But Don John had already made up his mind and announced his cordial concurrence with his papal and Venetian colleagues. The die was cast—it was to be war to the knife. All opposition then ended and the papal nuncio proclaimed a jubilee. With great ceremony, in his master's name, he bestowed upon the whole armament of the Holy League the Apostolical benediction, and announced anew the indulgences which in past ages had been conceded to the conquerors of the Holy Sepulchre.

On September 15, the unwieldy galleasses and galleons stood out from Messina, to be followed the next day by the three divisions of galleys. Ten days later, when at Corfu, it was learnt that a Turkish fleet under the Algerian corsair Uluch Ali, in the service of the sultan, had attacked the island, but had failed to take the fortress. From the prisoners captured during the raid Don John discovered that Uluch Ali had withdrawn to Lepanto (Naupactus) in the Gulf of Corinth (also called the Gulf of Lepanto).

As this was important news Don John immediately assembled a council of war and, after considerable opposition, he resolved to set out at once and bring the enemy to battle. The decision was a bold one, for not only did the sultan's fleet command the Mediterranean, but his army was overwhelmingly superior to any the Confederates could put into the field, and therefore a naval defeat would all but certainly lead to an outburst of invasions. As Sir William Stirling-Maxwell points out: "It was obvious that a wrong move, resulting in a disaster, would place Europe at the feet of the fierce Asiatic conqueror. But it was no less apparent that a timid and procrastinating policy, seeking to avoid a disaster, might have an effect, hardly less fatal, of resolving the great armament of the League into its original discordant elements, of breaking it up again into separate fleets, no one of which would be able to face the navy of Selim."[1] The truth is that the offensive alone could keep the Confederates together. It was *the* problem.

[1] *Don John of Austria*, Stirling-Maxwell, vol. I, p. 391.

On September 29, Don John with his division sailed ahead to Gomenizza on the Albanian coast, where he was met by a frigate of the vanguard and from her learnt that not only Uluch Ali but also Ali Pasha and 200 sail were at anchor at Lepanto. Don John did not await the arrival of the galleons, which were still far behind, but sent orders back to Corfu for Veniero and Colonna to join him with all speed.

To understand the battle which was soon to be fought, it is as well briefly to describe the main types of warships in use at this time. The galley was a single-decked vessel varying from 120 to 180 feet in length, with a beam of about twenty feet and a depth of hold of seven; she was propelled by sail or oars, but in battle always by the latter, and for a short spurt could move at six and a half knots. The Christian galleys mounted five bow guns, the Turkish three. The former had also a number of $4\frac{1}{2}$ pounders on each broadside; their planking was from three to four inches thick, and the rowers were protected by wooden mantlets, the Turkish were not. The galley was provided with a metal beak from ten to twenty feet long. In rough weather she was an indifferent fighting vessel. The galleon was propelled by sails only; she was a large vessel rising from the water-line a third of her length, and with her two gun-decks was a floating fortress. Between the above two came the galleasse, a ship half galley and half galleon, with lofty poop and forecastle, carrying from fifty to seventy pieces of ordnance, also four 20-barrel *ribauldequins* to cover the ship's waist against boarders. One of her main advantages over the galley was that she had a deck over her rowers. Her masts were lateen rigged and her bows proof against cannon shot. The brigantine and frigate were small half-decked, two-masted vessels, moved by sail or oars, and the cogs (transports) could carry 1,000 soldiers and their equipment.

Naval tactics in the Mediterranean consisted in manœuvring for position, followed by head-on assault in line abreast, outflanking and boarding, much as they had been at Salamis, Actium, and other ancient naval battles. To all intents and purposes battles at sea were land battles fought on water.

The following extracts taken from Alonzo de Chaves's *Mirror for Seamen*, written in 1530, are of interest:

"If you wish to board . . . let your small-arm men get in action, particularly those in the tops. The *afferrador* (man throwing grappling hook) should put the iron in the rigging or the forecastle where it will hold well, and the cable must be hauled in so as to keep it taut. Then the small-arms men must get busy without losing a shot. The men in the tops will empty their boxes of powder and tar, having lighted their matches and also throw the soap and oil to make the hostile decks slippery. . . . To repel boarders greased pikes are good (the grease was only near the head so that the enemy could not grip). Everyone will now fight with steel and fire-arms. Those with long-handled sickles will cut the enemy's rigging. Those with fire tubes on long handles will try to light the gear of the other ship. . . .

"On the other hand, if the enemy boards us, pikes and swords are the best weapons to repel him. The boarders' netting is an obstacle and, as the boarders try to get over it, we with our pikes from underneath should force him to jump into the sea. . . .

"Wounded men must be sent below, for they are in the way and intimidate the others. The dead men must be quickly thrown overboard to avoid dismay, so that everybody on deck is a fighting man."[1]

At Lepanto, Don John introduced certain notable changes. The most novel was the use he made of his galleasses as an advanced guard, and second to it that he had the beaks of his galleys removed, in order that the forecastle guns could be worked more freely. Added to these, he made far greater use of the arquebus than the Turks, and to stimulate his crews he ordered that all his Christian galley slaves should be unfettered and armed and promised them their freedom should they fight bravely.

By October 3, except for the galleons and great ships, the whole of the fleet of the League had assembled at Gomenizza, and from there Don John stood out again, and passing by Prevesa – the scene of the battle of Actium – on October 4 the fleet cast anchor off Cape Ducato. The fleet sailed again the same evening, but because of foul weather most of the day following was spent in the harbour of Phiskardo in the island of Cephalonia. Here it was that, from a passing brigantine, the news of the fall of Famagusta and the hideous death of Bragadino was received. The tidings could not have come at a more opportune moment, for they filled every Christian breast with a burning desire to avenge the disaster and the crime.

At Cephalonia an unlooked for trouble occurred which nearly

---

[1] (4) Quoted from *Naval Warfare under Oars 4th to 16th Centuries*, Vice-Admiral William Ledyard Rogers (1939), pp. 144–146.

wrecked the entire expedition. A Spanish officer on board Veniero's galley insulted some Venetians and the quarrel which resulted led to a fight in which several men were killed. Beside himself with fury and without reference to Don John, Veniero had the culprit and his associates seized and strung up at the mast's head. When he heard of this Don John lost his temper and was about to put Veniero under arrest, which would probably have resulted in the Christians flying at each other's throats, when Colonna wisely intervened and prevailed upon John to rescind his order. Nevertheless the latter refused to have anything further to do with Veniero and communicated with Barbarigo instead.

Delayed by another bout of bad weather, it was not until two o'clock on the morning of Sunday, October 7, that the fleet stood out again, skirting the Kurtsolari Islands. Soon after seven o'clock, Don John in his flagship the *Réal* (*Royal*) joined Doria's squadron which was ahead and then nearly out of the channel between the island of Oxia and Point Scropha, immediately north of the entrance of the Gulf of Patras.

Meanwhile, on September 27, the Turkish fleet had concentrated at Lepanto, and on October 3 or 4 Ali Pasha assembled a council of war. Its more noted members were Pertau Pasha, the commander of the troops – really boarding forces; Hassan Pasha, son of Barbarossa, the former viceroy of Algiers; Mahomet Sirocco Pasha, governor of Alexandria; Hamet Bey, governor of Negropont (Euboea); and Uluch Ali, now viceroy of Algiers, who by birth was a Calabrian. Through his spies, Ali had complete knowledge of his enemy's strength and movements, and since the sultan's orders were to assume the offensive the council decided to meet the approaching Christian fleet. On October 6 the Turkish fleet left the shelter of the fortresses of Lepanto, ran through the narrows and cast anchor off Galata, some fifteen miles west of Lepanto. There Ali learnt from a scout that the enemy was at Phiskardo.

Long before daybreak the next morning the Turks were again under way, and were only ten miles distant from their enemy when Don John caught up with Doria off Point Scropha. Half an hour later, the look-outs in the fighting tops of the *Réal* and Doria's *Capitana* (flagship) reported two sail to the east. Next, eight more appeared over the horizon, and a few minutes later the whole Turkish fleet came into sight. At once Don John ordered a cannon shot to be fired and the banner of the League run up in the *Réal* – the signal that the enemy had been sighted.

At the sound of the signal gun, each captain began to clear his galley for action, while the principal commanders boarded brigantines and repaired to the *Réal* to receive Don John's final instructions. Some were still against a battle, because defeat so far from their base would mean total ruin. But Don John's mind had for long been made up, and he said to his officers: "Gentlemen, the time for counsel is past, and the time for fighting has come", and with these words he dismissed them.[1]

As soon as they had returned to their ships the fleet was brought into the order of battle agreed upon at Messina; but, to compensate for the lack of the galleons – still far behind – the strengths of the divisions were slightly altered.

To Barbarigo, in command of the left wing, Don John allotted 63 galleys, and ordered him to sail with his left close to the Aetolian shore, in order to prevent the enemy outflanking him. To Doria, in command of the right wing, he allotted 64 galleys; 63 galleys were left for the central squadron, his personal command. Further, he instructed Colonna in the papal flagship to take station on his right, and Veniero, in the Venetian flagship, to do the same on his left. Also he increased the reserve squadron under the Marquis of Santa Cruz from 30 to 35 galleys, and instructed him to sail in rear of the central squadron and to support any part of the line which gave way.[2] The six galleasses were left in pairs, as agreed, each pair to take station three-quarters of a mile in advance of each of the three forward squadrons in order to disorganize the Turkish formation before the clinch. With his line of battle, between 6,500 and 7,500 yards in length, drawn up, he boarded a fast brigantine and inspected his fleet. When he caught sight of Veniero on his quarter-deck, forgetting the past and remembering only the moment, he waved so friendly a greeting to him that it wiped out the memory of the difference between them. Then the crews of every ship knelt in prayer, "the decks gleaming with prostrate men in mail".

While the Christians made ready, the Turks also prepared for action. Ali Pasha drew out his vessels in an immense crescent stretching from the northern shore of the gulf toward its southern

---

[1] *Don John of Austria*, Stirling-Maxwell, vol. I, p. 405.
[2] The names of the ships and those of their commanders are given by Admiral Jurien de la Gravière in his book *La Guerre de Chypre et la Bataille de Lépante* (1888), vol. II, pp. 52–59.

shore. Like Don John, he divided his fleet into three squadrons: he himself in the centre with 87 galleys and eight galliots; on his right Mahomet Sirocco, with 54 galleys and two galliots; and on his left Uluch Ali with 61 galleys and 32 galliots; eight galleys and 21 galliots he held in reserve.[1]

About 9'30 o'clock, when the fleets slowly approached each other, Ali Pasha straightened out his crescent formation, for he was surprised to find the galleasses stationed in front of his enemy's line of battle. Nervous at this unexpected use of these formidable ships, Pertau Pasha urged him to make a retrograde movement to entice the enemy to pursue and so to disorder his line – a common Turkish trick. But Ali refused to do so, because he considered that it would not be consistent with the order he had received from the sultan to attack at sight. Therefore the advance continued, the Turks shouting and screaming, when suddenly a glitter swept their enemy's line: Don John's soldiers had risen from their knees and were standing by their battle stations.

About half-past ten, when the battle opened, the position of the two fleets was as follows: The Christian left wing was slightly ahead, with its left at some distance from the Aetolian shore, because Barbarigo, unacquainted with the coast, was afraid that his galleys might run upon shoals. On its right, the central squadron was nearly abreast. But because the Turkish left wing extended beyond the Christian right wing, fearing envelopment, Doria moved the right squadron diagonally outward with the result that a gap of a mile or more developed between his extreme left and Don John's extreme right. The four galleasses of the left wing and centre were in position three-quarters of a mile in front of their respective squadrons; but the two allotted the right wing were still off Point Scropha. The reserve squadron, under Santa Cruz, was also in position, its galleys surrounded by brigantines ready to transfer troops to the three forward squadrons as the fighting might demand. At the same time, the Turkish right wing, under Sirocco, was also slightly in advance of the central squadron under Ali, and Uluch Ali, commanding the left wing, moved outward diagonally in order to conform with Doria's manœuvre. The general result of the several movements was that the battle developed into three separate actions: first between Barbarigo and Sirocco; next, about half an hour later,

---

[1] These are Admiral Jurien de la Gravière's figures (vol. II, pp. 109–118). A galliot was a small galley.

between Don John and Ali; and lastly, an hour later still, between Doria and Uluch Ali.

At half-past ten, when the Turkish right wing came within range of the two left galleasses, so destructive a fire was opened from them that Sirocco's squadron was thrown into confusion, its right wing forced towards the Aetolian shore. But because they were well acquainted with the coast, its pilots were ordered to close their galleys inshore and to turn Barbarigo's left flank. Barbarigo saw their intention and realized that where there was water enough for the Turkish galleys, there would be sufficient for his own, so he inclined his squadron toward the shore and took in flank all but six of seven of his enemy's galleys, which succeeded in getting in rear of him. At the time, Barbarigo's right wing, under Marco Quirini, was unengaged because Sirocco's left wing had set about to follow his right wing. Seizing the opportunity, Quirini swung his galleys round and fell upon Sirocco's rear like "a closing door". Meanwhile Barbarigo's galley had been engaged by five Turkish ships, which assailed her with shot, bullets and showers of arrows, one of which mortally wounded Barbarigo in the eye. Loss of command at once led to confusion, which worsened on the fall of his nephew, Marco Contarini, who was killed immediately after he took over command. At length Frederigo Nani, who succeeded Contarini, rallied the left of the squadron, and, assisted by Quirini, together they drove the whole of the Turkish right wing against the shore. The Turks abandoned their galleys and took to the land, and with the Venetians on their heels were hunted down and exterminated. The victory of the Christian left wing was complete, not a single Turkish vessel escaped, and Sirocco, mortally wounded, was taken prisoner.

About half an hour after Barbarigo and Sirocco engaged, the two galleasses ahead of Don John's squadron opened so effective a fire that Ali's galleys broke into groups, and rowed furiously away from them. Meanwhile a slow stroke was maintained by Don John's galleys, and to the strain of pipes and clarions, they advanced in perfect line; the bulk of the Turkish shot passed over them. Closing in on one another, the two squadrons met head-on; the Turkish galleys suffered severely from the superior gunfire of the Christian, whose gunners were given freer play because the beaks of their ships had been removed. Ali ordered his helmsman to steer straight for Don John's flagship, the *Réal*, and when the prow of his galley crashed against the *Réal* its beak became entangled in her rigging. Ali had on board 400 picked janissaries, and close astern of him were ten galleys and two galliots, the nearest of which were linked to his ship by ladders, up which

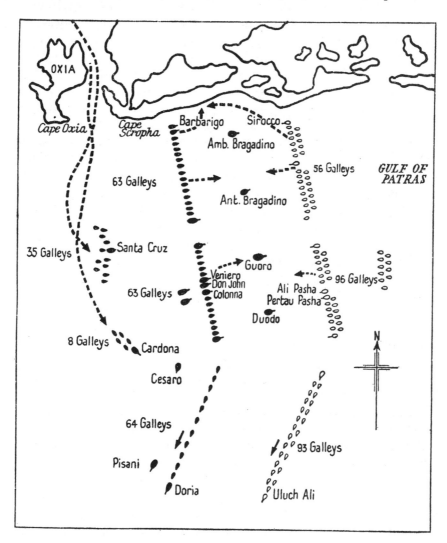

34. BATTLE OF LEPANTO, 1571

reinforcements were called when wanted. Don John also had several galleys astern of him with reinforcements.

Along the whole centre of the line, the battle now became general; the galleys of both sides closed in toward the struggle between the two flagships. Twice Ali's men boarded the *Réal*, only to be swept back by the fire of her 300 arquebusiers; and twice Don John's men boarded Ali's flagship as far as her mainmast. Meanwhile Veniero threw men aboard the *Réal*, and Santa Cruz, who was everywhere feeding the fight, came up with 200 fresh men to support her. About the same time—it was now nearly one o'clock—Colonna, who had overcome Pertau's galley, which was on fire, put his own vessel alongside Ali's and swept her deck with musketry. A third assault was then made from the *Réal*, during which a ball struck Ali in the forehead, and he fell on the gangway between the rowers.[1] At once he was seized by a soldier of Málaga, who cut off his head, ". . . *elle fust mise sur le bout d'une picque en sign de trophée; ce que estonna les turcs, et anima les Chrestiens*".[2] The Turkish flagship was then stormed and captured, and after further desperate fighting the whole of the Turkish centre was routed.

Meanwhile, it will be remembered, when at about 10.30 a.m. the battle opened on the left between Barbarigo and Sirocco, and when Don John was slowly approaching the central Turkish squadron, Doria's squadron was edging southward, and because of this an ever-widening gap was in process of development. Simultaneously, Uluch Ali's squadron was also moving southward, but as he commanded 93 galleys and galliots to Doria's 64, he could afford to do so at less risk.

Though it would appear that Uluch Ali's original intention was to turn his opponent's right flank, the opening out of the gap presented him with the choice of two additional manœuvres: either to move directly on Doria's squadron and to envelop both its flanks, or, by changing his course from south to north-west, to row through the gap in the Christian line, as Alexander had ridden through the gap in the Persian at Arbela, and to fall upon its rear. An able tactician, he saw that a crisis was approaching in the centre and decided on the latter manœuvre. He suddenly changed course and rowed all out through the gap toward Don John's right, which was held by Giustiniani, Prior of Messina and admiral of the small Maltese fleet. Bearing down upon Giustiniani, he overwhelmed his galleys, stormed them and massacred their crews. Next he took the Prior's galley in tow and hoisted its banner on his own ship.

[1] There are various versions of his end.
[2] *Œuvres Complètes de Brantôme*, vol. ii, p. 128.

Don Juan de Cardona, with eight Sicilian galleys of the reserve squadron, was hurrying to Giustiniani's assistance when, in his turn, he was attacked by sixteen of Uluch Ali's galleys, and the fiercest encounter of the whole battle was fought. Cardona was mortally wounded, and of the 500 soldiers on his galleys only 50 remained unwounded. Others suffered even greater loss. "In the *Florence*, a Papal galley, not only many knights of St. Stephen were killed, but also every soldier and slave; and the captain, Tommaso de Medici, himself severely wounded, found himself at the head of only seventeen wounded seamen. In the *San Giovanni*, another vessel of the Pope, the soldiers were also killed to a man, the rowing-benches occupied by corpses, and the captain laid for dead with two musket-balls in his neck. The *Piamontesa* of Savoy had likewise lost her commander and all her soldiers and rowers."[1]

Meanwhile Doria, who realized the mistake he had made, was rowing all out toward the fight; but before he could arrive the Marquis of Santa Cruz had come upon the scene with what remained of his reserve galleys, and at the same time Don John, who had been engaged in capturing prizes from the defeated Turkish centre, ordered the tow ropes to be cut, collected twelve galleys, and set out to help Santa Cruz. Fearing to be overwhelmed, Uluch Ali abandoned his prizes, and flying the banner of the Order of St. John which he had taken from Giustiniani's flagship, with thirteen of his galleys he rowed across the bows of Santa Cruz's ships and headed for the island of Santa Maura. By nightfall he gained Prevesa, and thirty-five more of his galleys, breaking away eastward, returned to Lepanto. At first Don John wanted to follow him, but the fine weather showed signs of breaking and it was decided to seek shelter in the harbour of Petala. There the fleet and its prizes arrived by nightfall.

No sooner had the ships been anchored or beached than accusations of treason were preferred against Doria. It was alleged that through his hatred of the Venetians he had not wanted the battle to be decisive. The simpler explanation that he was outmanœuvred would seem sufficient to account for the sorry part he played.

In spite of his blunder or defection, the victory was overwhelming, and credit for it is due, first to Pope Pius V, without whose persistence the League would never have been formed, and

---

[1] *Don John of Austria*, Sir William Stirling-Maxwell, vol. I, p. 420.

secondly to Don John. The employment of his galleasses was masterly, and though they were too cumbersome to manœuvre against galleys, the deadly effect of their gunfire showed that the age-old supremacy of the oar-propelled warship was at an end. Lepanto was the last of the great galley battles, which, tactically, remained much as they had been in classical and pre-classical times. Henceforth sail and broadside fire were to replace oar and head-on attack. Thus, from the point of view of naval history, Lepanto ended an epoch. Further, success was also due to Don John's decision to mix the galleys of the squabbling members of the League, and had he not done so, it is probable that the battle would never have been fought.

The losses suffered were exceptionally heavy, as was normal in galley battles; for once contact was made escape was most difficult, and between Turks and Christians quarter was rare. Out of some 172,000 combatants—84,000 Christians and 88,000 Turks—the Christians lost about 15,000 officers and men killed, wounded and drowned;[1] twelve of their galleys were sunk and one captured. The Turkish losses were estimated at 113 galleys wrecked and sunk, and 117 captured; 30,000 men killed, 8,000 taken prisoner, an unknown number drowned, and 15,000 Christian galley slaves freed.[2] In addition, Don John took 274 small cannon and an immense plunder; for the Turkish commanders carried about with them the bulk of their portable wealth. On Ali Pasha's ship 150,000 sequins were found, and on another galley 40,000.

When, on October 17, a galley named *The Angel* swept into Venice and announced the victory, the news was received with an outburst of religious fervour not witnessed since the first crusade. Throughout Christendom it spread from city to city and village to village, carrying with it the message that the dreaded Turk had been defeated. The pope instituted a perpetual festival in honour of the day, which is still annually observed in Rome. Painters, sculptors, and poets vied with one another to glorify the victory, and for years the wonder of the battle was a constant topic of Christian conversation. In 1591, James VI of Scotland, then a boy of twelve or thirteen, dedicated a poem to its fame, and more

---

[1] Among the wounded was Miguel Cervantes, then in his twenty-fourth year. In *Don Quixote* he mentions the battle.

[2] For various estimates see *Don John of Austria*, Sir William Stirling-Maxwell, vol. I, pp. 440–441. Though these figures are not exact, in all probability they are not exaggerated.

than three centuries later G. K. Chesterton wrote another, probably the most martial of them all:

> In that enormous silence, tiny and unafraid,
> Comes up along a winding road the noise of a Crusade.
> Strong gongs groaning as the guns boom far,
> Don John of Austria is going to the war.
> Stiff flags straining in the night-blasts cold
> In the gloom black-purple, in the glint old gold,
> Torchlight crimson on the copper kettle-drums,
> Then the tuckets, then the trumpets, the cannon, and he comes.

When the news of the disaster was received in Constantinople, Brantôme tells us, "all the councillors of the Porte and all his generals were so stunned that had they seen but fifty Christian galleys approaching, they would have abandoned the town".[1]

This is what Don John hoped for in the next year's campaign, when he set out on his return to Corfu. There he left the Venetian squadron under Veniero, and sailing on with the Spanish and papal squadrons, arrived at Messina on November 1, where the fleet was dispersed for the winter. On May 1, 1572, Pius V died, and from that moment life left the League. Nevertheless in June that year the Spanish and papal squadrons reassembled at Messina in preparation to rejoin the Venetian squadron at Corfu.

Meanwhile Selim built a new fleet of 150 galleys, and, what is notable, he added to it eight galleasses. But the vessels were hurriedly built of green timber; their guns were so hastily cast as to be worthless; their captains and seamen were raw, and their oarsmen untrained. Had the fleet of the League been boldly handled, there can be little doubt that a second Lepanto or its equivalent could have been won.

But this was not to be. Again France was the stumbling-block; not only did Charles IX foment an insurrection in the Spanish Netherlands, but during the winter of 1572–1573, he sent his ablest diplomatist, the bishop of Acqs, to Constantinople, with instructions to use every effort he could to bring about a peace between the Turks and Venetians. Further, Charles's aim was to gain control of Algiers, and this threat to Spain caused Philip II to retain half his fleet at Messina under Don John, while the other half and the papal squadron with Colonna in supreme command proceeded to Corfu to join the Venetians. Two abortive

---

[1] *Œuvres Complètes de Brantôme*, vol. II, p. 133.

campaigns followed; the first off Capes Malea and Matapan in August, in which Uluch Ali–the new Turkish commander-in-chief–refused battle and withdrew. The second was in October off Navarino, with Don John in command, when Uluch Ali again refused battle.

Next, while all three members of the League prepared for the 1573 campaign, the end of the League came. Through the machinations of the bishop of Acqs, secretly and with no reference to their allies, on March 7, 1573, the Venetians concluded a separate peace with the Turks. When, exactly a month later, this settlement was made public, Don John, then at Naples, at once hauled down the banner of the League and hoisted the Spanish flag.

The battle of Lepanto did not break the back of Ottoman naval power, it did not recover Cyprus, and it did not lead to the policing of the Mediterranean by Spain. Though a tactical victory of the first order, because of the dissolution of the League, strategically it left the sultan the victor. But morally it was decisive, for by lifting the pall of terror which had shrouded eastern and central Europe since 1453, it blazoned throughout Christendom the startling fact that the Turk was no longer invincible. Hence onward to the Battle of Zenta, in 1697, when Eugene, Prince of Savoy, drove in rout the army of Sultan Mustafa II into the river Theiss, and thereby finally exorcized the Turkish threat to Europe, though there were to be many ups and downs, never was the full prestige of Suleiman the Magnificent to be revived. His reign marks the summit of Turkish power, and it was the day of Lepanto which broke the charm upon which it rested.

# Index